D0646990

War Without Garlands
Operation Barbarossa 1941/42

War Without Garlands
Operation Barbarossa 1941/42
Robert Kershaw

SARPEDON
New York

This book is dedicated to my three sons Christian, Alexander and Michael.

Published in the United states of America by
SARPEDON
An imprint of Combined Publishing

ISBN 1-885119-71-2

For sales or rights inquiries, please contact Combined Publishing Inc., 476 West Elm Street, Conshohocken, PA 19428.

Also published in the United Kingdom in 2000 by
Ian Allan Publishing Ltd, Terminal House, Shepperton,
Surrey TW17 8AS.
ISBN 0 7110 2734 X

Half title page:
A forward artillery observer watches as one of the fortress magazines at Brest-Litovsk erupts into flames.

Title page:
A typical scene as German infantry move through a blazing village.

Picture credits:
All pictures are from the author's collection. Every effort has been made to trace original copyright holders of pictures.

Contents

Glossary, Abbreviations, Rank Comparisons

9AGSSt . . . . .Ninth Army Collection Point

Abteilung (pl -en) . . . . . . .Most often a battalion-sized unit; but also a unit, a section, a detachment or a department

AFV .Armoured fighting vehicle

APC . . . . .Armoured personnel carrier

Armee . . . . .Army formation

Armeegruppe . . . . .Army Group

Armeekorps .Army Corps

Artillerie . . . . .Artillery

Aufklärung . . . . .Reconnaissance

Auftragstaktik . . . . .German mission-orientated command philosophy

Bataillon . . . . .Battalion

Batterie . . . . .Battery

Befehlstaktik . . . .The alternative to *Auftragstaktik*, a detailed orders command philosophy

Befehlsstand . . . . .Command Post

C-in-C . . . . .Commander-in-Chief

Eisenbahntruppen . . . . .Railway troops

Fähnjunker .Officer-cadet

Fallschirmjäger . . . . .Paratroop

Feldgendarmerie . . . . .Military Police

Feldpost . . . . .Mail from the field

Flak . . . . .Anti-aircraft artillery

Flakkorps . . . . .AA Corps

Flakstand . . . . .Anti-aircraft position

Fliegerdivision . . . . .Air Division

Fliegerkorps .Air Corps

Frhr . . . . .Freiherr

Front . . . . .Used in a general sense by the Germans and to designate units by the Russians

Führungsabteilung . . . . .HQ detachment

Gebirgsjäger . . . . .Mountain infantryman

Geschütz . . . . .Gun/rifle — so *Geschütze* = rifleman

Geschwader . . . . .Wing. The German wing usually had three Gruppen (c65 aircraft) each of three or four Staffeln (9 aircraft rising to 16 later in the war) and a Stab (HQ flight)

GKO . . . . .Russian State Defence Committee

Grosstransportraum . . . . .Lorry-carrying capacity

HE . . . . .High explosive

Hitlerjugend . . . . .Hitler Youth

I/IR135 [= 1st Company of IR135] . . . . .Ist Battalion of Infantry Regiment 135

Ic . . . . .Intelligence officer

Jagdgeschwader (JG) . . . . .German fighter wing

Kampfgeschwader (KG) . . . . .German bomber wing

Kampfgruppen . . . . .Battle groups

Kanonier . . . . .Gunner

Keil . . . . .Wedge

Krad Schütze . . . . .Motorcyclist

Kriegsmaler . . . . .War artist

Kriegstagebuch (KTB) . . . . .War diary

Landser . . . . .British 'Tommy' equivalent

Lebensraum . . . . .Living space

Leichte . . . . .Light

LSSAH . . . . . . .1st SS Division 'Leibstandarte Adolf Hitler'

Luftflotte (pl –n) . . . . .Air Fleet

Luftwaffe . . . . .German Air Force

Nachrichten . . . . .Signals

NKVD . . . . .Russian Secret Police

Nummer (Nr) . . . . .Number (No)

Oberarzt . . . . .Battalion doctor

Oberkommando der Luftwaffe (OKL) . . . . .Luftwaffe High Command

Oberkommando der Wehrmacht (OKW) . . . .Armed Forces High Command

Oberkommando des Heeres (OKH) . . .Army High Command

Operation 'Otto' . . . . . .Attack on Russia later redesignated 'Barbarossa'

Operation 'Taifun' . . . . .Operation Typhoon

PAK . . . .*Panzer Abwehr-Kanone* — anti-tank gun

Panje (Fahrzeug/Wagen) . . . . .Horsedrawn (vehicle/wagon)

Panzer . . . . .Armour; gepanzert = armoured

Panzer Keile . . . . .Armoured spearhead-wedges

Panzergrenadier .Infantryman who road into battle in an APC

Panzergruppe . . . . .Panzer group; the ones involved in 'Barbarossa' were Panzergruppen 1 (von Kleist), 2 (Guderian), 3 (Hoth), 4 (Hoepner)

Panzerjäger . . . . .Anti-tank

Panzerwaffe . . . . . . .Overall word for the German tank arm

Pionier . . . . .Engineer

PoW .Prisoner of War

Propaganda-Kompanie (PK) . . . . . . .Propaganda Company

PzKpfwI, II, III, IV . . . . . .German *Panzerkampfwagen* (tank) designations

Ratas . . . . .Russian fighter-bomber

Reichsarbeitsdienst (also *Arbeitsdienst*) . . . . .Labour Service

Reichsbahn . . . . .German national railways

Reichswehr . . . . .German army

Rifle Corps	Russian infantry unit (Corps)
Rifle Divisions	Russian infantry unit (Division)
RM	Reichmarks
Rückwärts	Rear
SA	*Sturm Abteilung* or Nazi party 'brownshirt'
Sanitätsgefreiter	Medical corporal
Schützen Regiment	Infantry regiment
Schwerpunkt	Main point of effort
Sondermeldung	Special announcement
SPs	Self-propelled guns
Stalin organs	Katyusha rocket-launchers
STAVKA	Russian High Command
Stosstrup	Unit of assaulting troops configured for a particular mission, eg mix of infantry, engineer, heavy weapons

Stukageschwader (StG)	German dive-bomber wing
Panzerkampfwagen (PzKpfw)	Tank
Trost	Logistics
Untermenschen	Sub-human (ideological word used of non-Aryan races
Verbrauchssatzen	Logistic 'units'
Vernichtungskrieg	War of annihilation
Vorausabteilung	Lead element
Wehrmacht	All-encompassing word for all German armed forces
Weltanschauung	World outlook (philosophy)
Wochenschau	Weekly news show (radio/TV report)
Zerstörer	Destroyer — as in Bf110 *Zerstörer* twin-engined heavy fighter
ZG	*Zerstörergruppen*

COMPARISON OF RANKS

ENGLISH	GERMAN	SS
Army	Heer	-
Field Marshal	*Generalfeldmarschall*	-
General (Gen)	*Generaloberst* (GenOb)	*Oberstgruppenführer*
General	*General der Infanterie/Artillerie/Panzertruppe/Kavallerie*, etc	-
Lieutenant General (Lt-Gen)	*Generalleutnant* (GenLt)	*Obergruppenführer*
Major General (Maj-Gen)	*Generalmajor* (GenMaj)	*Gruppenführer*
Brigadier (Brig)	no equivalent	*Brigadeführer*
Colonel (Col)	*Oberst* (Ob)	*Standartenführer*
Lieutenant Colonel (Lt-Col)	*Oberstleutnant* (Oberstlt)	*Obersturmbannführer*
Major (Maj)	*Major* (Maj)	*Sturmbannführer*
Captain (Capt)	*Hauptmann* (Hptm)	*Hauptsturmführer*
Lieutenant (Lt)	*Oberleutnant* (Oblt)	*Obersturmführer*
2nd Lieutenant (2Lt)	*Leutnant* (Lt)	*Untersturmführer*
Regimental Sergeant-Major (RSM)	*Hauptfeldwebel*	*Stabsscharführer*
Sergeant-Major	*Oberfeldwebel*	*Oberscharführer*
Company Sergeant-Major (CSM)	*Feldwebel* (FW)	*Scharführer*
Sergeant (Sgt)	*Unterfeldwebel*	*Unterscharführer*
Corporal (Cpl)	*Obergefreiter*	*Rottenführer*
Lance Corporal (LCpl)	*Gefreiter*	*Sturmmann*
Private (Pte)	*Schütze* (or *Oberschütze* for a senior private)	*SS-Mann*
Royal Air Force	Luftwaffe	
Marshal of the RAF	*Reichsmarschall*	
Air Chief Marshal (ACM)	*Generalfeldmarschall*, also *Generaloberst*	
Air Marshal	*General der Fliegers*, etc	
Air Vice-Marshal (AVM)	*Generalleutnant*	
Air Commodore (Air Cdre)	*Generalmajor*	
Group Captain (Gp Capt)	*Oberst*	
Wing Commander (Wg Cdr)	*Oberstleutnant*	
Squadron Leader (Sqn Ldr)	*Major*	
Flight Lieutenant (Flt Lt)	*Hauptmann*	
Flying Officer (Flg Off)	*Oberleutnant*	
Pilot Officer (Plt Off)	*Leutnant*	

Introduction

Nobody has written a definitive 'soldier's' account of Operation 'Barbarossa'. Academic historians and survivors writing on the Russo-German war of 1941–45 generally concentrate on military operations and have often ducked uncomfortable moral issues, or concentrated on one area to the exclusion of the other. I read with interest Paul Kohl's comments retracing the footprints of the invading Army Group Centre during a historical pilgrimage through Russia in the 1980s.[1] Of 35 Wehrmacht veterans he contacted to assist in the project, only three admitted to having participated in excesses during the conflict. At the other end of the extreme is the *Vernichtungskrieg* (War of Annihilation) public exhibition travelling the length and breadth of present-day Germany seeking to publicise and lay clear blame for war guilt on the Wehrmacht. The significance is that the present-day *Bundeswehr* (the Federal Republic of Germany's Army) developed from the Wehrmacht after the war. There is no shortage of epic and heroic tales from German survivors, who rarely saw an atrocity. Conversely the equally stirring Russian rhetoric of the 'Great Patriotic War' tells a similar tale of heroism from a political and ideological perspective. An honest account is that of a Wehrmacht veteran who admitted during a TV interview, 'if some people say that most Germans were innocent, I would say they were accomplices'.[2]

There are varying degrees of accountability in war and they need to be examined. War guilt has been painstakingly examined by social democratic academics assessing the culpability of American soldiers fighting in Vietnam, Frenchmen during post-colonial conflicts in Algeria and the British in the Falklands. Moral issues are not as black and white as some learned authors would have us believe. Even UN and NATO soldiers have recently discovered in the Balkans that moral responsibility during conflict is a little blurred around the edges. The Russo-German war was fought between two totalitarian and ideologically motivated enemies, which produced a degree of 'peer pressure' upon combatants, frequently misunderstood by modern democratic historians who have never experienced it. Helmut Schmidt, a former German war veteran and later German Chancellor, once rounded on academic historians during a newspaper interview, pointing out they should not accept every document suggesting war guilt at face value.[3] Not every German at the front, he insisted, was a witness to atrocities.

Documents are truths in the purist sense. Perception is also truth because it is an imperative that causes us to act. This is then why attempts are made in this book, through personal, letter and diary accounts, to narrate, observe and identify the beliefs and concerns that motivated the soldiers. They are about perceptions that became truths in themselves.

How can one explain or indeed reconcile the Christian statements of soldiers, seemingly decent men, about to go to war, with the systematic maltreatment and murder of Soviet PoWs and non-combatants? That war is a brutal process and corrupts its participants is not the sole explanation. There was an undercurrent of emotion impacting on incidents that caused brave men to act in a criminal way. Only by viewing these 'snapshots' of experience can one identify the emotions, perceptions and motivation of soldiers fighting a pitiless war in a strange land. The title 'War Without Garlands' is a play on a *Landser* expression used to describe this war. Soldiers referred to it as '*Kein Blumenkrieg*', a war without flowers. Quite literally flowers were not thrown in salute by an adoring public, as in the case of triumphant parades in Berlin, acknowledging Blitzkrieg victories after the campaign in the West.

This book accepts that war is an intensely personal experience. Memories of conflict come in momentary glimpses or 'snapshots', and that is the style adopted. Concentrating on the five human senses brings a form of immediacy to the events being narrated. In addition, one must assess the soldier's psyche through a medium of practical experience, placing ideological influences within a rational perspective. This is attempted by interpreting extensive diary and letter accounts.

It is important to measure the impact of these events, because, of some 19 to 20 million soldiers who fought for the Wehrmacht, about 17-19 million fought in Russia. These men were to form the basis of the future state established in present-day Germany, numbered among the most enlightened and democratic in the world. The book is an examination of the beginnings of a crucible of experience that was to influence these men throughout their adult lives.

The spelling of individual personalities and place names has been difficult to unravel from the multiplicity of Russian, German and English sources through which I worked. Many of the latter have changed since the end of the war. In general I have used the English version or German in the absence of an alternative.

Every effort has been made to trace the source and copyright holders of the maps and illustrations appearing in the text, and these are acknowledged where appropriate. Most are my own. Similarly the author wishes to thank those publishers who have permitted the quotation of extracts from their books. Quotation sources are annotated in the notes that follow the text. My apologies are offered in advance to those with whom, for any reason, I have been unable to establish contact.

I am particularly indebted for information and documents provided by Bundeswehr colleagues and contacts from within various NATO HQs, who assisted in the book's long research and gestation period. My thanks also go to: the Panzerschule at Münsterlager and the Pionierschule at Munich; to Herr Michael Wechtler for access to a remarkable collection of documents and an informative 45th Division video chronicling the fall of Brest-Litovsk and to Dr Kehrig from the Bundesarchiv at Freiburg who assisted with important contacts, including Franz Steiner who enabled access to information and former members of the 2nd (Vienna) Panzer Division. Sheila Watson, my agent, has been very patient, gently reminding me during a series of overseas postings and operational tours that this book will never finish of its own accord.

My wife Lynn enabled the project to come to fruition by supporting me throughout. In typing the manuscript she applied her impressive eye for detail, clarity and grammatical accuracy. Any errors remaining are those I refused to change!

Without her, this book would quite simply never have been written.

Salisbury 2000

Chapter 1
'The world will hold its breath'

'I can imagine the surprise and, at the same moment, dread that will overcome you all. But you need have no worries, everything is so well prepared here, hardly anything can go wrong.'

Gefreiter, artillery regiment

SATURDAY, 21 JUNE 1941

The young NCO glanced up from his letter, the warm breeze of the Lithuanian plains wafting gently across his cheek. The weather was close and sultry. He continued to write:

'I have a feeling that in the morning, or the one after, things are going to happen that will make the world sit up and take notice again. Moreover I suspect these events will not pass me by without some impact. Hopefully the near future will bring Final Victory a further step closer.'

His unit, the 6th Infantry Division,[1] was one of 120 divisions poised along a demarcation line stretching between the Gulf of Finland and the Black Sea. An air of expectancy hung over this host, numbering some three million soldiers.

Leutnant Hermann Witzemann, a 26-year-old platoon commander, sat in a tented camp amongst his men, concealed in the forests beside the River Bug near the Soviet fortress of Brest-Litovsk. A beautiful summer day was drawing to a close. Scotch pines began to wave in the freshening evening wind. The sun's rays penetrated the branches. 'The blue sky was stretched over them like a tent,' he observed. 'We stood on the eve of momentous events,' he confided in his letter, 'of which I would also play a part.' The unknown was unsettling. 'None of us knew whether he would survive what was coming.' War appeared inevitable. A new campaign was about to begin, but where? Unease before battle permeated everything: 'After long conversations, questions and doubts we were serene and relaxed. As always, the last word that might have prompted differences was dropped.'[2]

Ital Gelzer further north occupied 'a multi-coloured tent city under tall Scotch Pines'. He felt himself fortunate. As a guest of the Intelligence platoon commander he could actually stand up in his tent. 'Very comfortable when dressing,' he remarked. With a bright lamp and a covering over the floor it was cosy at nights, if the temperature did not drop too much. His access to maps was of particular significance. They gave some clue of coming events. Knowledge within a welter of rumour always gave a soldier authority. 'All over the edge of the map that I am using now are arrows, pointing in the direction of Lemberg [Lvov],' he wrote in his letter. Little had been finalised. During the evenings he played the harmonica between the camp fires, singing Swiss songs. His thoughts, like many others', dwelt on loved ones on the eve of battle. 'I think of you all dispersed around,' he wrote, 'and hope that eventually one day, there will be a postwar period during which one can ponder a future different from that our parents experienced.' Enforced inactivity was frustrating. 'Have I ever waited so long as these past days?' he wrote. Rumour fed on rumour. 'The news of the

treaty with Turkey arrived; if it had been Russia, I could similarly have accepted it after the motto "*credo quia absurdum*" [I believe it because it is absurd].' Gelzer finished his literary correspondence with a conspiratorial flourish. 'When you read these lines we'll all know plenty. We're on the march this evening.'[3] He was not to know it, but the arrows on the map indicated his future final resting place: Borysychoi, north of Lemberg. He would be dead within four days.

Leutnant Witzemann steeled himself for the coming conflict. His letters reveal an idealistic yet religious man:

'God the Father grant me strength, faith and courage beneath whining bullets, under the impact of artillery and bombs, vulnerable in the face of enemy tank attack and the horror of creeping gas. Thanks be for love. Thy will be done.'

He was not to survive the first 24 hours.[4]

Deception measures for the coming operation, as yet unbriefed, were immense. They needed to be. Seven armies were massing along the 800km-long sector of the Russo-German demarcation line in Poland. Four Panzergruppen and three Luftwaffe Luftflotten were poised ready to go: 600,000 vehicles, 750,000 horses, 3,580 tanks and self-propelled guns, 7,184 artillery pieces and 1,830 aircraft.[5] Two workers observing German activity around Maringlen airstrip in Poland had already guessed the likely reason. Jews and Poles had been obliged to build the runways by forced labour in 1940. Jan Szczepanink said, 'I did everything that was ordered. If I was ordered into the wood to fetch timber — I fetched it. If I had to transport building materials for the barracks, I got on with it.' The sinister implication of measures taken to disguise progress was not lost on them.

'When the Germans finished the runway they let the grass grow and grazed cattle on it. It looked more like pasture than an airfield. White clover on the runway provided good grazing. The hangars were constructed by driving tree trunks into the ground. Hanging over this was wire or a green net overlaid with foliage. As leaves dried out they were replaced with fresh.'

Over 100 airfields and 50 dispersal strips had been built in Poland alone as part of the eastern build-up. Both Szczepanink and his friend Dominik Strug, looking on, were under no illusions. 'Everybody knew, they knew,' both said, 'that this was preparation for war against Russia.'[6]

By early June, Oberleutnant Siegfried Knappe's artillery battery had arrived in East Prussia. Exercising around Prostken near the Russian border, Knappe and the other battery commanders were invited to conduct a map study to 'determine the best positions for our guns in the event of an attack on Russia'. Their battalion commander insisted it be done 'carefully'. The existence of the Russo-German Non-Aggression Pact was cited in response, but they were reassured, 'it is just an exercise.' The positions were duly determined. Thereupon the battery commanders were ordered to send work details of soldiers dressed in civilian clothes to load 300 rounds of ammunition onto carts and transport them to their assigned gun positions. 'Your men are to look like farmers doing farm work, and your ammunition is to be camouflaged after you unload it,' instructed their battalion commander. The realisation sank in. One of the battery commanders asked: 'When are we going to invade, Major?' This caused acute embarrassment to their battalion commander, obviously labouring under security constraints. 'It is a purely hypothetical situation. But we have to make it look as real as possible,' he said. Civilian clothes were borrowed from local farm families and the ammunition concealed under brushwood in the reconnoitred positions.[7]

Tanks moved up under the cover of darkness. The forward elements of the 1st Panzer Division departed its garrison at Zinthen near Königsberg on 17 June. They were ordered to march only by night. Officer reconnaissance teams dressed as civilian hunters and farmers went forward to inspect the former German-Lithuanian border closely. Once the division was complete in its assembly areas, further movement by armoured vehicles was forbidden.[8] Schütze Albrecht Linsen, living in a hidden encampment near Wladowa on the high west bank of the River Bug, recalled that 'any activity outside barracks was regulated by strict orders on camouflage'; duties were conducted under cover of trees. Routine continued, not enthusiastically 'but with growing tension'.[9] There was collective awareness of impending events, but as yet no precise direction. Gerhard Görtz, another infantryman, speculated:

'We ourselves became aware around 20 June that war against the Russians was a possibility. There was a feeling in the air. No fires were allowed, and one could not walk about with torches or cause any noise. At least something was fairly clear — we were shortly to embark on a campaign!'[10]

Affectionate letters from home reflected even greater unawareness of what was happening. One wife wrote to her husband Heinz:

'Are you on a big exercise? You poor tramp. Oh well, hopefully things will soon get started so that the peace, long awaited, will finally come, when we can be man and wife, or better still, Daddy and Mummy.'[11]

At midday on 21 June Gefreiter Erich Kuby, a signaller, confided to his diary: 'I am on duty and little is going on.' His newspaper *Die Frankfurter Zeitung*, although only a week old, had nothing new to say. Kuby had surmised what might happen, but nothing had been confirmed. Interestingly, the padre had begun to conduct services that same afternoon.[12]

'FORGET THE CONCEPT OF COMRADESHIP'

Eleven months before, General Franz Halder, the German Army Chief of Staff, had hastily jotted down the essence of a high level conference conducted by Adolf Hitler at the Berghof. The invasion of Britain appeared improbable. 'To all intents and purposes the war is won,' Halder wrote. Factors that Britain may have hoped would change the situation needed to be eliminated. Such hope could only be provided by Russia and the United States. Remove Russia and 'Britain's last hope would be shattered'. Mastery of Europe and the Balkans was the issue. The elimination of Russia would remove the United States too, because Japan's power in the Far East would increase tremendously as a result. Halder scrawled an interim

conclusion: 'Decision: Russia's destruction must therefore be made a part of the struggle. Spring 1941.'[1]

Hitler's decision to invade Russia was not purely, or indeed primarily, motivated by his desire to knock Britain out of the war. Ideological considerations were the imperative powering conflict. These had been outlined in rambling and turgid form in *Mein Kampf* as early as 1925. Beneath the street dialogue terminology, of which Hitler was an acknowledged master, was a sinister causal chain that could only result in war against the Soviet Union. Race was the basic determinant of human civilisation. At one end of the spectrum stood the German nation, the embodiment and bastion of the Aryan race. At the lower end were the Jews, a parasitic and degenerative influence that threatened to destroy civilisation. German supremacy would be achieved first by destroying domestic political enemies and then by foreign conquest, eliminating the victors of World War 1. To reach their full potential, Aryan Germans needed to expand the geographic bounds of the Reich into the east, gaining *Lebensraum* (living space). The eventual aim was to create a German Empire from the Urals to Gibraltar, free of Jews, in which the *Untermenschen* (sub-human races) like Slavs would be subjected to Helot-like serfdom.

By 1941 a substantial portion of the German population, including much of the officer corps, fully subscribed to this philosophical conception. Halder took notes at a two and a half hour meeting of some 200 high ranking officers and generals in the Führer's office in Berlin during which 'colonial tasks', once the east had been subjugated, were discussed. Russia would be broken up: northern Russia to Finland, with protectorates established in the Baltic states, Ukraine and White Russia. Halder noted:

'Clash of two ideologies. We must forget the concept of comradeship between soldiers. A communist is no comrade before or after the battle. This is a war of extermination... We do not wage war to preserve the enemy.'

He recorded a series of brutal, yet hardly debated, directives under the precursor, 'This war will be very different from the war in the West.' The war against Russia would involve 'extermination of the Bolshevist commissars and the communist intelligentsia'.

The principles the staff officers were enjoined to embrace were to be reflected in future high command directives. 'Commanders,' Halder wrote, 'must make the sacrifice of overcoming their personal scruples.'[2] Many did.

Generalfeldmarschall von Brauchitsch, the German Army Commander-in-Chief, released a series of directives two months later to the rest of the Wehrmacht, defining their freedom of action in the coming war. *The Treatment of Enemy Inhabitants in the 'Barbarossa' Operational Zone*, released in May, was secret, and could only be communicated to officers. In essence it directed 'pacification' measures against any resistance in newly occupied areas, 'which was to be eradicated promptly, severely and with maximum force'. Troops were given the 'duty and right' to 'liquidate' irregulars and saboteurs 'in battle, or shoot them on the run'. Collective reprisals would be exacted from villages where resistance occurred. The infamous Commissar Order of 6 June was preceded by the introduction that 'in a war against Bolshevism, handling the enemy according to humane rules or the Principles of International Law is not applicable'. Communists were not to be treated as conventional PoWs, 'they are hitherto, whether in battle or found conducting resistance, in principle, to be shot immediately'. They were identified to soldiers as wearing a special badge 'with a red star with an embossed golden hammer and sickle, worn on the arm'.[3]

The *Oberkommando der Wehrmacht* (OKW) and *Oberkommando des Heeres* (OKH) were issuing decrees that dispensed with Germany's international and legal obligations. These were military directives, not SS orders. Senior generals — including Erich von Manstein, Walther von Reichenau and General Erich Hoepner — issued parallel directives. Hoepner reminded his troops in the Panzergruppe 4 that, 'it is the old battle of the Germans against the Slav people, of the defence of the European culture against Muscovite-Asiatic inundation, and the repulse of Jewish Bolshevism'. No quarter was to be given in the coming pitiless battle:

'The objective of this battle must be the demolition of present-day Russia and must therefore be conducted with unprecedented severity. Every military action must be guided in planning and execution by an iron resolution to exterminate the enemy remorselessly and totally.
In particular, no adherents to the contemporary Russian Bolshevik system are to be spared.'[4]

There were soldiers, particularly those educated since Hitler came to power, who accepted this Nazi *Weltanschauung* conception of world order. To these men, the signing of the August 1939 Nazi-Soviet Non-Aggression Pact with an implacable ideological foe, made good sense, despite philosophical reservations. The Führer had shown himself to be a wily foreign policy opportunist, negating the need to conduct a war on two fronts, unlike the catastrophic example of 1914–18. The *Wochenschau* newsreel, seen in German cinemas, showing Ribbentrop's historic flight to Moscow to sign the pact, exudes the same atmospheric quality to audiences as Chamberlain's waving a piece of paper for peace following his flight to Munich the year before. It appeared that Adolf Hitler had an almost visionary grip on world events. 'The Führer has it in hand,' was a simplistic and comforting notion for soldiers unschooled and politically naïve so far as world events were concerned. In common-sense terms there appeared no need to attack the Soviet Union.

German-Russian diplomatic relations since 1918 were very much characterised by national self-interest, often clouding the ideological divide. Both nations defeated in World War 1 resented the presence of the emerging Polish state. Secret military exchanges, even before the Treaty of Rapello in 1922, enabled German firms, via a bogus company established in Berlin, to manufacture aeroplanes, submarines and weapons of all kinds, including tanks and poison gas, on Russian territory. The Reichswehr had no intention of turning a benign eye to a German communist presence despite this assistance, which was aimed partly to influence it. Communism was brutally suppressed in Weimar Germany. The rise of the Nazi party increased the ideological divide and links were severed. Self-interest reversed the trend in the need for an accommodation desired by both Hitler and Stalin in August 1939. Even apart from the diplomatic and military aspects, the Soviet Union exported substantial amounts of raw materials and agricultural produce to Germany under the pact's protocol. Quantities of grain, oil derivatives, phosphate, cotton, timber, flax, manganese ore and platinum were regularly despatched. Germany was also dependent upon transit rights through Russia for the import of India rubber and soya. By 22 June some 1,000,000 tons of mineral oil had

been delivered.[5] Sonderführer Theo Scharf with the 97th Infantry Division, forming part of Army Group South, observed:

'There was obviously a vast concentration of troops in progress toward the 1939 demarcation line between Germany and the USSR. Discussions, speculations and bets were rife. On the one hand it seemed obvious that something was going to happen with the Soviets. On the other hand oil tank trains rolled continuously westward, past us, from the oil fields on the Soviet side.'

There appeared little point to invasion rumours despite obvious visual substance. Scharf ruefully admits, 'I still owe some long vanished Leutnant a bottle of champagne for my wager that we would never attack the USSR.'[6]

Soviet Foreign Minister Molotov visited Adolf Hitler in Berlin in mid-November 1940, an event given much fanfare and some prominence in German public newsreels. The public would have felt less comforted if they had been aware of the real issues. One month before the visit, planning for 'Otto' (later redesignated 'Barbarossa') was well under way. Halder exuberantly noted that Russia's calculation that it would profit from Germany's war with Britain 'went wrong':

'We are now at her border with 40 divisions, and will have one hundred divisions later on. Russia would bite on granite; but it is unlikely that she would deliberately pick a quarrel with us.'

'Russia is ruled by men with horse sense,' he scrawled as Hitler commented on the likely substance of future Russian resistance.[7] Molotov was a ruthless diplomat of Bismarckian proportions. Romania and Hungary had joined the Axis, leading Molotov to believe that Germany was violating the spirit of the August 1939 pact. The German Tripartite Pact Alliance with Italy and Japan, although aimed allegedly at the United States and Britain, did not convince Russia. Not surprisingly, and contrary to media coverage, the visit was a disaster for German-Soviet relations. Paul Schmidt, Hitler's personal interpreter, described the vitriolic dialogue hidden from public view, claiming that Molotov:

'...was blunt in his remarks and did not spare Hitler at all. Very uncompromising, hardly smiling at all, reminding me of my mathematics teacher, with hostile spectacles, looking at his pupil Hitler and saying: "Well, is our agreement last year still valid?"
'Hitler, who thought it was a mistranslation, said, "Of course — why not?" Molotov said: "Yes, I asked this question because of the Finns. You are on very friendly relations with the Finns. You invite people from Finland to Germany, you send them missions there, and the Finns are a very dangerous people. They undermine our security and we will have to do something about that."
'Whereupon Hitler exploded and said, "I understand you very well. You want to wage war against Finland and this is quite out of the question. Listen — do you hear me — impossible! Because my supplies of iron, nickel and other important raw materials will be cut."'

Schmidt concluded: 'it was a very tough, almost heavyweight championship, in political discussion.'[8] Whatever the public perception, there appeared little holding the two ideologies together except for short-term national self-interest. Both countries mistrusted each other. Hitler and his dinner guests greatly relished the tale carried by his physician, Dr Karl Brandt, that Molotov's Soviet Foreign Ministry staff had all plates and silverware boiled before use, for fear of German germs.[9] But public perception was important, if only in deception terms. Halder scrawled a note after the meeting: 'Result: constructive note; Russia has no intention of breaking with us. Impression of rest of the world.'[10] The weekly transmission of the German *Wochenschau* relayed the type of message cinema audiences in Germany wanted to hear:

'The Berlin discussions were transacted in an atmosphere of joint trust and led to mutual understanding in all important questions of interest to Germany and the Soviet Union.'[11]

'THE FÜHRER HAS GOT IT ALL IN HAND'

Soldiers in the divisions gathering in the east were not totally insensitive to a gradual deterioration of relations. One Leutnant wrote home in early March:

'Do you know what I have picked up? That now for the first time since we have had closer relations with Russia, the Russians have not been represented in the Leipziger Messe [International Industrial Exhibition]. Last autumn and summer he held all the cards, big style, in Leipzig and the Königsberg Baltic Sea Messe also. And when you follow the foreign press statements over our invasion of Bulgaria, you would have noticed that this time Moscow was not included. Now we're negotiating with the Turks to get into Syria where the Tommies have got one of their strongest armies. And do you think the Russians are going to keep quiet? That will be the day!'

Despite all these 'interesting developments' the junior officer concluded 'there is no use in cracking our heads over it, the main point is inescapable. Final Victory will be ours.'[1] Another soldier confided in a similar letter the same month:

'A Russian General, in a drunken state, stressed that Poland had been trampled over in 18 days, it would take eight days to do us! [ie Germany] That's what one is able to say in the Mess today! Well and good, we are not so well informed about Russia (terrain, army, barracks, airfields, etc) as we were over Poland, Holland, Belgium and France, and now over England. Anyway, not to worry, the Führer has got it all in hand.'

This certainly appeared to be the case according to observations by rank and file. A whole communications network had developed pointing eastwards. 'Barbarossa', the code name for the envisaged invasion of Russia, was planned with typical Teutonic precision. 2,500 trains transporting the first echelon to the east had already been despatched by 14 March. The build-up continued inexorably: 17 divisions and headquarters moved from Germany and the West between 8 April and 20 May. Nine further divisions went over the following 10 days. Between 3 and 23 June, 12 Panzer and 12 Panzergrenadier divisions were moved from the interior of Germany from the west and south-east. The total was to rise to some 120 divisions on the eve of 'Barbarossa'. 'The imposing vastness of the spaces in which our troops are now assembling cannot fail but strike a deep impression,' wrote Halder on 9 June. 'By its very nature it puts an end to the doctrine of defeatism.'[3] Hauptmann Alexander Stahlberg, a Panzer officer, commented:

'In June there came an order which clearly showed us what to expect. Every soldier, from simple private to commanding officer, had to learn the Cyrillic alphabet. Everyone had to be capable of reading Russian signposts and Russian maps. That told us something — but had not Hitler and Stalin ceremoniously signed a non-aggression pact less than two years ago? Had not Hitler received Molotov in November of the previous year, to discuss — it had filtered through later — the partition of the British Empire?'[4]

Leutnant F. W. Christians was convinced the forthcoming mission was to secure the oil wells at Baku against possible British attack. As they would, therefore, because of the pact, be passing through 'friendly territory', he packed his extra summer dress uniform and cavalry sabre.[5] 'There were some rumours around we were perhaps going through Russia to Pakistan,' declared Eduard Janke, a *Krad Schütze* (motorcycle soldier) in the 2nd SS Division 'Das Reich'. Nobody knew.

'There were calls for German help but these were rumours, nobody believed it was fact. We asked the platoon commanders: "So where are we off to?" — "No idea," was the response.'[6]

'Where are we going?' asked Götz Hrt-Reger with a Panzer reconnaissance unit. 'To Turkey? To Persia? To Africa?' There were no answers. The vehicles continued to motor on eastwards. 'We knew nothing when we started out,' he said. They reached Berlin, but still carried on.[7] Possibilities began to emerge as they entered East Prussia. Stahlberg's unit, the 12th Panzer Division, began to assemble in the forests at Suwalki in the same province. 'The closer we came to the Russian frontier, the more densely the regiments massed. The numbers of troops mustering exceeded anything we had seen before.'[8] Comprehension began to dawn collectively. Gerner Hälsmann's regiment 'assembled in an area 70–80km west of Warsaw. We were there for about four weeks and trained intensively,' he remarked. 'Before then we had received small dictionaries — small books, to learn a little Russian. I hardly did any,' he said, 'except to learn "*Ruki wjerch!*" — hands up!'[9]

All along the Russo-German demarcation line in Poland troops began to be increasingly aware of the imminence of a massive new campaign. 'So many troops are about here,' wrote home one Gefreiter as early as April, 'who share a like fate to ours, and their numbers still increase daily.' Another commented, 'You couldn't be bored here because the roads are overflowing with the military. What are the next few days going to bring?' Hopefully some improvement, because he declared with some exasperation:

'whether it's going to amount to yet another war within the year? I am just about fed up with the war, and would rather do something else as spend yet another year gadding about in uniform.'[10]

Planning for 'Barbarossa' occurred selectively, initially on a strict 'need to know' basis. Hitler declared his intention on 31 July 1940, after which preparations started. Major Karl Wilhelm Thilo, a young staff officer working in the operations section of OKH, recorded in his diary how on 21 September OKH in Fontainebleau declared:

'On the order of the Führer, Russia is to be photographed from the air up to 300km beyond its borders; preparations for invasion. I myself have to work on a mission for the German Military Attaché in Moscow to reconnoitre routes and communications for three spearheads.'

Eleven days later Thilo recorded that the German Military Attaché on Russian autumn manoeuvres 'states that everyone there is expecting war against Germany in 1941; after England it will be Russia's turn'.[11] General Günther Blumentritt, the Fourth Army Chief of Staff, commented that neither the commander — Generalfeldmarschall von Kluge — nor his staff received any indication of a possible war with Russia until January 1941.[12] Planning then continued apace, unabated until the execution in June. Halder had by the end of the same month encapsulated the mission: 'Commit all available units' (he foresaw 144 divisions on 29 January) and 'crush Russia in a rapid campaign.' He noted the main imperatives shaping the execution. 'Space' stretching to the Dnieper — the initial phase line — was the equivalent in distance from Luxembourg to the mouth of the Loire. 'Speed. No Stop!' Halder noted. The dependency would be on motorised transport, not railways. 'Increased motorisation' must result compared to the French campaign of 1940; he foresaw the need to create 33 mobile units.[13]

During spring 1941 more and more divisions were moved to the east and preparations intensified as the skeleton staffs of the senior commands began to establish themselves in situ. 'A strange atmosphere prevailed during these months,' commented General Blumentritt. Many of the senior staff officers had fought as junior commanders in Russia in 1914-18 'and we knew what to expect,' he declared.

> 'There was uneasiness both among the staff officers and in the divisions. On the other hand duty demanded precise and detailed work. All books and maps concerning Russia soon disappeared from the bookshops.'[14]

Evidence of this precision has survived in contemporary documentation and maps relating to the operation. Atlases were produced with special wallet editions showing distances to Moscow, highlighting Red Army barracks, industrial installations, rail networks, power, hospitals and local government. Tactical information indicating terrain 'going', temperatures, snowfall, incidence of mist and other meteorological details was given in tabular and map form. Painstaking preparation including photograph albums even showed which buildings were to be demolished in Moscow, while booklets mapping towns in White Russia showed a sinister yellow line, highlighting the main through-routes to Moscow.[15] Blumentritt observed:

> 'In particular, Napoleon's 1812 campaign was the subject of much study. Kluge read General de Caulaincourt's account of that campaign with the greatest attention: it revealed the difficulties of fighting, and even living in Russia . . . we knew that we would soon be following in Napoleon's footsteps.'

Two historical invasions had penetrated the depth and vastness of Russia: Charles XII of Sweden, defeated at Poltava in 1709, and Napoleon's invasion of 1812. The latter was of particular interest because it took the proposed German direct route to Smolensk. Accounts of these campaigns were read

avidly. 'I remember that Kluge's desk at his Warsaw headquarters was usually laden with such publications,'[16] remarked the Fourth Army Chief of Staff. Previous invasions had been defeated by long marches, shortages of supplies, tenacious resistance by the inhabitants and the awful Russian winter. They were food for thought and prompted foreboding. Nisbet Bain had written in 1895 of the severity of the Russian winter of 1708 that fatally weakened Charles XII's Swedish Army, where 'in the vast open steppes of the Ukraine . . . birds dropped down dead from the trees and wine and spirits froze into solid masses of ice.' Hilaire Belloc described the change of weather experienced by French sentries in 1812 in terms of being stalked by a living beast:

> 'What they felt as the night advanced was a new thing to them . . . a thing no Westerner among them had yet known — the winter advancing from out of Asia, from the frozen steppes . . . It came through the thick fog like something sentient . . . Men talk of having breathed that night an air itself freezing, and of having felt the rasp of that air so that they could only breathe through the coverings over the mouth.'[17]

Many of the German officers who had fought in Russia during World War 1, now commanding formations, had cause to ponder their first-hand experience of the tenacity of the Russian soldier.

German planners, however, believed that potential historical similarities were outweighed by the technological and ideological differences applying now. German racist beliefs, fundamental to the 'Barbarossa' conception, spawned miscalculations. The capacity of resistance of the Soviet Union, its population and industrial potential was measured in Slav sub-human terms. All that was required according to Hitler was to 'kick in the door and the whole regime would collapse like a house of cards'. 'The Russian is inferior,' noted Halder recording a Führer conference on 5 December 1940, and 'the Army lacks leadership'. A short Blitzkrieg campaign was sure to succeed: 'when the Russian Army is battered once, the final disaster is unavoidable,' he predicted.[18]

Hitler's previous respect for the Red Army had mellowed following its disastrous performance in the Russo-Finnish war of 1939. There was awareness of the inner turmoil Stalin's purges had visited on the Soviet officer corps. Intelligence pointed to the shortage of experienced commanding officers. German attachés graded the Russian higher officer corps as 'decidedly bad', a 'depressing impression' and that 'compared with 1933 [the] picture is strikingly negative. It will take Russia 20 years to reach her old level.'[19] Few military observers had been impressed, furthermore, by the Red Army's recent annexation of eastern Poland in concert with the Wehrmacht in 1939. A young artillery NCO taking part in the 'farewell' parade from Brest-Litovsk on 22 September that year commented upon the motorised procession that paraded before General Guderian and a Russian brigadier-general, remarking:

> 'The Soviets made a right poor impression. The vehicles, above all the tanks, were — I must say — a collection of oily junk.'[20]

Planning for Operation 'Barbarossa' tended, as a result, to concentrate on operational aspects, with less regard paid to the logistic effort required to sustain the three massive spearheads envisaged. Generalleutnant Paulus co-ordinated the effort from

September 1940. It was anticipated the Soviets would defend along a line of the Dnieper–Berezina–Polotsk, north of Riga in the Baltic states. Three German army groups were formed to pierce it: one to the south and two to the north of the Pripet Marshes lying between them. Hitler's primary objectives were economic, allied to a general desire to trap and swiftly destroy the Red Army in the west of Russia, before it could escape. *Lebensraum* dictated the need to annex the rich Ukrainian grainlands and the industrial area of the Donets basin, and eventually the Caucasian oil fields. Von Brauchitsch, the Commander-in-Chief, and his Chief of Staff, Halder, were motivated by an operational imperative: destroy the Red Army; economic prizes would follow.

Army Group Centre, some 51 divisions strong, commanded by Generalfeldmarschall von Bock, provided the *Schwerpunkt* (main point of effort). As the most powerful of the two army groups north of the Pripet Marshes, its task was to encircle the enemy west of the upper Dnieper and Dvina near Minsk, thereby preventing an eastward escape. Apart from strong infantry forces, it contained the bulk of the mobile formations: nine Panzer, six motorised and one cavalry divisions forming Panzergruppen 3 and 2 under Generals Hoth and Guderian. Army Group North, a much smaller formation of 26 divisions commanded by Generalfeldmarschall von Leeb, was to attack Leningrad, link up with the Finns and eliminate all Russian forces from the Baltic. Its Panzer spearhead of three Panzer and two motorised divisions forming Panzergruppe 4 was commanded by General Hoepner. Army Group South's 40 divisions, commanded by Generalfeldmarschall von Rundstedt, supported by 14 Romanian divisions and a Hungarian corps, was to attack out of Poland, supported by the five Panzer and two motorised divisions of Panzergruppe 1, led by General von Kleist. Its aim was to cut off enemy forces east of Kiev. Some 22 divisions, including two Panzer, were held in reserve across the front. The bulk of the armies, despite the inclusion of the mobile Panzergruppen, consisted of infantry. Armoured spearheads were expected to dictate the pace, otherwise they would advance at the same speed as Napoleon's infantry almost 130 years before.

There appears to have been only a loose connection between logistic and operational planning. Hitler's perception of Jewish-Bolshevik decadence led to generalisations concerning Soviet vulnerabilities and weaknesses. By November 1940 German logisticians were calculating they could at best case supply German forces within a zone approximately 600km east of the start-line. Yet strategic planners were setting objectives up to 1,750km beyond the frontier, and anticipating only six to 17 weeks to attain them. The planners and the Führer were expecting the norms achieved by the Blitzkrieg campaigns conducted in Poland, the Low Countries and France. The German soldier appeared capable of anything and had, indeed, already demonstrated so. Failure was a remote and as yet untested experience. Hitler confidently announced, 'when "Barbarossa" is launched, the world will hold its breath.'

TOMORROW 'WE ARE TO FIGHT AGAINST WORLD BOLSHEVISM'

'All the preparations indicated an attack against the Soviet Union,' declared Schütze Walter Stoll, an infantryman. 'We could hardly believe it, but the facts made the whole issue indisputable.' It was not a welcome prospect. 'We always retained the faint hope that it would not come to this,' he said. Officers had been summoned to an early morning conference on 21 June. Such activity normally preceded something special. It did.

'*At 14.00 hours the whole company paraded. Leutnant Helmstedt, the company commander, grim-faced, stepped forward. He read the Führer's proclamation to the Wehrmacht — now we knew the reason for all those secret preparations over the previous weeks.*'[1]

Unteroffizier Helmut Kollakowsky, another infantryman, received the news in similar fashion.

'*In the late evening our platoons collected in barns and we were told: "the next day we are to fight against World Bolshevism". Personally, I was totally astonished, it came completely out of the blue, because the treaty between Russia and Germany had always been in my mind. My enduring memory on my last home leave was of the Wochenschau [equivalent of Pathe-Newsreel] I had seen, reporting the treaty was settled. I could not imagine that now we would fight against the Soviet Union.*'[2]

Although suspected by enquiring minds, the announcement of the impending invasion caused universal surprise among the rank and file. 'One could say we were completely floored,' confessed Lothar Fromm, an artillery forward observation officer. 'We were — and I must emphasise again — surprised and in no way prepared.'[3] Siegfried Lauerwasser, attached to a Luftwaffe unit moving up to his assembly area by train, was not informed. 'We had no idea where we were going,' he said, and tried to work it out by peering through the train window. 'Then at a station the sign was in Polish.' That night they reached their destination: brand-new 100-man barracks. A photo-intelligence officer guided them to their quarters. Once Lauerwasser and his comrades were gathered together, the officer, unable to contain himself, confided:

'*I'm not supposed to tell you boys, but at 04.00 it starts! [Es geht los!] We were shocked. What will happen to us? Then with dawn came the realisation there will be an attack and an invasion of Russia — and what emotions we had!*'[4]

'We learned that the attack, Operation "Barbarossa", was on, only a few hours before it started,' commented Eduard Janke, with the 2nd SS Division 'Das Reich', 'and that in a few hours we would be off.'[5]

Knowledge of the decision was in many ways a relief. Uncertainty itself engendered nervousness. 'The long wait is a real burden,' complained a Gefreiter, 'to which we have all been sentenced.'

'Let's get on with it' was the pervasive emotion. The sooner the war got going again, the earlier it would finish. 'When will the next battle come?' wrote the same NCO. Letters home reflected such nervous anticipation. 'We live each day and hour with tension,' another wrote.

'*I can tell you much later. A lot of it will be incomprehensible. Hours waiting make the nerves taut, but it will eventually contribute to the victorious finale! And that one certainly wants to see pass us by as soon as possible.*'[6]

Many, perhaps the majority, simply viewed the decision with equanimity. They were soldiers after all. Officers and NCOs were confident and combat experienced. Some chose not to reflect and took it in their stride. Previous campaigns had been short, sharp and successful. 'We were all strongly convinced that this war would also not last long,' declared Gefreiter Erich Schütkowsky, a *Gebirgsjäger* (mountain infantryman).

'Personally, I already had a funny feeling as we cast our eye over large unfolded Russian maps, and Napoleon's fate came to mind. But these thoughts were soon banished with time. We had already experienced momentous successes, so nobody at this stage was contemplating defeat.'[7]

'Why are you losing hope that all this will not be over quickly?' enquired one Gefreiter in response to home mail. 'Once the thing with the Russians is in the bag, my hopes will be rising ever more.'[8] Hauptsturmführer Klinter, a company commander in the 3rd SS Division 'Totenkopf', reacted with mild surprise to the announcement, and with a casual acceptance typical of many soldiers' reactions to world political events. 'The war with Russia will begin early morning at 04.00 hours,' he declared, adding laconically 'with Russia? . . . against Russia.' He would simply get on with it. 'It took a while before it had sunk in, and then we thought it through.' There had been numerous previous examples when the Führer's political and military perceptions had been proved correct. His fatalistic acceptance was typical of an SS soldier: 'there was no room then for doubts or thoughts.'[9] Optimism and quiet resignation generally followed the initial surprise. Benno Zeiser, under training as a driver in a transport unit far from the front, voiced the type of idealistic fervour easily conjured up in the rear.

'The whole thing should be over in three or four weeks, they said, others were more cautious and gave it two or three months. There was even one who said it would take a whole year, but we laughed him right out. "Why, how long did the Poles take us, and how long to settle France, eh?"'[10]

The final evening waiting on the Russo-German demarcation line in Poland is permanently etched in the memories of many who reflected these may be their final hours. Artillery Oberleutnant Siegfried Knappe saw that, 'a few kilometres away, the village that would be our first objective lay sleeping, bathed in the comfort of soft moonlight'. He likened it to a beautiful painting. 'The strong scent of pine needles permeated my consciousness as I wandered among the 180 men of my battery, checking things out.' The prospect of combat clears the senses like a drug, throwing truths into sharp relief.

'I became more aware of the men as individuals than I had ever been before. Some were timid, others were brash; some were gloomy, others easily amused; some were ambitious, others idlers; some were spendthrifts, others misers. The diverse thoughts that lay behind their helmets as they waited for battle only they could know . . . One soldier was humming softly to himself in meditation. Some were no doubt full of foreboding, and others were thinking of home and loved ones.'

Knappe was totally confident. 'The men were strong and sure of themselves.'[11] Veterans had their doubts but emotions were kept tightly under control. Hauptmann Hans von Luck, having survived the French campaign, followed the truism common to all soldiers when faced with the next. 'Everyone tries to mobilise his mental forces,' he explained, 'and is ready to suppress negative experiences and assimilate even the slightest positive ones.' After all, the French campaign 'could not have turned out better,' but 'the euphoria of the past months had given way to a rather sober view'. His belief was that 'even the young ones, those schooled in National Socialism, doubted that Russia could be defeated with idealism alone'. The following morning, therefore, they would do what soldiers had done from time immemorial prior to going to battle: 'we set our minds on the present and were ready to do our "duty".'[12]

Such duties now focused the mind. Heinrich Eikmeier's 88mm Flak gun was positioned next to the River Bug in the central sector.

'During the evening before the war broke out, large numbers of telephone lines were laid to the gun; and in the morning there were many high ranking officers about, many of them unknown, including several generals. We were told our gun would provide the signal to open fire. It was controlled by stopwatch, exactly when the time was determined. When we fired, numerous other guns, both left and right would open up. Then war would break out.'

Eikmeier considered much later: 'whether we fired the first shot in Army Group Centre — or for the entire Russian campaign — I do not know!'[13]

Leutnant Hans-Jochen Schmidt's unit occupied its assembly area within a depression at dusk. 'Every man received 60 rounds of live ammunition,' he remarked, 'and the rifles from then on were loaded.' The soldiers were tense; 'nobody thought of sleep.' Troops at this final stage of preparation for battle invariably consider loved ones, lying motionless, awaiting the signal to move up to assault positions. Schmidt's men received a particularly poignant reminder of home. A radio receiver was broadcasting music.

'In the Reich one did not know what was going on, and the radio played a lively dance tune which touched us to the core of our souls.'

The reality of their situation refocused their attention once again. 'The march route had come alive with vehicle after vehicle.'[14]

In Germany the weather had been hot. Berlin slept peacefully although hectic activity continued in the main army headquarters. The civilian population had no idea what was going on. 'In addition to the already numerous rumours in circulation, new ones crop up daily with more and more detailed information,' revealed a classified SS *Secret Report on the Home Political Situation*. It even quoted the rumour of a possible launch date of an offensive against the Soviet Union on 20 May; another tied Hitler's visit to Danzig with a secret meeting with Molotov 'on the high seas to settle the conflict between Germany and Russia by diplomatic means as in 1939'. Baltic volunteer battalions were alleged to be forming in Berlin. The rumours, the report claimed, 'are caused predominantly by letters from soldiers at the Russian front.'[15] There was awareness at home that letters were not reaching husbands and loved ones, but the sinister implication of a pending new campaign was missed. One wife wrote to her husband on 17 June, with a touching optimism still prevalent:

'Darling, I hope you have got my letter. It is obvious from the way you are writing that you have received no post. Dearest love, that I cannot understand. Immediately I arrived back in Rheydt I wrote to you. That was on 8 June. Hopefully you will get it soon. But Josef you need not be sad, our wonderful time has yet to come. I will stay patient and wait for you.'[16]

Another wife tragically missed her husband's departure to the east before an anticipated weekend together. She continues in an inconsolable tone, apologising for the mistakes, because she is so devastated:

'When I telephoned, a female voice said that you had departed that morning at 0830. I thought that my heart would stop, my darling, it is worse than I thought it would be. Tell me whether it was as bad for you and excuse the blots, they are tears!'[17]

Topics concerning everyday life were the primary issues discussed: 'Tommy' air raids and clothing and ration cards. Most letters contained universal and understandable fears:

'My loved one, I'm keeping my fingers crossed, you must and you will come back to your beloved wife and children. Darling, I hope you are not ill, how are your poor feet? My dear, I think of you day and night, because I can imagine how it will be for you if you are on a long march . . . You fight and must fight on to rescue your wife and children; we can thank you if the bombs fail to strike . . . I will never forget you, and will always remain true . . .'[18]

Norbert Schultze, a Berlin composer, returned home at about midday on Saturday, 21 June, after an exhausting series of engagements, only to be summoned back immediately to the radio station by his director. He was tasked, with another colleague, Herms Niel, to participate in a competition 'to write the German Nation's signature tune for the Russian campaign'. They had two hours, after which the Propaganda Minister Goebbels, who had written the text, would make his choice. Both composers were shown into a room with a grand piano. Schultze won; Goebbels selected his tune and said 'and then I would like to request that you participate in producing the concluding piece to our Russian fanfare'. 'I beg your pardon?' enquired Schultze. 'Yes, don't you know?' responded Goebbels. Schultze did not. 'No, I have heard nothing over the last few days. I have been inundated with work and composing.' The Propaganda Minister played a record: Liszt's *Les Préludes*. It had already been played three times on the wireless, but Schultze had never heard it. 'Put that on the end,' said Goebbels, 'it will precede all the radio announcements.'[19] It was the primary signature tune for forthcoming *Wochenschau* cinema newsreels and became the fanfare preceding important High Command announcements. It was to be the overture informing the German public they were at war with the Soviet Union. An artillery NCO wrote home:

'And now to the situation. In three hours we will relay fire commands by radio which the batteries will receive to open fire on the Russian positions, that will destroy everything. You will meanwhile be peacefully asleep whilst we of the first wave will start the invasion of enemy territory. In any case, towards morning you, too, will know that the hour has arrived and you will be thinking of me even though this letter will not have arrived. I can imagine the surprise and at the same moment, dread, that will overcome you all. But you need have no worries, because everything is so well prepared here, hardly anything can go wrong.'[20]

All along the frontier with the Soviet Union and occupied areas German troops began to move up to their final assault positions. 'I was with the leading assault wave,' announced Helmut Pabst, an artillery NCO with Army Group Centre. His diary reveals snapshots of the final moments. 'The units moved up to their positions quietly, talking in whispers. There was the creaking of wheels — assault guns.' Such images remained permanently etched in the memories of survivors for the rest of their lives. Finally the infantry deployed. 'They came up in dark ghostly columns and moved forward through the cabbage plots and cornfields.'[21] Having reached their final attack positions, they spread out into assault formation. Men lay in the undergrowth listening to the sound of insects and croaking frogs along the River Bug, straining their ears to hear sounds from the opposite bank. Some were breathless, tense, waiting for the release of the opening salvo.

Rearwards, by the airstrip at Maringlen in occupied Poland, Dominik Strug, the Polish labourer, recalled, 'it was two o'clock at night when the engines started to turn over.' The air base was humming with activity, subdued lights showed here and there and the smell of high octane became apparent as clouds of exhaust began to disperse on the breeze. He went on, 'We didn't have a clue what was going on. Later we learned the Germans had started a war against the Russians.' Spectre-like black shapes lumbered into the air, gathered and began to move purposefully toward their objectives. Strug, gazing into the distance, attempted to discern some pattern to this activity. They flew eastward. 'Everything went towards Brest [-Litovsk], Brest, Brest . . .'[22]

Chapter 2
'Ordinary men' — The German soldier on the eve of 'Barbarossa'

> **'This drill — Ach! inhuman at times — was designed to break our pride, to make those young soldiers as malleable as possible so that they would follow any order later on.'**
> *German soldier*

'ENDLESS PRESSURE TO PARTICIPATE'

Every conscript army is a reflection of the society from which it is drawn. The Wehrmacht in 1941 was not totally the image of the Nazi totalitarian state: it had, after all, only recently developed from the Weimar Reichswehr. It was, however, in transition. The process had begun in 1933. Progress could be measured in parallel with the economic and military achievements of the Third Reich. Blitzkrieg in Poland, the Low Countries and France had brought with it heady success. The German *Wochenschau* newsreel showing Hitler's triumphant return from France showed him at the height of his power. Shadows thrown up by the steam-driven express train, Nazi salutes from solitary farmers en route juxtaposed against the sheer size of hysterical crowds greeting his return in Berlin have a true Wagnerian character. Children dressed in *Hitlerjugend* (Hitler Youth) uniforms wave gleefully from lampposts. Adoring breathless women are held back by SS crowd-controllers. Goering, standing with Hitler on the Reich Chancellery balcony, is visibly and emotionally impressed by the roaring crowd whose cheering dominates the soundtrack.

The Wehrmacht's morale, bathing in this adoration, was at its height. *Wochenschau* pictures of the French victory parade in Berlin, with close-ups of admiring women, and the pathos of a solitary high-heeled shoe left in the road as the crowd is pushed back from flower-bedecked troops, say it all. The troops were jubilantly received. Organisations and private people 'render thanks to our deserving soldiers', the newsreels opined. The wounded and those on leave received a torrent of presents and invitations. These were the good times. Schütze Benno Zeiser remembered on joining the army in May 1941:

> 'Those were the days of fanfare parades, and "special announcements" of one "glorious victory" after another, and it was "the thing" to volunteer. It had become a kind of super holiday. At the same time we felt very proud of ourselves and very important.'[1]

Success bred an idealistic zeal, producing an over-sentimental outpouring of the Nazi *Weltanschauung* that in modern democratic and more cynical times would appear positively alien. Leutnant Hermann Witzemann, a former theology student, marching with an infantry unit eastwards from the Atlantic coast, grandly announced to his diary:

> 'We marched in the morning! Over familiar roads billeting in familiar village quarters. Infantry once more on French roads, Infantry in wind and rain, tired and irritable in wretched quarters, longing for the homeland all the time. The Reich's Infantry! German Infantry. I lead the first platoon! In nomine Dei! [In God's Name!]'[2]

The postwar generation has had enormous difficulties reconciling and identifying with soldiers who clearly believed in God on the one hand and were seemingly decent human beings, yet on the other appeared receptive to a racist philosophy that enjoined them to disregard international law and the laws of armed conflict. One German soldier after the war, removed from the prevailing conditions that shaped and moulded him, gave an exasperated and often misconstrued view of the '*Landser*' (the German equivalent of the British 'Tommy') on the eve of 'Barbarossa':

> 'For me, it was a matter of course to become a soldier. Voluntary — not obliged to eh! If I hadn't been called up I would have reported voluntarily in '39. But not because of patriotism. I must say, all this sense of mission and "hurrah!" That wasn't it at all. It was a family thing. My father was strict, but right.'

An element of racism formed an integral part of the society that had developed from the Imperial period, subdued to some extent during the Weimar Republic but more overt after 1933. He continued:

> 'I was convinced we had to turn the Bolsheviks back. It has taken two World Wars — more! During peacetime alone the Bolsheviks had taken a human toll of eight million people. There you are! I found it shameful [he raised his voice angrily] that the German soldier is characterised as a murderer!'[3]

To comprehend this statement, one must penetrate and attempt to identify some of the aspects and atmosphere that characterised the Nazi social fabric. Its outward manifestation was to reflect and impact upon the character and conduct of the German soldier. The soldier was under peer pressure to conform to the commonly accepted prejudices of his fellows, which had the effect of intensifying them. In a letter a month before the invasion of Russia, one conscript related a conversation with his parents:

> 'While eating dinner the subject of the Jews came up. To my astonishment everyone agreed that Jews must disappear from the earth.'[4]

Those disagreeing with such a notion were unlikely to identify themselves by standing apart from the crowd and speaking up. Indeed, the whole ethos of army service was about subjugating oneself to the whole. Such unquestioning obedience was likewise required by the Nazi state which the soldier served. It was, therefore, a question of individual choice and personal ethics in an environment demanding corporate obedience. The state in time insidiously corrupted values, which, if they were not changed, were effectively subdued. Margot Hielscher, an actress, explained:

'I lived in Friedrichstrasse near the Kurfürstendamm
[in Berlin] *and many Jewish citizens lived in this district, so I experienced how they were treated by the shopkeepers and customers inside the shops. It was shameful. More shameful was the way we behaved. We were cowardly. We — unfortunately — simply turned away or failed to hear anything.'*[5]

National Socialism exploited all the modern means at its disposal to institute social change — in particular the media of radio and film. Both were cheap. The Nazi regime ensured radio receivers were mass-produced and offered at little cost, while the cinema was popular and readily available. A breathless pace of change was achieved from 1933 onwards. Modern ideologies tended, in any case, to blur the process of choice and action. This was particularly the case for the young, many of whom were to be conscripted into military service. 'There was no time to catch one's breath, no time to reflect, no refuge from the endless pressure to participate.'[6]

Some three million German soldiers and their allies were poised to attack the Soviet Union on 22 June 1941. How aware were they that there was some choice regarding the values they were ordered to compromise? Some 17–19 million Germans were eventually to serve on the Russian front from an overall total of 19–20 million under arms. Although all were old enough to kill as combat soldiers, they were completely naïve in terms of political awareness. Many actually reached adulthood during their service, but their only experience of politics was within a totalitarian state. They have since often been morally judged by historians who had only ever been exposed to the principles and values of the modern democratic constitutional state. Both conceptions are poles apart in terms of a common shared experience. Max Kuhnert, a German cavalry trooper, recalled the stultifying transition from civilian to military life. Even with six months' *Arbeitsdienst* behind him, where 'we had comradeship and learned discipline' with a healthy life, the shock when it came was considerable:

'For the first six months it was almost unbearable; we felt that we had lost our identity as slowly but surely we were moulded into soldiers. Politics never entered into it — in fact, no one in the army was allowed to vote.'[7]

Political choice is irrelevant when the vast majority of the population has no conception of what can or should be put in place of a totalitarian state. History also suggests[8] that brutal dictatorships inspire certain patterns of behaviour among people that in normal circumstances would be considered unusual, unappealing or even repulsive. Siegfried Knappe, serving as a young officer in 1938, recalled the impact of the *Kristallnacht* (pogrom conducted against the Jews in Berlin) among his fellows. 'We did not talk about it in the barracks,' he said, 'because we were ashamed that our government would permit such a thing to happen.' Reluctance to discuss such sensitive issues was not unusual. Knappe admitted: 'strong anti-Semitism

had always been just beneath the surface in the German population, but no one I knew supported this kind of excess.'[9] A revealing statement, indicative of the then prevalent flaw within the German character, true for officers and soldiers alike. Anti-Semitic excess was not even identifiable as such to many. Helmut Schmidt, a young Luftwaffe Flak officer serving with the 1st Panzer Division poised to invade Russia, has succinctly summed up the dilemma. His age group, he reasoned after the war, had no standard to measure themselves by, declaring:

'My generation and those that followed, the young people [who were conscripted] *had absolutely no yardstick to measure themselves by. We were therefore offered up* [to Hitler] *with no hope.'*[10]

Personal standards and individual moral resilience were, therefore, in conflict with accepted peer pressure. There was not a general collective or even total acceptance of Nazi standards; many simply chose to pursue the line of least resistance. Such a course may not even have involved conscious reflection. All one had to do was 'join in', which the Nazi *Weltanschauung* philosophy enjoined all to do. Knappe claimed Hitler's 'hatred of the Jews made no sense to any of us, and we just wanted to distance ourselves from the ugly side of his character'.[11] It was easier, indeed safer, to do nothing. This tied in with the soldiers' universal earthy philosophy of 'not volunteering', neither should anyone 'stick his neck out'. Inge Aicher-Scholl exemplified the consequences of an alternative course. Her brother and sister were to be executed two years later as members of the 'White Rose' Resistance Group to Hitler. On being arrested and questioned by the Gestapo, she was under no illusion where alternative philosophical paths might lead:

'I was only 19 at the time, and it was such a shock that from then on I was always afraid. I was afraid of anything that might lead to my being taken to prison again, and that was exactly what they wanted.'

She signed a paper agreeing that should she discuss her interrogation with anyone, it would provide grounds for a rearrest. It produced a persistent nagging fear. 'From that day on,' she said, 'I was afraid of prison, and this fear made me very timid and passive, just completely inactive.'[12]

Hauptmann Klaus von Bismarck, a battalion adjutant in Infantry Regiment 4, remembers he was shocked on receiving the Commissar Order. Communist Party officials, namely political commissars, captured serving with the Red Army, were to be shot.

'I rebelled against it and said, "No. I will not follow such an order." Numerous friends decided to support my view and that was what I reported to my CO. He simply received the report with a grim expression. He seemed a very decent sort to us.'

Infantry Regiment 4, waiting in its assembly area as part of the invasion force, was, as Bismarck described, 'a conservative regiment, still for the most part distinguishable as part of the 100,000-man army of the Weimar period'.[13] Hauptmann Alexander Stahlberg of the 12th Panzer Division heard about the Commissar Order from his cousin, Henning von Tresckow, a staff officer in HQ Army Group Centre. 'That would be murder!' was his assessment. His cousin concurred:

'The order is just that and for that reason we are not allowed to give it to the troops in writing, but you will receive it by word of mouth before the attack begins and will still have to pass it on by word of mouth to the companies.'

Appalled, Stahlberg asked from whom the order came. 'From the man to whom you gave your oath [Adolf Hitler]. As I did,' responded his cousin 'with a penetrating look'. Oberstleutnant Heinrich Becker, his commanding officer, formally briefed the Commissar Order to his officers and was met by a 'deathly silence'. Before dismissing them, Becker warned:

'There is reason to remind you of The Hague Convention on Land Warfare. I am now speaking of the treatment of prisoners and wounded. Anyone who abuses prisoners and wounded I shall have court-martialled. Do you understand me, gentlemen?'[14]

They did. Von Bismarck in Infantry Regiment 4 had determined not to shoot commissars because as a soldier and Christian he could not see why Wehrmacht people should despatch others simply because they possessed an alternative view of the world. They were all officers and took their own individual rather than collective decision on how they intended to conduct themselves during the coming campaign.

There were others with an equally robust alternative view. Unteroffizier Wilhelm Prüller with Army Group South confided to his diary on 22 June, following the announcement of the impending invasion:

'The fight between communism, which is rotting so many peoples, and National Socialism was bound to come. And if we can win now, it's better than doing it later.'

Anti-Semitism was never far beneath the outwardly decent demeanour of the majority. He noticed the Jews in Tschenstochov and other large towns 'are herded together', and that every man and woman is obliged to wear a white arm-band with a blue star of Zion on it. 'That's the way it should be in the whole world!' he confided. There was scant sympathy shown by the majority of German soldiers for the plight of the Polish population in the occupation zone. 'The people in general,' Prüller observed, 'are in a very depressed state.' They walked with heads down. Huge queues formed everywhere for food. 'The Poles won't have a very rosy time of it!'[15] he commented. Nor indeed would the Russians.

'ORDER AND DUTY' AND THE FÜHRER
'Order and Duty' were vital prerequisites demanded of the German soldier. He was familiar with them, because they were established Germanic qualities. The Nazi state harnessed Prussian virtues to its own ends. It was not a question of unthinking, unconditional obedience. They involved self-discipline and self-mastery: willingness to accept the consequences before God and man of one's own actions, whatever the cost. It was a philosophy that could be, and was, cynically exploited. It started at youth. Henry Metelmann, training as a recruit when the Russian campaign began, commented:

'Even though my father hated everything connected with the Nazis, I liked it in the Hitler Youth. I thought the uniform was smashing, the dark brown, the black, the swastika and all the shiny leather.'

Roland Kiemig, as a 14-year-old Hitler Youth, reflected, 'everywhere there was a certain regimentation. You didn't just walk around uselessly, you marched.' All this had a certain purpose. Metelmann's view was that training in the Hitler Youth 'meant the army was able to train us more speedily'. Therefore, 'when we were finally let loose on the Panzers, we knew what it was all about.'[1] Kiemig's basic training on entering the army subjected him to a rigorous regime that clouded his perception of values. They were replaced with those the army wished him to retain.

'They kept us on the run, they harassed us, made us run, made us lie down, drove us and tormented us. And we didn't realise at the time that the purpose was to break us, to make us lose our will so we'd follow orders without asking, "Is this right or wrong?"'[2]

There was rarely resistance to such a process. Götz Hrt-Reger, a Panzer soldier, explained it was 'totally normal training in how to be a social being'. They experienced the shock impact any soldier undergoes in the transition from a relatively sheltered civilian life to the rigours of basic military training. 'Of course,' remarked Hrt-Reger, 'if anybody — let's say — misbehaved, there would naturally be consequences.'[3] German recruits ran round in circles, frog-jumped, hopped up and down, drilled with full equipment, ran — threw themselves down — got up, and were made to repeat the process. 'Whenever I see a man in uniform now,' recalls Panzer soldier Hans Becker,[4] 'I picture him lying on his face waiting for permission to take his nose out of the mud.' The aim was to wear the recruit down until he responded automatically with no resistance. It worked. Kiemig realised that:

'This drill — Ach! inhuman at times — was designed to break our pride, to make those young soldiers as malleable as possible so that they would follow any order later on.'[5]

The decision to invade Russia was not likely, therefore, to generate anything more than superficial discussion, as also their personal moral conduct in that campaign. Leutnant Hubert Becker explained:

'We didn't understand the Russian campaign from the beginning, nobody did. But it was an order, and orders must be followed to the best of my ability as a soldier. I am an instrument of the State and I must do my duty.'

Discipline was ingrained. The corruption of values implicit upon acceptance of the Commissar Order was not a subject open for discussion. Many soldiers would agree with Hubert Becker's opinion voiced after the war. They knew of no alternative.

'We never felt that the soldier was being misused. We felt as German soldiers, we were serving our country, defending our country, no matter where. Nobody wanted such an action, nobody wanted a campaign, because we knew from our parents and the descriptions of World War 1 what it would entail. They used to say, "If this happens again, it will be fatal." Then one day I was told I had to march. And opposition to this? That didn't happen!'[6]

Faith in the Führer motivated German soldiers poised to invade Russia. The oath of the soldier 'Ich schwöre . . .' was made to Adolf Hitler first, then God and the Fatherland. Henry Metelmann recalled after swearing the oath, 'we had become real soldiers in every conceivable sense.' Metelmann's background and experience was representative of millions of German soldiers waiting on the 'Barbarossa' start-line. 'We were brought up to love our Führer, who was to me like a second God, and when we were told about his great love for us, the German nation, I was often close to tears,' he wrote. Disillusionment would follow, but in 1941 Hitler was at the height of his powers. Idealism and gratitude for seemingly positive achievements sustained popularity despite setbacks to come. Metelmann recalled with some affection what he felt the Nazis had delivered:

'Where before we seldom had a decent football to play with, the Hitler Youth provided us with decent sports equipment, and previously out-of-bounds gymnasiums, swimming pools and even stadiums were now open to us. Never in my life had I been on a real holiday — father was much too poor for such an extravagance. Now under Hitler, for very little money I could go to lovely camps in the mountains, by the rivers or near the sea.'[7]

The Weimar Republic proclaimed in 1918 had borne the burdens of a lost war. It was for many of its citizens simply a way-station for something better. Values such as thrift and hard work had been made irrelevant by inflation. Martin Koller, a Luftwaffe pilot, pointed out: 'My mother told me, when I was born [in 1923] a bottle of milk cost a billion marks.'[8] The economy, characterised by high unemployment, low profits and negative balances of payment through the 1920s, appeared to be saved by the advent of the Führer. Bernhard Schmitt, an Alsatian, summed up the feelings of many Germans who voted for Hitler when he said:

'In 1933–34 Hitler came to power like a knight to the rescue; we thought nothing better could happen to Germany once we saw what he was doing to fight unemployment, corruption and so on.'[9]

Even Inge Aicher-Scholl, later to lose a brother and sister to the state, said:

'Hitler, or so we heard, wanted to bring greatness, fortune and prosperity to this Fatherland. He wanted to see that everyone had work and bread, that every German become a free, happy and independent person. We thought that was wonderful, and we wanted to do everything we could to contribute.'[10]

Even when events turned sour, Hitler's soldiers continued to believe in him. Otto Kumm, serving in the Waffen SS, admitted: 'Sure, we had some second thoughts at the end of the western campaign in 1940, when we let the British get away, but these didn't last long.' Nobody questioned the higher leadership; indeed, the Führer's soldiers believed in him. Kumm's doubts 'were superficial and didn't cause us to question Hitler or his genius'.[11]

The German army on the eve of 'Barbarossa' was confident in itself and its Führer. Grenadier Georg Buchwald stated: 'we had done well in France',[12] an impression shared by Hauptmann Klaus von Bismarck, who opined: 'We were highly impressed with ourselves — our vitality, our strength and our discipline.'[13] Victory over France had also changed sentiments back home. Herbert Mittelstadt, a 14-year-old, was astounded to hear his mother refer to 'our wonderful Führer' after the French victory. In his view, 'despite her various and special religious beliefs she must have pondered the matter over a period, that all would turn out positive, and that the war could be won.' His father had spent three years at the front in World War 1, and had 'probably always suffered a little with the trauma of the defeat'.[14]

Stefan Thomas, a medic and social democrat, was approached by an old veteran political campaigner who admitted that perhaps they were 'in the wrong party'. Thomas had cause to reflect: 'my father had lain three long years in the mud of Champagne before Verdun in World War 1, and now in 1940, one saw France fall apart in a three to four weeks' Blitzkrieg.'[15]

This confidence was reflected in the cameraderie and demeanour of the soldiers. As in all armies, *'Thema Eins'* (theme one) was women. Events, therefore, worked to their advantage. Panzer NCO Hans Becker remembered the 'magical' effect war decorations had on the girls.

'They loved to be seen out with an old campaigner, and what did it matter if his pay stretched no further than one evening a week at a local dance hall or cinema!'[16]

Landser jargon, 'soldier talk', adapted tactical military expressions to describe their relationships with women. *Annäherung*, the approach to an objective, was to 'trap a bird'. *Ranrobben*, to 'get stuck in now', 'frontal attack' and 'emergency landings' provided graphic conventional military descriptions of developing relations with the opposite sex.

Wehrmacht soldiers had never had it so good. One Panzer NCO dressed in black uniform, on losing his girlfriend's ring in a cinema, had his money refunded on explaining his predicament to the manager. The latter, acutely embarrassed, apologised on behalf of the teller who had mistaken his black uniform for the Hitler Youth! Unteroffizier Jürgen E., apprehended by an attractive girl on home leave, was enticed to join her in a flat. Hardly believing his luck he shyly followed. On entry the lights came on, and he found to his astonishment that he had been 'captured' by the young lady for a party. She won the competition she was engaged in, and the young NCO was awarded the prize within weeks. The lady became his wife.

Two signallers, Karl Heinz Krause and Hanns Karl Kubiak, based in eastern Prussia, were despatched to Berlin to pick up spare radio parts required for the forthcoming Russian campaign. Krause struck up an amorous relationship with a young cook named Bertha. Kubiak was persuaded to write romantic letters on behalf of the less than literate Krause, in exchange for a share of the resulting food parcels, regularly despatched by the cook. Even when both were subsequently wounded in Russia, Krause kept the relationship going to ensure the continuity of much appreciated resupplies, claiming he had received wounds to both hands. Bertha thankfully continued to be compassionate. Soldiers, as ever, made the most of opportunities between life and death.[17]

'PREPARED... TO FACE WHAT IS COMING!'
THE GERMAN ARMY, JUNE 1941

Conquering France in six weeks had been a military achievement of some magnitude, but in a number of respects the campaign had been unique. Many allied divisions were obliged to undergo their baptism of fire in mobile situations for which they were unprepared. General von Kluge's Fourth Army campaign evaluation, coolly detached, admitted victory had transpired under special circumstances. Factors such as the poor morale of the French Army, complete German air superiority, exceptionally favourable weather and the double surprise of the employment of massed tanks and aircraft all conspired to produce resounding success.[1]

German tactical principles were particularly sound. *Auftragstaktik*, a philosophy of mission directives giving subordinates maximum freedom of action in pursuing clearly identified tasks, enabled initiatives, once grasped, to be retained. General Erich von Manstein, a corps commander, similarly assessed that success was due to the enemy's inability to defeat German tanks. The lesson to derive for the future was that other nations would similarly mass their tanks, motorise their infantry and aggressively use their air forces to support ground combat.[2] There would be no more cheap victories. After the painful initial ordeal of combat, many French divisions fought well after Dunkirk, even against hopeless odds. By the end of the campaign in the West the German Army had lost one quarter of its total tank strength — 683 tanks were lost — and 26,455 men were killed, 111,640 wounded and 16,659 missing in action.[3] It had not been a total walk-over.

The German Army officer corps meanwhile had retained a healthy respect for the Red Army. If the experience of World War 1 was any indication, a fight with the Russian Army would be a serious affair. Its soldiers had always demonstrated innate combat toughness with the ability to endure great hardship. Their tactical doctrine, not dissimilar from the German, was aggressive. Von Kluge's assessment was that, although his Fourth Army motorised forces had performed well in France, they were not tough enough for Russia. They needed to be more aggressive in the attack.[4]

On 20 March 1941, he directed that training should concentrate on hardening the soldiers, since in Russia they would be without even the simplest comforts. Men and horses had to practise long-distance marches, be prepared to cope with chemical and biological weapons, and anticipate assaults, when they came, to consist of several and deep waves of infantry supported by tanks and artillery. German infantry weapon co-ordination would have to improve if ever they were to defeat such attacks. Soldiers needed to be tougher to cope with the inevitability of close combat and overcome their present aversion to fighting at night. The Russians, described as 'children of nature', revelled in night combat. Despite shortcomings, the Red Army was better equipped than the Wehrmacht's previous victims. German soldiers would have to copy the Spanish and Finnish infantry precedents of attacking tanks with explosive charges. The coming war would not be conducted on roads as in the West; limitless space and massive forest areas would need to be reconnoitered and cleared. German headquarters staffs would now be vulnerable. Normal security precautions would not suffice. Headquarters personnel should become familiar with their side-arms and expect to use them.[5] For some, it was a daunting prospect.

As successful as the German Army had been, its hasty expansion had resulted in organisational problems and insufficient training. Overall fighting ability appeared to have even declined. This was reflected in low marksmanship standards, a disinclination for close combat, night and forest fighting, and reluctance to exercise and bivouac in the field and dig entrenchments.[6] Hitler's policy of spending lavish sums of money on military barracks had softened his soldiers. Accommodation demonstrated just how much the German soldier of 1939 was spoiled and pampered compared to his 1914 counterpart. Modernised versions of these barracks are still in use today.

The infantry, although unable to set the pace of the coming campaign — which would be the task of the motorised formations — still constituted the bulk of the fighting power of the German Army. Only it could fix and destroy the pockets of resistance planned to be surrounded and held by the motorised formations until they caught up. Yet the German infantry was badly in need of a period of reform and consolidation following a series of conflicting demobilisations and reconstitutions. Lessons from the French campaign had been clear. More motorisation and effective reconnaissance units were urgently required. The pace of the campaign had been much influenced by the speed of infantry marching on foot. Infantry divisions spearheading advances in France created ad hoc motorised advanced battalions by pressing captured vehicles, including civilian, into service.

A more effective anti-tank gun was required to replace the 37mm 'door-knocker', so called because of its inability to penetrate allied tanks, as well as better use of artillery and artillery observation units. The reorganisation of the German infantry arm was now a conceivable option if captured French equipment was used. In the midst of the French campaign, Hitler officially directed the army to reduce in strength to 120 divisions, while concurrently expanding its mobile element to 20 Panzer and 10 motorised divisions.[7]

The resulting demobilisation provided the army with a reserve supply of weapons and equipment. Ten weeks later Hitler reversed the decision, calling for an expansion up to 180 divisions, to pursue the Russian campaign. With only 11 months remaining to the invasion, time and energy were devoted to creating new units and operational planning. Any hopes of modernisation — motorising infantry and artillery, introducing new weapons and standardising tables of organisation and equipment — were gone.

Occupying Europe and garrisoning the flanks and rear of the proposed invasion led to the identification of commitments which the German General Staff assessed would require the army to field 208 divisions by June 1941. There were other agencies also competing for the army's increasingly scant resources of manpower and equipment. Goering's Luftwaffe expanded its ground combat capabilities after the fall of France. On 3 December 1940 Hitler directed the creation of a parachute corps using the army's 22nd Infantry Division as an air-land nucleus. Two months before, 4,500 army paratroopers and 20,000 rifles and pistols were absorbed. British bombing raids over the Reich required the army — on Hitler's insistence — to turn over 15,000 Flak guns and 1,225 officers in the summer of 1940 to Luftwaffe air defence. On 8 November 1940 Hitler further ordered the expansion of the Waffen SS from two and a half to four divisions, and the SS Regiment 'Leibstandarte' to a full brigade. This prompted army officers to complain the SS were a 'wandering arsenal' led by men who had never seen combat, and that these weapons would be better served by 'Third Wave' conscripted divisions of World War 1 veterans. At the end of August 1940 Hitler ordered the army to release 300,000 metal workers back into the armaments industry. To expand to 180 divisions, the army drafted the age groups of 1919, 1920 and 1921. They began basic training in August 1940. They would finish one month prior to the Russian campaign.[8]

Hitler's instructions to double the number of motorised divisions was virtually unachievable. In May 1940 there were 10 Panzer divisions; this was expanded to 19 by June 1941. Tank numbers in individual divisions were halved to achieve the reorganisation. Obsolete PzKpfwIs and PzKpfwIIs were recalled because German tank production was still very low, at under 200 per month. Instead of fielding a Panzer division with 324 tanks as in 1939, the 1941 divisions invading Russia were to number about 196 tanks (in reality, due to serviceability, between 150 and 200). Creating 10 new tank divisions required the army to remove more lorries from the infantry; even so, one Panzer division was solely equipped with captured French vehicles. The German infantry would therefore march even more short-handed than before. Some divisions were totally reliant upon captured Czech and French artillery and anti-tank guns. There was no standard organisation for the swiftly raised infantry motorised divisions. These were basically rifle regiments (equivalent to modern weak brigades) with two battalions of lorried infantry and one of motorcycles; sometimes there was a mechanised battalion riding in armoured half-tracks.

Rapid expansion diluted quality. The German infantry of 1941 differed little from that of 1939. Practically none of the reforms suggested at the end of the French campaign were carried out. The Panzer divisions were more numerous, had more medium tanks — PzKpfwIIIs and IVs — but were weaker than their 1939 counterparts. Delivery of new vehicles within the reorganisation phase continued right up to the very last moment, some even to the assembly areas preceding 'Barbarossa'. Leutnant Koch-Erbach, a company commander in the 4th Panzer Division, took delivery of his 37mm anti-tank guns mounted in half-tracks 'shortly before 22 June 1941'.[9] The SS Panzergrenadier Brigade 'Leibstandarte Adolf Hitler' started the campaign with 2,325 vehicles of which 240 were captured. Over 1,200 vehicles were to break down quickly due to lack of replacement parts.[10] The 20th Panzer Division had been obliged to occupy its assembly area in East Prussia in May 1941 short of many vehicles. Replacements arrived, according to the official unit history, 'in parts, and initially only a few days before the start of the attack'.[11] The logistic system was straining to cope, and the campaign had yet to start.

The 98th Infantry Division had been demobilised after the French campaign and then reconstituted in February 1941. Training began in earnest, 'but "what is to happen to the 98th Division?" was a question that occupied everyone'. Moreover it appeared that the 'industrial holidaymakers' — those temporarily demobilised — had forgotten much 'during the interim period'.[12] It demonstrated that German soldiers were ordinary men. As in all armies, soldiers were subject to and (reluctant, even if they wished, to resist) peer pressure. Conscript soldiers were positively discouraged from being independently minded. The system operated as teams to be effective *en masse*. This was a factor of training. The soldiers for their part did not want 'to stick their neck out'. So nobody was going to debate the Commissar Order. The German soldier believed in his superior officers and the Führer, who had already demonstrated economic, diplomatic and, more recently, military prowess. If they were to invade the Soviet Union, well, the Führer knew his business and had it in hand. Soldiers were comfortable with *Befehl und Gehorsam* (law and order) and the 'soldierly' concept of duty. His officers were confident that, in spite of the difficulties confronting him, the individual German soldier was innately superior to his Soviet counterpart.

The 120 German divisions poised on the border of the Soviet Union on 22 June 1941 represented potentially the most lethal striking force yet seen in the history of warfare. They were in terms of technology and tactical proficiency far superior to their opponents and were to attack with the benefit of surprise and timely concentration of force. In ideological commitment they possessed a fervour and enthusiasm that would never again be matched by succeeding German armies. The cream of German youth was going to battle: 75% of the Wehrmacht's total field army and 61% of its air force. Oberleutnant Dr Maull, the battalion adjutant of Infantry Regiment 289, was awarded the Iron Cross just before he departed for Russia. He wrote to his wife:

'I have always striven through personal example to achieve the ideal. Such standards have never been more necessary than in the army today. I am totally prepared, ready above all else, to face what is coming!'[13]

What was to transpire was to alter the map of Europe for decades to come.

Chapter 3
The Soviet frontier

| **'It was the very picture of tranquillity.'** |
| *Soviet officer* |

'THERE WAS NO INFORMATION...'

Within the Soviet hinterland the Russian Army was on the move. Lines and lines of tanks stood motionless on railway flatcars waiting in open fields near the frontier area. Some 4,216 wagons loaded with ammunition were threading their way towards the frontier network; 1,320 trainloads of lorries puffed and hissed their way towards border objectives. The LXIIIrd Rifle Corps, 200th and 48th Rifle Divisions were still in transit as were many other units in the middle of June. A huge consignment of maps alone filled 200 railway wagons in the Baltic, Western and Kiev Special Military Districts. Possibly the largest-scale train movement in Russian history was under way, much of it unnoticed by German reconnaissance, all of it moving westward.[1]

About 170 Soviet divisions were within operational distance of western Russia, from a total of perhaps 230–240 divisions under arms, but not all at war strength.[2] These belonged to the First Strategic Echelon; 56 were already deployed directly on the frontier and 114 further back. Ten Soviet armies were located within four Military Districts running north to south (**see map**). To the north was the Baltic Special Military District with the 26 divisions of Eighth and Eleventh Armies, which included six armoured divisions. Next in line south were Third, Tenth and Fourth Armies, belonging to the Western Special Military District. It had 36 divisions, of which 10 were armoured. The Kiev Special Military District with Fifth, Sixth, Twenty-sixth and Twelfth Armies had 56 divisions, of which 26 were armoured. To the south was the Odessa Special Military District with a further 14 divisions including two armoured. Behind these forces to the north lay the Leningrad Military District with the Fourteenth, Seventh and Twenty-third Armies. They faced a proposed new German front of 1,800km stretching from the Baltic to the Black Sea.

On Friday, 13 June 1941, Moscow radio broadcast an unusual and incongruous TASS report which was printed in the Communist Party organ the next day. It stated:

> *'The rumours of Germany's intentions to tear up the* [Russo-German Non-Aggression] *pact and to undertake an attack on the USSR are without any foundation* [and are] *clumsy propaganda by forces hostile to the USSR and Germany and interested in an extension of the war.'*[3]

On the day this communiqué was issued, 183 Soviet divisions were in transit. Between 12 and 15 June orders were given to the western military districts to move all divisions stationed within their interiors closer to the state frontier. The entire First Strategic Echelon of 114 divisions began to concentrate directly in the border belt; an additional 69 divisions belonging to the Second Strategic Echelon began preparations and movement in secrecy and under cover towards the western frontier. Maj-Gen N. I. Biryukov, the commander of the 186th Rifle Division stationed in the Ural Military District, recalled:

> *'On 13 June 1941 we received a directive of special importance from District Staff according to which the division must move to "a new camp". The address of the new quarters was not communicated even to me, the division commander. Only when passing through Moscow did I learn that our division was to be concentrated in woods to the west of Idritsa.'*[4]

All the divisions of the Ural Military District received similar orders. The first elements of the 112th Rifle Division began moving by rail. Then the 98th, 153rd and 186th Divisions started to move. All troop movements were conducted in secret. Similar redeployments simultaneously took place within all the internal military districts of the Soviet Union, inside the Kharkov, North Caucasian, Orel, Volga, Siberian and Archangel Military Districts. A total of eight complete armies was thereby formed.[5] Five immediately and secretly moved to the Ukraine and Belorussia. The operation took up the entire spare capacity of the national rail system to achieve it and even this was insufficient for a concurrent simultaneous move of all armies. Soon some 860,000 reservists were crammed inside railway wagons on the move. Colonel I. Kh. Bagramyan, the head of the Kiev Military District operational department, recalled the frantic activity required to take the XXIst Rifle Corps under command. Its one mountain and four rifle divisions numbered 48,000 men. They undertook a gruelling 16,000km rail journey from the Far East. 'We had to provide quarters for almost a whole army in a short time,' he said. 'At the end of May echelon after echelon started to arrive.' Resources were stretched to the uppermost.

The whole of the First Strategic Echelon of the Soviet Army was being secretly reinforced. Activity on the frontier zone was not concerned solely with digesting the arrival of these large reinforcing formations; much regrouping along frontier districts also took place. Under the guise of changing summer camps, units drew closer to the frontier. The 78th Rifle Division in the Kiev Special Military District 'on the pretext of training exercises' according to the district official history 'was moved out to the state frontier'. Colonel Bagramyan recalls the instruction to move all five of his district's rifle corps to the border on 15 June, stating 'they took with them everything necessary for active operations.' In the Odessa District, Maj-Gen M. V. Zakharov, the Ninth Army Chief of Staff, oversaw the movement of the 30th and 74th Rifle Divisions on the same day. They 'assembled in woods to the east of Bel'tsy under the pretext of training exercises'.[6]

There is some controversy over possible Soviet offensive intentions in the summer of 1941. One view, based upon the massive rail deployment of troops under way, totally absorbing the rail network and to the possible detriment of the harvest, was that Stalin foresaw a full concentration of Soviet troops on the frontier by 10 July. Prior to the Russo-German Non-Aggression Pact, only divisions and corps had existed in Soviet frontier districts. Between August 1939 when it was signed and April 1941, the number of armies on the Soviet western border increased from none to 11. Three more arrived during May together with five airborne corps. Stalin could have assembled

23 armies and more than 20 independent corps if Hitler had not invaded on 22 June.[7]

Whatever the outcome of the debate, what is clear is that the Soviet build-up of forces on the western frontier by June 1941 was following a distinct and planned development. Third Soviet Army in the Grodno region, following reinforcement by the XXIst Soviet Rifle Corps, had an army boundary only 80km wide, with seven rifle divisions with an average divisional frontage of only 6.6km, when 10km might be considered normal. Apart from being the strongest unit compared to its sister formations along the western border, it had, unusually, a self-sufficient independent tank brigade in addition to its mechanised corps.

This army was clearly configured in an offensive stance. In essence Third, Tenth and Fourth Soviet Armies, numbering 36 divisions with 10 armoured, did present a possible offensive threat to East Prussia. Tenth Army's air force units were located near the border, while all the logistic bases and camps of the entire Western Special Military District were located well forward. Ten million litres of petrol were cached forward in Brest-Litovsk alone,[8] directly on the new German/Russian demarcation line.

Part of this apparent Soviet offensive stance is explainable by the practicalities and difficulties of deploying Soviet forces from the interior to the west, compared to the German build-up, capable of more rapid achievement because of the denser road and rail network on their side of the border. Soviet military doctrine from the 1930s considered that future conflict would involve armies numbering millions of men. Offensives need not necessarily await the complete mobilisation of these millions. There should be troops on the frontier, able to enter enemy territory on the first day of war. These would disrupt enemy mobilisations while covering their own. Marshal of the Soviet Union M. W. Tukhachevski, instrumental in formulating this doctrine before his execution during the Stalinist purges, advocated 'invasion armies' stationed near the frontier. These forces should cross the border immediately following mobilisation. Mechanised formations ought to be deployed within 50–60km of the belt to enable this. Factors such as these were influencing the form-up and deployment of the First Strategic Echelon near the border, well under way by June 1941.

Stalin's personal experience serving with a military district during the German advance into southern Russia in 1918 suggested to him that any future German blow would be delivered in the same region. A number of indicators supported such a premise, encouraging and probably accounting for much of the intense military activity between the Russian interior and the frontier in May–June 1941. It appeared unlikely to the Russians that Germany was sufficiently equipped at this time to attack the Soviet Union along her entire western border. Germany would be dependent upon and desire the economic resources of southern Russia. To seize them would require the capability to engage in deep operations maximising space, and penetrating with massive forces. Russia would need to block this move and attack elsewhere. A particularly favourable jump-off point might be the Bialystok salient in the Western Military District in Belorussia and possibly from Lithuania. Occupying such option areas in force would enable the pursuit of Russian *realpolitik*, applying the politics of pressure in future relations with Germany.[9]

As the Red Army deployed towards the western frontier in June 1941, it did not dig trenches and anti-tank ditches, neither were obstacles and barbed wire barricades erected. There was no perception of immediate threat. Divisions secreted themselves in woods near the frontier, exactly as the German units were doing on the opposite side. The crucial difference was that the massive force the Germans had assembled was ready for action. The Soviet force was not.

Even now German units positioned in woods across the frontier were striving to assess and gauge their future opponents. Officer observation posts were set up to observe the border area using scissor telescopes. Hauptmann Heinz-Georg Lemm, a company commander in the 12th Infantry Division, poised to advance with Army Group North, scanned Soviet positions near Gumbinnen in East Prussia. He commented:

'We received only poor information on the enemy and terrain in the area of attack . . . we had been able to recognize that the Russians had high wooden guard-towers, and had been able to observe the relief of the sentries and their supply procedures.'

Trenches were visible 800–1,000m behind the border. Information was sketchy. Aerial photographs revealed some Russian field artillery. The German assessment was they could anticipate a delaying action from two Soviet regiments from prepared positions. 'The maps we received,' Lemm complained, 'were poorly printed and provided hardly any information on altitudes, road conditions and forest vegetation.'[10] Likewise, Hauptmann H. J. von Hoffgarten, training in east Poland with a motorcycle infantry company from 11th Panzer Division, recalled that, even when training ceased on 19 June, 'there was no information on the Russian Army or on the impending campaign'.[11]

Despite the apparent lack of information available to troops at the front, the Wehrmacht's appreciation of Soviet strength facing it, two days before the offensive, was reasonably accurate in outline. *Abteilung Fremde Heer Ost des Generalstabes des Heeres* [the General Staff section analysing eastern theatre enemy forces] had identified a total of 154 rifle divisions, 25.5 cavalry, 10 tank and 37 motorised divisions in Europe. There were, in addition, seven or eight parachute brigades. In Asia it identified a further 25 rifle divisions, eight cavalry, and five tank or motorised brigades.[12] The location of staff headquarters and, in particular, mechanised units was generally known. The assessment, however, lacked depth, and rough assumptions concerning the potential effectiveness of German unit organisations versus Red Army formations were wide of the mark. Figures were broadly accurate, perceptions were not.

The Wehrmacht was to assault with a strength of 3.6 million men — just over three million German soldiers, the remainder Romanians, Finns and Hungarians. In support were 3,648 tanks and self-propelled guns, 7,146 artillery pieces and 2,510 aircraft. Opposing them in the Western Military District were 2.9 million Soviet soldiers with 14,000–15,000 tanks with at least 34,695 artillery pieces and 8,000–9,000 combat aircraft.

Right:
Strength ratios on the eve of 'Barbarossa' on 21 June 1941, showing the direction of likely points of main effort by both sides. Two Army Groups, North and Centre, were physically separated from Army Group South by the Pripet Marshes. The Russian stance of 'Invasion Armies' exercised a degree of *realpolitik* against Romania, which had allied itself to the Axis. This was the finest and technically most proficient force Germany had ever committed to battle. Blitzkrieg was to be tested against its most determined and best-equipped opponent to date.

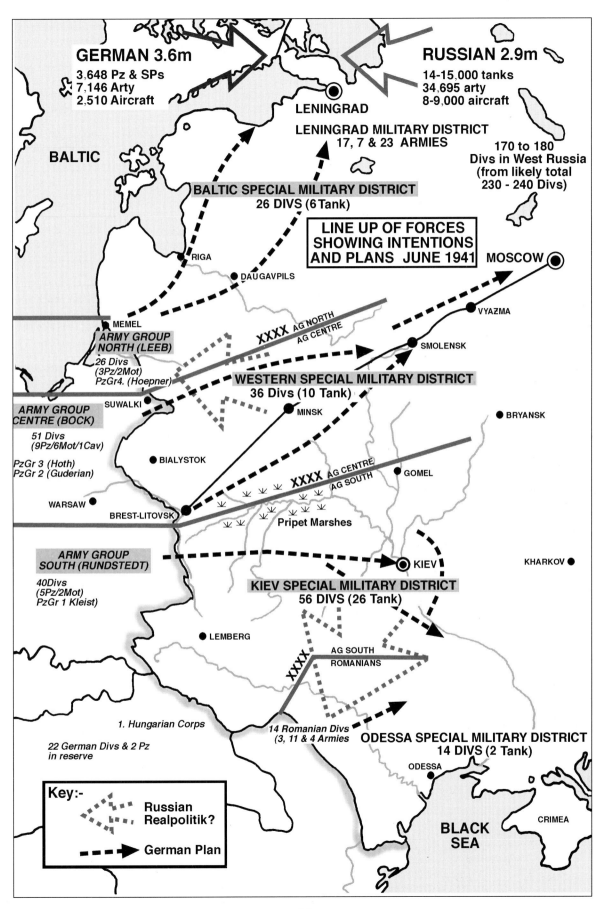

GERMAN 3.6m
3,648 Pz & SPs
7,146 Arty
2,510 Aircraft

RUSSIAN 2.9m
14-15,000 tanks
34,695 arty
8-9,000 aircraft

LENINGRAD

BALTIC

LENINGRAD MILITARY DISTRICT
17, 7 & 23 ARMIES

170 to 180
Divs in West Russia
(from likely total
230 - 240 Divs)

BALTIC SPECIAL MILITARY DISTRICT
26 DIVS (6 Tank)

LINE UP OF FORCES
SHOWING INTENTIONS
AND PLANS JUNE 1941

MOSCOW

RIGA

DAUGAVPILS

MEMEL

XXXX AG NORTH
AG CENTRE

VYAZMA

ARMY GROUP
NORTH (LEEB)
26 Divs
(3Pz/2Mot)
PzGr4. (Hoepner)

SUWALKI

SMOLENSK

WESTERN SPECIAL MILITARY DISTRICT
36 Divs (10 Tank)

ARMY GROUP
CENTRE (BOCK)
51 Divs
(9Pz/6Mot/1Cav)

PzGr 3 (Hoth)
PzGr 2 (Guderian)

MINSK

BRYANSK

BIALYSTOK

XXXX AG CENTRE
AG SOUTH

GOMEL

WARSAW

BREST-LITOVSK

Pripet Marshes

ARMY GROUP
SOUTH (RUNDSTEDT)
40Divs
(5Pz/2Mot)
PzGr 1 Kleist)

KIEV

KHARKOV

KIEV SPECIAL MILITARY DISTRICT
56 DIVS (26 Tank)

LEMBERG

XXXX AG SOUTH
ROMANIANS

1. Hungarian Corps

22 German Divs & 2 Pz
in reserve

14 Romanian Divs
(3, 11 & 4 Armies

ODESSA SPECIAL MILITARY DISTRICT
14 DIVS (2 Tank)

ODESSA

Key:-
Russian
Realpolitik?

German Plan

BLACK
SEA

CRIMEA

Of the German Panzers, 1,700 were completely inferior to Russian tank technology. Only 1,880 German tanks within the armoured spearheads were capable of combating the mass of even the older types of the 14,000–15,000 Russian tanks they expected to meet. Soviet industrial potential to make good losses was also grossly underestimated by Wehrmacht planners. Innate superiority in qualitative, racial (ie belief in racial superiority), combat experience, military organisational and technological terms was deemed to be sufficient to deal the required crushing blow in a short campaign. So confident was the Wehrmacht that after September, based upon a reckoning of anticipated casualty levels, there would be no reserves of manpower available in October.[13] Serious consideration of possible withdrawals or the likelihood of a winter campaign was not contemplated or assessed. The Wehrmacht was about to attack its most heavily armed opponent to date with fewer misgivings than when it had launched its western offensive, then with some trepidation.

Lack of knowledge was feeding a false bravado. In the 20th Panzer Division sector it was remarked that, contrary to the plethora of information available prior to the western campaign, 'not once were briefings received over troop strengths, to say nothing of enemy organisation tables or their equipment'. All that was issued were out of date reports or 'rough estimates'. Observation of forward Soviet positions revealed sentries stripped to the waist who had laid down their weapons and taken off boots and socks. 'This was taken as an indication of slack discipline within the Red Army.'[14]

General Heinz Guderian's Panzergruppe waited either side of the Soviet fortress of Brest-Litovsk on the River Bug. Following a visit to his forward units on 20 and 21 June, Guderian concluded:

'Detailed study of the behaviour of the Russians convinced me that they knew nothing of our intentions. We had observation of the courtyard of the Brest-Litovsk citadel and could see them drilling by platoons to the music of a military band. The strongpoints along their bank of the Bug were unoccupied. They had made scarcely any noticeable progress in strengthening their fortified positions during the past few weeks. So the prospects of our attack achieving surprise were good and the question therefore arose whether the one-hour artillery preparation which had been planned was now necessary after all.'[15]

The General decided not to cancel it.

Heinrich Eikmeier's artillery unit situated next to the River Bug continued to monitor the far bank. They were in position to observe the rail traffic that crossed the Bug to the west of the Brest-Litovsk citadel. Flowing across this bridge was much of the economic rail traffic agreed within one of the protocols of the Russo-German Non-Aggression Pact. 'On 21 June,' Eikmeier recalls, 'we were told that the next morning the war with the Soviet Union would go ahead.' But to their amazement they observed:

'Despite this, at six o'clock a goods train loaded with either wheat or coal passed over the Bug river to Russia. We could not understand the point of delivering up these locomotive crews as victims. Actually we were somewhat uncertain over whether it was right or wrong. Was it going to be war or not?'[16]

Nothing had changed. Within a few hours the war would begin.

'WE'VE NEVER HAD SUCH A SITUATION . . . WILL THERE BE ANY INSTRUCTIONS?'

Across the river in Brest, life went on much as before. It was a stiflingly hot summer. Colonel Il'ya Grigoryevich Starinov, a mine specialist and a military engineer department head, arrived in Brest on 19 June. He was due to attend manoeuvres with the troops of the Soviet Western Border District. Starinov saw that:

'The streets were blossoming with young girls and women in bright dresses. Ice-cream vendors screeched at passers by. "It's going to be very hot here!" At a trolley stop on Mayakovsky Square, a young fellow dressed in an Apache shirt was trying to pick up a leggy girl, but she had just turned up her sweaty nose and kept a haughty silence. A trolley sailed majestically along past beautifully decorated windows, flower stalls, and carefree crowds on the evening sidewalks . . .'[1]

Following famine, forced collectivisation and civil war, there had been peace in Russia for a few years. Some rebuilding was taking place. In a closed totalitarian society, the population had no idea of the momentous events about to unfold. An increase of military strength in border areas had simply resulted in the appearance of more uniformed soldiers. This was not so unusual. There were now no food shortages and in Minsk the shops were full. Milk and bread were plentiful. These were the 'good times' that some were to later recall. Natalie Shirowa recalled the prevailing atmosphere. People were relaxed and enjoying the weather:

'I remember the hot summer. We lived in wooden houses then, today they are of stone. But in those days we had two-storey houses, and when the weather was so hot, the people simply went out into the open. They fetched their mattresses and feather beds with them and slept under the sky. There was no rowdyism, people lived together then with some understanding.'

Clothing was even more fashionable in Minsk than it is now. There were fashion shows, cinemas and the shops were full. Natalie Shirowa emphasised, looking back:

'I must say that there was a great variety of things to buy in the shops. I remember I had a pair of leather boots that cost 36 roubles. My father earned 700 roubles then, so all in all we felt we led comfortable lives.'

Normal life continued. Football matches featured 'Locomotive' versus 'Spartakist' Minsk. There were sports parades. A degree of contentment was being felt in those areas beginning to create wealth again. The Soviets were proud of the establishment of the new border in Poland, which had recovered for Russia ground lost in 1918. Confidence that had faltered during the war with Finland was returning.[2]

Along the Soviet western border, however, there was a paradoxical sense of tension at odds with the heat wave that had engulfed the region by 20 June. Engineer Colonel Starinov in Brest-Litovsk observed:

'It was another marvellous sunny morning. The sun shone down on the heaps of coal along the railway track and on the stacks of glistening new rails. It was the very picture of tranquillity.'

Starinov, on exercise, had already heard reports 'about

German spies and aircraft violating our borders'. The TASS announcement of 14 June, castigating such rumours as 'propaganda' inspired by those hostile to the Soviet Union, had contributed to a lessening of tension but still did not account for the disturbing activity apparent on the other side of the River Bug. Starinov was informed by the Fourth Army Engineer Chief, Colonel A. I. Proshlyakov, that the Germans had been bringing up equipment to the western side of the River Bug all through June. Camouflage screens had been erected in front of the open sectors in their lines and observation towers. An artillery colonel told him that the TASS announcement had not changed the situation on the German side of the border, 'but our troops had begun to relax'. Nodding toward soldiers carrying suitcases along the Brest railway station platform, he remarked ironically:

'Not so long ago these guys were sleeping with their boots on, and now they're getting ready to go off on leave! Why? The TASS announcement!'[3]

Soviet military archives clearly demonstrate that the commanders of the respective military districts bordering the frontier were aware of the German build-up. Reports from troops stationed on the border were giving clear indications of an impending German attack. Although mobilisations of interior districts were producing a partial deployment toward the western frontier, no concrete measures were ordered by the Soviet General Staff to raise readiness postures on the border itself. Indeed, where measures were taken on the initiative of individual staffs, they were ordered to be reversed.[4]

The background to this bizarre response is explained by Dimitrij Wolkogonow, then serving as a lieutenant, but later to become a general and historian. Stalin thought the war would occur much later than was to be the case. In discussion with his closest advisors 20 days previously he announced that 'evaluation of intelligence suggests we cannot avoid war. It will probably begin early next year.' Soviet perception, Wolkogonow feels, was moulded by Stalin's view.

'Stalin was like God on earth. He alone said, "the war will not happen now." It was his isolated belief, and he wanted to believe it. And what is particularly important is that he was totally clear in his own mind that the Red Army was unprepared for war.'

Some 85% of Soviet officers serving in the Western Military District had only been in their appointment for a year; a direct consequence of the bloody purges of 1937–38 which had all but obliterated the officer corps. Stalin's view prevailed. Nobody would dare question it. Wolkogonow commented:

'It is likely that Stalin's deception over the outbreak of war was directly related to the earlier suppression of information he did not want to hear. What should not happen was therefore unlikely to occur.'[5]

Logical developments, however, continued their inexorable course. On 20 June Kuznetsov, the commander of the Third Army in the Western Special Military District opposite the German Army Group Centre, reported the Germans had cleared the barbed wire on their side of the frontier north-east of Augustovy, near one of the border crossings. The forested area of the Suwalki region had been particularly tense, suited as it was for the passage of agents moving in both directions. German reconnaissance had been active in this area, producing detailed overviews of tracks, the road network, the state of bridges, Soviet defence positions and field landing strips for aircraft. The removal of the wire was clearly an indication of impending attack.

Similar suspicious activity had been identified on the border of the Kiev Military District. Nikolai Kirillovich Popel, the Chief Political Officer of the VIIIth Mechanised Corps, attending the usual Saturday evening entertainment in the Red Army Garrison House, was not enjoying the party. He was totally preoccupied with distracting and disturbing developments. 'What's happening now on the opposite bank of the San river?' he constantly asked himself.

'No, it wasn't a premonition. How many times afterwards did I hear of that night "my heart told me" or "my mind felt it"? Neither my heart nor my mind told me anything. It was just that I — like many of the senior officers in the frontier formations — knew more facts than I could explain.'

The commander of the Sixth Army, Lt-Gen Muzychenko, decided to split up a running artillery competition. Only one regiment was allowed on the range at the same time. Infantry were also surreptitiously moved from barracks to fortified areas. The VIIIth Mechanised Corps was placed on high alert at dawn on 22 June by the Twenty-sixth Army commander, Lt-Gen Kostenko. The corps commander, Lt-Gen D. I. Ryabishev, was informed to 'get ready and wait for orders'. He confided to Popov, his political officer, 'I don't know what this means, but anyway I've given the order to stand to, and commanded the units to go out to their areas.' Staff officers alerted by the call-out appeared at headquarters to man their desks. They carried 'alarm-cases', so called by families, holding two changes of underwear, shaving gear and a small stock of food; the minimum necessary to go off to war without returning home. Popov noticed:

'The staff officers were grumbling. Really, what can be more unpleasant than an alarm on the eve of Sunday. The day is spoiled, the plans which the family has been making all week are broken. How could they not grumble!'

Popov was concerned. 'Our corps was not ready to fight.' They were in the process of regrouping. Newer KV and T-34 tanks were still arriving to replace obsolete T-26, T-28 and T-35 tanks. Some had arrived that week. The new arrivals lacked repair equipments and spare parts. 'How could our minds reconcile themselves to beginning a war in such unfavourable conditions?' Popov opined.[6]

Back in Brest, the weather conditions were idyllic. Colonel Starinov declared:

'On the warm evening of 21 June 1941, the staff officers of the Fourth Army, which was covering the approaches to Brest, were following a typical Saturday routine.'

Starinov's exercise had been cancelled, so 'we wandered around the picturesque town for a long time'. Georgij Karbuk, also in Brest that night, described how:

'On Saturday, the day before the war, we met with friends in the park. It was about ten or ten-thirty in the evening. Many people were in the park. In fact, it was the only place where you could get together. Orchestras and brass bands played, people danced, and we were happy. It was lovely and pleasant.'

But lurking beneath this carnival atmosphere 'was a certain tension within the town'. Like the anxiety prevalent along the frontier, a paradoxical feeling of pending unpleasantness was incongruously juxtaposed with glorious weather. Karbuk noticed as the evening wore on that:

'Groups of men in uniform began to surface. They all seemed alike, and attentive. They entered the park. We stayed at the entrance, and everything carried on with the bands playing. Just as we were leaving the park, within five to ten minutes, the electric lights suddenly went out. That had never happened before. We continued on further to Pushkin street, about half a kilometre away, and the lights went out there, too. Only a few lights remained now in the street, where at the cross roads there were a few groups. Later we discovered this had been caused by infiltrating German saboteurs.'[7]

Nothing further happened. Karbuk returned home and went to sleep. Meanwhile, to the north in the Third Army area there was a sudden and wild outbreak of shooting in the darkness. Tension, which had already been high in this forested border region, now manifested itself in gunfire, as German 'Brandenburger' soldiers from ZbV 800 dressed in Russian uniforms clashed with Soviet outposts they were attempting to infiltrate.[8]

Colonel Nikolai Yeryomin, a staff officer in the 41st Rifle Division, was awoken at 02.00 hours on Sunday, 22 June. He was concerned as he hurried from his small house in the camp. 'Ever since I had been stationed here, near Lvov,' he declared, 'this was the first time the frontier guards had called me out at night.' The summons appeared serious. Picking up the telephone, he heard a worried voice:

'Comrade Colonel, this is the commandant of the Lyubycha-Krulevkaya sector speaking. All along the state boundary the posts of my sector are reporting unusual behaviour by the Germans. Troops and armour movement can be heard on their side. Our listening posts have discovered that infantry has been massing since dusk. We've never had such a situation and I decided to report to you. Will there be any instructions?'[9]

At the same time telephone lines between the staff of the Fourth Army and the Western Special Military District, and to some divisions, were reported cut. Despatch riders were sent out until contact was re-established at 03.30 hours.[10]

Ninety minutes before, the General Staff of the Red Army released Directive Number 1, which raised the defence posture of the western military districts. It tersely announced:

'During 22. and 23.6.1941 a surprise attack by the Germans on the fronts of the Leningrad Military District, the Baltic, Western, Kiev and Odessa Special Military Districts is possible. Attack could be preceded by provocative actions.'

Troops were instructed not to react to provocations, 'which would enormously complicate the issue'. Nevertheless, all the districts were placed on the highest alert 'in order to meet an eventual surprise attack from the Germans or their Allies'. Marshal Timoshenko, the People's Commissar for Defence, the head of the Red Army, signed the order. During the night gun positions on the border were ordered to be camouflaged, and aircraft dispersed and also hidden before dawn. Troops were to occupy battle positions, disperse and camouflage themselves. Air defences were alerted in border areas, but not allowed to mobilise additional conscript soldiers. 'Black-out' measures were introduced at key objectives of military importance and in the cities. Timoshenko ended by stating: 'no further measures are to be taken without special directives.'

The message was telegraphed throughout the night. It reached the Kiev Special Military District at 02.30 hours on 22 June. The commander of the Western Military District received a copy at about 03.30 hours. Relayed onward to army staffs, Fourth Army HQ in Kobrin near Brest was contacted at 04.15 hours.[11]

H-hour for the German assault was set for 03.15 hours.

Colonel Nikolai Yeryomin with the 41st Rifle Division near Lvov heard:

'The hollow rumble of many aircraft engines, swelling and then dying down again, vibrated over the camp, approaching from the west and sinking in the east. There was no doubt that they were warplanes, and heavy bombers at that . . .'

Disturbed, Yeryomin sought to pass on this worrying information. 'For some inexplicable reason,' he related, 'I could not contact headquarters.' A pale dawn was already appearing in the east; Sunday, 22 June, the longest day of the year. Suddenly the teletape began to tick. 'I reported the flight of the aircraft and the behaviour of the Germans on the frontier,' he said. Back came the disappointing if not entirely unexpected response: 'Do not fire. Carry on with your observations. I shall at once report to the Chief of Staff. Wait for instructions.'

What was he to do now? The field telephone rang. It was a call from the frontier sector. An urgent metallic voice announced:

'Comrade Colonel, the Germans have opened fire along the entire front of my sector. They have crossed the state boundary. My posts are in action.'

It was four o'clock in the morning. Yeryomin recalled:'breaking the stillness, the reverberations of the first salvoes of gunfire reached us from the frontier'.[12]

Chapter 4
H-Hour 03.15

THE RIVER BUG... BREST-LITOVSK

Gerd Habedanck, a war correspondent, moved forward with the 45th Infantry Division. Its objective was the Russian fortress at Brest-Litovsk.

'We came from Warsaw through heat, dust and jam-packed roads to the Bug. We passed tracts of woodland bristling with vehicle parks, artillery batteries in villages and radio relay stations and headquarters staffs under tall fir trees.

'Silently, absolutely silently we crept up to the edge of the Bug. Sand had been strewn across the roads so that our hob-nailed boots made no sound. Assault sections already grouped moved along the road edges in mute rows. Outlines of rubber dinghies were discernible as they shuttled along, raised up against the light of the northern sky.' [1]

Joining the battalion headquarters in an old bunker, part of the original western defences alongside the Bug, Habedanck looked across the river where, 100m away, Russians sat in similar casemates. What might they be thinking? 'One could clearly hear them speaking on the other side,' he observed, while 'further within [the fortress] a loudspeaker sounded'. [1]

Rudolf Gschöpf, the division chaplain, had held a final service at 20.00 hours. He now watched the doctor and medical orderlies dig shelter-trenches alongside the forward dressing station of the IIIrd Battalion of Regiment 135. They presently retired to a small house nearby and chatted together, welcoming any distraction from the rising tension. At 02.00 hours they glanced with surprise at the passage of a Russian goods train, 'certainly with goods as part of the German–Russian economic agreement of 1939', puffing up clouds of steam into the night air as it crossed the four-span railway bridge into Germany. This incongruous reminder of peacetime was entirely at variance with the bustling activity around the heavy mortar that was being loaded in preparation outside their house.

'On the other side in the citadel, inside the houses, the barrack objectives and casemates, all appeared to be sleeping unconcerned. The waters of the Bug lapped peacefully while a tepid night lay over territory where, in a few blinks of an eye, death and destruction would break out.' [2]

General Guderian's Panzergruppe 2 had been ordered to cross the Bug on either side of the Russian fortress at Brest-Litovsk. Because the border demarcation line between Germany and the Soviet Russian zone in Poland was the River Bug, the fortress defences (which had already been conquered by the Wehrmacht during the 1939 Polish campaign, and subsequently withdrawn) were split. The citadel on the outskirts of the city was occupied by the Russians, while the old outer forts on the west side were in German hands.

Before the invasion of Russia Guderian was aware that 'the supreme German command did not hold uniform views about the employment of armoured forces'. Panzer generals wanted their armoured divisions at the forefront of the attack right from the start, to avoid the confusion of mixing tanks with slower foot soldiers. Other arms of the service were of the opinion that initial assaults should be spearheaded by infantry divisions after heavy artillery preparation. Tanks would then exploit after the infantry had broken through to a specified point. The fortifications of Brest-Litovsk might be out of date, but Guderian's view was that 'the combination of the Bug, the Muchaviec [rivers] and water-filled ditches made them immune to tank attacks'. Therefore an infantry corps was placed under command, one division of which, the 45th, was to assault Brest directly. Guderian concluded that:

'Tanks could only have captured the citadel by means of a surprise attack, as had been attempted in 1939. The requisite conditions for such an attack did not exist in 1941.' [3]

The fortress of Brest had been built in 1842. It consisted of four partly natural and partly artificial islands situated at the confluence of the Bug and Muchaviec rivers. In the centre was the Citadel Island, surrounded concentrically by three others: the western Terespol Island (referred to subsequently in the text as West Island), the northern Kobrin Island (North Island) and the Cholmsker Island to the south (South Island). The central 'keep' or citadel was ringed by a massive two-storey wall, easily defensible with 500 casemate and cellar positions, which doubled as troop accommodation. These positions were also connected by underground passages. Inside the walls were numerous other buildings including the 'white house' officers' mess and the garrison church. The thick outer walls provided good protection against modern artillery. The West, North and South islands provided an outer defence belt, which supplemented the citadel, with 10m high earthwalls. These were studded with bastions or old casement forts complete with towers, such as the *Nordfort* (North Fort) and *Ostfort* (East Fort) on the North Island. In all, some 6km of defence works ringed the fortress.

The objective, however, possessed an Achilles' heel. It had been built originally for all-round defence. Following the 1939 Polish campaign, the fortress network was split by the demarcation line separating the German and Soviet zones of occupation. The most relevant section, the forward defences facing west, were already in German hands. Moreover, only three gates allowed access to the 6km defensive ring in keeping with the original defence concept, adding to the reaction time required to man the fortress in the event of an alert. Maj-Gen Sandalov, the Soviet Fourth Army Chief of Staff, calculated this might take three hours, during which time the defenders would be vulnerable to considerable casualties. Only 2km of the ring faced westwards, now the main direction of threat, with room for only one infantry battalion and a half battalion of border troops. It is likely that on the night of 21 June there were about seven battalions from the 6th and 42nd Soviet Rifle Divisions in Brest in addition to regimental training units, special units and some divisional artillery regiments. [4]

They would be directly faced by nine German infantry battalions with a further 18 operating on their flanks. XIIth Infantry Corps, under the command of Generalfeldmarschall Kluge's Fourth Army, had been tasked to surround the fortress and clear a path for the vanguards of Panzergruppe 2. The inner flanks of the two Panzer corps forming it (XXIVth and XLVIth) were to be protected as they passed either side of the fortress. XIIth Infantry Corps intended to attack with three infantry divisions forward: 45th Infantry Division against Brest-Litovsk in the centre, with 31st Division left (north) and 34th Division right (south).

The 45th Division had three regiments (130th, 133rd and 135th) of three infantry battalions each. Its primary tasks were to capture the citadel, the four-span railway bridge over the Bug, five other bridges crossing the Muchaviec south of the town of Brest and secure the high ground 7–8km east of the town. This would open up the Panzer *Rollbahn* (main route) identified for Panzergruppe 2 to march eastwards towards Kobrin.

The division attack plan was based on two primary attack axes: north and south. The northern prong of a pitch-fork thrust was to attack across the West Island to the citadel, then through the North Island to the eastern side of the town of Brest. Two battalions from

Regiment 135, supported by two armoured train platoons, were earmarked for this task. Meanwhile, the southern prong would assault south of the River Muchaviec across the South Island with Regiment 130. The five Muchaviec bridges were to be taken by an assault-pioneer *coup de main* force mounted within nine assault boats. One battalion was held as divisional reserve and the three battalions of Regiment 133 were to be held back as corps reserve. Nine light and three heavy batteries of the division's artillery, supported by a group of nine heavy mortars and two 60cm siege guns would provide a pulverising five-minute preparatory surprise bombardment, before switching to nominated targets. The two flanking infantry divisions, the 34th and 31st, would also contribute to the initial barrage. A specialised, and until now secret, unit Nebel Regiment 4 (ZbV Nr 4) was to support the attack with newly developed Nebelwerfer multiple-barrelled rocket launchers. 'Hardly a mouse would survive the opening bombardment,' was the assurance given to the assault groups.[5]

There was no lack of confidence. Leutnant Michael Wechtler with the reserve regiment assessed that the operation would probably be 'easy', noting that the first day's objective was set 5km east of Brest. Having viewed the fortifications from a distance, the corporate view was that it appeared 'more like

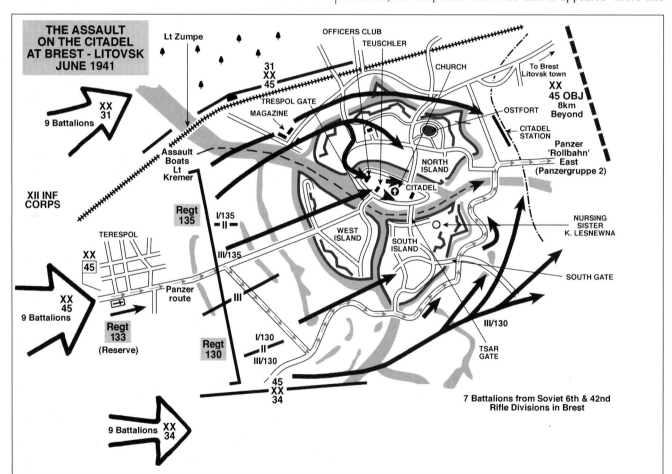

Above: The fortress at Brest-Litovsk was built across four islands at the confluence of the Muchaviec and Bug rivers. Its all-round defence design was adversely affected by the haphazard establishment of the Russo-German demarcation line in 1939. Nine German infantry battalions conducted the break-in assault across the islands either side of the citadel and a further 18 advanced on the flanks. The northern prong with Regiment 135 attacked through West Island, and a battalion was soon cut off in the citadel while a further assault broke into North Island. Regiment 130 attacked Southern Island and bypassed the fortress further south of the River Muchaviec. Nine assault boats entered the river to the west to capture the five bridging points in successive *coup de main* operations. It was a microcosm of the coming experience on the eastern front. An operation anticipated to last one day did not cease until German forces had formed the Smolensk pocket, nearly half way to Moscow, almost six weeks later.

normal barracks accommodation than a fortress'.[6] This optimism is reflected in the fact that only two of nine battalions, or 22% of the infantry force, would be in direct contact with the enemy to deliver the first blow. Three others would, meanwhile, b, deploying while four waited in reserve.

The 45th Infantry Division was a veteran formation of the French campaign, where it had lost 462 dead. Like many other infantry divisions massing on the frontier, the soldiers were optimistic and well rested. While billeted in Warsaw prior to the campaign, soldiers were given the opportunity to sightsee. Many took snapshots from open horse-drawn tourist carriages. Training had been pleasant. Crossing water obstacles had been the theme. Expertise in negotiating high riverbanks in assault formation and attacking old fortifications was practised. Conditions had been idyllic. Bathing trunks were worn during off-duty moments. Watermanship often deteriorated into high-spirited splashing and clowning with races between rubber dinghies. Inventive one-man rafts were pelted with rocks, soaking the grinning occupants. There was only mild conjecture over the purpose of the training.

As they left Warsaw for the 180km approach march to the assembly area, the band of Regiment 133 played. An initial downpour of rain soaked everyone, but spirits rose again when it was replaced by a continuation of the heat wave. The march was demanding but carefully managed in 40km stages, with bathing opportunities in the lakes en route. It ended 27km from the border, where the regiments were billeted in cosy village quarters. The last of the captured French champagne was consumed with gusto and final letters written home. *Scheinwerfer* (searchlight) units were formed by squads of men who had elected to shave their heads prior to the coming campaign (they were nicknamed 'shiny-heads'). Final 'squad' photographs were snapped inside the heavily camouflaged wood bivouacs. Few of these groups, it was realised, would ever muster complete again. Then in the early hours of 22 June the soldiers moved up to their final assault positions.[7]

Shortly before 03.00 hours, Chaplain Rudolf Gschöpf stepped out of the small house in which he had been waiting. 'The minutes,' he remembered, 'stretched out interminably the nearer the time to H-hour approached.' Dawn was beginning to emerge. Only the routine noises of a peaceful night were apparent. Looking down to the river he saw:

'There was not the slightest evidence of the presence of the assault groups and companies directly on the Bug. They were well camouflaged. One could well imagine the taut nerves that were reigning among men, who, in a few minutes, would be face to face with an unknown enemy!'[8]

Gerd Habedanck was abruptly awoken by the metallic whir of an alarm clock inside his vehicle. 'The great day has begun,' he wrote in his diary. A silvery light was already permeating the eastern sky as he made his way to the battalion headquarters bunker down by the river. It was crowded inside:

'A profusion of shoving, steel helmets, rifles, the constant shrill sound of telephones, and the quiet voice of the Oberstleutnant drowning everything else out. "Gentlemen, it is 03.14 hours, still one minute to go."'

Habedanck glanced through the bunker vision slit again. Nothing to see yet. The battalion commander's comment, voiced yesterday on the opening bombardment, still preyed on his mind.

'It will be like nothing you have experienced before.'[9]

AIR STRIKE... FIRST LIGHT

The pilot of the Heinkel He111 bomber kept the control column pulled backwards as the aircraft continued climbing. He glanced at the altimeter: it wavered, held, then continued to move clockwise past 4,500–5,000m. The crew were signalled to don oxygen masks. At 03.00 hours the aircraft droned across the Soviet frontier at maximum height. Below was a sparsely inhabited region of marsh and forest. Even had the rising throb been discernible from the ground, nobody would have linked it to an impending start of hostilities.

Kampfgeschwader (KG) 53 had taken-off in darkness south of Warsaw, steadily climbing to maximum height before setting course to airfields between Bialystok and Minsk in Belorussia. Dornier Do17-Zs from KG2 were penetrating Soviet airspace to the north toward Grodno and Vilnius. KG3, having taken-off from Demblin, was still climbing between Brest-Litovsk and Kobrin. The aircrew scanning the darkened landscape below for navigational clues were hand-picked men, with many hours' night-flying experience. These 20–30 aircraft formed the vanguard of the air strike. The mission was to fly undetected into Russia and strike fighter bases behind the central front. Three bombers were allocated to each assigned airfield.[1]

They droned on towards their targets. Below, the earth was shrouded in a mist-streaked darkness. Pin-pricks of light indicated inhabited areas. Ahead, and barely discernible, was a pale strip of light emerging above the eastern horizon. There was little cloud. Only 15 minutes remained before H-hour.

Behind them, in German-occupied Poland, scores of airstrips were bustling with purposeful activity. Bombs were still being loaded and pilots briefed. Aircraft engines burst into life, startling birds who flew off screeching into the top branches of trees surrounding isolated and heavily camouflaged landing strips.

Leutnant Heinz Knoke, a Luftwaffe Messerschmitt Bf109 fighter pilot based at Suwalki air force station near the Russian frontier, watched as groups of Junkers Ju87 Stuka dive-bombers and fighter planes from his own unit slowly took shape in the emerging twilight. There had been rumours of an attack on Russia. 'That appeals to me,' he confided to his diary that night. 'Bolshevism is the arch-enemy of Europe and of western civilisation.' Orders came through earlier that evening directing that the scheduled Berlin-Moscow airliner was to be shot down. This created quite a stir. His commanding officer took-off with the headquarters flight to execute the mission, 'but they failed to intercept the Douglas'.

Knoke had spent the earlier part of the night sitting in the mess discussing the likely course of events with other pilots. 'The order for shooting down the Russian Douglas airliner,' he wrote, 'has convinced me that there is to be a war against Bolshevism.' They sat around waiting for the alert.[2]

'Hardly anybody could sleep,' recalled Arnold Döring, a navigator with KG53, the 'Legion Condor', 'because this was to be our first raid.' Aircrews had been up since 01.30 hours, briefing and preparing for a raid on Bielsk-Pilici airport. The aerodrome was thought to be full of Soviet fighter aircraft. As they hurried 'like madmen' about the airfield, attending to last-minute preparations, they were aware of 'a glare of fire and a faint strip of light that signalled the approaching day'. Although these aircraft were not part of the vanguard force, already airborne, they still faced the difficulty of taking-off and forming up in the dark. 'So many things went through my mind,' Döring recalled. 'Would we be able to take-off in darkness, with fully laden machines, from this little airfield, where we'd only been a few days?'

The Luftwaffe was confident with its task but ,inevitably on the eve of combat, there was nervous trepidation. Hans Vowinckel, a 35-year-old bomber crew member wrote to this wife:

'I have not quite said what I truly feel, and really wish to say. Already there is insufficient time off to write. You will come to understand later why this is the case. So much remains unsaid. But basically I think you know exactly what I want to say!'[3]

Planning for this crucial air strike, which aimed to guarantee the requisite air superiority needed to support the ground force attack, had been going on at the Gatow Air Academy near Berlin since 20 February 1941. Generalfeldmarschall Albert Kesselring, the commander of Luftflotte 2, was given overall command of the Luftwaffe forces earmarked for 'Barbarossa'. Hitler, convinced of the innate inferiority of the Soviet Union had been 'stunned' by early reports presented on the Red Air Force.[4] Luftwaffe Intelligence (Ic) reports assessed the total strength of the Red Air Force to be 10,500 combat aircraft, of which 7,500 were in European Russia and 3,000 in Asia. Only 50% of these were reckoned to be modern. The number of aircraft they might expect to encounter over the front, not including transport and liaison assets, was estimated at 5,700. Some 1,360 reconnaissance and bomber types and 1,490 fighters were believed to be operational. These could be reinforced during the first half of 1941 by 700 new fighters. These formed part of a modernisation and re-equipment programme which would also update 50% of the bomber fleet but not increase its overall numbers. In support, the Red Air Force could depend on 15,000 fully trained pilots, 150,000 ground personnel and 10,000 training aircraft.[5]

The Luftwaffe, by contrast, on 21 June had 757 bombers operational from a total of 952, 362 of 465 dive-bombers, 64 Messerschmitt Bf110 *Zerstörer* fighters (the Bf110 *Zerstörer*, or destroyer, was a heavy fighter) and 735 of 965 conventional fighters, in addition to reconnaissance, sea, liaison and transport types.[6] Despite the Soviet superiority — they had three or four times the number of Luftwaffe aircraft — Luftwaffe staffs assessed overall enemy combat effectiveness would be much smaller. Because of the size of the operational area to be overflown and scepticism over Russian training and command and control capabilities, it was thought the Soviet air divisions would not to be able to mount joint operations with their ground forces. Luftwaffe General Konrad briefed Halder, the German Army Chief of Staff, selectively on the Red Air Force. Fighters were rated inferior to Luftwaffe variants and were described as 'fair game for German fighters' — as were the bombers. Red Air Force training, leadership and tactics were belittled. Halder commented in note form that Soviet leadership skills were 'hard and brutal, but without training in modern tactics, and mechanical, lacking adaptability'.[7]

German planning was characterised by this subjective rather than objective appreciation of capability. On 22 June 1941 Luftwaffe staff estimated that only 1,300 bombers and 1,500 fighters were fully operational in European Russia, this from an overall assessment of 5,800 aircraft. Moreover, radio intercepts had identified the assembly of some 13,000–14,000 aircraft in western Russia.[8] General Jeschonnek, the Luftwaffe Chief of Staff, had earlier briefed Halder that 'the Luftwaffe expects concentrated attacks against our spearheads, but thinks they will collapse owing to our superior technique and experience'. All faith was placed in the effectiveness of the pre-emptive strike, which aimed to catch the Red Air Force vulnerable and at peace on the ground. 'Russian ground organisations, being organic to operational flying units,' Jeschonnek explained, 'are clumsy and, once disrupted, cannot be readily restored.'[9]

Kesselring's mission was clear:

'My orders from the C-in-C Luftwaffe were primarily to gain air superiority, and if possible, air supremacy, and to support the army, especially the Panzer groups, in their battle with the Russian Army. Any further assignments would lead to a harmful dissipation and must at first be shelved.'[10]

Contrary to the planning priorities that had been accorded the Luftwaffe for the invasion of the West, the army this time was to have final say on the timing of H-hour. It was set for 03.15 hours on 22 June. The decision had emanated from a heated and protracted debate between the General Staffs of both land and air forces. 'My Geschwader, to get into formation and attack in force, need daylight' observed Kesselring. 'If the army persists in marching in darkness, it will be a whole hour before we can be over the enemy's airfields, and by then the birds will have flown.' The army had to assault at first light to achieve maximum tactical surprise, but thereafter wanted the Red Air Force kept at bay. Generalfeldmarschall Fedor von Bock, commanding Army Group Centre, responded: 'the enemy will be put on his guard the moment your aircraft are heard crossing the frontier. From then on the whole element of surprise will be lost.' Zero hour was fixed at daybreak against the wishes of the Luftwaffe 'for very convincing ground tactical reasons,' recalled Kesselring. 'This was a great handicap to us, but we managed to overcome it.'[11] The compromise was selective pre-emptive night attacks conducted by specially trained crews. These should cause sufficient mayhem on the ground to delay any concerted response before the arrival of the main strike waves.

Sixty per cent of the Luftwaffe's strength was deployed along the frontier with the Soviet Union on 22 June: 1,400 of its 1,945 operational aircraft, of which 1,280 were serviceable. They were assembled in four Luftflotten, warming up or training over airstrips dispersed across the new front. Luftflotte 1 would support Army Group North; Luftflotte 2 with 50% of the strike force, was to attack with Army Group Centre. Luftflotte 4 would operate over Army Group South and Luftflotte 5 would fly in the north from Norway. All told there were 650 fighters, 831 bombers, 324 dive-bombers, 140 reconnaissance and 200 transports and other variants. To the south, the Romanian Army was supported by a further 230 aircraft, including Hungarian and Slovakian machines; 299 Finnish aircraft would join later.

The force, however, was completely outnumbered by the enemy. German estimates of Red Air Force strengths were out by at least a half. Only 30% of the total European Russian element had been located. Fighter figures were misrepresented by half and bombers by a third. Nevertheless, the Luftwaffe was convinced it could deal with the threefold superiority it had identified by its own qualitative superiority and a devastating pre-emptive strike.[12]

Arnold Döring took-off in darkness with KG53 which managed, despite difficulties, to form up in the restricted visibility. They headed toward Sielce airport in order to rendezvous with their fighter escort. 'However,' to their dismay, 'our fighter friends were nowhere to be seen,' Döring declared. Crews anxiously scanned the skies from their cockpits. 'That is rich, we thought.' There was no alternative but to press on. 'After a slight change of course,' he recalled, 'we flew on stubbornly towards the target.'[13]

In Berlin the day had been oppressively hot and close. Josef Goebbels, the Minister of Propaganda, burdened with the knowledge of the onslaught, found it difficult to concentrate on routine. He was, nevertheless, confident.

'The business of Russia is becoming more dramatic by the hour,' he confided to his diary. Russian protests concerning German frontier overflights were studiously ignored. 'Molotov has asked for permission to visit Berlin, but has been fobbed off. A naïve request,' Goebbels wrote, which 'should have been made six months ago. Our enemies are falling apart.'

During the afternoon Goebbels hosted a visiting Italian delegation at his home at Schwanenwerder. The guests were invited to watch a recently released American film — *Gone with the Wind* — which all found impressive. Despite all this social activity, Goebbels admitted, 'I cannot relax sufficiently to give it my full attention.' His colleagues at the Ministry were informed about the coming operation. 'At home it is so close as to be almost intolerable,' Goebbels complained. 'But the entire world is waiting for the cleansing storm.' As his guests watched the long film to its conclusion, the Minister ordered his Ministry officials out to his house 'so that I have them close at hand'.

A telephone call from the Führer summoned him to the Reich Chancellery. Shining lights and open windows in the various army headquarters nearby provided mute testimony to the activity going on to finalise last-minute preparations for the impending attack. The code word 'Dortmund', confirming H-hour at 03.30 hours, was given at 13.00 hours. Should an unexpected delay occur, it would be postponed by a further coded message 'Altona'. Nobody seriously expected Altona to be transmitted.

Hitler briefed Goebbels on the latest developments. Wladimir Dekanosow, the Soviet Ambassador in Berlin, had made representations about illegal reconnaissance flights across the border, but had received yet another evasive response. After discussion it was decided that the time for reading the proclamation of war over the radio should be set for 05.30 hours. The international press and correspondents would receive their summons after 04.00 hours. 'By then,' Goebbels noted, 'the enemy will know what is happening, and it will be time that the nation and world were informed as well.' Meanwhile, the inhabitants of both Moscow and Berlin slept on, blissfully unaware of impending events.

Goebbels left Hitler at 02.30 hours, noting: 'The Führer is very solemn. He intends to sleep for a few hours. And this is the best thing that he can do.' He drove on to his own ministry building, noting 'outside on the Wilhelmplatz, it is quiet and deserted. Berlin and the entire Reich are asleep.' It was still pitch dark when he arrived to brief his staff. 'Total amazement in all quarters' was the response, even though 'most had guessed half, or even the whole truth'. They set to work immediately, notifying and mobilising the radio, press and newsreel cameramen. Goebbels glanced repeatedly at his watch. '03.30 hours. Now the guns will be thundering. May God bless our weapons!'[14]

Over the primary Russian fighter bases immediately behind the newly forming *Ostfront* (Eastern Front), trios of aircraft from KG2, KG3 and KG53 had arrived undetected. It was still dark, but a shimmering strip of light was now floating on the eastern horizon. The independently operating wings began their descent. By 03.15 hours they were roaring in at low level. Hundreds of SD2 2kg fragmentation bombs began to trickle from open bomb bays, invisible against the night sky. They fell among serried ranks of aircraft, neatly parked wingtip to

wingtip with personnel tents situated close by. It was peacetime. The Russian aircraft were neither camouflaged nor dispersed. Last-minute alerts had been to no avail. The small bombs were adjusted to explode either on impact or above ground. Within seconds, crackling multiple explosions began to envelop the lines of aircraft as light flashes illuminated the sky. Each bomblet had a blast radius of up to 12m. Airframes were lacerated and slashed by the release of 50–250 particles of shrapnel. A direct hit had the impact of a medium anti-aircraft shell. Punctured fuel tanks, ignited by subsequent detonations, produced multiple swirling fireballs, jetting dense clouds of boiling black smoke into the night sky. The result was total chaos. Attempts to combat fires by dazed ground crews were inhibited by vicious delayed-action explosions, which further demoralised and added to casualties. There was no guidance from superior headquarters. Individual stations coped as best they could.

It took some four hours for situation reports to get out. Third Soviet Army HQ in Grodno, north-west of Bialystok, called the Western Special Military District Chief of Staff:

'From 04.00 hours, there were aviation raids of three to five aircraft each every 20 to 30 minutes. Grodno, Sopotskin, and especially army headquarters were bombed. At 07.15 hours Grodno was bombed by 16 aircraft at an altitude of 1,000m. Dombrovo and Novy Drogun are burning. There are fires in Grodno. From 04.30–07.00 hours there were four raids against the Novy Dvor airfield by groups of 13 to 15 aircraft. Losses: two aircraft burned, six were taken out of action. Two men were seriously and six lightly wounded. At 05.00 hours the Sokulka airfield was subjected to enemy bombing and machine gunfire. Two men were killed and eight wounded.'[15]

Back at Suwalki air base in Poland, Stuka dive-bombers and Messerschmitt Bf109s converted into fighter-bombers were lining up and jockeying for position in the half light of dawn. Leutnant Heinz Knoke remembered the general alert for all Geschwader sounded at 04.00 hours. 'Every unit on the airfield is buzzing with life,' he recalled. With all the activity came an increasing awareness of the scale of this operation. 'All night long,' Knoke declared, 'I hear the distant rumble of tanks and vehicles. We are only a few kilometres from the border.' Within one hour his squadron was airborne. Four fighter aircraft in Knoke's Staffel, including his own, were equipped with bomb-release mechanisms. They had practised for this mission weeks ahead. 'Now there is a rack slung along the belly of my good "Emil", carrying 100 2.5kg fragmentation bombs,' he declared. 'It will be a pleasure for me to drop them on Ivan's dirty feet.'

The objective was a Russian headquarters situated in woods to the west of Druskieniki; it was to be a low-level pass. As they skimmed treetops 'we noticed endless German columns rolling eastwards'. As he looked up, he observed bomber formations 'and the dreaded Stuka dive-bombers alongside us, all heading in the same direction'.[16]

Kesselring's Luftflotten, using the ambient light of dawn, were now flying in formation, intent on delivering the main blow following the initial spoiling attacks. The first strikes were made by 637 bombers and 231 fighters penetrating Soviet airspace shortly after first light. Their objectives included 31 airfields.[17]

Arnold Döring, the Luftwaffe navigator flying in formation with KG53, flew over the River Bug frontier at 04.15 hours. Pilots and crew clinically went about their business.

'Quite relaxed, I made a few adjustments to our course. Then I looked out of the window. It was very hazy down below, but we could make out our targets. I was surprised that the anti-aircraft guns had not yet started up.'[18]

The formation started its bombing run. All along the Eastern Front from the North Cape to the Black Sea, waves of Kesselring's four Luftflotten crossed the border and immediately went into the assault. Stuka dive-bombers descended shrieking onto more easily identified targets, while medium bombers carried on to more distant objectives. Fighter-bombers bombed and strafed Soviet airfields. 'We could hardly believe our eyes,' reported Hauptmann Hans von Hahn, commander of the 1st Staffel of Jagdgeschwader (JG) 3 operating against the Lvov area to the south. 'Row after row of reconnaissance planes, bombers and fighters stood lined up as if on parade.'[19]

Döring's Heinkel He111 lifted as it dropped its bombs. Down below, the navigator observed:

'Smoke clouds, flames, fountains of earth, mixed with all sorts of rubble shoots into the air. Blast it! Our bombers had missed the ammunition bunkers to the right. But the lines of bombs continued along the length of the airfield and tore up the runway. We'd scored two hits on the runway. No fighters would be able to take off from there for some time.'

Other bomber groups would soon unleash their bombs over the same target. He glanced back, 'as we climbed again', and 'I could see that about 15 of the fighters on the runway were in flames as well as most of the living quarters.' They set course back to base. This had been their first bombing mission. 'We'd been so successful,' he reported 'that there was no longer any need to carry out the second raid we had planned on the airfield.'[20]

These early morning successes were not achieved without loss. In Poland, Siegfried Lauerwasser, a combat cameraman, was filming aircraft as they returned to their bases. 'That's how it started,' he stated, running the film for television after the war. Within a few hours it became apparent some crews were missing. It was 'a great surprise,' he said, 'when we were told "so and so" had not returned, and we waited'. They were not coming back. 'What a shock. Comrades, friends, human beings gone — with unknown fates — people you had lived with for days and months together.'[21] This was to be an often repeated experience.

The most devastating pre-emptive strike in the short history of air warfare was gathering momentum.

THE SHORTEST NIGHT OF THE YEAR . . . H-HOUR

Leutnant Heinrich Haape, medical officer of III/IR18, stood with his battalion commander, Major Neuhoff, and Adjutant Hillemanns on the crest of a small hill on the south-eastern border of East Prussia. They were peering into the darkness ahead, trying unsuccessfully to pick out recognisable features on the pitch-black Lithuanian plain stretching before them. Five minutes remained to H-hour.

'I glanced at the luminous dial of my wrist watch. It is exactly 3 a.m. I know that a million other Germans are looking at their watches at the same time. They have all been synchronised.'

Haape was sweating slightly. This was more from the 'awful tenseness of these fateful minutes' rather than the sultry night. He noticed:

'A man lights a cigarette. There is a barked command and the glowing end drops earthward, sparks on the ground, and is stamped out. There is no conversation; the only sounds the occasional clink of medal, the pawing of a horse's hoofs, the snort of his breath. I imagine I can see a faint blush in the distant sky. I am eagerly searching for something on which to fix my eyes and divert my thoughts. Dawn is breaking. In the east the black sky is greying. Will these last seconds never tick away? I look again at my watch. Two minutes to go.'[1]

The shortest night of the year was nearing its end. Although at ground level all was shrouded in a murky darkness, the sky was taking on a distinctly lighter hue.

Erich Mende, an Oberleutnant in the 8th Silesian Infantry Division, remembered a last-minute conversation with his commanding officer shortly before going into action. 'My commander was twice as old as me,' he said 'and had already fought the Russians as a young Leutnant on the Narwa front in 1917.'

'"We will only conquer our deaths, like Napoleon, within the wide Russian expanse," he pessimistically predicted. As by 23.00 hours there had been no revision of the original H-hour, they realised the attack would begin at 03.15 hours. "Mende," he said, "remember this hour, this is the end of the old Germany. Finis Germania!"'

Mende, however, was unmoved. He explained how 'amongst the youngsters there was optimism, because of the way the war had gone already. We did not share the doubts voiced by the older men, nor myself, those of my commander.'[2]

A testimony to the vast scale of the impending campaign was the variation of H-hours required to cater for the spread of daybreak along the 3,000km front. Dawn would appear in Army Group North's sector first at 03.05 hours. In the Central Army Group it was anticipated at 03.15 hours, in the south at 03.25 hours. All eyes along the massive front followed the progress of minute hands on watches. These final moments were to prove both interminable and unforgettable to men facing the prospect of imminent death or mutilation.

Hauptmann Alexander Stahlberg, with the 12th Panzer Division, remembered:

'We were sitting in our vehicles in deepest darkness. Many men had simply lain down on the ground in the forest. We could not sleep.
'Towards three o'clock, the NCOs went from one vehicle to another, waking up the soldiers. The drivers pressed their starters and slowly the columns rolled out of the forest, like the gradual emptying of a car park after some sporting event. This new 12th Panzer Division made an impressive sight when, crossing open country, one could see the whole body of 14,000 soldiers with their vehicles.'[3]

Walter Stoll, an infantry radio operator, positioned nearby on the Bug, remembered frantic last-minute preparations.

'Now we had to get a move on. Strike tents, load vehicles, continue to roll up some [signals] line, receive iron rations and ammunition. We even got chocolate, cognac and beer. Everyone helped each other.'

As they moved up, the roads became increasingly clogged with artillery moving into their final positions. '28s, 15s, 21cm mortars, there was no end.' They marched across log-corduroy roads, through sand and woods to their assembly areas. In a village jammed with self-propelled assault guns, they discarded equipment except that required for action. Vehicles were left behind. Infantry squads began to shake out in assault formation.[4]

Gefreiter Erich Kuby, sitting in his Horch vehicle on the edge of a wood, observed: 'it was a beautiful morning, cool and clear, with dew on the meadows.' Following the hustle and bustle of the previous week the 'calm before the storm lay over the land'. Hardly a single vehicle was moving in his sector. All lay motionless awaiting the attack. After receiving the order to drive forward, Kuby noticed the emerging dawn. 'The sky was yellow and red, the outline of the woods silhouetted in black and presently also the Panzers, waiting in long lines.' The tranquillity of the scene, with battle shockingly imminent, made a deep impression. 'There was not a single restless line within the picture,' displayed before him.[5]

Senior German officers assembled at vantage points to witness the anticipated spectacle of the opening bombardment. General Guderian, commander of Panzergruppe 2, drove to his command post, an observation tower located south of Bohukaly, 15km north-west of Brest-Litovsk. 'It was still dark when I arrived there at 03.10 hours,' he noted.

General Günther Blumentritt, Chief of Staff to von Kluge, the commander of Fourth Army, was standing in 31st Infantry Division's sector nearby. From there 'we watched the German fighter planes take off and soon only their tail lights were visible in the east'. As zero hour approached, 'the sky began to lighten, turning to a curious yellow colour. And still all was quiet.'[6]

In the 20th Panzer Division sector near Suwalki, the northern prong of Army Group Centre, the 'typical tension prior to the beginning of an offensive' reigned. Rows and rows of tanks waited, motionless, seemingly floating on mist or long dew-strewn meadow grass. Occasional scraping-sounding movements of shadowy figures could be discerned on turret tops as commanders stood to gain a better view forward, scanning with binoculars through an emerging twilight. A few minutes before 03.00 hours swarms of Stuka dive-bombers, followed by more bombers, began to fly up from behind their assembly areas.[7]

With two minutes to go, Leutnant Haape with Regiment 18, like many others, began to think of his wife.

'My thoughts turn to Martha, linger with her. She will be asleep, as will the sweethearts — and the wives and mothers — of millions of other men along this vast front!'[8]

Gefreiter Erich Kuby, with Army Group South, composed a last-minute letter to his wife while waiting in his vehicle in the dark. He predicted the emotional impact coming events would have upon her and his child.

'Now you know [about the invasion] as even I. That means at this moment — but not yet — because you will certainly still be asleep as the declaration of the Russian War is read out at 07.30 hours. But soon Mrs Schulz will turn up and you are going to be shocked. Then you will take Thomas into the garden and tenderly tell him that I will come back again.'[9]

The unsettling immediacy of their present predicament occupied all minds. Heinrich Haape reconciled himself with the thought that at least his wife was mercifully unaware. 'This night is as a thousand others, and that is how we wish it to be.' But for the waiting soldiers an uncertain future beckoned. 'We will march,' Haape accepted. There was one minute to go, 'And tomorrow night, where the horizon burns, there the war will be.'[10]

Down by the River Bug Heinrich Eikmeier watched as the first 88mm round slid easily into the breech of his Flak gun, nicknamed 'Ceaser'. All around, officers peered intently at stopwatches. Eikmeier took up the slack on the firing lanyard and waited. Would his be the first round to herald the new campaign on the *Ostfront*?

Ludwig Thalmaier with the *Geschützkompanie* (heavy weapons company) of Infantry Regiment 63 fitfully tried to sleep in a lorry, concealed in a wood. He had a light fever. Later recording diary impressions, he saw that:

'The grey dawn comes earlier here than in Germany. The birds began to chirp, a cuckoo called. There — precisely at 03.15 hours — the German artillery suddenly began to shoot. A rumbling filled the air . . .'[11]

Gerhard Frey, an artillery gunner, observed that:

'Punctually at 03.15 hours the first report ripped through the stillness, and at the same moment all hell broke loose! It was a barrage unlike anything we had heard before. Left and right of us flashed the muzzles of countless cannon, and soon the flickering flames of the first fires on the other side of the Bug became apparent. Men there were experiencing this awful onslaught of fire in the middle of peacetime!'[12]

Artillery Oberleutnant Siegfried Knappe had previously studied his target, the village of Sasnia on the Central Front, in bright moonlight. The tranquil scene was transformed.

'I could see our shell bursts clearly from our observation post, as well as the oily black and yellow smoke that rose from them. The unpleasant peppery smell of burned gunpowder soon filled the air as our guns continued to fire round after round. After 15 minutes we lifted our fire, and the soft pop-pop-pop of flares being fired replaced it as red lit up the sky and the infantry went on the attack.'[13]

Back on the artillery firing line, the noise was intimidating. Kanonier Werner Adamczyk with Artillery Regiment 20 described what it was like crewing a 150mm gun battery:

'Standing next to the gun, one could feel the powerful burst of the propellant's explosion vibrate through the whole body. The shock wave of the explosion was so powerful that one had to keep one's mouth wide open to equalise the pressure exerted upon the eardrums — an unopened mouth could cause the eardrums to be damaged.'[14]

Infantry and some armoured vehicles began to move forward. Soldiers advanced with trepidation and mixed feelings. Götz Hrt-Reger with an armoured car unit animatedly recalled the start of 'Barbarossa' in a later interview:

'Of course you're scared. You were ordered to move out at 03.30 hours and naturally you had certain feelings that set your stomach churning, or you're afraid you know. But there's nothing you can do. That's why I didn't want to give orders but rather follow . . .'[15]

The three German army groups closed onto a frontier stretching from Memel on the Baltic south to Romania on the Black Sea. Many of the images of this dawning of the longest summer day of the year were captured on *Wochenschau* movie newsreels. Spectacular film footage was shown to German cinema audiences within one week of the event. They showed flares hanging in a dark sky already streaked with dawn. Tracer fire curls lazily over a single-span railway bridge, flashes of explosion beneath reflect briefly on the outline silhouette of advancing infantry. On the Russian side, wooden watch-towers alongside the Bug burn furiously, like flaming torches, lighting up the sky above the dark mass of the opposite bank. Smoke rises majestically into the air, expanding languidly into an inky smudge, staining the light of an emerging dawn. Stark black outlines of soldiers laden with combat gear are discernible, moving swiftly through meadow grass and briefly silhouetted crossing the high riverbanks of the Bug. They pause and lie down as the pick-pock of opposing echoing rifle fire pins them down.

The *Wochenschau* images atmospherically convey an aura of menacing power and progress to their audiences, as combat vehicles and soldiers pass the distinctive stripe-patterned frontier marker posts. Cameras linger on scenes of flaming destruction. Repeated shots of artillery muzzles punching through and recoiling back inside camouflage nets that jerk convulsively, raising dust, with each concussive report of the gun, add to the aura of pitiless technological dominance. Birds, panicked by explosions in the target area, fly around the periphery of rising clouds of dirty coloured smoke. Lines of motionless Panzers, filmed awaiting the call forward, underscore a constant theme of latent lethality.

All along the 800km line of the River Bug, *Sturmgruppen* (assault parties) dashed across bridges and overwhelmed surprised Russian guards before they could detonate demolition charges. Rubber dinghies ferried across infantry assault groups, followed soon after by parties of engineers constructing the first pontoon bridges.

In Generalmajor Nehring's 18th Panzer Division sector near Pratulin, numbers of tanks simply drove down the bank of the Bug and disappeared underwater. Infantry nearby watched in amazement as tank after tank slid beneath the surface of the water like grotesque amphibians. These tanks, belonging to Ist Battalion Panzer Regiment 18 had originally been trained and equipped to wade underwater from ramp-mounted ferry boats built in preparation for Operation 'Seelöwe' (sea lion), the proposed invasion of England. In October 1940 the venture was cancelled, then resurrected in part for the foreseen amphibious assault crossing of the Bug.

The 'U-Boat' tanks were fitted with 3m steel pipes which protruded from the surface of the water as they waded across the river bottom, enabling the crew and engines to breathe. Exhausts were fitted with one-way valves and gun turrets were insulated by air-filled bicycle inner tubes. Bubbles from the exhaust were obliterated by the moving current. Total surprise was achieved as 80 of these Panzer amphibians emerged on the far bank, rapidly establishing a deep bridgehead. Russian armoured cars that had begun to menace landed infantry were quickly despatched.[16]

'The east is aflame,' announced Leutnant Haape, observing the progress of the assaulting spearheads. Infantry mainly led the way. Many of these men were still coming to terms with the surprise they had inflicted on the Russians. Gefreiter Joachim Kredel, a machine gunner in Infantry Regiment 67 of 23rd Division, had hours before queried his company commander's reading of the Führer Order. 'Soldiers of the *Ostfront*,' it had announced. Kredel turning to a friend asked: 'Did the company commander actually say *Ostfront*?' Feldwebel Richard von Weizsäcker (a future President of the Federal Republic of Germany), nearby with Regiment 9, refused to believe, right up to the point of going into action, that Hitler would seriously go to war against the Soviet Union. Leutnant von dem Bussche, a platoon commander in the same regiment, thought:

'Funny, almost exactly 129 years before, the Emperor Napoleon, supported by the Prussian Corps under General Ludwig Yorck, had started the great Russian campaign. We all know what happened to them. Will we do better?'

Soldiers sought to allay their acute uneasiness by engaging in purposeful last-minute checks. Rifle loaded and safety catch on? Uniform buttons done up? Helmet strap not too tight — or too loose? Hand-grenade arming mechanism screw easy to turn? Have I got an uninterrupted line of sight to the soldier nearby?[17] They awaited the signal to advance. Ernst Glasner wrote in his diary while waiting on the edge of the Bug:

'Involuntarily we counted the seconds. Then a shot tore through the stillness of this summer Sunday on the new Eastern Front. At the same moment a thundering, roaring and whining in the air. The artillery had begun.'[18]

Feldwebel Gottfried 'Gottlieb' Becker had counted off the final seconds, observing the railway embankment that was his first objective. As they ran forward, 'the echoes of explosions mixed with the incoming whine of new salvoes'. Becker and his platoon were astonished when they reached the embankment without once coming under fire. Only single shots rang out as the first German motorised column began to trundle down the road to his right; with that, worries vanished. The opening attack had proved unexpectedly smooth. Becker had reached his first objective without losing a single man.

Nearby, Gefreiter Kredel with Regiment 67 stormed forward as fast as his legs could carry him, his machine gun sloped across his shoulder. This was his first time in action. Propelling him was the sage advice of a veteran who had assured him 'the first wave gets through mostly unscathed, because the enemy is surprised. That's why those that follow get the full punishment.' Kredel thought it strange the way bullets whistled by one's helmet. He saw a wooden Russian observation tower reduced to matchwood by a direct hit from an anti-tank gun. 'Pieces of wood and Russians whirled through the air, and fell like toys to the ground.' Simultaneously the Germans' artillery dropped short and fell among their own ranks. 'Wounded cried out, and curses of "idiots — pay attention!" became mixed with the detonations of shells.'[19] Fire shifted abruptly forward, as if in response to these recriminations.

The campaign was already exacting its first toll of dead. Leutnant Hubert Becker with Army Group North remembered:

'It was a hot early summer day, and I had no inkling. We were walking across a meadow and came under artillery fire. That was my baptism of fire — a very strange feeling. You're told to walk there, then next to you comes an inimitable sound. There is a feeling that any minute you might be full of holes, but you get over that. Standing next to me was my commanding officer and you had to play the hero. You couldn't just lie down, which would have been easier. And then over there lay a German soldier. His hand was raised in the air which made his wedding ring shine in the sun, and his head — a little reddish and puffed up — had a mouth with lips full of flies. That was the first dead man I had ever seen in my life.'[20]

Gefreiter Joachim Kredel stormed forward with the 67th Infantry Regiment, still mindful of the likely retribution that must soon come to this attack, which had obviously achieved surprise. Casualties up until now had been light. His platoon commander, Leutnant Maurer, observed with satisfaction as

Kredel repeatedly hosed bursts of MG34 fire across the aperture of a Soviet bunker barring progress. There was a short pause of some seconds. No answering fire. 'Move! Bypass it!' cried the platoon commander, and soldiers scrambled around the flanks of the silenced bunker. It was a nerve-racking moment, the calculated instant of exposure.

On the far side of the fortification, Maurer and the lead elements relaxed from their tense crouching stance to a more upright position and continued to move forward. The burst of fire that spat out from the rear of the overrun position killed Maurer instantly and an NCO with two accompanying soldiers. Suspecting just such a ploy, the Russians had moved their machine gun to the rear of the bunker. Now the shock of the enormity of this first major loss sank in.

Unteroffizier Voss took command of the platoon, and with the support of a direct-firing anti-tank gun, managed with his soldiers to scramble up onto the roof of the bunker. Secure from the Russian beaten zone of fire, the position was held in thrall as the remainder of the company stormed by. Voss, marooned on the roof, could not get at the Russian soldiers inside. They held this 'tiger by the tail' the whole night long. Only a few isolated pistol shots punctuated the nervous waiting period. They were too tense to sleep. Much later, at daybreak, Kredel and Voss's group were evacuated from their exposed position and ordered to rejoin the company. A section of assault pioneers was brought up to reduce the menace with explosive charges.[21]

Surprise had been achieved. The campaign was barely hours old, yet men had already endured experiences that would haunt them for the rest of their lives. Years after these events, Karl Unverzagt, a *Fähnjunker* (officer-cadet) in a Panzergrenadier division, quietly reflected, pipe in hand, that 'we had shot into a scene where there had been dancing, drinking and singing, with people dressed in riding boots.' His unit had burst in upon this celebration. 'It was awful what our shells had done, something I will carry with me for the rest of my days — it was so terrible.'[22] Josef Zymelka, an engineer, said:

> 'Over there, behind the Bug, stood an isolated house. I reckon it was a Customs post. In the early days, before war broke out, we had even swam there, and in the evenings I had always sung "a soldier stands on the banks of the Volga." Before long, the Russians had also begun to sing, like in peacetime . . . After the attack I saw that the house was burning. Within four hours I was inside. On entry I saw that the soldiers — there were about 12 of them — had all been shot. They lay amongst burning, half collapsed rafters. They were the first dead I had ever seen.'[23]

At 04.55 hours XIIth Army Corps reported to Fourth Army HQ that 'until now, the impression is the enemy has been totally surprised'. The corps pointed to Soviet radio intercepts which were asking 'what should we do?' among other things.[24]

There had been Soviet troop movements prior to the German onslaught. German comment on this and reactions regarding Soviet preparedness are mixed. Committed National Socialists such as Leutnant Hans Ulrich Rudel, a Stuka pilot who participated in the opening raids, left little room for doubt. His unadulterated view was that 'it is a good thing we struck.' Based on in-flight observations, he later wrote:

> 'It looks as if the Soviets meant to build all these preparations up as a base for invasion against us. Whom else in the West could Russia have wanted to attack? If the Russians had completed their preparations, there would not have been much hope of halting them anywhere.'[25]

Leutnant Erich Mende, advancing with the 8th Silesian Infantry Division in the central sector, believed 'the Red Army positions were prepared for attack, not defence. We had, according to one view, pre-empted an assault by the Red Army.' In the fullness of time, he felt: 'to support this view directly is wrong. But on the other hand, quite possibly such an operation could have taken place within a few months or a year.'[26] Bernd Freytag von Lorringhoven, a Panzer officer serving on the staff of General Guderian's Panzergruppe 2, said after the war:

> 'At that time we had nothing to support the present view, often repeated, that the Russians planned an attack themselves. It became quickly apparent the Russians had adopted a defensive stance and were partly prepared when the German assault began. Infantry divisions were mainly positioned on the border, while the armour was located further to the rear. If they had been required for an attack, they would have had to be positioned closer to the border.'[27]

Whatever the intention, there had certainly been large-scale Soviet military deployments prior to 22 June. Perception often has paramountcy over facts, and will influence decisions in war. Infantryman Emanuel Selder was in no doubt that 'at no time' on the eve of the offensive 'could anyone seriously calculate the Russians were going to strike first'. His view was that 'the Red Army was totally surprised by the attack.' Unimpressed by any 'preventive war hypothesis', Selder noted that the Russians in some areas had absolutely no artillery support. 'Like us,' he pointed out during interview, the Russians constructed camps within woods near the border.

> 'But contrary to our bivouacs, theirs were not camouflaged. They were even showing lights with hanging portraits of Stalin and red flags. All this is basically contrary to the widely held impression that, despite these factors, the Russians were equipped for an attack.'[28]

This view is echoed by examination of the radio logs of attacking German vanguards. XIIth Corps in the central sector near Brest-Litovsk was reporting by 06.15 hours to Guderian's Panzergruppe 2 that 'according to radio intercepts and statements from captured officers, the enemy appears completely surprised. Maximum offensive effort by all corps is ordered.'[29]

Lines of motionless Panzers awaiting information from attacking infantry — *Sturmtruppen* — began to erupt into a haze of blue exhaust-shrouded activity. Dust began to rise as tanks lurched forward and clattered and squeaked toward newly constructed pontoons, or captured bridges. Leutnant F. W. Christians, moving with a Panzer division in Army Group South, remembered how young soldiers were already impressed at the extent to which the battlefield was 'dominated by our artillery and Luftwaffe'. Another aspect was also evident. Bodies from both sides were already lying by the roadsides. 'There was also a bitter side to this advance,' he remarked, 'the first dead', which 'gave the young soldiers a foretaste of what to expect'.[30]

DAYBREAK . . . BERLIN

The Soviet Ambassador in Berlin, Wladimir Dekanosow, had been attempting to contact the German Foreign Minister, Joachim von Ribbentrop, without success. Valentin Bereschkow, his First Secretary and interpreter, recalled: 'It appeared that the Reich's Foreign Minister was not in Berlin, but was at the Führer's headquarters.' Dekanosow, irritated, had been denied access. He was still unable to protest against the German border overflights.

'THE INVASION'

Right:
Swarms of Ju87 Stuka dive-bombers take-off in the early morning twilight of 22 June from secret pre-prepared landing strips in Poland. The air assault came as a total surprise. By dusk the Soviet Air Force had lost 1,811 aircraft and was rendered virtually ineffective.

Left:
Bombs burst across the runways of a Russian airfield north-west of Bialystok during the massive first light pre-emptive air strike. White pointers indicate neat lines of Soviet aircraft, parked as for peacetime.

Below:
German troops advanced across a 1,200km front. Rubber dinghies in the first wave river assault cross the River Bug. Troops watchfully observe craft nearing the far bank. The tension is palpable. As yet no fire is being returned.

Right:
Further south, crossing the River Prut in Romania.

Left:
German infantry under fire advance cautiously from bridging points.

Below:
German soldiers crossing a repaired bridge in the early morning mist of 22 June. Frontier markers are to the left. To their right a 20mm anti-aircraft gun maintains a watch for Soviet aircraft.

Above:
Soviet civilians listen pensively to the announcement of the German invasion broadcast across public address systems. They look up, seemingly uncomprehending; it is a stunning surprise.

Right:
Moscow 10 minutes after noon, listening to the news that Germany has declared war on the Soviet Union. 'It caused real anguish,' admitted a bystander, 'a feeling at the pit of the stomach.'

Above:
A gateway to the citadel at Brest-Litovsk with its fire-blackened windows bears grim testimony to the intensity of fighting to subdue this 'Verdun of the East'. It was the third time, including World War 1, that German soldiers had stormed the fortress.

Right:
'Wake up it's War!' Shock and fear are clearly reflected in the faces of these stunned Russian soldiers taken in the first minutes of the surprise attack on the Soviet fortress at Brest-Litovsk. Many did not even have time to get dressed.

Left:
At 10.00 hours on the first day at Brest-Litovsk, when these pictures were taken, one German infantry battalion from 45th Division was already cut off in the citadel. Pockets of Soviet resistance were forming behind them. German soldiers supported by a machine gun *(below)* are hurling grenades at forward Soviet positions covered by riflemen.

Left:
Further along the same trench they are supported by light infantry mortars. Crews crouch to avoid concussion from the mortar on firing.

Left:
A sequence of photographs showing a bunker system overrun by German infantry. Artillery, direct fire from self-propelled guns and flamethrower teams would precede the final entry by assault pioneer infantry groups — shown here — scrambling into the interior to finish off the surviving defenders. Each man in the group has a set predetermined task.

Right:
Once inside the strongpoint, the steel-plate entry doors are blasted open with satchel charges which are thrown into place. The soldiers are moving forward cautiously through the smoke caused by the detonation. At the front are grenadiers armed with canvas bags stuffed with stick grenades. These are lobbed into the interior of the bunker while riflemen follow on to protect them and deal with the defenders.

Left:
The group is picking its way through the wreckage of the entrance. Note the grenade bags attached to the hips of the lead man.

Right:
Covered by the riflemen above, the killing group armed with machine pistols moves in to subdue the occupants.

Above:
An indication of the number of men required to storm a bunker. One by one the fearful defenders are pulled out and disarmed.

Left:
Exhausted prisoners squat listlessly to one side as more of their comrades are dragged into the daylight. The rest of the 'Sturmgruppe' will be attacking the next bunker.

Above: South of the Pripet Marshes infantry paddle across the River Styr, silhouetted by the blazing wreckage of the bridge denied them.

Above: Capturing such bridges was often the key to a successful Blitzkrieg advance. This unusual picture shows a group of smiling Brandenburg Regiment 'commandos' posing on a captured lorry and wearing Russian uniforms prior to a raid. There were spectacular successes. Failure, on the other hand, due to an unlucky compromise or insufficient reinforcement, was equally total. The unit would be wiped out.

In the German Foreign Office, Erich Sommer, a Russian-speaking interpreter, was informed by his legation head, Herr Strack, to call Bereschkow at the Soviet Embassy. Ribbentrop would see the Russian Ambassador now. Sommer and Strack drove off to the Russian Embassy to escort the Soviet delegation back. Before they left, Strack informed Sommer that war was to be declared against the Soviet Union, 'but it had yet to be done'. As the official car drove along the Wilhelmstrasse on the return journey, the sun was only just beginning to rise. The occupants were preoccupied with their thoughts over the coming interview. Dekanosow felt at last he may be able to deliver his long-overdue protest. Sommer recalled his ironic remarks as the car glided past familiar Berlin landmarks. 'It promises to be a beautiful day,' the Soviet Ambassador said.[1]

Josef Goebbels, the Reich's Propaganda Minister, was anticipating the forthcoming radio proclamation and press conference. 'Radio, press and newsreel are mobilised,' he wrote in his diary: 'Everything runs like clockwork.'[2] Telephones had been ringing since 03.00 hours summoning the press. 'What is it this time?' many asked. Had the British decided to give up? Was the victorious Wehrmacht announcing a new objective? Cars sped through the dew-covered *Tiergarten* (zoo) towards the press conference room. It seemed it would be yet another hot stifling day.

Dekanosow and Bereschkow were led in at 04.00 hours to see Foreign Minister Ribbentrop. Erich Sommer, present as interpreter, witnessed all that transpired. The Foreign Minister was leaning lightly on his desk. Dekanosow attempted to raise the issue of certain 'infringements' affecting both nations but Ribbentrop did not take the matter up. Instead he indicated to his envoy Schmidt who began to read a memorandum 'in which,' Sommer said, 'the Soviet Union was accused of systematically dismantling German-Soviet co-operation'. As Bereschkow and Sommer were about to interject to translate, the Soviet Ambassador stopped them. For nearly half an hour Schmidt continued reading, itemising Soviet border infringements both in the air and on the ground. The Memorandum continued:

'Unfortunately, because of these unfriendly and provocative actions on the part of the Soviet Union, the German Government is obliged to meet the threat with all available military means.'

Sommer observed that, significantly, 'the Memorandum did not end with a declaration of war. Hitler had expressly directed that the words "declaration of war" were not to appear in the text.'[3]

Bereschkow could hardly believe what he heard. The Soviet Union was allegedly threatening Germany. In fact a Soviet attack was pending. Hitler had to protect the German people. Therefore, already — two hours before — German troops had crossed the border.

Ribbentrop stood up and offered the Soviet envoy his hand. 'The Ambassador,' Bereschkow said, 'was very nervous, and I think even a little drunk.' Dekanosow, not surprisingly, ignored the gesture. 'He declared that the German invasion was an aggression and the German Reich would soon very much regret launching this attack.' Sommer saw the Soviet Ambassador 'go red as a lobster and clench his fists'. He repeatedly said: 'I regret this so much.'

As Bereschkow followed his ambassador from the room, Ribbentrop unexpectedly approached him and whispered close to his ear that 'he was against this war. He still wanted to convince Hitler not to begin a war which he himself viewed as a catastrophe for Germany.' Bereschkow was unmoved. He was damning in his interpretation of these events after the war, declaring: 'in fact, there was no actual diplomatic declaration of war'. 'Stalin strove,' he believed, 'right up to the last moment, to avoid the war.' Diplomatic norms had been perverted, in his view, to maximise the military impact of surprise. He stated during interviews:

'We had not evacuated any Soviet citizens from Germany. Even family dependents and children were still there. All German families had been evacuated from Moscow before 21 June, with the exception of some embassy staff. There were still about one hundred German diplomats in Moscow at the outbreak of war, whereas in Germany something like a thousand remained. It is absolutely clear that when someone initiates an attack, first of all, he evacuates his people. That was not the case with us.'[4]

Shortly after the painful interview, at 05.30 hours Ribbentrop announced to the world's press that the war was already two hours old. Only 21 months previously he had returned from Moscow with his greatest diplomatic triumph: the German-Soviet Treaty of Friendship.

Meanwhile Liszt's *Les Préludes* sounded as a fanfare across countless wireless sets in the Reich. 'The High Command of the Wehrmacht announced the news of the invasion of Russia to the German people,' Goebbels grandly wrote in his diary:

'The new fanfare sounds. Filled with power, booming and majestic. I read the Führer's proclamation to the German people over all stations. A solemn moment for me.'

Afterwards he drove home to his Schwanenwerder lake residence in Berlin. 'The burden of many weeks and months falls away,' he wrote: 'A glorious wonderful hour has struck, when a new empire is born. Our nation is making her way up into the light.' Goebbels had every reason to feel pleased with himself. A diplomatic and military triumph was now in the offing. Surprise for this new campaign had most certainly been achieved. At Schwanenwerder the sun was now up 'standing full and beautiful in the sky'; he allowed himself 'two hours of deep, healing sleep'.[5]

By the time he awoke, on the new *Ostfront*, artillery NCO Helmut Pabst was already feeling a hard-bitten veteran. He wrote in his diary on 22 June:

'The advance went on. We moved fast, sometimes flat on the ground, but irresistibly. Ditches, water, sand, sun. Always changing position. Thirsty. No time to eat. By ten o'clock we were already old soldiers and had seen a great deal: abandoned positions, knocked out armoured cars, the first prisoners, the first dead Russians.'[5]

Josef Deck with Artillery Regiment 71 near Brest-Litovsk vividly remembers a Feldwebel talking in subdued tones on the way to their final firing positions. This NCO did not share the Reich Propaganda Minister's optimism. His view was that:

'A war was beginning in the East before that in the West appeared won. Moreover it had occurred to him that Germany had already once before come to grief in a two-front war.'[6]

Chapter 5
The longest day of the year

THE FIRST SOVIET POCKET IS FORMED — BREST-LITOVSK

Georgij Karbuk had listened to the pleasant melodies of an orchestra in Brest-Litovsk the night before. As dawn broke on 22 June he was rudely awakened by his father. 'Get up,' he declared, 'it's war!' Karbuk was immediately aware of the sounds of battle. 'It was not a case of hearing single shots,' he remembered, 'it was a whole barrage. The artillery firing on the fortress.' Out in the street soldiers were running. 'What's up?' the Karbuks asked. They said: 'Can't you see?, It's war!'[1]

Maj-Gen A. A. Korobkov, the commander of the Fourth Soviet Army, hastily despatched a situation report from his headquarters in Kobrin to the Western Special Military District in Minsk. Released at 06.40 hours, it read:

'I report: at 04.15 hours on 22 June 1941 the enemy began to fire on the fortress at Brest and the region of the town of Brest. At the same time enemy aviation began to bomb the airfields at Brest, Kobrin and Pruzhany. By 06.00 hours artillery shelling intensified in the region of Brest. The town is burning . . .'[2]

'We youngsters did not want to believe in a war,' admitted Georgij Karbuk, 'it was something too far away for us.' Suppressed suspicions were overtaken by the grim reality of events.

'We had a foreboding that war would soon break out. We had certainly seen the Germans behind the Bug, but in spite of this we did not want to believe it. Then when we saw the first wounded and dead lying on the pavement and all the blood — we had to believe that now there would be war.'[3]

Katschowa Lesnewna worked as a nursing sister in the surgical hospital located within 36 buildings on the South Island. 'Immediately with the initial bombardment,' she said, 'the buildings forming the surgical clinic went up in flames, as did the others.' There was outrage. 'We thought the Fascists would spare the hospital;' she complained, 'there was a large red cross painted on the roof. At the same time there were the first wounded and dead.'[4] Wooden buildings burned furiously.

Unteroffizier Helmut Kollakowsky, a German infantry NCO, spoke in awe of the opening bombardment:

'Someone told us that at 03.15 hours an overwhelming barrage would come, and it would be so strong, that we would be able to cross the Bug unhindered. It is impossible to contemplate any resistance after such an opening bombardment.'[5]

Gerd Habedanck observed the preliminary barrage secure within the battalion HQ bunker of one of the 45th Infantry Division's assaulting units. They heard a single artillery report break the stillness, then:

'We had barely heard it when the earth shook, boomed and rolled. Strong draughts of air blew into our faces . . . I risked a quick look outside the casement. The sky over us was lit up bright red. An infernal whistling, droning and crackle of explosions filled the air. Young willows were bent over as if in a storm . . . It is still not yet quite light and thick clouds of smoke darken the sky.'[6]

Wochenschau German newsreel cameramen were on hand to record the destruction. The films show mushrooms of smoke jetting up from the flash of impacts on the citadel walls; in the foreground, German artillery observers wriggle into better positions to see. Targets smothered in explosions disappear behind clouds of ground-hugging smoke and dust. Here and there, larger-calibre shell strikes abruptly shoot up huge geysers of smoke towering above the rest.

Chaplain Rudolf Gschöpf with 45th Division recalled: 'as 03.15 hours struck, a hurricane broke loose and roared over our heads, to a degree never experienced before or indeed later in the war.'[7] Hermann Wild was in a dinghy precariously weighed down by 37mm anti-tank guns. Alongside Infantry Regiment 130, he was part of the southern attack axis assaulting across the River Bug, and he saw 'the air filled with metal at a stroke'. Sheltering in a slit trench, 'one was shoved from side to side by the rhythmic explosion and concussion of shells'.[8] Most of Wild's company achieved the crossing during the short opening bombardment. The plan appeared to be working. Gschöpf described how:

'This all-embracing gigantic barrage literally shook the earth. Great fountains of thick black smoke sprang up like mushrooms from the ground. As no counter fire was evident at that moment, we thought everything in the citadel must already have been razed to the ground.'[9]

Gerd Habedanck's battalion began the assault river crossing of the Bug. His subsequent correspondent's account atmospherically re-created the scene:

'One boat after the other slid into the water. There were excited cries, splashing and the howling of assault boat engines. Not a shot from the other bank as blood red flames dance in the water. We jump on shore and press forwards.'[10]

Gefreiter Hans Teuschler, in the second assault wave of Infantry Regiment 135, was with the northern axis. He watched the rubber dinghies of the first wave enter the river at 03.19 hours. Artillery fire lashed the ground ahead, creeping forward in 100m jumps every four minutes, coinciding with the time it was estimated each wave would need to cross the river. 'The sky was filled with bursting shells of every calibre,' Teuschler observed. 'It was an awful roaring, exploding, crackling and howling as if hell was actually about to come on earth.' Even the attacking soldiers were intimidated. 'An uncanny feeling came over us all,' the NCO admitted.[11]

The two-pronged assault on the citadel of Brest-Litovsk was pressed home furiously. Two battalions (I and III) from Infantry Regiment 135 penetrated the North and West islands on the northern axis, while to the south two other battalions from Regiment 130 (I and III) attacked the South Island, attempting to bypass Brest town further south, following the line of the River Muchaviec. The imperative was to secure bridges for the Panzers. Leutnant Zumpe's 3rd Company sprinted across the four-span railway bridge to the north. They passed the customs post through which, barely an hour before, the last goods train from Russia had rolled. They took fire from a dug-out. Soldiers continued to skirmish forward until a dull thud signified it had been despatched with explosives by accompanying assault pioneers. An urgent survey of the bridge's superstructure revealed a demolition charge on the central pier. This was disconnected and dropped into the river. Zumpe flashed a green light toward the home bank. German armoured cars began to cross immediately. Within 15 minutes of the start of the assault XIIth Corps Headquarters received the anticipated signal: 'Railway bridge secured intact'.[12]

Leutnant Kremer's amphibious *coup de main* force of mixed infantry and assault pioneers from Regiment 130 and Pionier Battalion 81 had barely manhandled their nine assault boats into the water when they were engulfed by the same hurricane of fire that was plastering the opposite bank. A carpet of crackling detonations spurted multiple geysers from the river intermingled with fountains of mud and huge clods of damp earth which were ejected into the pale sky. Bitter-smelling clouds of grey cordite smoke wafted along the riverbank in the deathly calm that followed. Four of the nine boats were a complete wreck, floundering and settling in shallow water.

Bodies began to snag among the reeds lining the riverbank. Wounded soldiers shrieked for assistance. Hermann Wild, attacking upriver, remembered losing his close friend Muller to this unexpected strike. 'I had spoken with him only five hours before the assault,' he said: 'Even then he was already troubled by a premonition of impending death.'[13] Now he would never speak to him again. German artillery, likely the newly employed secret Nebelwerfer multi-barrelled mortar Regiment, had dropped short: 20 men were dead or hideously mutilated.

Kremer reorganised the survivors. Delays and the mind-cloying shock of the artillery strike stifled momentum, but they continued with the mission. Five surviving assault boats motored eastwards along the River Muchaviec toward the first bridge objective. To their left rose the imposing two-storey-high walls of the citadel fortress. Before long a storm of scything, splashing fire spat out from its dominating walls. Two more boats riddled with holes were swamped in the vicinity of the north bridge linking the West Island to the citadel. Survivors struggled ashore to the Citadel Island where they were to remain pinned down for two days. Leutnant Kremer had lost two-thirds of his force in the first few hundred metres. He rallied the surviving three boats and pressed onward toward the first two bridges. These were secured by 03.55 hours, jointly supported by a landward attack pressed home by the 'Stosstrupp Lohr', also from Regiment 130. Leutnant Lohr's group fired from the riverbank while Kremer's remaining trio of vulnerable boats carried on. The third 'Wulka' bridge was captured at about 05.10 hours. Kremer was elated. He insisted on raising a swastika flag over the bridge, his final objective, to mark the accomplishment of the mission that had cost his force so dearly. Lohr advised him not to expose himself but Kremer

recklessly persisted. As the flag was raised the hapless officer violently jerked backwards, mortally wounded, struck in the head by a single sniper's bullet.[14]

The northern axis of the 45th Infantry Division's attack made good progress. The IIIrd Battalion, having penetrated thick bushes and barbed wire on the high banks of the West Island, pushed on through parkland dotted with buildings burning furiously from the artillery bombardment. The 37mm PAK (anti-tank) guns were manhandled along by crews spearheading and supporting the advance. Presently the pronounced landmark of the Terespol tower, already considerably holed by shellfire, came into view as did also the tall two-storey walls enclosing the citadel. Shortly after 04.00 hours German troops penetrated this inner bastion utilising a dead ground approach enabled by the low north bridge. The flow of the German advance parted either side of the garrison church inside the walls. The northern prong had already pierced the fortress's keep.

Meanwhile the southern fork of the division's advance had gained swift admittance to the South Island via the south gate. German machine gun posts were established on the high earth walls that overlooked the island to cover the advance to the Tsar's Gate, the southern bridge entrance to the citadel. Hermann Wild's gun crews tore hands and bruised limbs manhandling their 37mm anti-tank guns onto heavy-duty rubber dinghies. 'The marshy approaches to the river made it difficult,' he said, 'but on the other side it was even worse!' Terrain east of the River Bug was a morass of water-filled ditches and swamp. 'In places the anti-tank guns sank up to their axles in mud,' complained Wild. 'We were pushed extremely hard to keep the momentum of the advance going.'

Lines of straining infantrymen pulled the PAKs over the high banks and down into the South Island. The wide 'camp road' through the middle was strewn with a carpet of leaves and branches scythed down by artillery fire. As they trundled their guns north along this route they passed groups of Russian corpses strewn at the road's edge. Many wore underclothes or were only partially dressed. 'The first Russian prisoners came up,' Wild remembered. 'They had very few or practically no clothes at all. One could see they had been totally surprised!'[15] Soon the 37mm guns were in action against light Russian armour.

Further to the south-east the IIIrd Battalion, bypassing the town of Brest, was winding its way around knocked-out obsolete Russian tanks. Counter-attacks by these and light amphibious tanks had either bogged down in the marshy ground or were destroyed by guns. Back at division headquarters, situation reports passed on by these lead units indicated clear success.

Timofei Dombrowski, a Russian machine gunner, excitedly described how 'again and again huge volumes of fire' engulfed his unit. 'The Luftwaffe from above, and at ground level everything that an army had at its disposal — mortars, machine guns — and all at the same time!' The implication of all this was sinisterly clear.

'We were positioned directly along the line of the Bug, and we could see the complete advance on the other side, and immediately grasped what that meant. Germans — it was war!'[16]

There were normally 8,000 Soviet soldiers stationed in the fortress of Brest-Litovsk, but only 3,500 were present at the time of the attack. It was a weekend, Sunday morning in peacetime, and many soldiers were on leave.[17]

The fortress was a small community in its own right. Next to the barracks and magazine was a school, a kindergarten and hospitals. Families lived alongside the soldiers. Nikitina Archinowa, the wife of a Russian officer in the *Ostfort*, remembered:

'Early in the morning I was woken up with my children by a terrible noise. Bombs and shells were exploding. I ran barefoot with my children into the street. We only had the opportunity to throw on a coat, and what a dreadful scene outside. The sky above the fortress was full of aircraft dropping bombs on us. Totally distracted women and children were rushing about looking for a place to hide from the fire. Before me lay the wife of a lieutenant with her young son; both had been killed.'[18]

The animated rhetoric and suppressed excitement characterising these postwar interviews with Russian eyewitnesses give some indication of the shock, surprise and fear activated by the sudden and unexpected German attack. A Russian policeman at Brest railway station, Nikolai Yangchuk, stated:

'At 04.00 hours when the German artillery began to fire from behind the Bug, we all reported, as ordered, to the station. Lieutenant Y. gave the orders to distribute weapons and defend the station.'

They moved down to the Bug bridge and saw German troops were bearing down on them. 'A great avalanche with no start or finish.' These men appeared lethally bent on their destruction. 'They had their sleeves rolled up, hand-grenades stuck in belts and machine pistols hanging from their necks or rifles at the ready.'[19] Dombrowski, defending on the river line, declared: 'some of our people ran away faced with this mass attack'.[20]

Wassilij Timovelich, a Russian engineer, accounted for the apparent ease with which the outer Soviet defences were overrun. 'Our fortifications were very well built,' he explained, modelled on their Maginot and Siegfried line predecessors. 'But the bunkers were not finished, and had yet to be occupied by their military crews.' The transfer of the Russian border westward into the Polish–Soviet occupation zone in 1939 negated much of the effectiveness of the original Russian frontier defences. Repositioning was still going on. 'Only 14 cupolas were enclosed by fortifications,' Timovelich estimated, 'and patrolling soldiers made certain nobody went inside. But,' he logically asked, 'who would want to do so? This was a border area!' The sector was not on alert. 'Troops were seldom inside the bunkers,' because there was no need; consequently, 'we slept in tents in the summer'. These tents dotted around the defence belt were overrun in the initial German rush. Many of the sleeping soldiers within were killed before they even realised they were at war. Surprise was complete. 'Soon an intense rate of fire' raked the unsuspecting bivouacs 'and bullets went whizzing through the tents. There were many direct hits,' Timovelich explained. 'Tents were riddled and human bodies flung out.' The defenders, confused and befuddled by sleep, had scant opportunity to defend themselves. Nikolai Yangchuk echoed this view:

'We had too few rifles. A reinforcement of one thousand men suddenly arrived and they were sent into battle. "Don't we get any rifles?" they asked. "Get to the front," they were told. "You will find some weapons there".'

There was no alternative but to move forward and lie in the trenches. 'There they waited until someone was killed,' Yangchuk soberly testified, 'before they got their rifles.'[21]

The initial German assaults profoundly shocked the garrison. Grigori Makarow, a driver in a Soviet infantry division, said:

'I felt in the first moments what war meant. All around me were dead and wounded friends and dead horses . . . German infantry came from the railway and began to penetrate into the fortress.'

Georgij Karbuk in Brest town said that 'after a few hours the first tanks drove through the town, followed by motorcycle troops, then the infantry'.[22] The Panzers were beginning to move.

The 45th Infantry Division sent a stream of optimistic situation reports to XIIth Corps headquarters. At 04.00 hours, 45 minutes into the attack, it was claimed: 'Thus far, still no enemy resistance'. A number of bridges were secured: the key railway bridge and another bridging the southern entrance to the citadel. Yet 'still there was no noteworthy enemy resistance'. At 04.42 hours '50 prisoners of war were picked up dressed only in shirts, because they had been surprised while asleep'. Momentum built up, additional bridges and fort emplacements fell into German hands. Three hours after H-hour, XIIth Corps was informed 'that the division believes it will soon have occupied the North Island'. Resistance was becoming more apparent with 'enemy armoured attacks between the bridge and the citadel' but the situation was in hand. Within five hours bypassing Panzer spearheads announced good progress, supported by effective Stuka dive-bombing attacks on 'Rollbahn 1', the main axis of advance.

At 08.35 hours, however, a more sober appraisal admitted that, 'there was still hard fighting going on in the citadel'. By 08.50 hours XIIth Corps began to realise that the 45th Infantry Division thrust into Brest was not mirroring the pace of flanking formations bypassing the built-up area. It was decided to commit the corps reserve — Infantry Regiment 133 — to alleviate a situation where 'thus far two battalion commanders and a company commander have been killed, with one regimental commander seriously wounded'. By 10.50 hours the pessimism was more pronounced. 'The fighting for the Citadel is very hard — many losses,' it was reported. 'We are going to try and lay smoke on the objective.' The attack against the citadel was bogging down.[23]

Gefreiter Hans Teuschler crossed the River Bug as part of the second wave with the 10th Company, Infantry Regiment 135. His unit advanced through the West Island 'without noticeable difficulty' across gardens, through isolated enemy positions, and soon reached the inner Citadel Island. They crossed over the bridge dominated by a huge gate, the entry to the inner keep of the fortress. Directly opposite was a long extended building with four great gates 'which were defended by Soviet machine gunners and riflemen who had now overcome the first shock of surprise'. Fighting began in earnest. Each gate had to be grenaded into submission. 'The square in front' of the building, Teuschler observed, 'was cloaked in thick smoke, punctured by fresh shell bursts and covered with rubble, which at least offered some possibility of cover.' Attacks by light Russian armour were beaten off. The 10th Company advanced to a further gate where other assault groups and battalion support elements were assembling, concentrating for the next phase of the attack. They filed onward, picking their way around the massive garrison church. III/IR135 was now deep within the citadel and on the point of achieving its objective.[24]

To its left I/IR135, forming the other prong of the northern attack axis, had traversed the North Island and was attempting the break into the citadel from the east. The southern advance was doggedly clearing routes through the South Island and bypassing the town of Brest even further south. The pitchfork thrust into Brest-Litovsk had impaled itself deeply into the enemy's defences on both axes. All indications suggested that the harm inflicted was mortal. No suggestion of any setback was apparent to XIIth Corps commander until 11.00 hours; 45th Infantry Division staff were, however, expressing misgivings within three to four hours of H-hour.

'It soon became clear between 05.30 hours and 07.30 hours that the Russians were bitterly fighting especially hard behind our forward attacking companies. Infantry operating with the 35 to 40 tanks and armoured cars based inside the citadel began to form a defence. The enemy brought his sharpshooting skills to bear, sniping from trees, rooftop outlets and cellars in multiple engagements, which soon caused us heavy losses among officers and NCOs.'[25]

Having penetrated the citadel, III/IR135 was pinned down in the vicinity of the church and partly surrounded by Russians. Reinforcements attempting to follow up through the West Island were slowed to crawling pace, picking their way forward with extreme difficulty. Commanders were being struck down by snipers with depressing rapidity. Hauptmann Praxa and his artillery battery commander, Hauptmann Krats, were killed attempting to co-ordinate the move forward. Major Oeltze, commanding I/IR135 trying to break into the citadel from the eastern side, was struck down alongside his artillery forward observer Leutnant Zenneck. The advance was steadily denuded of its leadership. The Terespol bridge leading into the citadel became impassable. Russian infantry, having overcome their initial shock, were now manning the citadel walls. Anyone moving in the open was shot.

As the day wore on the sun grew increasingly hot. Russian resistance around the church and officers' mess inside the citadel perceptibly increased. Walking wounded soldiers began to stumble back across the bridges, many bandaged and half undressed, always under fire. By midday the division's attack was visibly faltering. The subsequent post-action report explained:

'During the early morning hours it became clear that artillery support for close quarter fighting in the citadel would be impossible because our infantry were totally enmeshed with the Russians. Our own line was in a tangle of buildings, scrub, trees and rubble and could hardly be identified as it ran partly through Russian resistance nests or was in places surrounded. Attempts to engage the enemy directly with individual heavy infantry weapons, anti-tank guns and light artillery often failed due to poor visibility, the danger to our own troops and primarily the thickness of the fortress walls.'

A passing battery of self-propelled guns was commandeered and employed to no effect. Infantry Regiment 133, the corps reserve, was moved forward after 13.15 hours to the South and West islands, but was unable to influence the situation because:

'New forces reappeared after a short time, where the Russians had been driven or smoked out. They emerged from cellars, houses, pipes and other hiding places, shooting accurately, so that our losses rose even higher.'[26]

Gefreiter Hans Teuschler, near the church inside the citadel, was directing the fire of a light machine gun from an abandoned Russian anti-aircraft position. Using binoculars, he had barely discerned muzzle flash from a casemate 300m away when the number two on the gun shouted urgently 'Get down!' The sniper round slammed into Teuschler's chest as he attempted to do so. Spun around by the massive force of the impact, he remembered drowsily trying to squeeze the hand of the machine gunner lying alongside him, to give an indication of life that might be ebbing away. Thoughts of God and home welled up in his mind before blacking out. On regaining consciousness later he was confronted with a bleak scene:

'On the forward edge of the Flak position was the half-constructed tripod of a heavy machine gun. Behind it lay its gunner, mortally wounded, gasping with a severe gunshot wound to the lung. His eyes were glazed over and he groaned with pain and thirst. "Have you anything to drink Kamerad?" he asked me. I passed him my canteen with difficulty. To my right the machine gunner sat bolt upright, unmoving. There was no response when I spoke to him. In the immediate vicinity a sad concert of cries from the helpless wounded could be heard from all sides. "Medic, medic. God in Heaven, help me!" The sniper had been particularly effective in his work.'

Teuschler, nearing the end of his strength, weakly struggled to extricate himself from the top of an uncomfortable ammunition box, upon which he had fallen backwards after being shot. 'My chest felt as heavy as lead,' he admitted, 'and my shirt and tunic were soaked in blood'. He placed a field dressing on his chest to 'build up a crust' to match that which had congealed over the exit wound on his back, where he had lain on the box. His senses, dulled by shock, barely enabled him to complete the process. But having achieved it 'he felt himself rescued and began wandering through a wonderful dream world'.[27] He was delirious. All the time the sun beat mercilessly down.

At 13.50 hours Generalleutnant Schlieper, the commander of 45th Infantry Division, on the North Island observing the faltering attack from a vantage point in Infantry Regiment 135's sector, resigned himself to the inevitable. The citadel would not be taken by infantry attack alone. Generalfeldmarschall von Bock, the commander of Army Group Centre, had visited the XIIth Corps Command Post 40 minutes before, and came to the same conclusion. At 14.30 hours it was decided to withdraw the 45th Division vanguard elements who had already penetrated the citadel. The move would have to be conducted under the cover of darkness. Once a clear combat demarcation line had been established, the Russian garrison could be reduced by systematic and directed artillery fire. Commander Fourth Army confirmed the decision. The division log explained the reasoning:

'He did not want any unnecessary casualties; traffic on the "Rollbahn" and railway line already appeared possible. Enemy interference to this should be prevented. In general, the Russians should be starved out.'[28]

It was a depressing start to the campaign for 45th Division: 21 officers and 290 NCOs and men had been killed in the first 24 hours.[29] This represented two-thirds of the entire losses suffered during the preceding six-week French campaign.

The XIIth Corps requested additional support from self-propelled guns and flamethrowers. Mopping up was unlikely to be achieved by artillery alone.

Across the River Bug, the decisions being enacted at headquarters had no impact upon the intensity of the fighting raging in and around the citadel as dusk settled. The outline of the garrison church was barely discernible, shrouded by the dust and smoke of battle. Some 70 German soldiers, still holding Russian prisoners, were cut off. There was radio contact, but intermittent. Fresh salvoes of artillery fire howled over the headquarters and began to flash and crackle in the dying light. This appeared no easy task.

'ONLY 1,000KM AS THE CROW FLIES TO MOSCOW'

'Thank God! It's started up again!' wrote a *Wochenschau* newsreel cameraman on his calendar.[1] The tension of the previous weeks had broken at last. 'It appears that we brutally surprised the Russians early this morning,' confided 28-year-old Ulrich Modersohn in a letter to his mother. Modersohn, serving with Army Group South, described how:

'It was never possible for him to muster any worthwhile resistance. Our artillery and Stuka fire must have been pure hell for him. By midday assault bridges were across the Bug and ready. Now our troops are rolling over into Russia. This afternoon I saw how the earth shook and the sky hummed . . . Everything is following the set plan.'[2]

First-day impressions recorded by soldiers reveal elation at the extent of success and atmospheric descriptions of conflict often just out of sight. Robert Rupp, a Berlin school teacher in civilian life, wrote: 'The thunder of artillery woke us at 03.15 hours. 34 batteries are firing.' He was observing the River Bug border from the edge of a wood 7km away:

'Soon villages were burning and white Very flares climbed high. The front raged like a lightning storm. Grey stripes climbed up into the sky if Flak fired and dispersed slowly. An aircraft fell burning to the ground. The sky, which to begin with was red and clear, became tinged with purple and green. A huge smoke-cloud stood behind the low base-line silhouette of the ground and turned slowly to the right. I tried to sleep a little but managed only a doze.'[3]

Oberleutnant Siegfried Knappe observed the infantry assaults that advanced following the pause in the opening artillery barrage in the Army Group Centre sector:

'As the infantry moved forward, the morning darkness was filled with the sounds of shouting, the crack of rifle shots, the short bursts of machine guns, and the shattering crashes of hand-grenades. The rifle fire sounded like the clatter of metal-wheeled carts moving fast over cobblestone streets. Our infantry overran the barbed wire the Russians had erected on each side of their no-man's land and stormed the guard towers and pillboxes the Russians had built immediately beyond the death strip.'

Short bitter fire-fights took place with an enemy who often stood his ground even though surprised. 'Our men took as prisoners those Russians who surrendered and killed those who resisted,' commented Knappe. A bottle-neck of retreating Russian soldiers was decimated at a bridge in Sasnia, the objective, by Stuka dive-bomber support. Knappe, a veteran of the French campaign, confronted with the sight of the first dead bodies, declared: 'although I was no longer shocked by the sight, I had not become accustomed to it either.' The advance rolled irresistibly eastwards. Knappe's unit, the 87th Infantry Division, was preceded by Panzer formations. 'We took Sasnia and Grajewo the first day,' he declared, 'and then started the long road to Moscow.'[4]

Progress was evident along the entire 3,000km front. Curizio Malaparte, an Italian war correspondent with Army Group South standing on the banks of the River Prut, watched the advance of a mechanised division near Galatz.

'The exhausts of the Panzers belch out blue tongues of smoke. The air is filled with a pungent, bluish vapour that mingles with the damp green of the grass and with the golden reflection of the corn. Beneath the screaming arch of Stukas the mobile columns of tanks resemble thin lines drawn with a pencil on the vast green slate of the Moldavian plain.'

He was held up for two hours as the column rumbled by. 'The smell of men and horses gives way to the overpowering reek of petrol,' he remarked. Traffic control at crossroads was conducted by groups of 'stern, impassive *Feldgendarmen*' (military police). Lorried infantry followed the tanks. 'The men sat in strangely stiff attitudes; they had the appearance of statues.' The open trucks filed by, raising huge columns of dust, which settled upon the weary infantrymen hunched in the back. 'They were so white with dust,' observed Malaparte, 'they looked as if they were made of marble.'[5]

Leutnant Alfred Durrwanger, commanding an anti-tank company in the 28th Infantry Division attacking from East Prussia near Suwalki, said: 'When the battle began, we found the Russians surprised, but not at all unprepared.' His men crossed the Soviet border with a sense of foreboding. 'There was *no* enthusiasm,' he declared, 'not at all!' The prevailing atmosphere 'was rather a deep feeling of the immensity of that enterprise, and the question immediately arose: where and at which place would there be an end to the operations?'[6]

This was a question asked by many German soldiers at the outset of the campaign. Some were arrogantly confident; one Leutnant in the 74th Infantry Division wrote:

'I tell you in advance that in four to five weeks time the swastika flag will be wafting over the Kremlin in Moscow, and that moreover we will have Russia finished this year and Tommy on the carpet . . . Ja — it is no secret, when and how, that we will be in Moscow within four weeks with our as yet undefeated Wehrmacht. It is only 1,000km from Suwalki as the crow flies. We only need to conduct another Blitzkrieg. We only know how to attack. Forward, onward and again forward in concert with our heavy weapons raining fire, cordite, iron, bombs and shells — all on the heads of the Russians. That's all it needs.'[7]

Another infantry Oberleutnant declared that, unlike his comrades, he was not surprised at the outbreak of war 'which he had always prophesied'. He rationalised that 'after this war with Russia, and that in Arabia, Iraq, Syria, Palestine and Egypt, is over — which I believe will be in a short time — then Ribbentrop [the German Foreign Minister] will need only to send a single German soldier to England to negotiate' the peace. Whatever the outcome, he sarcastically continued, 'perhaps we will all have to go over [to England] but we will have at least secured our rear with five to six air fleets and 10,000 Panzers.'[8] Others were fortified by ideological conviction. 'Na, what do you think of our new enemy then?' wrote an infantry Feldwebel. 'Perhaps Papa will recall how I spoke about the Russian army during my last leave, emphasising even then that it's not possible to maintain lasting friendly relationships with the Bolsheviks,' commenting sinisterly: 'There are too many Jews there.'[9] Not all members of the invading army were so patriotically motivated, as anti-tank gunner Johann Danzer recalled:

'On day one during our first break one of the company's soldiers shot himself with his own rifle. He put the rifle between his knees, placed the muzzle in his mouth and squeezed off. For him, the war with all its pressures was at an end.'

Danzer's experiences on this first day bore mute testimony to the horrors his suicidal comrade sought to avoid. After the opening bombardment he and his anti-tank gun crew 'could see absolutely nothing at first, except for powder smoke. But as this began to disperse, and it got lighter, the devil broke loose from the Russian side.' The PAK crew of five and commander had to drag their 37mm anti-tank gun into the attack, maintaining the same pace as the infantry advancing alongside. Four additional infantry soldiers were earmarked to assist so they could keep up. 'Our immense load became, as a consequence, the primary target for enemy fire.' The first burst of Russian machine gun fire tore the entire group apart. 'Three men were killed instantly,' said Danzer, 'all the others were severely wounded and I was the only one left uninjured.'[10]

After the crust of Russian resistance was broken by the infantry, on the frontier the Panzers began to clatter through the breaches and penetrate the hinterland. Their passage was not totally unimpeded. 'I found myself on the Eastern Front encountering what seemed to be a different and terrible race of men,' declared Hans Becker,[11] a Panzer crew man with the 12th Panzer Division. 'The very first attacks involved sharp, fierce fighting.'

Seventh Panzer Division achieved an initial deep penetration. Border defences were weak in relation to what had been reported by intelligence, 'and enemy artillery never emerged in any consequential strength'. By 12.45 hours on the first day the bridge spanning the River Neman at Olita was captured intact, falling victim to a determined swiftly advancing vanguard. The bridgehead was immediately counter-attacked by Russian heavy tanks supported by infantry and artillery. During this first tank-on-tank battle of the Russian campaign, 82 Soviet tanks were shot into flames.[12] Karl Fuchs, a tank commander in Panzer Regiment 25, wrote home:

'Yesterday I knocked off a Russian tank, as I had done two days ago! If I get in another attack, I'll receive my first battle stripes. War is half as bad as it sounds and one thing is plain as day: the Russians are fleeing everywhere and we follow them. All of us believe in early victory!'[13]

Olita village burned furiously. Numbers of German tanks smouldered along the roads leading into it. Rubber treads on road wheels formed miniature flaming hoops. Many had turrets blown clean away. All had been picked off during the advance by dug-in Russian tanks. Seventh Panzer Division almost immediately burst out of its bridgehead on the other side of the River Neman, but Oberst Rothenberg, the commander of Panzer Regiment 25, was to call the engagement 'the hardest battle of my life'.[14]

The weather on this first attack day was, as the 7th Panzer Division official history declared:

'. . . particularly favourable for fighting, and over the following days. It was dry, the sun shone, roads and tracks were easily negotiable, and even the terrain off roads and paths, normally swampy, had dried out and was drivable for both tracked and wheeled vehicles.'[15]

Gefreiter Erich Kuby summed it up with some irony in his diary: 'This is truly Hitler war weather,'[16] he declared. The official history of the 20th Panzer Division, also with Panzergruppe 3 under Generaloberst Hoth, commented on the impact the heat was having on accompanying marching infantry regiments, which traversed considerable stretches on the first day, some as far as 50km. Assessments of Soviet strength on the border proved exaggerated. Three hundred prisoners, including 20 officers and 10 lorries, were captured on 22 June. Deeply rutted sand tracks caused unexpectedly high levels of fuel consumption. Shortages resulted when wheeled fuel tankers found they were unable to keep up in the hot sandy conditions. Columns began to stretch out. 'The long slow division line snaked along dry shifting tracks in the summer heat,' recorded the division history, 'raising clear dust-cloud outlines, offering a promising target for enemy bombers.' Six air attacks fell on these lines of erratically moving vehicles on the first day alone.[17]

WHERE WAS THE RED AIR FORCE?

'We were not bothered at all by the Red Air Force,' remarked Leutnant Michael Wechtler. His men, lying in reserve with Regiment 133, awaited the call forward to Brest-Litovsk. They basked in the sun in an open meadow seemingly oblivious to air attack, awaiting further orders.[1] Leutnant Heinz Knoke, a Bf109 fighter pilot flying with JG52, had already attacked his early morning Russian headquarters objective. Total surprise was achieved:

'One of the huts is fiercely blazing. Vehicles have been stripped of their camouflage and overturned by the blast. The Ivans at last come to life. The scene below is like an overturned ant-heap, as they scurry about in confusion. Stepsons of Stalin in their underwear flee for cover in the woods.'

Five or six more strafing runs were conducted over the camp and headquarters. Light Flak began to open up and was immediately suppressed. 'An Ivan at the gun falls to the ground,' Knoke observed, 'still in underwear.'

His flight arrived back at Suwalki fighter base at 05.56 hours, managing a turn-round within 40 minutes before returning to their previous objective, guided 'by the smoke rising from the burning buildings'. After systematically raking the target the wing was refuelled and rearmed again; this time it took 22 minutes. By the end of the day Knoke saw that:

'Thousands of Ivans are in full retreat, which becomes an utter rout when we open up on them, stumbling and bleeding as they flee from the highway in an attempt to take cover in the nearby woods. Vehicles lie burning by the roadside after we pass. Once I drop my bombs on a column of heavy artillery drawn by horses. I am thankful not to be down there myself.'

By 20.00 hours Knoke's squadron was flying its sixth mission of the day. The Luftwaffe, the most modern arm of the Wehrmacht, had many technically trained young Germans in its ranks. They had, in the main, been educated by a National Socialist regime extolling the virtues of modern technology and racial purity. Air attacks as a consequence were pursued with pitiless ferocity. Knoke admitted:

'We have dreamed for a long time of doing something like this to the Bolshevists. Our feeling is not one of hatred, so much as utter contempt. It is a genuine satisfaction for us to be able to trample the Bolshevists in the mud where they belong.'[2]

A Luftwaffe Unteroffizier based at Lyon wrote home the day following the invasion. His pragmatic comments are tinged with similar racist overtones. 'Yesterday we stood close to the map and thought through all the possible contingencies we could face.' Identifying the problems, they mockingly concluded: 'It would be better if we're never stationed with the General Staff.' *Weltanschauung* still jaded the NCO's reasoning process. 'Everything that belongs to Jewry stands on one front against us. The Marxists fight shoulder-to-shoulder with the big financiers as was the case in Germany in 1933.' Surprise at the invasion announcement was tinged with a degree of quiet optimism. 'Who would have thought that now we would be up against the Russians,' he declared, 'but if I recall correctly, the Führer has always done the best he could.'[3]

The efficacy of this statement was borne out by an increasing realisation of the success of the pre-emptive air strike. Flights of gull-winged Stuka dive-bombers were at that moment peeling off, sirens wailing into the attack. Junkers Ju87B Stukas were the main providers of close air support to the army. Leutnant Hans Rudel had by the evening of the first day 'been out over the enemy lines four times in the area between Grodno and Volkovysk.' His targets were large numbers of tanks together with supply columns that the Russians were bringing up to the front. 'We bomb tanks, Flak artillery and ammunition dumps supplying the tanks and infantry,' he wrote.[4]

War correspondent Hans Schaller described the cockpit view of just such a dive-bombing attack. Observing a Stuka flight below, he described how:

'They are just changing their course. I cannot hear them above the noise of my own machine; they seem to be flying quietly and noiselessly above the landscape like sharp-eyed birds of prey, eager to claim their victim. One of the dive-bombers is already leaving the formation! The machine tilts to one side, begins to dive and plunges down through a milky wall of cloud towards the objective, hurtles down steeper and steeper. Stands on its head, dives almost perpendicularly and now the tension of the pilot has reached its climax.'[5]

This mode of attack, although not precision bombing, was the most accurate that technology could achieve at the time. Pilots laboured under uncomfortable G-force pressures varying from 4g to 12g for one to six seconds depending how the pilot levelled from his dive.[6] Hauptmann Robert Oleinic, a Stuka training instructor, explained:

'A dive speed of 480kph placed enormous strain on the system. The dive brake set at this speed prevented the machine from breaking up in the air, enabling the pilot to get it under control again. The pressure while levelling out was so intense that pilots occasionally experienced a temporary misting sensation that could last a few seconds. That meant for a moment he blacked out.'[7]

Leutnant Rudel commented on the cumulative physical strain dive-bombing had upon Stuka pilots during the opening weeks of the Russian campaign. Take-off was at 03.00 hours in the first few days with the final landing often after 22.00 hours. 'Every spare minute,' he stated, 'we stretch out underneath an aeroplane and instantly fall asleep.' When scrambled, 'we hop to it without even knowing where it is from'. Prolonged stress caused them to go about their business 'as though in our dreams'.[8]

Soviet Air Force reports were soon referring to impending catastrophe. Third Army Air Force commander informed his Western Front higher command that:

'At 04.00 hours on 22 June 1941 the enemy attacked our airfields simultaneously. The whole of the 16th Bomber Regiment was put out of action. The 122nd Fighter Regiment suffered heavily, the 127th Fighter Regiment to a lesser extent.'

A paralysis of command and control developed. Frantic requests for information were despatched. The report continued:

'I request that you report where the 122nd and 127th Fighter Regiments have been transferred and give us their call signs and wave numbers. I request that you reinforce us with fighters for the fight against the air enemy.'[9]

Fourth Soviet Army reported similar setbacks. 'The enemy is dominant in the air; our aviation regiments are suffering great losses [of 30–40%].'[10]

The staff of the Soviet Tenth Army was told by the 9th Air Division that by 10.29 hours all its fighters at Minsk had been destroyed. At 10.57 hours, 28 minutes later, the 126th Fighter Regiment in the same division asked permission to destroy its logistic stocks at Bielsk and retreat so as to evade likely capture. Bielsk, the staff ominously noted, was 25km inside the border.[11]

Soviet Air Force units were mauled as they took-off from runways. At Bug near Brest-Litovsk a single Soviet fighter squadron attempting to 'scramble' was bombed while still in motion on the ground. Flaming wrecks skidded into each other in a fiery mêlée and were left to burn out on the airfield boundaries. Reckless courage displayed by Soviet bomber crews to stem the onslaught was to no avail. 'It seemed to me almost a crime to allow these floundering aircraft to be attacked in tactically impossible formations,' commented Generalfeldmarschall Albert Kesselring commanding Luftflotte 2. On the second day he described how 'one flight after another came in innocently at regular intervals, as easy prey for our fighters'. His final caustic comment was: 'It was sheer "infanticide".'[12]

Hauptmann Herbert Pabst from Stuka Geschwader 77 saw a Soviet air raid on his base shortly after returning from a sortie. Black mushrooms of smoke suddenly burst up from the airfield boundaries with no warning. Six twin-engined enemy machines could be observed making a wide curving turn away, heading for home. Simultaneously two or three minute dots, German fighters, were sighted converging rapidly.

'As the first one fired, thin threads of smoke seemed to join it to the bomber. Turning ponderously to the side, the big bird flashed silver, then plunged vertically downwards with its engines screaming. As it crashed a huge sheet of flame shot upwards. The second bomber became a glare of red, exploded as it dived, and only the bits came floating down like great autumnal leaves. The third turned over backwards on fire. A similar fate befell the rest, the last falling in a village and burning for an hour. Six columns of smoke rose from the horizon. All six had been shot down!'

Pabst added: 'They went on coming the whole afternoon', but all were knocked out. 'From our airfield alone we saw 21 crash and not one got away.'[13]

The German pre-emptive air strike hit 31 airfields during the early morning hours of 22 June. Sorties thereafter were directed against suspected Soviet staff headquarters, barracks, artillery and bunker positions and oil depots. Defending Soviet fighters tended to keep their distance, turning away after an initial burst of fire. Leutnant Rudel was clear the Russian 'Rata' J15 was inferior to the German Bf109s. Whenever they appeared, 'they are shot down like flies,' he reported. Heinz Knoke claimed on 22 June there was 'no sign of the Russian Air Force the entire day'. Therefore, 'we are able to do our work without encountering opposition'.[14] The reason was clear. By the end of the first morning the Soviets had lost 890 aircraft, of which 222 were shot down in the air by fighters and Flak and 668 destroyed on the ground. Only 18 German aircraft failed to land after the initial attacks. By that night the Soviets had lost 1,811 aircraft: 1,489 on the ground and 322 shot down. German losses rose to only 35.[15]

Between 23 and 26 June the number of Soviet airfields attacked reached 123. By the end of the month 4,614 Soviet aircraft were destroyed at a cost of 330 German. Of these 1,438 were lost in the air and 3,176 caught on the ground. Total Luftwaffe air supremacy had been achieved. Generalfeldmarschall Kesselring recalled the 'reports of enemy aircraft destroyed in the air or on the ground totalled 2,500; a figure which the Reichsmarschall [Goering] at first refused to believe!' Pilot reports by the very nature of the mêlée of air combat were prone to exaggeration. 'But when [Goering] checked up after our advance, he told us our claim was 200 or 300 less than the actual figure.'[16] In fact the claims had been under-assessed by some 1,814 aircraft.

Damage inflicted on completely unprepared Russian airfields was enormous. Soviet pilots and ground crews had been asleep under canvas when the first attacks swept in. Aircraft were not camouflaged and stood in densely packed rows at border airfields. Bomber squadrons were not stationed in depth within the hinterland and were mostly unprotected by flak. When they finally rose in swarms to do battle, their ponderous non-tactical and unprotected formations were savaged by attacking German fighter wings. JG3, commanded by Major Günther Lutzow, shot down 27 attacking Soviet bombers in 15 minutes, without losing a single aircraft.[17] As a consequence, senior army and Luftwaffe generals were euphoric in the first week of the campaign. Generalmajor Hoffmann von Waldau, Chief of the *Führungsabteilung* of the Luftwaffe General Staff, claimed 'full tactical surprise' had been achieved, reckoning on 'battle-winning success'. This view was shared by General der Flieger Frhr von Richthofen, the commander of the VIIIth Fliegerkorps in Kesselring's Luftflotte 2, who believed at the end of June that the mass of the Red Army's attack armies had been annihilated. Two

weeks later he stated, 'the way to Moscow was open.' Eight days, he felt, was all that was required.[18]

Premature as this comment may have been, air supremacy was assured. The Soviet Air Force, however, was not totally destroyed, although it had been dealt a crushing blow. Most of the aircrew baling out from stricken bombers did so over their own territory. They would live to fight another day, as also the crews of machines destroyed on the ground, who could be reintroduced into the air battle at a later stage. Only 30% of the European Red Air Force had been located by the Luftwaffe during the planning and reconnaissance phase. Its overall assessment of potential was out by one half. Nine days after the pre-emptive strike Generalmajor Hoffmann von Waldau told the Army Chief of Staff, Halder:

'The air force has greatly underestimated the enemy's numerical strength. It is quite evident that the Russians initially had more than 8,000 planes. Half of this number has probably already been shot down or destroyed on the ground, so numerically we are now equal with the Russians.'[19]

He privately confided to his diary on 3 July that the surprise attack had hit a massive Russian deployment. The high numbers previously dismissed as propaganda now required careful reassessment. 'The matériel quality is also better than expected,' von Waldau admitted. Continued success was dependent upon maintaining the current massive Russian attrition rate with 'minimal own losses'. But a sinister development was already apparent: 'The bitterness and extent of mass resistance has exceeded all we had imagined.'[20]

The first indication of this was when Soviet pilot Sub-Lieutenant Dimitri Kokorev of the 124th Fighter Regiment deliberately rammed a Messerschmitt Bf110 during a dogfight over Kobrin. He had run out of ammunition. Both aircraft spiralled earthwards. Near Zholkva another Polikarpov I-16 pilot, Lieutenant I. Ivanov, directed his propeller into the tail of a German Heinkel He111 bomber. Kokorev was to survive; Ivanov did not. Nine Russian pilots reportedly resorted to suicidal ramming tactics on the first day. One exasperated Luftwaffe Oberst declared: 'Soviet pilots were fatalists, fighting without any hope of success or confidence in their own abilities and driven only by their own fanaticism or by fear of the commissars.'[21] The Germans were winning the air battle, but their opponents, despite the one-sided nature of the dogfights, could still be unpredictably lethal.

The Luftwaffe had the Russian tiger by the tail. Mass resistance tinged with an element of fanaticism was pitted against a tactically deadly but smaller foe. Only by constantly achieving the same level of crippling losses could the Luftwaffe expect to win. 'Success is axiomatic to inflicting very high casualties relative to minimal own losses,' von Waldau calculated, 'but first greater numbers need to be annihilated'.[22] German control of the air was complete by dusk on the first day. From now onwards Luftwaffe units concentrated on supporting the ground advance.

Arnold Döring flying with KG53 was strafing and bombing the roads north-east of Brest-Litovsk leading toward Koboyn. His comments encapsulated the Luftwaffe's new intent. 'In order to leave the road intact for our own advance,' he said, 'we dropped the bombs only at the side of the road.' Their target was massed enemy columns of tanks, motorised columns with horse-drawn carts and artillery in between, 'all frantically making their way east'. The result was pandemonium.

'Our bombs fell by the side of the tanks, guns, between vehicles and panic-stricken Russians running in all directions. It was total panic down there — nobody could even think of firing back. The effect of the incendiary and splinter bombs was awesome. With a target like this there are no misses. Tanks were turned over or stood in flames, guns with their towing vehicles blocked the road, while between them horses thrashing around multiplied the panic.'[23]

DUSK . . . 22 JUNE 1941

'As the men marched the dust rose until we were all covered in a light yellow coating,' remarked Leutnant Heinrich Haape with Infantry Regiment 18, part of Army Group Centre. 'Men and vehicles assumed ghostly outlines in the dust-laden air.'[1] Steady progress had been achieved during this, the longest period of daylight in the year. 'Our divisions on the entire offensive front,' noted General Franz Halder, 'have forced back the enemy by an average of 10-12km. This has opened the path for our armour.'[2] Hoepner's Panzergruppe 4 had captured two bridges across the River Dubysa intact in Army Group North's sector. Units were achieving penetrations averaging 20km.[3] General Guderian's Panzergruppe 2 in the centre made startling progress: 17th Panzer Division covered 18km; 18th Panzer to its right drove 66km north of Brest-Litovsk. South of the town, 3rd Panzer Division penetrated 36km, 4th Panzer 39km and the 1st Cavalry Division 24km.

The pace had been hectic. Robert Rupp wrote in his diary after crossing the River Bug: 'Further drive at speed into the darkness. Dust often so thick that one could hardly see the vehicle in front any more.'[4] The vanguard of XIIth Army Corps, the detachment 'Stolzmann', reached the Bereza Kartuska area one day later, an advance of 100km.[5] Hoth's Panzergruppe 3 forced the River Neman near Olita and Merkine scattering enemy resistance. It created full operational freedom of movement in so doing; there was no tangible enemy line in front of it. Hoth was poised to break out. Further south, von Kleist's Panzergruppe 1, part of Army Group South, was approaching the River Styr; patrols were already across the River Prut. The frontier crust appeared broken. All bridges on the Bug and other river frontiers were captured intact. Halder concluded:

'Tactical surprise of the enemy has apparently been achieved along the entire line. Troops were caught in their quarters, planes on the airfields were covered up, and . . . enemy groups faced with unexpected developments at the front enquired at the HQ in the rear what they should do.'

The OKW report for 22 June reported an 'overall impression that the enemy, after having overcome initial surprise, took up the battle'. Chief of Staff Halder likewise concurred; 'After the first shock,' he wrote, 'the enemy has turned to fight.'[6]

Infantry following up the main border-breaching assaults were beginning to feel the consequence of this. In Army Group Centre, III/IR18, numbering some 800 men, was fired upon by a Soviet rearguard. It consisted merely of a Soviet Commissar and four soldiers, who aggressively defended a hastily improvised position in the midst of a cornfield. German casualties were negligible. 'I didn't expect that,' battalion commander Major Neuhoff confided shakily to his medical officer, Leutnant Haape. 'Sheer suicide to attack a battalion at close quarters with five men.'

It left an uncomfortable feeling of insecurity. Veterans of the previous French campaign the year before were accustomed to enemy surrender once they were outmanoeuvred. These tactics were unfamiliar. 'We were to learn that those small groups of Russians would constitute our greatest danger,' declared Haape. High-standing corn provided ideal cover for small stay-behind groups, prepared to fight on, even after the main body of Russian forces had been pushed back. 'As a rule they were fanatically led by Soviet commissars and we never knew when we should come under their fire.' German units were subjected to nuisance raids the entire day. Haape's battalion was ambushed twice in the morning. A Hauptmann from a neighbouring unit admitted later the same day: 'That's happening all over the countryside'. Exasperated, he complained: 'These swine build up ammunition dumps in the cornfields and then wait until our main columns pass before they start sniping.'[7]

By contrast the German general staff was not too displeased at this Soviet tendency to turn and fight. 'There are no indications of an attempted disengagement,' Halder reported. The Russian command organisation 'is too ponderous to effect swift operational regrouping in reaction to our attack, and so the Russians will have to accept battle in the disposition in which they were deployed'. The aim was to destroy the Russian armies as far west as possible. Halder's diary entries exude a certain smug confidence. The plan was working. 'Army groups are pursuing their original objectives,' he noted. 'Nor is there any reason for a change. OKH has no occasion to issue any orders.'[8] The campaign was developing satisfactorily.

Blitzkrieg for the ordinary soldier at the front, however, was not fitting this tidy conception of order and progress. At the end of this interminably long summer's day Leutnant Haape was taxed by the grim task of providing assistance to the injured who had already fallen in the apparently faultless execution of the task. Progress at troop level was not so obvious. Faced now as a medical officer with the onerous task of clearing up the physical and psychological carnage, Haape felt exasperated, even indignant. He remonstrated:

'In how many fields and woods and ditches were German soldiers dying, waiting for help that would not come — or that would be too late when it did arrive? Surely, I thought, the army could have made better arrangements to deal with the hellish mix of confusion, terror and despair that was left behind by the relentless forward march of our storm troops. The organisation of the fighting troops and the paraphernalia of war seemed to have been worked out with amazing precision, but there appeared to have been a criminal disregard of the necessities behind front line troops. Surely it would even have been better to advance more slowly if it would have given us time to find and treat our wounded and bury our dead.'[9]

The victors had suffered in the process. Even less compassion was expended on the vanquished as the first 24 hours of a conflict that was to last nearly four years drew to a close.

Chapter 6
Waiting for news

'Bets have already been made, not on the outcome of the war, but on the date it will end.'

Secret SS report

THE HOME FRONTS... VICTORY WILL BE OURS! GERMANY

Outwardly, Sunday 22 June appeared a normal day in the Reich. Some 95,000 voices roared appreciation at a thrilling football cup final being played out at the Berlin Olympic Stadium. Many Germans, ignoring the distraction of world events, immersed themselves in an exciting game of football, the highlights of which were replayed in German cinemas the following week. Rapid Wien, the first *Ostmark* (non-German) team to play in a German final since the Austrian *Anschluss*, met the defending champions and favourites FC Schalke 04. The German team, leading 3–0 at the 70-minute point, lost 3–4 in the final few minutes to a suddenly resurgent Austrian team. It was a breathtaking performance and totally unexpected result. National reverses in wartime had been rare until now. Theirs was different.

Reportage of sporting conflicts was preferable to listening to the depressing news broadcast across the Reich hours before. Goebbels' radio speech shocked the German nation. One housewife in Hausberge Porta wrote:

'Ja, and then I switched on the radio and heard — "the most recent news report from the Eastern Front" — and joined the ranks of those already deeply disturbed in Germany. Turning on the radio early this morning and completely unprepared to listen to the Führer's proclamation left me totally speechless.'[1]

Another gentleman, Herr F. M. living in Neuwied declared:

'When I heard the National Anthem played with Goebbels on the radio this morning I thought some good news was going to be reported. But, on the contrary, it was the opposite . . . Now one can understand the previously incomprehensible — why the army was in the East. Both of us will face some different weeks. You soldiers will have to fight and hold while we at home need to wait and hope. Once again we live in troublesome and uncertain times.'[2]

Distractions beyond football matches were concentrating minds. Charlotte von der Schulenburg's husband, already at the front, had left her alone at home with four young children, aged between four months and six years-old to support. Domestic pressures were building up. She pointed out:

'One must remember in those days that people needed ration and clothing cards. It was already becoming a problem. There were only a few vegetables and a little fruit, and that was already coming from the garden.'[3]

The war had hit the Reich holiday industry. The *Münchener*

Neuesten Nachrichten (Munich's Latest News) commented in an article on 1941 tourism that large numbers of Swiss hotels were faced with closure because 60% of their customers had previously been foreign tourists.[4] War kept people at home in Germany. Soldiers on leave preferred to spend their precious final furlough at home with their families. Hotels were overfilled, but not with holiday-makers. Most were commandeered by the state for military hospitals, convalescent homes for the wounded or for children evacuated to the country to avoid British bombers as part of the *Kinderlandverschickung* programme. Actress Heidi Kabel, commenting on the growing frequency of air raids, which had grown more menacing since 1940, expressed her concern.

'My husband and I worked in the theatre. We had a son and often took him with us. It was serious but not as bad as later in Hamburg, but we were worried. We always took him and he slept in a wardrobe. It was always OK.'[5]

Local threats are often perceived to be more significant than epic impersonal events shaping history. One infantry Oberleutnant, despite optimism that the coming campaign would be short, was concerned more for his wife's vulnerability to air raids, than of impending combat. 'These things unsettle me less,' he wrote home, 'than the fact you poor women and children have to stay in cellars night after night.' Euskirchen, his home town, 'is revisited time after time,' yet, he asks his wife, 'you don't write about casualties?'[6] She doubtless preferred not to worry him.

Although the government wished to promote an air of normality, there was scepticism in the Reich over the announced invasion. 'It was a very serious moment,' recalled Charlotte von der Schulenburg. 'War had always a deep horror for me', and with a husband at the front it was 'an extremely worrying event'.[7] Gefreiter Erich Kuby's wife, Edith, writing to her husband on the day the news broke, similarly expressed concern:

'This is the first actual war letter! My God, right at the end [of leave] you had already thought of this possibility, and now you are in the middle of it! Hopefully your luck will hold and nothing bad will happen.'

The new campaign appeared more sinister than those which had preceded it. 'The Russian wastes,' Edith wrote, 'will bring a different type of war from that in France, because a "forward point" is hardly discernible.' She despairingly finished her letter saying, 'all the time it occurs to me how awful war is, and you are now in it.'[8] The significance of these unfolding events was not lost on children. On her way to fetch the Sunday morning milk with her uncle, grandfather and father, 12-year-old Marianne Roberts heard the radio news that German troops had crossed the Russian frontier. The implications were immediately apparent. Marianne's uncle Mattes, Pionier Gefreiter, who had already fought in the Polish and French campaigns, broke the complete silence that had ensued. 'Now we have lost the war,' he simply announced. Marianne said:

'Not a word was passed. Everyone kept their silence. From this day onwards I knew there would be no Final Victory'.[9]

Her uncle departed for Russia immediately and was killed shortly after near Smolensk. Within three years her father was dead also. Four days after the outbreak of the Russian war, the classified *SS Secret Report on the Home Political Situation* stated:

'The reports on the war that have recently come in unanimously confirm that the initial nervousness and dismay especially noticeable around women lasted only a few hours and as a consequence of a comprehensive information campaign has given way to a generally calm and optimistic attitude.'[10]

Leutnant Helmut Ritgen, a Panzer regiment adjutant, regarded himself as a mathematician. So optimistic was he of the outcome of the approaching campaign that he began to calculate potential leave dates. The importance revolved around his future marriage.

'I tried to compute the length of our campaign by the duration of the past campaign in Poland and France in relation to the strength of the opposing forces, distances and other factors. My conclusion was that the war would be over at the end of July. I set my wedding day for 2 August.'

He omitted a crucial factor from his equation — the Russians. Optimism there most certainly was. The same secret SS report continued:

'The population's mood had changed to the extent that today Russia is generally considered an inferior military foe. That a military victory over Russia will soon be forthcoming is common knowledge to every citizen in this war to a greater extent than in any other previous campaign. The optimism of most of the population is so great that bets have already been made, not on the outcome of the war, but on the date it will end. In this context the most popular time limit for the duration of the war is six weeks!'

Helmut Ritgen's fiancée was to wait two more years for her wedding. Marga Merz's experience was different. Her fiancé was conscripted, like her two brothers, into the army in 1940. But the wedding never took place. He was killed within days of the opening of the Russian campaign. She was totally overwhelmed.

'I was howling and blowing my nose throughout the year. Clearly when you think you have built up your life, truly started to live and have someone — and then something else comes along . . .'

The remainder of her war years passed 'like a terrible dream'.[12] Similar tragedies were to occur ten-fold in Russia.

VICTORY WILL BE OURS! RUSSIA

Sixteen-year-old Ina Konstantinova lived near Kastin, northeast of Moscow. She confided to her diary on the first day of war that 'only yesterday everything was so peaceful, so quiet, and today . . . my God!' Her thoughts were echoed by Yitskhok Rudashevski from Vilna on the Lithuanian-Russian border, who remembered how a cheerful conversation was interrupted by the sudden howling of an air-raid siren. 'The siren was so inappropriate,' he said, 'to the peaceful, joyous summer which spread out around us.' The first air raids began that same beautiful summer evening:

'It is war. People have been running around bewildered. Everything has changed so much . . . It has become clear to us all: the Hitlerites have attacked our land. They have forced a war upon us. And so we shall retaliate, and strike until we shall smash the aggressor on his home soil.'[1]

The outbreak of war profoundly shocked ordinary Russian people. At noon on 22 June in Moscow public address systems broadcast an announcement by Foreign Minister Vyacheslav Molotov from every street corner describing the German invasion. Contemporary Russian newsreels captured these anxious crowds gazing with concern at metal loudspeakers as if they might offer something of more substance than the metallic voice rasp of the same shocking news that had been delivered to the Reich hours before:

'At four o'clock this morning, without declaration of war, and without any claims being made on the Soviet Union, German troops attacked our country, attacked our frontier in many places, and bombed Zhitomir, Kiev, Sebastopol, Kaunas and some other places from the air. There are over 200 dead or wounded. Similar air and artillery attacks have also been made from Romanian and Finnish territory.'

Crowds listened restlessly, hands in pockets, thoughtfully pinching noses or abstractedly raising fingers to mouths as shocked minds came to terms with the import of the speech.

'This unheard-of attack on our country is an unparalleled act of perfidy in the history of civilised nations. This attack has been made despite the fact that there was a non-aggression pact between the Soviet Union and Germany, a pact the terms of which were scrupulously observed by the Soviet Union.'

Some individuals stared straight ahead, while others looked about to assess the impact the depressing speech was having on their fellows. Tense faces, pursed lips and shifting glances, manifested the sense of foreboding increasingly apparent to grim-faced audiences straining to catch every word.

Ina Konstantinova declared, 'I can't describe my state of mind as I was listening to this speech! I became so agitated that my heart seemed to jump out.' She, like countless others, was caught up in a patriotic fervour. 'The country is mobilising; should I continue as before? No! I ought to make myself useful to my Homeland.' She wrote fervently in her diary, 'we must win!'[2] Lew Kopelew, a Ukrainian studying in Moscow, was initially euphoric. A committed socialist, he admitted later:

'I was so stupid, I was pleased, because in my view the announcement seemed to presage a "holy war" in which "the German proletariat" would join us, and Hitler would immediately collapse.'[3]

His reasoning was based on the fact the German Communist Party in 1933 had been the largest voluntary communist organisation in the world.

Others expressed emotion in terms of pain. Jewgenlij Dolmatowski, later to become a Soviet Second Lieutenant, said, 'I tell you, seriously, it caused real anguish, a feeling at the pit of the stomach'. From that moment on he was inspired to serve his country. Kopelew was similarly convinced. 'My Homeland must be defended, and eventually Fascism come to a reckoning,' he concluded. As a fluent German speaker he suspected he might be considered suitable for recruitment for parachute missions deep into Nazi Germany. 'Stupid idea, eh?' he ruefully admitted to his interviewer.[4]

These impacts, however, were the very emotions to which Molotov's speech sought to appeal. 'The whole responsibility for this act of robbery,' the speech continued, 'must fall on the Nazi rulers'. There was a characteristic socialist input which gave some credence to Kopelew's opinion:

'This war has not been inflicted upon us by the German people nor by the German workers, peasants and intellectuals, of whose suffering we are fully aware, but by Germany's bloodthirsty rulers who have already enslaved the French, the Czechs, the Poles, the Serbs, and the peoples of Norway, Denmark, Holland, Belgium, Greece and other countries.'

There was scant comprehension, this early, the pitiless ideological methods the German armies would employ to prosecute the war. The attack was nevertheless clearly an aggression, a transgression of civilised behaviour. It must be stopped.

'The government calls upon you, men and women citizens of the Soviet Union, to rally even more closely round the glorious Bolshevik Party, around the Soviet Government and our great leader, comrade Stalin. Our cause is good. The enemy will be smashed. Victory will be ours.'[5]

With that the crackling speakers became silent. They later broadcast martial music. The declaration left people shocked and in some respects humiliated. There had been the Non-Aggression Pact. No demands had been made on the Soviet Union, the Germans had simply attacked. Maria Mironowa, a Russian actress, gravely recalled the impact of the surprise announcements:

'Suddenly the streets were flowing with people. Uncertainties were at the forefront. Nobody knew what to do next. I didn't know whether I ought to go to the theatre, carry on, or not go in. There were only a few people in the audience, practically nobody. In spite of all this no one comprehended how awful the war was going to be.'[6]

Sir John Russell at the British Embassy in Moscow declared, 'the shock was all the greater when it did come.' It was like a work of fiction.

'I had been out that particular night somewhere and I came home rather late and turned the radio on, and I got onto I think it was Rhykov or Kiev or somewhere like that. Accounts were going on of bombings and attacks and things which I thought was like an Orson Welles programme, like when he bombed New York [as part of an H. G. Wells' War of the Worlds interpretation] you remember? Then when we checked around we found it was real.'[7]

Elena Skrjabin, listening to Molotov's radio broadcast with her mother in Leningrad, suspected the effect of the transmission was not quite that intended. 'War! Germany was

already bombing cities in the Soviet Union'. She felt Molotov 'faltered' and the speech 'was harshly delivered as if he was out of breath'. The atmosphere conveyed suggested something dreadful threatened. People caught their breaths with a start as the news was announced. On the streets she saw:

'The city was in panic. People fell upon the shops, standing in queues, exchanging a few words, buying everything they could get their hands on. They wandered up and down the streets lost in thought. Many entered banks to withdraw their deposits. I formed part of this wave attempting to take roubles from my savings account, but I came too late, the cashier was empty.'

A palpable feeling of crisis reigned. 'Throughout the entire day,' Skrjabin felt, 'the atmosphere was tense and unsettled.'[8] A day before, journalist Konstantin Simonov had been summoned to the Party Broadcasting Committee and instructed to write two anti-Fascist songs. 'With that I decided that the war, which we all basically expected to happen, was very close.' He worked throughout the morning of 22 June until disturbed by a telephone call at 14.00 hours. The first thing he heard on lifting the receiver was, 'It's war.' Instructions followed to join the Soviet Third Army in the central sector near Grodno. He was to join a Front newspaper organisation. Unbeknown to him, it already lay within the shadow of the German advance. Uniforms were then issued. During the hectic fitting process he recalled, 'we were all very lively, perhaps too lively and certainly nervous'.[9]

Like the civilian population in Germany, the impressions of that fateful first day are indelibly stamped on Russian memories. Vladimir Kalesnik, a student living in halls of residence, was caught unawares as his door was flung open and a voice cried, 'It's war. It's war — get up!'

'We thought it was a joke, a game. We got going and were ordered to the Commissariat. We went in and every man received about ten call-up conscription and mobilisation orders. They had to be personally delivered. It all came so unexpectedly.'

Caught up in the patriotic fervour of the moment, young Kalesnik was not mature enough to comprehend fully the emotional implications of his work.

'As I handed them around I noticed how nervous the family became. I was astonished when men and wives began to weep. At the time, I thought them cowards. But I could never foresee how brutal and awful this war was to become.'[10]

Vladimir Garbunow living in the Urals remembered that Sunday 'was summer-like and warm, and we were not thinking about a war at all'. On his way home he saw people gathering in the streets listening to loudspeaker announcements. War had begun. Garbunow, like Kalesnik, was too young to comprehend its significance.

'It hadn't made us uneasy and we were not afraid. Hmm — now we are at war . . . The grown-ups wept and remonstrated among themselves . . . it was clear to them this was bad news. War would bring hard times, but we didn't understand.'

With the other 16- and 17-year-olds he reported to the Military Commissar and asked for permission to report to the front. Animatedly he recounted:

'But they responded, "We will call for you when it is necessary." Already very many had volunteered. Everybody, full of ideals, wanted to participate. Bombs had already exploded on this first day, buildings had collapsed and people killed — thousands. But this was no tragedy for me, not until later when the meaning of it all became apparent.'

Now an old man, and having experienced the war, it came back as he was interviewed. 'Yes,' he declared, visibly upset, 'it was difficult, very difficult.'[11]

Pjotr Aleksandrowitsch Lidow, a 35-year-old party official living in Minsk, was informed by a *Pravda* secretary at 09.00 hours that morning that his country was at war. Gazing through his apartment window he saw 'the town was completely quiet. Nobody knew anything. People were going into the parks and the countryside.' Lidow's life until that moment had been completely normal. Routine domestic issues occupied his mind. A Sunday drive with the children was planned and the only complication was 'what should one wear, should we pack the childrens' sun covers, will we be able to buy refreshment there or do we need to take drinks with us?'[12] Over breakfast he told his wife and children they were at war.

Vladimir Admoni from Leningrad was travelling on the express train between Ufa and Moscow on 22 June. A passenger who briefly got out at a station to buy something announced bluntly on his return, 'I think we are at war.' Aside from that he knew nothing. Admoni remembered 'all the other passengers except me immediately assumed it was a war against England.' The press at Stalin's instigation had been so 'Hitler friendly' during the Non-Aggression Pact period, that the English were branded the potential trouble-makers.[13]

Meanwhile, back at Minsk, Josef V., a documentary cameraman, remarked, 'The war had already begun, but here . . . it was quiet, nothing was happening.' Outside he noticed a policeman standing wearing an imposing white uniform with 'majestic shoulder epaulettes' and a white-pointed helmet. 'The police wore such a uniform in those days,' he said. As he began filming his street documentary panorama, real historical events began to unfold.

'I suddenly noticed aircraft flying over, as if in an air show I thought to myself. There were a lot, something like 20 in formation. I carried on filming and suddenly saw an explosion, and later as they came on I clearly saw black objects falling from beneath . . . then it dawned on me, they're bombs!'

Despite the explosions and the urge to take cover, Josef V. carried on filming 'the first action pictures of the first day of the war'. Suddenly he was seized by the collar and poked in the ribs. Totally engrossed in filming, he ignored the distraction until, unable to pan the camera any longer, he turned to face an unexpected assailant. It was the policeman, only now:

'His uniform was not white but full of dust and he had lost his helmet. His hair stood on end and his face was like straw. He prodded me again in the chest with his pistol and roared "Papers — or I'll fix you!" He was very excited. I showed him my ID card and he responded, "they're dropping bombs on us and you have nothing better to do than carry on filming!"'

Which is what he did, sincerely believing it was his duty to show cinema audiences the destruction being visited on the streets and buildings he filmed. It resulted in a misappreciation of the bureaucratic tenor that would be applied to his work. 'People in those days,' he said, 'were only used to seeing good things' on their cinema screens. Every ten minutes fresh swarms of aircraft passed over.

'I filmed it all, and every time I did I questioned whether I was doing the right thing. Later came the realisation that it was not only the policeman who thought like this. When the film material reached Moscow the decision was made not to use it. The Red Army was in retreat, cities were burning and the Fascists were taking Red Army prisoners. All this misery did not need to be projected on the screen . . .
The Directors took what they needed and the rest was consigned to the rubbish bin.'[14]

The fundamental difference between the German and Soviet home front experience at the outbreak of war was that Russian civilians were immediately caught up in ground fighting. So far as ordinary Germans were concerned, it was a distant event that one followed on the radio. Stephan Matysh, an artillery commander in the 32nd Russian Tank Division on the outskirts of Lvov, explained how, on the Saturday night before the war, 'each of us had his plans for Sunday. Each had his family cares.' All this was abruptly transformed. After the unexpected early morning air raids on barracks, garages, storehouses and officers' houses, 'many found they had lost their near and dear ones' and, as Matysh pointed out, 'many became orphans and cripples'. He, like many other Soviet officers, was constrained by his joint responsibility to look after civilian dependants while at the same time preparing for action with no warning. His division commander, Colonel Yefim Pushkin, issued orders for action and:

'While taking steps to get the division into full combat readiness in such a trying situation he did everything he could to save the families of the officers. The necessary number of lorries and parties of soldiers were detailed off to help load the luggage and send old folk, women and children, deep into the country.'[15]

The front situation at this stage appeared serious but salvageable. One Soviet staff officer, Captain Ivan Krylov, concerned at the build-up of a German advance toward Minsk, was assured the dangerous situation could be restored 'provided our troops fight to the end'. He stated:

'The men have been ordered not to die before taking at least one German with them. "If you are wounded," the order says, "sham death, and when the Germans approach kill one of them. Kill them with your rifle, with the bayonet, with your knife, tear their throats out with your teeth. Don't die without leaving a dead German behind you."'[16]

'DON'T DIE WITHOUT LEAVING A DEAD GERMAN BEHIND YOU'... BREST-LITOVSK

Savage fighting continued unabated into the second day at Brest-Litovsk. Grigori Makarow, a Red Army soldier, remembered:

'The whole garrison was without water because a shell striking the Terespol tower [at the entrance to the citadel] had destroyed the large water-tank. The power station had also been hit so there was no longer any light. The attack was beaten back with machine guns.'[1]

It became apparent to the German 45th Division on the same day that the original decision to withdraw selectively to clarify the front line situation and ensure the citadel was completely surrounded had simply resulted in the vacated positions being immediately occupied by Russians. From 05.00 hours German artillery pounded the citadel in concentric patterns at timed intervals. Care was taken to avoid hitting a beleaguered group of German soldiers, who were trapped with prisoners of war in the vicinity of the church. Gefreiter Hans Teuschler, severely wounded, lying nearby, recalled, 'never had I had a more burning desire to see the coming day'. After the pain, chill and uncertainties of the previous night 'the dear sun became too good to us. The heat rose until it was almost unbelievable.'[2]

Artillery harassing fire continued throughout the day. German gun crews removed their tunics and laboured on in shirtsleeves, presenting an incongruously peaceful appearance as manual labourers in braces. Infantry began to dig in systematically around the remaining Russian defence works. It was necessary to bury the dead quickly because of the oppressive heat. Small thickets of crosses began to appear, adorned with German helmets. They formed a sinister backcloth to passing dust-shrouded vehicle convoys bypassing the town and the fighting, on their way to 'Rollbahn 1' moving east.

Two German propaganda cars, fitted with loudspeakers, began transmitting on the North Island, using the prevailing wind direction to waft their surrender appeals across the citadel. Between 17.00 and 17.15 hours a murderous artillery barrage mushroomed off the enemy positions, after which the loudspeakers announced to survivors they had a temporary 90-minute amnesty within which to surrender. Some 1,900 Russians took the option and shakily emerged from the ruins. Nikitina Archinowa, the wife of a Russian officer near the *Ostfort*, described what happened:

'We women were taken with the children from out of the casemates and thrown outside. The Germans sorted us out and handled us as if we were soldiers, but we had no weapons, and led us off into captivity.'

Their German captors were in no forgiving mood. Forty-fifth Division had already radioed to XII Corps that morning that 'so far, 18 officers have been killed'. Casualties rose remorselessly. The influx of prisoners suggested 'the resistance capability of the Russians had been substantially reduced, and that a repeat of artillery fire and propaganda broadcasts would cause the citadel to fall without further losses'.[3]

Civilian captives were not courteously handled. Mrs Archinowa said: 'as we came over the bridges shells were being fired into the fortress'. The amnesty was over. Prisoners were made to lie down directly beneath the artillery pieces engaging the citadel walls. Archinowa explained:

'These were big guns. The Fascists laid us under the guns as hostages so that my husband and the other defenders would surrender. What should I do? It was awful. With every shot I thought my brains were going to come out of my head. The children began to bleed from the ears and mouth.'

Mrs Archinowa's daughter's hair turned grey. 'My son. then only five years old. was permanently deaf afterwards.' When the constant artillery pounding paused they got up and moved on. Firing recommenced as the newly displaced refugees stumbled along. Their overriding fear was that at any moment they might be taken out of the line and shot.[4]

That evening the propaganda broadcast cars were despatched to Infantry Regiment 133 on the South Island to build on their proven success. Their eerie metallic appeals began echoing around the city again as twilight descended. Once darkness fell, however, the Russians made renewed attempts to break out of the fortress to the north and east into the town. The division after-action report dolefully commented that 'the intense artillery and infantry fire from all sides opposing [break-out attempts] completely drowned out the volume of the loudspeakers'. It appeared the weaker-willed had already surrendered.

Mrs Archinowa, moving out of immediate range, said, 'we survived thanks to an old German soldier who had been detailed to look after us.' After they crossed the River Bug back onto Polish soil the soldier told them, 'I must report, and you — make up your minds. If you can get going — Go!' They dispersed and Mrs Archinowa took her children home. Her husband was not to survive the subsequent fighting for the citadel and the war was to take her mother, brother, son and daughter also. 'Practically my whole family was annihilated,' she lamented.[5]

On 24 June Gefreiter Teuschler and about 70 other soldiers cut off in the vicinity of the church were rescued by a foray from I/IR133, covered by a concentrated artillery bombardment. The battle for Brest-Litovsk encapsulated in miniature the approaching pitiless experience of the new Eastern Front. Heinz Krüger, a combat engineer, commented after the war:

'A fantastic thing, Ja? — the fortress at Brest-Litovsk. And the men that fought there, they didn't give up. It was not a question of a victory — they were communists — it was more one of annihilation. And it was exactly the same for them — we were Fascists! It was some battle! A few prisoners were taken, but they fought to the last.'[6]

It was anticipated the division objective could be taken within eight hours. Now it was the third day and there was scant prospect of surrender. Russians occupied the barracks and the so-called 'Officers' Mess' within the citadel, the eastern part of the North Island, part of the wall on the northern bridge (Werk 145) and the *Ostfort*. A decision was taken to reduce the remaining strongpoints with artillery to avoid further German bloodshed. Invasion traffic could still, with detours, be directed onto 'Rollbahn 1' moving east.

At 16.00 hours on 24 June, 45th Infantry Division announced: 'the citadel has been taken' and 'isolated infantry was being mopped up'. Optimistically, it was claimed 'resistance was much reduced'. A triumphant report at 21.40 hours the same evening announced, 'Citadel at Brest taken!' It was one of several misleading messages, commonplace in the confusion of war. Gunfire still reverberated around the city. The brief confirmation of 'false report' followed. The siege was about to enter its fourth bloody day.[7]

ACROSS THE DVINA . . . ARMY GROUP NORTH

Three German Army Groups — North (Leeb), Centre (Bock) and South (Rundstedt) — attacked into the interior of Russia along historically proven invasion routes, towards Leningrad, Moscow and Kiev. The northern approach had already been traversed by the Teutonic Knights, ironically re-enacting an epic film being shown to Russian cinema audiences at that time. Sergei Eisenstein's totalitarian cinematic masterpiece about 13th century warrior prince Alexander Nevsky portrayed a united Russian medieval peasantry combining to defend the city of Novgorod against the invading Knights of the German Teutonic Order in 1242. Its poignant depiction of events was not lost on its audience. The wardrobe of the attackers included distinctively shaped German helmets, and the presciently staged atrocities against Russian peasants stirred the same emotions subsequent brutalities would engender. The manner of the German defeat, its Knights swallowed up by the cracking ice of Lake Peipus in the dead of winter, was so prophetic in symbolic terms that the film had to be withdrawn within a year of release. It conflicted with the diplomatic intent of the Non-Aggression Pact signed with Hitler in 1939. The film was soon back on the screens.

Both the northern and central invasion routes had been used in part by Charles XII of Sweden. His army, defeated at Poltava in 1709, was destroyed by the following Russian winter. In 1812, Napoleon's Grande Armée thrust across Minsk and Smolensk to Moscow: it, too, collapsed in the Russian winter. The third, southern, route was separated from the other two army groups by the Pripet Marshes to the north of its area and the Carpathian mountains in the south. This road was the gateway to the Ukraine, the 'bread-basket' of Russia. Beyond lay the great industrial, mining and oil-bearing regions of the Donets, Volga and Caucasus. Few serious natural obstacles barred these approaches apart from some of the great Russian rivers. Even these were no serious impediment to suitably equipped mechanised forces. Blitzkrieg operations in the Low Countries had already demonstrated the ability of modern technology to overcome them. No serious military operations were contemplated within the swampy 65,000sq km expanse of the Pripet Marshes.

The Wehrmacht appeared to have mastered the operational art of war during its successful fast-moving campaigns in Poland, Scandinavia, the Low Countries and France. This previously unseen capability of waging 'joint' campaigns combining the synergy of land, air and maritime forces to direct overwhelming combat power in the right place at the right time was unprecedented. The *Schwerpunkt* (focus of effort) had to be properly supported by firepower and logistics. The scale and shape of the huge concentration of forces required to invade the Russian land mass from the west, or combine to oppose such an intent, needed careful and skilful operational planning. The German general staff excelled at the art. Such planning involves risk and some luck, and also a methodical prosecution of the aim within an accepted staff framework. This then confers a scientific ability to outweigh the intangible factors, those elements Clausewitz would describe as the 'frictions of war'. In directing massive armies there comes that decisive moment when forethought backed by meticulous planning and organisation enables the enemy to be outmanoeuvred operationally. This is achieved when the foe, in spite of realising what is likely to happen, is powerless to react. The aim is to penetrate the opponent's 'decision cycle', so that the time and space to execute operational counter-moves is denied him.

These preconditions had been achieved by German planning on the Soviet frontier by the third week in June 1941. Soviet defences were deployed linearly along its 4,500km front from the Barents Sea to the Black Sea. Fifty-six divisions were deployed to a depth of 50km to the front, with the second echelon and their tanks 50–100km behind. Reserve corps were

a further 150–400km from the frontier. It was too late to redeploy to meet German offensive concentrations — reserves were too far back. A 'checkmate' configuration had been set up on the frontier.

This was soon acknowledged by the Soviet initial contact reports that began to flood higher headquarters. The Soviet Third Army observed on the second day of the campaign that its right flank was being enveloped by the enemy, stating: 'We have no reserves at all, and there is nothing with which to plan a strike.' Extracts from the report reveal why: 'Our most available force — the 11th Mechanised Corps — suffered great losses in tanks, 40 to 50 in all, on 22–23 June 1941.'

The 56th Rifle Division was reduced to two scattered detachments numbering 700 to 800 men and the 85th Rifle Division 'suffered considerable losses'. The 27th Rifle Division was reduced by 40%, with units down to a quarter or a half of a combat unit of ammunition. Operational flexibility did not exist. 'Units that are on peacetime establishment have no transport.' The commander of the Third Army complained, 'I have had no front orientation for two days', and that 'in view of the fact that a number of walkie-talkies are out of order, I can communicate with you on only one walkie-talkie'.[1]

Counter-moves were doomed to failure before they could even begin. Soviet mechanised corps in the central area, required to block German advances between 22 and 26 June, faced long marches. These ranged typically from 80–100km for the IIIrd and XIIth Mechanised Corps and up to 200km for the IXth and XIXth Mechanised Corps. The VIIIth Mechanised Corps had to move 500km. The outcome was piecemeal commitments within a few hours of arrival or immediate and costly advances with no preparation. Gains were insignificant.[2]

Infantry fared even worse. The 212th Rifle Regiment on the right flank of the 49th Division in the Soviet Fourth Army area was facing the German IVth Army Corps. Following an alert at midnight on 22 June the unit slogged 40km through unbearable heat, fighting exhausting skirmishes en route to reach Siemiatycze, its stated objective to the north. Completely fatigued on arrival, they were required to counter-march another 40km after a short rest to Kleszczele, virtually back to their original start point. The soldiers were demoralised. Their situation was hopeless. Progress could be measured by their discarded equipment, notably greatcoats and gas masks, abandoned by roadsides along their route.[3]

Even with warning, Soviet frontier forces had neither the time nor resources to react. The operational paralysis engendered is a consequence of surprise and had featured in all previous German campaigns. At no point had the Polish or western armies been able to break out of the operational straitjacket to which they had been consigned by German strategy. There were, however, a number of fundamental differences to this new campaign. The Wehrmacht was attacking its most heavily armed and psychologically resilient opponent to date. He had been totally outmanoeuvred on the frontier but time, as with previous offensives in Poland and the West, was short. The German army and economy was geared for only a short war. Space was also different. The Soviet Union was limitless in comparison to the distances traversed during the western Blitzkrieg. A key precondition, neutralising the Red Air Force, had already been achieved. Only time would tell, once the impact of surprise wore off, whether the enemy would remain standing. In the west the French had fought valiantly and with some resilience after Dunkirk, but manoeuvre space had been irretrievably lost. In Russia it could be different.

Army Group North commanded by Generalfeldmarschall Wilhelm von Leeb was the weakest of the three army groups. The OKH 'Barbarossa' order of 31 January 1941 had directed it to destroy enemy forces in the Baltic theatre, and occupy the Baltic ports and Leningrad and Kronstadt, to deny the Russian fleet its bases. Neither of the other two army groups had such vast distances to cover and it had the least armour to execute the thrust. Leeb's one Panzer group, Panzergruppe 4 under Generaloberst Hoepner, consisted of three Panzer divisions, three motorised infantry and two foot infantry divisions. With two further army corps — XVIth and XVIIIth, consisting of eight and seven infantry divisions respectively — Army Group North was advancing with only 18 divisions, approximately half the size of Army Group Centre and South (including its Romanian divisions). It was directly supported by about 380 aircraft from Luftflotte 1.[4]

Unlike the Centre and South sectors, Army Group North was faced by a shallow rather than wide line of enemy positions. Russian deployment in the recently occupied Baltic countries was dispersed, and in greater depth. Enemy forces stretched back into the territory of the old Russian Empire with a large reserve of Soviet tanks east of Pskov. An encirclement strategy was not, therefore, feasible. Leeb — unlike the practice in the other army groups — kept his comparatively weaker Panzergruppe, the 4th under Hoepner, directly under command and at the centre of his advance. Surprise was to be achieved by exploiting superior speed and mobility. Each partial engagement aimed not at encirclement but rather a deeper and quicker thrust towards Daugavpils, Pskov and Leningrad, the eventual strategic objective. Panzers formed the apex of thrust lines with infantry following as best they could along the flanks, delivering attacks close to the point of the spear to maintain forward Panzer momentum. Daugavpils, with its two bridges over the wide River Dvina, was the immediate objective. The aim, having punched into the defences, was to push forward and maintain sufficient momentum to keep the enemy off balance.

Stiff frontier resistance was quickly broken so that, by the end of the first day, the 8th Panzer Division was already 80km deep into the hinterland, and succeeded in throwing a bridgehead across the River Dubysa. Confidence and progress was so good that at 19.55 hours on the first day the division reported, 'troops are advancing rapidly eastwards'. The quality of opposition was such that 'the Division has the impression that it has yet to come into contact with regular troops'.[5]

At 04.00 hours the next day, air reconnaissance identified strong Russian motorised columns moving north from an area north-west of Wilno toward an important road junction at Kedaynyay. The force, which included between 200 and 350 Soviet tanks, appeared to be bearing down on the 8th Panzer Division, leading LVIth Panzer Corps. It was the 2nd Soviet Tank Division. They passed through Kedaynyay and missed LVIth Panzer Corps but then struck the 6th Panzer Division of XXXXIst Panzer Corps at Rossieny, 60km away. Hoepner, the commander of Panzergruppe 4, took a calculated risk. Despite the power of the attacking Russian force — 300 tanks and comparable in artillery and infantry strength to the corps it was attacking — XXXXIst Corps was tasked to destroy it without reinforcement. The lead LVIth Corps division, 8th Panzer, was directed onwards to Daugavpils on the River Dvina as planned. Blitzkrieg was becoming reality.

Between June 24 and 26, the Soviet force, which included 29 heavy tanks of an unknown type, were surrounded and liquidated by XXXXIst Panzer Corps' large complement of Czech-manufactured light Pz Kpfw IIs and modestly gunned medium Pz Kpfw IIIs. German tactical superiority overcame the shock of encountering the new tank types. The decision not to divert the armoured apex from its aim paid off handsomely, for even as the tank battle at Rossieny died down, the forward elements of the 8th Panzer Division had the vital bridges across the River Dvina in sight. They were over 100km ahead of the main Army Group.

Hauptsturmführer Klinter from the 3rd SS Division 'Totenkopf', following up the armoured spearhead with his motorised infantry company, recalled:

'Heat, filth, and clouds of dust were the characteristic snapshot of those days. We hardly saw any enemy apart from the occasional drive-by of enemy prisoners. But the country had totally altered after we crossed the Reich border. Lithuania gave us a little taste of what we were to find in Russia: unkept sandy roads, intermittent settlements and ugly houses which were more like huts.'

A merciless sun bore down through the swirling dust raised by vehicles. 'The air,' Klinter remembers, as they approached Daugavpils, 'had that putrefying and pervasive burnt smell so reminiscent of the battle zone, and all nerves and senses began to detect the breath of the front'. They became aware of piles of discarded Russian equipment alongside the steep roadside embankments.

'Suddenly all heads switched to the right. The first dead of the Russian campaign lay before our eyes like a spectre symbolising the destructiveness of war. A Mongolian skull smashed in combat, a torn uniform and bare abdomen slit by shell splinters. The column drew up and then accelerated ahead, the picture fell behind us. I sank back thoughtfully into my seat.'[6]

Two bridges, road and rail, spanned the River Dvina, approximately 300m wide at this point. The bridges needed to be taken intact to maintain the eastern momentum of Army Group North. Oberstleutnant Crisolli's Kampfgruppe formed the division vanguard earmarked to attack Daugavpils. It consisted of a Panzer and infantry regiment (10th and 18th respectively), infantry motorcyclists and other motorised elements with artillery and the 8th Company of Lehr Regiment 800 'Brandenburg'. The Brandenburger company was ordered to attempt a *coup de main*.

Lehr Regiment 800, originally conceived as a special forces company, had already been employed as such during the previous Polish and French campaigns. Its role was to raid behind enemy lines, occupy and prevent demolitions or destroy key headquarters and objectives such as bridges. Directly subordinate to Admiral Canaris's Military Intelligence Headquarters, it was founded at Brandenburg in Berlin from the first Bau-Lehr Company. By the time of the Polish campaign the unit was 500-men strong, rising to two battalions which were employed during the Western campaign. They created confusion in enemy rear areas through sabotage, demolitions and raids in direct support of Blitzkrieg combined advances of paratroopers and Panzers. In October 1940 an entire regiment was formed which had within a year expanded to division size.[7] Eduard Steinberger from South Tyrol served with the unit and explained:

'The Brandenburg Division originally consisted of mostly non-Reich Germans — Sudeten Germans who spoke Czech, a few Palestinian Germans and volunteer Ukrainians. There were people from all over who mostly spoke other languages, but all units were under German command.'[8]

At the outset of the Russian campaign Oberleutnant Herzner commanded the Ukrainian 'Nightingale' battalion, recruited mainly from west Ukrainians released from Polish prisoner of war camps after the 1939 campaign. These formed part of the German advance toward Lemberg.[9]

Oberleutnant Wolfram Knaak, commanding the 8th 'Brandenburger' Company observing the Daugavpils bridges, had been wounded during a similar bridge raid near Kedaynyay. He was well aware of the risks involved operating so far forward of the vanguard battle group. 'When the commanders of the divisions we were assigned saw they'd got a company of Brandenburgers,' Steinberger remarked, 'they immediately put us with the advance units who would be the first to make contact with the enemy.'

Knaak split his company into two raiding groups, one each for the railway and road bridges. Steinberger described how these units might be configured for a mission. They could be up to half a company strong, 60–70 soldiers, or more usually platoon sizes of 20–30 men.

'We always operated in decoy uniforms. We wore all kinds — Russian ones for example — over our Wehrmacht uniforms. We had to be able to swiftly get rid of the cover uniform.'

The penalty, if they did not, was inevitable execution on capture. 'We generally played a situation by ear,' Steinberger said. In attempting to seize a bridge:

'We always drove over in captured Russian trucks, with one of us sitting on top while someone who spoke Russian, a Latvian or Estonian for instance, sat in the cab.'[10]

During the early morning hours of 26 June Knaak's group of captured Russian trucks began its tense drive, headlights on, toward both bridges, the spans of which could just be discerned with approaching daylight. The bridges, separated by a bend in the river, were about 1.5km apart. At Varpas, a village over 3km from the river, the parties diverged, each to its allotted objective. Left and straight on was the northern railway bridge, while the road crossing lay in a south-easterly direction to the right. Five Russian armoured cars parked by the road were overtaken by the railway group, which carried on to the main bridge span and judiciously halted, placing itself between these and additional Russian armoured cars on the bridge. During the resulting confusion, as the intention of these newly arrived trucks became clear, enemy gunners in the armoured cars were constrained against engaging the intruders for fear of hitting their own men. They moved off into the town to secure better fire positions. Meanwhile Feldwebel Kruckeberg deftly descended from the trucks to the bridge superstructure and began to cut suspected demolition cables.

Oberleutnant Knaak, having wound his way through unsuspecting civil traffic in the suburb of Griva on the southern riverbank to Daugavpils, drove up in the first of three trucks onto the road bridge. As they approached the western Soviet outpost they noticed the guards chatting to Russian civilians. With the prize tantalisingly within their grasp the action started. The nearest sentries were bayoneted but shots rang out. Now compromised, Knaak's truck, engine screaming, started to accelerate to the far bank. The remaining lorries in hot pursuit began to close-up behind.

As gunfire began to reverberate around the bridge and suburb of Griva, followed by eerie flashes and the thump of hand-grenades, the lead tanks of Panzer Regiment 10 began to move. They had driven up as close as they dared. Hatches were dropped on order from their commander, Oberstleutnant Fronhöfer, and they began a metallic clattering race through the built-up area of Griva. Civilian traffic scattered.

Oberleutnant Knaak on the road bridge gritted his teeth and urged his driver on. Behind, whining engines and clanking gears indicated he was not alone. A crack followed by the iridescent red-hot slug of an anti-tank projectile spat out from the far Russian bank and slammed into Knaak's truck, passing straight through, ejecting sparks and splinters of metal. The truck trundled to a halt out of control, Knaak sprawled dead inside the cab. A murderous fire jetted out from houses alongside the riverbank. German Panzers and infantry were, however, already visible on the bridge spans. An artillery shell crashed into the railway bridge producing a secondary detonation from part of the explosive charge. It was repairable, but for the moment tanks could not cross. The 'Brandenburgers' were pinned down. Steinberger described the typical dilemma once fighting broke out and decoy uniforms had to be jettisoned.

'Nobody could tell whether we were friend or foe, and the tanks following on often shot at their own people in the chaos. If a mission succeeded, we usually had very few casualties. But some missions went wrong, if for example, our own people were recognised by the enemy. Then almost everybody was wiped out.'

Leutnant Schmidt commanded the first Panzer platoon to cross the Daugavpils bridge. Soon the remainder of 9/Panzer Regiment 10 was engaged in intense fighting with Russian infantry attempting to scale the river embankment and place grenades on tank tracks to immobilise them. Duelling with anti-tank guns began up and down the streets as further Panzers and German infantry crossed the bridge and began to penetrate the town.

Fighting continued throughout the day and columns of smoke spiralled above the town as desperately mounted Russian counter-attacks vainly attempted to wrest control of the bridges back. Air raids conducted by Soviet twin-engined aircraft in a last-ditch effort to destroy the bridges were also unsuccessful. Soviet soldiers were constantly plucked from the bridge superstructures later that day, still attempting to reignite demolition fuses. The 9th Panzer Company destroyed 20 light Russian tanks, 20 artillery pieces and 17 anti-tank guns during its battles around the bridge entry points.

Army Group North had stormed the Dvina and had achieved a bridgehead. The way to Leningrad had been opened.

NO NEWS

At home in the Reich there was no news. After the initial invasion announcement the population was given nothing of substance for seven days. Daily OKW reports gave sparse information. There were no names or unit numbers and rivers and towns received no mention at all. Goebbels, the Minister of Propaganda, played his psychological instrument with adroitness. 'The public mood is one of depression,' he recorded in his diary on 23 June. 'The nation wants peace, but not at the price of defeat, but every new theatre of operations brings worry and concern.' Well aware of early campaign successes, he wrote on 25 June: 'We have still issued no details in the High Command Bulletin. The enemy is to be kept in complete ignorance.' He exploited the period of tension with consummate skill. The press was constrained from publishing big maps of Russia. 'The huge areas involved may frighten the public,' he claimed. Similarly he took a firm line against imprudent campaign length predictions widely pronounced by the Foreign Office. 'If we say four weeks and it turns out to be six, then our greatest victory will be transformed into a defeat in the end.' The Foreign Ministry appeared to compromise security. 'I've had the Gestapo take steps against one particular loudmouth,' he admitted.[1]

Quiet confidence began to replace the initial nervousness. Certainty of a rapid victory over Russia became the accepted view, a reversal of previous campaign experience. Rumours abounded, raising tension to a 'feverish' height. Over 100,000 Russian prisoners had allegedly been taken. The SS *Secret Report on the Home Political Situation* reported: 'Already on Tuesday [the third day of the campaign] one could hear in open conversation that 1,700 aircraft had been destroyed; by Wednesday this number had climbed to over 2,000.'[2] The public deduction derived from all this was general suspicion that German troops had in reality penetrated the Russian hinterland far deeper than hitherto reported. Large-scale maps of Russia completely sold out in bookshops. In Dresden it was rumoured German troops were only 100km from Moscow.[3]

Letters to the front reflected this concern at the news blackout. One wife wrote to her husband, seven days into the invasion: 'Sunday is upon us again, and you have probably experienced so much already. I didn't get any post today.'[4] A National Socialist mother wrote to her son from Brand on 28 June announcing the lifting of the postal ban, stating, 'I do not doubt for one instant that there will be a victory over these dogs, whom one cannot refer to as human beings'. Yet beneath the dogma there remained concern for her son at the front:

'In the morning we will hear through High Command Bulletins how much and where these barbarians have already been beaten. My dear boy! You know I am really concerned now, for you and Jos. Whenever you get a chance, give me a sign of life — a postcard would suffice.'[5]

Army Group Centre was the strongest in armour of the three army groups and its two Panzergruppen — 3 commanded by Hoth and 2 by Guderian — were committed to a huge encirclement operation. Army Group Centre sought to destroy as many of the Soviet forces as possible facing it in White Russia before they could disengage and escape into the depths of Russia. There, they might choose to stand and fight on the great natural obstacles of the Dvina and Dnieper rivers. The aim was to secure the 'land-bridge' between the headwaters of these two rivers — where the Minsk–Smolensk road passes en route to Moscow — as Napoleon did before them. As the massive Panzer thrusts by Army Group Centre gathered momentum, German air reconnaissance reported numerous enemy columns retreating eastward from the Bialystok region.

Simultaneously reports indicated an increase in the tenacity of local Soviet resistance, which Generalfeldmarschall von Bock, the commander of Army Group Centre, assessed might be to cover a withdrawal. The original 'Barbarossa' concept visualised Minsk forming the eastern edge of the first encircling movement towards the east. Bock expressed his preference to OKH that his Panzer groups should continue onward to Smolensk, 320km

beyond the start line, fearing strong enemy contingents might escape eastwards into the Berezina marshlands, escaping the ring due to close at Minsk.[6] OKH ironically faced the parallel dilemma it had experienced during the race to the English Channel after crossing the River Meuse the year before at Sedan in France. At what point, planners conferred, does a deep penetration become compromised by over-exposed flanks? OKH insisted on the junction of the two Panzergruppen near Minsk, in accordance with the original 'Barbarossa' plan. Panzergruppe 3 began to turn inward on 24 June. As a result, Soviet troops were pushed southward onto the flanks of Guderian's Panzergruppe 2. Fourth and Ninth German armies marching up their infantry on foot were ordered to destroy fast-forming Soviet stay-behind elements that could menace the advance of the follow-up forces needed to consolidate the Panzer advances.

By 25 June Army Group Centre was beginning to coalesce around two primary pockets: 12 Soviet divisions were already marooned in the Bialystok and Volkovysk areas; within four days another belt of 15 Soviet divisions was enveloped in the Minsk area. It was becoming apparent from countless local Russian counter-attacks that the enemy, almost instinctively, was going to fight for every foot of soil.

In Germany there were still no *Sondermeldungen*. These satisfying fanfares of music on the radio had been a distinctive feature of the preceding French campaign, heralding Wehrmacht victories. Edith Hagener wrote to her husband in the field:

'My Dearest,
We want to be very brave at this time and draw strength from the many beautiful years we have spent together. After the first perplexing sadness I have come quietly to my senses, because I need also to remain a happy mother to our children and a brave wife for you. Stay healthy my love. May dear God and my enormous love protect you. Your Edith.'[7]

Goebbels, better informed, enthused to his diary on 23 June:

'Brest-Litovsk taken. All the day's objectives reached. No problems so far. We are entitled to be very pleased. The Soviet Regime will crumble like touchwood. [He continued the following day] Our new weapons are carrying all before them. The Russians are emerging from their bunkers trembling, unfit for interrogation for a day afterwards . . . Everything is going to plan and better.'[8]

This information was unavailable to the general public. The only point they might identify with was Goebbels' comment on the prevailing weather. 'I am totally drained by the oppressive heat,' he complained. 'These are difficult days for our soldiers.'[9] One housewife, fretful at the absence of mail, expressed entirely different emotions:

'If only I knew how my love was getting on. Are you still in good health? Otherwise I hope you are well. I would gladly have fetched you something to eat and drink during this hot week. If I had to be outside in the heat as well, then you would not have been thirsty. Where are you my love? I so look forward to your next letter. Write to me as soon as you can. Perhaps you are near Brest-Litovsk, where there is certainly fighting going on.'[10]

She was correct. Fighting still raged within the disputed border city.

BREST-LITOVSK ... 'I WONDER HOW IT IS I AM STILL ALIVE!'

On the fourth day of the siege at Brest-Litovsk, combat teams from the three infantry regiments of the German 45th Division formed mixed groups of assault pioneers and infantry to reduce remaining strongpoints. Nebelwerfer multi-barrelled rocket launchers were in support. Helmut Böttcher, an assault engineer, recalled their bizarre impact on the enemy.

'A type of rocket was used. They didn't go far, but their impact was terrible. The worsy possible there was, I think, at that time. Everything within a circle of about three and a half metres was dead, caused by the air vacuum created, which collapsed all the lungs of humans and animals alike. It was awful. Generally one saw the people simply sat there, immovable, frozen like dolls — Ja! — many had marks, but some simply sat still on a chair or bench. Death was certain, and came very quick. Ghastly!'[1]

It was decided to clear the North Island before grappling again with the citadel. Immense difficulties were encountered from the start. Artillery support was impractical due to the confined nature of the areas to be reduced. 'Infantry weapons were ineffective due to the strength of the walled fortifications,' reported 45th Division staff, while 'heavy tanks or SPs (self-propelled guns), which might have made an impact, were not available'. The one remaining flamethrower belonging to Pionier Battalion 81 could not close up to the houses without armoured protection. Attempts were made to bring captured Russian tanks into action.

Newly constituted assault teams commenced mopping up the identified resistance points. Daja Dmitrowna, married to a Soviet artillery soldier, tearfully recalled the claustrophobic nature of the fighting:

'We were hidden in barrack cellars with no water or anything to eat the whole week long. When the Fascists stormed the fortress they threw smoke grenades into the cellar. I saw my children suffocating but could do nothing to prevent it. I have no idea how I manage to survive — purely by chance. I wonder how it is I am still alive!'[2]

Close-in fighting for these enclosed built-up areas was brutal. Trapped Russians, expecting to be shot on the spot if taken prisoner, even fought back with knives. Grigori Makarow, a Red Army soldier, recalled how attack directions conducted with tear gas 'were indicated by the noxious clouds rising in the air'. Women and children were trapped within the same choking casemates as desperately resisting Russian soldiers. Makarow saw 'a small youngster, dead. He had suffocated in the gas. His mother had covered his face with a fur glove, to protect him.' Their position was hopeless. 'There were many wounded,' said Makarow, 'but no disinfectants; gangrene took hold therefore very quickly and many of the injured died.'[3]

Leutnant Schneiderbauer, of 45th Division's 50mm Anti-tank Platoon, was ordered to move his guns forward to assist in the reduction of citadel strongpoints. As the platoon advanced across the South Island he noticed:

'The whole route showed the bitter fighting that had taken place here over the first few days. Buildings were for the most part destroyed and brick rubble, and dead Russians and horses covered the roads. The oppressive stench of burning and corpses was all-pervasive.'

As the specially constituted assault groups began mopping up enemy-held buildings, 50mm guns provided fire support, shooting up windows and suspected hiding places. Snipers made the enterprise extremely hazardous. A propaganda company officer, ignoring exhortations to be careful, was shot. Extricating the casualty degenerated into a lengthy and dangerous task. Stretcher-bearers came under fire 'but by a miracle,' commented Schneiderbauer, 'managed to get back in one piece'. The remorseless process of wearing down the defenders continued. The anti-tank platoon commander watched as:

'Assault engineers got up onto the roof of the building block opposite us. They lowered explosive charges down with poles onto windows and firing positions, but only a few Russians gave up as a result. The majority sat it out in secure cellars and, despite the heavy artillery strikes, would take up the fire fight again after the demolitions had exploded.'

The German tactic was to utilise these brief respites offered by supporting fire and rush into the buildings. Schneiderbauer explained, 'we would go in between, packing and ramming boxes, crates and rubble into all the outlets to prevent the surrounded Russians from breaking out again from beneath the houses.' The monotonous cracks and thumps of demolitions carried on throughout the day.[4]

The so-called 'Officers' Mess' building in the citadel was a constant thorn in the side of mopping-up operations being conducted to clear the North Island. These were repeatedly exposed to enfilading fire. Assault Pionier Battalion 81 was ordered to reduce this flanking threat with demolition teams. Groups clambered onto the roof and again dangled massive explosive charges attached to poles, which were exploded opposite occupied windows. 'One heard the screams and moans of Russians wounded in the explosions' recorded the Division report, 'but they carried on firing.'[5]

Conditions in the Russian strongpoints were becoming intolerable. One nursing sister, Katschowa Lesnewna, described how:

'In the casemates we gave emergency aid to the wounded, injured children, soldiers and women. By then we had no bandages, medicines or water. Everything had been used up, above all, the water. We couldn't fetch water from the river, but we had to have it for the wounded!'

Georgij Karbuk explained the dilemma presented to defending Red Army infantrymen. 'The worse thing,' he said 'was the shortage of water'. Machine guns needed constant cooling to avoid jamming from hot expanded metal working parts producing friction. Lying alongside these same guns were the wounded, dying of thirst.

'Now what's the most important? Keeping the machine gun intact in order to rescue these people? If a machine gun went down, so indeed, did the whole group. All around, lay the wounded and dying, parched, thirsting for water. Families! Children! How many were dying of thirst! And nearby only a few steps away, two rivers.'[6]

Progress in German eyes appeared equally illusory. 'Only now,' wrote Generalfeldmarschall von Bock in his diary on 25 June, 'has the citadel at Brest fallen after very heavy fighting.'[7]

Yet the following day an insultingly huge explosion rocked the massive edifice that once housed the Communist Officer School. Pionier Battalion 81 had blasted its metre-thick massive brick side-wall with a prepared charge. Out were taken 450 dazed prisoners. The final impediment to the reduction of the North Island remained the *Ostfort*. All approaches to it were driven back with withering bursts of accurate machine gun fire. The men of 45th Division concluded 'the only option left was to oblige the Russians to give up through hunger and especially thirst. All other means were to be employed to accelerate this process of wearing him down, such as constant harassing fire with heavy mortars, preventing movement in trenches or houses, using direct tank fire, employing megaphone appeals to surrender or by throwing in surrender notices.'

The lack of water was virtually unsupportable for the defenders. Sister Katschowa Lesnewna witnessed 'how one of the nursing sisters from our ward was shot on the riverside meadow because she wanted to fetch water. I saw it with my own eyes. We could not recover the body. She lay there in the grass for eight days.' Any conceivable ploy to wear down defenders was employed. Georgij Karbuk said:

'The Germans set up huge searchlights on their bank and illuminated our side, turning night into day. Every bush was lit up, and if any of us attempted to go down to the river, even to fetch a tin can full of water, he was immediately taken out. Many of us ended up lying there.'[8]

The siege was now approaching its sixth day. A Russian deserter admitted that resistance, centring on the *Ostfort*, held some 20 officers and 370 men from the 393rd Anti-aircraft Battalion of the Soviet 42nd Rifle Division. They possessed a quadruple-barrelled AA machine gun, 10 light machine guns, 10 automatic weapons, 1,000 hand-grenades and plenty of ammunition and food. They could be expected to fight on. 'Water was short, but was extracted from boreholes in the ground.' There were women and children in the fort. 'The core of the resistance,' it was reported, 'appeared dependent upon a major and a commissar.'[9] Despite the round-up of several thousand prisoners the day before, German casualties rose inexorably. With them came an increasingly bitter frustration with the failure to end such pointless resistance.

Two incongruous-looking armoured vehicles were driven up by Panzer Platoon 28. One was a French Somua tank taken in the previous French campaign, the other a Russian tank captured in this one. Two other platoon tanks had already broken down. Nevertheless, both vehicles began systematically to shoot up loopholes, embrasures and windows in and around the *Ostfort*. 'The Russians became much quieter,' the division report observed, 'but still no sign of success.' Mopping up continued but was inconclusive. The Germans became perplexed and enraged at incredible acts of resistance performed by snipers who 'fired ceaselessly from the most amazing and impossible hiding places, from beneath dustbins and rubbish heaps'. They were winkled out in detail, but through it all 'firing from the *Ostfort* was always discernible'.[10]

Grigori Makarow, a Soviet soldier, recalled attacks mounted on 27 June by a 'troop of German chemical weapons'. They assaulted with tear gas. The defenders had sufficient gas masks but, as Makarow pointed out:

'They were too big for the small children. We wound them a few times at the top to tighten them up so the gas would not get in, but for one woman whose child was only a year and a half old, it was too late. He suffocated in the gas.'[11]

Such harrowing experiences served only to temper and add ferocity to resistance.

Ever more lethal combinations were employed against stubborn strongpoints. Helmut Böttcher, a German assault engineer attached to a flamethrower section, considered himself an ordinary soldier. The barbarous offensive capability he employed was perfectly normal to him, even if it makes uncomfortable reading to modern social democratic rather than totalitarian audiences. 'I was 19 years old,' he said, and 'have often thought about it, being labelled a murderer, but in war one is a hero.' Moreover, in war the bizarre becomes the norm. Böttcher's childhood was difficult but not remarkable. A product of the depression years, he said, 'at 14 years old one could say I was thrown out of home, and eventually sought a different type of experience through military service.' He had volunteered 'for this and that, but not for the flamethrowers. I was ordered to do that.' Army life offered new and different opportunities, and he tried them 'like many others'. Employment as a flamethrower operator at Brest-Litovsk was a disturbing experience. He rationalised it, saying:

'It is awful to think of such a job, but I should point out that flamethrower operators were never allowed to surrender. They were immediately shot.'

It was not an easy weapon to handle. Strapped to the operator's back was a cumbersome tank of inflammable liquid weighing over 21kg. This contained an adhesive mixture of viscous fuel which on spraying was designed to enmesh the victim in flame. The strength of the wind and its direction could transform it into a double-edged weapon which was, in any case, highly vulnerable to enemy fire. The operator needed to be part of a team protected by escorting infantry. Böttcher explained:

'The equipment itself produced a flame about 30m long at a temperature of 4,000°C. When one came up to an angled trench system the flame could be directed around corners, of course liquidating anything in there.'

The inflammable fuel was launched by compressed gas through a nozzle incorporating an igniter to produce a spray of flame against which there was absolutely no defence. Each tank carried sufficient for 10 single-second bursts of fire. They sucked out the oxygen in confined bunkers, scorching and collapsing lungs in cumulative pressure waves of intense heat. 'Most were burned immediately or at least blinded,' admitted Böttcher. 'These things were dreadful.'[12] Even today, in the preserved ruins of Brest-Litovsk, bunkers remain scarred by the characteristic starred-effect of molten stone. Black or dark red, they resemble a form of lava paste. Georgij Karbuk, a Russian in Brest at the time, remembered:

'The Germans deployed flamethrowers. They simply poked the nozzles into cellar windows and held them there. They avoided actually penetrating the cellars themselves. They held them there and burned everything. Even the bricks melted. Others threw grenades into cellars where families were hiding.'[13]

The sun bore down mercilessly throughout the sixth day of the siege. Most of the citadel and North Island had been cleared but the *Ostfort* tower still held out. Russian dead, swelling grotesquely in the blistering heat, were tipped into ditches and covered with lime and earth, to alleviate the stench. In the River Bug shallows, German dinghies were reaping a similar dreadful harvest of swollen German dead bodies snagging among the reeds. There seemed no limit to the interminable suffering experienced by the Russian defenders. 'Everything burned,' explained Katschowa Lesnewna, a surgical sister, 'the houses, even the trees, everything burned.' The condition of the wounded became increasingly critical:

'We used our underclothes as bandages. We had no water. The wounded shook . . . Although there was water next to us, it was under fire. Sometimes we got a bucket into it, but there were only a few drops to distribute. We risked our lives for it, but it was sufficient only to wet the lips of the wounded. They were desperate for it, and appealed — "Sister, sister, water", but we couldn't give them any.'[14]

During the morning of 28 June the surviving two tanks from Panzer Platoon 28 were reinforced by a number of repaired self-propelled guns. They continued to shoot up the windows and apertures of the *Ostfort*, but with no apparent result. An 88mm Flak gun was pulled forward and began to engage in the direct-fire mode. Again, there was no sign of surrender. To break the impasse Generalmajor Schlieper, the commander of 45th Division, despatched a request to the Luftwaffe airfield nearby at Malaszewieze to administer an aerial *coup de grâce* to this final stubborn strongpoint. Once the air attack was agreed, the forward German attacking elements had to be withdrawn to the outer fortress wall as a safely measure. Low cloud that afternoon caused the postponement of the solitary Luftwaffe mission. Reluctantly the investing ring was pulled in tightly again to prevent break-outs. Searchlights illuminated the walls all night. Any careless approach venturing too near the fort was immediately engaged by vicious bursts of automatic fire. Tracer continually spat out from this totally isolated outpost. Would it ever capitulate?

On 29 June the news blackout ended in the Reich.

Sondermeldung or special news bulletin 1, preceded by the Liszt 'Russian fanfare' announced that 'the Soviet Air Force had been totally destroyed'. Bulletin number 2 announced, 'the strong enemy border defences were in part broken, even on the first day'. Victory after victory received commentary in a series of statements that exuded satisfaction. 'On 23 June the enemy directed rabid counter-attacks against the vanguards of our attacking columns' yet 'the German soldier remained victorious'. Place names at last emerged. It was stated the fortress of Grodno had been taken after hard fighting. 'The last strongpoint in the Citadel at Brest-Litovsk was stormed by our troops on 24 June.' Vilnius and Kowno were taken. In all, 12 special bulletins were sonorously announced one after the other on 29 June.[15] 'Two Red Armies trapped east of Bialystok,' Goebbels gloated. 'No chance of a break-out. Minsk is in our hands.' Although a glut of information was released, the Reich audience was not totally feckless. Goebbels perceptively admitted to his diary:

'It is all too much at once. By the end, one can sense a slight numbness in the way they receive the news. The effect is not what we had hoped for. The listeners can see through our manipulation of the news too clearly. It is all laid on too thickly, in their opinion . . . Nevertheless the effect is still tremendous . . . We are back at the pinnacle of triumph.'[16]

His comment was echoed in an SS Secret Service report the following day which concurred that 'summarising the 12 Special Announcements within two or three reports would have been better received'. Despite the feverish anticipation of good news, the extent of the successes came as a general surprise. Media releases were 'almost unbelievable', particularly the numbers of Soviet tanks and aircraft destroyed. Rumours continued, because it became obvious from the *Sondermeldungen* dates that more would follow. 'With total lack of judgement,' the SS report commented, 'in some areas it was being wagered that the German Wehrmacht was likely to appear in Moscow on Sunday'.[17]

These were 'heady days'. More was to follow as the Blitzkrieg gathered momentum towards Smolensk.

Chapter 7
Blitzkrieg

'We hardly had any sleep because we drove through both day and night.'

Panzer platoon commander

THE 'SMOOTH' PERIOD . . . THE PANZERS

Generalfeldmarschall von Bock, the commander of Army Group Centre, felt exasperated as he turned his two Panzergruppen — 2 and 3 — inwards to complete the first major encirclement of the Russian campaign after being denied the greater prize at Smolensk. It was, nevertheless, a stunning achievement. 'I was still so annoyed by the order to close the pocket prematurely,' wrote von Bock in his diary, that when visited by Generalfeldmarschall von Brauchitsch, the Commander-in-Chief, his response to congratulations was a gruff 'I doubt there's anything left inside now!'[1] The 250–300km Panzer advance beginning to curl around the trapped Soviet forces was about to net some 27 Russian divisions.

Major Johann Graf von Kielmansegg, a Panzer commander with the 6th Division, later explained that the nature of the fighting on the ground belied the impressive achievements trumpeted to the world's press. It was no walk-over. The Soviet border defences were 'certainly surprised', he said, 'but not overrun'.[2] Leutnant Helmut Ritgen, serving in the same division, concurred.

'Since nobody surrendered, almost no prisoners were taken. Our tanks, however, were soon out of ammunition, a case which had never happened before in either Poland or France.'[3]

The 'smooth' period of the Panzer advance von Kielmansegg described 'lay between two parts':

'The first was the battles fought directly on the frontier — these were very very hard. Next came a blocking action on the so-called "Stalin Line", which was where Russian reinforcements were fed in. But to speak of "overrunning", even though Goebbels may have been asserting this, was an overstatement from the start.'[4]

The 'smooth' period was testimony to German tactical superiority, conferred by the collective experience of the previous successful campaigns. 'In three days I have slept for two hours and one attack has followed the other,' wrote war correspondent Arthur Grimm, advancing with elements of Panzergruppe 1 under von Kleist with Army Group South.

'The enemy cannot hold us and constantly attempts to pin us down in a major engagement. But we are always forewarned in time and bypass him in ghostly night drives.'[5]

An unpleasant surprise for the supremely confident Panzer troops was the quality of some of the Soviet equipments they soon faced.

On the second day of the campaign, in the 6th Panzer Division sector, 12 German supply trucks were knocked out, one after the other, by a solitary unidentified Soviet heavy tank. The vehicle sat astride the road south of the River Dubysa near Rossieny. Further beyond, two German combat teams had already established bridgeheads on the other side of the river. They were about to be engaged in the first major tank battle of the eastern campaign. Their urgent resupply requirements had already been destroyed. Rutted muddy approaches and a nearby forest infested with bands of stay-behind Russian infantry negated any option to bypass. The Russian tank had to be eliminated. A battery of medium 50mm German anti-tank guns was sent forward to force the route.

The guns were skilfully manhandled by their crews through close terrain up to within 600m of their intended target. Three red-hot tracer-based shells spat out at 823m/sec, smacking into the tank with rapid and resounding 'plunks' one after the other. At first there was cheering but the crews became concerned as these and another five rounds spun majestically into the air as they ricocheted off the armour of the unknown tank type. Its turret came to life and remorselessly traversed in their direction. Within minutes the entire battery was silenced by a lethal succession of 76mm HE shells that tore into them. Casualties were heavy.

Meanwhile a well-camouflaged 88mm Flak gun carefully crept forward, slowly towed by its half-track tractor, winding its way among cover provided by the 12 burnt-out German trucks strewn about the road. It got to within 900m of the Soviet tank before a further 76mm round spat out, spinning the gun into a roadside ditch. The crew, caught in the act of manhandling the trails into position, were mown down by a swathe of coaxial machine gun fire. Every shell fired by the Russian tank appeared to be a strike. Nothing moved until nightfall when, under the cover of darkness, it was safe enough to recover the dead and wounded and salvage some of the knocked-out equipments.

An inconclusive raid was mounted that night by assault engineers who managed to attach two demolition charges onto this still, as yet, unidentified tank type. Both charges exploded, but retaliatory turret fire confirmed the tank was still in action. Three attacks had failed. Dive-bomber support was requested but not available. A fourth attack plan was developed involving a further 88mm Flak gun, supported this time by light Panzers which were to feint and provide covering fire in a co-ordinated daylight operation.

Panzers, utilising tree cover, skirmished forward and began to engage the solitary tank from three directions. This confused the Russian tank which, in attempting to duel with these fast-moving and fleeting targets, was struck in the rear by the newly positioned 88mm Flak gun. Three rounds bore into the hull at over 1,000m/sec. The turret traversed rearward and stopped. There was no sign of an explosion or fire so a further four rounds smashed remorselessly into the apparently helpless target. Spent ricochets spun white-hot to the ground followed by the metallic signatures of direct impacts. Unexpectedly the Soviet gun barrel abruptly jerked skyward. With the engagement over at last, the nearest German troops moved forward to inspect their victim.

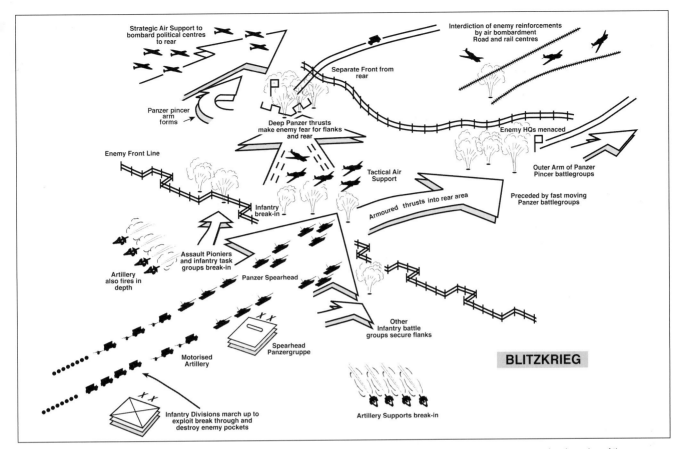

Labels in the diagram:

Strategic Air Support to bombard political centres to rear

Interdiction of enemy reinforcements by air bombardment Road and rail centres

Separate Front from rear

Panzer pincer arm forms

Deep Panzer thrusts make enemy fear for flanks and rear

Enemy HQs menaced

Enemy Front Line

Tactical Air Support

Outer Arm of Panzer Pincer battlegroups

Infantry break-in

Armoured thrusts into rear area

Preceded by fast moving Panzer battlegroups

Assault Pioniers and infantry task groups break-in

Artillery also fires in depth

Panzer Spearhead

Other Infantry battle groups secure flanks

BLITZKRIEG

Motorised Artillery

Spearhead Panzergruppe

Infantry Divisions march up to exploit break through and destroy enemy pockets

Artillery Supports break-in

Excited and chattering they clambered aboard the armoured colossus. They had never seen such a tank before. Suddenly the turret began to rotate again and the soldiers frantically scattered. Two engineers had the presence of mind to drop two stick grenades into the interior of the tank, through one of the holes pierced by the shot at the base of the turret. Muffled explosions followed and the turret hatch clattered open with an exhalation of smoke. Peering inside the assault engineers could just make out the mutilated remains of the crew. This single tank had blocked forward-replenishment to the 6th Panzer Division vanguard for 48 hours. Only two 88mm shells actually penetrated the armour; five others had gouged deep dents. Eight carbonised blue marks were the only indication of 50mm gun impacts. There was no trace at all of the supporting Panzer strikes, many of which had clearly been seen to hit.

The nature of the enemy armoured threat had irretrievably altered. General Halder wrote in his diary that night:

'New heavy enemy tank! . . . A new feature in the sectors of Army Group South and Army Group North is the new heavy Russian tanks, reportedly to be armed with 8cm guns and, according to another but untrustworthy observation from Army Group North, even 15cm guns.'[6]

This was the KV-1 (Klim Voroshilov) which mounted a 76.2mm gun. Its sister variant, the KV-2, although more unwieldy, did have a 15cm gun. In 1940, 243 of the former and 115 T-34 tanks had been produced, rising to 582 and 1,200 respectively by 1941.[7] The Russian-German tank balance was grossly distorted to the Soviet advantage in both quality and quantity. There were 18,782 various Russian tank types versus 3,648 German in 1941.[8] German Panzers in

Above: The prelude to a Blitzkrieg advance was the shattering of the enemy front at the main German point of effort, preceded by a joint artillery and air bombardment with an infantry break-in battle. The Panzers were then passed through to strike deep into the enemy rear, intimately supported by tactical air sorties and motorised artillery to overrun headquarters and break up logistic support areas. These armoured units moving at best speed would form pincer 'arms' which would then encircle and cut off retreating Russian forces, penning them into pockets to be subdued later by following marching foot infantry.

weight, main armament, operating distances and speed were generally inferior to Russian tanks.

The appearance of the 34-ton T-34 caused much consternation to the German Panzerwaffe. Developed in relative secrecy six years before, its 76mm gun was the largest tank armament (apart from the 15cm KV-2) then mounted. Its 60% sloping armour was revolutionary in terms of the increased armoured protection it offered against flat trajectory anti-tank shells, which often simply ricocheted off. Josef Deck, a German artilleryman with Regiment 71 in the central sector, complained that the 37mm standard anti-tank fire 'bounced off them like peas'.[9] Adapting the American Christie suspension system, the T-34, with extra-wide tracks and a powerful lightweight diesel engine, possessed an enormous relative power-to-weight ratio, conferring superior mobility on the Russian vehicles. It was to prove the outstanding tank design of the war, and was a formidable adversary, even in the hands of a novice. Alexander Fadin, a T-34 commander, remarked:

'As soon as you start the motor it begins throbbing, and you feel part of this powerful machine. You pick up speed and no obstacle can stop you. Nothing, not even a tree.'[10]

The vast majority of Soviet tanks, some three-quarters, were the T-26 series (approximately 12,000) while BT-2s, 5s and 7s made up a further 5,000. The remainder consisted of 1,200 T-34s and 582 heavier KV-1s and KV-2s. As a consequence 17,000 Soviet tanks were on an equal fighting footing or inferior to 979 PzKpfwIIIs and 444 PzKpfwIVs and superior to 743 PzKpfwIIs and 651 PzKpfw38(t)s, based on a captured Czech chassis. Other generally technically inferior or command variants made up the German difference with the notable exception of 250 Sturmgeschütz IIIs — assault guns made up of 75mm guns on a PzKpfwIII chassis — that operated in independent units. They were heavily armoured, with a low hard-to-target profile; they proved lethal Russian tank killers, normally employed in close support of infantry. German armoured superiority stemmed not from technology but from the combat edge conferred by their trained crews. German crews were larger: five within the PzKpfwIII and IV and even four inside the small PzKpfw38(t). Russian crews numbered four in heavy tank prototypes or less. Panzers operated within a comprehensive radio net whereas the Russians had few radios and hardly any below battalion level. Control was executed using signal flags. Responsiveness in rapidly changing circumstances was therefore cumbersome.

German Panzer crews were well versed in battle drills developed over several recent campaigns and many of their junior commanders had combat experience. Russian tank crews, by contrast, tended laboriously to follow crest lines to aid visibility and control, presenting themselves as easy targets. The Soviet tank arm caught unprepared in the middle of reorganisations and major operational redeployments to frontier areas was presented with conflicting tactical and command dilemmas. Many of the older Russian tanks, estimated at 29%, required total overhaul on the eve of the invasion and 44% were due routine servicing.[11] A key factor further bedevilling Soviet armour was the lack of air parity. Russian armoured columns were consistently and destructively harassed by the Luftwaffe while denied the accurate air intelligence freely available to their Panzer adversaries.

German tank crews were clearly shocked by the appearance of heavier and obviously superior Russian tanks. It did not square with the comfortable Untermensch (sub-human) perception of the Russians, fostered by overrunning squalid worker settlements early in the campaign. German cinema newsreels often poked fun at so-called 'paradises for Soviet workers', assuming German technological superiority was unassailable. Broadcasts in the Reich proclaimed German tank rounds 'not only penetrated once, but came out the other side of Russian tanks as well'.[12] Leutnant Helmut Ritgen of the 6th Panzer Division admitted after clashes with these previously unknown tank types that:

'That day changed the character of tank warfare, as the KV represented a wholly new level of armament, armour protection and weight. German tanks had hitherto been intended mainly to fight enemy infantry and their supporting arms. From now on the main threat was the enemy tank itself, and the need to "kill" it at as great a range as possible led to the design of longer-barrelled guns of larger calibre.'[13]

German crews entered Russia convinced of their innate technological and tactical superiority, proven in former campaigns. Tank gunner Karl Fuchs, crewing the relatively inferior PzKpfw38(t) with the 7th Panzer Division in the central sector, wrote to his wife at the end of June:

'Up until now, all of the troops have had to accomplish quite a bit. The same goes for our machines and tanks. But, nevertheless, we're going to show these Bolshevik bums who's who around here! They fight like hired hands — not like soldiers.'[14]

Curizio Malaparte, an Italian war correspondent advancing with a German armoured column in Bessarabia, described a group of Germans examining a knocked-out Soviet heavy tank four days later.

'They look like experts conducting an on-the-spot enquiry into the causes of an accident. What interests them most of all is the quality of the enemy's matériel and the manner in which that matériel is employed in the field . . . They shake their heads and murmur "Ja, ja, aber" . . . The whole secret of the German success is implicit in that "aber", in that "but."'[15]

Karl Fuchs declared more candidly to his wife, 'we have fought in battle many days now and we have defeated the enemy wherever we have encountered him.'[16] Victory jargon even became a feature of Wehrmacht slang. The BT-7 light Soviet tank was knocked out in such numbers it was referred to as the 'Mickey Mouse'. This was because the silhouette of both crew hatches, invariably left open on top of abandoned tank hulks, resembled the distinctive mouse ears of the famous Walt Disney cartoon figure.

FRONTIER TANK BATTLES

War correspondent Arthur Grimm rode with the 11th Panzer Division, part of Army Group South, toward the first major tank battle in the eastern campaign within 24 hours of the invasion. Columns of half-track SdKfz251 armoured personnel carriers festooned with infantry churned up dust as they lurched along heavily rutted village roads, 'when the reconnaissance group from our unit radioed that some 120 Soviet tanks had moved up in front of the village of Radciekow'. Engines whined and hummed into life as Grimm described 'their forward advance into the dawn twilight'. Shortly before 05.00 hours 'we drove through high cornfields as the early morning fog began to clear'. PzKpfwIIIs and IVs drove by, dark silhouettes floating across the surface of a sea of corn. They distinguished groups of Soviet tanks to their right which 'included the heaviest and most modern tanks in the world'.

On the other side of the dispersed village houses Grimm observed the dark tell-tale dots that were Soviet tanks moving about. At 05.20 hours the German assault drove into the left flank of these indistinguishable dots and, with a flash, a tall globule of black smoke rose slowly into the air and began to form into a dark ominous mushroom shape. The boom of the report carried across the intervening distance as the first Soviet tank erupted with a shot that 'penetrated its ammunition compartment'. The first tanks encountered were B-26 variants. Grimm, following closely behind the German tank advance, took photographs of scenes of blazing destruction around him. Dirty columns of smoke began to hang lazily in the air as tank after tank was hit.

'20-rounds were required to bring this heavy tank to a standstill', commented Grimm captioning a photograph which he took passing a blazing T-34 tank. Its gun was traversed rearward, to enable the driver to escape from his forward hatch. 'But this only lasted a few seconds before the remaining ammunition exploded in a blinding flash'. Grimm's reportage for *Signal*,[1] the German pictorial propaganda magazine, glossed over the desperate nature of the engagement as German tank gunners realised they were up against surprisingly heavy and unknown tank types. Leutnant Ritgen's observations of the 6th Division's encounter with KVs at Rossieny three days later were more honest:

'These hitherto unknown Soviet tanks created a crisis in

Kampfgruppe "Seckendorff", since apparently no weapon of the division was able to penetrate their armour. All rounds simply bounced off the Soviet tanks. 88mm Flak guns were not yet available. In the face of the assault some riflemen panicked. The super-heavy Soviet KV tanks advanced against our tanks, which concentrated their fire on them without visible effect. The command tank of the company was rammed and turned over by a KV and the commander was injured.'[2]

Despite the quality of the Russian tanks, tactical surprise and superior German battle drills began to tell. Alexander Fadin, a Soviet T-34 tank commander, described the spectrum of emotion a tank crewman would feel in such a battle:

'You get excited as you look for a target. The engine starts and the ground bumps up and down as you charge forward. You sight the gun and the driver shouts "Fire!"'

Spent shell cases clatter to the floor of the turret and begin rattling around, as with each concussion and recoil of the gun the fighting compartment fills with fresh cordite fumes. Fadin continued:

'When you hit a German tank in battle and blow it up, instead of firing at another tank, you open the hatch. You look out and make sure you got it!'[3]

German tank crews were coldly and professionally detached. Leutnant Ritgen surmised, 'the Soviet tank crews had no time to familiarise themselves with their tank guns or zero them in,' so soon after the invasion, 'since their fire was very inaccurate . . . Furthermore, the Soviets were poorly led.' Arthur Grimm observed that by midday on 23 June 'a dusty sea of black smoke from red and yellow flames had built up'. German reinforcements that had been brought up in support 'hardly needed to get into the fight and remained merely as spectators'. Leutnant Ritgen said the 6th Panzer Division's early frontier battles were not without crisis.

'One of our reserve officers — today a well-known German author — lost his nerve. Without stopping at the headquarters of his regiment, the division or the corps, he simply rushed to the command post of General Hoepner [the commander of Panzergruppe 4] to report that "everything was already lost".'

German tactical ingenuity began to level the odds. 'Despite their thick skin,' Ritgen explained, 'we succeeded in destroying some by concentrating fire on one tank after the other. "Aim at the hatches and openings!" we ordered.'

Grimm, the war correspondent, observed by 16.00 hours that afternoon 'the black smoke over the battlefield became ever thicker'. PzKpfwIV tanks had already ceased firing because they were being resupplied with ammunition. Panzer tactics varied according to crew initiative. 'Some enemy tanks were set on fire and others blinded,' Ritgen pointed out. 'If they turned around we found it was possible to knock them out from the rear.' Such lessons were being learned throughout the new Russian theatre.

Hauptmann Eduard Lingenhahl serving with Panzer Regiment 15 explained the heavy PzKpfwIV companies 'found mainly by chance' that quarter-second delayed action HE shells fired into the back of T-34 tanks either set the fuel or engine on fire, as blazing fuel poured through the air induction grating.[4] By 21.00 hours the battle was over. The 11th Panzer Division destroyed 46 tanks on the heights south-west of Radciekow

village alone. Contrary to the later propaganda coverage there was little complacency. Three days later Major Kielmansegg spoke to his 6th Division commander about the first encounter with heavy Soviet tanks at Rossieny. 'Herr General,' he said, 'this is a totally different war from that we have experienced with Poland or France.' It had been 'a hard battle with hard soldiers' and a number of officers had been badly shaken. 'Early panic,' Kielmansegg declared, 'was mastered finally only by the attitude and discipline of the officers.' He stated soberly:

'At the division level we saw, for the first time in the war, the danger of a serious defeat. This was one of the heaviest strains I experienced during the war.'

The only comfort he could derive was a report that one of the 'monster tanks' he had seen had been immobilised by a Leutnant placing a mine under its track.[5] Arthur Grimm's *Signal* report, not unexpectedly, ended on a high note.

'The Soviets left the battlefield after a duel lasting eleven hours. More than 40 Soviet tanks were destroyed. The pursuit continues. Only five of our own tanks were disabled.'[6]

Hard fighting near the frontier was followed by a relatively 'smooth' period of spectacular Panzer advances towards Minsk and later Smolensk. The pattern of these days, although less eventful, remained gruelling. Hyazinth Graf von Strachwitz — an Oberleutnant with Panzer Regiment 15 — declared, 'we hardly had any sleep because we drove through both day and night.'[7] The enemy was given time neither to rest nor regain the initiative. Anotoli Kruzhin, a Red Army captain facing the German onslaught opposite Army Group North, said:

'In the first days of the war the German Army was advancing very quickly. The state of shock, as it were, stayed with us for quite a long time. As far as I know the Soviets were not organised to fight until July or even the beginning of August. This was in the region of Staraya Russia, west of Novgorod. But before that, in July, the Soviet Army was retreating in such chaos that reconnaissance for the North-West front had to be provided by a special detachment. Not to find where the enemy was positioned, but Soviet units — their own army!'[8]

On the outskirts of Lvov, a similar picture was evident in the Russian 32nd Tank Division sector. Stephan Matysh, the artillery commander, had seen that superior T-34 and KV tanks had exacted many casualties. Russian tank crews were well aware of their superior armour, 'sometimes even ramming [German] tanks', but cumulative pressure was beginning to tell.

'The incessant gruelling marches and the continuous fighting over several days had taxed the tank crews to the utmost. Since the beginning of the war the officers and men had not had a single hour's rest and they seldom had a hot meal. Our physical strength was leaving us. We desperately needed rest.'[9]

Colonel Sandalov, the Soviet Fourth Army Chief of Staff, had established the Army HQ in a forest grove east of Siniavka. With no radio communications whatsoever, he was reliant on messenger traffic alone. He reported the outcome of consistent and crushing blows inflicted on his forces by Guderian's Panzergruppe 2 and Fourth German Army following its central route. Sandalov's 6th and 42nd Rifle

Divisions had already withdrawn eastwards with 'remnants [which] do not have combat capability'. The 55th Rifle Division, having unloaded from motor transport, was quickly pushed from its rapidly established defence line, 'unable to withstand an attack of enemy infantry with motor-mechanised units and strong aviation preparation'. No word had been heard of the 49th Rifle Division since the invasion. The XIVth Mechanised Corps, 'dynamically defending and going over to counter-attacks several times, suffered large losses in material and personnel', and by 25 June 'no longer had combat capability'. Paralysis afflicted the Soviet defence:

'Because of constant fierce bombing, the infantry is demoralised and not showing stubbornness in the defence. Army commanders of all formations must stop sub-units and sometimes even units withdrawing in disorder and turn them back to the front, although these measures, despite even the use of weapons, are not having the required effect.'[10]

Konstantin Simonov, on the Minsk highway under German air attack, remembered a Soviet soldier shell-shocked by the bombing fleeing down the road shrieking: 'Run! The Germans have surrounded us! We're finished!' A Soviet officer called out, 'Shoot him, shoot that panic-monger!' Shots began to ring out as the man whose 'eyes seemed to be crawling out of their sockets' fled.

'Evidently we did not hit him, as he ran off further. A captain jumped out in his path and, trying to hold him, grasped his rifle. It went off and, frightened still more by this shot, the fugitive, like a hunted animal, turned round and with his bayonet rushed at the captain. The latter took out his pistol and shot him. Three or four men silently dragged the body off the road.'[11]

A collapse appeared imminent.

PANZER VANGUARD

A typical vanguard for a Panzer division in open terrain would consist of a mixed battalion-strength force of light armour and motorcycle-borne infantry. These were the 'eyes and ears' of following units (see diagram) which might include a battalion or regiment of Panzers, supported by motorised infantry at similar strength, riding on lorries or Panzergrenadiers in armoured half-track open-compartment APCs (armoured personnel carriers). Bringing up the rear would be a battalion — or even up to a regiment — of motorised towed-artillery, to provide close fire support. Light Panzer armoured cars or tracked vehicles (PzKpfwIs or IIs) would drive either side of parallel moving columns, forming a protective screen to the flank. Such a lead element in total was termed a Vorausabteilung or vanguard combat team. It might vary in size from a battalion to a regiment plus.

Depending on terrain 'going', units would move in dust-shrouded columns, several kilometres long. Leading reconnaissance elements were often tactically dispersed on a broad front, but many follow-on units simply drove at best speed, spaced at regular intervals. Three columns might advance in parallel if sufficient routes were available. Often they were not. Map-reading in choking dust-covered and packed columns was difficult. Crewmen would sleep fitfully wherever they could, as they bumped and lurched along in vehicles. These Panzer Keile (armoured spearhead-wedges) might operate from roads or spread out in tactical formation if terrain and ground conditions allowed. In woodand or 'close

country' (bushes and scrub), the infantry would lead, clearing defiles, choke points or woodland, with tanks overlooking, prepared to give fire support. Open steppe-like terrain would see Panzers leading. War correspondent Arthur Grimm, following such a Vorausabteilung at the end of June, gave an atmospheric description of his observed axis of advance:

'The landscape stretches flat ahead with wave-like undulations. There are few trees and little woodland. Trees are covered in dust, their leaves a dull colour in the brilliant sunlight. The countryside is a brown-grey green with occasional yellow expanses of corn. Over everything hangs a brown-grey pall of smoke, rising from knocked-out tanks and burning villages.'

Panzer crewmen have a different battle perspective compared to infantry on their feet. Scenery, as a consequence of greater mobility, changes quickly and more often. Maps are read from a different vista in terms of time, distance and scale. Panzers quickly crossed maps. Infantrymen saw each horizon approaching through a veil of sweat and exhaustion. Following armoured formations made infantry feel more secure — often a false assumption, but it did mean that friendly forces were known to be ahead. A new horizon for the tank soldier meant an unknown and, very likely, a threatening situation. His was an impartial war, fought at distance. Technology separated him from direct enemy contact: he normally fought with stand-off weapon systems at great range. When direct fighting did occur, it was all the more emotive for its suddenness and intensity. Grimm stated:

'Scattered trees and wide cornfields are not pleasing to the eye, as they mean danger to us. Gun reports crack out from beneath every tree and from within every field of corn.'[1]

It was the accompanying supporting troops who closed with the enemy and saw him in the flesh. Anti-tank gunner Helmut Pole recalled the deep impression early Soviet resistance had upon him and his comrades.

'During the advance we came up against the light T-26 tank, which we could easily knock out, even with the 37mm. There was a Russian hanging in the turret who continued to shoot at us from above with a pistol, as we approached. He was dangling inside without legs, having lost them when the tank was hit. Despite this, he still shot at us with his pistol.'[2]

Little can be seen from the claustrophobic confines of a tank closed down for battle. Fighting was conducted peering through letter-box size — or smaller — vision blocks in a hot, restricted and crowded fighting compartment with barely room to move. Each report from the main armament or the chattering metallic burst of turret machine gun fire would deafen the crew and release noxious fumes into the cramped space. Tension inside would be high, magnified throughout by a prickling sense of vulnerability to incoming anti-tank round strikes, anticipated at any time. These projectiles were easily seen flying about the battlefield as white-hot slugs, with the potential to screech through a fighting compartment and obliterate all in its path. The kinetic energy produced by the strike set off ammunition fires, searing the fighting compartment in a momentary flash, followed by an explosive pressure wave blasting outward through turret hatches, openings or lifting the entire turret into the air. An external strike by a high-explosive (HE) warhead would break off a

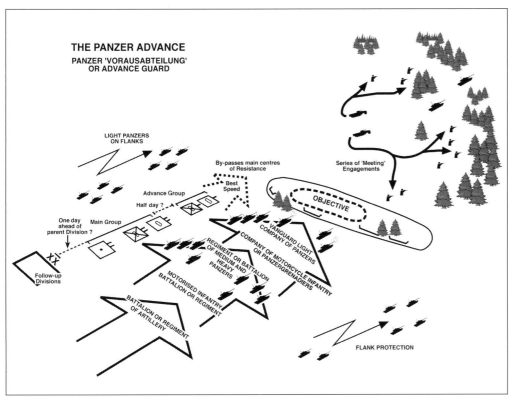

THE PANZER ADVANCE

PANZER 'VORAUSABTEILUNG' OR ADVANCE GUARD

LIGHT PANZERS ON FLANKS

By-passes main centres of Resistance

Best Speed

Advance Group

Half day ?

One day ahead of parent Division ?

Main Group

Follow-up Divisions

OBJECTIVE

Series of 'Meeting' Engagements

VANGUARD LIGHT COMPANY OF PANZERS

COMPANY OF MOTORCYCLE INFANTRY OR PANZERGRENADIERS

REGIMENT OR BATTALION OF MEDIUM AND HEAVY PANZERS

MOTORISED INFANTRY BATTALION OR REGIMENT

BATTALION OR REGIMENT OF ARTILLERY

FLANK PROTECTION

Left: A diagramatic representation of the Panzer advance. The vanguard — a light mixed force of Panzers and motorised infantry — would seek the line of least resistance. Once battle was joined, this lead element would 'fix' the objective while following heavier elements would manoeuvre, bypass, destroy or surround enemy resistance, relying upon later echelons to subjugate stay-behind elements. Fighting was generally in the form of meeting engagements shown top right) whereby junior commanders would exercise iniative to retain the tactical and operational momentum of the advance.

Below: Village clearanaces would occur once Panzer forces had isolated the settlements. Panzergrenadier infantry would be committed with tank fire support shooting them in from the flanks, at an acute angle to advancing troops. Artillery and Luftwaffe air support might be employed to precede the attack, prevent the insertion of Russian reinforcements and harass the eventual retreat. Achieving tactical momentum was of paramount importance.

Legend

1. Panzers and infantry split. Infantry lead attack on village.
2. Infantry dismount.
3. Panzers bypass and give fire support.
4. Panzer and anti-tank gun in direct fire support.
5. Infantry fight through village with man-handled anti-tank gun support.
6. Surviving Russians surrender or flee.
7. Grenadiers remount and with Panzers continue the advance.

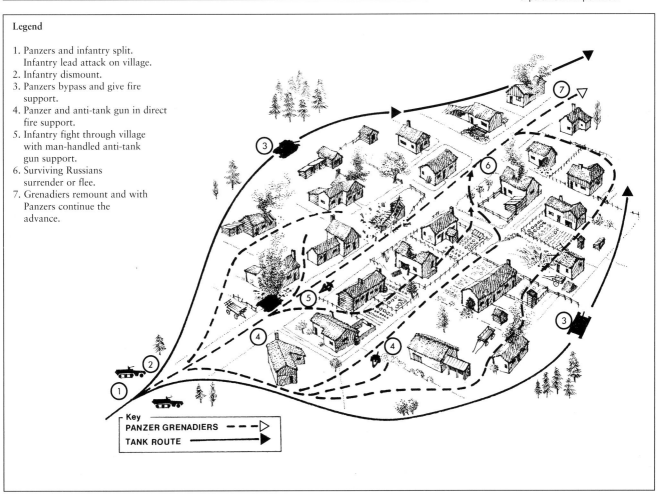

Key
PANZER GRENADIERS - - - ▷
TANK ROUTE ———▶

metal 'scab' inside; propelled by the shock of the explosion, this would ricochet around the cramped interior of the tank. The results were horrific. Flesh seared by the initial combustible flash was then lacerated by jagged white-hot shrapnel, which in turn set off multiple secondary explosions.

Tank crewmen were muffled to some extent from battle noises outside the turret, because the screams were dulled by the noise and vibration of the engine. Human senses were ceaselessly buffeted by violent knocks and lurches as the tank rapidly manoeuvred into firing positions. Dust would well up inside upon halting, and petrol and oil smells would assail nostrils during momentary pauses. A grimy taste soured mouths already dried of spittle by fear. Tank gunner Karl Fuchs from Panzer Regiment 25 admitted to his wife:

'The impressions that the battles have left on me will be with me forever. Believe me, dearest, when you see me again, you will face quite a different person, a person who has learned the harsh command: "I will survive!" You can't afford to be soft in war, otherwise you will die.'[3]

Fatigue and fear went hand in hand. Unteroffizier Hans Becker of the 12th Panzer Division spoke of Panzer battles at Tarnopol and Dubno:

'Where we had no rest for three days or nights: for rearming and refuelling we were withdrawn not by units but tank by tank and then hurled immediately into the fray again. I put one enemy tank out of action at Tarnopol and four at Dubno, where the countryside became an inferno of death and confusion.'[4]

Motorised infantry units alongside were subjected to the same persistent and physically demanding pressures. Hauptsturmführer Klinter, a company commander with the vehicle-borne SS 'Totenkopf' Infantry Regiment, which was part of Army Group North, remembered in the first few weeks of the Russian campaign that 'all the basic tactical principles we had learned appeared to be forgotten'. There was hardly any reconnaissance, no precise orders groups, or few accurate reports, because the situation was fast-moving and constantly changing. 'It was a completely successful fox hunt,' he said, 'into a totally unknown environment, with only one aim in sight — St Petersburg!'

Maps were either incorrect or inadequate. As a result, columns separated on the line of march would often drive off along the wrong route when they reached a junction. Road signing was in its infancy in a rapidly developing tactical situation. 'So every driver, in complete darkness, observing totally blacked-out conditions and at varying speeds, had to try to remain close together driving in tight columns.'[5] Driving continuously, day and night, in such conditions was nerve-racking and exhausting.

The speed of the Panzer advance may have been an elated 'fox hunt' but its rapidity produced problems of its own. Communications, although vital, were difficult to maintain. This was the experience of 7th Panzer Division columns on the Minsk–Moscow 'autobahn' at the end of June. On reaching Sloboda some 20km north-west of Minsk, they realised Russian units had become intermingled with their own vehicles during darkness. So confusing became the situation that columns of German, then Russian and then German units again were often passing each other, going in the same direction. On one occasion Russian lorries, 100m behind a German unit, overtook it and on realising their

mistake, panicked and drove back again at full speed, passing the bemused German column yet again.[6] War correspondent Bernd Overhues, travelling at an exhilarating 'autobahn' speed towards Minsk with the vanguard of a Panzer unit, recalled shots ringing out at night. A loud call warned, 'Soviet tanks up ahead!' Bullets suddenly whistled in all directions.

'What had happened? A number of small Soviet AFVs had joined the middle of the German column. It seems they had driven along together for a short stretch and then suddenly opened fire with a quadruple MG mounted on a lorry, shooting all barrels straight into the German vehicles. The sharp voice of a German officer icily restored order. The Soviet tank and lorry were shot into flames and put out of action.'[7]

Some of the 7th Panzer Division Vorausabteilungen advanced so quickly in chaotic pell-mell rushes that they became separated from the main bodies following on behind. As the unit itself related, 'again and again a wild outbreak of shooting would break out, which could only be clarified when the command "7th Panzer Division cease firing!" was given by radio.'[8]

Arthur Grimm's Vorausabteilung, clearing a cornfield of Soviet soldiers near Nowo-Miropol, unexpectedly detected an airfield to their right, obviously still in use.

'At that moment two enemy aircraft landed. The first escaped us, but we had a few seconds available for the second. Our tracer hit it full-on and it crashed on fire.'

A light 20mm Flak gun mounted on a half-track drove onto the airstrip and began shooting up the serried lines of aircraft. Soldiers gleefully disembarked with axes and grenades and began to wreck the remainder. Connecting wing struts were knocked off biplanes with axe-heads, tyres shot flat with pistols, fuselages grenaded and propellers lifted off and dropped to the ground. In all 23 aircraft were destroyed or disabled. The greatest prize was a still steaming field cooker. Requisitioned with relish, its contents were consumed on the spot. Loaves of bread and captured fresh rations were heaped on top of groundsheets and tossed into the German vehicles. The advance was quickly resumed, for once, with full stomachs.[9]

Tempo occasionally resulted in tragedy. Oberst Rothenberg, the distinguished and experienced commander of Panzer Regiment 25, a holder of the Pour le Mérite and Knight's Cross, was severely wounded by stray rounds exploding from a burning tank. He required immediate medical evacuation. His Panzer spearhead had advanced so rapidly it was cut off from the main body, marooning the wounded. Rothenberg, mindful of the vulnerability of his exposed forward position, rejected the offer of his division commander's Fieseler Fi156 Storch light aircraft or an eight-wheeled armoured car escort. Instead, he elected to be driven back in two light jeeps. The small group was apprehended by Soviet soldiers in the insecure zone immediately behind the advance, and Rothenberg was shot. The bodies were not recovered until a counter-attack was mounted the following day.[10]

The primary difficulty during lightning advances was in successfully co-ordinating maximum combat power at the chosen point of main effort — a tenet of Blitzkrieg. Leutnant von Hoffgarten, commanding Motorcycle Battalion 61 with 11th Panzer Division, advanced 510km in four weeks after crossing the River Bug at the start of 'Barbarossa'. Tanks generally led in open terrain, but there were situations, von Hoffgarten explained, that required:

'. . . still greater co-operation between the two arms. This happened in complex terrain and when facing river obstacles, minefields or enemy occupied villages. Both company commanders had to plan precisely the control of such a joint operation in advance. This was not so very easy because of the poor maps, on which usually only the main roads were drawn.'[11]

Depending on the effectiveness of enemy fire, riflemen might initially ride into battle mounted on tanks or by motorcycle. They would then dismount and close with the enemy, intimately supported by protective Panzer fire. Arthur Grimm with the 11th Panzer Division recalled attacking heavily defended villages in the Dubno area early in the campaign:

'Although the tanks could see no infantry in the open, the Soviet infantry remained hidden in the cornfields. German infantry trying to winkle them out were also invisible.'

Tank commanders, after being briefed, sketched the tactical plan on their maps in the early dawn hours. At 04.30 hours war correspondent Grimm started taking photographs as the motorcycle infantry, tasked with clearing the outlying village fields, began to drive by in a seemingly endless column of dark silhouettes. They bobbed and bumped along, rifles slung at the shoulder, raising a cloud of dust that began to merge with the low-lying early morning mist. Sunlight glinted on the metalwork of sidecars as they advanced under the protective dark outlines of tactically dispersed Panzer platoons. Commanders observing the advance formed part of the menacing silhouettes of the tanks.

After a short artillery or mortar preparation Panzer platoons would approach a village. The tactic was either to encircle or to flank the objective, pouring in fire from a distance at an acute angle to the infantry advance, closely supporting it (see diagram). The Panzer battle was detached, conducted over radio, and therefore remote and clinical. Although fast-moving, it remained nerve-racking. Watchful for opposing tanks or suspected anti-tank positions, fire would converge in tracer patterns, both automatic and tank fire, onto flimsily built houses whose thatched roofs quickly caught fire and blazed spectacularly. Throughout the action, figures would be seen dashing from house to house. Flashes, instantly observable, followed by the slower travelling 'crump' sound of stick grenades, signified the beginning of mopping-up operations to clear each dwelling. The sound of automatic fire rose and faded in concert with the movement of the distant toy-like running figures. It was impersonal, but not for the infantry. Grimm described the capture of the approaches to the village ahead:

'And then the awful work began, hand-to-hand fighting took place in the weak light of dawn. The fields were infested with enemy riflemen. Every metre of ground was fought over. The Soviet soldiers did not give up. Even hand-grenades did not bring them out of their hiding places.'

Tank guns cracked out supporting fire. Presently figures, some bearded, wearing flat caps and padded jackets, emerged with hands raised. Fear showed in their faces. Lines of prisoners were formed. Confusion over an uncharacteristically large number of civilians cleared when Grimm noticed that

many of the discarded Soviet knapsacks strewn about contained civilian clothes.[12]

Unteroffizier Robert Rupp, serving in a motorised infantry unit, described the aftermath of a typical village attack. Panzers were standing by, ready for action, alongside a reserve half-platoon of infantry, all watching two wooden houses blazing fiercely nearby. As the mopping-up group combed through houses, civilians drove cows out of harm's way, carrying possessions outside. Presently about 50 Russians were pulled out of isolated hiding places from barns and houses.

'One of them had his cheek torn open by a hand-grenade. He asked me for water and greedily slurped down some tea. A Major asked the Russians in their own tongue where the Military Commissar was, but he had already fled. The prisoners were a little happier and began passing around the Soviet star emblems from their caps. The wounded sat, unbandaged, for a long time in the street. They had to wait until the German wounded received treatment before being seen by the doctor. W. showed me his blood-stained hands, and boasted he had shot a few Russians. They had shot at him, he said.'

Later that afternoon he was awakened from an exhausted doze by the sound of shooting. Two prisoners of war had been shot and were being buried by their comrades. One had allegedly been firing dum-dum bullets (doctored rounds designed to splat on impact, causing grotesque wounds). The other apparently opened fire after signalling to surrender. 'One of them,' Rupp said, 'was still alive, because he continued to wheeze even beneath a thick layer of earth, which rose up as an arm worked itself up into the air.'

Four more Russians were ordered to dig another hole. For whom? wondered Rupp. The Russian who had earlier drunk his tea was led forward, made to lie in the hole, and shot by the Unteroffizier — the missing commissar. General Halder's pre-campaign remarks were becoming ominously prescient. 'A communist is no comrade before or after the battle. This is a war of extermination.' Such behaviour was by no means universally acceptable. Rupp pointed out:

'Differences of opinion over the shooting broke out. It was explained the motorcyclist battalion had shot the entire inhabitants of a village, women and children too, and cast them into graves they were made to dig themselves. This was because the whole village had been involved in an ambush that had cost the motorcyclists dearly.'[13]

Panzer soldiers might observe such incidents, but the momentum of meeting engagements kept them moving. Finishing off the enemy was infantry business. Their war was physically removed from the need to close with the enemy. A German staff officer serving with an armoured unit with Army Group South encapsulated the difference with his remarks to war correspondent Curizio Malaparte:

'He spoke as a soldier, objectively, without exaggeration, without using any argument not of a strictly technical order. "We take few prisoners," he says, "because they always fight to the last man. They never surrender. Their matériel can't be compared with ours; but they know how to use it."'[14]

It was an impersonal matter of suppressing enemy resistance. Battle took up only a fraction of the time expended during even eventful advances. Physical discomfort was the primary consideration.

'The roar of engines cleaves the red cloud of dust which covers the hills . . . Icy gusts of wind form sharp ridges in the thick dust. Our mouths are filled with sand, our eyes smart, our eyelids bleed. It is July, and the cold is intense. How many hours have we been on the road? How many kilometres have we travelled?'[15]

Leutnant Horst Zobel's tank platoon with the 6th Panzer Regiment, part of Guderian's Panzergruppe 2, travelled 600km between the rivers Bug and Dnieper over 12 days, covering some 50km per day.

'Sometimes we fought continuously in tanks for 24 hours. This was usually while we were on the march or detailed to a security mission. That does not mean a continuous 24 hours' fighting. Of course there were always places where the crew could rest or nap. They slept either in the tank or on the rear of the tank, which was pretty warm from the engine. Sometimes they dug holes underneath the tank which provided them secure rest uninterrupted by night bombers often flying over.'[16]

Tank crewmen shared everything. Comradeship was intense, forged sharing common dangers, enduring trying conditions and living intimately together within the confines of a Panzer. *Signal*, the glossy German news magazine (equivalent to the American *Life* picture publication) ran an atmospheric article entitled 'The Five from Panzer Number 11'. It described typical conditions among five crew members of a PzKpfwIV (heavy tank) from Panzer Regiment 15 (with the 11th Panzer Division).

'These five men, each from totally different practical backgrounds, represent a whole. Each one knows he is, and must be, reliant on the other. Each is a human being, with all the strengths and weaknesses all of us has; but taken together they are a feared and lethal weapon.'

The Panzer commander — 'Der Alte' (the old man) — was 21-year-old Leutnant Graf Hyazinth St___ (names withheld in the *Signal* article) [probably the Oberleutnant Hyazinth Graf Strachwitz referred to earlier], who had joined at the beginning of the war serving in the Yugoslav campaign prior to Russia. His father, from a distinguished family, was a Panzer battalion commander.

The gunner was Unteroffizier Arno B___ who, 'after every battle, stuck a cigarette in his mouth.' He was 25 years old with three brothers, all serving in the Wehrmacht, and two sisters. After the war he intended to be a technical salesman, 'preferably in Africa'. Inside the fighting compartment he was aided by the gun loader Adolf T___. He was an elderly 32-year-old ex-SA (Sturm Abteilung or Nazi party 'brownshirt'), married, with two young daughters. His first task after any engagement was to swab out the gun barrel.

Tank communications was the responsibility of the radio operator, Walter D___, who had worked on the railways before becoming a regular soldier. He had six brothers, five serving, the eldest of which was a Feldwebel.

Unteroffizier Hans E___, the 26-year-old driver, had earlier been a civil motor mechanic, a trade he intended to resume after the war. He was married and always carried a photograph of his four-year-old son in his pocket.

The five-man crew represented a 'presentable' microcosm of Reich society in *Signal* propaganda terms. Enlisted soldiers earned between RM105 and RM112.50 each month. This might be supplemented by a monthly family allowance of RM150. Most of them saved their money and sent it home. Factory workers by comparison earned an average of RM80 (or RM51.70 for women). It is not known whether this chosen crew survived the campaign. Their statistical chance of avoiding death or injury before the end of the war was remote.[17]

These were ordinary men. 'The first man of the crew who required a rest during a stop was the driver,' explained Leutnant Horst Zobel with Panzer Regiment 6. 'We had to care about him and he was seldom used as security or a sentry mission.' As a consequence, 'the tank commander,' like himself, 'regardless of rank, unless a company or battalion commander, had to share in those tasks.' Each depended on the other to survive. As Zobel stressed, in the attack 'the enemy is always the first to open fire. He fires the first shot and the crew must react.'[18] Everyday life followed a routine regimented by administrative and security tasks interspersed with the intense demands of acting as an integrated and focused team in battle. Typical routine in the 20th Panzer Division, according to one Panzer crewman, meant one was:

'. . . always extremely alert. Tanks were stationed forward as security outposts with officers peering through binoculars. The battalion HQ officer comes from regiment with new orders. A few people hastily eat a sandwich. Others lie about and talk about the attack they experienced that morning. Another writes a letter on the radiator bonnet of a vehicle. The commander attempts to work improvements to the camouflage. The adjutant tries to get signatures for paper returns but is fobbed off with the response: "we have no time in summer for the 'Paper War'."'[19]

Lurking behind such routine was not so much a morbid fear of death, rather a healthy regard for the unexpected. Catastrophe was something that happened to others and it was unhealthy to dwell upon it for too long. Götz Hrt-Reger, a keen amateur cine cameraman, describing scenes he had taken during the war from his armoured car, remarked:

'This was a shot through the side window showing the grave of our driver. I had just left the vehicle to operate the radio when it received a direct hit, killing the whole crew. Changing cars can be advantageous — eh?'

His view was that death struck in a haphazard way. There was scant time or scope to sentimentalise about its impact.

'It's pure chance if you're hit or not. You might consider it's tragic, but that is that. What more can you say? You could have been hit yourself and that's war. You can't expect a fighting unit to hang around tending each grave for a day, or think about the dead — because there are too many. If we had, then the German Wehrmacht would have made no headway at all!'[20]

ON TO SMOLENSK

The German Army was making headway but at some cost. The original conception of a great pocket extending from Bialystok to Minsk broke into several fragmentary pockets created during desperate fighting, first around Bialystok and then around Volkovysk. General Günther Blumentritt, Fourth Army Chief of Staff, explained:

'The conduct of the Russian troops, even in this first battle, was in striking contrast to the behaviour of the Poles and of the Western allies in defeat. Even when encircled, the Russians stood their ground and fought.'[1]

There were insufficient German troops in Panzer units to seal off the larger encirclement completely. Motorised units obliged by necessity to fight on or near roads were powerless to prevent Russian columns using forest tracks to slip away eastward at night. In the large trackless spaces between German units, Russian units were left unmolested. Confusion reigned in uncertain circumstances. During one battle the I/'Grossdeutschland' Regiment drove into a village on captured Russian trucks and fought a mobile engagement with Russian troops driving out with captured German vehicles. 'Everyone fired at everyone else — it was pure chaos,' related the unit historian.[2] The greatest pressure was on the eastern side of the pockets, the focus for Russian attempts to break out.

Commanders were presented with a dilemma. Panzers disrupted Soviet units by cutting their rearward communications, providing the optimum conditions for further advances. But because of the imperative to keep moving forward, they were unable to create solid rings around encircled Soviet forces. These pockets could only be closed and reduced by the 32 infantry divisions of Army Group Centre forced-marching their way forward. Unexpectedly bad roads and tough fighting on the edges of pockets with Russian formations which refused to surrender disrupted the previously assumed schedules of marching performance. Inevitably the gap between marching infantry and driving Panzers widened. The infantry was the substance of Wehrmacht fighting power; its role was to grind down and crush resistance. Panzer thrusts bludgeoned the enemy, but were incapable of inflicting the *coup de grâce*. Panzergruppen commanders strove to maintain momentum to exploit surprise and disrupt Soviet command and control. These were the basic conditions that ensured success. Von Bock confided his exasperation with High Command's apparent inability to recognise this basic tenet. He declared in his diary:

'They are even toying with the idea of halting the Panzer groups. If the latter happens, they will have failed to exploit the bloodily-won success of the battle winding down; they are committing a major error if they give the Russians time to establish a defensive front at the Dnieper and the Orscha-Vitebsk land bridge. In my opinion we have already waited too long.'[3]

It was becoming increasingly clear that manoeuvring alone onto tactically advantageous positions was not going to finish this enemy.

The Bialystok–Minsk battles fought from 24 June onwards were nearing conclusion on 8 July. They cost the Soviets an estimated 22 rifle divisions, seven tank and three cavalry divisions, and six motorised brigades. During the fighting two Panzergruppen, numbering nine Panzer and five motorised divisions, were employed to seal the pockets. These were joined by 23 more infantry divisions, which closed and annihilated them.[4] In short, 50% of the entire strength of Army Group Centre, 51 divisions, was tied to destroying units of its own comparable strength; a devastating blow. The experience in Poland and the West was that Blitzkrieg tactics achieved operational success once armies had been outmanoeuvred. Denied space and resources, the enemy's political will collapsed when faced with pointless casualties. Surrender invariably followed. In Russia established norms became perverted when Soviet units fought on in hopeless conditions with no prospect of success. Up to 50% of German attacking potential was thereby constrained during the first decisive phase without achieving the initial operational objective. This was the Smolensk land bridge, the historically significant jump-off point required to mount an offensive against the political heart of the Soviet Union — Moscow.

Although out of reach of German land forces, the Luftwaffe already had this operational prize firmly within its sights:

'Smolensk is burning — it was a monstrous spectacle this evening. After a two and a half hour flight we did not need to look for our objective; the blazing torch lit our way through the night from far away.'

Hans August Vowinckel's Heinkel He111 bomber avoided 'a spire' shape of searchlights and Flak before negotiating a series of wide curves and setting course for the city centre. 'The inside of the aircraft was as light as day,' he later wrote to his wife. As his aircraft flew over the River Berezina on its return, Vowinckel found himself reflecting upon Napoleonic history.

'Smolensk — once the point of destruction for a great conqueror; Berezina, where the downfall occurred. The sound of these names produce a strange historical thrill from the past. But they will not be repeated, their meaning has altered.'

It was a tiring flight, 9½ hours from taking-off at 18.00 hours until landing at 03.30 hours. Artillery fire could clearly be seen on the ground far below, where the advance continued unabated. On return to his home base Vowinckel ironically found time to read Friedrich Holderlin's *The Peace*. 'Everything that is important,' he wrote to his wife, 'is already in there.' But he was never to experience it. Two days later, flying in formation during a dogfight, a Russian fighter shot into flames by another German bomber collided with his aircraft from above. His commanding officer wrote to his wife explaining, 'the whole crew were likely killed in the crash.' As the incident occurred well beyond the advancing German line, he had sadly to conclude:

'The crash site cannot be investigated yet, and due to the expanse of the Russian area, we could not say for certain whether later he might be found.'[5]

When the Minsk pocket capitulated to Army Group Centre on 9 July, General Günther von Kluge was already far beyond, creating an even larger encirclement at Smolensk. His two Panzergruppen, 2 and 3, had continued moving considerable Panzer formations eastward, despite daily crises keeping existing pockets closed. It had been a calculated risk. On 3 July German Army Commander-in-Chief Walther von Brauchitsch, merged the two Panzerkampfgruppen forming Fourth (Panzer) Army, under von Kluge, rationalising the necessary command arrangements to achieve a breakthrough in the direction of Moscow. It was accepted the infantry would follow at best speed, but at a distance. Fourth Army units were taken under the new command of Second Army under General Maximilian Frhr von Weichs.

Panzergruppe 2 succeeded in forcing the River Dnieper either side of Mogilev at Stary Bykhov and Shklov, after hard fighting, between 10 and 11 July. Meanwhile Panzergruppe 3, following the line of the River Dvina between Polotsk and Vitebsk, was ordered to break into the region north of Smolensk. Vitebsk fell on 9 July, animatedly recalled by soldier Erhard Schaumann, who witnessed its fiery capitulation:

'Driving through Vitebsk we were suddenly surrounded by fire — to the left and right, and ahead of us — it was burning everywhere. So we turned around to get out. We thought we'd never get out of the burning city alive. I thought the trucks would blow up, it was so hot. But we were lucky. Then we attacked Vitebsk from the west. The Russians expected us to come in from the south. That's how Vitebsk was stormed.'[6]

Panzergruppe 3 pressed on, bypassing Russian forces on the Orscha–Smolensk road. It had, following intense fighting, set in motion the beginning of the Smolensk encirclement by 13 July. Two days later a bold surprise attack on the city itself resulted in its capture.

On 17 July a new pocket had been created around the Dnieper-Dvina land bridge containing about 25 Russian divisions centred on Vitebsk, Mogilev and the city of Smolensk. It was estimated some 300,000 enemy soldiers were inside. Von Bock's infantry formations were anything up to 320km behind the Panzer spearheads at this point, with many units still extricating themselves from mopping up the Minsk pockets. The Panzers and motorised formations of Fourth (Panzer) Army strung a noose around the highly dangerous Russian formations and hung on, tightening the pressure and waiting for the marching infantry to arrive. The grip was tenuous. On 18 July only six German divisions were in place against 12 Soviet divisions in the pocket.[7] Soviet pressure built up quickly from within and outside der Kessel (the cauldron). Everybody was now focused on the progress of the infantry. Where were they?

FINALE: BREST-LITOVSK

Even as the enormous pocket at Smolensk was being formed, the 45th Infantry Division had still to reduce the very first Soviet pocket that had been established on day one of the campaign.

At the end of June isolated resistance points had gradually succumbed to the German investment of Brest-Litovsk. German soldiers forced to engage in hand-to-hand fighting to clear confined spaces in the bitterly contested outposts took no risks. Casualties were heavy. Mercy was neither anticipated nor freely given. Medical Sister Katschowa Lesnewna from the surgical hospital on the South Island said:

'After being under siege for a week, the Fascists penetrated the fortress. They took out all the wounded, children, women and soldiers, and shot them all before our eyes. We sisters, wearing our distinctive white hats and smocks marked with red crosses, tried to intervene, thinking they might take notice. But the Fascists shot 28 wounded in my ward alone, and when they didn't immediately die, they tossed in hand-grenades among them.'[1]

At 08.00 hours on 29 June, the eighth day of the siege, the much-vaunted Luftwaffe sortie was finally flown. A single bomber dropped a 500kg bomb onto the Ostfort. It was intended that German lives would be saved by blasting defenders into submission. The resulting massive explosion caused only superficial damage to the brickwork. Preparations were made for a close-in ground attack the next day, using incendiary devices. Barrels and bottles were filled with a mixture of petrol, oil and fat. These were to be rolled into the fort's trenches and ignited with hand-grenades and Very pistols. Nobody relished the task. The Luftwaffe was given one last chance.

The solitary bomber returned and languidly circled the fortress while final aiming instructions were radioed to it. All attention focused on the Ostfort. Soldiers moving through the devastated wasteland of surrounding parkland and on the scarred walls of the citadel paused and gazed skyward. Another 500kg bomb whistled into the fort with minimal impact. The scene had taken on a relaxed, almost bizarre troop trial atmosphere. Cameras rolled to capture the moment on film. Interested spectators from the 45th Division headquarters staff gathered on the roof of a nearby building to watch. Circling above, the lone Luftwaffe bomber steadily came on line and lobbed a solitary 1,800kg bomb. The black cylindrical speck descended with slow effortless ease until it struck the corner of the massive ditch-fronted wall. A violent crack and boom echoed around the streets of Brest. Windows shattered and the whole population started as a huge pall of smoke spurted up above the stricken fort. This time there was massive damage, signalling the end for the survivors. Russian soldiers began to emerge from the fort: there were women and children among them. By dusk, some 389 men had surrendered.[2]

During the early morning hours of 30 June the Ostfort was searched and cleared of Russian wounded. German bodies, which had been pathetically sprawled for days around the fort's deadly apertures, were finally recovered. Jets of bright flame marked by incandescent eruptions of black smoke marked the progress of flamethrower teams burning and incinerating likely hiding places rather than risk a look inside. Victory appeared complete. The town and fortress of Brest-Litovsk had been cleared. Panzer 'Rollbahn 1' moving eastward and the Warsaw–Brest railway were open to uninterrupted convoy traffic. Elements from two Soviet divisions, the 6th and 42nd, with over a hundred officers and 7,122 NCOs and men, were captured. In addition, 36 tracked and 1,500 badly damaged vehicles of other types were taken, along with 14,576 rifles, 1,327 machine guns and 103 artillery pieces of various calibres. Although victory appeared total, and the Panzer spearheads were already hundreds of kilometres into the Russian interior, psychologically it was an empty result.

PK-cameramen filmed the last exhausted Russian survivors as they emerged from the devastated Ostfort. Dirty and bandaged, they looked directly and unashamedly at the cameras. Adopting a relaxed stance, smoking cigarettes, they exuded a grim confidence that was not lost on their captors, and probably not the message intended for the cinema audiences in Germany who would later view the weekly *Wochenschau* newsreel. The 45th Division report stated, 'they were in no way shaken, appearing strong and well fed, giving a disciplined impression.' The major and commissar who had maintained resistance to the last were never found. They had committed suicide.[3]

The 45th Infantry Division had entered the Russian theatre as a veteran formation, having lost 462 men in France. Its chaplain interred 482 men in the first divisional cemetery of the Russian campaign at Brest-Litovsk, including 32 officers. Another 30 officers and about 1,000 other ranks were wounded.[4] Some 2,000 Russian dead were actually found in the vicinity of the citadel and fortresses, but it is estimated as many as 3,500 may have died. The experience of the 45th Division at Brest was to prove a microcosm of the fate soon to befall its sister divisions in Russia. It lost more men during this initial action in the east than it lost during the entire campaign in the west the year before. It was a sobering calculation. The 45th Division became part of the newly formed Second Army on 3 July and marched eastward far behind the renamed Fourth (Panzer) Army, with which it had started the campaign.

Even after 30 June, and following 45th Division's departure, German soldiers needed to be alert in the vicinity of the fortress, because isolated sniping continued. Frustration at this 'unfair' — to the German mind — form of guerrilla warfare was vented on innocent bystanders. Gefreiter Willi Schadt, a motorcycle NCO from the 29th Motorised Division, recalled how Unteroffizier Fettenborn from his company shot dead 15 defenceless civilians in Brest, 'before,' as the perpetrator explained, 'these red swine start something'. The hapless victims were forced to dig their own graves before execution.[5]

Security had improved little by mid-July. Helmut K___[6] a 19-year-old Reichsarbeitsdienst driver employed in Russia immediately after the invasion, wrote to his parents about continuing resistance in Brest. Even as the battle at Minsk was concluded he wrote on 6 July that 'the citadel was still held' and pockets of resistance were still active. 'Twice the Reds had hoisted a white flag, and every time a company of Waffen SS were sent in, the doors were slammed in their faces.' Driving close to the citadel walls with another truck, Helmut narrowly missed being killed during a reprisal Stuka dive-bombing raid. The strike was only 300–400m away, and 'if I am truly honest, I wet my pants a little,' he confessed. On 11 July two German officers were shot in the streets of Brest. Helmut K___ wrote again the following day, complaining:

'There are tunnels beneath the earth in a 3km stretch from the citadel to the barracks, inside which the Russians are still sitting. Our unit is in the barracks. The streets are often strewn with scattered nails. We have already patched up our tyres many times . . . our troops are already 300km ahead en route to Moscow.'[7]

Even today, messages carved into concrete by bayonets in cellars and casemates throughout the old fortress of Brest-Litovsk are preserved. 'Things are difficult, but we are not losing courage,' reads one. Another proclaims: 'We die confidently July 1941.' 'We die, but we defended ourselves. 20.7.41.' is crudely scratched elsewhere.

Isolated shooting incidents carried on throughout July. Few people knew about these lonely deaths.[8]

'THE PANZERS'

Left:
The view from the commander's turret: a monotonous bumpy drive across the interminable — and here, cloudy — steppe, watchfully observing the progress of the rest of the armoured column.

Below:
A pause on the steppe. The tank commander observes the rest of the Panzer company regrouping in a gully prior to action. Despatch riders and *Kübelwagen* move between vehicles as crew members confer.

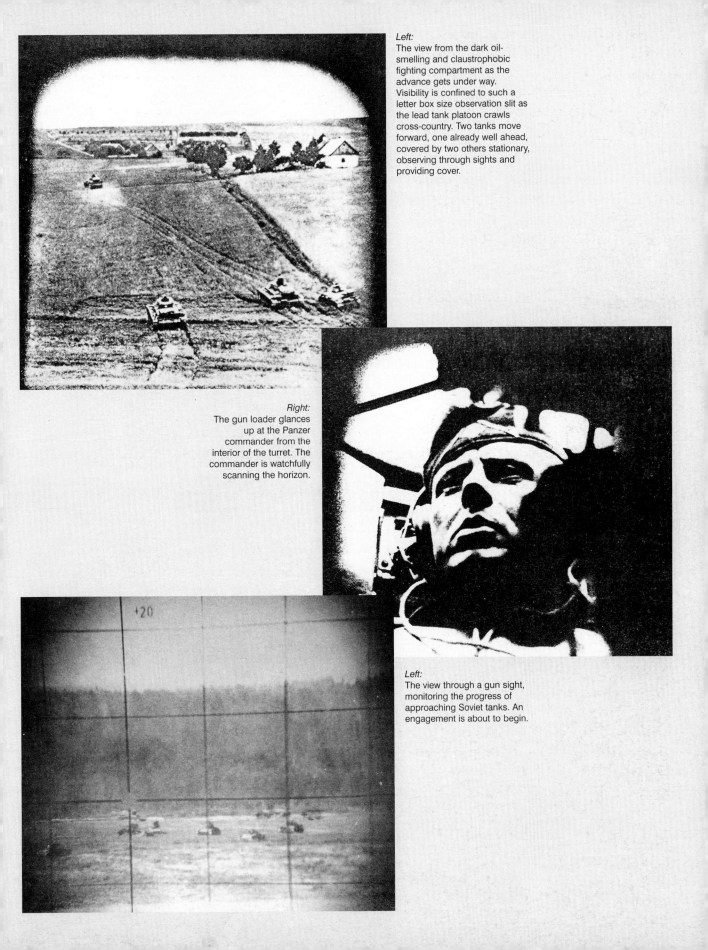

Left:
The view from the dark oil-smelling and claustrophobic fighting compartment as the advance gets under way. Visibility is confined to such a letter box size observation slit as the lead tank platoon crawls cross-country. Two tanks move forward, one already well ahead, covered by two others stationary, observing through sights and providing cover.

Right:
The gun loader glances up at the Panzer commander from the interior of the turret. The commander is watchfully scanning the horizon.

Left:
The view through a gun sight, monitoring the progress of approaching Soviet tanks. An engagement is about to begin.

Left:
Battle is joined. The
gunner's view of the
first strike on a light
Russian tank at close
range in a cornfield.
Success cannot be
judged at distance
unless smoke is visible.

Below:
On other occasions, as
in the case of this
Soviet T-34, a colossal
explosion will result if
its ammunition
compartment is hit.
Compression from the
detonation has
launched the turret
high into the air, visible
in the left foreground.
The subsequent chain
reaction of multiple
explosions can cause
an armoured vehicle
virtually to disintegrate.

Above:
War correspondent Arthur Grimm filmed the first major tank battle of the eastern campaign with the 11th Panzer Division near the village at Radciekow. On receiving news of a concentration of 120 Soviet tanks nearby, armoured half-tracks start their engines and move off into the dawn twilight.

Right:
They drive through high cornfields as early morning mist is burning off. The PzKpfwIVs have sighted a Russian concentration to their right. The tanks appear to 'float' on the corn.

Above:
The black dots are Soviet tanks and the Panzer *Keil* (wedge) has driven into their left flank. At 05.20 hours the first Russian tank spectacularly explodes as a German shot tears into its ammunition compartment.

Above right:
Soviet artillery fire begins to straddle the Panzers as they encircle enemy tanks ahead. Grimm continues to photograph the battle, now fragmenting into a series of sharp swiftly fought meeting engagements.

Right:
The view from the commander's cupola, passing the burning wreckage of a heavy and as yet unknown (T-34) modern tank type.

Right:
Grimm claimed up to
20 rounds were
needed to finish off
this blazing tank.

Above & right:
The column continues its
tortuous advance among
the debris of the destroyed
Russian tank unit.

Left:
A fiery sea of red and yellow flames had engulfed the Soviet tank formation by 12.00 hours. One of the Panzer crew members hangs out of the turret to view better the heat-shimmering scene of absolute destruction.

Left:
By 16.00 hours the sky above the battlefield had turned black. Grimm reported 40 enemy tanks were destroyed.

Below:
German tanks poised at the edge of a Russian pocket. After regrouping they will establish a thin picket line. This could well involve Panzergrenadiers in village-clearing.

Right:
The SdKfz251 was one of the most effective armoured infantry personnel carriers of the war. Crew visibility was considered more important than overhead protection. Most motorised infantry still travelled in lorries.

Below:
Conditions in the back were cramped and crowded, but less so as casualties inexorably mounted. Personal effects and requisitioned items such as food competed for room with as much ammunition as they could carry. Note the commander sits forward, monitoring the progress of activity ahead through binoculars.

Above:
Troops dismount under cover from tanks for a village-clearing operation. Tanks often provided fire support from the flanks.

Left:
A village clearance observed from the flank by another armoured personnel carrier. Progress can be discerned as each new house bursts into flame. The physical and psychological demands placed on mounted infantry were immense. One soldier complained: 'motorised transport is only there to make certain we poor Panzergrenadiers are brought up against the enemy more often than our fellows in the infantry divisions . . . so that we have the dubious advantage of being in action more often'.

Chapter 8
Smolensk

'We wished that the Russians would make a stand — anything, a battle even, to relieve the monotony of this ceaseless, timeless tramping.'

German infantry officer

THE INFANTRY

On 8 July 1941 the Fourth (Panzer) Army staff had established their headquarters at Borisov on the River Berezina. Problems lay ahead. It was vital, in order to avoid the catastrophic implications of the developing gap between Panzers and infantry formations, to hurry the foot soldiers forward. General Günther Blumentritt declared:

'A vivid picture which remains of these weeks is the great clouds of yellow dust kicked up by the Russian columns attempting to retreat and by our infantry hastening in pursuit.'[1]

The Smolensk pocket offered the tantalising prize of effecting much of the destruction of the western group of Soviet Armies originally planned, as well as securing the vital 'land bridge' for the eventual advance on Moscow. At Borisov there were traces of Napoleon. A few kilometres north, almost 130 years before, Napoleon's Grande Armée had been compelled to cross the frozen River Berezina during the winter of 1812, and suffered appalling casualties doing so. It was not an auspicious omen. General Blumentritt, the Fourth Army Chief of Staff, noticed, 'when the water is clear the remains of the props driven into the river bed to support the bridges built by the French engineers are still visible'.[2] The German bridges had been built. They awaited the arrival of the infantry.

Further to the rear, Harald Henry, a 22-year-old foot soldier, was marching forward with an Army Group Centre infantry regiment 'in scorching heat with rest stops whereby one slept like the dead'.[3] Leutnant Heinrich Haape, a doctor with Infantry Regiment 18, recalled the briefest of rests by night during early campaign days:

'The hour and a half's sleep had done more harm than good. It had not been easy to awaken the dog-tired men. Our bones were cold, muscles stiff and painful and our feet were swollen. We pulled on our field boots only with great difficulty.'[4]

German infantry equipment had altered little since the turn of the century. Each soldier still wore traditional calf-high jackboots and fought with a modified 1898 rifle. He carried in excess of 30kg of gear, on top of which might be added rations, reserve ammunition and components for machine guns and mortars. Harald Henry complained:

'I don't know exactly how heavy our equipment is, but in addition to all of it there was a thick woollen blanket, an ammunition box that could drive one crazy and that lamentable packet with the books in it I should have sent back.'[5]

Soldiers on the march quickly discarded extraneous items or left them in regimental transport. The pack, usually transported separately, would hold a blanket, stove, tent poles, rope, spare underwear and clothes, toiletries, a 'fat' box (for cooking) and personal effects. Standard marching equipment weights would be about 14kg. The leather harness would hold together pouches for 60 rifle rounds, a spade, gas mask (often discarded, but its carrier utilised to carry other effects), water bottle, bread basket containing some bread and meat or sausage, a small fat tin and bayonet. The helmet, weighing 1.5kg, was not worn marching, but would be attached by its chin strap to the harness equipment. The rifle, another 4kg weight, would be slung on or across the shoulder.

Every soldier carried an aluminium identity disc around his neck pressed into two halves, which were snapped off if he became a casualty. One half would go to the unit chaplain if the soldier were killed, or to the administrative unit. Small bread bags and tunic pockets bulged with all the other necessities and comforts each soldier felt he needed to carry. These items became fewer as march distances increased. 'All the roads in this land are uphill,' declared one veteran. 'The countryside is flat, but all roads go up regardless of which horizon they are leading to.' This phenomenon 'represents little more than the earth curvature with its constantly disappointing "false crests".'[6] A typical infantry regiment's march routine would be to wake the soldiers at 02.45 hours in order to be on the march by 03.15, when it was becoming light. Morale so early in the morning, with the prospect of a further brutal day of forced marching, was rarely good. Harald Henry lamented:

'We only had a little sleep. Once, when we finally managed to secure accommodation in a barn, our section [squad] was assigned to sentry duty, and we spent yet another night in a soaking meadow.'[7]

Sleep was a precious and often elusive commodity. Personal equipment was pulled on and all straps and accoutrements secured. Unnecessary clothing would be placed in packs and handed across to be ferried by the regiment's logistic transport (the *Trost*). Some companies marched as many as 50km in one day. One veteran calculated a single step covered 60cm — 'one took shorter or longer paces, but this was the average' — so 50km meant an estimated 84,000 paces.[8]

Breakfast was a hasty affair, perhaps a cup of tea or ersatz coffee with bread, butter and some jam or a can of liver-sausage. After the order 'prepare to move', there was still time to crack and drink a raw egg. Companies would then begin to form up on the road in the half-light of dawn. At first, soldiers strode energetically along the route, with rifles properly slung as the sun slowly rose. Within an hour or two rifles and weapons were festooned haphazardly about the body. Fingers began to worry absent-mindedly at swinging helmet rims fastened to belts or dangling from rifles. Artillery Oberleutnant Siegfried Knappe said:

'Our feet sank into the sand and dirt puffing dust into the air so that it rose and clung to us. The horses coughing in the dust produced a pungent odour. The loose sand was nearly as tiring for the horses as deep mud would have been. The men marched in silence, coated with dust, with dry throats and lips.'[9]

Feet already bruised by rutted roads began inexorably to rub on boots. Friction with each step produced blisters and calf-high boots became excruciatingly hot. Such discomfort stymies interest in all but the most immediate issues. Leutnant Heinrich Haape with Infantry Regiment 18 observed white puffs of smoke in the sky — Flak — as Russian aircraft flew overhead.

'But the marching men had no eyes for something which was not their war. Each man's war at this stage was circumscribed by the next few steps he would take, the hardness of the road, the soreness of his feet, the dryness of his tongue and the weight of his equipment. Beckoning him on was the thought of the next halt. Just to stop, to have no need to put one foot in front of the other for a few hours, was the dream of every man. There was no singing, no joking, no talking that was not strictly necessary.'[10]

After five hours of such exertion, one observer remarked:

'the repetitive rhythm of the march had produced a mask of monotony on every face; a cigarette would dangle in the corner of the mouth. Smoke would not be inhaled, the aroma would simply waft around the marching soldier.'[11]

During brief halts stabbing pains from disconcertingly soft and malleable blisters now swelling and bursting were apparent. Stiffening limbs began to ache. Friction burns in the crutch of the trouser might necessitate readjustments of equipment and rearrangement of clothing. This left less time to relax or drink. Sweat was everywhere, soaking between arms and legs, streaming down backs and faces, making leather harnesses pinch and rub skin. Shoulders burdened by heavy weapons or containers ached with constant pressure of applied weight. Sticky wet hair caused a clammy itching and irritation if the helmet had to be worn.

Harald Henry declared, 'the dust covered us all uniformly; blond men had dull-white brilliant hair, black hair made the men look like Frederick the Great's soldiers with light powdered wigs, others had their hair tousled like negroes.' Soaking wet uniforms took on a cardboard consistency as they became impregnated with rising dust. Fluid did not come only from sweat, there were 'sometimes even tears', Henry confessed. 'Tears of helpless rage, of doubt and pain over these unbelievable demands placed upon us.'[12] Bayonets irritatingly slapped the hip with each step. The day, even by late morning, was unbelievably long.

With luck, the main company meal appeared at midday, carried on so-called *Goulash-kanonen* (soup cannon). These horse-drawn mobile kitchens on wagons were the most important company support vehicles in the battalion *Trost*. It would rumble forward. The cauldron, filled with vegetables and available meat early in the morning, stewed as they marched, with a capacity of either 175 litres of fluid or two smaller 60-litre containers. A glycerine lining prevented the contents from burning. This simple but very functional vehicle developed an unforeseen morale role during long campaigns. It became the accepted collection point for infantry companies, a rallying area where psychological bonding took place. Units which had suffered considerable casualties in retreat or failed attacks were pulled together with difficulty by officers of the *Feldgendarmerie* (military police). Field cookers provided focal points where fragmented units or dejected survivors would gather for mutual comfort. Letters were handed out here and news or announcements given in its vicinity. Most importantly it catered for the soldiers' fundamental need to confide in each other, proving a haven in an otherwise hostile environment and one of the few locations offering respite from the normal day's pressures. The midday meal on the march, invariably the main meal and often the only sustenance, provided the essential respite that kept tired columns moving for yet another half day. An hour's rest was generally ordered.

'And then everyone sank into a sleep of total exhaustion. Motorcycles racing by do not disturb the sleepers, one of whom has made a pillow of his helmet, lying so comfortably up on it that it seemed like an eiderdown. Sleeping, even within the background sound of the guns, is a soldierly virtue, because he knows the day is yet long.'[13]

Bodies would have to be reluctantly coaxed to get working again. Company commanders forced columns along in these conditions by the power of their personalities. Pressure was applied to encourage soldiers to close the inevitable gaps that appeared between company columns. Although a young man's profession, many infantry battalion and company commanders were ex-World War 1 veterans. Despite this, feet reduced to burning raw flesh were kept moving between clenched teeth and wan faces. Oberleutnant Knappe continued to force the pace toward Minsk:

'As we marched, low hills would emerge from the horizon ahead of us and then slowly sink back into the horizon behind us. It almost seemed that the same hill kept appearing in front of us. Kilometre after kilometre. Everything seemed to blur into uniform grey because of the vastness and sameness of everything . . . Fields of sunflowers stretched for kilometre after kilometre after weary kilometre.'[14]

An officer with the Potsdam 9th Infantry Regiment recalled that the next days 'meant marching, marching and again marching and the heat was always unbearable'. They plodded forward in columns of threes.

'"Come on men, grit your teeth, the gap to the next company is much too big," announced one company commander, whereupon conversations that had just started died and were replaced by the monotonous clatter of gas mask cases, field spades, hip bayonets and ammunition belts. The view of the marchers sank and remained on the back of the man ahead.'[15]

Few of the fatigued soldiers took much notice of their immediate surroundings. They focused haphazardly on feet, the end of a rifle, swinging equipment and on the back of the man ahead. Losing themselves in personal thoughts or maintaining a psychological vacuum enabled them to endure pain and discomfort more easily. Leutnant Haape remembered how 'the sun sank slowly through the dense clouds of dust that we left in our wake. And into the darkness our march continued.'

Skirmishes with the enemy might almost be welcomed as a release from the monotony. Adrenaline would surge and after an outpouring of fear and nervous energy there would be a strength-sapping relapse as the steady eastward slog was resumed.

'We wished that the Russians would make a stand — anything, a battle even, to relieve the painful monotony of this ceaseless, timeless tramping. It was 11p.m. before a halt was called at a big farmhouse. We had covered close on 65km that day!'[16]

There was only about three hours' sleep before preparation for the next day's march began. Personal administration or letter-writing could occur only during this period. Some soldiers would have to stand sentry. There was never enough time to rest properly. All along the three army group fronts the infantry strove to catch up with the Panzers. By 1 July the 6th Infantry Division had covered a 260km stretch in Army Group North's sector from Memel to Riga — 10 days traversing bad roads and fighting en route. The 98th Infantry Division marched 40-50km each day between 9 and 30 July in the central sector.[17] Its official history described the *Rollbahn* as 'seemingly endless, no wayside trees and totally devoid of shade. Wide and dead straight, it stretched ahead to the horizon disappearing way into the distance.'[18] Harald Henry wrote home:

'Nobody can convince me that any non-infantryman can imagine what is taking place here. Think of the most brutal exhaustion you have ever experienced, direct burning sunlight, weeping sores on your feet — and you have my condition not at the end but at the beginning of a 45km march. It takes hours before your feet become insensitive to the painful wounds at each step on these roads which are either gravel or sand at the edges.'[19]

Numerous factors accounted for this remarkable stamina. Service in the Hitler Youth and *Arbeitsdienst* often included long route marches. This was also an age when everybody walked. Boys walked to school and adults to work. The transport and communications revolutions of the late 20th century had yet to come; people were fitter and psychologically disposed to walk long distances to work or for pleasure. None the less, this does not prepare the body for the brutal forced-marching required in war. Some motivation would have come from stoic veterans of the previous French campaign. It was clear that sabre-like Panzer slashes across the Low Countries could be blunted by prolonged heavy resistance or indeed snapped off if over-extended.

One such event had occurred at Arras on 21 May 1940 when a determined British flank attack had taken advantage of a developing Panzer-infantry gap. Panzer advances were dangerous because they unhinged the defence after plunging into the depth of the enemy hinterland. They ignored threats to the flanks because the enemy was more concerned with the vulnerability of their own and the rear. Terminal lethality in German Blitzkrieg terms was conferred by marching infantry. It was their fighting power which ensured eventual annihilation and a decisive outcome. Veterans sensibly assumed casualties might be reduced if the momentum of the advance convinced the enemy further resistance was pointless and surrender. Infantry following close on Panzers sensed that the nearer they were to the Panzers the less fighting would be required. With luck, the tanks would do it for them. This was motivation indeed. 'A powerful and shocking impression was left by our

Panzers and Stukas from the destroyed armies on the follow-on march routes,' declared Harald Henry, marching toward Mogilev in the central sector.

'Huge craters were left by Stuka bombers always precisely accurate along the edges of roads. Their air pressure had lifted the biggest and heaviest tanks in the air and turned them over. Our Panzers had settled the rest after the surprise bombing attacks, and we marched for 25km along a scene of unbelievable destruction.'[20]

'As we march the enemy continues to withdraw eastwards,' observed Leutnant Heinrich Haape with Infantry Regiment 18. 'It seems as if our battalion is never to catch up with him.' The monotony of the march transcended everything, even the approaching horror of combat. So far as Haape was concerned, it appeared 'as if our war is to be an uninterrupted marathon march to the Urals, perhaps even further'.[21]

'These marching hours were endless,' declared Harald Henry, marching on to the Dnieper river, '25 or 30km alongside smashed and burned out tanks, vehicle after vehicle, onward past skeletons of totally shot-up and fire blackened villages'. He had a sensitive eye for the incongruous picture of tiger-lilies blooming in the gardens of gutted buildings within 'black and ghostly surrounding walls'. These forced marches were no victory parade. They were a remorseless brutal and physical ordeal required of the infantry to keep up with the Panzers. Casualties apart, they exerted their own psychological toll. 'One breathed in the distinctive characteristic smell this campaign had already permanently etched on my mind,' admitted Henry, 'a mixture from burning, sweat and horse carcasses.' Strong sunlight swiftly transformed bodies into grotesque black shapes.

'The most dreadful [sight] was the horses completely bloated and eviscerated, with their intestines spilled out and muzzles bloodily torn off. Overall there hung the stench of destruction: a disturbing mixture of the abattoir and putrefaction pervading the air with a stagnant decadence over our column. The worst was a pig gnawing with noisy relish at a horse carcass, because we realised the logic of the food chain meant we would one day taste some of this horse flesh ourselves.'[22]

Slowly but surely the massed German infantry formations closed up on the Panzer advance. 'We are happy, we can laugh at the dust, the heat, the thirst — for only another 30km marching lies ahead,' declared Leutnant Haape. 'Our vanguard and the Panzer units are already involved in heavy fighting.' There was to be a battle. Resistance on the east bank of the Dvina river was stiffening by the hour. 'At last the war is waiting for us!' proclaimed Haape exuberantly.

'The column swings cheerfully along the road. There is point to the marching, and the objective is only a few kilometres away.'[23]

Closing with the enemy, the realisation that one must kill or be killed was a different and more emotive experience for the infantryman. 'As a soldier in action,' remarked Leutnant Hubert Becker after the war, 'I know that others will die, that I might die — might get killed at any moment.' Individuals mastered pre-battle fears in their own intensely private way. 'Killing,' Becker explained, 'that word, was never used; it was never a topic for us.' Nevertheless it had to be faced.

'During attacks, when the Russians charged or when we advanced, we would be extremely fearful and uneasy. One didn't know whether one would survive the next minute.'[24]

The physical burden was part of this psychological pressure. Infantry soldier Harald Henry's experience was typical. Having marched 25km by day, he spent the night standing guard with other members of his infantry section in a soaking meadow. His following day was 'also very demanding'. There was a few hours' rest during the afternoon before marching resumed to an objective 44km distant. When at midnight a halt was declared, they were fired upon as they rested. This resulted in a series of manoeuvres and counter-marching for two and three-quarter hours, having discarded packs, so as to attack the enemy. 'But for me,' said Henry, 'that meant carrying a 30lb ammunition box.' A largely uneventful night action ensued, following the collateral damage produced by fighting up ahead with an occasional burning tank lighting up the night. They did not close with the enemy, but did expend a lot of nervous energy at the prospect of doing so. Henry complained:

'The effort required for this attack with its rapid advances was immense, and now, with dawn coming up, the second part of our 44km long stretch lay before us. I was totally drained and worn out with absolutely no reserves of strength remaining.'[25]

The burden on motorised infantry units, far ahead with the Panzers, was no less unremitting. They had to drive constantly, fight a containment battle, then continue the advance with the same bleak prospect of relentless meeting engagements. These produced a steady, but increasingly apparent, casualty toll. Hauptsturmführer Klinter, commanding a motorised 3rd SS Division 'Totenkopf' platoon near Daugavpils, recalled Russian infantry attacks at 05.00 hours, following an eventful night. Countless figures in earth-brown uniforms surged toward their position 'like an avalanche — or more accurately like an unstoppable stream of molten lava'. Artillery support was not available; there had been no resupply of shells.

'Ever closer came the earth-brown flood. Even closer and uglier was the rifle and machine gun fire whining about our ears. Enemy artillery fire grew even heavier. And then, they were 100m — 60m — 30m away. A shrill and, until then, unprecedented nerve-racking "Hurrah!" rang out like a thunderclap. And then they began to fall here and there as our machine guns began their work. They were into my sector on the right . . . Dull thuds from hand-grenade explosions rang out and then they all ran back.'

Casualties among Klinter's men were heavy; a section commander was down.

'Totally exhausted, we fell back from the parapets and into the trenches. We lay on the ground as if we were dead, from the physical and psychological pressure.'

Having hardly gathered their composure, three hours later a further massive assault began. Ammunition this time sputtered to a desultory halt. There was nothing left. Onward came the earth-brown wall of Russian soldiery with barely 50m to go. 'We clutched our spades and hand-grenades tighter,' said Klinter, at the prospect of close hand-to-hand fighting. Suddenly a loud 'whooshing' sound sped over their heads.

Anxious faces glanced skyward, attempting to follow the sound of this invisible displacement of air, in time to see high fountains of earth shooting up in the ranks of the Russians just ahead.

'Again and again, howling rushes passed just over us. The enemy attacking waves were flayed, lacerated and smashed. Bodies and weapons were spun high into the air. Crushed people and pulverised equipments produced terror, panic — and then flight.'

The German supporting artillery had conserved what little ammunition it had for just such emergencies and delayed to the last possible moment. The line was held. Klinter said:

'Half dead with exhaustion, we squatted down in our trenches, semi-intoxicated with feverish nerves. Slowly, very slowly we quietened down. Hunger and thirst afflicted us again.'

The enemy retired. After a short interval Klinter's men received a brief break and some water. Later that afternoon, after an ammunition resupply, the company was committed to an attack. There had been neither food nor rest.

The pursuit was carried out on foot in temperatures of 28°C, even in the shade. Before long the company was pinned down by fire behind a railway embankment. The men were at the end of their physical and psychological resources. Pressing bodies into the ground and intimidated by the sights and sounds of battle, 'tongues were glued to palates swollen thick from dust, heat and thirst'. The realisation that they were trapped inside a strawberry patch dawned only slowly. At first one or two figures, and in time the entire company, were crawling around the embankment seeking out and hungrily devouring ripe strawberries. 'And now,' Klinter recalled, 'the first laughter began to cackle out.' Such an incongruous scene, even in such a bizarre setting, was not without a certain ribald appeal.

Their suffering was still not over. By 22.00 hours that night, the objective had been secured. As if by prearranged signal the thunderstorm, which had threatened throughout the sweltering humid day, burst upon them. 'There was no cover and no tents; sweat-soaked, exhausted and now without rations for 72 hours,' Klinter said, 'the men stood in streaming rain throughout the pitch-black night.' Defensive positions laboriously dug in this mud and slime were not completed until 03.00 hours. At dawn, having dried out, they marched back 14km to the village of Kraslawa, where their motorised transport had waited. The pursuit continued in lorries. Exhausted soldiers piled into the back of lurching and bumping transports and tried to sleep. Officers and drivers had to stay awake. At every halt the officers had to get out and scan the skies for Soviet aircraft;[26] and with good reason.

Obergefreiter Jaeschke from the 18th Panzer Division recalled watching a dogfight from his Panzer column on the *Rollbahn* (the main road). The aircraft were 'flying in such a wild mêlée,' he said, 'that one could not work out which side one was watching.' Soon fat-bellied Russian biplanes began falling from the sky, burning and exploding in the fields on both sides of the column. At this point 'they received an icy shock'. A German fighter exploded in the air while another, fully ablaze, crashed into the ground a few metres away from the *Rollbahn*.

'The burning fuel gushed out in a fiery flood across the road and caught an armoured half-track. The crewmen, poor devils, jumped out like living flaming torches onto the road.

Another Messerschmitt lined up for an emergency landing ahead of us, but one of the thick-bellied beasts with a red star got behind the Me. and shot it into pieces just as it approached the ground.'[27]

Russian air attacks were a constant irritant. Leutnant Hubert Becker, an artillery officer with Army Group North and a keen amateur cine cameraman, filmed one such raid. 'We were seriously harassed by Russian fighter-bombers,' he complained, 'which attacked our emplacement and shot us up.' His men managed to shoot down an aircraft with small arms because they had no anti-aircraft guns in support.

'Immediately cheering burst out. We were overjoyed to have got this villain. It had not even been possible to go to the "John" — terrible eh! Sitting in your foxhole all the time [enduring the strafing] is hardly a bed of roses, so we fired by volleys, hoping to hit him.'

He filmed the blazing aircraft wreckage afterwards, including the mangled remains of the pilot. Screening the incident to postwar audiences raised a level of pathos inconsequent to those who had actually beaten off the air attack. 'I looked at that scene feeling well pleased,' Becker admitted, 'at having managed to destroy a hornet . . . You see,' he stated blandly, 'it had been pestering us. He might have killed five men — really.'[28]

Hauptsturmführer Klinter's SS 'Totenkopf' unit, meanwhile, still exhausted, spent the next night preparing a position in swampy woodland. There was little peace during the night because they received a warning order, requiring battle preparation, to conduct an attack which was to last the entire day. It finally succeeded when two Sturmgeschütz assault guns shot them onto the objective at dusk. Having endured three days of intense combat, there was at last an opportunity to rest. But as Klinter laconically pointed out, 'if one wants sleep, and further, has managed to procure a quiet post in order to get it, then you can bet that position will most certainty be relieved'; and so it transpired. Elements of the 290th Infantry Division moved up to occupy the line the very night they could practically have achieved some sleep. A 10km return march ensued, stumbling over poor Russian roads in pitch darkness. There was still no food. After all their efforts over the previous few days the SS platoon commander complained: 'what was the point of belonging to a fully motorised unit when one always had to march, and almost invariably when the vehicles were most needed?' His was the sarcasm of a typical Panzergrenadier veteran:

'Motorised transport is only there to make certain we poor Panzergrenadiers are brought up against the enemy more often than our fellows in the infantry divisions. Before and after battle we always have to march just as far and of course fight, so that we have the dubious advantage of being in action more often.'

At 03.00 hours they reached their trucks and half-tracks and set off, within the hour, to continue the pursuit in the direction of Opotschka. They were in action again by daylight.[29] The cumulative grind of this physical and psychological toll had the same impact, marking the steady deterioration of the marching infantry formations. Klinter's experience encapsulated the remorseless killing power of the German infantry. It was now to be applied against the Smolensk pocket.

THE SMOLENSK POCKET

As the motorised vanguards of Panzer divisions struck substantial Russian resistance, meeting engagements ensued. Infantry or Panzers would move up in combination while artillery and Luftwaffe air support was called forward to break up the crust of the opposition. Areas of stubborn resistance were simply bypassed and subsequently encircled to maintain the momentum of the advance. Armoured advance guards would wheel left and right of the discerned threat and attempt to come together at an identified point further east to close the pocket. The area enclosed was termed *der Kessel* (the cauldron), an apt description. Closing the pocket was a complicated and dangerous manoeuvre requiring the need to recognise and co-ordinate firepower with fast-moving Panzer units which were directed onto virtual collision courses. Timing and communication was all important. Coloured Very flares were often fired into the air as a crude verification of friend or foe. Confused fighting led to clashes between units on the same side — something that the fast-moving pace of battle made almost inevitable.

The formation of the Smolensk pocket, and the subsequent battles that were fought between 11 July and 11 August 1941 to close it, typified and illustrate the nature of the fighting being conducted at this point in the Russian campaign. The Bialystok and Minsk encirclement battles that started on 24 June ended only three days before the ring around the massive Smolensk *Kessel* coalesced. They had been tying down 50% of Army Group Centre's fighting assets, 23 infantry divisions as well as Panzer and motorised formations. These units, mopping up final resistance, had to be pushed eastward in sufficient strength to embrace and crush the new enclave containing the largest Soviet force entrapped to date. On 18 July only seven German divisions were holding down 12 surrounded Soviet equivalents. The Russians not only sought to break out. They were also being reinforced by fresh units from the east, which sought to break in to extricate their own men.

Keil und Kessel tactics were applied to achieve the German encirclement and destroy the Red Army in western Russia. The *Keil* (wedge) was the penetration hammered into the Soviet front by four Panzergruppen, one each to the north and south and two in the centre. Enemy forces were encircled within concentric rings to form *der Kessel*. The first outer ring achieved by Panzer vanguards isolated the enemy before the Panzers then turning inward to establish dispersed security pickets (**see diagram**). These were in effect 'buffers', whose role was to beat back enemy forays into the pocket. Heat was applied in a terminal sense to bring the cauldron to the boil by the foot infantry divisions marching up. On arrival they formed a second inner circle around the trapped Soviet units and squeezed. German infantry supported by artillery faced inwards, containing repeated Soviet attempts to break out, until the trapped units were inexorably worn down and liquidated. Motorised and Panzer formations meanwhile held the outer ring, simultaneously parrying enemy relief attacks while preparing to continue the advance east once the fate of the pocket was sealed.

Tactics, which had proved successful during the earlier western campaigns, proved inappropriate when applied to this fiercely stubborn and less compliant adversary in the east. Inadequacies in German defence doctrine, already identified by senior commanders after the victorious Polish and French campaigns, became apparent again. Although Blitzkrieg doctrine depended on 'lightning' advances supported by close Luftwaffe air support, ultimate success depended on how fast the marching infantry could cover ground before they closed with the enemy, and how

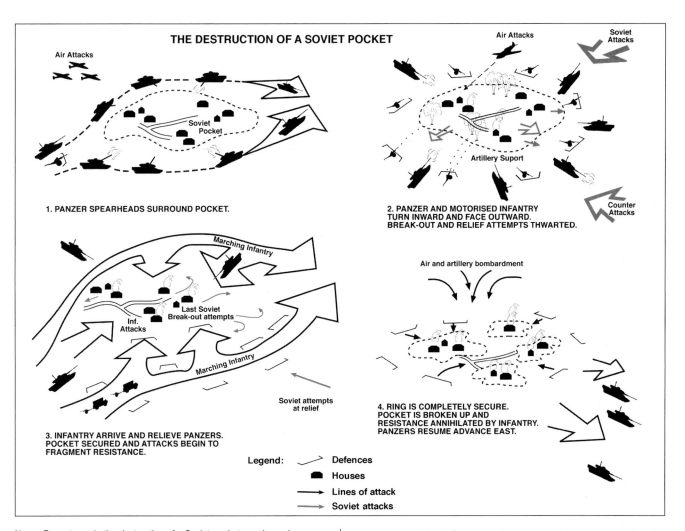

THE DESTRUCTION OF A SOVIET POCKET

Air Attacks

Soviet Pocket

1. PANZER SPEARHEADS SURROUND POCKET.

Air Attacks

Soviet Attacks

Artillery Suport

Counter Attacks

2. PANZER AND MOTORISED INFANTRY TURN INWARD AND FACE OUTWARD. BREAK-OUT AND RELIEF ATTEMPTS THWARTED.

Marching Infantry

Inf. Attacks

Last Soviet Break-out attempts

Marching Infantry

Soviet attempts at relief

3. INFANTRY ARRIVE AND RELIEVE PANZERS. POCKET SECURED AND ATTACKS BEGIN TO FRAGMENT RESISTANCE.

Air and artillery bombardment

4. RING IS COMPLETELY SECURE. POCKET IS BROKEN UP AND RESISTANCE ANNIHILATED BY INFANTRY. PANZERS RESUME ADVANCE EAST.

Legend:
- Defences
- Houses
- Lines of attack
- Soviet attacks

Above: Four stages in the destruction of a Soviet pocket are shown here diagrammatically. 1. Panzer spearheads first encircle and cut off Soviet forces. 2. The perimeter, once formed, faces inwards and outwards to prevent break-out attempts and block external Russian counter-attacks seeking to free or reinforce encircled forces. 3. The arrival of the foot infantry divisions with their heavy artillery would herald the subsequent annihilation of resistance. Concentric attacks are mounted to harass the pocket as the perimeter is hermetically sealed. The Panzer screen is meanwhile withdrawn and continues its eastward advance. 4. Infantry attacks supported by artillery break the pocket into digestible fragments which are reduced in turn.

effectively the Panzers could defend while waiting for them. Much of the fighting, apart from the skirmishing involved establishing pocket perimeters, became a matter of sheer infantry will-power to contain and destroy increasingly desperate cut-off Russian units inside. Robert Rupp, a motorised infantry soldier serving with Army Group Centre, encapsulated the nature of pocket fighting in a diary entry of 31 July. 'One is concurrently defending during every attack,' he wrote, 'perhaps even more than when defending.'[1]

German Panzer divisions may have been fearsome in the attack but they were less formidable when tied to static defensive tasks because they were short of infantry. An up-to-date Panzer operations manual, published just six months before the campaign, devoted 26 pages to the 'Attack', but only two paragraphs covered 'Defence'.[2] Units not only lacked time when hastily organising defensive pickets, but also lacked the expertise needed to produce the sort of co-ordinated defence in depth

recommended in infantry training manuals. Motorised units skilled in the art of mobile warfare did not have the eye for ground that experience conferred when selecting defensive positions. A young infantry Leutnant with the Ist Battalion of Panzergrenadier Regiment 'Grossdeutschland' explained the dilemma of having to create a defensive position near Smolensk by night:

'The battalion had taken up a so-called security line spread improbably far apart. This was something new for us; we had never practised it. There was no defence, only security. But what if the enemy launched a strong attack?'[3]

In France or Poland motorised units had generally superimposed a hasty and *ad hoc* screen consisting of primarily security pickets around an encircled enemy force. It did not work in Russia. Generalfeldmarschall Fedor von Bock, commanding Army Group Centre, wrote with exasperation at the inevitable consequence on 20 July as the battles around Smolensk gathered momentum:

'Hell was let loose today! In the morning it was reported that the enemy had broken through the Kuntzen corps at Nevel. Against my wishes, Kuntzen had sent his main fighting force, the 19th Pz Div, to Velikiye Luki, where it was tussling about uselessly. At Smolensk the enemy launched a strong attack during the night. Enemy elements also advanced on Smolensk from the south, but they ran

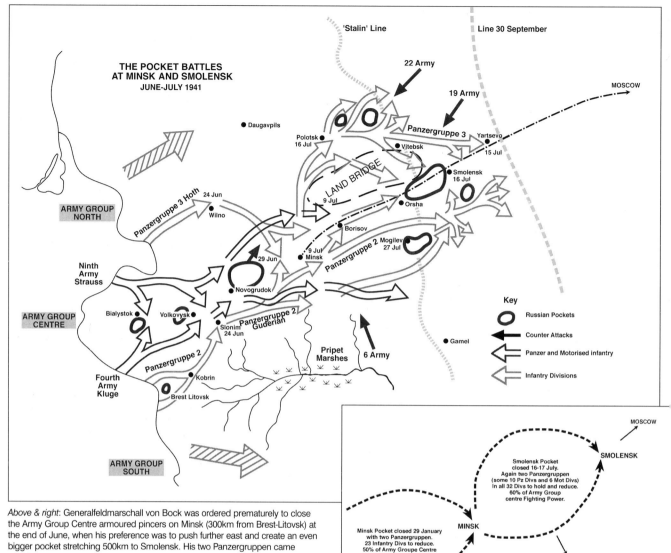

'Stalin' Line   Line 30 September

22 Army

19 Army

MOSCOW

Panzergruppe 3

Daugavpils

Polotsk 16 Jul

Vitebsk

Yartsevo 15 Jul

Smolensk 16 Jul

Panzergruppe 3 Hoth   24 Jun

LAND BRIDGE 9 Jul

Orsha

ARMY GROUP NORTH

Wilno

Borisov

Mogilev 27 Jul

Panzergruppe 2

Ninth Army Strauss

29 Jun

9 Jul Minsk

Novogrudok

ARMY GROUP CENTRE

Bialystok   Volkovysk

Slonim 24 Jun

Panzergruppe 2 Guderian

Panzergruppe 2

Pripet Marshes

6 Army

Gamel

Fourth Army Kluge

Kobrin

Brest Litovsk

Key

⬤ Russian Pockets

⬅ Counter Attacks

⇐ Panzer and Motorised infantry

⇐ Infantry Divisions

ARMY GROUP SOUTH

MOSCOW

SMOLENSK

Smolensk Pocket closed 16-17 July. Again two Panzergruppen (some 10 Pz Divs and 6 Mot Divs) In all 32 Divs to hold and reduce. 60% of Army Group centre Fighting Power.

MINSK

Minsk Pocket closed 29 January with two Panzergruppen. 23 Infantry Divs to reduce. 50% of Army Groupe Centre Fighting Power.

KIEV

Above & right: Generalfeldmarschall von Bock was ordered prematurely to close the Army Group Centre armoured pincers on Minsk (300km from Brest-Litovsk) at the end of June, when his preference was to push further east and create an even bigger pocket stretching 500km to Smolensk. His two Panzergruppen came together at Minsk, employing 23 German infantry divisions after the initial encirclement on 29 June. 50% of Army Group Centre's fighting power was thus tied up until the pocket capitulated on 9 July. Nevertheless, sufficient momentum had been achieved by the remainder of Army Group Centre to close the Smolensk pocket on 17 July. The Russians unexpectedly fought on, tying down 60% of the army group's offensive fighting power until 11 August. Despite staggering Soviet losses, the Blitzkrieg momentum had run out of steam just beyond the Smolensk 'land bridge', the jumping-off point for any assault on Moscow.

into the 17th Pz Div and were crushed. On the southern wing of the Fourth Army the 10th Motorised Division was attacked from all sides and had to be rescued by the 4th Panzer Division. The gap between the two armoured groups east of Smolensk has still not been closed![(4)]

Hubert Goralla was a *Sanitätsgefreiter* with the 17th Panzer Division caught up in the desperate fighting alongside the Minsk–Moscow *Rollbahn* leading into Smolensk. Russian break-out attempts were on the point of collapse.

'It was absolutely pointless. The [Russian] wounded lay left and right of the Rollbahn. The third attack had crumpled in our fire and the severely injured were howling so dreadfully it made my blood run cold!'

After treating their own wounded, Goralla was ordered forward with two grenadier medics to deal with the Russian casualties 'lying as thick as herring in a box' in a hollow off the road. The medics, who were wearing Red Cross armbands, approached to within 20m of the hollow when the Russian wounded began to shoot at them. Two medics collapsed and Gefreiter Goralla waved those following behind to crawl back. As he did so:

'I saw the Russians coming out of the hollow, crawling and hobbling towards us. They began to throw hand-grenades in our direction. We held them off with pistols we had drawn from our holsters and fought our way back to the road.'

Later that day the same wounded were still persistently firing at the road. A staff captain threatened them back with a pistol and stick. They took no notice. 'Ten minutes later,' said

Goralla, 'it was settled.' A Panzergrenadier platoon went into the attack and cleared the area around the road.

'Every single wounded man had to be fought to a standstill. One Soviet sergeant, unarmed and with a severely injured shoulder, struck out with a trench spade until he was shot. It was madness, total madness. They fought like wild animals — and died as such.'[5]

Containing the Smolensk pocket, in the face of such pressure, became an obsession for von Bock. 'At the moment,' he wrote on 20 July, 'there is only one pocket on the Army Group's front! And it has a hole!'[6] The Panzer ring holding it, lacking strong infantry support, was extremely porous. Without the attached Luftwaffe anti-aircraft batteries, originally configured to protect the Panzers against air attack, the defence situation would have been even more alarming. High-velocity 88mm Flak guns were switched from air defence to the ground role. An example of their effectiveness is revealed by 7th Panzer Division's defensive battle tally against 60–80 attacking Russian tanks on 7 July. Just under half — 27 of 59 enemy tanks — were knocked out by Flak Abteilung 84. Of the remaining 29 kills, 14 were knocked out by five other infantry units and 15 by the division's Panzerjäger Abteilung (also equipped with Flak guns).[7]

On 21 July von Bock grudgingly acknowledged the pressure the enemy was applying to his closing ring, 'a quite remarkable success for such a badly battered opponent!' he admitted. The encirclement was not quite absolute. Two days later Bock complained, 'we have still not succeeded in closing the hole at the east end of the Smolensk pocket.'[8] Five Soviet divisions made good their escape that night, through the lightly defended Dnieper valley. Another three divisions broke out the following day. Unteroffizier Eduard Kister, a Panzergrenadier section commander, fought with the 17th Panzer Division near Senno and Tolodschino against break-out attempts mounted by the Sixteenth Soviet Army.

'They came in thick crowds, without fire support and with officers in front. They bellowed from high-pitched throats and the ground reverberated with the sound of their running boots. We let them get to within 50m and then started firing. They collapsed in rows and covered the ground with mounds of bodies. They fell in groups, despite the fact the ground being undulating offered good protection from fire, but they did not take cover. The wounded cried out in the hollows, but still continued to shoot from them. Fresh attack waves stormed forward behind the dead and pressed up against the wall of bodies.'

Schütze Menk, serving in a 20mm Flak company with the 'Grossdeutschland' Regiment, described the desperate need to keep all weapons firing in the face of such suicidal mass assaults.

'Our cannon had to be fed continually; flying hands refilled empty ammunition clips. A barrel change, a job that had to be done outside the protection of the armour plate, was carried out in no time. The hot cannon barrel raised blisters on the hands of those involved. Hands were in motion here and there, calls for full clips of ammunition, half deaf from the ceaseless pounding of the gun . . . there was no time to feed hidden fears by looking beyond one's task, the Russians were unmistakably gaining ground.'[9]

Kister maintained it was a totally unnerving experience. 'It was as if they wanted to use up our ammunition holdings with their lives alone.' His sector was attacked 17 times in one day.

'Even during the night they attempted to work their way up to our position utilising mounds of dead in order to get close. The air stank dreadfully of putrefaction because the dead start to decompose quickly in the heat. The screams and whimpering of the wounded in addition grated on our nerves.'

Kister's unit repelled another two attacks in the morning. 'Then we received the order to move back to prepared positions in the rear.'[10]

Pockets were not only porous, they moved. As Red Army units continually sought to escape, German Panzers had frequently to adjust positions to maintain concentric pressure or bend as they soaked up attacks. 'Wandering pockets' complicated the co-ordination of hasty defence and especially the reception of march-weary reinforcing infantry units moving up to form the inner ring. Infantry divisions moving behind Panzergruppen fared particularly badly. They were often obliged to change direction at little notice onto secondary routes to avoid Panzer countermeasures rapidly manoeuvring along the primary or supply arteries. Movement in such fluid situations was perilous, as described by Feldwebel Mirsewa travelling with one 18th Panzer Division convoy:

'Suddenly they were there. Even as we heard the engine noises it was already too late. Soviet T-26 and T-34 tanks rolled, firing uninterruptedly, parallel to our supply convoy. Within seconds all hell had broken loose. Three lorries loaded with ammunition driving in the middle of the column blew up into the air with a tremendous din. Pieces of vehicle sped over us, propelled on their way by the force of the explosions.'

Men cried out and horses stampeded in all directions, running down anything that stood in their way. Suddenly the Russian tanks changed direction and swept through the column, firing as they went.

'I will never forget the dreadful screams of the horses that went under the tracks of the tanks. A tanker lorry completely full with tank fuel burst apart into orange-red flames. One of the manoeuvring T-26 tanks came too close and disappeared into the blaze and was glowing incandescently within minutes. It was total chaos.'

A 50mm PAK was rolled up from the rear and quickly immobilised two of the heavier T-34 tanks, hitting their tracks. Both began to revolve wildly, completely out of control in the surreal battle now developing. Meanwhile, the lighter and faster T-26 types had shot every vehicle in the column into flames. Bodies of men who had attempted to flee their vehicles were strewn across the road. 'I heard the wounded cry out,' recalled Mirsewa, 'but not for long, as the Russian tank clattered up and down over the dead and injured.' A platoon of Panzergrenadiers with additional anti-tank guns drove up and swiftly set to work. At first the unmanoeuvrable T-34s were despatched. The scene began to resemble Dante's 'Inferno' as the T-26s still engaging the burning vehicles were attacked.

'The crack of detonations mixed with the tearing sound of huge tongues of flame. Metal parts whirled through the air.

In between, machine guns hammered out as the grenadiers first engaged tank vision slits before their destructive high explosive charges were brought to bear. The chaos intensified into an inferno. Everywhere tanks were exploding into the air. Burning steel colossuses melted alongside our blazing supply column forming a long wall of flame.

'The heat radiating across the road and reaching our position was hardly bearable. Worse of all, though, was the sight of numerous dead from our column lying in the road. Just as well our people back home will never get to know how their boys met their deaths.'[11]

Containing 'wandering pockets' appeared an insurmountable problem. Von Bock reacted belligerently to the 'Führer's ideas on the subject, the gist of which was that for the moment we should encircle the Russians tactically wherever we meet them, rather than with strategic movements, and then destroy them in small pockets'.[12] This implied Blitzkrieg sweeps should be subordinated to minor tactical actions. With it came the realisation that the increasing gap developing between Panzers and infantry was annulling the previously proven benefits of a combined arms advance. Panzers were not robust in defence while infantry were insufficiently protected on the move.

The Soviets, sensing this weakness, attacked the outside of the Smolensk ring to exploit the vulnerability. The attempts, however, were unco-ordinated and lacked tactical sophistication. But in terms of naked aggression and totally uncompromising resistance, the Panzer divisions were sustaining punishment far beyond that meted out by any foe thus far in the war. Von Bock lamented the appearance of new Russian build-ups, 'in many places they have tried to go over to the attack' even as he closed the Smolensk pocket. 'Astonishing for an opponent who is so beaten,' he admitted, 'they must have unbelievable masses of material, for even now the field units still complain about the powerful effect of the enemy artillery.'[13] The next day the Smolensk pocket was sealed.

The battle continued for another 14 days. At its height the Wehrmacht fielded elements of 32 divisions consisting of two Panzergruppen with 16 Panzer and motorised (and one cavalry) divisions and 16 infantry divisions. This was 60% of the fighting power of Army Group Centre. Some 50% of its strength had been expended holding the Bialystok–Minsk encirclement perimeters between 24 June and 8 July. The same troops had then to march further eastward to embrace the even greater Kessel at Smolensk and participate in the battle that raged between 11 July and 10 August. Trapped inside were the Soviet Sixteenth, Nineteenth and Twentieth Armies. By 8 July OKH calculated it had destroyed 89 of 164 Russian divisions identified.[14] At this point Blitzkrieg momentum had petered out. There were no further German formations of appreciable operational size available to continue eastward until this pocket was annihilated. Breathtaking though the victories were, the price was now becoming apparent, even to the highest commanders at the front.

Two days after the closure of the Smolensk pocket, von Bock noted in his diary that 'powerful Russian attacks are in progress on almost the entire front of Ninth Army' and that '40 batteries [of artillery] have been counted at one place opposite its eastern front'. A Soviet penetration was even reported south of Beloye. 'The fact is,' concluded von Bock, 'that our troops are tired and are also not exhibiting the required steadiness because of heavy officer casualties.'[15] The German Army at the end of July was beginning to conclude the vast battles of encirclement that had been designed to destroy Soviet forces in western Russia. Only now was the Pyrrhic nature of this achievement becoming apparent, hidden within sensational Sondermeldungen at home.

On 21 July, 7th Panzer Division reported a strength of 118 tanks, which indicated 166 had been knocked out (although 96 of these were under repair).[16] One battalion of Panzer Regiment 25 was temporarily broken up to keep the other two at effective strength. Most of the tank crews survived. It is interesting to compare the lot of Panzers and infantry fighting in the same formation.

Panzer gunner Karl Fuchs was exuberant prior to the battle of Smolensk. 'Our losses have been minimal and our success great,' he wrote to his wife Madi. 'This war will be over soon, because already we are fighting against only fragmented opposition.'[17] Six days later he wrote:

'For the time being I am in a safe spot. If only I had some water to wash myself! The dirt and the dust cause my skin to itch and my beard is growing longer and longer. Wouldn't you like to kiss me now! I am sure you can see the dirt on the paper on which I write.'

On 15 July he anticipated, 'I would imagine that within eight to ten days this campaign will be over.' Soldiers often prefer to offer a sanitised version of experiences writing to their families. They confirm they are alive and in good health and generally like to predict future prospects with some optimism. Karl Fuchs was typical of the soldiers of his generation. Two days later he exuberantly described how:

'Yesterday I participated in my 12th attack. Some of these attacks were more difficult than others. With 12 attacks under my belt, I have now caught up with the boys who had a head start in France! You can imagine that I'm very proud of this achievement.'[18]

Fuchs wrote what he thought his wife would expect to read. The rotation of tank crews for rest referred to 'in a safe spot' was likely the result of tank casualties and battle fatigue. Diary entries, expressed in private and only selectively released, are often more frank. An infantry officer serving in Fuch's division wrote more candidly the following week:

'The faces of the youngsters exude the same image as First World War veterans. Long beards and the filth of these days make many of them look older than is the case in reality. Despite the pleasure at sudden Russian withdrawals, one notices this change in the faces of the soldiers. Even after washing again and shaving the chin — something difficult to describe is from now on different! The first days at Yartsevo have certainly left an impression.'[19]

Panzer Regiment 7 was deployed at the eastern end of the Smolensk pocket, directly in the path of Russian divisions attempting to escape. General Halder caustically commented in his diary:

'Four [German] divisions are advancing eastward from the west, pushing the enemy against the eastern block formed by only four battalions of the 7th Panzer Division which is also being attacked by the enemy from the east. We need hardly be surprised if 7th Panzer Division eventually gets badly hurt.'[20]

The Panzergrenadier Regiment 'Grossdeutschland' was under similar pressure. Repeated surprise encounters in confused situations caused a steady drain of casualties. Commanders had

'POCKET FIGHTING'

The Panzers held the pocket perimeters, fighting to contain the enemy until the arrival of the marching infantry. The following sequence of photographs illustrates a PzKpfwIII duel with a light Soviet tank across a railway level crossing near Miropol in July 1941.

The first shot cracks out, stripping the dust from the railway embankment as it tears toward the solitary Soviet tank, whose turret has turned to engage.

Above: The PzKpfwIII advances and stops short of the stricken enemy tank. Two crew members jump out and dash forward the last few metres to investigate, armed with machine pistols.

Above: Meanwhile the only surviving Russian crew member stumbles towards them with his hands in the air.

Right: The inquisitive crew crawl over the light armoured tank. The first shot had smashed its running mechanism, the second had set it on fire.

Above:
Inside the pocket, battle is joined as German infantry, here under fire, begin village clearances to annihilate Soviet resistance in a series of attacks to break up the pocket.

Right:
One infantryman commented he spent more time in the defence, containing pockets, than he ever did in the attack. A hasty meal is taken between engagements.

Right:
A German infantry anti-tank team has destroyed a Soviet tank on the road just outside Smolensk with a direct hit. The detonation has blown the turret from the hull.

Left:
Wehrmacht victory jargon labelled the 13.8ton Russian BT-7 light tank the 'Mickey Mouse'. Its 20mm of armour made it easy prey to virtually every German anti-tank gun variant. Hundreds remained littering the battlefield, with both escape hatches left open, producing the distinctive Walt Disney mouse silhouette.

'Pak nach vorn!' — 'Get the anti-tank guns forward!' Pockets were initially only lightly held by German advance guards. Anti-tank guns such as these 50mm PAK38 guns were constantly called forward to deal with sudden crises, often having to deploy to unprepared positions. These were tense moments requiring strict fire discipline from crews who needed to keep their heads and, if possible, engage from the flanks as shown here. This crew is receiving clear direction as to which target to engage.

'Treffer!' — 'A direct hit!' Despite confusion occasioned by noise, smoke and fear, crews needed to retain their nerve and pick off the immediate threat. Disciplined tension gives way to jubilation once it is realised the attack has been stopped.

Soviet prisoners emerge from woodland inside a pocket. They apprehensively wave surrender leaflets that assure them their lives will be spared, and are motioned forward by their captors. Many were eventually to die in captivity.

to react to swift situation changes with no clear information about the enemy. It produced a cumulative toll.

'No one could say during the advance whether one would see heavy fighting within the next hour, or whether Russian troops would be on the roads during the hours of darkness. This constant tension strained men's nerves to breaking point. The resulting over-exertion left them somewhat indifferent, almost resigned to accept everything as it arose. It also explains the losses among officers and NCOs, which were dreadfully high at the outset of the campaign.'[21]

It was to get worse. From 23 July the Ist Battalion 'Grossdeutschland' Regiment fought defensive battles near Yelnya and Smolensk along the Kruglowka railway embankment. For five days the unit was attacked by masses of Russian infantry desperate to flee the pocket. 'GD' grenadiers were generally paired to each foxhole. The official historian relates how 'many spent the day next to a dead comrade. No one could help the wounded while it was still daylight.' At night the dead were laid out behind a shack wall to the rear of the position.

'They had all died from head or chest wounds. That meant all were standing in their holes and firing at the enemy when they were hit. In so doing they had to expose their upper torsos or at least their heads. They knew the likely consequence of this. Can a man do more, or be stronger?'

At night they heard calls, shouts and the clatter of vehicles as the enemy manoeuvred in preparation for fresh assaults. During the fourth night of the defence the battalion was informed it could not be relieved. They had to hold on for longer, because infantry units earmarked to relieve them were needed elsewhere.

'Now what were we going to do? Several Grenadiers overheard the message. Their reaction was "Man, that's totally impossible." The tension mounted. It spread through the position like poison. Several men wept, others immediately fell asleep. Most sat still in their holes. Our eyes were red from the heat, smoke and lack of sleep.'

The relief delay resulted in a number of Russian penetrations during the heavy fighting that continued in all company sectors. Russians shared holes with dead grenadiers in trenches often only 20m away from the surviving German outposts. Eventually during the night of 26/27 July, after five days of uninterrupted fighting, the remnants of the battalion were withdrawn behind a German machine gun battalion that set up a new line 1,000m behind them. One company, the second, lost 16 dead and 24 wounded. Elements from three Russian divisions had been attacking in their sector. Despite this temporary reprieve the regiment was kept in the line a further 23 days.

On 5 August 1941 Generalfeldmarschall von Bock announced the conclusion of the battle at the Dnieper, Dvina and Smolensk. The trapped Russian divisions were destroyed. Booty, he announced, included 309,110 prisoners, 3,205 captured or destroyed tanks, 3,000 guns and 341 aircraft, and the count was still going on.[22] The announcement was of scant interest to the remaining soldiers of the 'Grossdeutschland', finally pulled out of the line for a much needed, albeit brief, rest.

'We lay in the meadow dozing in sunshine and relishing every breath . . . Within eight days we would be in a hole again in combat and perhaps in 14 days already dead. But nobody was crippled by such thoughts. Instead we lived life more consciously, also more simply. We just lived. In contrast, in peacetime one merely passed the days.'[23]

For the German infantry, these weeks and days were becoming increasingly short.

'DO NOT CRY' . . . SOVIET DEFEAT IN THE WEST

'A terrible misfortune has befallen this country,' announced Ina Konstantinova to her diary in mid-July. 'The Germans are already so near . . . They are bombing Leningrad and Mozhaisk. They are advancing toward Moscow.' A sense of foreboding was now beginning to erode the initial popular emotion and outraged patriotism that had accompanied the invasion. 'How troubled our life has become!' wrote Konstantinova. Aircraft were constantly taking-off from the nearby Kashin airfield north-east of Moscow. Military detachments of tanks and anti-aircraft guns were observed moving through the streets. Things were different. 'Even the atmosphere has changed somehow,' she lamented. 'What does the future hold in store for us?'[1] Her concern was echoed by Soviet staff officer Ivan Krylov:

'Smolensk! Smolensk in danger. The way to Moscow, the great highway followed by the army of Napoleon, was once again the invasion artery. But it was only 10 July, hardly three weeks from the beginning of hostilities. I began to think that the fighting abilities of our forces must be lower than . . . imagined.'[2]

Russian units were retreating in front of an apparently inexorable German advance. Common to any examination of Soviet military staff documents covering this early period is recognition of the stultifying impact of Luftwaffe air attacks, a dearth of knowledge of the actual limit of German advances and confusion following on from a total breakdown of communications with alarming reports of appalling losses. Commander Fourth Army reported to the commander of the Western Front as early as 30 June that:

'All my resources are exhausted. I ordered to hold to the last, but there is no certainty that the line will be held.'

As his XXXXVIIth Rifle Corps attempted to withdraw to the River Ola, the general declared 10 hours later:

'The only means of fighting is the medium tank detachment. Manpower has lost its meaning on the given route. We have no means of support at our disposal . . . It is necessary to cover the Mogilev, Bobruisk Highway using front forces, since there are no units at all on this direction.'[3]

In by far the worst situation were hapless Soviet units cut off in ever-shrinking pockets. Kesselschlacht — the German term for pocket fighting — was apt. A Kessel (cauldron) was quite literally boiled until life within was extinguished. It was a methodical, slow operation causing terrible casualties to both sides. Tank soldier Alexander Golikow wrote to his wife, while he was engaged in fighting around Rowno against German Army Group North units:

'*Dear Tonetschka!*

I don't know whether you will be able to read these lines, but I do know, for certain, this will be my last letter to you. A bitter and deadly battle is being fought at this very moment. Our tank has been knocked out and all around us are the Fascists. We have tried to beat off their attacks the whole day. The road to Ostrov is covered with bodies in green uniforms . . . Two of us — Pawel Abramow and I, remain. You will know him, I have written about him. We do not expect to be rescued. We are soldiers and have no fear of dying for our homeland.'[4]

Once the initial Panzer screen was thrown around an intended pocket, Soviet units would march and counter-march within, attempting to get out. Lack of intelligence and nothing to brief to soldiers made this phase seem particularly aimless to those trapped inside. J. Jewtuchewitsch's unit was moved from Leningrad to engage the German Army Group North advance in July.

'They put us on lorries and propelled us in a completely different direction . . . We have been moving for a few days now from place to place. Sometimes we look for the battalion, they on occasion us . . . During one such move we covered a 94km stretch.'

Uncertainty was all-pervasive. Jewtuchewitsch remembered driving through the streets of Leningrad with civilians dolefully following their passage, 'uncertainty in all eyes, unease about us and we also about ourselves'.[5] Major Jurij Krymov serving on the Soviet West Front confessed similar reservations to his wife. 'It is now 19 days since I have heard anything from you or the others'. Newspapers were unavailable, only radio. He had no idea how his wife was living in Moscow and was not optimistic. 'Due to the war and the need for women to work (because here there seem to be a lot) I am beginning to be concerned for your welfare,' he wrote. Conditions inside cut-off pockets quickly deteriorated. Alexander Golikow continued the letter to his wife:

'I am sitting in a misshapen tank shot through with holes. The heat is unbearable and I am thirsty. There is not a single drop of water. Your picture is lying on my lap. As I look into your blue eyes I feel better — you are with me . . . I have thought of you since the first day of the war. When will I return to you and press your head to my breast? Perhaps never.'[6]

Krymov complained, 'it is not so much the danger or the risk of losing one's life, rather the absence of the most elementary things'. Everyday life was burdensome:

'We go without water for days and eat badly and irregularly, having to sleep in defensive positions that one previously would have thought unthinkable. It was all down to filth, heat and the strain.'[7]

Soldiers completely unaware of the real situation had no option but to follow orders. German soldiers dismissed this as a 'herd mentality', which often led to mass suicide attacks against their positions. Confusion bred doubt feeding on fear. Russian officers offering a course of action, a solution, or order from chaos would appeal to soldiers faced with no visible alternatives. Survival drove men to attempt the bizarre. They were simply human beings worn out by tension and physical exertion. Konstantin Simonov, a Russian war correspondent, described the difficulties officers had to band men together into companies and battalions after they had first been disorientated by the shock of the German invasion and then under constant air attack since it began. 'Nobody knew one another,' he said, 'and with the best will in the world, it was difficult for people either to give or take orders'. He had not eaten or drunk for two days. 'My eyes were drooping from tiredness and hunger,' and his face 'was burned to a shining iridescence by the sun'.[8] Dimitrij Wolkogonow, a Soviet Lieutenant, described how:

'On the radio it was given out that our army was resisting bitterly in some region, and then suddenly a day later we heard that the German Army had already penetrated 50–70km further eastward. And I must further say that it was not only the simple soldier who had no clear impression of what was going on in these pockets, characterising the war at this stage, because there was no clear picture in the STAVKA High Command. Stalin constantly demanded new situation reports, but nothing could be usefully reported.'[9]

The outcome was predictable. Soviet Engineer Colonel Il'ya Starinov believed early offensives taken against the German attack were counter-productive and 'produced negligible results. But the losses inflicted on our troops were extraordinarily heavy'. He concluded, 'the unjustifiable attempts to go over to the offensive at a time when we should have been organising our defences only exacerbated a situation that was already bad.'[10] All available news was negative. 17-year-old Sinauda Lischakowa was living in at Vitebsk when the Germans marched in. As a fledgling partisan she had access to a radio. The radio news from Moscow 'was most distressing at that time,' she stated. 'The Germans were already saying then, in 1941, repeatedly: "Moscow Kaputt. Stalin Kaputt. The war will soon be over," but naturally we did not believe it.'[11]

Desperate measures were ordered by officers to try and escape encirclement, because they were acutely aware of the consequences of failure. Commissar 'dual authority' was restored to Red Army units on 16 July. On 27 July an order sentencing nine senior officers to death was read out to all officers and men. The condemned included the Signals Officer of the Western Front, blamed for the catastrophic breakdown of communications, and the commanders of the hapless Third and Fourth Armies as also the commanders of the 30th and 60th Rifle Divisions. Engineer Colonel Starinov himself was briefly placed under arrest while he was supervising a bridge demolition across the River Dnieper on the Minsk highway. He was not surprised. Mistakes were not tolerated. Despair and confusion reigned among Western Front staff as, he said, 'the arrests took the ground right out from beneath people's feet. No one could be sure of living to see the next day.' The nihilistic ordeal of the 1937 state-conducted purges remained all-pervasive. 'Even strong-willed experienced officers,' Starinov explained, 'who had never cracked in the toughest situations, completely lost their self-control, at the appearance of people in the green garrison caps of the NKVD (Secret Police).'[12] Men fought on in hopeless circumstances as a consequence. Alexander Golikow further wrote to his wife:

'Our tank shook with the impact of enemy shots, but we were still alive. We have no more shells and are short of bullets. Pawel is shooting at the enemy with the turret machine gun while I "take a breather" and chat with you [ie to a photograph]. *I know this will be the last time. I would like a long chat but time is too short . . . It is good to die when you know somewhere there is a person who will think "It is good to have been loved".'*[13]

It became quickly apparent to the Russian population, reeling from the surprise of the invasion, that the war was going badly. German correspondent Paul Kohl retraced the invasion route to Moscow 40 years after the attack. During his investigative historical tour in 1985 he was questioned by a 70-year-old woman in Gross Prussy, south-west of Minsk: 'Why did the Germans do this? We had a non-aggression pact with you. Why did you invade us?'[14] Surprise characterised the responses of the Russian people he met who had experienced the war, along the former invasion route. Alevtina Michailowna Burdenko heard war had been declared in a radio broadcast. Thereafter she had enormous difficulties returning to her home town at Baranowa, some 210km east of Brest-Litovsk. Every train was attacked from the air, and any still running were reserved for military transport. She managed to board a train three days later but the locomotive and a number of carriages were destroyed during a strafing attack, and 'many passengers were killed'. The only remaining option was to walk home to her village, which she did, 'constantly shot at by low-flying aircraft'. The village, however, had been overrun by the Wehrmacht on 25 June.

'When I arrived in Baranowa in the evening, the town was full of German soldiers — the jack-boots, the sentry posts — all over there were control points. My husband was no longer there when I got home! Taken away! I never saw him again!'[15]

The town of Sluzk, further east, was occupied the following day. Sonja Davidowna declared:

'On the same day they marched in they announced strict laws. All Communists and Komsomol members were to report without delay in order to be registered. Whoever went in could naturally bid life "Adieu". Anyone supplying provisions to Soviet soldiers or partisans was immediately shot. A curfew was imposed. Anyone found on the streets after 18.00 without an identity pass was immediately executed.'[16]

Minsk, the capital of Belorussia, was occupied on 28 June, seven days after the invasion. Its fall was preceded by savage air raids. When W. F. Romanowskij emerged from his cellar shelter he was confronted with a horrific scene.

'What a sight! Burning houses, debris and ruins. Bodies lay in the streets all around. People tried to flee the town during the bombardment but were not able to get out quickly enough, because the streets had been blocked with debris. Those caught in the open were annihilated by low-flying German aircraft.'

When the Germans marched in, the city had 245,000 inhabitants. Three years later only 40,000 remained and the town was 80% destroyed. A strict curfew was imposed from the start, as also were measures against supporting 'political commissars', the 'Red Army' and 'saboteurs'. Romanowskij described how life in the occupied city took on a totally different hue.

'There were SS and police patrols day and night with sudden house searches. People were arrested on the slightest pretext, disappearing into Gestapo cellars and then whisked off to be shot. An atmosphere of constant fear reigned in the city.'[17]

The Jewish Minsk ghetto was established in a district to the west of the city on 19 July, encapsulating the area where most Jews had been living at the time of the invasion. Two days before, the Germans had driven into the settlement of Kirowski, south-west of Mogilev on the Smolensk road. 'It was very interesting for us children,' remarked Georgia Terenkerwa — 10 years old at the time — who saw 'sparkling helmets and the uniform shoulder straps' and 'officers in their open saloon cars'. Within two hours the initial wave of soldiers had passed through. 'At midday they came again.' These newly arrived soldiers were of a totally different type.

'We had six children in the family. There was a hollow disbelief in the village as they began to shoot people. Nobody took it on board to flee. Everyone was surprised. I remember it all precisely. I was in front of the school as the Fascists started killing our neighbours. Shortly before it began, I had even seen in front of our house — it was about 100m away — my mother was standing gossiping with our neighbour's wife. Then the soldiers came, forced their way into the house and then I heard the shots. I do not know how it was I managed to survive.'[18]

Surprise at the stunning extent of early German advances was universal. Panzer vanguards entered Russian towns while trams still ran. German motorised units were even cheered by civilians as they drove through, mistakenly believed to be their own troops. Wera Kulagina visited Vitebsk, which was occupied by Panzergruppe 3 on 9 July, coming from a neighbouring village accompanied by her elder sister. 'As we arrived,' she said, 'we noticed the mood in the town was a lot more oppressive and uneasy than that before in the village.' They looked around. 'The town was blazing and the streets empty of people.' The reason soon became apparent. 'Only the Germans moved about undisturbed and freely through the town, like conquerors.' Fear was all-pervasive. 'We felt something was not right here.' As the bridge across the River Dvina had been blown up, Wera Kulagina's sister would not be able to go back to work. They quickly retraced their steps to the village. The inhabitants were totally oblivious to what had been going on nearby.

'When we got back to the village and reached my mother, the Germans had yet to pass through. She did not believe us. As we told her we had already seen the Germans on the Dvina she would not take it in. She could not comprehend that the town was occupied.'[19]

Stalin began to emerge from the apparent initial paralysis imposed by the shock of the attack on his country and populace. He addressed the nation by radio on 3 July. His listeners found the speech to be extraordinary. Stalin spoke in an entirely unprecedented tone and manner, precisely encapsulating the atmosphere and emotional appeal needed to explain this crisis. One civilian, Boris Preobazhensky, recalled its dramatic impact long after the war.

'The first thing we heard was the clinking of a glass against the jug, and then water was poured into the glass. You could hear it so clearly. The water poured out. Stalin took a gulp and then he began to speak: "Comrades, citizens, brothers and sisters," those first few words brought us so close to him, as though it were our own father speaking.'[20]

This paternal appeal struck a sentimental chord with the Soviet people, unused to being addressed in such a manner by their leader. Stalin, while understating territorial losses, admitted the gravity of the situation, declaring: 'a serious threat hangs over our country'. Advantage had been lost to the Germans because the Non-Aggression Pact had been 'perfidiously violated'. The enemy was 'cruel and merciless', Stalin claimed, but there could 'be no room in our ranks for whimperers and cowards'. State production would be put on a war footing. 'The Red Army and Navy and the whole Soviet people must fight for every inch of Soviet soil, fight to the last drop of blood for our towns and villages.'

The famous 'scorched-earth' instruction was issued alongside an order to prosecute 'partisan war' in the rear of the enemy.[21] Measures described included the State Defence Committee set up to deal with the rapid mobilisation of all the country's resources. It was realised that the existing state machinery was inappropriate to prosecute the war effectively. On 10 July Stalin combined the formal title of Head of Government with the post of Supreme Commander, which the Supreme Soviet formalised on 7 August. The State Defence Committee (GKO) included Stalin, Voroshilov, Beria, Molotov (Foreign Affairs) and Stalin's party deputy, Malenkow. The STAVKA (High Command) was subordinated to it, having also been reorganised to include Stalin, Molotov and Voroshilov from the party and an army element including Timoshenko, Budenny, Shaposhnikov and Zhukov. The General Staff, extended to oversee all branches of the armed forces, was subordinated to the STAVKA on 8 August. Stalin, in so doing, elevated himself to all the highest appointments in the Soviet state, party and army. Victory or defeat rested on his shoulders alone.

Similarly on the same date three Soviet Fronts were established: North-west, nominally under Voroshilov, West under Timoshenko and South-west under Budenny. These corresponded to the three German Army Groups attacking them. The measure further rationalised the command of reinforcements and supplies that GKO was mobilising for defence.

This defence was already in a parlous state. German OKH assessed on 8 July that it had eliminated 89 of 164 identified Russian rifle divisions and 20 of 29 tank divisions. It concluded, 'the enemy is no longer in a position to organise a continuous front, not even behind strong terrain features.'[22] The Soviet plan appeared to be to counter-attack incessantly to keep the German advance as far to the west as possible and thereby slow progress by inflicting heavy casualties.

Stalin's toneless admittance of great but not insurmountable problems to his population on 3 July suggested not weakness but great strength. The bitter truth, though understated, was out. At least the Soviet people felt that their feet, despite apparent imbalances, were firmly on the ground. The resolve of the Soviet population was stiffened. 'Every night Moscow is subjected to air raids,' wrote Ina Konstantinova on 5 August. 'The enemy troops are coming closer and closer. How awful! But never mind, they will soon be stopped.'[23]

The grandiose heroism that permeates the official Soviet 'Great Patriotic War' version of events is out of place to students of history at the beginning of the 21st century, accustomed to the grainy realism of immediate on-the-spot TV news reportage. There was then a strong perception of duty reinforced by nationalism which could be drawn upon — a feature still evident in European conflict today. Soviet infantry machine gunner Timofei Dombrowski explained, 'yes, it was our duty to defend the Motherland . . . there was also patriotism, and we were in a very serious position.' His view as a soldier was uncomplicated. Russia had not started the war, and up until this moment his battles had been fought to stay alive. 'We had to defend ourselves,' he said. 'We had not been the attackers, and we were permanently surrounded.'[24]

Tank crewman Alexander Golikow's last letter to his wife was found next to his corpse inside a knocked-out Russian tank on the Ostrov road.

'I can see the road, green trees and colourful flowers in the garden through the holes in the tank.

'Life after the war will be just as colourful as these flowers, and happy . . . I am not afraid to lay down my life for this . . . do not cry. You will likely not be able to visit my grave. Will there indeed be a grave?'[25]

Nobody knows. The only certainty is that the letter was recovered by German soldiers searching the shell-scarred hulk.

'THE INFANTRY'

The following sequence of photographs records a day's march of 50km by a typical foot infantry company recorded by war correspondent Hilmar Pabel.

Right:
It has been estimated that 50km translates into 84,000 paces of about 60cm each. An infantryman's view of the march, head down observing each step, puffing dust into the air.

Left:
Awaiting the order to step off, each man drinks from a raw egg he has commandeered the night before. Yawning and grim-faced, many will be nursing burst blisters, as yet another day of foot-slogging beckons.

Right:
The company
occasionally
raised a song
as they set off.

Below:
Note the two men in the foreground, who
were to become casualties later in the day.

Left:
It is now daybreak,. The soldiers stretching out with long paces are disciplined, with rifles uniformly slung as the dust begins to rise after the dampness of early morning dew.

Right:
An hour later and still morning, the pace is beginning to take its toll. Rifles are slung more carelessly about the body to alternate the weight for comfort. Hands are idly playing with helmet straps.

Left:
Five hours later and the
column is still marching.
Faces reflect a uniform mask
of monotony. A cigarette
dangles loosely from the lip,
it is not inhaled, the tobacco
smoke lingers around the
marcher. The dust and grime
accentuate relief lines on
faces contorted by the
concentration of effort.

Right:
Constant wiping
smears dirt lines
across faces as the
soldiers strive to
keep the stinging
salt perspiration
from their eyes.

Right:
There are skirmishes and enemy alarms during the march. After one such engagement the two men previously identified at the front of the column become walking wounded. They seek the dressing station to the rear. One has had his face slashed by a bullet. He carries the rifle of his comrade who has been shot in the hand and hip.

An hour's rest is ordered at midday. Exhausted and with empty water bottles, the soldiers pass around a pitcher of sour milk offered by a friendly farmer. They each take one mouthful and collapse on the ground and go to sleep, many too tired even to eat.

Above:
The scene at sunset: faces are grotesquely masked with white dust as the soldiers limp and press on through golden clouds of dust reflecting the final rays of the sun.

Right:
Sweat has penetrated the woollen tunics and their hair is a straw-like sticky mess. As darkness descends in the humid half light a fine drizzle begins to fall. Helmets come off and sleeves are rolled up to capture every glistening drop of moisture denied them the whole day.

Left:
Day's end.

Below:
A platoon commander tiredly contemplates his men, who have fallen asleep in their order of march.

Bottom:
A typical scene on the infantry division line of march. The motorised column has priority on the road and has obliged the infantry to march alongside in the ditch. A Panzer is on flank picket duty.

Chapter 9

Refocusing victory conditions

> **'And now it seemed we were to turn away from our greatest chance to get to Moscow and bring the war to an end. My instinct told me that something was very wrong. I never understood this change in plans.'**
>
> *German soldier*

THE LONGEST CAMPAIGN

The day after Army Group Centre announced it had finally closed the Smolensk pocket, its commander received depressing news in the form of a new Führer directive. Von Bock confided bleakly to his diary: 'the Army Group is being scattered to the four winds.'[1] Advance notice had been received four days before:

'. . . which divides my Army Group into three parts. According to the instructions I am to divert one group of forces, including Panzer Group Guderian (Pz Gr. 2) southeast to Army Group South, a group without tanks is to go towards Moscow, and Panzer Group Hoth (Pz Gr.3) is to be diverted north and subordinated to (von Leeb's) Army Group North.'[2]

Splitting the effort was anathema to a professional commander conditioned and trained to plan and ruthlessly adhere to a single aim. A disconnect between aim and reality had been evident in 'Barbarossa' planning from the start. The loose correlation between operational and logistic planning was based upon Hitler's ideological premise that a 'kick in the door' would be sufficient to collapse the Soviet Union 'like a house of cards'. 'Barbarossa' Directive Number 21 issued in December 1940 gave only a broad outline to the conduct of operations. It aimed to create a barrier against Asiatic Russia on the line between Astrakhan on the Caspian Sea and Archangel in the Arctic. Apart from the need to annihilate the main enemy forces, there was no absolute strategic plan or objective to which all operations were subordinate. Three primary invasion objectives were identified: the coal and iron fields of the Donets Basin in the south, the capital Moscow in the centre and Leningrad to the north. One army group was assigned to each, with Panzergruppen to spearhead the way. Few plans in practice survive their inception on crossing the start line, and focusing the continuation of effort is invariably the next problem.

The decisions faced by the Führer and his High Command at the beginning of August were unprecedented. No German campaign during this war had lasted so long. Obergefreiter Erich Kuby with the 3rd Motorised Division recalled a disgruntled infantry NCO muttering they were not 'sprinting any longer as in the Polish autumn and French May (campaigns), they had been hard on the go for five weeks now'.[3] Blitzkrieg in the West and Scandinavia lasted six weeks, Poland was conquered in 28 days, the Balkans took 24 days and Crete was overwhelmed in 10.

An intangible and unremarked watershed was passed on 2 August. The Wehrmacht was used to success, often against heavy odds and suffering casualties, but quickly. Little attention was therefore paid to the passing of a milestone that was to be superseded by momentous events to follow. Victory in Russia, whatever the propaganda aspirations, was never seriously thought achievable in six weeks by rational planners. But the tempo was beginning to falter. Vacillation and indecision became increasingly apparent at the Führer's headquarters. The Wehrmacht had indeed 'kicked in the door', but there was little prospect of the Soviet edifice collapsing. One German housewife writing to her husband at the front mused, 'when one hears in the reports what losses the Russians have had already, one can hardly imagine how he has kept up the fight for so long'.[4]

General Halder made no mention in his diary at the six-week point that the campaign had exceeded the duration of the western Blitzkrieg. His only comment was that the logistic situation regarding shoes and clothing was 'tight'. Winter clothing would require consideration alongside the 'clamour for lost replacements' by Panzer and infantry divisions. A considerable deficit had by now emerged between casualties and these replacements. Army Group South received only 10,000 reinforcements to compensate for 63,000 losses while Army Groups Centre and North were short by 51,000 and 28,000 men respectively.[5]

Six weeks into the campaign Generalfeldmarschall von Bock was lamenting the difficulties of holding the Smolensk pocket perimeter. 'We are at the end of our tether just now trying to prevent Soviet units escaping,' he wrote. It was a far cry from the euphoric conditions that had existed in France barely one year before. Von Bock observed a perilous situation, commenting on signs of increasing strain. 'The nerves of those burdened with great responsibility are starting to waiver,' he said. Victory might be near but a terrible price was already apparent. The VIIth and Vth Corps were 'proud of their success' but had 'suffered considerable casualties, especially in officers'.[6]

The common perception among German soldiers was less that of pending victory, more a dawning realisation that the road ahead was going to be hard. One soldier in the 35th Infantry Division wrote home on 19 August:

'Today is Sunday, but we didn't notice. We are on the move again some 50km north-eastwards. At the moment we are part of the Army reserve — and high time — we have already lost 50 in the company. It shouldn't be allowed to continue much longer otherwise the burden will be really heavy. We normally have four men on the [anti-tank] gun, but for two days at a particularly dangerous point, we only had two. The others are wounded.'[7]

The longevity of the campaign was developing a sinister parallel to Napoleon's 1812 experience. A transport battalion Gefreiter presciently wrote, 'If we ended up here in the winter, something the Russians would dearly have us do, it would not do us a lot of good either.'[8] Another infantry soldier with

Army Group Centre complained the following day, 'our losses are immense, more than in France'. His company had been fighting around the Moscow *Rollbahn* since 23 July. 'One day we have the road, then the Russians, and so it goes on, day after day.' Victory did not appear imminent. On the contrary, time and intense combat was corroding the courage of the soldiers, in particular pessimism regarding life expectancy.

'I have never seen such vicious dogs as these Russians. Their tactics are unpredictable and they have an inexhaustible supply of tanks and material etc.'[9]

Unteroffizier Wilhelm Prüller, in a motorised infantry regiment accompanying the 9th Panzer Division with Army Group South, was dipping deeply into his courage bank at the six-week point. On 4 August his battalion lost four officers among 14 dead, 47 wounded and two missing, all within 24 hours.

At Temovka his captain was shot through the head just after he left his side to cross a street. His close friend Wimmer from another company was killed the same day. 'I'm so sorry for his wife,' Prüller wrote in his diary, 'especially since she's going to have a baby in October.' Wimmer he remembered — and this was a 'funny thing' — had always been 'quite sure nothing would happen to him'. Next, Prüller's friend Schober was struck by a grenade splinter which penetrated his head below the left eye. He fell 'dead on the spot' at a place Prüller had barely vacated. Two others had already been killed at the same inauspicious place and a third comrade also fell, all within the space of a few hours. Prüller's diary entry that night encapsulated the lot of the German infantryman in the sixth week of the campaign. 350 men had perished in his battalion over five weeks. At this point the year before in France it had been finished. He wrote :

'At 22.00 I lie down, dog tired on some straw. It was a terrible day. But again luck was with me. How long will it last?'[10]

Von Bock's fear of being 'scattered to the four winds' reflected the unparalleled scale as well as unprecedented length of the new campaign. In Poland in 1939 the front expanded from a 320km-wide start line to an area of operations 550km broad at its widest point. Depth did not become a problem to the 41 infantry and 14 Panzer and motorised divisions that were committed because the campaign was over within 28 days. The spring 1941 Yugoslav and Greek campaign involved 33 divisions, of which 15 were Panzer or motorised, advancing over narrow geographically constricted frontages, but to a depth of 1,200km. It was finished in 24 days. The western Blitzkrieg beginning in May 1940 was the Wehrmacht's supreme test. Three army groups, totalling 94 divisions including 10 Panzer divisions and 46 in reserve, advanced on a broad 700km front across Belgium, Holland and France. A decisive victory resulted in six weeks (see map on page 119). These examples paled into relative insignificance compared to the scale and ferocity of the Russian campaign. The operation dwarfed its predecessors in terms of time and scale.

The 'Barbarossa' invasion front was double that of the Western campaign and expanded a further one third in six weeks from over 1,200km at the start to a breadth of 1,600km. This time 139 divisions were committed. More Panzer and motorised formations were employed than in France, but the 19 Panzer divisions were smaller in size. By late autumn 1941 the

front had broadened almost three-fold incorporating the Karelian Peninsula and Baltic states, stretching 2,800km from Murmansk to the Black Sea. Navigation problems dogged the advance from the beginning. Max Kuhnert, a cavalry NCO, said on crossing the border with Army Group South in June:

'I had to be careful not to take the wrong route, for many units had branched off in different directions. There were no roads as such in the west, only field tracks established by tanks and all the other traffic.'

It seemed as though the invading armies were immediately swallowed up by the vastness of the terrain. 'I went strictly by compass,' commented Kuhnert, 'occasionally checking the divisional insignia on the vehicles going east.'[11] To place the scale of the expanding front in relative context, it could be assumed that a widely stretched division might defend a 10km frontage. The new front would therefore require 280 divisions; but only 139 were theoretically available. Geographical hindrances such as the Pripet Marshes and Carpathian Mountains would restrict manoeuvre space. In reality, combat probably only occurred physically over a 1,000km frontage, and then only haphazardly. German divisions moving forward over the difficult roads that formed a primitive network probably advanced sweeping an area about 3km wide. Most combat formations would elect to concentrate in depth, forcing routes on narrow fronts. German progress, in a sense, could be pictured as three arrow shots — the army groups — fired into an empty but expanding funnel. An advance into the depth of the Soviet Union meant also that divisions had to remain behind to guard vital communication and supply routes, and reduce isolated Russian pockets. As a consequence, forces in the advance were constantly diminishing while the land area to be conquered doubled in depth and tripled in width. At the 2,800km-wide point the front was 1,000km deep.

The sheer scale of the objective was becoming part of the problem. If the Russian colossus could not be overwhelmed by the body blows being administered, a rapier *coup de grâce* might be the solution. In short, the conditions required to achieve victory needed to be reconsidered.

CONDITIONS FOR VICTORY

As a rapid Russian collapse did not materialise, Adolf Hitler and his army planners were obliged to reconsider uneasily the future focus as the width and depth of the Russian land mass unfolded before them. One German Army photographer wrote in the Ukraine, 'we have no more maps and can only follow the compass needle to the east'.[1] There were no road signs and few landmarks enabling Germans to calculate their bearings across the limitless steppes of the eastern Ukraine. Patrols and despatch riders simply asked the women and old men in the fields for directions. Poor planning and a degree of unit directional floundering resulted in these vast uncharted territories.

General Halder admitted on 11 August that 'the whole situation makes it increasingly plain that we have underestimated the Russian colossus'. The enemy's military and material potential had been grossly miscalculated. 'At the outset of the war, we reckoned with about 200 enemy divisions. Now we have already counted 360'. These divisions may be qualitatively inferior to the German and poorly led, 'but there they are, and if we smash a dozen of them, the Russians simply put up another dozen'.[2] As a consequence, German staffs had enormous difficulty reconciling their

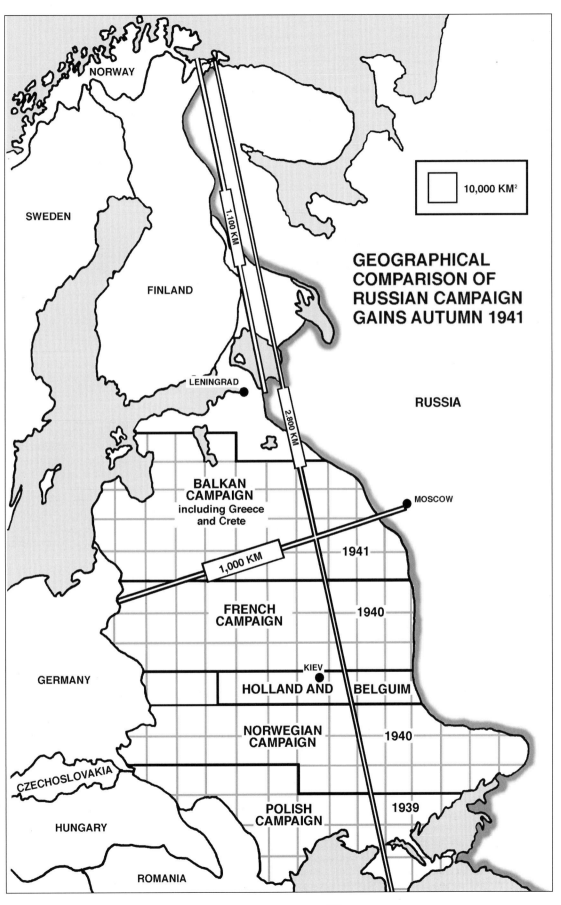

GEOGRAPHICAL COMPARISON OF RUSSIAN CAMPAIGN GAINS AUTUMN 1941

10,000 KM²

NORWAY

SWEDEN

FINLAND

LENINGRAD

RUSSIA

1,100 KM

2,800 KM

BALKAN CAMPAIGN
including Greece and Crete

MOSCOW

1,000 KM

1941

FRENCH CAMPAIGN

1940

GERMANY

KIEV

HOLLAND AND BELGUIM

NORWEGIAN CAMPAIGN

1940

CZECHOSLOVAKIA

POLISH CAMPAIGN

1939

HUNGARY

ROMANIA

Left:
A diagrammatic representation of the vast area covered by the eastern campaign compared to previous shorter operations in the West and Balkans. Poland was conquered in 28 days, the Balkans in 24. The campaign in the West ended at the six-week point. Army Group Centre was lamenting its losses and commenting upon the difficulty of holding Russian forces inside the Smolensk pocket six weeks into the Russian campaign. Resistance at the very first pocket to be established, at Brest-Litovsk, ended only one week before.

victories against tangible achievements. The Russians were obstinate. They would paradoxically fight bitterly to the death in one instance and surrender en masse at the next. The cumulative impact of such victories thus far, at considerable cost, seemed merely to be the attainment of 'false crests'. Although the summit might be tantalisingly ahead, planning fatigue tended to obscure the best means of achieving the most direct route to the objective: that of total victory.

Hitler's controversial change of direction introduced at this stage of the campaign is often discussed with the benefit of a strategic hindsight not available to those executing decisions. It is these contemporary perceptions influencing such deliberations that ought to be considered. One school of thought opined that the Wehrmacht, stretched to its physical limit advancing into an ever-widening land mass, should concentrate its resources against one objective at a time. Generalfeldmarschall von Bock and his Panzergruppen and army commanders Kluge, Guderian and Hoth gave united support, to von Brauchitsch, the Wehrmacht and his Chief of Staff Halder in making Moscow the primary target. Hitler, almost perversely it seemed, elected to concentrate operations against Leningrad to the north and the Ukraine in the south. Moscow would fall as a consequence of this pressure directed against the flanks. Political and economic reasons were cited for this diversification of effort. Führer Directive Number 33, issued initially on 19 July, outlined the concept of future operations. Army Group Centre was to be divested of its two Panzergruppen — 3 (Hoth) and 2 (Guderian) — which were to be diverted from Moscow to co-operate with von Leeb and von Rundstedt in advances north to Leningrad and south to Kiev. Vacillation and confusion followed during a subsequent 'Nineteen-day Interregnum' (4–24 August) as commanders debated or fought their preferred operational concept at conferences. Führer Directive 34A followed on 7 August when OKW and OKH, after conferring with Jodl and Halder, persuaded Hitler of the need to resume the advance on Moscow. This was, however, rescinded three days later when renewed resistance at Leningrad frightened Hitler into insisting Hoth's Panzergruppe 3 move north to assist von Leeb. Hitler resolved to strike southward toward Kiev. He was not deflected by a spirited presentation from Guderian, recalled from the front to brief at Rastenburg on 23 August, arguing the Moscow option for von Brauchitsch and Halder. Recriminations among the top commanders exacerbated the already vitriolic debate. Hitler, backed by Feldmarschall Keitel, Jodl, Chief of the Operations Staff, and Schmundt, his chief Adjutant, patronisingly stated, 'my generals know nothing about the economic aspects of war.' Political, military and economic reasons were given for deflecting the advance southward into the Ukraine. Soviet air force bases in the Crimea could menace the Romanian Ploesti oilfields, economically vital to the German war effort. They had therefore to be neutralised.

Following three weeks of inertia the *Ostheer* (army of the east) was to resume the attack with a full-blooded offensive to the south. Urgency was provided by the need to conclude the Kiev operation in sufficient time to redirect an assault on Moscow before winter. The Russians, who anticipated an assault on Moscow, were astonished to see instead an attack suddenly directed to the south.

The controversy over the importance of Moscow was bound up in the army staff debate of what to do, now that the Soviet regime was prepared to fight on despite catastrophic reverses. What were the preconditions for victory in this new and not previously considered scenario? Options to circumvent the impasse might be to capture cities to create a political impact or capture ground for economic acquisition. The economic option was not seen as a rapid war-winning strategy. Gaining popular support, a measure that proved particularly effective in 1917–18, was not seriously considered due to its ideological unacceptability to the Führer. In any case it would take too long. Annihilating the Red Army remained an unfulfilled aspiration. None of the proposed strategies appeared to be working. Leningrad, the 'cradle of Bolshevism', was an attractive objective to Hitler, a 'party' man, who appreciated the ideological fibre the Communist Party conferred on the regime. Communism resided in the cities and built-up areas, not necessarily in the countryside. Panzer Leutnant F. W. Christians remembered, as his unit crossed the Ukrainian border in the middle of summer, 'we were greeted with real enthusiasm'. It was an emotive appeal never exploited. 'They did not just bring salt and bread,' the traditionally hospitable Ukrainian form of greeting, 'but also fruit and eggs,' he declared. 'We were warmly greeted as liberators.'[3] Such a psychological undercurrent was irrelevant in the Blitzkrieg context, because it had no immediate significance for military operations. The ideological end-state was, in any case, to enslave these people for the economic benefit of the Reich. A more positive outcome from a change in the direction of attack would be to strike an unexpected blow with potentially damaging consequences for the Soviet southern salient bulging westwards. A Cannae was envisaged.

Hitler's decision caused real anguish to the High Command at OKH. Halder complained:

'I regard the situation created by the Führer's interference unendurable for OKH. No other but the Führer himself is to blame for the zig-zag course caused by his successive orders, nor can the present OKH, which now is in its fourth victorious campaign, tarnish its good name with these latest orders.'[4]

But in a number of respects the Army High Command was the victim of its own confidence. There was a gulf opening up between aspiration and reality commensurate with the physical gap developing between the headquarters at the front and rear. Senior staff officers had only a limited perception of the rigours and deprivations endured by officers and men on the new Russian front. Bickering over dwindling reserves of reinforcements and logistic assets to replenish faltering Panzer advances continued; OKW and OKH were becoming complacently spoiled by a seemingly automatic flow of victories. Complaints from spearhead commanders, who repeatedly produced triumphs despite dwindling resources, not surprisingly tended to be shrugged off. Somehow, whatever the declared limitations, the German soldier managed.

Junior officers and soldiers at the front commented on the change in the direction of advance, but theirs was an uncomplicated view. They were concerned less with strategy, rather the imperative to survive or live more comfortably in a harsh environment. German soldiers were used to sudden and unexpected changes in direction. These were generally accepted without much comment because the Führer and 'higher-ups' invariably 'had it in hand'. Rapid changes in the direction of the *Schwerpunkt* (main point of effort) or in risk-taking had saved the day on many an occasion in France and Crete, for example. The German soldier was conditioned to instant and absolute obedience.

Major Bernd Freytag von Lorringhoven recalled Guderian's return from the fateful conference at Rastenburg on 23 August, after the General had failed to secure the Führer's compliance for a continuation of the drive on Moscow. 'We were all very astonished,' he said, '. . . when Hitler had convinced him it was more important to push southwards into the Ukraine.'[5] Hauptmann Alexander Stahlberg was similarly perplexed to learn the 12th Panzer Division was to be redirected against Leningrad.

'The order to discontinue our advance towards Moscow and go over to a defensive position had been a shock. What strategy was intended? The word had gone round at once that it had come from the highest level, that is from Hitler himself.'

Within a few days, he explained, 'the riddle was solved', so far as the 12th Panzer Division was concerned. 'Moscow was no longer the priority, Leningrad was to be taken first.'[6] Major von Lorringhoven remarked after the war that the decision 'is difficult to comprehend under conditions that would be prevalent today'. One simply did not question orders. He added thoughtfully:

'One must try to imagine the fixed hierarchy that existed, a strong conception of the importance of the chain of command. It was very difficult to pose alternatives outside this convention.'

To question the change of direction was incomprehensible;'for practical purposes that was simply not possible,'[7] said von Lorringhoven.

Some soldiers have since remarked on the change, in postwar publications. Artilleryman Werner Adamczyk was informed his unit was to be diverted towards Leningrad.

'I had a chance to look at a map of Russia. It showed the distance between Smolensk and Leningrad to be about 600km. On the other hand, the distance from where we were to Moscow was less than 400km. And we were really making progress — prisoners from the Smolensk encirclement were still passing by every day. Definitely the Russians confronting us on our way to Moscow had been beaten. And now, it seemed we were to turn away from our greatest chance to get to Moscow and bring the war to an end. My instinct told me that something was very wrong. I never understood this change in plans.'[8]

Leutnant Heinrich Haape, with Infantry Regiment 18 on the Central Front, made similar calculations.

'We had marched 1,000km from East Prussia, 1,000km in a little over five weeks. Three-quarters of the journey covered; a quarter still to do. We could do it in a fortnight at the most.'

There was then a pause in the normally incessant stream of marching orders. Until 'on 30 July we received the incredible order to prepare defensive positions'.[9] Many postwar personal accounts point to this abrupt dispersal of effort 'to the four winds' with hindsight as sealing the eventual outcome of the campaign. The 'nineteen-day interregnum' between 4 and 24 August, which one eminent historian claims 'may well have spared Stalin defeat in 1941', is not a theme in contemporary diary accounts and letters home.[10] Ordinary soldiers may comment on plans after the event, but during conflict it rarely occurs to them. Soldiers did what they were told. Most of their letters reflect a desire to get the campaign finished. If this warranted a change in the direction of attack, then so be it. Survival and conditions at the front are what they wrote about.

Optimism was tempered with an increasing frustration at the way the campaign was being drawn out. 'If this tempo is maintained,' wrote a Düsseldorf housewife to the front, 'then Russia's collapse will not be long in coming.'[11] An Obergefreiter declared on 8 August that 'since this morning the battle is now raging for the cradle of the Bolshevist revolution. We are now on the march to Leningrad.' Despite bitter resistance from 'committed communists', and facing rain and storms, the advance 'could not be held up by them'.[12] Another infantry Gefreiter with Army Group South wrote on 24 August, 'the enemy fought bitterly at several positions but, nevertheless, had to fall back with heavy losses'. Many of his comrades 'were left dead or wounded on the battlefield. This war is dreadful,' he lamented.[13] There was more frustration at the requirement in the centre to go over to the defensive and engage in static positional warfare than comment about the opening thrust to the south. 'I'm already fed up to the eye-teeth with the much vaunted Soviet Union,' declared an Unteroffizier from the 251st Infantry Division.

'Day and night we have to live in shell holes and protect ourselves against shrapnel. The holes are full of water and lice and other vermin are already crawling out.'[14]

It might have been 1917. Another infantry Gefreiter from 256th Division complained, 'it was better last year, by the beginning of July the war with France was already over and the first people were beginning to go on leave'.[15] Common to many letters is recognition of the imperative to finish the campaign quickly in order to survive. Bernhard Ritter, a 24-year-old motorised infantry soldier, attempted to come to terms with the psychological toll the war was exacting by expressing his private innermost thoughts to his diary. He wrote on 19 August:

'Which direction will the war cast us next? How will it go? We hope that another decisive battle will be fought soon and that we will be part of it.'

Ritter, like many front-line soldiers, sought to distance himself from the pain and anguish of losing friends in order to maintain emotional equilibrium. It was not easy. Ritter came across the graves of two former comrades in the rear. They had all ridden in the same vehicle. He subconsciously tried to rationalise his feelings of regret.

'One understands the implications exactly. He was on my side, a fraction of a distance away — that one could feel totally and unsentimentally. It was the normal course of events, even if one hardly knew the other man.'

The graves would remain behind the advance. 'One of the simple secrets of life that war teaches us,' reflected Ritter, was that buried inside those plots 'was something from our own souls'.[16] Harald Henry, still enduring tortuous forced marches with Army Group Centre, wrote on 18 August:

'It would be no overstatement to declare "a dog could not go on living like this," because no animal could stoop to live any lower or more primitively than us. All day long we hack ourselves under the ground, crawl into narrow holes, taking sun and rain with no respite and try to sleep.'

He wrote another letter four days later, during the static 'interregnum' period, as the future strategic direction of the campaign was being discussed. 'Yesterday was a day so immersed in blood, so full of dead and wounded, so blasted by crackling salvoes and shrapnel from shells and the groans and shrieks of the wounded, that I can no longer write about it.' Casualties within Henry's unit were high. 'Old Unteroffizier Grabke and many other friends are dead,' he said. 'It was a miracle I was relieved from this heavy fighting in the afternoon and so far have not been injured.'[17] The strategic implications of a change in the direction of advance were of no consequence to men who sought to survive the next day. Soldiers and families at home simply wanted the fighting to stop. 'Is the Russian still not finished off?' wrote a mother to her son at the front:

'We had hoped you would be able to settle any doubts. My dear son! I have put in a few pieces of paper [ie in the envelope]. Perhaps you haven't got any writing material to give us at least a sign of life. Yesterday I got some post from Jos. He is OK. He wrote — "I passionately wanted to be part of the attack on Moscow, but now would now be more pleased if I could get out of this hellish situation."'[18]

The Germans had underestimated their Russian opponents. This inability to finish off an apparently reeling foe formed the background to vacillating strategies. Nobody, it seemed, was able to identify a war-winning solution. The soldiers left it to the generals who in turn tended, with failure, to blame Hitler. There had been a misappreciation between the Russian national and 'Soviet' identity. Hitler assumed the innate 'rottenness' of the Soviet Bolshevik ideology would result in the rapid collapse of the regime. He and his generals preferred to apply the experience of 1917 to the outcome of the campaign. A more meaningful example was Napoleon's experience of 1812.

German victory over Tsarist Russia during World War 1 and the treaty signed at Brest-Litovsk in 1918 was followed by further German advances into the Baltic states, Poland, Belorussia, the Ukraine and Crimea. The Russian Army buckled under the strain of a two-pronged military and propaganda offensive that exacerbated tensions and disharmony in Imperial Russia. Many Wehrmacht officers and soldiers had served in this war, which presaged the total collapse of the Imperial Russian State. Although the successful methodology of its joint military-propaganda prosecution was not reapplied in 1941, generalisations were nevertheless made on its likely outcome based on World War 1 lessons.

The precedent of 1812 was arguably more significant. The fact that Russia did not surrender to Napoleon even after the capture of Moscow, before winter, had not escaped Adolf Hitler. It is debatable whether Moscow was so crucial to the survival of the regime. Stalin in his 3 July speech harnessed the emotive appeal of nationalist 'Mother Russia' to protect the homeland. 'I see Russian soldiers standing on the threshold of their native land' against 'the dull, drilled, docile brutish masses of Hun soldiery plodding on like a swarm of locusts,' he said.[19] Grigori Tokaty, a refugee White Russian teaching at Moscow Military Academy, recalled at this moment of crisis:

'In that very situation something else appeared among us. The tradition of Borodino. Borodino is the place where Napoleon was defeated. This suddenly released feelings appearing from nowhere that helped to unite the people.'[20]

Dismantling Russian factories and relocating them further eastwards beyond the reach of the Luftwaffe suggested surrender was not imminent, whether Moscow fell or not. When the front was only 80km from Vitebsk in early July, 2,000 of 5,000 workers from the 'Flag of Industrialisation' textile factory were moved to Saratow, several hundred kilometres further east. During the journey, constantly dogged by air raids, the workers learned their city had been overrun by the German advance.[21]

Russian resistance remained unbowed. The only logical means of achieving victory must be to break her armies. The advance to the south decided by Hitler had the potential to achieve a gigantic encirclement operation that might result in the annihilation of several Russian armies. It was beginning to develop sinister parallels with the crushing victory achieved by Hannibal's Carthaginians over Rome at Cannae in 216BC.

A CITY 'PULSING WITH LIFE' . . . LENINGRAD

Generalfeldmarschall von Leeb's Army Group North accelerated its rate of advance along the Baltic coast as Army Group Centre completed the destruction of the Smolensk pocket. General Hoepner's Panzergruppe 4, with three Panzer and three motorised divisions, provided the spearhead, flanked on the Baltic coast by Generaloberst von Kuchler's Twenty-eighth Army to the left and Generaloberst Busch's Sixteenth Army to the right. Crossing the River Dvina signalled the piercing of the old 'Stalin Line' that had run along the previous Latvian/Russian Border. The 1st Panzer Division reached Ostrov on 4 July. Pskov fell three days later, opening rail and road connections that led to Leningrad. Spectacular encirclements were not a feature of this advance because, unlike Army Group Centre, the Panzer spearheads had to negotiate difficult terrain — lakes, forests and rivers — from the very start. Even so, by mid-July Solzy and Novgorod had been taken, enabling the smallest of the three Army Groups to stand on the River Luga, the last remaining physical obstacle before Leningrad. It had achieved an advance of 750km by the time Army Group Centre occupied Smolensk. On 10 July Field Marshal Mannerheim's Finnish Karelian Army invaded the USSR from Finland and began to advance south-east down the Karelian isthmus towards Lake Ladoga and Leningrad.

Army Group North battered its opposing forces so effectively and captured Lithuania, Latvia and most of Estonia so quickly that Soviet forces were denied freedom of manoeuvre. With the capture of Leningrad imminent Generalfeldmarschall von Leeb received instructions on 15 July that 'the immediate mission is not to capture Leningrad but to encircle it'.

Generaloberst Reinhardt's XXXXIst Panzer Corps broke into open country beyond the River Luga on 8 August in a move which seemed to presage a Soviet collapse. The Luga, 100km from Leningrad, was in effect the outermost ring of the city's defence. Rolf Dahm, a radio operator in a German infantry division, commented:

'As I see it today we had practically reached Leningrad almost without a fight. We moved forward from our jump-off attack positions and encountered virtually no resistance.'[1]

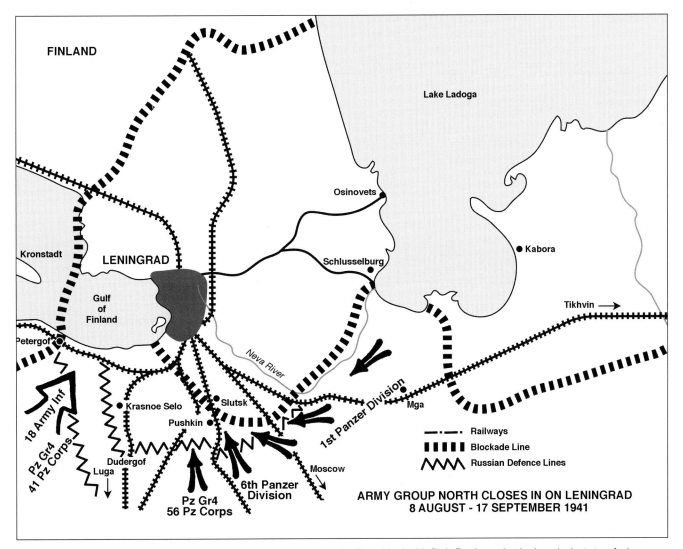

FINLAND

Lake Ladoga

Osinovets

Kronstadt

LENINGRAD

Schlusselburg

Kabora

Gulf of Finland

Tikhvin →

Petergof

Neva River

18 Army Inf

Krasnoe Selo

Slutsk

1st Panzer Division

Mga

Pz Gr4 41 Pz Corps

Pushkin

Dudergof

Luga

6th Panzer Division

Moscow

Pz Gr4 56 Pz Corps

— · — · — Railways

❚❚❚❚❚ Blockade Line

〜〜〜〜 Russian Defence Lines

**ARMY GROUP NORTH CLOSES IN ON LENINGRAD
8 AUGUST - 17 SEPTEMBER 1941**

Between 14 and 18 August, however, Russian forces attacked following urgent prompting from Moscow. The counter-offensive was extravagant and poorly co-ordinated. Masses of cavalry, lorried infantry and inexperienced reserves were put into costly frontal attacks that did at least slow some of the momentum of the German advance. General Erich von Manstein's LVIth Panzer Corps, prevented from reinforcing its sister XXXXIst Corps in the Panzergruppe, marched and counter-marched during three critical weeks of fighting across the dried-out marshes of the upper Ilmen river. Men and machines were exhausted.

The Luftwaffe, ranging far ahead of German mobile units, had been responsible for much of the success. Lieutenant J. Jewtuchewitsch's Russian 64th Engineer Battalion, operating south of Leningrad, was totally intimidated by repeated air raids. Driven out of a barn by an early morning Messerschmitt Bf110 strafing attack, he saw the surrounding buildings soon enveloped in flames. 'One tried to make oneself tiny,' he later wrote, 'completely invisible' to escape the attention of the predatory aircraft. Pauses between strafing and bombing runs which continued nearby were occupied 'with jokes and forced laughter, trying to convince each other we were not frightened'. They were. The platoon commander, Muschtakow, ordered them to run into nearby woods and take cover. Jewtuchewitsch and five men ran the

Above: Von Leeb's final offensive against Leningrad prior to transferring armour to Army Group Centre for the coming Operation 'Taifun' (Typhoon). The impetus was soaked up by three primary lines of defence placed before the city. These had 1,000km of earthworks, 645km of anti-tank dishes, 600km of barbed wire and 5,000 pillboxes. First Panzer division attacked south-west along the line of the River Neva while 6th Panzer Division pushed northwards following the main rail link from the south. Schlüsselburg and the outer southern city suburbs were captured and a vital rail link to Tikhvin cut. The city was completely encircled by land from the middle of September 1941.

gauntlet of a 'rain of machine gun fire' across an open field chased by a Bf110. Even inside the wood they did not feel safe. 'The edges,' Jewtuchewitsch described, 'were raked with methodical persistence by bombs and machine gun fire.' Having been blown from a depression by the force of a bomb blast, he heard a plaintive cry for help from Lissizyn, one of his soldiers, a few metres away. 'Come to me, over here, over here,' he shrieked. Jewtuchewitsch staggered towards the source of the screaming, concussed and disorientated from the explosion. He was confronted with the dreadful sight of his companion with no legs and a gaping stomach wound, 'something which would remain long in my memory,' he said. There was no option but to leave him behind. Rallying the survivors, he rejoined the battalion later that night. There was no rest, and at dawn the air attacks started again.[2]

At the beginning of September a determined German assault was mounted against Leningrad. Geography posed problems in encircling a city protected to its rear by the enormous expanse of Lake Ladoga. It would not be possible to close the northern side of the ring effectively. Extensive and concentric defence lines faced the direction of German attack. These were thrown around the city by the Leningrad command, which mobilised the city population to construct 1,000km of earthworks, 645km of anti-tank ditches and 600km of barbed wire entanglement linked by 5,000 pillboxes. Over 300,000 members of the Young Communist League and 200,000 civilian inhabitants, including as many women as men, achieved this extraordinary effort of labour.[3] Stalin's 'Mother Russia' appeal to elicit the population's help in stemming the 'Fascist horde' was bearing fruit.

Von Leeb ordered an all-out assault on the city preceded by a triple-wave Luftwaffe bombing attack. Nine days of savage fighting followed, during which the attacking German divisions closed onto the three lines of the city's defence. The 1st Panzer Division followed the left bank of the River Neva south-west into the city while 6th Panzer, straddling the main railway to Leningrad, pushed up from the south. Tank commanders suffered considerable casualties because, after weeks of mobile operations, they were slow to adapt tactics to unfamiliar wooded and urban terrain. Four successive commanders of the 6th Panzer Division became casualties during the first day of the assault.[4] On 8 September Schlüsselburg was taken and the outer suburbs to the south of Leningrad occupied. With this, the city of nearly three million inhabitants, with its vital rail link to Tikhvin lost, was completely encircled and cut off.

The 1st Panzer Division reached and penetrated the Dudergof height defences 10km south-east of Leningrad. Only one of its battalions remained at over 50% effective strength. By 16.00 hours on 10 September Height 167 — the 140m topmost point of the ridge south-east of the city — had been scaled by the attackers. Daniel Granin, a Soviet volunteer, described how:

'On the heights above Leningrad we came under air attack which caused heavy casualties. The rest of the soldiers in my unit scattered and I was left alone — without an army. So I boarded a tram car and drove back home, with my machine gun and hand-grenades. As far as I was concerned, and I had no doubts, the German army was going to be in Leningrad in a few hours.'[5]

On the left flank of the XXXXIst Panzer Corps, Eighteenth Army infantry edged their way across the valley. Once the Russian guns and observers were cleared from Height 167, entry into the suburban districts of Slutsk and Pushkin could be attempted. Krasnoye Seloe, south-west of the city, fell on 11 September. Hans Mauermann, an artillery observer moving forward with one of the assaulting infantry divisions, recalled:

'Our company had in fact stopped a tram car that had driven out of Leningrad, and ordered the passengers to get out. We considered whether or not to hang on to the driver, so they could drive into Leningrad the following day.'[6]

Russian Lieutenant Jewtuchewitsch despaired. Soldiers in his unit had recently arrived from the reserve and were untrained.

'We march from place to place the whole time. Can one still label them a Regiment? People had only rifles and pathetically few machine guns. No medics! What is that supposed to be? We haven't any grenades either! In reality that is no military unit, it's "cannon-fodder".'

His experience was typical of the many untrained and disintegrating Russian units caught up in the maelstrom of the German advance. 'Our company has been rubbed out once again,' he wrote, 'and we have landed in the rear of the enemy and are being hunted through the wood like animals, trying to get across the German-occupied road to break out and join the others.' They were separated from their Commissar Jermakow in the trees and had been unable to regain contact. That night Lieutenant Jewtuchewitsch wrote his last diary entry.

'Shooting and Panzers everywhere. We are now faced with a serious dilemma — what is going to happen? Will I be able to write again tomorrow in this book? If not, would the person who finds this diary pass it with a loving kiss and my last word "Mama!" to: Leningrad, Prospect 25. October, House 114, Flat No 7. To Jewtuchewitsch, Anna Nikolajewna . . .'

Jewtuchewitsch had said goodbye to his mother barely two months before.

'With a sad feeling I looked at my poor Mother's ever-loving face and thought: what a difficult life she has had, what had life ever given to her that was ever any good? Here she sits beside me, my old mother, keeping back her concern, hardly able to keep back the tears. She made the sign of the cross over me.'

After a final sad meal his mother and sisters had accompanied him to the barrack gates before he left. 'I said a quick goodbye and with a lump in my throat, holding back the tears, I kissed them all.'

German soldiers searching among the bodies decided the small book taken from the dead Soviet lieutenant might be of military significance. It was passed on to company headquarters.[7]

By the fourth day of the all-out German assault on Leningrad it became clear that further progress was not possible without substantial reinforcements. A limit of exploitation was declared on the Peterfog–Pushkin road. Street-fighting was slowing the tempo of the advance and continued for a further five days before it began to abate. The arrival of Soviet General Zhukov, previously dismissed as Chief of Staff by Stalin because of his frank advice on the developing Kiev crisis, energised the defence. Zhukov was well practised in the value of combined operations and ordered the saturation of the enemy with jointly interacting artillery, mortar and air support. This and the depth of the defence lines soaked up the impetus of the Panzer advances. Large numbers of medium and heavy mortars proved as lethal as artillery inside the close ranges over which the battle was fought.

Other factors also diluted the German effort. The bulk of Generaloberst Hoepner's Panzergruppe 4 was ordered to transfer once again to Army Group Centre and prepare for the assault on Moscow. Likewise, the Finnish advance along the Karelian Isthmus had halted. Marshal Carl Gustav Mannerheim, the Finnish leader, resolved to reconquer only that land he believed justifiably belonged to Finland. Despite the apparent nadir of Soviet fortunes, he did not wish to be held hostage to any future resurgence. The impact at the front from these developments was dramatic in some sections. Rolf Dahm, forward with an infantry division, recalled:

'Suddenly there was this stop. We're not going on further. I naturally thought, "Why not?" Then later the Führer Befehl [Directive] came. Our command probably considered the problem we would have taking over a city of a million inhabitants that would have to be fed throughout the winter. Better to stay in front of it and try and starve the inhabitants into submission.'[8]

German soldiers ensconced on the Dudergof heights were treated to the panoramic sight of the city of Leningrad only 12km away with its golden cupolas and towers bathed in sunlight. Warships could be seen in the port, shelling targets to their rear. It was a tantalising, and at the same time confusing, experience for officers and soldiers alike, unaware of what was impeding the final assault. Realists such as Walter Broschei correctly guessed why:

'In the middle of September we reached a chain of hills 8km from the Gulf of Finland and 20km south-west of Leningrad town centre. In the distance the city pulsed with life. It was bewildering — trains ran, chimneys smoked and a busy maritime traffic ran on the Neva river. We had 28 soldiers left from 120 normally in the company and had now been gathered into so-called "combat" battalions — unsuitable to attack Leningrad.'[9]

Artillery Forward Observer Hans Mauermann likewise had few illusions about the likely outcome of any further costly attacks. He breathed a sigh of relief.

'Then suddenly it was — halt, which, actually, was met with some satisfaction. Every day it had been attack, with all its uncertainties and not knowing what might happen. From the perspective of even further hardship this was very much welcome. The emotion swung between a shame we had not pulled it off to thank God we did not have to go in there.'[10]

Generalfeldmarschall von Leeb mounted this spoiling attack despite the order to transfer his Panzer strength back to the Central Front. But it had not succeeded. There was now no alternative to the Führer's original intent articulated during the euphoric and successful early phase of 'Barbarossa'. Halder had stated on 8 July:

'It is the Führer's firm decision to level Moscow and Leningrad, and make them uninhabitable, so as to relieve us of the necessity of having to feed the populations through the winter. The cities will be razed by the Luftwaffe. Panzers must not be used for the purpose.'[11]

Even before von Leeb's final attempt to 'bounce' the city on 6 September, Halder had already declared the previous day 'our objective has been achieved'. The area, as promulgated by Hitler, 'will now become a subsidiary theatre of operations'. Von Leeb was denied his victorious entry into the city. He was, in any case, aware of approaching operational limitations which would be to support a main drive against Moscow from mid-September. 'True, it will be a hard job for the Northern wing,' explained Halder, responding to von Leeb's request to retain Reinhardt's Panzer Corps and VIIIth, 'but the scheme underlying our directive remains the only possible solution.'[12] Hitler's aim to encircle the city and reduce it by bombardment and starvation was as consistent as it was calculated.

Once the envelopment of the city was complete, various strategies were discussed at army command level as to how best to reduce its fabric and annihilate the inhabitants. The speed and success of the German advance left the city ill-prepared to withstand a siege. Even before the final German assault, the Leningrad State Defence Committee had identified the city's available reserves on 27 August as 17 days'-worth of meals; vegetables for 29 days, fish for 16, meat for 25 and butter for 28 days.[13] The decision was taken to increase supplies, but the rail link was cut by the German advance before it could be actioned. Meanwhile, a series of chilling secret measures had been identified by the Land Defence Department of the Supreme Wehrmacht Staff at OKW on 21 September.[14] Assessments ranged from treating the city like those already taken, to erecting an electrified fence around it to form a huge concentration camp. Women, old people and children would be allowed to evacuate. Another solution was to present the city to the Finns. Workable scenarios were stymied by the sheer scale of the problem combined with the imperative to avoid epidemics being passed on to German troops. Enormous reserves of manpower would further be needed to enforce the proposed measures.

The eventual solution was to suggest to the world that Stalin had declared the city a fortress. It could then be hermetically sealed and reduced by artillery and air attack. When the city, ripe from hunger and terror, was about to collapse, certain 'gates' would be opened and the masses within released to burden the administration of the Soviet hinterland. Once the remaining fortress defenders had been weakened, probably in the spring, the city could be stormed. The survivors would be imprisoned and Leningrad razed to the ground. Subsequently the land area north of the Neva might be handed over to the Finns. This modern 'Carthaginian' solution was delivered to Adolf Hitler. He, in turn, directed Generaloberst Jodl, Chief of the *Wehrmachtführungs* Staff, and von Brauchitsch on 7 October that:

'Any capitulation of Leningrad or later Moscow is not to be accepted, even if offered from the other side.'[15]

Johannes Haferkamp, an infantry soldier who served on the Leningrad front, succinctly expressed the resulting dilemma after the war:

'You have to imagine, the Russians knew the Germans had erected an impenetrable ring around Leningrad. All its inhabitants had been sentenced to death through hunger and disease. What efforts could the Russian Army now take on to free the city? What other measures might they take to provide the population with provisions? The population was inevitably going to starve to death and that was the real intent of our higher command.'[16]

Leningrad's intended fate mirrored those pitiless ideological measures that were planned for prisoners of war and the populations of occupied areas even before the campaign started. Extracts from the Diary of the Quartermaster Department of Twenty-seventh Army laying siege to the city reflect the same intent. In responding to a question in early October over what measures were foreseen to feed the population should this be required, it cited shortages in the Reich and the bland justification, 'it is better our people have something and the Russians go hungry.' Two days later the Army Quartermaster was requested to feed 20,000 mainly factory workers in the German-occupied suburb of Pushkin.

'It can only be recommended that work-capable males be interned in prison comps. The provision of rations from army sources for the civilian population is out of the question.'[17]

Official documents clearly confirm the uncompromising intentions of the German High Command. They were articulated with a degree of logic that would appeal to the self-preservation interests of soldiers. Starving the inhabitants of Leningrad into surrender made perverse tactical and operational sense. 'That Leningrad has been mined and will be defended to the last man has already been announced by Soviet radio,' stated Army Group North in its war diary in early October. 'Serious epidemics are anticipated. No German soldier need place a step inside the place.' If the population can be forced to flee into the Russian hinterland through artillery and bombing, 'the chaos in Russia would be even greater, the burden on our administration and the exploitation of the occupied eastern provinces made even lighter'.[18]

The opinions of German soldiers surveying the city from the Dudergof heights for artillery bombardment were not so starkly objective. Front-line soldiers invariably present simple interpretations of events, untroubled by later academic debates.

When an Obergefreiter who served with the 9th Luftwaffe Field Division manning the line near Schlüsselburg visited Leningrad as a tourist 40 years later, he was asked if his conscience was troubled by later events. He responded:

'I do not feel guilty. It was war then. We had to fight just like every Russian soldier, and the Russians fought as heroically as we did.'

He accepted the subsequent long siege had been 'senseless', but pointed out the imperative was to win and finish the war.

'The city burned every day and every night. We observed the fires all the time. The capture of Leningrad could not be abandoned because this was a symbolic city for us as well. The city's fall was important because then practically the whole of the northern sector would have been in our hands. But it was already getting difficult for us. I was a volunteer then and had signed up for 12 years. We fought for our system in just the same way the Russians fought for theirs.'[19]

The official documents portray an unemotional perspective, exposing the analysis and clear intent of the German High Command. The perceptions governing the soldiers enacting that intent are equally important. Difficult questions were asked. The commander of the 58th Infantry Division accepted he would have to order his troops to fire upon any mass break-out attempt by the city's inhabitants, but felt certain realities could not be ignored. Troops would obey orders, but 'whether they would retain the nerve to fire upon repeated outbreaks by women, children and harmless old men, he had his doubts. Every man has his own interpretation of what constitutes human decency. German soldiers were under immense political, ideological and military duty pressures to compromise previously held values. The commander's view, courageously expressed, was that his soldiers were clearly aware of the need to intern Leningrad's millions where they were. But the danger was, 'the German soldier may thereby lose his inner morality, and after the war they would not wish to worry about legal proceedings as a result of their actions.'

It was not only the commander of the 58th Division who had misgivings. Civilians were being forcibly evacuated from the areas occupied by German soldiers encircling the city, and from the army rear area security zone, then dispersed into outlying villages. Several thousand refugees were moved along the Krasnogwardeisk–Pleskau road. They were mainly women, children and old men. Nobody knew where they were to go. The Official Army Group North Diary admitted:

'Everybody had the impression that these people would sooner or later die from starvation. The scene had a particularly negative impact upon German soldiers employed working on the same road.'[20]

It had not been like this in France the year before.

'THE RUSSIANS'

Right: Exhausted Russian infantry await the next onslaught. Although totally outmanoeuvred and surprised, the tenacity of Russian resistance exacted an unexpected price which was eventually to check the German Blitzkrieg.

Below: Russian troops fall back and wait for ferries to cross a river. Nearly all their equipment has been abandoned and there is only makeshift provision for the wounded.

Above:
The Russian T-34 was a technological shock for German soldiers, convinced through propaganda that they were attacking a primitive and inferior country. They appeared in greater numbers during counter-attacks from forested areas west of Moscow in the autumn and winter of 1941. The following sequence of photographs charts the progress of an infantry-mounted T-34 counter-attack.

Left:
Infantry scramble down from the tank and go into the attack.

A KV-1 drives on to crush a Russian cottage housing a German strongpoint . . .

. . . reducing it to a splintered wreck.

A T-34 counter-attack viewed through the driver's vision block — German soldiers run for their trenches as the attack converges on their position.

The 37mm anti-tank gun was contemptuously referred to as the 'door knocker' by their German crews, here about to be overrun by the advancing tank.

Both are hit by artillery fire . . .

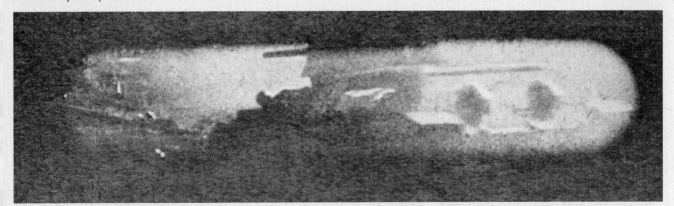

. . . as other T-34s converge on the position. One tank track would be locked to swivel the tank on the spot, crushing the gun and collapsing the trench onto its crew.

Female Soviet prisoners. German soldiers imbued with National Socialist 'Motherhood' ideals were genuinely shocked when confronted by women in uniform. It further accentuated their suspicion that they were fighting in an alien environment.

Chapter 10
A war without garlands

> **'If some people say that most Germans were innocent, I would say they were accomplices. As a soldier I was an "accomplice".'**
>
> *German soldier*

'BETTER THREE FRENCH CAMPAIGNS THAN ONE RUSSIAN'

Fritz Köhler, a 20-year-old veteran of the French campaign, entered the town of Roslavl south-east of Smolensk on 3 August following a successful attack. Oil and petrol supplies had been torched by the Russians prior to leaving. 'Unfortunately,' he wrote in his diary that night, 'there is practically nothing in this city to "liberate".' Gazing at the inferno of fire and smoke around him he declared, 'it was a lot better in France.'[1]

Nine days later, Obergefreiter Erich Kuby, on sentry duty with Army Group North, peered watchfully from 'foxhole 4' in a rain-soaked forest. His duty period was two hours by night or three by day before relief. Ahead lay a dead Russian soldier, one of several killed blundering into their position the night before. The body — some 5m away and covered only with a sprinkling of earth — reeked. Kuby resolved to bury him deeper during the next rest period. 'Better three French campaigns than one Russian' was the often-repeated catch-phrase voiced by the troops. 'French beds and the lustrous surroundings were missed.' The good days were over. 'The expectation of finding both in Leningrad in the near future,' reflected Kuby, 'was replaced by foxhole positions 1, 2, 3 and 4 and so on.'[2]

Kuby and Köhler were articulating a viewpoint fast becoming prevalent among the soldiers on the new Eastern Front. This was *Kein Blumenkrieg* — quite literally 'a war without garlands'. No glory as there was after the war in France the year before, when victory parades on homecoming were deluged by clouds of flowers tossed by adoring wives and girlfriends while a grateful Reich cheered. Newsreels now mocked 'so-called "Socialist Workers' Paradises"' in the newly occupied areas. Cameras dwelt on rickety filthy balustrades overlooking slum housing for Soviet city workers, while the commentary announced:

> *'The mindless uneducated masses are cannon fodder for the Soviets. In just five days German soldiers have been shown a picture of the Soviet paradise which defies all description. This explains why Russia felt the need to cut itself off from the rest of the world!'*[3]

Much of the new *Ostheer* would have preferred that it remained so.

Russia was an unknown. Veterans of the French Blitzkrieg realised there was neither champagne, wine nor booty, nothing to 'liberate'. The pitiless and total nature of the conflict quickly differentiated it from any other campaign experienced thus far. Any feeling this was a 'just' war was diluted by the pressure of excesses dubiously excused by National Socialist Lebensraum rhetoric extolling the survival of the fittest. Contemporary paternal and social democratic societies find it difficult to transfer their experience to the uncompromising ideological framework within which this war was conducted. The army

that fell upon Communist Russia believed in Christ: 95% of the German population in 1939 had declared itself Christian, or from a religious order. Of 75.4 million (from 79.4 million) who had professed the faith, 41.9 million were Protestant and 31.4 million Catholic.[4]

Although cynical historians of religious wars would not regard this as auspicious, the Wehrmacht prosecuted the war with soldiers who had Christian caring families at home. Historical experience suggests that periods of protracted conflict are often accompanied by a certain corruption of standards of human decency. This assiduous process is often not immediately apparent to the combat soldier embarking on a campaign. Soon he is exposed to successive emotional experiences that trigger indefinable and often unrecognisable behavioural changes. It can begin by looking for battlefield souvenirs at one end of the spectrum to picking up useful military items such as binoculars and weapons and then even to stealing money and valuables from the dead at the other. This may be explained away by an incontrovertible logic that suggests a corpse has no need of possessions. Looting can in turn deteriorate to rape and organised plunder and later to murder, should the enemy get in the way.

The excesses of SS Einsatzgruppen behind the German front lines are well documented. Four of these special mobile units was formed and trained in the late spring of 1941 specifically to support Operation 'Barbarossa'. The core of the groups were provided by Heydrich's Security Police (Gestapo and Kripo) as well as from the intelligence apparatus (Security Service or SD), supplemented by small units of Waffen SS (the military branch of Himmler's SS). By the middle of July convincing military successes hinted at the likelihood of total victory. Hitler, as a consequence, ordered the intensification of the planned pacification programme due to be conducted behind the rear of the advancing German armies. Security Police battalions were also attached to the Einsatzgruppen. A sociological survey carried out on one of these — Reserve Police Battalion 101 — revealed their unremarkable manning. In fact they were labelled 'ordinary men', consisting mainly of prewar police recruits rather than reservists. They came predominantly from the Hamburg area, considered by reputation to be the least Nazi-orientated of German cities. The soldiers were from less privileged backgrounds, 65% working class, while 35% were thought to be lower middle class. By virtue of age, all had been taught before the Nazi period but the majority were party members by 1942. According to their researcher, Christopher R. Browning, they did 'not seem to have been a very promising group from which to recruit mass murderers on behalf of the Nazi vision of a radical utopia free of Jews'.[5]

War crimes, nevertheless, influenced the nature of fighting on the Russian front. The relevance had been recognised by the commander of the 58th Infantry Division laying siege to Leningrad in October 1941. The German soldier, he warned, was in danger of losing his 'inner morality'.[6] That this can degrade combat sustainability has been demonstrated by French soldiers in Algeria serving during the past colonial civil war and by American troops in Vietnam. Malaise induced by seemingly pointless, yet officially sponsored, violence reduced the justification of prosecuting the Russian war to German soldiers to one of mere survival. One veteran, Roland Kiemig, claimed after the war:

'I saw no executions, [but] I heard from people who did. It was no secret. They [the Russians] perished and many of them were killed through hard labour and other methods; that was clear. They weren't resettled, they were systematically . . . decimated.'[7]

Another soldier, transport Gefreiter Hans R., gave a sobering description of mass shootings he witnessed during the advance into Russia. Accompanied by his companion Erich, the company commander's clerk, they saw 'men and women and children with their hands bound together with wire being driven along the road by SS people'. They decided to investigate. Aged 93, some 40 years later, his description of what happened was delivered in a precise monotone which consciously suppressed the obvious emotion he felt. Outside the village they came across a pit, 3m deep and 2.5m wide. Along its 150m length were hundreds of people, on foot and standing in open-backed lorries. 'To our horror we realised they were all Jews,' he said. The victims were tumbled into the ditch and made to lie in rows, alternately head to foot. Once a layer was in place, two SS men moved either side of the ditch with a Russian machine pistol firing automatic bursts into the backs of heads. Single shots rang out afterwards as they strode along the line finishing off the wounded.

'Then people were again driven forward and they had to get in and lie on top of the dead. At that moment a young girl — she must have been about 12 years old — cried out in a clear piteous shrill voice. "Let me live, I'm still only a child!" The child was grabbed, thrown into the ditch, and shot.'[8]

The official attitude to brutality was permissive. Common decency in such circumstances was a matter of personal inclination. Right and wrong were clouded by ideological imperatives that were administratively applied. The impact of the Commissar Order, for example, became apparent through the conduct of numerous units shortly after the campaign began. Bruno Schneider from 8/IR167 was told by his company commander, Oberleutnant Prinz:

'Red Army prisoners of war are to be taken only in exceptional circumstances, in other words when there is no other choice. In general captured Soviet soldiers are to be shot and this applies even to women serving in Red Army units.'

Schneider said, 'the majority of soldiers from my unit did not follow this bloody order as closely as was required.'[9] Individual inclinations were applied with variable results. Martin Hirsch, a 28-year-old NCO from 3rd Panzer Division, was castigated by a soldier from another unit while bandaging a badly wounded Russian during fighting around Brest-Litovsk. 'What are you doing here?' he was asked. 'I told him I was bandaging a soldier' but 'he said it was not my job to look after these Untermenschen [sub-humans]'. Hirsch chose to ignore him. 'He told me he would report me, but I never heard anything more from him.' His view was that he was 'quite a callous Nazi, and I was pleased that I never caught sight of him again'.[10]

In the German Sixth Army with Army Group South the Commissar Order had been passed down to battalion level. Killings after the advance began were common enough to be unremarkable. Twenty-four hours into the campaign, Panzergruppe 1 reported to the IC (Intelligence officer) of Sixth Army that both XXXXVIIIth and IIIrd Corps had each taken one political commissar prisoner 'and handled them appropriately'. According to a 62nd Infantry Division report, nine alleged civilian irregulars and one political commissar, captured in woods north of Sztun, 'had been dealt with appropriately as per the ordered directive'. Further shootings followed: 298th Infantry Division despatched a commissar on 1 July and 62nd Division shot five, and nine more the next day. The XXXXIVth Corps killed another with one further committing suicide after capture. Commissar executions in Sixth Army became routine: 122 had been 'despatched' during partisan operations in LIst Corps' area by the end of the battle of Kiev. Shootings of 30 or so individuals were occurring throughout the advances.[11]

Soldiers became accustomed to the killings, which altered values, transitioning to a form of group insanity. Combat soldiers, however, rarely kill for uniquely political or ideological convictions. Operation reports by the *Einsatzgruppen* and other official documents provide factual data and are designed to impress those elements in the higher commands who did possess ideological conviction. Whether they were representative of the Wehrmacht as a whole is debatable. The truth lies in between and is not as clear-cut as academics, quoting solely from documents, might suggest. Helmut Schmidt, a Flak officer, declared in an emotive interview after the war that not all soldiers were completely aware of what was happening. 'Other people had different experiences from those generally quoted in many documents,' he stated.[12]

No one is disputing the written official evidence or that atrocities occurred, but whether such experiences were universally shared at all times and at every sector of the front is not so certain. This alternative view shared by Schmidt (who was there) suggests soldiers were too young for political and ideological reflection. They were completely engrossed in the mind-numbing activity of surviving combat while enduring considerable physical hardship. Only much later did the extent of the crimes committed become hideously apparent. As such, they were unsuspecting 'victims' themselves of the totalitarian nature of the society to which they belonged. Soldier Roland Kiemig claims the truth dawned only after he had been captured by the Russians himself.

'As a prisoner of war the Russians called me "Fascist". I heard of the extent of German crimes for the first time in the camp, not only in Russia but also in the concentration camps. We had not known about that. We didn't believe it at first and thought it was a little over-exaggerated. They typically referred to us as the "Fascist hordes". But when they presented credible evidence, one did start thinking.'[13]

There was no time to think in action. In the ranks they became the victim of the common bonding required of soldiers to face adversity, and of a form of National Socialist 'peer pressure'. Both pressures were sufficient to stifle individual predilections and often conscience. As Kiemig further explained:

'You mustn't forget I'm 66 now, I was 17 or 18 then, a different person. I wasn't strong enough then. It was a kind of machine from which there was no escape — for anybody. 'What could I have done then? I could have done — what? What way out was there then? It was your duty to serve. If you didn't like it, then you were punished, and I did not want that.'[14]

Rudi Maschke, serving with the Pomeranian 6th Infantry Regiment, was even more emphatic. 'Not following these orders,' he stated, referring to the Commissar Directive, 'would have cost us our lives ourselves.'[15] Kiemig said, 'you could get locked up and charged with a military offence'. National Socialism demanded unambiguous conformity. It preached, moreover, that only the strong should survive in a fundamentally competitive society. 'If you were a "softie",' said Kiemig, 'you would be treated very badly, ridiculed even, and I didn't want that either.' The only recourse was to conform.

'I wanted to stay in between. You might say that wasn't a crime. But if some people say that most Germans were innocent, I would say they were accomplices. As a soldier I was an "accomplice".'[16]

What made soldiers accomplices?

THE PRESSURES ON THE GERMAN SOLDIER

Fear for the German soldier was the same as for all fighting men through the ages: would he survive the next battle sound in body and mind? There was no shortage of time to dwell on the dubious prospect during the long journey to the front. This might last weeks as the advance progressed deep into Russia. Hospital trains offered the first disenchanting glimpse of what lay ahead, passing the troops as they moved forward on their painstaking journey to the rear. German soldier Benno Zeiser, a driver in a transport unit, started with a naïve view. During training, he and his fellows had been served a diet of victory proclamations on the radio, which led him to believe arrogantly that:

'Any fool knows you have to have losses, you can't make omelettes without breaking eggs, but we were going to fight on to victory. Besides, if any of us did stop a bullet, it would be a hero's death. So hurrah, over the top, come on, charge, hurrah!'

His first glimpse of a hospital train returning from the front quickly dispelled his 'hurrah' patriotism. 'The orderlies began bringing in chaps with limbs missing, uniforms all blood, a mass of bandages, the linen soaked red on legs, arms, heads, trunks, and bloodless agony — distorted faces with sunken eyes.' One of the soldiers on the train told them what to expect:

'According to him it was pretty grim. The Reds were fighting desperately and we had had heavy losses. All the same, the advance was continuing swiftly, but it was at a price which made it clear we could not tell how long it would all be as, apart from anything else, the Russians had more men than we, many more.'[1]

Psychological pressure builds up as the soldier approaches the front. The first visible sign is often sight of the enemy's dead. Many young soldiers had never seen a corpse before. Werner Adamczyk, with a 150mm artillery battery near Minsk, became morbidly fascinated at his guns' handiwork. 'The repulsive scene caused me to shake; nevertheless, I found the guts to walk around,' he said. 'What I saw then was even more cruel.' War quickly stripped the veneer of propaganda. Foxholes around him were filled with dead Soviet soldiers. 'I shuddered and turned around to walk back to the truck' admitting, 'the reality of death was just too much to take'. He was troubled. What he had witnessed contradicted earlier briefings that suggested the Russian soldier was 'poorly trained and not very much inclined to heroism'. Indeed:

'It became clear to me that they must have been willing to fight to the very end. If this was not heroism, what was it? Did the communist commissars force them to fight to the death? It did not look like it. I did not see any dead commissars.'

Before long the German soldier realised the Russian fighting man was infinitely better than his superiors would like him to believe. 'With this realisation,' admitted Adamczyk, 'my dream of going home soon receded.'[2] German soldier Benno Zeiser was also taken aback at the sight of his first dead Russian. 'Only such a very short time before, this must have been a living human being,' he reflected. 'I thought I would never get rid of the thought after that.' *Kriegsmaler* (official war artist) Theo Scharf, advancing with the 97th Division with Army Group South, 'passed a Red Army soldier, seemingly asleep in the roadside ditch, but covered in thick dust, face and all'.[3] It was the first of many corpses they would all see. Familiarity bred a form of indifference with the passage of time. Benno Zeiser saw more and more Russian dead. 'And it was not long before I found myself merely feeling they were lumps of soil which belonged to the earth they lay on and that they might have been there since ages ago.' It was less upsetting to view them as if they 'never had been alive at all'.[4]

Viewing one's own dead was different, engendering an emotive mixture of bitterness, torment, fear and a feeling of acute loss. Werner Adamczyk recalled burying his first two friends in the battery. 'That was the end; they were no more. I stood there in anguish'. Both had been blown to pieces in an exploding ammunition truck.

'I was indeed sorry for the families of these two men. It could have been me. With rising emotions I visualised the reactions of my family and friends, if that had happened to me. For the first time in my life I fully realised what love and affection really meant.'[5]

Zeiser felt 'it was worse when you saw the first one in our own field grey . . . and you stare at him, lying there in the same uniform you wear yourself, and you think that he too has a mother and a father, perhaps sisters, he may even have been from the same parts as yourself.'

Prolonged exposure to the stark realities of combat corrupts the accepted codes of normal behaviour. Dead bodies became unremarkable. Zeiser continued:

'In time you even get used to that. You just don't really take it in at all when there are more and more who are dead but they are all in German uniform. So in the end you come to reckon yourself on a level with all those others, Russians or Germans alike, lying dead in their various uniforms; you yourself then turn into just one of the creatures who never really did live, you are just another lump of earth.'

The bizarre tenuously develops into the norm. Violence and death, cruel behaviour and the taking of life became unremarkable behaviour. Killing, on or off the battlefield, lay outside this category. Although 'normal' behaviour on or around a battlefield is a paradoxical misnomer, killing human beings — dispensing death — was a searing emotional experience. The impact in psychological terms is unpredictable. Such uncertainties are the only constant in this bizarre and fast-changing environment. Fear is the result.

'Then one day, you're right up against it. You are chatting with one of your mates when suddenly he folds up, just settles in a heap, and is stone dead. That is the real horror. You see the others stepping over him, just as anybody steps over a big stone he doesn't want to catch his heel on, and you see your mate's death no differently from any of the others that are dead — those whom you've already learned to think of as never really having lived, as being just lumps of earth.'

This was the supreme pressure on individual soldiers. Not just dying but worse, becoming a meaningless and soon forgotten official statistic. Zeiser explained:

'That's when you get the horrors and after that it is always a nightmare; it never, never stops, the real fear of being wiped out, the fear of merciless nothingness, the fear of thinking any moment you may be one of those who never were living creatures.'[6]

Fear of becoming a casualty was accentuated by the 'strangeness' of the very land the Wehrmacht had invaded. Families at home would have no idea where it was and what it was like, where they died. War correspondent Felix Lützkendorf, serving with an SS unit in the Ukraine, wrote:

'This land is endless, beneath an endless sky with roads trailing endlessly into an incalculable distance. Each village and town seems just like the one that preceded it. They all have the same women and children standing dumbly by the roadside, the same wells, the same farmsteads . . . If the column comes off the road and moves on a compass bearing across fields, we look like lost world circumnavigators seeking new coasts beyond these oceans.'[7]

War developed into a form of pseudo-tourism to many German soldiers, whose previous knowledge of the world had been cycling or walking to the next village or town. One soldier had described his campaign experiences in France in May 1940 in terms of a 'Strength through Joy' trip comparable to prewar sponsored Nazi party outings. Another soldier, writing in the assembly area before the start of the Russian campaign, described how his 'long journey up to the edge of the Russian border' had 'enabled him to view half of Europe' at no effort or expense to himself. Russia, however, offered few attractions. Three weeks into the Russian campaign a Gefreiter complained, 'It's not like it was in France here. We had everything we wanted there; here, there is absolutely nothing.'[8] Another soldier observed cryptically that they had exchanged their previous 'Polack's (Polish) shacks' for Russian 'dog kennels'.

'Yesterday we moved out of our beautiful quarters and are now lying in a cursed lousy shack, with more filth than I have ever seen'.

Physical conditions matched the rigours of campaigning. Soldiers accustomed to well-appointed barracks in Germany became increasingly depressed as the operation dragged on, outpacing the length and discomforts of all previous campaigns. 'These immense plains, huge woods with a few dog kennels here and there, make a dissolute impression,' wrote one soldier. It was 'uninteresting to the eye', with 'sad-looking wooden huts, forests and marshes. Everything,' he said, 'seemed to lose itself in an endless expanse.'[9]

As the advance continued, so did apprehensions. 'Orientation in Russia is as difficult as it is in the desert,' remarked one soldier. 'Only you do not see the horizon — you are lost.' Another commented:

'The immense space was so vast that we had many soldiers who became melancholy.
'Flat valleys, flat hills — flat valleys, flat hills, endless, endless. There was no limit. We could not see an end and it was so disconsolate.'[10]

'Where is this endless war driving us?' asked 33-year-old Günther von Soheven, fighting on the southern front.

'There is no identifiable objective in terms of space across countryside stretching ever further away. Even more depressing, the enemy is becoming even more numerous, even though we have offered up huge sacrifices'.

Soldiers were becoming homesick. 'The distances grow immeasurably,' concluded von Soheven, 'but our hearts remain close.'[11]

Determination to finish the campaign was, however, matched by an equal Russian stubbornness to fight on. It was not difficult to dehumanise an enemy who chose to resist fanatically within an alien landscape for no logical reason despite apparent defeat. National Socialist propaganda sowed the insidious seed, which fell upon the receptive minds of soldiers already exposed to racist doctrine. Unteroffizier Wilhelm Prüller, a motorised infantryman with the 9th Panzer Division, wrote on 4 July, 'we have heard the most horrible things about what the Russians are doing to our prisoners'. The 8th Company of his Schütze Regiment 11 was badly mauled in a Russian ambush and lost 80 men. 'The wounded Kameraden were worked over by the Russians with gun barrels until they were dead.' Prüller's anti-Semitic comments depersonalised the enemy. Like many German soldiers, he was surprised to encounter Russian women in uniform. Inside a Russian pocket they came upon 'women, completely nude and roasted,' who 'were lying on and beside a [destroyed Soviet] tank. Awful.' He indignantly concluded, 'it's not people we're fighting against here, but simply animals.' American soldiers similarly dehumanised their Japanese foes in the Pacific Theatre, and later the Vietcong in Vietnam in the 1960s and 1970s; a reaction, therefore, not unique to purely totalitarian societies. Prüller later observed, 'among the Russian dead there are many Asiatic faces, which look disgusting with their slit eyes'. He was impressed by the strangeness of it all. In a park in Kirovograd the soldiers bathed in a small pond. 'It's curious to see the Russian women shamelessly undressing in front of us and wandering around naked,' he wrote. 'Some of them look quite appetising, especially their breasts . . . Most of us would be quite willing to . . . but then again you see the dirty ones and you want to go and vomit. They've no morals here! Revolting!'[12]

Tank gunner Karl Fuchs with the 7th Panzer Division offered a similarly maligned view of Russian prisoners of war to his wife:

'Hardly ever do you see the face of a person who seems rational and intelligent. They all look emaciated and the wild, half crazy look in their eyes makes them appear like imbeciles. And these scoundrels, led by Jews and criminals, wanted to imprint their stamp on Europe, indeed on the world. Thank God that our Führer, Adolf Hitler, is preventing this from happening.'[13]

German *Wochenschau* newsreels viewed in July dwelt on portrait shots of Mongol prisoners of war and other Asiatics. The commentary poked fun at 'a small sample of the particularly horrible types of sub-human Bolsheviks'. These sentiments were reflected in letters sent home from the front. One signaller wrote:

'We are deep in Russia in the so-called "paradise" which calls upon [German] soldiers to desert. Terrible misery reigns here. People have been unimaginably oppressed for two centuries. We would rather all die than accept the torment and misery these folk have had to put up with.'[14]

Over-confidence upon meeting an allegedly 'inferior' foe, based purely on racist criteria, bred a contempt during the early stages of the campaign that was soon punished.

At the end of June 1941 III/IR9 was wood-clearing around a road north-east of the city of Bialystok, near the village of Krynki. A young Panzerjäger Leutnant, despite warnings to the contrary, arrogantly insisted on pushing ahead of the road clearance through woods probably infested with Russian soldiers. The Panzerjäger platoon pressed on and was barely out of sight of the supporting German infantry before the vehicles were heard to stop. Inhuman shrieks of pain soon rent the air, interspersed with shouted commands in Russian. Major Haeften, the infantry company commander, ordered a hasty assault to rescue the ambushed anti-tank platoon. The lead platoon led by Feldwebel Gottfried Becker encountered a scene of carnage they 'could only gradually, very slowly, allow to sink in'. They were sickened by what they saw. 'Here and there a body jerked convulsively or danced around in its own blood.' The nearer the rescuing troops approached the macabre scene, the greater their appreciation of the atrocities visited upon the wretched Panzerjäger.

'The majority of the German soldiers had their eyes gouged out, others their throats cut. Some had their bayonets stuck in their chests. Two soldiers had their uniform jackets and shirts ripped apart and their naked stomachs slit open, glistening entrails hung out of the bloody mass. Two more had their genitals cut off and laid on their chests.'

German soldiers 'stumbled as if in a trance' onto the road to survey a scene of utter desolation. 'The swine,' muttered one soldier while another retched into the road; a third man stood and stared, his body shaking as he silently wept. News swept quickly through the division. The regimental commander had objected to the Commissar Order, but the next political commissar captured was handed without scruple to the military police and shot.[15]

The Russian soldier, previously accorded scant respect, became on object of fear. He responded in kind to the excesses inflicted on him and his people. 'I was always afraid of the Russians,' admitted German soldier Erhard Schaumann with Army Group Centre, 'not only because of that mass of humanity, but because they were so close to nature.' Russian soldiers were the master of their environment, the forests and swamps, and were particularly adept at night fighting. 'Whereas we,' Schaumann said, 'by virtue of our culture, were unable and hardly suited to react to everything like an animal, close to nature.'[16] Ignorance of the enemy bred fear which, in turn, encouraged inhuman behaviour; as Panzer soldier Hans Becker commented, 'bestiality breeds bestiality'. He felt, 'there is no defence for the fantastic atrocities which we inflicted on their race.'[17] Roland Kiemig, another German soldier, conjectured after the war:

'If I was attacked like the Russians by the German "hordes", and to them we were simply "Fascist hordes", which is how we did partly behave, then I would have fought to the last.'[18]

On 1 July 1941, nine days after the start of the campaign, 180 German soldiers belonging to Infantry Regiment 35, Infantry Regiment 119 and artillerymen were captured in a sudden Russian counter-attack on the Klewan–Broniki road in the Ukraine. They belonged to two motorised infantry formations which blundered into a superior Soviet force of one and a half divisions and were overwhelmed. The prisoners, most wounded, were herded into a clover field alongside the road and ordered to undress. Gefreiter Karl Jäger hurriedly began to pull off his tunic having 'had to hand over all valuable objects, including everything we had in our pockets'. Prisoners were generally compliant in this initial phase of capture, in shock and concerned for their lives. The wounded soldiers had difficulty undressing. Jäger recalled a fellow NCO, Gefreiter Kurz, struggling to undo his belt because of an injured hand. To his horror he saw 'he was stabbed behind in the neck so that the bayonet came out through his throat'. Shocked, the other soldiers frantically removed their tunic jackets. Another severely wounded soldier was kicked and clubbed around the head with rifle butts. Totally cowed, the German prisoners were shoved north of the road in groups of 12 to 15 men. Many were half-naked and 'several completely naked,' recalled Jäger. Oberschütze Wilhelm Metzger said, 'the Russians . . . grabbed everything we had, rings, watches, money bags, uniform insignia, and then they took our jackets, shirts, shoes and socks.' Private Hermann Heiss had his hands roughly tied, like many others, behind his back. They were then forced them down into thick green clover by the Russian soldiers. Heiss described how:

'A Russian soldier stabbed me in the chest with his bayonet, at which point I turned over. I was then stabbed seven times in the back. I did not move any more. The Russians evidently assumed I was dead . . . I heard my comrades cry out in pain and then I passed out.'

'Suddenly the Russians started to shoot at us,' said Private Michael Beer. Bursts of automatic and machine gun fire swept through the separated groups of tied-up and semi-naked German prisoners. Karl Jäger, led north of the road, started with surprise as shooting broke out among the groups following behind. 'Panic reigned after the first shots, and I was able to flee,' he said. Hand-grenades were tossed in among groups of officers and NCOs who had been singled out for special treatment. They suffered appalling injuries.

The next morning soldiers and Panzers from the 25th Division combed through the field: 153 half-naked bodies were found, their pale white skins pathetically outlined against a background of lush green clover. One group of 14 soldiers had their genitals hacked off. Among the corpses was a severely wounded Hermann Heiss. He was comforted by German soldiers. Glancing around the scene of total devastation, he 'saw the head of my comrade' who had screamed out in pain 'was split open . . . Most of the others were dead' or later died of their wounds. There were only 12 survivors.

Open trucks were driven up and stacked high with half-naked corpses. They were a jumble of tangled limbs grotesquely stiffened into untidy rigor mortis. Sunlight glinted from the hobnails of distended boots spilling over the side flaps of the lorries which had been lowered to accommodate them. A soldiers' cemetery was established outside the church in Broniki. The effect on the soldiers of the 25th Division obliged to tidy up the scene of the massacre can be imagined.[19] They quietly resolved to avenge their comrades.

Eye and genital mutilations were inflicted with such frequency on German prisoners during the early part of the campaign that it increased unease even further at the prospect of possible capture by the enemy. The rapidity of Blitzkrieg often punished reckless advances, so that prisoners of war were not solely a Russian phenomenon. Over 9,000 German soldiers were reported missing in July, 7,830 in August and nearly 4,900 in September 1941.[20] Although the death rate of Germans falling into Russian hands was to decline later, at this stage 90% to 95% perished.[21] These numbers pale into insignificance compared to the fate of millions of Soviet PoWs, but they were enough to promote unease among German soldiers. Captured Soviet documents revealed the fate of some German PoWs. One Soviet 26th Division report dated 13 July 1941 observed 400 enemy dead had been left on the battlefield west of Slastjena and 'some 80 Germans had surrendered and were executed'. Another captured company-level report, submitted by a Captain Gediejew on 30 August, referred to enemy dead, captured guns and mortars and '15 wounded men who were shot'.[22]

Russian radio intercepts and documents provide a wide spectrum of reasons for disposing of German PoWs. Enemy soldiers who fought rather than surrendered and troublesome wounded were often shot. Unexpected tactical developments or a lack of transport to carry prisoners away might also seal their fate. Summary execution during interrogation might occur as a result of refusing to give military information or to encourage others to talk. German excesses, in short, were matched by a like response. Food was always short and therefore not readily available for prisoners. Rewards were also offered for inflicting high German casualties. Executing Nazis and officers also happened, manifesting outrage through 'tit for tat' killings. Resistance to the German foe was, in any case, to be prosecuted totally. A Soviet Fifth Army document dated 30 June revealed:

'It has frequently occurred that Red Army soldiers and commanders embittered by the cruelties of the Fascist thieves . . . do not take any German soldiers and officers prisoner but shoot them on the spot.'[23]

The practice was criticised for wasting intelligence as well as discouraging the enemy to desert. Maj-Gen Potapov commanding Fifth Soviet Army ordered his commanders to explain to soldiers that killing PoWs 'is detrimental to our interests'. Prisoners, he emphasised, were to be properly processed. 'I categorically forbid shootings on individual initiative,' he ordered. Another document captured from the Soviet XXXIst Corps, signed by the Chief Commissar of the propaganda department on 14 July 1941, revealed 'prisoners have been strangled or stabbed to death'. It argued 'such behaviour towards PoWs is politically damaging to the Red Army and merely strengthens the will of the enemy to fight . . . The German soldier, when he is captured, ceases to be the enemy,' it stated. The aim was 'to take every measure necessary to capture soldiers and especially officers'.[24]

However, the reality at troop level was that Russian soldiers — like their German adversaries — had been equally and quickly brutalised by the pitiless ideological nature of the

fighting. Soviet PoW interrogations conducted by the Germans at Krzemieniec in July 1941 found:

'No general order has been given to kill all German officers, NCOs and men upon capture. The shootings and torturing to death of German soldiers are explained by captured Soviet soldiers, commissars, officers and doctors as stemming from individual or special orders. These are given to the troops by commissars or officers or both. A junior commissar stated that such orders are given primarily by battalion and regimental commanders to whom commissars are accountable.'[25]

Any doubts about what might happen upon capture by the Red Army were dispelled by the publicity that accompanied the capture of the Polish-Ukrainian city of Lvov, by the 1st Gebirgsjäger Division on 30 June 1941. Four thousand corpses were found in various stages of decomposition inside the still burning Brygidky prison and the former Samarstinov military prison. The NKVD had begun executing their inmates, primarily Ukrainian intelligentsia, within two days of the outbreak of war. Pogroms followed later, carried out by Ukrainian and Polish citizens against local Jews. The SD and SS contribution was to add a further 38 Polish professors and at least 7,000 Jews to the grim tally. Initially, however, public focus was on the disturbing crime perpetuated by the Russian Secret Police. German propaganda capitalised on an event made more convincing by the genuine horror the shooting engendered.

Maria Seniva's husband was imprisoned by the NKVD. She said:

'There was a message on the radio from the Germans. It said "wives, mothers, brothers, sisters, come down to the prison." I got to the entrance, I can't remember which one. People were standing round on all sides of the gates. I could see the bodies through it. They were lying in the courtyard in rows . . . I walked up and down the rows and I stopped to look at one of the dead bodies, it was covered by a blanket. I lifted the blanket and there he was, I'd found him. [She cries at this point.] I don't know what had happened to him, but his face was all black. He had no eyes, nothing there, and no nose.'

Jaroslaw Hawrych, similarly emotionally distraught, recalled finding her brother-in-law among 'hundreds, thousands' of corpses laid out by rows in the courtyard.

'I wouldn't have recognised him, he was half naked. There were signs of wounds on his body, and his face was swollen all black and blue. He was shot through the head and his hands were tied with a piece of rope. The only way I recognised him was when I saw the sock. He had a sock on his foot, one sock coloured in stripes. I recognised my mother's knitting.'[26]

A medical Gefreiter with the 125th Infantry Division wrote home about the extent of 'Jewish-Bolshevist cruelty which one would hardly deem possible':

'Yesterday we went through a huge city and by a prison. It stank of corpses even from a long distance away. The smell was hardly bearable as we approached it. Inside lay 8,000 civilian prisoners, not even all shot, but beaten and murdered — a bloodbath which the Bolsheviks set up shortly before withdrawing.'[27]

The soldiers were much influenced by what they had seen. It impacted upon both morale and morals. 'If the Soviets have already murdered countless thousands of their own unprotected citizens and Ukrainians,' wrote one NCO, 'bestially mutilating and killing them — what will they then do to Germans?' His own prescient opinion was, 'if these beasts, our enemy, ever come to Germany there will be a bloodbath the like of which the world has never seen.'[28]

The publicity surrounding the Lvov atrocity, reported in German newsreels and newspapers, accentuated the suspicions and unease already aroused within the public at home. Their concerns were transmitted to their menfolk serving at the front, magnifying the isolation and pessimism beginning to emerge at dubious personal prospects should the campaign become even more protracted. A Düsseldorf housewife confessed to her husband:

'We get some indication from the Wochenschau [newsreels] what it seems to be like in the East, and believe you me those clips have produced such dread that we prefer to close our eyes while a few scenes roll by. And the reality — what's it like for you? I don't think we will ever be able to imagine.'[29]

Classified SS Secret Service observations confirm the Ukrainian murders at Lvov 'produced a deep impression of disgust' during the second week of July. 'It was often asked what fate must our own soldiers expect if they become prisoners, and what are we doing on our side with the Bolsheviks "who already are no longer human?"'[30]

'KEIN KINDERGARTEN KRIEG'. PRISONERS AND PARTISANS

Tens of thousands of prisoners were shown on the newsreels to cinema audiences in the Reich as commentaries gloated over victories. Of every 100 PoWs shown, only three would survive.

The first problem on being taken prisoner was to survive the engagement. The intensity of fighting often precluded this. The consequences of failure in tank-infantry engagements, for example, were normally fatal. German anti-tank NCO Kurt Meissner described what normally occurred:

'All the crews were killed as they baled out and no prisoners were taken. That was war. There were times when such things happened. If we felt we could not collect or care for prisoners then they were killed in action. But I do not mean that they were killed after being taken prisoner — never!'[1]

The two biggest encirclement battles had netted 328,000 prisoners at Bialystok and Minsk during the first weeks of the advance and then another 310,000 were taken at Smolensk. General von Waldau, Chef des Luftwaffen-Führungsstabes, calculated that just short of 800,000 prisoners had been taken by the end of July. This was to rise to 3.3 million by December.[2] Perhaps two million Soviet PoWs are estimated to have perished in the first few months alone.[3] Artillery Leutnant Siegfried Knappe was astonished at the phenomenal numbers giving up:

'We had started taking prisoners from the first day of the invasion. The infantry brought them in by the thousands, by the tens of thousands and even by the hundreds of thousands.'[4]

Coping with such masses produced a pressure of its own. The 12th Infantry Division, for example, captured 3,159 PoWs between 31 August and 8 October 1941, which in numerical terms constituted about one quarter of its own effective strength of 12,000–13,000 men. The 18th Panzer Division, spearheading advances with Army Group Centre, took 5,500 Red Army prisoners during the first five weeks of the campaign, while its strength was reduced from 17,000 to 11,000 by August.[5] Few soldiers were, therefore, available to guard prisoners totalling about the equivalent of 40% of the division's own formed strength. Panzer units ahead of the infantry had to maintain the advance, hold down encircled pockets and secure masses of prisoners with ever-dwindling tank and infantry numbers.

The sheer scale of the problem can be measured against German infantry division strengths. By the end of July the Germans had to administer 49 enemy division equivalents in terms of medical care, transport and rations in addition to their existing order of battle. One single German division required 70 logistic tons per day of supplies, of which one third constituted rations.[6] There were insufficient logistic resources available to maintain the advance and even less for PoWs. Little thought, apart from grim ideological intent, was given to the sudden and unexpected influx of prisoners. Artillery Leutnant Hubert Becker declared after the war:

'It is always a problem because no war manual says what you do with 90,000 prisoners. How do I shelter and feed them? What should one do? Suddenly there were 90,000 men who gave up coming to us in a never ending column.'[7]

Schütze Benno Zeiser, with a special duty Company, witnessed the outcome of officially sponsored neglect:

'A broad earth-brown crocodile slowly shuffling down the road towards us. From it came a subdued hum, like that from a bee-hive. Prisoners of War, Russians, six deep. We couldn't see the end of the column. As they drew near the terrible stench which met us made us quite sick; it was like the biting stench of the lion house and the filthy odour of the monkey house at the same time.'[8]

It was a problem that could not be ignored. Even if one German soldier was allocated to secure 50 men each, 18 battalions or six regiments were needed to administer the 800,000 PoWs taken by the end of July alone, a figure that would increase to three million by the end of the year. The requirement is not just to guard the prisoners; they have to be medically treated, fed and transported. Leutnant Knappe correctly surmised control had been lost. 'I wondered at first,' he wrote, 'whether we were prepared to care for so many of them, and as the numbers continued to grow I was sure we were not.' The resulting appalling conditions were to physically enact the planned ideological intent by default. 'Our supply line did well just to keep the German Army supplied.' Commented Knappe, 'we could not possibly have anticipated so many prisoners.'[9]

Dehumanisation was the result. 'Many Germans had closed their hearts to such sights,' admitted Pionier Leutnant Paul Stresemann. 'If I had known the rest of it . . . I think I would have run away.' Despite the suffering, Stresemann argued, 'I can say that in all my army service I never saw a single atrocity.' Circumstances in themselves were creating insufferable conditions. 'Of course, when so many prisoners are taken as in Russia there is bound to be some chaos in feeding etc, for everything was in a terrible mess.'[10] Knappe thought 'the prisoners seemed apathetic and expressionless. Their simple uniforms created the impression of a huge dull mass.'[11] Benno Zeiser recoiled from the horror of this institutionalised disregard:

'We made haste out of the way of the foul cloud which surrounded them, when what we saw transfixed us where we stood and we forgot our nausea. Were these really human beings, these grey-brown figures, these shadows lurching towards us, stumbling and staggering, moving shapes at their last gasp, creatures which only some last flicker of the will to live enabled to obey the order to march?'[12]

Soldiers tend not to dwell overly long on upsetting sights, and the German troops were no exception, preoccupied as they were by the need to survive. Leutnant Paul Stresemann claimed, 'I had no idea that many of the poor devils would end up starving or dead in the west after they had been marched away in vast columns many, many kilometres long.'[13] Siegfried Knappe explained, 'it was a terrible situation, but it was not that they were neglected — it was just not possible to feed them in such numbers and still feed our own troops.'[14]

He was wrong. The policy was deliberate. It was tenuously excused by pointing out the Soviet Union had not ratified the Geneva Convention Agreement of 1929 relating to prisoners. Germany, however, was bound to the general international law relating to nations, which required humanitarian treatment of PoWs in the absence of a standing agreement. Both the USSR and the Third Reich had ratified the Geneva Agreement covering wounded in 1929 obligating a clear duty to care for the sick and wounded.[15]

An OKW order on 8 July 1941 covering first aid for PoWs directed 'Russian medical personnel, doctors and medical supplies are to be used first' before the German. Wehrmacht transport was not to be made available. OKH insisted on further limitations two weeks later 'to prevent the Homeland being flooded by Russian wounded'. Only lightly wounded prisoners who could be capable of work after four weeks were allowed to be evacuated. Those remaining were consigned to 'improvised PoW hospitals' staffed 'primarily' with Russian personnel using 'only' Soviet medical supplies. The directives were followed without question. Generaloberst Hoepner, commanding Panzergruppe 4, concurred 'it was a matter of course that German medics treat Russian wounded after the last German wounded have been handled'. The 18th Panzer Division, part of Generaloberst Guderian's Panzergruppe 2, ordered 'in no circumstances' were Russian wounded prisoners to be treated, accommodated or transported alongside German wounded. They were to be moved in 'Panje' wagons (horse-drawn carts).[16]

Soviet prisoners taken in the pocket battles were not only in a state of shock, many were wounded and injured. At this initial stage and thankful to be alive, they were often so tired and intimidated they did not consider escape. They depended upon sustenance from their captors while at this physical and psychological low point. This was the phenomenon that kept the massive PoW columns together. Leutnant Hubert Becker, a keen amateur movie cameraman, filmed such a concentration of PoWs and described the pictures after the war:

'They gathered in a valley and had their wounds dressed. Nurses were moving about. The majority were badly wounded and in a bad state, half dead with thirst and resigned to their fate. It was terrible, the lack of water in the dry shimmering heat of the scorching Steppe. Prisoners fought for even a drop of water. Some of their people, retaining a strong sense of discipline, fought them back so

that the healthy ones, best able to walk, would not drink all the water. Then those who needed it most could get the few drops available.

'These people were so numb and happy to have escaped the inferno that they hardly noticed the camera. They didn't even see me!'

Becker, wryly pondering the fate of this mass of humanity filling his camera lens, admitted 'what eventually became of these many, many, many soldiers I don't know, and it is better that one does not know'.[17] Some did what they could. One doctor working with the Ninth Army Collection Point (9AGSSt) spoke of 'islands of humanity in an unbridgeable sea of PoW misery'. Nobody was able to cope. Requests for supplies, rations and medicines were completely ignored. At one camp near Uman in August 1941, some 15,000 to 20,000 Soviet wounded lay under the open sky. Schütze Benno Zeiser, guarding such a camp, gave an indication of what such neglect created:

'Nearly every day we had men die of exhaustion. The others would take their dead back to camp, to bury them there. They would take turns carrying corpses and never seemed in the least moved by them. The camp graveyard was very large; the number of men under the ground must have been greater than that of those still among the living.'[18]

Thousands of prisoners perished during the forced marches from the front, the wounded succumbing first. So many were shot around the vicinity of Vyazma, later in the campaign, that the commander of the rear area was uneasy about its impact on enemy propaganda.[19] Sixteenth Army instructed its formations on 31 July not to transport PoWs in empty trains returning from the front for fear of 'contaminating and soiling' the wagons. The 18th Panzer Division warned its units on 17 August 1941 against allowing prisoners to infect vehicles with lice.[20] Schütze Zeiser claimed:

'We gave them whatever we could spare. There were strict orders never to give prisoners any food, but it was to hell with all that. We were pretty short ourselves. What we did give them was like a drop of water on a hot stove.'[21]

Conditions by early November 1941 could be described as catastrophic. Korück 582, a rear area security unit supporting Ninth Army, took over Army PoW Collection Centre 7 at Rzhev from its forward formation at the end of the month. Each single-storey accommodation block, measuring 12m by 24m, sheltered 450 prisoners. Disease was endemic because there were only two latrines for 11,000 prisoners. These had consumed all vegetation within the barbed-wire perimeter long before. Prisoners were subsisting on bark, leaves, grass and nettles until eventually isolated cases of cannibalism were reported. Watchdogs received 50 times the ration of a single Russian prisoner.[22] Inevitably typhus broke out in the autumn of 1941. The Health Department of the White Russian (Weissruthenien) General Commissariat recommended all infected prisoners be shot. This was rejected by the responsible Wehrmacht authorities 'on the grounds of the amount of work it would entail'.[23]

Such treatment was not without moral and morale implications for their captors. It accentuated the 'dehumanisation' of the foe which made the execution of such excesses more bearable. Soldier Roland Kiemig explained after the war:

'We had been told the Russians were sub-human Bolsheviks and they were to be fought. But when we saw the first PoWs we realised that they weren't sub-human. When we shipped them away and later used them as "Hiwis" [helpers], we realised they were absolutely normal people.'

There may have been doubts about the 'justness' of their cause, but they were not widespread. 'We knew this was no defensive war, forced on us,' admitted Kiemig, 'it was an idiotic war of aggression and a glance at the map showed it could not be won.'[24] Pressure manifested itself in other insidious ways. Schütze Benno Zeiser stopped his friend Franzl beating Soviet prisoners. He said:

'Let me be! I can't bear any more of it! Stop looking at me like that! I'm clean barmy! I'm plum loony! Nothing but this bloody misery all the time. Nothing but these creatures, these wretched worms! Look at them wriggling on the ground! Can't you hear them whimpering? They ought to be stamped out, once and for all, foul brutes, just wiped out.'

Franzl had suffered a nervous breakdown. 'You must see it,' he said, 'I simply can't stand this any longer!'[25]

National Socialist propaganda had 'dehumanised' the enemy even before the campaign had begun. Russian commissars were separated from soldiers on capture and executed. Maltreatment and the indiscriminate shooting of Russian PoWs was not solely the result of specific orders from above, neither was it necessarily conducted in a disciplined manner. Division and other records indicate that 'wild' and often indiscriminate shootings of Soviet PoWs began during the very first days of the campaign. Senior officers objected to this on discipline rather than morality grounds. The fear was that excesses might lead to anarchy in the ranks and intensify bitter Russian resistance. General Lemelsen, the commander of XXXXVIIIth Panzer Corps, rebuked his troops in an order three days into the campaign, complaining:

'I have observed that senseless shootings of both PoWs and civilians have taken place. A Russian soldier who has been taken prisoner while wearing a uniform and after he put up a brave fight, has the right to decent treatment.'

He did not, however, question the 'ruthless action' the Führer had ordained 'against partisans and Bolshevik commissars'. Soldiers interpreted his directive so liberally that a further directive followed within five days to curb their exuberance.

'In spite of my instructions of 25.6.41 . . . still more shootings of PoWs and deserters have been observed, conducted in an irresponsible, senseless and criminal manner. This is murder! The German Wehrmacht is waging this war against Bolshevism, not against the United Russian peoples.'

Lemelsen was perceptive enough to grasp that 'scenes of countless bodies of soldiers lying on the roads, clearly killed by a shot through the head at point blank range, without their weapons and with their hands raised, will quickly spread in the enemy's army'.[26]

Excesses were commonplace. Gefreiter Georg Bergmann, with Artillery Regiment 234 near Aunus at the end of August, on the northern Finnish front witnessed the bizarre spectacle of unit vehicles driving by at high speed with Russian prisoners perched on the engine bonnet or mud-guards. 'Most fell off because of the tremendous speeds and were "shot whilst trying to escape",' he said. Infantry Gefreiter Jakob Zietz spoke of six Russian PoWs captured by his 253rd Infantry Division company, who were press-ganged into carrying their ammunition near Wilikije Luki. 'They were totally exhausted as a result of the heat and their efforts and fell to the ground, unable to march any further.' They were shot. Others died clearing mines or transporting ammunition forward into the front line.

During the evening of 27 August, thousands of Soviet PoWs were jammed into a prisoner collection point at Geisin near Uman. The compound was designed to hold only 500 to 800 persons, but with each passing hour 2,000 to 3,000 prisoners arrived to be fed and then sent onward to the rear. No rations arrived and the heat was stifling. By evening 8,000 were packed into the camp. Oberfeldwebel Leo Mellart, one of the 101st Infantry Division guards, then heard 'cries and shooting' in the darkness. The sound of firing was obviously heavy calibre. Two or three 85mm Flak batteries nearby had engaged a grain silo inside the barbed wire perimeter with direct fire, 'because the prisoners had allegedly tried to break out'. Mellart was later told by one of the watch-keepers that 1,000–1,500 men had been killed or severely wounded.[27] Poor organisation and administration had resulted in chronic overcrowding, but the Stadtkommandant of Geisin was not prepared to risk a break-out.

There was no place in the ordered German military mind or tactical doctrine to deal with civilian irregulars. This had historically been the case during the Franco-Prussian War of 1871 and was repeated again during early occupation phases of World War 1. German soldiers considered it wrong or somehow 'unfair' for the enemy to continue fighting in the rear after having been overrun or encircled, fighting on in a hopeless situation. In Russia, unlike previously in the west, the enemy refused to follow the convention of orderly surrender. Irregulars were termed 'bandits' in German military parlance and treated as such. Thousands of Russian soldiers found themselves cut off from their parent formations during huge encirclement battles. On 13 September 1941 OKH ordered that Soviet soldiers who reorganised after being overrun and then fought back were to be treated as partisans or 'bandits'. In other words, they were to be executed. Officers of the 12th Infantry Division received guidance from their commander:

'Prisoners behind the front line . . . shoot as a general principle! Every soldier shoots any Russian who is found behind the front line and has not been taken prisoner in battle.'[28]

Such a command would not be considered unreasonable to soldiers sympathetic to the convention that warfare should be open and fair, giving the edge, of course, to German organisational, tactical and technological superiority.

German soldiers were incensed by snipers. Driver Helmut K___, writing to his parents on 7 July, complained his unit transporting material from Warsaw to the front had suffered 80 dead, '32 of them from snipers'.[29] Resulting repressive measures raised the level of violence. There was virtually no partisan activity in the Ukraine following the invasion apart from stay-behind Red Army, Communist officials and NKVD special groups. After the encirclement battle at Kiev, partisan operations in the Army Group South area considerably increased. In the Army Group Centre area partisan groups were to control 45% of the occupied area, but initially activity was on a small scale.[30] Sniping was the initial manifestation of resistance. During the advance to Leningrad, artillery soldier Werner Adamczyk was fired upon by people who were 'not in uniform' and 'not shooting too badly'. He was surprised and indignant:

'Now it seemed we would also have to fight civilians! It was enough to fight the Russian Army. Now we could not even trust civilians any more.'[31]

Any resistance in rear areas was always referred to as by 'bandits' or 'civilians'. Karl D___ wrote in his diary at the beginning of July:

'To our right were wheatfields. Precisely at that moment a civilian fired out of the corn. The field was searched through. Now and then a shot rang out. It must be snipers. There are also Russian soldiers who have hidden in the woods. Time and again shots sounded off.'[32]

Another soldier, Erhard Schaumann, described how:

'The Russian population hadn't fled but stayed in underground bunkers, as we realised much later. We received highly accurate incoming mortar fire where our unit was encamped, which caused very heavy losses. There must be some Russians [observing] nearby, we thought, to be aiming so well.'

On investigation they hauled out many people from the earth bunkers. Schaumann became reluctant to explain the subsequent course of events.

Schaumann: 'Ja — they were brought in, questioned, then I'd hear . . .'
Interviewer: 'Where were they taken?'
Schaumann: 'To the battalion or regimental commander or division commander, and then I'd hear shots and knew they had been executed.'
Interviewer: 'Did you see that too?'
Schaumann: 'I did.'
Interviewer: 'Did you participate?'
Schaumann: 'Do I have to answer that? Spare me this one answer.'[33]

Peter Petersen remembered an old school friend, an SS Untersturmführer, on leave from the front. He had received 'a terrible bawling out' from his superiors for his reluctance to shoot prisoners. His personality, Petersen observed, had completely changed from his school days.

'He was told that he would learn this was no Kindergarten war. He would be sent to take command of a firing squad where he would be shooting partisans, German deserters, and who knows what else. He told me that he had not had the courage to refuse to obey this order, since he would have been shot.'[34]

An atmosphere of uncertainty reigned behind the front. Soldiers felt beleaguered and isolated. Korück 582 — a rear-area security unit operating behind Ninth Army — was responsible for 1,500 villages over an area of 27,000sq km. It had only 1,700 soldiers under command to execute this task. No support was forthcoming from Ninth Army, which had been 15,000 men short at the start of the campaign. Partisan activity encompassed 45% of its operational area. These security units were often commanded by old and incompetent officers aged 40–50 years, compared to a front-line average age of 30 years. Korück 582 battalion commanders were almost 60 years old and their soldiers were poorly trained. Feelings of vulnerability and prevalent danger existed in these zones which, paradoxically, could be as active and dangerous as the front line.[35]

Walter Neustifter, an infantry machine gunner, said, 'you always had to keep partisans in mind'. Atrocity fed on atrocity.

'They had fallen upon the whole transport and logistic system, undressed the soldiers, put their uniforms on and passed all the captured material around with a few rifles. So, to frighten them, we hanged five men.'[36]

Peter Neumann, an officer in the 5th SS Division 'Wiking', following a revenge massacre after partisan atrocities against German soldiers, explained:

'We of the SS may be ruthless, but the partisans also wage an inhuman war and show no mercy. Perhaps we cannot blame them for wishing to defend their own land, but all the same, it is clearly our duty to destroy them . . . where does true justice lie? If such a thing even exists.'[37]

'When we marched into the Soviet Union,' declared Hans Herwarth von Bittenfeld, a junior infantry officer, 'we were regarded initially as liberators and greeted with bread and salt. Farmers shared the little they had with us.' All this changed with the self-perpetuating vicious circle of atrocities and revenge attacks. Villages were caught helpless in the middle. 'The disaster was the Nazis succeeded in driving people who were willing to co-operate with us back into the arms of Stalin,' he said. Von Bittenfeld's view was 'we lost because of the bad handling of the Soviet populace'. Russian 'Hiwis' that worked with the Wehrmacht were not all pressed labour. 'The idea originated,' he explained, 'from the soldiers, not the General Staff.'[38]

Atrocities were an inescapable fact of life on the Eastern Front. Leutnant F. Wilhelm Christians also spoke of being 'greeted with real enthusiasm' in the Ukraine. 'But behind the Panzers came the SD Security troops' which was 'a very sad and grim experience'. In Tarnopol, Christians recalled, 'Jews were driven together, with the help, I must also say, of the Ukrainians, who knew where their victims lived. 'My general's reaction when I reported this to him was that it was forbidden, with immediate effect, for any member of his division to participate in these measures.'[39]

There were a myriad factors that caused German soldiers to participate in or ignore excesses. They were isolated in a strange land, beset by numerous pressures and had of course to enact the disciplined violence expected of soldiers at war. Most had never left Germany or even been beyond their home districts before. They were then subjected to a form of group insanity. War corrupts, whatever the political beliefs, and a high level of culture is not necessarily a guarantor of civilised values. SS officer Peter Neumann with the 5th SS Division 'Wiking' recalled how a friend dispassionately executed a group of Russian ITU civilians. (These were Isspraviteino Trudovnoie Upalvelnnie — the Central Administration of Corrective Training — responsible for sending people to concentration camps.) He shot them with his Mauser rifle. Neumann observed:

'These characters were by no means saints, and probably had no hesitation in sending any poor devil guilty of some minor offence off to the mines in Siberia. But all the same I stopped for a moment rooted to the spot by Karl's amazing cold-bloodedness. His hand didn't even tremble.

'Is it possible that this is the same fellow I once saw, in short pants, playing ball on the sands down by the breakwaters of the Aussen-Alster in Hamburg?'[40]

Most soldiers would say that only those who were there truly understand the dilemma. The same men would have been labelled the 'boys next door' by their contemporaries. Police Battalion 101, responsible for grim excesses, was manned by unremarkable and 'ordinary men'.[41] After a soldier has killed, it is correspondingly easier the next time. There are criminal types in any cross-section of society that form part of the dark inexplicable make-up of human kind. Soldiers are not excluded. Indeed, condoned violence on the battlefield presents opportunities to those emotionally susceptible to evil and destructive acts. Artillery Obergefreiter Heinz Flohr saw mothers obliged to witness the execution of their own children at Belaja-Zerkow in the summer of 1941. 'I had to ask myself,' he said, visibly moved, 'are these human beings committing such acts?' Rape was also not always ideologically repulsive. Gefreiter Herbert Büttner stopped a medical Feldwebel molesting a Russian girl, but the same Feldwebel humiliated a group of Jews later by shaving half their beards and hair during a forcible eviction.[42]

Dehumanising the enemy provided an emotional safeguard of sorts. If the enemy are not people but *Untermenschen* (sub-human), it matters less what happens to them. Soldiers adrift in a sea of violence within a lethal environment were answerable only to their company commanders and those immediately in charge nearby, nobody else. Perhaps it is unrealistic to expect combat troops to make moral choices. Faced with impossible human dilemmas, it is invariably easier to obey orders. Those unable to recognise there was a choice were ideologically and frequently officially absolved of the responsibility.

Dr Paul Linke, an infantry medical officer, had always thought the commissar shooting order a 'latrine house rumour' until his battalion commander ordered his close friend, Leutnant Otto Fuchs, to shoot one. Fuchs, a lawyer in civilian life, had his stuttering ethical protest silenced by his superior officer. 'Leutnant Fuchs, I do not wish to hear another word,' he said. 'Get out and carry out the order!' The quick-thinking doctor offered to accompany his hapless friend in his sad duty, and promptly led him to the corpse of a Soviet soldier he had earlier discovered in a ditch nearby. The Russian commissar was encouraged to change clothes and bury the corpse in his commissar uniform and then allowed to slip back to his own lines. Two pistol shots fired into the earth disguised the act. Linke 'hoped it was clear to the [commissar] that both of us would be shot should this ruse ever be discovered'. The Russian gratefully disappeared into the night. The young doctor 'felt the risk to maintain his honour as an officer was worth it — we do not shoot defenceless prisoners,' he said. Fuchs had to report to his battalion commander and confirm the execution order had been carried out. 'I'm sorry Fuchs,' he admitted. 'I did not want it either. In the final analysis I delegated my responsibility for the order to you.'[43] Common decency in the final resort was a matter of personal inclination. Some soldiers actually relished the culture of violence, but for the majority, the main bonding factor was the solidarity of the group with whom they lived. Survival depended upon one's comrades. Right and wrong was not the issue, rather that there were variations in the degree of wrong.

Leutnant Peter Bamm, another medical officer, with Army Group South, observed that the Jewish massacres after the fall of Nikolaev were not approved by front-line soldiers, who felt that their victories 'gained in grim and protracted battle' were being used by the 'others' — the SS and SD. 'But it was not an indignation that sprang from the heart.' After seven years' domination by the SS and SD, moral corruption 'had already made too much progress even among those who would have denied it vigorously'. Protest was nullified by actions directed against families back home, as in the case of the wife of an Oberst in his division. Russian atrocities also had an impact upon the maintenance of emotional integrity. Soldiers would do whatever was required to survive. 'There was no blazing indignation,' Leutnant Bamm admitted. 'The worm was too deep in the wood.'[44] There could be no turning back now. Should the enemy ever reach the Reich, there would be the devil to pay.

A degree of ethical disintegration resulted from atrocities which had a negative impact upon the moral component of fighting power within the Ostheer. Ideals, even those directed toward the ideological ends of National Socialism, were compromised. The Christian army that invaded Russia was behaving in the manner of the Teutonic Knights of the 13th century, portrayed in Eisenstein's film *Alexander Nevesky*. This had an immediate appeal to cinema audiences in an oppressed and threatened Soviet nation. Paradoxically, it diluted fighting power because officially sponsored brutality raised questions of a fundamental and compassionate nature, which led to a questioning of motive. This in turn affected willpower. At the same time the enemy's moral component was strengthened. These indignities massively increased the resolve to resist. The German soldier began to realise in the absence of guaranteed success, for the first time in this war, that his very survival may be at stake. Conversely the Russian soldier knew he had no recourse but to fight to the bitter end. It was a pitiless prospect.

Unteroffizier Harald Dommerotsky, serving in a Luftwaffe unit near Toropez, was a witness of 'almost daily executions of partisans, by hanging, by the security service of the SS'. Enormous crowds — predominantly Russians — gathered. 'It may well be a human characteristic,' he remarked, 'this apparent predilection to always be present when one of your own kind is rubbed out.' It made no difference, he continued, 'whether it was the enemy or their own people'. Public hangings in Shitomir often resulted in cheers as lorries drove off leaving victims pathetically hanging in the market place. One witness described how gaily-dressed Ukrainian women would hold up their children to see, while Wehrmacht spectators would bawl 'slowly, slowly!' so as to be able to take better photographs.[45]

In Toropez a huge gallows had been erected. Lorries would drive forward, each with four partisans standing in the back. Nooses would be placed around their necks and the lorries driven off. Dommerotsky remembered the occasion when only three instead of four bodies were left dangling at the end of the ropes. The victim was sprawled on the ground, his rope broken. 'It made no difference,' the Luftwaffe NCO remarked, he was hauled up onto the lorry and pushed out again. The same happened again. Undeterred, his executioners repeated the ghastly process and yet again the victim fell onto the ground, still very much alive.

'My friend standing beside me said: "It's God's judgement." I could not work it out either and only responded: "Now they will probably let him go."'

They did not. As the lorry drove away for the fourth time the rope snapped taut around the victim's neck, and he kicked his life away as the exhaust smoke dispersed. 'There was no wailing,' Dommerotsky remembered, 'it was sinisterly quiet.'[46]
This was Kein Blumenkrieg — *a war without garlands.* *

* Literally no flowers were thrown — eg at a victory parade.

'A WAR WITHOUT GARLANDS'

Above:
'*Es war kein Blumenkrieg*' — 'A war without flowers,' declared veterans, alluding to the flower-bedecked victory parades, shown here, that followed the French and earlier Blitzkrieg successes.

Right:
The reality was better expressed by the face of this hard-bitten veteran enjoying a final draw on a cigarette before going into action.

Left:
A 'Leibstandarte-Adolf Hitler' SS Sturmgeschütze (Assault gun) commander is wounded and carried from the field of battle on his first day in action. The equivalent of three divisions' worth of officers were killed in the first seven days of the campaign.

Right:
The end of a day's hard fighting for men of the SS 'Das Reich' division near Smolensk in August 1941. Faces bear the imprint of tension and fatigue.

Left:
The so-called 'Yelnya look' was a reflection of the combat exhaustion exhibited by those who fought on this particularly hotly contested sector of the Smolensk pocket. This is the face of the victor, not the vanquished.

Above:
These men awkwardly stand in front of the body of their dead company commander. Such losses were not simply emotional: to lose a veteran commander was to reduce one's life expectancy, as he would probably be replaced by a less experienced officer.

Above right:
This man's 78th Division company was overrun at the end of June 1941, with 48 men killed and wounded in a single day. He is the sole survivor of an infantry section of nine men. His vacant stare leaves much unsaid.

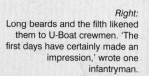

Right:
Long beards and the filth likened them to U-Boat crewmen. 'The first days have certainly made an impression,' wrote one infantryman.

Above: The post represented an emotional reaching out to home, and its distribution was the highlight of the day. Panzer crewmen receive their post.

Above: A rare moment to relax and catch up with home news.

Right: It needed two to four fit men to look after every wounded soldier. One-third of the veteran element of the *Ostheer* was either dead or wounded by the end of September 1941. They were the 'cream' — men who led and fought directly at the front.

Right:
A Panzer Unteroffizier crew member sprawled dead, with his uniform ablaze, across the glacis plate of a PzKpfwIV. He was probably killed baling out after his tank had been hit. The spare track hung across the front provided additional frontal armoured protection.

Below:
An unusual picture of an early German prisoner being interrogated by Soviet officers in the Ukraine in July or August 1941. At this time in the war his chances of survival in Soviet captivity were only 5%.

Left:
'We hanged five men to frighten them,' wrote one German soldier. Public executions of so-called partisans could be conducted in an almost fairground atmosphere, with ghoulish onlookers taking photographs. This picture was found on the body of a German soldier.

Below:
A familiar scene as a village is torched during an anti-partisan sweep. Both sides burned shelter to deny it to the other, whatever the consequences to the civilian population.

Left:
An SS officer wrote, 'we cannot blame them for wishing to defend their own land, but all the same, it is clearly our duty to destroy them.' This is the aftermath of a Russian massacre of German prisoners at Broniki in the Ukraine only nine days into the campaign. They were stripped, then bayoneted, shot and grenaded to death. 'Where does true justice lie? If such a thing even exists?' asked the same SS officer.

Below:
The aftermath of a partisan ambush on an isolated German detachment in White Russia. The occupants are stripped of their uniforms and the bodies were often mutilated.

Left:
Soviet prisoners are transported to the rear from Kharkov in open railway wagons in late October 1941. There is snow on the ground. Some 20% will freeze to death before they reach their destination.

Below:
Soviet prisoners at Stalag XD at Wietzendorf near Hamburg in the autumn of 1941. The barracks have yet to be built so the prisoners have dug holes in the ground to protect themselves from the elements.

Chapter 11
'Kesselschlacht' — victory without results

'We will have to annihilate everything before this war is going to end.'

German soldier

CANNAE AT KIEV

On 20 August the Eastern Front presented a fascinating picture. Lead elements of Army Group Centre had occupied Yelnya, south-east of the Minsk–Smolensk–Moscow highway, holding a salient that appeared to point at the Russian capital. Some 600km due south on roughly a straight line, Army Group South had reached the River Dnieper at Kremenchug. This represented the forward wedge of a German front shaped like an isosceles triangle. Its western apex lagged 550km behind the leading eastern elements. Concentrated within the triangle was the entire South-west Soviet Army Group situated south of the Pripet Swamps. Few commanders since Hannibal had ever enjoyed the prospect of achieving an operational double envelopment. Concept here verged on actuality.

On a hot August day in 216BC, an outnumbered Carthaginian force of 40,000 men commanded by Hannibal Barca surrounded eight Roman legions during the battle of Cannae. A feint toward the centre resulted in the double envelopment of the Roman Army of 86,000, twice the size of the Carthaginian force. Seventy thousand Roman legionaries perished, unable to escape. History appeared to be repeating itself more than 2,000 years later. Soviet Marshal Budenny's South-west Army Group was inside an enormous salient 240km wide that extended from Trubchevsk in the north to Kremenchug on the River Dnieper to the south. Kiev lay at the western extremity of the bulge. The conditions for a Cannae-like battle of encirclement were recognisable at this point, but only to those with a visionary operational view. Marshal Budenny had about a million and a half soldiers in this area, elements of eight armies, located mainly at Uman and Kiev itself.

Hitler's controversial strategic directive to change the main axis of advance southwards was planned as a double encirclement. A preliminary inner ring was to be created by three manoeuvring German infantry armies. Second Army was to advance south-east from Gomel, Seventeenth would strike north from Kremenchug, while the Sixth Army fixed Russian attention on the centre at Kiev. The outer ring was to be formed by Generaloberst Guderian's Panzergruppe 2 driving south from Trubchevsk with 500 Panzers to make contact with von Kleist's 600 tanks of Panzergruppe 1 attacking north from Kremenchug, 200km east of Kiev. It was a carbon copy of Cannae. Carthaginian infantry lured the Roman legions into the heart of their concave formation in the centre, while cavalry, the precursor of the Panzers, smashed the wings and then enveloped the committed Roman infantry from the rear. The aim was not to defeat but annihilate the enemy.

As the German plan unfolded, the Russians appeared paralysed and incapable of decisive action. Nobody saw the awesome trap opening. Instead of withdrawing behind the natural defensive line of the River Dnieper, Marshal Budenny reinforced those very areas, like Uman south of Kiev, which were to be engulfed by the German spearheads even before the main battle commenced. General von Kleist's Panzers entered Novo Ukraina on 30 July, cutting the Kiev–Dnepropetrovsk railway line, isolating Uman from the rear. The only route left open to the Soviet Sixth, Twelfth and Eighteenth Armies lay south-eastward along the River Bug to Nikolaev on the Black Sea. The *Kessel* (cauldron) thus formed leaked until closed by the German infantry divisions of Eleventh and Seventeenth Armies marching up from the west and south-west, which relieved the Panzers. Fifteen Soviet infantry and five armoured divisions were trapped and destroyed in a pocket that netted 103,000 PoWs. Its reduction was complete by 8 August. One German artillery battery pounding the encirclement fired more ammunition in four days than it had expended throughout the entire six weeks in France during 1940.[1]

An idea of the magnitude of distances covered during these tactical envelopments can be gauged from the progress of one of the Panzer spearhead divisions. Ninth Panzer Division, belonging to von Kleist's Panzergruppe 1, was at the end of the pincer that closed the Uman pocket. Setting off at Belaja-Zerkow, it swung down from the north to link with German infantry from the Ist Gebirgsjäger Corps. Between 24 and 30 July it captured 747 PoWs, destroying two tanks and eight guns en route before grappling with the enemy. By 5 August it had knocked out 33 tanks and 116 guns, taken or destroyed 1,113 trucks and captured 11,000 PoWs during an advance of 185km. A further tactical sweep occurred between 7 and 26 August through a series of Ukrainian industrial and communications centres between Kirovograd and Dnepropetrovsk on the River Dnieper. The distance covered was 490km, greater than the distance from London to Paris and slightly less than from Paris to Amsterdam in the Netherlands. A further 65 guns and over 16,000 PoWs were taken *en route*.[2] This latest advance opened up the possibility of a Cannae-like pocket. To the west the front was concave in shape, while the sinister spindly fingers of Panzer advances reflected on maps were reaching out to envelop the Soviet flanks. Fingers poised at Roslavl in the north and Kremenchug in the south needed only to close in order to spring a gigantic trap. They were some 600km apart.

The experience of these fast-moving German columns alternated between routine interspersed with sudden isolated skirmishes. Nothing was permitted to interrupt the flow of operations. Food was eaten on the move. Curizio Malaparte, an Italian war correspondent, described how:

'In this fluid type of warfare there is no time for meals. One eats when one can. Every soldier carries with him his ration of black bread and marmalade and his thermos of tea. Periodically, even during the heat of battle, he will take a slice of bread from his haversack, spread it with marmalade, raise it to his mouth with one hand, while with the other he grips the steering wheel of his lorry or the butt of his machine gun.'[3]

Fighting varied in intensity. Activity for the most part was clinically observed from a safe distance through binoculars. Incidents spluttered to life here and there, clouding the overall picture. Malaparte described a skirmish between his armoured column and Russian rearguards, which typified the haphazard and indistinguishable nature of such mobile engagements.

A Soviet tank opened fire on the column. 'I hear distinctly the clatter of its tracks,' he wrote, but nobody was aware of what was going on. 'It seems to be sniffing the air, trying to locate an invisible trail leading though the corn.' Battle was joined, but its progress and outcome was indistinct:

'[The Russian tank] starts firing with its machine guns, but half-heartedly, as if it merely wanted to test them. It advances swiftly down the slope toward us, then, without warning, it describes a wide half-circle and doubles back on its tracks, blazing away with its cannon. One could almost believe that it was looking for someone, that it was calling someone.'

The Russian infantry attack that followed was similarly surreal:

'Presently some men emerge from the corn and proceed to wander about the hillside, making no attempt to conceal themselves. Others emerge at various points. All told they must number about a hundred. Evidently this is some rearguard detachment or perhaps a detachment that has been cut off from the main body. The men seem to hesitate. They are seeking a way of escape.'

Leutnant Weil, the officer accompanying Malaparte, unlike the majority, knew the plan. 'Arme Leute [poor fellows] — poor bastards,' he said. The Russian soldiers spotted the Panzer column and advanced down the hill towards it, firing as they came.

'Then suddenly they vanish. There must be a dip in the ground at that point, a depression in the hillside. Around the tank can be seen the tiny chunks of turf thrown up by the shells of our mortars. The stutter of machine gun fire spreads along the flank of the column like a message tapped out in morse. Then some German soldiers appear over to our right, walking with their heads down, firing at the Russians. They advance in a line, blazing away with their sub-machine guns. An anti-tank gun fires a few rounds at the Russian tank. And now the outlines of two Panzers appear on the brow of the hill, immediately behind the Russian tank.'[4]

Scores of such flanking and minor tactical encirclements made up the flow of the German Panzer advance. They were unstoppable, but progress was not necessarily easy.

Occasionally there was time for pathos. After the skirmish, Russian bodies alongside the knocked-out tank were checked for signs of life. 'There's nothing we can do,' concluded the medical orderly.

'One of the Germans looks around for some flowers; there are only red flowers in the corn, a species of poppy. The soldier hesitates before these flowers, then he gathers an armful of corn, with which he covers the faces of the two dead Russians. The others look on in silence, nibbling hunks of bread.'

Interestingly, Malaparte observed he did not bother to cover the faces of the Mongolian soldiers.[5]

Despite the signs of impending encirclement at Kiev and the consequent likelihood of a catastrophic situation developing on the southern front, Stalin rejected suggestions that Russian troops be withdrawn to more defensible positions. On the contrary, he sought to increase the already over-manned Ukrainian capital garrison, being prepared to strip other sensitive sectors of the front to do so. German moves were interpreted as a diversionary feint to focus attention away from Moscow, the main objective, which he expected to receive an all-out attack prior to the autumn rains. A speedy resolution of the immense and technically complex issues which the German side would have to solve to create an envelopment was beyond the comprehension of Soviet staff officers with far less experience. There was, indeed, no historical precedent — which may have stimulated suspicion — to compare. Michael Milstein, an officer on General Zhukov's staff, gave his view on the impending catastrophe after the war:

'Firstly, the German Army had a colossal and overwhelming superiority. Secondly, we lacked the necessary combat experience. The third factor was Stalin's interference, which like Hitler [later] was to have tragic consequences for the German Army's advance. In this instance it appeared we did not withdraw from the area in time.'[6]

The potential for catastrophe was not appreciated. Zhukov was relieved as Chief of the Red Army General Staff and down-graded to a reserve front at Leningrad for having the temerity to suggest surrendering Kiev and withdrawing the exposed South-west Front to more defensible positions. Marshal Budenny, who commanded this sector of the front, was given an unambiguous order: 'not a step backwards, hold and if necessary die'. Dimitrij Wolkogonow, a young Soviet staff officer, assessed the likelihood of anyone questioning such an order:

'All dictators are similar in certain respects. Victories are explained in terms of genius and of personal merit. But when dictators experience defeat, they attempt to pass the guilt to those executing their orders — the generals, for example.'

Stalin had already relieved about 100 military commanders in 1941, including an array of generals. General Pavlov was removed after the initial catastrophic week on the western frontier and was arrested alongside Klimowskich, the front signals commander, with one other army commander and several other generals. They were executed. Wolkogonow summed up, pointing out that 'Stalin forced his military commanders to produce successes through such stern measures.'[7]

On 9 September Col-Gen Michael P. Kirponos, commanding

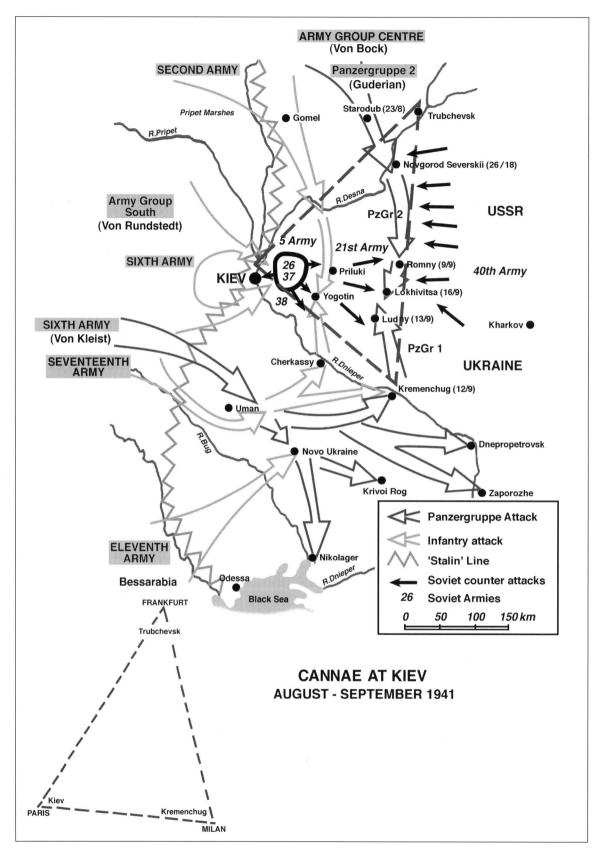

ARMY GROUP CENTRE
(Von Bock)

SECOND ARMY

Panzergruppe 2
(Guderian)

Pripet Marshes

R.Pripet

Gomel

Starodub (23/8)

Trubchevsk

Novgorod Severskii (26 / 18)

USSR

Army Group
South
(Von Rundstedt)

R.Desna

PzGr 2

SIXTH ARMY

5 Army

21st Army

KIEV

26
37

Priluki

Romny (9/9)

40th Army

38

Yogotin

Lokhivitsa (16/9)

SIXTH ARMY
(Von Kleist)

Ludny (13/9)

Kharkov

SEVENTEENTH
ARMY

Cherkassy

R.Dnieper

PzGr 1

UKRAINE

Kremenchug (12/9)

Uman

R.Bug

Novo Ukraine

Dnepropetrovsk

Krivoi Rog

Zaporozhe

Panzergruppe Attack

Infantry attack

'Stalin' Line

ELEVENTH
ARMY

Nikolager

R.Dnieper

Bessarabia

Odessa

Black Sea

Soviet counter attacks

26 **Soviet Armies**

0   50   100   150 km

FRANKFURT

Trubchevsk

CANNAE AT KIEV
AUGUST - SEPTEMBER 1941

Kiev

PARIS

Kremenchug

MILAN

Above: The drama of the 'Cannae' fought at Kiev unfolded on an unprecedented scale, as shown on the representative scale of the pocket indicated by the triangle on the map. Guderian's Panzergruppe 2 from Army Group Centre pushed southwards, linking up with von Kleist's Panzergruppe 1 coming up from the south. Five Soviet armies were annihilated, generating hope again in Germany that the war might be won that year. But it was a victory without decisive results, achieved at considerable German cost. The Russians fought on.

Soviet forces around Kiev, was ordered by Marshal Budenny, the front commander, to begin preparing for an 'orderly phased withdrawal' to escape the approaching encirclement and prepare to counter-attack. Stalin was familiar with this theatre of operations, having served there in 1918. He took close interest, having determined to fight in its defence. As a precaution he ordered the evacuation of industrial plant eastwards. He further conferred regularly with the Kiev High Command hierarchy, and installed a telegraph machine in the Kremlin for this purpose. Kirponos, Budenny and Nikita Khrushchev, the political commissar commander (and later Soviet premier) constantly raised the issue of withdrawal at these conferences. Alexander M. Wassiliwski, Stalin's Deputy Chief of the Red Army General Staff, recalled his ruler 'flying into a rage' on hearing of the 'absolute necessity' to give up Kiev recommended by his commanders. Orders were issued to cancel the withdrawal set in motion. 'Take all possible and impossible measures,' he ordered, 'to defend Kiev.' Two days later Kirponos appealed again for flexibility, but Stalin was uncompromising. He adamantly declared:

'Kiev is not to be given up and the bridges are not to be blown without STAVKA authority. Kiev was, is and will be — Soviet. No withdrawal is allowed. Stay and hold, and if necessary die! Out!'

Kirponos, at the other end of the telegraph, responded with a tired resignation. 'Your orders are clear — out. Farewell.'[8]

Generaloberst Guderian's Panzergruppe 2 had started south on 23 August on a blisteringly hot summer day. Armoured columns began raising immense clouds of impenetrable dust. The 3rd and 4th Panzer Divisions moved with the 10th Motorised Infantry Division, supported directly behind by the 2nd SS Division 'Das Reich'. They attacked due south. The 3rd Panzer Division was typically subdivided into three mixed *Kampfgruppen* (battle groups) of Panzers, motorised infantry and artillery with anti-tank units. Primitive sandy road conditions reduced progress to no more than 70km before columns had to be refuelled. After 40km the lead battle group — Kampfgruppe 'Lewinski' — passed the first road sign bearing the distinctive Cyrillic characters which indicated they were entering the Soviet Socialist Republic of the Ukraine. General Guderian's initial response on hearing his army was to move into the Ukraine and then back toward Moscow was, 'I doubt if the machines will stand it, even if we are unopposed.'[9] Encirclement battles at Minsk and Smolensk had already exacted a considerable toll. His Panzer divisions were on average only at 45% effective strength. Exceptions were the 10th Panzer Division at 83% and the 18th at 57%.[10]

The troops, nevertheless, were in buoyant mood. Roads were firm with few swampy areas and the weather was sunny and clear. It was Sunday, typical 'cavalry weather' or in other words 'Panzer weather', according to the 3rd Division official historian. After three hours' driving, a Russian transport column was surprised and caught on the road. The enemy abandoned their *Panje-wagons* and fled into the sunflower fields. As the Panzer spearhead breasted another rise they came across a huge column of Russian lorries passing left to right. The line of vehicles consisted of artillery batteries, logistic units, engineers, tractors, *Panje-wagons* and mounted Cossacks riding security supported by two armoured cars. Lead Panzers shot a gap through the column and the spearhead passed on through the stream of milling Russian vehicles.[11]

On 24 August an advance battle group from the 3rd Panzer Division captured the 700m-long bridge spanning the River Desna at Novgorad Seversk. So rapid was the assault that the Pionier platoon commander was overtaken by the lead Panzer company as he removed high explosive charges from the bridge and tossed them into the water. Having crossed, strong resistance was encountered from units of the Twenty-first Soviet Army. Its commander was becoming increasingly alert to the sinister implications of this powerful Panzer force, driving south-east, well over 200km east of Kiev.

The 2nd SS Division 'Das Reich' captured another bridge on the division's right flank at Makoshim, after a daring assault by its motorcycle infantry reconnaissance battalion. Stuka dive-bomber air support had been frustratingly delayed. As the SS soldiers began to prepare the bridgehead against inevitable Russian counter-attacks, the missing Stukas appeared and howled into the attack, dive-bombing their own troops. Forty Waffen SS soldiers were killed.[12]

Between 25 August and 7 September the 3rd Panzer Division fought a number of heavy battles south of Sostka, advancing only a further 55km south.

Generalfeldmarschall von Bock, the commander of Army Group Centre, monitoring Guderian's progress from afar, was becoming increasingly frustrated at the imposed redirection of his main armoured thrust away from Moscow. Army Group Centre's stalled infantry were now enduring intense punishment from Russian counter-attacks directed at the Yelnya salient, where some ground had to be given up. On 30 August he sullenly confided to his diary, 'the idea of an offensive on my front thus appears to be dead'. He noted the next day, 'the Panzer group [Guderian] is being attacked on both flanks and is in a difficult situation'. On 2 September Guderian was demanding more forces to support his southern advance, following the loss of the 10th Motorised Infantry Division bridgehead south of the River Desna. 'Guderian's description of the situation was so pessimistic,' declared von Bock, 'that I had to decide if I should propose to the Commander-in-Chief of the Army [Halder] that the armoured group be pulled back across the Desna.'

Even the Führer felt the tension emanating from this ambitious enterprise. Guderian, he insisted, should be concentrating his forces for the drive south. Generalfeldmarschall Keitel telephoned von Bock twice on 4 September and stated, 'if the Army Group and the Commander-in-Chief of the Army don't intervene with orders, the Führer will do it.' Guderian became so headstrong and irritated at the perceived lack of support from his army commander that von Bock felt, 'I finally had to ask for his relief.' On 5 September he admitted, 'I cannot hide my worries about new difficulties with this outstanding and brave commander.'[13] Tension was not a solely Russian prerogative. On the following day, the weather broke. Torrential summer storms turned the roads into a quagmire. *Kriegsmaler* Theo Scharf observed, 'half an hour of deluge would turn the unmade roads in the rich red soil into knee-deep melted chocolate, bogging down every vehicle, except the fully tracked ones.'[14] Movement began to grind to a halt.

General Halder visited von Rundstedt's Army Group South headquarters on 7 September and agreed final details for a plan involving both Army Group South and Army Group Centre. It directed that all enemy in the Kiev–Dnieper–Desna bend were to be destroyed and the city of Kiev taken. The Panzer envelopment shaping up like Cannae 2,000 years before was imminent. Guderian was to continue his 12-day-old thrust southward to Romny and Priluki with Second Army (infantry) covering his right flank. Army Group South's Seventeenth Army would pin Soviet forces on the lower Dnieper below Cherkassy and establish a bridgehead across the river at Kremenchug. Von Kleist's Panzergruppe 1 was to drive northward and link up with Guderian in the Romny-Lokhvitsa area. Six Soviet armies could then be cut off and isolated. Generalfeldmarschall Walther von Reichenau's Sixth Army was to cross the 650m-wide River Dnieper opposite Kiev and attack the now encircled enemy forces in the city. Panzergruppe 1 was down to 331 armoured fighting vehicles, which was 53% of its campaign start-state.[15] By 12 September he was over the River Dnieper and the race northwards to link up with Guderian was on.

Panzergruppe 2, on the other side of the pocket being created, struggled desperately to maintain the momentum of its southern advance. Surprise had initially paved the way. Soviet General of Engineers Tschistoff, who had been tasked to construct a defensive obstacle along the River Desna, directed his train from Moscow into Novgorod-Severski on 3 September. It had already been in German hands for eight days. On the following day General Model, commanding the spearhead German 3rd Panzer Division, which had penetrated to 16km north of the River Sejm in Krolevec, was handed a selection of captured maps. They had been removed from the body of a crashed Soviet airman, shot while attempting to escape. Analysis of the material revealed 3rd Panzer lay directly on the boundary between the Soviet Twenty-first and Thirteenth armies and that ahead a gap loomed between the opposing enemy forces. Two days' fighting through stubborn resistance 'in every village' in driving rain followed. A bridgehead was thrown across the River Sejm at Malnja. By 9 September Model's division was a further 25km south. An advanced detachment with the division Panzerjäger battalion, reinforced with a medium Panzer company (PzKpfwIIIs), a light tank platoon and a company of motorised infantry, was created from the dispersed spearhead element to push on alone. Major Frank, its commander, was given a simple directive: 'thrust forward as far as possible'. Behind him the 3rd Panzer Division regrouped and concentrated for a deliberate division attack, due to commence at 06.00 hours on 10 September. Every soldier was informed this was the final dash required to link with Panzergruppe 1, advancing towards them from the south. Rain began to soak the columns as the attack toward Romny started.

Panzergruppe 2 reached and crossed two bridges north and south of the city of Romny, establishing a bridgehead over the River Sula. Initially unaware of their presence, violent local Russian counter-attacks developed in the built-up area and around the bridges; 25 air attacks were directed against the 3rd Panzer Division strung out along muddy roads. Fuel trucks had to be towed through impassable boggy areas by engineer half-track tractors to refuel Major Frank's advance detachment. On 12 September, with the appearance of clearer weather, the small group was ordered to test the route further south to Lokhvitsa.[16] Generalfeldmarschall von Bock was satisfied to note that 'resistance has collapsed in front of the Second Army and Panzergruppe 2'. Success appeared to beckon:

'At the request of Army Group South, Panzergruppe 2, which is stretched out over more than 200km, was instructed to advance on Lokhvitsa as well as Priluki and Piryatin, in order to link up there with the tanks of Army Group South which early this morning set out toward the north from Kremenchug.'

There was palpable tension at von Bock's headquarters.

'At noon came news that the enemy is streaming east out of the more than 200km-wide gap between Kremenchug and Romny in dense columns. Immediately afterward, three telephone calls were received from Army Group South within a half hour, asking if Lokhvitsa had been reached yet!'[17]

Panzer Unteroffizier Hans Becker was enduring the harsh reality of executing his commander's intent from a more human perspective on the ground. 'The advance had been growing steadily slower and slower,' he said, 'the number of casualties larger and larger.' He had destroyed six Russian tanks from his own Panzer PzKpfwIV during a single day's action until his tank was immobilised by a strike on the right-hand track. With no infantry in direct support, the crew decided to blow up the Panzer to prevent it falling into enemy hands. 'The score was six to one and we were without a scratch between us,' commented Becker ruefully. Within a day the crew was in action again, this time manning a reserve Panzer. 'We felt ill at ease,' he confessed, because there had been no time to paint the barrel with rings commemorating the crew's tally of tank kills. Although merely a superstition, it was important to them. The new tank was also a PzKpfwIV but it 'was unfamiliar in small ways, and all of us were suffering from the after-effects of the previous evening's combat,' he said. During the four and a half hours of subsequent fighting, the new Panzer despatched 'two enemy tanks up in flames'.

As they broke off the action 'there came a heart-catching crack and jolt'. Becker instinctively realised this was not superficial damage. 'The morning's ill-omens had been justified.' They had received a direct strike on the right rear corner. The Panzer burst into flames. Two of his five-man crew were dead, 'sprawled in a corner, covered with blood'. The survivors hauled the bodies through the hatch to prevent them being burned. Unusually, the Panzer did not explode, but there was no alternative but to abandon the scorched but repairable hull to the enemy. Running, dodging and weaving, the three remaining crew members started back to their headquarters using a brief lull in the enemy fire. Once clear, Becker described how 'dejectedly we plodded back four or five kilometres, smoking cigarettes to steady our nerves'. Their appearance was bizarre. All had been splattered with blood from their dead comrades and the splinters that had ricocheted around the Panzer interior as the incoming round had struck home. Depressing news awaited them when they reached their company headquarters. Two complete crews had failed to return. Their seriously wounded company commander was doggedly manning his post and listened to their unfortunate situation report before being evacuated to hospital himself. Victory had been as costly as defeat. Becker reflected, 'glory grows with the passing of time, and the best battles are battles long ago.'[18]

Even the soldiers fighting in the field could sense the climax to this battle was fast approaching. Cavalry Feldwebel Max Kuhnert, riding reconnaissance for infantry regiments, recalled 'latrine news' or gossip 'that a large encirclement was in progress around Kiev, the capital of the Ukraine, since air activity had increased and we were urged to march faster'. The implication merely inspired resignation. 'This meant less rest for everyone, including our horses.'[19] As before, the infantry struggled to match the pace of the Panzers. Units on foot, particularly those in transition between battle areas, requisitioned whatever transport was available. Theo Scharf, marching with the 97th Infantry Division, 'estimated the division [column] reached a maximum [length] of about 60km, with hardly anybody on foot'. Quartermasters did not necessarily approve, but turned a blind eye. Soldiers simply took what horses and wagons they needed. On nearing the combat zone, Scharf said, 'the illicit requisitioning and trappings, the rubber plants and canary cages, all melted away and the soldiers' boots were back on the ground.'[20]

At midnight on 14 September, XIVth Panzer Corps with Panzergruppe 1 ordered its spearhead division, 9th Panzer, to take the railway station at Romodon, 138km north of the Dnieper crossing at Kremenchug. It received further supplementary orders the next day to block Soviet advances east of Mirgorod and advance north to seize a crossing over the River Sula and link up with Panzergruppe 2 driving south on Lokhvitsa. This was where it was proposed the spearheads should meet. Two battle groups formed for the task: one artillery-heavy for the blocking order and a second with Panzers and motorised infantry to achieve the link-up. This was the final spurt to achieve the encirclement. The Panzer battle group advancing north to Senca began to overrun large numbers of Soviet lorries, including one column of 50 trucks. Captured Soviet soldiers in the vehicles were completely shocked, convinced they were moving in a totally secure rear area. By midnight on 15 September Kampfgruppe vehicles of the 9th Panzer motorised infantry were approaching the railway station at Senca. Ahead lay the River Sula.

Three days before, Major Frank's vanguard unit of Guderian's Panzergruppe 2 had overwhelmed Soviet defences along a road just east of the same river during the evening twilight. During the subsequent hours of darkness they drove a further 45km undetected through Soviet territory. An undamaged bridge over the same meandering river was captured 2km north-east of Lokhvitsa. Heavy fighting developed until the arrival of the first substantial battle groups forming part of the 3rd Panzer Division deliberate attack. As night fell on 13 September, the soldiers camouflaged their vehicles behind haystacks and underneath stooks of corn. Officers closely observed the silhouetted outline of Lokhvitsa, clearly identifiable now from the high ground upon which they had paused. The scene was thrown into golden relief by the dying rays of the setting sun. On inspection:

'Dust and smoke clouds were seen rising above the houses, machine gun rounds were whistling through and cracking artillery impacts could be discerned. There was now no doubt. The forward element was directly behind the Russian front. Only a few kilometres away was the spearhead of Army Group South.'[21]

Frank's battle group, combined with the leading 3rd Panzer Division battle group, fought its way into Lokhvitsa at 05.00 hours the following morning. The large north bridge across the tributary of the River Sula, which ran through the main city, was seized in a *coup de main* assault. German motorised infantrymen clambered over six Soviet heavy anti-aircraft guns which were lined up wheel to wheel, filling the street and pavements 200m beyond the bridge. There was virtually no resistance. The Soviet crews were asleep.[22]

Confusion reigned as the two converging German army group spearheads groped towards each other in a mêlée of fighting, closing in from both the north and south. The 3rd Division battle group pushed on.

'Oberleutnant Warthmann gave the order: "Panzers — advance!" The Kampfgruppe trundled forward into a deep depression and fired at the shocked Russians who were killed as they suddenly emerged from the darkness. Ahead lay a small water-course blocking the way. The vehicles sought a crossing point and noticed a bridge. As the Oberleutnant's Panzer III drove up to it they realised it had been demolished. Grey ghost-like figures leaped to their feet at this point, covered in clay with stubble on their chins, and they waved and waved — soldiers from 2nd Assault Engineer Company of 16th Panzer Division [Army Group South].'

Shortly after, Guderian's headquarters received a short radio message: '14 Sep 1941, 18.20 hours, Panzergruppen 1 and 2 establish contact.'

The grimy soldiers indicated the way across the small stream. Oberleutnant Warthmann's Panzer ground its way over and turned toward Lubny. The rest followed. Presently they pulled alongside other armoured vehicles with a white 'K' (Kampfgruppe 'Kleist') painted on the front and rear mudguards. Their own vehicles had the white 'G' denoting the Kampfgruppe 'Guderian'. By 09.10 hours on 15 September the 3rd and 9th Panzer Divisions established conclusive physical contact at Lokhvitsa in the central Ukraine. Stretching out to the west lay five Soviet field armies within this initial tenuous ring.[23]

Von Bock announced the same day: 'the ring has closed around the enemy in front of the inner wings of Army Groups South and Centre'. 'The battle at Kiev,' he declared, 'has thus become a dazzling success.' Hannibal at Cannae won his battle but failed to defeat Rome. Von Bock thought in parallel. A huge victory was in the offing:

'But the main Russian force stands unbroken before my front and — as before — the question is open as to whether we can smash it quickly and so exploit this victory before winter comes that Russia cannot rise again in this war.'[24]

To achieve this the Soviet field armies embraced by the Panzer wings had now to be annihilated. Although the potential strategic reward matched the experience of Cannae, the scale was entirely different. On a hot day in August 2,000 years before, 120,000 men fighting on foot and horse faced each other in an area measuring 1.5km by 1.75km. They died at the rate of 100 per minute.[25] At Kiev on the first day of the link-up, three German infantry armies and two Panzergruppen had trapped five Russian armies in a huge triangle with sides 500km long encompassing an area of 135,500sq km.[26] The same tactics were being applied in a totally different technological age over the massively greater distances appropriate to modern armoured warfare. The triangle covered an area that would today link Paris, Frankfurt and Milan. Euphoric German newsreels portrayed the area as lying between Stettin in the north of the Reich, Cologne in the west and Munich to the south. Seeking to escape this trap were between a half and three-quarters of a million Russian troops, at least 665,000 men from 50 divisions. The scale of killing was also different in modern warfare. At Cannae, 50,000 Romans were lost in a single afternoon. In the battles around Kiev the Russians lost an average of 8,543 soldiers each day for 64 days.[27]

German field commanders were under no illusion that the hardest part had yet to come. The Russians would fight. Generaloberst Guderian visited Major Frank's observation post near Lubny on the morning of the successful encirclement. 'A fine view could be obtained over the countryside,' he later wrote, 'and Russian supply columns were to be seen marching from west to east.' He spoke with Oberstleutnant Munzel, commander of the 6th Panzer Regiment belonging to the 3rd Panzer Division. Prior to 'Barbarossa' the regiment numbered about 198 tanks. 'On this day,' Guderian observed, 'Munzel had at his disposal only one Panzer IV [heavy], three Panzer IIIs [medium] and six Panzer IIs [light tanks armed with 20mm cannon], that is to say ten tanks were all that was left of a regiment.' It was an ominous portent of the Pyrrhic nature of a victory yet to be confirmed and, as Guderian commented, gave 'a vivid picture of how badly the troops needed a rest and a period for maintenance'.[28] Surrounding such a massive Russian force had been a decisive achievement. The scale of this pocket dwarfed any previous experience in the history of warfare.

As at Smolensk and earlier encirclement battles, the *coup de grâce* had to be administered by the infantry divisions. They did not relish the prospect of such killing unless it meant a shortening of the campaign. Günther von Scheven, a 33-year-old infantryman, instinctively appreciated what this would mean. 'There is no rest,' he wrote home. 'Always the same marching through woodless areas and along endless roads, column after column. Horse, rider and guns like spectres in thick clouds of dust.' Having marched over 2,000km, he was approaching the extremes of physical and psychological endurance. 'The last few days of combat are taking a toll of my courage,' he admitted. 'One cannot encompass the destruction of so many lives.' He had already experienced 'the wild despairing break-out attacks the Russians attempted, surprising even for us, right up to our front with tanks, infantry and Cossacks'. The 'experience of death is awful,' he lamented, 'like a new form of baptism'. Günther von Scheven had fought the earlier encirclement battles south of Uman. His conclusion was both cynical and laconic: 'probably,' he said, 'we will have to annihilate everything before this war is going to end.'[29]

It was a depressing prospect.

THE REDUCTION OF THE KIEV POCKET

As in the earlier encirclement battles, the Panzer ring faced inward, toward the pocket interior, and outward, establishing pickets to repel Soviet relief attempts. They awaited the arrival of the infantry divisions. Between 16 and 19 September the German Second and Seventeenth Armies — respectively from the north and south — closed in upon Yagolin, the inner encircling ring objective. Sixth German Army, meanwhile, carried out a concentric assault upon the city of Kiev, advancing broadly from the west. It was the third largest city in the Soviet Union and fell after bitter fighting on 20 September, a depressing blow to Russian morale. Some 35 German divisions began to compress the sides of the pocket. Before long the original triangle had shrunk to a smaller version about the size of an area between Munich, Stuttgart and Würzburg in Germany, or likewise Caen, Le Mans and Paris. At this point the manoeuvring was over. The methodical dismemberment and killing of five trapped Soviet armies began.

On 19 September 33-year-old Soviet Major Jurij Krymov wrote a letter to his wife Anka. Surrounded by sleeping soldiers, he pored over the letter in fading evening light, utilising the flickering flame of a lamp and throwing grotesque shadows onto the white clay walls of the shed where he sat. Opposite was his commissar. He had been four days without sleep.

'*How is it that we come to be inside a pocket? One could offer a long explanation, but I do not feel like it. Until now it's not exactly clear. No one is going to argue about one point. All around, wherever you look there are German tanks, sub-machine guns or machine gun nests. Our unit has already been defending on all sides by the fourth day, within this circle of fire. At night the surrounding ring is clear to see, illuminated by fires that light up the horizon, which here and there give the sky a wonderful yellow hue.*'

Krymov had not written to his wife for some time. There had been 'no chance to send a letter'. Now appreciating the gravity of the present situation, he felt 'a written letter might somehow get through to you, an unwritten one would clearly disappear without trace'. He glanced at the soldiers all around, sleeping with full equipment, rifles and machine guns cradled in their arms, only belts unbuckled for comfort, and laboriously attempted to write in the poor light. He described the battlefield night sky about him: 'wonderful golden twigs,' he wrote, created by flares 'grew vertically into the darkness'.

'*These star-like embers of light crept — then abruptly somersaulted — over the vastness of the Steppe and were then extinguished, until another broke out, high up, in another position.*'[1]

As the Germans drove into the pocket, sub-pockets were created, which in turn were smothered in hard fighting. Jewgenlij Dolmatowski, with a Russian press company, was isolated in just such an enclave. 'We were surrounded, I believe, by soldiers called grenadiers,' he said. Few asked for quarter which was not freely given. 'It ended in hand-to-hand fighting,' continued Dolmatowski, 'during which I was thrown to the ground, and virtually held down by my hands and feet.' He likened the desperate mêlée to 'fighting like children' but 'actually, it was to the last'. They were totally out-fought. 'I have never had such a thrashing in my life,' he admitted, 'even as a child — never!' Afterwards 'we were then taken off to the prison camps'.[2]

Russian units marched and counter-marched through the confusion inside the pocket, constantly seeking a way out. Local inhabitants, aghast at the prospect of impending German occupation, looked on in despair. Major Krymov described the scene on evacuating a village as they retired deeper into the shrinking pocket.

'*Anxious, serious faces of collective farmers. Soft words from the women. Clipped phrases from the officers. Engine sounds. Horses neighing. "Heads up comrades, we'll be back"* . . . *"Back soon"* . . . *"Come back"* . . . *"How are we going to defeat the Germans?"* . . . *"Now if we don't come, others will, take care"* . . . *"A little fresh water for my field flask?" "Thank you"* . . . *"We'll be back, if not us, then others just as good. And the German parasites will go down like flies"* . . . *"Take care friends!" "No, not farewell, simply goodbye."*'

As logistic units attempted to march towards the centre of the pocket, combat units reorganising and regrouping for a break-out marched the other way. Units became entangled. 'The pocket has been constricted to an appalling degree,' observed Krymov, 'nobody can move now, in any direction.' The decisive phase of the battle was anticipated within hours.

'Without doubt the soldiers will break out of the pocket, but how, and at what price? This is the issue that preoccupies the various unit commanders.'[3]

Belated attempts to break out of the pocket during the night of 17/18 September were broken up by the Germans.

The Luftwaffe was meanwhile engaged in two vital tasks: tactical air-ground support for the advancing Panzers and interdicting the area of operations to block all Russian approaches to the pocket. Major Frank's 3rd Panzer Division advance guard, for example, which achieved the decisive link-up at Lokhvitsa, was protected from a Soviet tank formation by Stuka dive-bombers which broke up an advance menacing one of its tenuously held bridgeheads.[4] For four weeks the Luftflotten systematically attacked all Soviet rail communications converging on the area of operations from the east and north-east. The northern part of the pocket was covered by Luftflotte 2's IInd Fliegerkorps, while Vth Fliegerkorps from Luftflotte 4 attacked in the south. Strafing and bombing attacks were mounted against stations, bridges, defiles and locomotives and trains. Soviet reinforcements for Marshal Budenny's armies were blocked and lines of retreat disrupted. Fearful punishment was meted out to Russian vehicle traffic jams unable to manoeuvre within the pocket.[5]

Bad weather hampered close formation attacks, which were substituted by isolated and group sorties. These kept railway lines in the battle area permanently cut. Repeated Bf110 strafing runs cut 20 to 30 trains marooned along one section of railway track to ribbons. Large formation-size Russian units did not appear on the roads until forced to concentrate in order to break out. As soon as they committed themselves, they were — in the words of the Luftflotten commander — 'relentlessly attacked with devastating results'.[6] Gabriel Temkin, serving in a Russian labour battalion, remembered:

'The Luftwaffe's favourite places for dropping bombs, especially incendiary ones, were forested areas close to main roads. Not seeing, but expecting, and rightly so, that the woods were providing resting places for army units and their horses, German planes were bombing them, particularly at nightfall.'

Pure birch forests, which, Temkin confessed, 'I never before or after saw,' were consumed in the flames. 'The burning greyish-white trees were turning reddish, as if blushing and ashamed of what was going on.' As he observed the inferno he became aware of a peculiarly pungent smell. 'For the first time,' Temkin said 'I smelled burnt flesh.' He was unable to distinguish whether it was men or horses.[7]

Stuka dive-bombers were employed to shatter resistance in the pocket. Between 12 and 21 September, Vth Fliegerkorps flew 1,422 sorties, dropping 567,650kg of bombs and 96 incendiary Type 36 devices. Results were impressive: 23 tanks, 2,171 vehicles, 6 Flak batteries, 52 railway trains and 28 locomotives were destroyed. In addition, 355 vehicles were damaged and 41 put out of action alongside 36 trains. Railway lines were cut in 18 places and a bridge destroyed. Soviet losses included 65 aircraft shot down and 42 destroyed on the ground. Luftwaffe losses, by comparison, were slight, with 17 aircraft destroyed and 14 damaged, costing 18 missing aircrew and 9 dead.[8]

German infantry divisions moved in to eliminate any remaining resistance. On 19 September Fritz Köhler's motorised infantry unit was still north of the River Desna. At midday he heard the radio *Sondermeldung* that the link-up with Army Group South had been achieved and four Soviet armies surrounded. After an afternoon of 'routine work' they heard a further announcement that the city of Kiev had fallen. Three days later he was in action with an advance guard hastily dug in to repel break-out attempts near Lokhvitsa. As six T-34 tanks moved towards them, Köhler realised they 'had been seen'. His lorry-borne unit had only recently dismounted and consequently 'had not dug in very far'. German 37mm anti-tank and 105mm field guns directly engaged the tanks, but the 'rounds ricocheted straight off'. One German gun after the other was knocked out during the unstoppable advance, which drove over and crushed wrecked guns and the bodies of the hapless crews. The last German guns abruptly withdrew, leaving the infantry unprotected. Köhler nervously glanced above the parapet of his shell-scrape as:

'The tanks drove right up next to our position. We experienced some very uncomfortable minutes. One crunched by about five metres from my foxhole and even stopped now and again. I hunched myself up and made myself as tiny as possible, hardly breathing. Finally the armoured vehicle drove on, but it was a moment I will certainly never forget.'

The threatened section of the line was restored with the arrival of 88mm guns and Pioniers who laid mines. Köhler commented, 'luckily there were no [enemy] infantrymen sitting on the tanks, otherwise few of us would have seen that evening'.[9]

The German 45th Division, already badly mauled at Brest-Litovsk, began to arrive at Priluki, 120km east of Kiev, on the eastern edge of the pocket. Like so many other divisions, it had endured a steady attrition rate as it marched eastward. At Brest-Litovsk it had lost more men than during the entire French campaign. Between 1 and 6 September, 40 more soldiers were killed and a further two officers and 23 men between 9 and 13 September. Pouring rain slowed their rate of advance to 4.5km per day. They were under the command of Second Army advancing on the pocket from the north. Its commander relayed the situation in an order of the day on 10 September:

'Bitter enemy resistance, terrible roads and constant rain have not stopped you . . . This advance has enabled you to contribute to the possible realisation of a battle of annihilation, which will begin within the next few days. We will surround the enemy from all sides and destroy him.'[10]

As the 45th Division entered the line the outline of the pocket had been reduced to a diameter of about 40km. It was subsequently attached to Sixth Army belonging to Army Group South, forming part of a group of eight German divisions tasked with forcing the beleaguered surviving Russian divisions to surrender. On 20 September 45th Division was set astride the Yagolin gap on the eastern side of the perimeter, which became a focal point for Russian escape attempts. As the first battalions started arriving on 22 September, the Russian attacks began.

Cavalry Feldwebel Max Kuhnert had also arrived at the periphery of the ring surrounding the Kiev pocket. The perimeter, he could see, 'was closing fast, but this only made the Russian forces in and around Kiev all the more determined to throw everything into the battle'. Positioned behind a Panzer division, Kuhnert admitted, 'luckily for us' only 'strays of the

Russian armour got through'. He ruefully reflected, 'we were then in a fine pickle', and 'wished myself many kilometres away'.

'We were utterly helpless in those situations. Warfare against tanks we had hardly practised because it was not our job on horseback. The best we could do was to get out of the way, seeking cover in the wooded areas, and hope for the best.'[11]

Massed Soviet break-out attempts often resulted in thinly distributed German mobile units being surrounded themselves. These were reduced to adopting an *Igel* (literally island or hedgehog) all-round defence position, from which they fought for their very lives. Walter Oqueka participated in the earlier Uman encirclement, and was a crew member of a 20mm Flak 38 mounted on a half-track chassis. His unit's role was air defence, not to fight the 'grey-green colossus' Soviet tanks that suddenly appeared on their front.

'"T-34" — hissed the gun commander between tightly compressed lips. The T-34, we had all heard about these tanks, amazing things — which meant not good for us. We were hardly likely to win any prizes with the 37mm "Wehrmacht door-knocker" [anti-tank gun], and certainly not against these monsters. How were we supposed to knock out these great lumps with our pathetic [20mm] calibre?'

Oqueka's battery commander, Oberleutnant Rossman, ordered them to concentrate automatic fire on the tracks of the advancing T-34s. Nobody was optimistic as to the likely outcome, but there remained little else they could do. Oqueka 'clenched his teeth and decided they would sell their skins as dearly as possible'. They held their fire until the tanks had approached to within 200m. A burst of fire smashed the track of the leading T-34, which began to turn helplessly around on the same spot. Guns were then ordered to concentrate fire at the turret. Even before the first magazine emptied, the turret lid flipped open and a white flag appeared. The Russian crew clambered out and were taken prisoner. Meanwhile the cone of 20mm fire was switched to the left and another T-34 similarly disabled.

Instead of surrendering, the crew of this vehicle chose to fight with small arms as they emerged. They were cut to pieces by multiple impacts of 20mm cannon explosions which sparked and spluttered around the hull. Other tanks met the same fate. Crews were scythed down at any sign of resistance. The rest of the T-34s turned back. It was inconceivable to Oqueka and the other gun crews that their insignificant calibre cannon could have triumphed against tanks considered the heaviest and best of their type. 'Our nervous tension was released in a triumphant yell,' Oqueka exclaimed, 'as if we were eight-year-old kids playing cowboys and indians!'

They moved forward curiously to examine the results of their handiwork and discovered that, apart from cut caterpillar treads and damage to drive and sprocket wheels, there was nothing to explain the abrupt abandonment of the tanks. 'Not until the prisoners were questioned did the riddle become clear,' explained Oqueka. The answer lay in the resonant din produced by multiple 20mm strikes on cast steel turrets, which had the effect of transforming them into 'huge bells'.

'Continuous explosions on the turret had produced a hellish noise which had grown louder from explosion to explosion. The sound had swollen beyond the realms of tolerance and had virtually driven the crews insane.'

Oqueka recalled the example of executions of indicted criminals in ancient China. Hapless individuals were incarcerated inside a huge bell which was hammered outside until the unfortunate victim expired. The 20mm gunners appreciated they were not totally defenceless when facing heavy tanks. Oqueka claimed his battery disabled 32 T-34 tanks before the end of the year, employing similar tactics.[12]

Other German sectors on the Kiev perimeter were not so fortunate. On the right wing of the 45th Infantry Division, Infantry Regiment 133 experienced 'a lunatic and reckless cavalry attack which rode through our machine gun fire'. They were followed by 'mass human-wave attacks, which we had not experienced until now'. Cossacks galloped through German outposts with drawn sabres, slashing down with such force that troops caught in the open had their helmets cleaved through to the skull. A segment of this epic Tolstoyian charge reached as far as the division headquarters at Yagolin before it was stopped. Behind the cavalry came a tightly compact triple-wave infantry assault, supported by heavy artillery fire. Four tank and three lorry-mounted infantry platoons were amongst them, suicidally driving directly against the division line. As they dismounted when blocked by a railway line atop an embankment facing the German positions, they were subjected to a withering storm of fire from co-ordinated artillery, anti-tank, machine gun and small arms fire. 'The dead,' according to the division report, 'covered the length of the embankment in countless masses.' Among them were women in uniform.

On 24 September the tidal wave of suicide assaults shifted against the 44th Division to the right and south of 45th Division. Russian troops exploiting inter-division boundary gaps penetrated into the rear positions, falling upon the logistic and artillery units that stood in the way. The 6th Battery of Artillery Regiment 98, occupying high ground at point 131, fired directly into waves of attacking Russian infantry, creating huge gashes in the advancing crowds. Undeterred, the remorseless mob swept into the German gun positions where furious hand-to-hand fighting developed. One German artillery piece was captured and hauled around to fire at its own division headquarters, wounding horses but missing personnel. At this moment in the struggle, one of those curious paradoxes of war occurred. While the chaotic and savage mêlée continued around the gun positions of 6th Battery, hardly 100m away columns of Russian infantry marched by moving eastwards, with rifles at the shoulder, as if on parade, oblivious to what was going on. They would have made all the difference and widened the breakthrough if they had been deployed to support the penetration struggling on their flank. The 45th Division padre, watching this in disbelief, remarked 'they did not take the slightest notice of the clear route on offer over there, they were on another mission!'[13]

Fearful losses on both sides became increasingly apparent as the pocket was compressed. 'I could not avoid seeing the truckfuls of young corpses,' recalled Max Kuhnert following the advance. They were German.

'It was just ghastly, and those were only a few from our immediate area. Blood was literally running down the side from the floorboards of the trucks, and the driver was, despite the heat, white as a sheet.'

Strewn along the roadsides were dismembered corpses. German soldiers were visibly affected at the sight of uniformed female Russian casualties. Kuhnert, inspecting a knocked out '60-tonner' tank, saw that the flames had burned away the clothes of the driver and another crew member, a woman, hanging half out of a side door. She was probably a tank crew member but Kuhnert, uncomfortable with the concept of women fighting in uniform, surmised, 'the Russians had apparently been so confident of their breakthrough that one had taken his wife or sweetheart into the large tank.' Kuhnert was eating iron rations, which often contained a small tin of pork. As he prised it open with the tip of his bayonet and took his first mouthful, it coincided with the awful stench emanating from the tank.

'Maybe I was simply too tired and the last few days for me as for many others, had been just too much. We had been in battle for 12 days; it was enough for anybody. Even so, for years to come whenever I tried to eat or wanted to eat tinned pork, I just couldn't.'[14]

He was violently sick.

The reduction of the Kiev pocket was a battle of annihilation. As the Soviet divisions were cut to pieces, German casualties rose also. 'Whose turn would it be today?' was the unasked question vexing tired infantry as they roused themselves from a few hours' sleep, often in woodland, before resuming the advance. 'Pain, hunger and thirst took second place now,' said one soldier, 'with the ice-cold breath of death brushing our cheeks and sending shivers down our spines.' It took five days to reduce the pocket. On the fourth day, 45th Infantry Division was attacking a heavily wooded feature in the Beresanj area, pushing westwards toward Kiev. Heavy hand-to-hand fighting developed near Ssemjonowka against Soviet soldiers unusually armed with sub-machine guns and automatic weapons. There was no surrender.

Bundles of grenades bound together were hurled at the German attackers for maximum effect. One concentrated charge wiped out an entire machine gun crew. All night long the Russians repeatedly attempted to break out. By first light about 100 corpses could be counted, sprawled around the perimeter of one of the lead companies. A body inspection revealed 25 were officers and commissars and another 25 were NCOs. The wood where the enemy had been concentrated was raked by heavy artillery time and again until all resistance ceased: 700 PoWs including a Soviet army corps general emerged.

Even areas already overrun had to be systematically combed. It was a slow, methodical and remorselessly bloody process. 'Survival became the only thing that mattered,' declared Kuhnert. 'One could actually become jealous of others who got wounded, not badly mind you, but just enough to get them home or away from this place of slaughter, stench and utter destruction.' All the countless haystacks and straw huts that dotted the landscape had to be laboriously checked. Hiding inside were cut-off enemy groups who continued to pick off single German soldiers or vehicles. A 'reconnaissance by fire' was instituted to overcome the problem. The shelters were shot into flames. The 45th Division chaplain described the surreal scene:

'If it were not necessary to contribute further to the fury of war one might have admired the countless dazzling columns of fire that made up this grandiose spectacle of illumination. In between, the infantry fanned out in wide skirmish lines and finally cleared the area of the last remnants of its defenders. Here and there the last magazine was fired off or a grenade thrown from haystacks already on fire.'[15]

Unteroffizier Wilhelm Prüller with Infantry Regiment 11 was pursuing fleeing Russian columns in vehicles mixed with tanks. German Panzer and motorised companies had become intermingled with the enemy 'in the intoxication of this fabulous chase'.

'There ought to be some newsreel men here; there would be incomparable picture material! Tanks and armoured cars, the men sitting on them, encrusted with a thick coating of dirt, heady with the excitement of the attack — haystacks set on fire by our tank cannons, running Russians, hiding, surrendering! It's a marvellous sight!'

Prisoners were flushed out from beneath haystacks or lying between furrows in the fields. 'Shy, unbelieving, filled with terror, they came,' gloated Prüller. Resistance by 'many a Bolshevik' was regarded as 'stupid pig-headedness'. They were shot on the spot.[16]

By the fifth day Russian resistance was visibly collapsing. Col-Gen Michael P. Kirponos, commanding the Kiev troops, perished alongside his staff when his column failed to break through the German ring. Very few Soviet units escaped. Marshals Budenny, Timoshenko and their senior political commissar, Khrushchev, were flown out of the pocket by air. M. A. Burmistrenko, a member of the war council and Secretary of the Central Committee of the Ukrainian Communist Party, and the Chief of Staff of the Soviet Army Group, General Pupikov, were killed, as were most members of the General Staff. One single cavalry unit led by Maj-Gen Borisow managed to exfiltrate with 4,000 men.[17] Although masses of Soviet PoWs were rounded up, they did not readily surrender. Gabriel Temkin, serving in a Soviet labour battalion, admitted 'although officially a taboo in the Soviet press, the PoW issue was a public secret'. The Russian public was aware huge numbers of prisoners had been taken. 'We were told both how the Nazis were mistreating them, which was indeed a fact, and what the Soviet punishment for letting oneself become a PoW was, which was also true.'

Commanders who surrendered were considered deserters, the consequence was their families could be arrested as forfeit. Likewise, families of Red Army soldiers taken prisoner would be denied government benefits and aid. 'Falling into the enemy's hands was considered almost tantamount to treason,' Temkin explained. Exoneration was achievable only if one was incapacitated by wounds, killed, or later escaped. The capture of Stalin's own son, Yakov, produced a poignant irony. 'The Germans,' Temkin said,' were dropping leaflets with his photo over cities as well as over railway stations and Red Army groupings.' Many soldiers had already witnessed the random and apparently officially sponsored shootings and ill-treatment of prisoners. Stalin's son later died in a concentration camp. Temkin had no illusions. 'I could not get out of my mind the fear of falling into their hands,' he confessed. 'I dreaded it more than being killed.'[18]

Major Jurij Krymov had already resigned himself to the inevitable. He received notification at 02.00 hours that the enemy were 4km from his left flank. There was no room inside the crowded shed with his sleeping soldiers, so he went outside. 'The whole horizon was illuminated in red with everywhere the damn clatter of machine gun fire.' It was apparent that 'even with the best will in the world we are not going to get out of this'. A further depressing report revealed contact had been lost with the neighbouring unit to his left. Beleaguered from all sides, 'they were being overwhelmed by events'. His commissar, who had supported him throughout, interrupted his melancholic train of thought, passing him two biscuits. 'I had absolutely no idea where he had got them from,' he said, 'but he had not eaten them, he had brought them to me.' Krymov's letter to his wife stopped at this point. He was killed three days later.[19]

Leutnant Kurt Meissner was watching yet another despairing Soviet attack on the hard-pressed German ring. 'This great mass of singing humanity had only been told to break out in our direction,' he said. He and his men were new to combat and afraid. They had never seen anything like this before.

'They came on in a shambling, shuffling gait and all the way they were calling out in this low, moaning way, and every so often they would break out into this great mass cry of "Hurraaa! Hurraaa! Hurraaa!".'

Meissner and his men, covering a vast and flat sector, fired and fired until a wall of corpses built up, behind which still, advancing Russians began to shoot back. Thousands more came on, pushing beyond the bloody barrier and trying to rush the German positions. Meissner's men quickly fell back and took up new positions to avoid being overrun. Now blocked, the Soviet tide sought to break through in another direction. As they did so, the Germans poured a murderous fire into their flanks. Meissner admitted:

'I was in a sweat, very hot and frightened. Then a strange thing happened, and this was even more extraordinary: the whole mass of surviving Russians — and there were still thousands of them — simply stopped dead about a kilometre from us as if on order. We wondered what was happening and then saw through our glasses that they were discarding all their equipment. Then they turned about to face us. All the enormous sacrifice they had made had been in vain. They simply sat down on the spot and we received orders to go in and round them up.'[20]

On the fifth day it ended. German soldiers moved warily across to take the surrenders. Meissner recalled, 'we moved over hundreds of dead, dying and wounded, they had no apparent organisation for dealing with the latter. Russki — Komm!' was the first order preceding nightmarish forced marches to the rear and PoW camps.

The battle of Kiev spluttered to an end on 24 September 1941. A doctor from the 3rd Panzer Division surveying the battlefield reported:

'A chaotic scene remained. Hundreds of lorries and troop carriers with tanks in between are strewn across the landscape. Those sitting inside were often caught by the flames as they attempted to dismount, and were burned, hanging from turrets like black mummies. Around the vehicles lay thousands of dead.'[21]

Sergeant Ivan Nikitch Krylov, a demoted Soviet staff captain, witnessed the final days in the pocket.

'The Germans outnumbered us, their munitions were practically inexhaustible, their equipment without fault and their daring and courage beyond reproach. But German corpses strewed the ground side by side with our own. The battle was merciless on both sides.'[22]

Six Soviet armies — the Fifth, Twenty-first, Twenty-sixth, Twenty-seventh, Thirty-eighth and Fortieth — were either wholly or partially destroyed and 50 Soviet divisions were removed from the Soviet order of battle as a consequence. The German news service announced the pocket contained 665,000 Russian prisoners, 884 tanks and 3,718 guns. Soviet sources record that 44 divisions and six brigades with 12 defended localities participated during the Kiev defensive operation conducted between 7 July and 26 September. A total of 700,544 casualties are admitted, of which the greater part — 616,304 — were irrecoverable losses.[23]

The battle, as Krylov suggested, was not completely one-sided. Feldwebel Max Kuhnert's unit suffered heavy casualties but, as a colleague pointed out, 'our losses are nothing like the poor devils of the battalions'. The IInd Battalion and reconnaissance unit on his right flank was much reduced: 'motorcycles with sidecars were standing or lying on the primitive track and there were bodies everywhere'.[24]

Chaplain Rudolf Gschöpf's 45th Division had received a comparable mauling to that already received at Brest-Litovsk. Three infantry Regiments lost 86, 151 and 75 men respectively; 40 others died at the division dressing station and 40 more were scattered elsewhere. In total the division lost 40 officers and 1,200 NCOs and men. This represented half a regiment's complement of officers and a battalion and a half of men. A service was held over the graves, freshly covered in flowers, and the military band played before the division departed the battlefield. Gschöpf commented, 'it was the last time our music corps were able to play their instruments during this war.'[25] Vehicle shortages had dictated the instruments be sent home to make space for essential stores. The war was losing its heraldry; lethality and objective usefulness were all that was left.

The German press was jubilant. The *Völkischer Beobachter* crowed: 'An Army of One Million Wiped Out!' and 'End of the Kiev Catastrophe'. The *Frankfurter Zeitung* declared simply: 'Five Soviet Armies Annihilated'.[26] For over a month there had been no *Sondermeldungen* relayed to the population since the heady days of Smolensk. The third anniversary of the start of World War 2 had passed, bringing with it an inevitable questioning of what had been achieved and, more significantly: what remained to be done? Interest in the Russian War had not been attracting the previous banner headlines. Secret SS situation reports briefed to Himmler at the beginning of September stated, 'the already overlong campaign in the east is viewed by much of the population with a certain disquiet.'[27] Victory at Kiev changed all this. Attention once again focused on Russia. Popular interest surged to the previous 'Barbarossa' invasion levels. 'Recently held convictions that static positional operations had developed and that a severe winter campaign is in the offing have slipped into the background,' observed reports.[28] A German housewife living near Nuremberg wrote:

'Another public announcement was issued today saying the Russians appear to be breaking up around Kiev and 50 divisions have been destroyed. Father said that would be an even greater blow because of the amount of material taken there as well. The Russians with their great masses are impervious to human losses, but they will not be so quick to replace all the equipment.'[29]

German infantry with Army Group South were less sanguine. It was they who had to mop up the mortally wounded Soviet armies, easily written off by the press, as if surrounding them was all that was required. Finishing off the Kiev pocket had been a hazardous enterprise. Thirty-five

German divisions, including six Panzer and four motorised, had been required to execute this Cannae. They represented about one-third of the strength of the original 'Barbarossa' invasion force — a massive effort. Soldiers felt and recognised the immense strain. An Obergefreiter with the 98th Infantry Division wrote, 'we have had 75% losses in our company'. He anticipated the arrival of replacements in a few days. 'But I believe if they do arrive sooner, as is invariably the case, we will already have been relieved and moved on before they even get here.' Replacements never seemed to arrive.[30]

Another Unteroffizier, with the 79th Infantry Division, wrote he 'had got through the pocket fighting east of Kiev well enough'. He hoped 'that after this battle they would be taken out of the line, but, even though we have shrunk to a tiny band, sadly, it was out of the question'. They were already marching toward Kharkov. 'I have strong reservations,' he confessed, 'whether we will see an end to the war in Russia this year.' The outlook appeared pessimistic. 'Russia's military might is certainly broken, but the land is too big, and the Russians are not thinking of surrender.'[31] His view was echoed by that of a Gefreiter with the 72nd Infantry Division, who declared in a letter that 'the campaign against Russia began today, three months ago'. He had then surmised 'the Bolsheviks would be ripe for surrender within at least eight to ten weeks'. German soldiers, he reflected, were more used to a Blitzkrieg — a tempo campaign. Progress had been as rapid as in France when considered in manpower and material terms. 'Only this morning,' he wrote, 'we heard by chance that near Kiev for example, 600 guns were destroyed and 150,000 men taken prisoner . . . What about those for numbers! . . . Russia is almost inexhaustible!' But there was, he pointed out, a fundamental difference between the French and Russian campaigns. In the west:

'After the penetration of their defensive lines and encirclement, their armies saw further resistance as senseless genocide. They surrendered to save their people. It's another case here. We're not fighting against the Russian people but against the Bolshevik world menace, which has enslaved them.'

In short, 'there would be no armistice forthcoming from the Russians'.[32]

Generalfeldmarschall von Bock became impatient to begin the promised thrust against Moscow as soon as the encirclement at Kiev had been achieved. The move south had been a distraction from his main effort. He had been miserly with resources, husbanding the main forces within Army Group Centre for as long as possible, reluctant to assist Guderian in the tactical possibilities he opened up as operations progressed. As these forces moved further south he became correspondingly geographically removed from what he clearly considered to be the overdue main effort: an assault on Moscow prior to winter. Throughout the Kiev encirclement battles his diary reflected his frustration and concern. On 20 September, the day after the formation of the pocket, he wrote:

'The build-up in my front lines can't be concealed from the enemy in the long run. I must reach a decision: should I wait for the bulk of the promised forces or should I not? In spite of the difficulty of the attack, I am leaning toward "risking something" and attacking as soon as the most necessary units are in place.'

On 24 September he observed, 'it is clear that the Russians are withdrawing forces from in front of my front to prop up their threatened northern and southern wings. It is time!'[33]

As ever, the soldiers in the field were blissfully ignorant of this intent. Panzerjäger Ernst Victor Meyer was enjoying the same sunny day to the east of the Kiev pocket. Writing to friends back home, he admitted his virtual ignorance of the true situation.

'As always we know practically nothing about objectives and intentions. So for now, we are totally unaware what should become of us. Another "Kessel" pocket [Kiev] has been "finished off" and for the moment our task completed. Now where are we off to?'[34]

Theo Scharf, moving through cornfields with the 97th Infantry Division toward Kharkov, recalled, 'the yellow ripe cornfields could now be picked out of their own tall, stalky forests.'[35]

It was autumn.

Chapter 12
'Victored' to death

'I considered whether I ought to write a letter to [my wife] Maria, so that it would be in my pocket, should I never get to go home.'

German soldier

OBJECTIVE MOSCOW

Führer Directive Number 35 was issued on 6 September as Guderian's Panzergruppe 2 battled southward to begin the closure of the Kiev pocket. Code-named 'Taifun' (Typhoon), the operation aimed at the defeat and annihilation of the Russian forces blocking the road to Moscow 'in the limited time which remains available before the onset of the winter weather'. Following the encirclement and destruction of the Red Army facing Army Group Centre, Generalfeldmarschall von Bock would 'begin the advance on Moscow with [his] right flank on the Oka [river] and [his] left on the upper Volga'.

Army Group Centre was to become the *Schwerpunkt* (main point of effort) in this last push before the end of the year. Von Bock issued his attack order on 26 September,[1] even as the final blows were being administered to the disintegrating Kiev pocket. In order to provide Army Group Centre with the appropriate force and penetrative power commensurate with its *Schwerpunkt* role to achieve the objective, Army Groups North and South were directed to transfer important forces to von Bock's control. Hoepner's Panzergruppe 4 was to be detached from Army Group North and Panzergruppe 2, fighting around Kiev, from Army Group South. Von Bock would have three Panzergruppen under command: these two and Hoth's Panzergruppe 3, at that moment supporting von Leeb's assault on Leningrad. Three marching infantry armies — the Ninth, Fourth and Second — would follow behind the Panzer forces.

The attack plan aimed at a double armoured encirclement which would close their pincers east of Vyazma, bringing the Panzer spearheads to within 160km of Moscow astride the main road leading from the west. Guderian's Panzergruppe 2 (now renamed Second Panzer Army) was tasked to attempt an envelopment south-east of Bryansk, by advancing north-east from its present position at Kiev to effect a junction with the Second Infantry Army moving due east. Staff preparation now focused on the requirement to amass the necessary force and matériel.

The war in the east was approaching a climax. On the German side Army Group Centre had nearly two million (1,929,000) soldiers at its disposal, facing one and a quarter million Russian defenders. Over one-third of the forces on both sides formed the logistic and rear area security 'tail' supporting the operational 'teeth' forward. In reality some 1,200,000 German 'fighters' were to engage 800,000 Russian, a ratio of broadly eight German to every five Russian soldiers.[2] This was not sufficient for the conventional military wisdom of a ratio of three to one, to ensure a realistic chance of success for attack against defence. Overall figures are less important, however, than tactical and operational excellence, which is required to create the necessary force ratios that ensure success at a given time and place at the front. Surprise is one factor ensuring this, but it becomes subject to an effectiveness 'fade' once the operation is underway.

Such a point had arguably been reached in the eastern campaign. The Red Army was configured in a quasi-offensive stance at the outset of 'Barbarossa' and was 'checkmated' in the wrong place when the German attack began. Massive defeats and encirclements at Minsk and Smolensk bore testimony to the benefits of the surprise achieved. With Leningrad besieged and the armies at Kiev annihilated by a further unexpected move, only one clear German objective remained. This was Moscow. The only remaining conundrum was 'when?'

Surprise is a two-edged weapon and applies to both sides. Captured Soviet West Front documents give an insight into the tactical and technical surprises inflicted by the German onslaught during the initial invasion phase. 'Use of infantry forces strongly supported by heavy-calibre infantry guns and anti-tank weapons, with motorcycle troops and the application of deeply echeloned Panzer attacks, in close co-operation with the Luftwaffe', according to the documents, had considerable impact, 'thereby deceiving the intent of eventual encirclement, and with good fire control on the move.' A lesson of the previous short campaigns, which was missed due to the rapidity of the Polish and Balkan operations, but partly reflected in the greater German casualties suffered during the latter part of the French campaign, was that, with experience, Blitzkrieg could be blunted. Shortfalls discerned and commented upon by the German General Staff,[3] following the six-week French campaign, were not identified by the enemy until it was too late.

The Russians, with space to react, were given time to learn. They had already noted the difficulty of matching the infantry pace to Panzers. Night defence was invariably poor, as also the reaction of motorised and Panzer elements to unexpected attacks, especially when they were resting on roads or in villages. These had 'weakly defended outposts that can be easily overwhelmed during the attack', the report read. It was deduced that wide-ranging night attacks to harass the Germans, by destroying material and inflicting casualties, was likely to have considerable impact. But German officers arrogantly surmised they held the tactical edge. Generalmajor Nehring, commanding the 18th Panzer Division, calculated from an examination of captured staff maps that he would require a 15-day logistic capability to sustain the forthcoming attack.[4] This would suffice to reach Moscow, or just short of it, when a further decision dependent on the situation would be necessary. Estimates of Russian strength had been 171 divisions prior to the campaign, which was revised to 200 shortly after and then to 360 divisions within six weeks.[5] Surprise had been mutual.

The effectiveness of surprise was diluted over time. New factors started to emerge. Halder foresaw the approaching dilemma as early as 11 August:

'The time factor favours them, as they are near their own resources, while we are moving farther and farther from ours. And so our troops, sprawled over an immense front line, without any depth, are subjected to the incessant attacks of the enemy. Sometimes these are successful, because too many gaps must be left in these enormous spaces.'[6]

In mid-September he wrote to his wife that 'the shame of it is that time is frittering away, and time is the stuff of victory.'[7] Time, distance and the unexpected ferocity of resistance had a cumulative impact upon the *Ostheer*. Commanders retained confidence because the Wehrmacht had yet to lose a battle during this war. Two factors, however, interacted in reducing the qualitative impact of a barely sufficient attack-to-defence ratio. They were faltering logistics and an army that was, in its own words, 'victoring itself to death' (*Totsiegen*).[8]

A LOGISTIC 'TRIP-WIRE'

The original 'Barbarossa' concept surmised that the Russian field armies would have to be defeated in western Russia, within 500km of the border, to realise the plan. OKH calculated that the distance from the frontier to Smolensk should be covered in one mighty leap, followed by a pause, during which time the rail network would be extended to catch up. Covering the resupply gap, meanwhile, would necessitate a balance of tracks, wheels and rail transport. The reality was that tracks — the Panzers — rapidly outstripped the marching armies which were reliant upon horse-drawn transport.

Logistics was based upon the army's *Grosstransportraum* (lorry carrying capacity), which was truck columns supplying the 33 'fast' divisions and their supporting troops and headquarters. There were 144 divisions to be supplied in total. The sanguine expectation was that the 300km drive to Smolensk could be covered by a six-day 600km round-trip by lorries, including loading and unloading. Each division would

receive only 70 tons per day through this method, of which well over one-third would consist of rations. Concentrating only on the 'fast' divisions would denude the remaining 111 divisions. 'Fast' divisions encircled the pockets, but the slower divisions still required substantial logistic support to reduce them. Potential for problems existed even before the 300km intermediate Smolensk objective was reached. The 500km line (from the frontier) beyond it represented a form of intangible 'trip-wire' that would snag any offensive and cause it to falter. At worst case it might collapse. German field-post letters home had already frequently alluded to shortages of equipment, food and manpower replacements at the front.

A fundamental tenet creating a 500km logistic check was the technological inferiority of lorried transport compared to rail in 1941. The French Blitzkrieg, despite the convincing perception given by newsreels of powerful motorised German columns portrayed in the propaganda film *Sieg im Westen* (Victory in the West), was not reality. Indeed, the earlier campaigns had irretrievably damaged the motorised lorry fleet, now reliant upon captured stocks. Even if these fleets had existed, they would have been inferior to rail. No fewer than

Below: The Logistic 'trip-wire' was the limit of the *Ostheer*'s strategic logistic sustainability, beyond which an offensive aimed at Moscow could not be achieved unless supported with a rail-based transport network. The lorried tactical carrying capacity, *Grosstransportraum*, was the only element able to keep up with the fighting spearheads. The lorry fleet, as also combat vehicles within the fighting formations, had been decimated by the eve of Operation 'Taifun' at the beginning of October 1941.

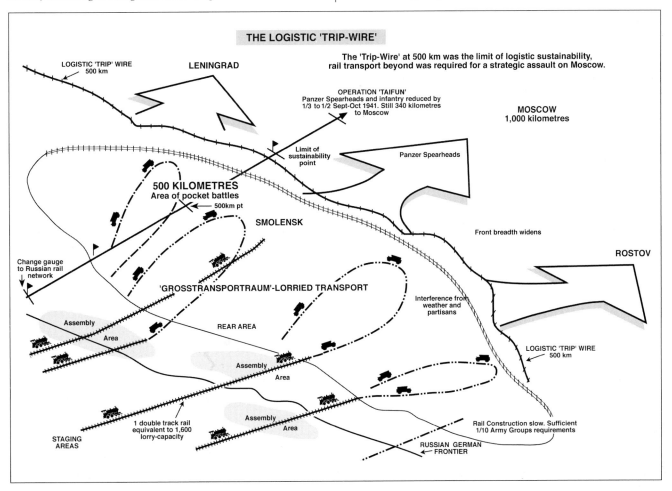

THE LOGISTIC 'TRIP-WIRE'

The 'Trip-Wire' at 500 km was the limit of logistic sustainability, rail transport beyond was required for a strategic assault on Moscow.

LOGISTIC 'TRIP' WIRE 500 km

LENINGRAD

OPERATION 'TAIFUN'
Panzer Spearheads and infantry reduced by 1/3 to 1/2 Sept-Oct 1941. Still 340 kilometres to Moscow

MOSCOW 1,000 kilometres

Limit of sustainability point

Panzer Spearheads

500 KILOMETRES
Area of pocket battles
500km pt

SMOLENSK

Front breadth widens

ROSTOV

Change gauge to Russian rail network

'GROSSTRANSPORTRAUM'-LORRIED TRANSPORT

Interference from weather and partisans

Assembly Area

REAR AREA

Assembly Area

LOGISTIC 'TRIP' WIRE 500 km

1 double track rail equivalent to 1,600 lorry-capacity

Assembly Area

Rail Construction slow. Sufficient 1/10 Army Groups requirements

STAGING AREAS

RUSSIAN GERMAN FRONTIER

1,600 lorries were needed to equal the capacity of one double-track railway line over the 500km distance. Motorised transport further devoured material in its own right, requiring fuel, drivers and personnel, spare parts and maintenance. Consumption relative to the payload carried placed railways in the ascendancy as the most efficient primary carrier at distances in excess of 320km. Lorry columns were a tactical rather than strategic asset.

Some 40% of Wehrmacht divisions were equipped with captured French motorised vehicles at the outset of 'Barbarossa'.[1] Panzer division reorganisations prior to the campaign created more units from virtually the same number of tanks, forming 19 Panzer divisions from nine. The creation of the additional 'fast' divisions resulted in a corresponding demotorisation of units and services in infantry divisions, which had meanwhile expanded from 120 to 180. The newly created motorised units were experiencing enormous difficulties by late summer, due to wear and tear.

Technical transport reports from the SS Panzergrenadier Division 'Leibstandarte Adolf Hitler' (LSSAH) offer an instructive snap-shot of the problems experienced by a relatively well equipped motorised unit. The LSSAH started the eastern campaign with an inventory of 3,403 vehicles, 240 of which were captured. Many of the same vehicles had already been used for campaigns in Austria, the Sudetenland and Bohemia-Moravia, and most of them had been employed in Poland, France, Greece and the Balkans, and now Russia. No regular or complete refurbishment of vehicles occurred between the French and Balkan campaigns before 'Barbarossa'. OKH simply ruled that fairly worn parts — those with an assessed 5,000km of life — were to be reinstalled. By the autumn most vehicles had averaged 8,000km and supply and special-duty variants had surpassed 12,000km. Fine dust on all roads caused numerous break-downs. There were no new filters to remedy the situation, so cylinders and pistons wore out early. Reliance on low-grade oils caused piston-rod failures requiring a complete overhaul to repair damage. Shortage of spare parts resulted in 'junking' otherwise repairable vehicles, which were cannibalised to keep the remainder of the fleet moving. By 10 October the Motor Transport Officer was predicting catastrophic fall-out rates: 493 vehicles had broken down, 160 were immobilised awaiting spare parts and, he assessed, 250 more vehicles would likely break down within the next 500km.[2] This was the situation on the eve of the final German offensive at the end of the year.

The IIIrd Panzer Corps, part of Generaloberst von Kleist's Panzergruppe 1, reported only 142 of 338 Panzers available for action on 17 October, and 3,100 of a total of 4,300 vehicles in running order. The report complained, 'the vast majority of vehicles are worn out'. By the time the corps reached Dnepropetrovsk:

'Units had clearly reached the high point of their technical performance capacity. Instead of refurbishment, patching took place! Five hundred kilometres have been added in the meantime, not counting the trips on the battlefield and the rides back for supplies.'[3]

German advance routes and Russian avenues of retreat were carefully combed for usable parts from wrecked trucks. The LSSAH Division Engineer claimed only 50% of his motor transport fleet was fully serviceable at the end of August. Search groups seeking vehicle parts actually fought engagements with their Soviet counterparts for possession of burned-out vehicles.[4]

The Ostheer's motor-vehicle fleet was experiencing serious difficulties. Only 1,000 trucks were allocated to Wehrmacht land forces each quarter to make up losses. This was insufficient to replace those lost through normal wear and tear, never mind enemy action. Fuel was in short supply, and could not be procured as in France by filling up at civilian petrol stations. Russian petrol had a high octane content and could only be used in German vehicles after the addition of benzol, mixed at specially constructed installations. Provision of spare parts was critical. German units in Russia used no fewer than 2,000 different vehicle types. Army Group Centre, the Schwerpunkt for the coming offensive, needed over one million spare parts to support it.[5]

The Eastern Army lacked homogeneity because its motor vehicles were concentrated within a small number of units. Priority was given to these 'fast' Panzer and motorised divisions for breakthrough and exploitation. Infantry forces normally opened the attack paving the way for Panzer break-ins following along afterwards to subjugate enemy units encircled by the fast forces. Ironically this required 75 infantry divisions to be issued 200 Panje horse-drawn carts to supplement their Grosstransportraum. Fast units were checked at about 500km from their start point due to the requirement for lorries to return empty to reload. They had also to carry their own fuel. On average they were driving 2km (because of the need to manoeuvre tactically) for every kilometre of enemy territory conquered.

Technical problems were exacerbated by the absence of metalled roads. Few were anticipated, and these were expected to be low-grade. The reality was even worse, as the small number of metalled roads became degraded within three days of the campaign start, through the volume and pressure of traffic. Heavy rain transformed them into quagmires, and deep sand and dust pushed fuel expenditure up by 30% in dry weather. Raids by groups of cut-off Russians also exacted a considerable toll. Losses were approaching 25% within 19 days of the invasion, rising to one-third within Army Group Centre alone a week later.[6] Columns of marching infantry moving up to relieve the Panzers complicated the problem by bringing resupply convoys to a complete standstill. Junkers Ju52 transport airlifts of petrol had to be substituted within 48 hours of the beginning of the campaign to keep Panzer spearheads moving.

Some of the reality of these statistics is revealed through the diary of a German driver with a transport unit at the end of September. He was often away from his company for three to four days at a time. His 6-ton (French) Renault 'was very good up to a point,' he wrote, 'but not for these roads'. Accidents were common. He carried rations, petrol or ammunition as cargo. On one occasion:

'...transporting munitions we were under fire all day, from 05.00 until 19.00. It was a real "pleasure" with whistling bullets and exploding shells. One man was killed and eight wounded in our ammunition column, but our "blue-eyed [ie lucky] boys" got through.'

Mud and the danger were all pervasive. 'It is forbidden to drive at night,' he explained, 'because there are too many ambushes.'[7] Driving conditions were harsh. Kanonier Mutterlose, serving with the SS 'Leibstandarte's 2nd Artillery Regiment, complained:

'What did I know of our front situation? We sat in our vehicles shrouded in clouds of dust with parched throats and dry lips. We strove to look far ahead because the countryside was as flat as a table. Nothing interrupted the eye.'

Driving by night, in columns, was even worse. Mutterlose noticed the driver:

'. . .was having a bad time of it now. His primary concern was the vehicle ahead of us, whose tail-lights were not functioning. Hans sat far forward hunched over the steering wheel, his eyes drilling through the darkness. Sometimes we could not see a thing because of all the dust, other times there was just a silhouette of the vehicle in front.'

Mutterlose clambered onto the running board and attempted to remedy the problem by steering the driver through signals and shouts. The inevitable happened. 'Suddenly, I noticed the vehicle ahead of us had stopped.' He screamed 'Halt!' but it was too late. As the lorry skidded into the one in front, Mutterlose was catapulted into the road. 'In the silence that followed I could only hear the trickle of radiator water running out into the dirt.' This ominous sound was the precursor of the driver's nightmare: to be left behind alone by the road. The SS column drove by, guided around the crippled truck by flashing torch-light. A long lonely vulnerable night followed until they received a tow into a nearby village for repair. They were promptly ambushed by a group of cut-off Russian soldiers. The truck was blazing furiously by the time they were rescued by another German unit, which had also detoured to resolve its repair problems.[8]

Incidents such as these, combined with other frictions, could make life unbearable and fray nerves. Haphazard resupply had a negative impact on morale. Feldwebel Max Kuhnert vividly recalled a dark march by night, chilly and pelting with rain. The soldier's tent-sheets had not kept them dry. An offer of hot tea, brought up by resupply with a rum included, 'was music to our ears'.

'It was a total disaster and an everlasting shame to our regimental field kitchen staff. Nobody could drink the stuff; not only did it smell evil, but it tasted revolting. Those clots. They had put tobacco instead of tea in the kettle, which was a very large one at that, to hold some 30–40 litres. Then they had put sugar in it, and the precious rum. For quite some time nobody forgot those agonising minutes of disappointment and anger.'[9]

Even before the *Grosstransportraum* reached its 500km practical limit of operations, it was clearly labouring under cumulative pressures made worse by time and distance. Under the prevailing technical conditions of 1941 even the Wehrmacht, a moderately modern and certainly innovative force, remained dependent upon rail transport for strategic reach — just as their predecessors had in 1917.

'Barbarossa' planning was not decisively influenced by the existing road and rail network, but the need to keep operations supplied did influence route consideration. The initial concentration of divisions for the invasion could be achieved only by intensive use of the rail network in German-occupied Poland. Surprise was achieved by transporting the Panzer and motorised divisions last, a tangible indicator of the coming invasion if they had been moved prematurely. Once the offensive began, the fundamental problem was that Russian railways did not conform to the German gauge. Only the railways had the strategic logistic carrying capacity to reach beyond the 500km 'trip-wire' point.

Ideological arrogance leading to an illogical deduction of Russian weakness encouraged German planners to assume the Führer's 'kick in the door' would suffice to bring down the Soviet Union like a stack of cards. A decisive victory was anticipated within the 500km belt immediately to the east of the border. *Eisenbahntruppen* (railway troops) therefore neglected to spend the winter of 1940 exercising the conversion of Russian railways to standard European gauge and were not adequately prepared. Priority was given to the more pressing task of extending the Polish network in anticipation of the German concentration. This resulted in an over-capacity, which was ironically applied to assist in the 'Final Solution' extermination of European Jewry. Even when the invasion began, railway troops had low transport priorities. Equipped with inferior and captured French and English vehicles, they were not able to keep up with the advance. Only one-sixth was motorised and two-thirds had no vehicles at all. They were poorly supplied with fuel by the army groups, and their signals and communications assets could only stretch to 100km.[10] Their numbers were not appropriate to the immense demands they faced. In recognition of this they were supplemented in early July with men from the German *Reichsbahn* (national railways).

As the army groups penetrated the Russian hinterland, the railway troops worked feverishly to restore damage and convert lines to the German gauge. By 10 July 480km had been completed but only about one-tenth of the load capacity required was reaching the army groups.[11] Russian rail-track was lighter than German variants and supported by one-third fewer sleepers, which prevented running heavy locomotives over converted track. Soviet locomotives were larger, their water stations further apart, and many had been destroyed. Russian coal, it was discovered, could not be burned efficiently in German engines without German coal or petrol additives. Damage to signal equipment and rolling stock, bridges and engine sheds, and the elementary point that one double track can carry more capacity than two single ones, reduced German logistic planning figures to theoretical aspirations.

Resupply bottlenecks occurred at the exchange-transfer points between German and Russian railway gauges. A 'catastrophic' situation developed at Schaulen in Army Group North's area on 11 July, when instead of an anticipated three-hour turn-round, some trains took 12, 24 or even 80 hours to unload. Hopeless congestion resulted. Some trains were actually 'lost' in the confusion. Army Group North calculated it needed 34 trains per day (carrying 450 tons each) to meet operational requirements. The maximum achieved on only exceptional occasions was 18. Ninth Army, serving with Army Group Centre, complained it was receiving only one-third of its daily entitlement of trains in early July.[12]

The majority of Soviet division deployments on the eve of war had, by necessity, been by train. Gabriel Temkin, serving in a Russian labour battalion shortly after the outbreak of war, had experienced the German Blitzkrieg through Poland at first hand. He noticed the difference in effect of Luftwaffe attacks on the Russian rail network:

'In Poland the Luftwaffe had managed in the first few days, if not hours, of the war to disorganise the railway transportation system completely. This was not the case in Russia, fortunately. Because of the distances here (in Russia) *and the lack of an alternative transportation system — there was little movement of supplies by trucks — having a functioning rail system was a sine qua non for the Red Army to retain its fighting ability.'*

After air attacks, railway soldiers immediately cleared the debris and completed rudimentary repairs so that 'trains were moving again, slowly, stopping quite often, but moving'. German logistic pressures were insignificant compared to those experienced by Russian armies enduring bottlenecks under relentless air attack the whole time. In addition, the Soviet rail network was engaged in the migration of whole factory complexes complete with workers. These were transported eastward as countless troop trains moved west. Temkin remarked that his mail continued to arrive from his fiancée even 'during this chaotic time'. Despite being slow and sporadic the military postal service continued to deliver to the front. 'The trains were moving,' Temkin emphasised, 'the freight cars often damaged and half-burned but moving.' In the face of seemingly endless military reverses Temkin pointed to the value of small achievements: 'to me it was an encouraging sign,' he said.[13]

The jump-off point for the projected final German assault on Moscow was over 600km from Brest-Litovsk, and little over half-way to Moscow. The German railway network was labouring even at this distance. Generalfeldmarschall von Bock, commander of Army Group Centre, estimated he needed 30 trains per day during August to replenish current consumption and build up stocks for the forthcoming Moscow attack. On average only 18 arrived, although he was promised 24. Even after the conversion of the railway gauge to Orscha and Smolensk by 16 August and other improvements, the objective of 30 trains per day was never achieved. Von Kluge, the commander of Fourth Army, declared on 13 September that 'with growing distances, the army is almost completely dependent on the railways'. Although current consumption was met, the build-up of offensive stocks was less certain. 'The army lives from hand to mouth,' he admitted, 'especially as regards the fuel situation.' The Ninth Army commander was less compromising, commenting the following day that its transport 'was insufficient to support the coming operations'.[14]

Some progress was achieved in September but only limited stocks of *Verbrauchssatzen* (logistic 'units') could be amassed to support the pending offensive. It was not possible to amass the 'buffer' stocks desired: 27 trains were needed daily in September to shunt units into place and locate material forward. Only 16 could be mustered before 22 September, although 27 delivered up to 30 September, producing a limited build-up of stocks. OKW estimated 29 trains would be needed daily during October but could only confirm 20. It was anticipated that November and a cessation of activity due to winter conditions would lessen the requirement to a much reduced three trains daily in order to move winter clothing and equipment.[15]

In any event it was not enough. Material shortages constantly featured in letters sent home from the front. Secret SS Home Front situation reports, monitoring the impact of these letters, referred to the concerns mothers and wives were expressing about the harsh conditions endured by their menfolk at the front. Supply shortages were a feature of correspondence during August and September, together with apprehension at the approach of winter. Observers reported *Feldpost* letters revealed 'soldiers had to endure enormous difficulties because resupply, and with it the supply of combat troops, appeared very difficult'. Within weeks of the final offensive it stated, 'relatives of soldiers serving in the east are much preoccupied today with the accommodation and supply difficulties of German soldiers for the coming winter'. This, in contrast to the very optimistic views expressed at the beginning of the campaign, was now having a cumulative impact. 'Growing difficulties with resupply' was a recurring theme, along with the 'unimaginable huge reserves the Soviet Army possessed in men and material'. There was pessimism over 'the almost certain likelihood of not achieving a decisive outcome in the foreseeable future'.[16]

Army Group Centre was teetering on an intangible logistic trip-wire extending some 500–600km east of the German border from north to south. Motorised transport was designed to keep the 'fast' Panzer and motorised divisions replenished, filling the supply vacuum created as railway construction units sought to close the gap and catch up. Generalmajor Gereke, the Chief of Army Transportation, estimated one railway battalion could change Russian to German track gauges at a rate of 20km per day. Smolensk had been reached, but not the capacities required to stockpile for the coming offensive. Army Group North, able to capitalise on the more sophisticated Baltic rail network, had already reported 84 combat incidents between its railway construction troops and stay-behind Russian troops, suffering 162 casualties in the process.[17]

Overland vehicles, tracked or wheeled, did not offer a solution. The new offensive would start in the autumn with the prospect of worse weather than that already experienced during the closing stages of the battle of Kiev. OKH announced a deficit of 38,000 vehicles on 16 August. Panzer units were on average 50% short, with corps troops and headquarters already 25% down. Infantry divisions with comparably fewer vehicles, and mainly horse-drawn at that, had lost one-quarter of their motorised fleets. The mobile columns required to spearhead the final Blitzkrieg were between one-quarter and one-third below their previous capacity. This time there would be no surprise; the remaining vehicles were worn out and weather prospects were bleak.

The Panzer situation was serious by late summer. At the beginning of September 30% had been destroyed and 23% were under repair. About half of the Panzer divisions foreseen for Operation 'Taifun' had only 34% of their tanks in service. Panzergruppe 1, reduced to 50%, was to continue the advance in the south. Von Bock retained the three remaining Panzergruppen. Generaloberst Guderian's renamed Second Panzer Army had been reduced to a 45% average even before the Kiev encirclement battles. Its 10th Division was at 83% but its 18th was down to 57%. After the battle Guderian's force was reduced to 25% in addition to being badly located some 200km south of the Smolensk-Moscow axis. Its 9th Division — having begun the campaign with 157 Panzers — had only 62 tanks with 67 under repair. Overall the three Panzer corps forming Second Panzer Army (with five Panzer divisions) mustered 252 tanks. General Hoth's Panzergruppe 3 was down to an average of 45% of its strength at the beginning of September and Hoepner's Panzergruppe 4 to between 50% and 75%.[18]

A feverish period of repair and transfer of reserve Panzers forward to the front was undertaken (125 of the 181 tanks available were already positioned at Orscha and Daugavpils). Repair was slow because major overhauls were still being conducted in the Reich. This necessitated a two-way additional journey to and from the front. Logistic difficulties further stymied the transfer process, so that the readiness states of the severely pressed Panzer force could only be raised a further

10%. Guderian's Second Panzer Army, for example, had been promised 100 new Panzers: it received only 50 in time; the remainder were despatched to Orscha, 200km away, by mistake.[19] By 15 September, Army Group Centre had 1,346 serviceable tanks for the forthcoming operation; this was from the 2,609 the divisions theoretically had at their disposal at the outset of the campaign.[20]

Mal-location did not just affect Second Panzer Army, obliged now to advance north-east, an additional 100–200km, instead of due east along the Smolensk–Moscow road. Panzergruppe 3 had to relocate 600km from Leningrad via Luga, Pskov and Nevel to join Army Group Centre south-east of Velizh. Large numbers of Panzers and self-propelled guns broke down during the rapid three to four-day administrative march. Service support vehicles were obliged to move northward from the Panzergruppe assembly area to recover many of these vehicles, denying vital last-minute support to the remainder prior to the offensive. Artillery gun numbers were reduced as a result of half-track prime movers breaking down and a shortage of spare parts.

The logistic brake was applying remorseless attrition. 'Panzergruppe 3's main supply point in the Ribshevo area in no respect carried sufficient supplies to feed a far-reaching attack later on,' admitted Oberst Hans Röttiger, the Chief of Staff of XXXXIst Panzer Corps. Fuel and ammunition were particularly short, as also spare parts for Panzers and artillery towing vehicles. On the eve of battle the corps possessed between 50% and 75% of its strength, about one to one and a half divisions. Its 1st Panzer Division was down to 90 Panzers, having begun the campaign with 154 tanks.[21] Army Group Centre was about to embark on the last thrust on Moscow, although it was over half way with 340km to go, with under half (48%) of its serviceable Panzer strength and without the benefit of surprise.

Luftwaffe Luftflotte 2 HQ, located in woods near Smolensk, was considerably reinforced in anticipation of the coming offensive. The VIIIth Fliegerkorps was moved from the Leningrad front at the end of September and attached to the left wing of the gathering Panzer spearheads to support Panzergruppen 3 and 4. The latter was also reinforced by the IInd Flak Corps configured in the ground role. Only Flak artillery calibres were capable of dealing with Soviet heavy tanks with some certainty. The Ist Flak Corps was placed on the right wing to support Fourth Army and Second Panzer Army. In addition to the relocation of the VIIIth Fliegerkorps, 1StG, 77StG and 26JG, formerly committed in the Kiev area, arrived at airfields in Army Group Centre's area of operations. Once again Luftflotte 2 was positioned to support the army group with massive sortie rates. Meanwhile the 'Legion Condor', KG53, began to attack installations in the greater Moscow area from the night of 1 October. Generalfeldmarschall Albert Kesselring, commanding Luftflotte 2, described the envisaged concept of operations:

'Our air-ground support fighters, following a practice which had already become axiomatic, were to blast a path for the army divisions. Our heavy bombers were to seal off the battlefield to the rear.'[22]

As with the Panzers, the Luftwaffe air situation had changed. There would be no unexpected pre-emptive attack. The front now stretched from Leningrad to the Black Sea, having expanded from 1,200km at the beginning of the campaign to a width exceeding 2,000km. Prior to the Kiev encirclement,

OKW had calculated respective air strengths (from fighters, bombers and reconnaissance aircraft) to be 1,916 German aircraft against 1,175 Russian. Soviet factories had been steadily making good the damage meted out by the Luftwaffe's surprise June air-strikes. A comparison of relative operational strengths on 6 September reveals a German 7% shortfall of bomber and dive-bomber strengths, and an almost 2:1 inferiority of medium- and long-range fighters. The figure was based on an assessment of 1,710 Soviet combat and 1,230 training aircraft, with a further 350 ready in factories. Creative accounting was applied by German planners, who assumed a best case figure of 40% for operational Russian aircraft availability.[23]

German letters from the front, supported by diary and eyewitness accounts, testify to the frequency if not lethal impact of constant Soviet air raids up to and including successive Russian defeats at Minsk, Smolensk and Kiev. These were not confidence-building features during the run-up to the final autumn offensive. Generalfeldmarschall Kesselring confided:

'Preparations for a fresh assault were pushed on from 15 September with coldly calculated ardour. My old friend from Metz days, General Hoepner, commanding Panzergruppe 4 — apparently impressed by the lack of success of Army Group North [at Leningrad] — had little confidence.'[24]

Kesselring observed that the successful Kiev encirclement battles and optimistic expectations of Operation 'Taifun' encouraged OKW to anticipate success. Commanders' doubts, he commented, were to some extent allayed 'by the spirit of the front-line troops'. OKW was pinning its last offensive hopes on the almost mythical ability of the German soldier to snatch victory from apparently impossible conditions. They had yet to lose a campaign. There was total faith in their capability to master this last test. The *Ostheer*, however, had changed its intrinsic character since the heady opening days of 'Barbarossa'.

'TOTSIEGEN' . . . "VICTORED' TO DEATH

By the third week of the Russian campaign total casualties had exceeded those of the entire French Blitzkrieg in 1940. Officers were perishing during the initial period at the rate of 500 per week (524 died between 22 June and the beginning of July), with 1,540 officer casualties occurring in the first seven days of the offensive. This figure represented the combined officer establishments of three German infantry divisions.[1] At the end of July, even before the end of the battle of Minsk, almost 17% more German soldiers had died in Russia than in France. Total losses were 181,000 killed, wounded and missing, compared to 154,754 for the entire French operation. By the end of September the Germans had lost 518,807 casualties, or over three times the losses suffered during the six-week French campaign.[2]

Despite having inflicted three to four million casualties on the Russian army, the cost — at over half a million men — was sufficient to have a fundamental impact on the structure of the original *Ostheer*. The Wehrmacht was achieving a Pyrrhic victory. As early as 11 July, the 18th Panzer Division had been reduced to 83 operational tanks representing 39% of its initial start state. It lost 2,279 men, 13.3% of its strength, in almost 20 days. By the end of the month this figure was approaching 20% and required two Panzer regiments to combine to form one with only 600 men in its two battalions. The division commander ominously warned such losses should not be allowed to continue, 'Wenn wir uns nicht totsiegen wollen' ('if we do not intend to victor ourselves to death').[3] A succession of such victories between June and the beginning of October was affecting the very fabric of the Ostheer. Already seriously injured, the losses of officers, NCOs and men were burning out the seed corn of Blitzkrieg.

The horror of becoming a casualty was all-pervasive. All-encompassing shock is the premier emotion engendered as a projectile tears through vulnerable human tissue. German medical doctor Peter Bamm, serving in an infantry division with Army Group South, described the impact:

'A man — a human being — is wounded. In the split second in which he is hit he is hurled out of the fighting machine and has become, in an instant, utterly helpless. Up to that moment all his energy was directed forwards, against an enemy . . . But now he is thrown back on himself: the sight of his own blood restores him to full self-awareness. At one moment he was helping to change the course of history: at the next he cannot do anything even for himself.'

Following shock there is pain and fear. The wounded were often condemned to lie unattended for hours during intensive fighting before they could be recovered.

'Hours afterwards night falls. Grey fear envelopes him. Will he bleed to death? Will he be found? Is he going to be hit again? Are the Germans retreating? Will he be captured by the Russians?'[4]

If fortunate, the casualty will be dragged or carried back to a shell crater or primitive dug-out where the company aid post offers the first possibility of medical assistance. The regimental medical officer might apply a bandage, a splint or a tourniquet, or give an injection to ease pain. Afterwards the soldier would be laid down somewhere to await the arrival of an ambulance, which would take him to a field dressing station, the next stage in the evacuation chain.

Soldier Erhard Schaumann described the process for those who had not survived this far. 'You'd take half the [metal ID] tag [snapped in two halves, part for the unit and the other left on the man], and that meant the Feldwebel could notify the relatives.' Corpses were buried 'wherever you had a chance, beside a railway or in the woods, and quickly, to prevent epidemics breaking out'. Every soldier was equipped to do this. 'We all had a little spade,' he said, 'on the back of the belt-order.'[5] Those surviving treatment were carried further back to ambulances. A long crowded journey would follow, squashed together with other wounded in semi-darkness, punctuated by the sound of groans. The next time the stretcher was lifted would be into the glare of a hospital theatre lamp prior to surgery.

Dr Paul Rohwedder recalled occasions when his field dressing station was overwhelmed by a sudden influx of casualties. 'It was a tough mission,' he said, describing the aftermath of one action, 'a big burden on us, we buried 63 men. Most of them were dying as they came in.' During such surges of activity, 'we operated day and night'.

'The contacts were short, you'd get masses of wounded then it was all over. We had 1,200 [casualties] inside 48 hours. That's the sort of number you would get over six months in a big [peacetime] clinic. There were seven doctors and one pharmacist, the others were novices who had no idea and

had to be trained. One had to improvise in order to do all that, and we did.'[6]

This pressure of work was not untypical. During a 12-day period in August 1941, the 1st Medical Company of the 98th Infantry Division dealt with 1,253 wounded near Korosten in Army Group Centre's sector.[7]

The next stage of the medical evacuation process was transfer to a field hospital, either in the occupied areas or the Reich, where the wounded could recover and convalesce. 'As the soldiers were as a rule tightly disciplined,' explained Dr Rohwedder, 'the hospital [with its comparative freedoms] was a big break for them.' Morale would rise: 'They were happy, feeling "now I'm in hospital someone will care for me".' Men still succumbed to their injuries, even this far along the chain. 'There were certain nice phrases you'd use to notify the relatives,' said Rohwedder, like 'died peacefully, etc'. A patriotic sense of duty kept the doctor motivated. 'In any war there will be associated losses,' he mused long after the event. 'That can be very painful, but as a doctor and a soldier — a patriot — you've got to stand that.'[8]

Medical Officer Peter Bamm described the medical evacuation chain as:

'A grim conveyor belt which brought the debris of battle to a human repair shop. We could show no sympathy; we couldn't afford to. We should soon have been exhausted and totally unfit for work.'

It was difficult to be completely divorced emotionally from what was going on. Caring for the wounded exacted an intangible and remorseless mental toll.

Leutnant Bamm treated a young soldier seriously wounded during a heroic action against a Soviet pillbox complex which captured the admiration of the whole regiment. 'This story of unparalleled bravery by a handful of infantry,' he said, 'had become a legend in less than a day.' One of the patients was a former student from a technical college in southern Germany, with hideous mutilations to both hands. He bore his detailed and painful examination 'with stoic indifference'. Bamm found it difficult to suppress sympathy for such a poignant case.

'To lose both hands! A student! And 22 years old. The thought flashed suddenly through my mind that he would never again be able to caress a girl's body.'

Three days after the amputations the student's clumsy inability to detonate a hand-grenade with his bandaged stumps resulted in a failed suicide attempt. Gangrene set in which meant the uninfected parts of the remaining arm had to be removed 'in order to save the life that had become worthless to its owner'. Bamm handed over his patient when the unit moved on. He never saw him again. 'The members of our operating group learned from this case,' reflected the disheartened doctor, 'that a hundred successful operations are valueless in the face of one such failure.'[9] Casualty statistics posed an emotional strain beyond measured shortfalls of battle strengths. They badly affected morale.

German officer casualties in the first five weeks of the campaign were extremely high and represented 5.9% of the total.[10] They could not be easily replaced. Officer training lasted 14–18 months. At platoon level, they were often replaced by veteran senior NCOs. An indication of the scale of losses can be gauged from the fact that a typical infantry division had 518 officers on its unit establishment. By the end of July, 2,433 had been killed and 5,464 wounded, an equivalent casualty rate of more than 15 divisions' worth of officers. Nearly 15 more division equivalents were lost in August, but the figure fell to half of this — seven division equivalents — in September. On the eve of the Moscow offensive the *Ostheer* had lost one-third of its officer strength (a total of 37 division equivalents from 117 divisions) which had started the campaign.

These men represented the tip of the spear, the experienced elite of the combat arms: mainly infantry, artillery and Panzer. Many were at the height of their professional prowess, — commanders who had led in Poland, France, the Low Countries and the Balkans. It was these men who were required to think and act in the 'operational' dimension — leaders who took crucial decisions in terms of time and space, following *Auftragstaktik* (a mission-orientated command philosophy). German officers were schooled to achieve objectives while affording subordinates a high degree of freedom of action in their execution. A commander was given the requisite resources — Panzers, artillery or air support — to achieve a mission. How he did it was up to him. This style of command conferred an intrinsic advantage over Soviet commanders accustomed to receiving *Befehlstaktik* (detailed orders). Initiative in their case was circumscribed by painstaking control by senior commanders over its execution. Not only were resources granted, the commander was told in detail how to fulfil his mission. *Auftragstaktik* requires a commander to take independent action and apply creative judgement. Imaginative steps involving risk if necessary can be taken to achieve the desired goal. Time and again German junior officers applied tactical excellence in achieving encirclements or complicated tactical manoeuvres through joint co-ordination with other ground arms and the air force. Remarkable and surprising results were achieved against a more numerous foe. But there was a price to pay, and it was exacted by a fanatical enemy.

Officer deaths, particularly of those sharing the risks and stresses of their subordinates, magnified the sense of dismay felt by the troops when they fell. Experienced officers were important to fighting men who measured survival prospects against the life-span of proven commanders leading from the front. Veteran commander casualties influence tactical and operational flexibility, the very quality that confers battle-winning effectiveness. Officers were planners. They handled communications, the effective two-way passage of orders from above and below which produces success. Responsibility for synergising the effect of combined arms between tanks and aircraft, or infantry and artillery, or together, lay with them. Officers embodied leadership and direction through their very presence — important to men confused at the pace and direction of battle. A strong personality in control of events at the local level conferred the bedrock of stability and motivation needed to keep soldiers moving. Consequently it came as a shock, with repercussions at several levels, if they fell in battle. They were responsible for so much. Coping with the abrupt loss of a leader could cost momentum in the attack or reduce sustainability in defence. General Halder commented on 'remarkably high officer casualties' only three days into the campaign, compared to the 'moderate' losses of wounded and killed. In early July he remarked again on the higher proportion of officer casualties, which by then were 6.6% of total deaths compared to the previous experience of 4.85% in France and 4.6% in Poland.[11]

There is no logical reason for this beyond a spirit of sacrificial patriotism. Nazi ideology extolled group values over the individual. 'You are nothing, *Dein Volk* [your people] are everything.' Wagnerian mythology was pervasive in propaganda and documentary newsreels. Soldierly virtues were extolled through images of tight-lipped heroes against a backcloth of stirring music taken from film director Leni Riefenstahl's *Triumph of the Will*, and the 1936 *Olympia* documentary. *Feldzug in Polen* alongside *Sieg im Westen* glorified modern war, chronicling the campaigns in Poland and France. Blitzkrieg was presented through realistic and gritty campaign footage juxtaposed with victory parades in Berlin where the victorious troops were bombarded with flowers and bouquets by adoring females. The colloquial *Blumenkrieg* expression (literally a 'war of flowers') originated from these mass celebrations of success. Idealistic young officers became imbued with a desire to match these epic precedents. As the new campaign was expected to be short, there would be only a fleeting opportunity to prove themselves. Many paid the ultimate price. Although the *Alte Kameraden* (veterans of previous campaigns) had gloried in public adulation, by the middle of August the war was assuming more a mantle of Wagnerian tragedy rather than triumph. Realisation dawned that the campaign would be no walk-over. Casualty levels assumed horrific proportions.

There is, in any case, a fine dividing line between courage and self-preservation. This is illustrated by an interview between Dr A. Stöhr, a wartime veteran and psychiatrist, and an infantry company commander, who described a typical experience in a 'tight corner'.

'I returned to my position having left battalion headquarters just as a Russian attack came in. My men were streaming back towards me in uncontrolled flight. I beat them back into their positions with the ornamental cane we used to carry at Wolchow [peacetime barracks]. We were able to repel the assault. Later, I and a number of soldiers were decorated for this successful defensive action.'

Subsequent remarks by the same officer reveal an insight of the imperatives that drive commanders and soldiers to acts of courage under duress. He admitted:

'I would rather have joined my men in flight but as an officer I could not. This was due on the one hand to the likely [disciplinary] consequences, while on the other, I was frightened of being considered a coward. Later rationalising my conduct I realised I took this course of action because it was the most effective. We had far more chance of surviving in the position than in flight. It is probably likely, therefore, I hurled my soldiers back into their trenches out of fear of the consequences.'[12]

The commander of IIIrd Panzer Corps, General der Kavallerie Eberhard von Mackensen, believed the scale of officer casualties was undermining the effectiveness of his corps. Its 'fitness for action,' he claimed, was 'only a fraction of what it had been before Kiev, for example'. Many of his officers, including numerous 'combat leaders', had perished. 'In some cases it is more than half.' Across the corps 25% to 35% of officers had been lost and over 10% of the soldiers. 'Specialist' casualties were having a significant impact upon his combat effectiveness. Von Mackensen explained, 'that has a more profound effect on a motorised rather than infantry unit.'[13]

The ability to think on one's feet during combat was expected, but to a lesser degree, from NCOs. These junior leaders were essentially trainers and movers of troops, commanding sections or squads of up to 10 men in the infantry, or a small element — a Panzer or artillery gun — in the other arms. Casualties often resulted in elevation to platoon command if there were no officers left. There was less of a leadership gulf between NCOs and soldiers compared to officers. NCOs provided the deputy commanders, but more often the 'administrators' preparing for combat. This involved making things work, feeding and caring for soldiers, with minor but cumulatively important supervisory tasks such as ammunition resupply, organising sentry rotations or controlling an important weapon or technical capability.

NCO losses were fearsome. One analysis of casualty figures in an infantry (Schützen) regiment with the 11th Panzer Division reveals 48 deaths prior to Operation 'Taifun', with 79 by the end of the year and 210 wounded. The effective full strength of a company would normally lie between 150 and 170 men. Intense periods of combat coinciding with peaks of fighting in July and August reveal the majority of casualties to have been NCOs and senior soldiers. Of 29 killed in July, all but one were within this category, as were 11 of 13 killed in August.[14] Numbers of wounded were on average three times that of fatalities.

A typical infantry division numbered 518 officers, 2,573 NCOs and 13,667 men. NCOs represented 18.8% of the whole. Evidence suggests — as in the case of Infantry Regiment 110 — that NCO casualties were much higher than soldiers. Even accepting a low estimate of 20% casualties of the whole, an interpretation of OKW casualty figures (see Appendix 2) suggests the manning equivalent of at least 13 divisions' worth of NCOs had been lost in killed, wounded and missing by the end of July. In August 15 division equivalents were lost and nearly 11 in September. By the start of the Moscow offensive nearly 39 division manning strengths had become casualties or about one-third of all the NCOs (from 117 divisions) who had started the campaign. Therefore, about one-third of the veteran leaders of the Ostheer had perished even before the final offensive of the year. Such an abrupt changeover has implications for tactical flexibility and operational effectiveness. The blood-letting in the ranks was on an even grander scale.

Gerhard Meyer, serving in an artillery unit, claimed the battles around the River Dnieper crossings of 23 July 'cost blood on blood' in a 'high priced to-and-fro of constant fighting around four positions'. His division was reduced to less than half its strength and 80% of the officers had perished. He wrote despairingly:

'To believe, amidst the smell of decaying bodies, that this life has a beginning and end, and is the only purpose and reason for our existence is totally unacceptable. It seems idiotic to me that there is still no order in this world.'

Three weeks later Meyer reported 'two-thirds of the division has now been rubbed out', and his commander was wounded and had been captured by the Russians. The division was on the defensive.

'As I traversed the dreadful "street of misery", a straight track leading from the gun position to the administrative area on my way to wash, I noticed holes had already been freshly dug among the rows of graves to left and right.'

One of these holes was earmarked for his friend, a signals section commander, who had also come from Würzburg, his home town. They had been sitting together talking about old times when he got up to retrieve his coat spread out to dry 15m away. He 'waved back to me' Meyer said, 'and at that moment was struck in the head by a shell splinter'. His battery commander, a father with three young sons, was also interred there. Meyer was reminded of 'the old song about the blood-red dawn lighting the way to an early death, which became comprehensible for the first time'. He confided to his diary, 'whoever is not a soldier would not understand'.[15]

Unteroffizier Robert Rupp, equally despondent, wrote in his diary on 12 July:

'Many of the others seem particularly cheerless.
I considered whether I ought to write a letter to Maria [his wife], so that it would be in my pocket should I never get to go home.'

Two days later the company dead were piled on a lorry, which had to be towed into their position because it had been disabled by a strike in the radiator. 'H. was there,' he noticed, 'with his wedding ring on the finger.' One of the Unteroffizier section commanders told him, 'it looks like the whole of his squad had been taken out'. He had 'three dead, four seriously wounded and the others were at least badly injured'. Morale was low; 'everyone is very gloomy, very quiet,' said Rupp. The dismal task of sorting through the possessions of the dead and wounded followed. Private things were separated from military. Shaving utensils and writing materials were shared out among the other soldiers because they were short. 'It is sad work,' he confessed. Pocket fighting had exacted a serious toll. The company was being led by a Leutnant one month later (normally a Major's appointment). Another Leutnant was wounded within 24 hours of his arrival at the front. He had confided to one of Rupp's friends that 'the company commander insisted on senseless sacrifices, but I am not going to be considered a coward'. It was a particularly dismal incident. The company commander had been wounded in the leg and his company pinned down. 'Wait here you cowards,' he had called out. 'If I could still run I would soon show you how to attack.' Thirteen more men were wounded to prove him wrong. Even the company commander's batman was shot in the stomach and another soldier through the nose. 'One hundred and sixty-two men have been taken-out so far,' said Rupp, 'not including the sick.'[16] This meant that, taken from a company fighting establishment of 176, often in reality much lower, very few veterans survived from those who had crossed the border on 22 June. These were depressing survival statistics.

There were approximately 16,860 soldiers in a German infantry division. By the end of July casualty figures reveal that the equivalent of 10 full divisions had been lost. August was even worse, with 11.6 divisions, and a further 8.3 divisions were removed from the order of battle before the end of September. The Ostheer was indeed 'victoring itself to death'. Before the onset of Operation 'Taifun' at the beginning of October, nearly 30 divisions' worth of casualties had been lost. This figure exceeded the entire strength of Army Group North's 26 divisions, which had been sufficient to fight to the gates of Leningrad. These losses represented three-quarters of the size of Army Group South, now in the Ukraine, and three-fifths that of Army Group Centre in June.

Dry statistics do not encapsulate the full significance of the negative impact upon those remaining. Pressure was moral, psychological and physical, all cumulative in their effect. The moral and psychological character of the *Ostheer* was intangibly but perceptibly changing. Faith remained in the Führer's ability to see the campaign through to a successful conclusion, but *Feldpost* letters written by educated and articulate soldiers were beginning to question the extent of the sacrifice relative to the value of the objective. One soldier, writing to his former schoolmaster, apologised for not answering his letters for two months. His 'bad conscience' was quoted as part reason.

'The contrast between what you are saying and what I could tell you is so crass I feel unable to write without being under considerable moral pressure.'[17]

The gulf between front and home was virtually insurmountable. It applied pressure in two directions. Front soldiers were reluctant to reveal the reality of their experiences for fear of worrying their loved ones. Conversely, those at home had no idea what they endured. Infantryman Harald Henry, although prepared to reveal his innermost thoughts to his diary, struggled with any imperative to inform those at home.

'Mother writes how much knowledge of our suffering torments her. Should I not write at all, simply offering greetings each time and that I am still in one piece? If so, who knows where I have already been!'[18]

A number of factors enabled the *Ostheer* to endure privation and enormous casualties. The realities of war produced increasing cynicism alongside growing experience. Dr A. Stöhr, for example, recalls 'actually witnessing a case during the Polish campaign when a German infantry company stormed the citadel at Brest-Litovsk singing the German National Anthem'. His veteran judgement was that patriotism combined with tactical training, repeated so often it became automatic, kept the German soldier going:

'One did what one practised a hundred times. Take cover! You give fire support — I will move! Jump up — go! Orders were to be followed above all else. The natural survival mechanisms to hesitate were turned off by this automatic process.'[19]

Patriotism continued and was rationalised as 'duty'. It did, however, became tempered with a more realistic appraisal of what should constitute 'sacrifice'.

Another motivation was so called *Halsschmerzen*. This so-called 'sore-throat' affliction was suffered by heroes who aspired to the Knight's Cross, Germany's highest order for bravery, worn at the throat. Its holder, whether officer or soldier, was entitled to a salute by all ranks. The medal was implicit recognition: 'I have proved myself.' Knight's Cross holders were less inclined to avoid tight situations because collective peer pressure anticipated results. Nazi propaganda extolled the concept of a 'nation of heroes'. The resulting by-product was a crop of veterans who mastered their lethal craft. One former soldier described them as:

'Those soldiers who were called "excellent chaps or fellows". They were men who recognised their calling and

carried out the tank- and bunker-busting required of them. They led the assault teams or long-range patrols, being hauled in or volunteered freely when the situation was especially precarious. Their names were known throughout their units.'

Killing was their expertise, and as such they were bizarrely appreciated in the same vein that football or racing-car heroes are feted in peacetime. Veteran A. Stöhr remarked, 'they were not particularly unique because every other man also risked being killed himself all the time'. War also changed men. Veterans remarked that the scale alternated between sensible types, who overcame their fear, to insensitive psychopaths, who, because they lacked imagination, knew no fear. Alongside doubters fought fanatic 'Hitlerites', to whom everything was the same. Stöhr recalled a Feldwebel whose bride was killed before his eyes during an allied bombing raid. From that moment on he became a 'hero', whose reckless courage won him the right to wear a string of tank victory badges on his sleeve, proof he had destroyed seven tanks single-handed in combat. At his throat hung the Knight's Cross, 'a hero,' Stöhr remarked, 'because his own life had become unimportant'.[20]

Hardship at the front was a physically cumulative and psychologically wearing process. Fewer surviving soldiers meant more to do — notably sentry and other security duties — for those remaining. There is also universal comment in *Feldpost* letters and diaries from soldiers about the filth, dust, mud and lice and other discomforts on the Russian front. Obergefreiter Erich Kuby wrote typically in his diary on 19 August, 'I slept miserably in a soaking bed and developed a headache. Since 22 June I have spent every single night in the open.'[21]

Fresh food, which had been reasonably plentiful in the summer, became increasingly difficult to commandeer in the autumn. Haphazard marching routines punctuated by unexpected periods of sustained or intense fighting meant soldiers ate poorly, and when they could. Incessant hard marches with poor food produced intestinal complaints and diarrhoea, which by the fourth consecutive month of the campaign was draining physical reserves. Natural body resistance was on the decline, colds and fever commonplace, further raising the susceptibility to disease. The prospect of enduring a Russian winter in the open became both depressing and alarming to soldiers at the front and their concerned relatives at home.

A 'Leibstandarte-SS' medical report surveying supplies reaching combat troops revealed their nutritional value was on average 'more than a quarter below what they should have received'. In particular, 'the supply of fat is always remarkably low', as also the intake of vitamin C. Summer foraging had compensated for the shortfall but, by late autumn and winter, opportunities to supplement this meagre diet fell away. This eventually 'led to considerable numbers of men being taken out of service due to illness'. Harsh conditions and insufficient resupply reduced core body resistance to face the approaching winter. The 'Leibstandarte' doctor wrote:

'Aside from a reduction in body weight, one is further aware of an increased susceptibility to disease and a tendency for these to last longer with more pronounced effect. The cause, as with the generally noticeable prolongation of wound healing times with a tendency to develop complications, can be ascribed to reduced body resistance caused by insufficient nutrition.'[22]

Casualties and harsh physical demands were starting to erode the moral component of the *Ostheer*'s fighting power. A sociological transformation was to occur during the coming winter. The supremely committed idealistic army that had crossed the demarcation line in eastern Poland on 22 June was undergoing change. Many of its commanders, including junior officers and NCOs, had been veterans of World War 1. The youngest were in their early 40s, serving both with the *Kampftruppen* (combat arms) and staffs. They were less able to endure the drawn-out hardships of a campaign which was totally unlike France, where they had been able to purloin comfortable billets at will. Cumulative physical and psychological pressure alongside the attrition of incessant combat, with still no prospect of victory four months into the offensive, exacted a toll. Atrocities were removing much of the idealistic gloss from soldiers who originally considered they were participating in a 'crusade against Bolshevism'. Leutnant Peter Bamm referred to the original volunteers of 1914 as 'a fellowship apart', adding, 'they greeted each other with an old-fashioned and traditional courtesy.'

'These old soldiers, who as beardless striplings had been the heroes of Verdun and the Somme, now that they were adult men and not easily ruffled attempted to preserve chivalrous traditions in this war too. The younger soldiers were less sceptical and thus more courageous; but theirs was the courage not of probity but of fanaticism.'

Hauptmann Klaus von Bismarck described his own Infantry Regiment 4 as 'conservative', claiming 'there were no Nazis with us in Kolberg' (their original garrison town). But later, 'I noticed from about 1941 onwards, how far the leadership at the top had already been successful in infecting the army [with Nazism] — ever more'. Leutnant Bamm described the development as a 'rot that during the course of the years had slowly infected the army like a creeping thrombosis'. As the 1914–18 generation of soldiers were killed or succumbed to nervous and physical exhaustion, they were replaced by less competently trained but less compromising and younger men. These men had either been educated under National Socialism, or owed their recent advancement to it. Von Bismarck pointed out:

'There were many reactivated officers in my own regiment who had "muddled through" during the Weimar period. That means once proud officers who had lived many years beneath their socially expected standing. Then all of a sudden they had been elevated again by the "Führer". These people were the willing instruments of Nazi politics.'[23]

Traditional reservist commanders, such as Leutnant Haape's battalion commander in Infantry Regiment 18, a World War 1 veteran, were beginning to feel the strain of incessant combat. Haape noticed how easily he fell asleep on occupying quarters as the weather grew colder. 'It had become noticeable,' he observed, 'that the strains and stresses of these days were beginning to affect him more than the rest of us, and his responsibilities seemed to weigh more heavily on him by the day.'[24] An important strata of collective experience in the *Ostheer* was becoming worn out.

Heavy casualties produced a spiral of mutual concerns that applied both to soldiers at the front and to their relatives and loved ones at home. Rumours of heavy casualties prompted the despatch of emotional letters to the front which could be equally devastating to the soldiers receiving them. 'My dearest and good Helmut,' wrote one wife on 21 September:

'I am already totally unsettled having had no post from you since 31 August. Perhaps something will arrive in the morning because nothing was there on Sunday today . . . It's really difficult to stay calm. I think I ought to write to your Hauptmann again, that I want to have a child, because I was born to be a mother. A man offered to get me out of my embarrassment from compassion. But you do not have to worry my dear "Papa", I could never go behind your back. I would never be able to face you again . . . I have to make do with only a quarter of a gram of butter the whole week . . . I have no peace of mind. People at work have already noticed I hardly ever smile.'[25]

Black barrack-room humour was often the only antidote to emotional pressures such as these. Soldier Hanns-Karl Kubiak described the plight of his friend, Obergefreiter Gerhard Scholz, when he discovered during an unexpected home leave that his wife 'had not precisely followed the marriage vows' as anticipated. The sardonic response of his comrades to the divorce that followed was to poke fun at the propaganda theme requiring men to defend their homes and families. Scholz obviously 'no longer needed to fight for his wife at home'.[26]

Concerns for families left at home, beginning to endure the threat of Allied night-time bombing, created further nervous tension at the front. Berlin housewife Ingeborg Tafel wrote to her husband on 15 September:

'There have been four air raid warnings already since you departed. We can reckon on the "Tommies" [British air raids] coming today, because the sky is brilliantly clear.'

Three weeks later she told her husband about the emotional effect of her young brother's death.

*'A letter finally arrived from Gerhard today. So shocked was he at the news of the death of his little brother that he cried shamelessly like a kid. He crawled into his tent while shells were whistling over him feeling totally empty and apathetic. He beseeched his mother to look after herself because she was all that was left to him in the world making life worth living.
— Darling, let everything go well with you and return safely to us all.'*[27]

Todesanzeigen (death notices) produced rashes of black crosses across newspaper pages announcing the *Heldentod* (heroes' death) of those 'fallen for the Führer and Fatherland'. There was depression in the Reich. Secret SS home front reports recalled Hitler's Sportpalast speech of the previous year which hinted the war should be over in 1940–41. 'Now one is faced with a further year of war with new fronts and a further expansion of the conflict,' the report read. The general tenor was: 'who would have thought the war would have lasted so long?' and, 'it has already lasted two years'. Yet another anniversary of the beginning of the war (1 September) had passed, 'and still no end in sight'.[28] Actress Heidi Kabel recalled the impact of the casualty notices published in the press:

'Terrible, friends and then colleagues went missing and nothing was ever heard of them again . . . There was no patriotic "gung-ho" hurrah feelings like in World War 1 over how the war was going. It never happened like that.'[29]

Observations of home front morale assessed 'the population is beginning to take the view that the war in the east will not end as quickly as was anticipated following early successes'. Rumours fuelled by numerous *Feldpost* letters quoted high casualties among certain identified units. 'Death notices in the newspapers,' read one report, 'in particular a number of publicly known personalities who have died, exacerbate the extensive public concern over German losses in the east.' The 1st SS Division 'Leibstandarte Adolf Hitler' had reportedly 'lost 60% of its strength'; another rumour claimed 'officer casualties in all units were way beyond all expectations'. In one town it was alleged 23 men had perished from a community of only 3,000. SS Home Front reports observed, 'the population is becoming increasingly convinced from front reports that Soviet resistance appears not to be decreasing and that clearly the enemy has further huge reserves of matériel available.'[30]

The handling of death notices attracted intense criticism, as revealed by one lengthy SS Home Front survey. It criticised an insensitive and inefficient bureaucratic system responsible for gross errors. Probate wills were being returned stamped 'Fallen for Greater Germany', before families had even been officially informed by the Wehrmacht Army Office. Suffering was, in any case, unavoidable. Hildegard Gratz in Angerburg recalled 'the first "black letter" for our family' came with the advent of the Russian war. Her brother-in-law had perished on the very first day of the campaign.

'Suddenly everything changed. The radio carried on broadcasting news of victories. But the daily papers carried endless columns of death notices.'[31]

Such inconsistencies were not lost on the population. Rumours intensified as black stories abounded. A wake organised at St Ingbert on the basis of a witness report sent by letter from a comrade who had witnessed the 'death' was cancelled after a hospital notification that the 'deceased' had survived. Some 'killed in action' letters of condolence were thoughtlessly composed, graphically describing the wounds that led to death and sometimes even the duration and extent of suffering. 'Two particularly crass cases were reported from Düsseldorf,' noted the SS Home Front survey. A death notice inserted through a letter box with normal mail when there was no answer resulted in a housewife discovering her husband had died as she sorted through routine correspondence while her children were present. Another unfortunate mother was handed her tragic news at the tram stop, with her children, while the unsuspecting postman continued on his round. She screamed and fainted in the street. The SS report recommended numerous humane changes to procedure.[32]

'Being a postman suddenly became an unpleasant occupation,' commented Hildegard Gratz. 'He became the bringer of bad news.'

'There were these terrible letters, and the postmen told stories of pitiful scenes of grief. The postman came to dread his round if ever there was one of those black-edged letters to be delivered. It wasn't just a question of witnessing grief and suffering. The official line was that women were bearing their news "with proud grief" but many of the women in their despair screamed out curses on this "damned war". This was a risky business, such people were supposed to be reported.'

The war was sucking the very vitality from normal life. 'Three young women went around our village in black that autumn of 1941,' said Frau Gratz. 'I had danced at their weddings, and they at mine.'[33]

On 18 September the press announced the death of Generaloberst Ritter von Schobert, the commander of the Eleventh Army, killed six days before when his Fieseler Fi156 Storch light aircraft force-landed in a minefield. 'Just imagine how high casualties among officers and men must be,' was the public perception, 'if even an army commander is killed'.[34] Casualties produced a nagging unease throughout the Reich during August and September. Rumours were temporarily allayed on 22 September when the 'Announcement of Eastern Campaign Losses' was revealed: about 86,000 had died and almost 22,000 were missing. The figures were reasonably accurate (87,489 and 19,588 respectively). Conjecture had varied from 200,000 at the low end of the scale to one million as the worst case. The figures 'have in one blow,' according to the official assessment, 'settled the uncertainty'. Although viewed as costly at first, they were eventually accepted as an inevitable expense for 'the harshness of the battle against Bolshevism'. People temporised, claiming they were lower than World War 1 losses with far greater success to show for it. Interestingly, the 'wounded' totals were not given: they numbered 302,821. Soviet casualty figures were, in any case, calculated as far higher, with 1.8 million prisoners taken and reportedly 3–4 million dead.[35]

The impact of German losses was tearing away at the very fabric of the *Ostheer*. The cream had likely already perished. Even the SS, who had begun this battle supremely confident and motivated, were expressing doubts. The commander of the 4th SS Infantry Regiment 'Der Führer' wrote:

'The campaign in the east had begun with unspeakable harshness. We were all firmly convinced of the necessity of this battle, all believed in our leaders and in our own strength and were in no doubt that we would emerge victorious from this confrontation.

'But in spite of all the confidence, in spite of all our self-confidence, a feeling of isolation crept over us when we — following the army's armoured spearheads — advanced into the endless expanses of Russia. We did not share the unfounded optimism of many who hoped that they might spend Christmas 1941 at home. For us the Red Army was the big unknown, which we had to take seriously, which we could not underestimate. The goal of this struggle lay in the unforeseeable future.'[36]

Army Group South, which would support the right flank, had similar misgivings. The commander of its IIIrd Panzer Corps reminded the commander of Panzergruppe 1, Generaloberst von Kleist, that 'it is psychologically wrong to drive a unit that has proven its fitness'. More than half of his combat leaders had fallen in some units and his Panzers were reduced from 338 to 142. 'The vast majority of all vehicles are worn out,' he lamented. His comments concerning the fighting power he was able to muster were more significant. 'Morale,' he explained, 'is weighed down' by the increasing frequency of Russian air raids and the apparently inexhaustible reserves of Russian ammunition. Both factors 'will only increase as the Russians move back to their unattacked positions and reach their stocks of ammunition and matériel'. His men were depressed 'by the fact that the final goal seems out of sight'. Moreover 'the number of men out of commission proves that the Russians are by no means "beaten" as it might appear in the big picture' — a statement all the more significant coming, as it did, three weeks after the annihilation of several Russian armies in the Kiev pocket. The men were worn down. 'Readiness for action for the personnel can only be achieved with a few days of rest outside the area of Russian fire.' So far as 'material' was concerned, 'no full readiness can be expected anymore'.[37]

One artillery NCO serving with Army Group Centre expressed his foreboding more succinctly. 'God save us from a winter campaign in the east,' he wrote. 'It is very cold here already and it rains practically every day.'[38] Infantryman Harald Henry noted in his diary on the eve of Operation 'Taifun' that even 'at the beginning of this new offensive we had no rest for 44 hours having been incessantly on the march'. Pressure was beginning to tell:

> 'You couldn't imagine how it is with endless nights with no cover or coats in a half-open barn or even digging in under the open sky! One cannot even unfasten one's equipment if the enemy is nearby. You have to sleep through the awful cold, battered again by icy storms tonight like the one before, already soaked by freezing rain, with your marching pack still attached to your back.'[39]

The German infantryman was at the end of his tether, as was also the fighting power of the *Ostheer*.

A DYING ARMY

The fighting power of an army can be broken down into three components: the conceptual, physical and moral.[1] The conceptual is 'how' the campaign is to be fought and includes the strategy and operational and tactical plans to support it. Successful Blitzkrieg was dependent upon the flexibility conferred by the *Auftragstaktik* concept of mission command tactics. Up to one-third of the veteran leadership of the *Ostheer*, its officers and senior NCOs, had perished by the eve of Operation 'Taifun'. These were veteran combat leaders, men who had been killed leading from the front. Although they represented one-third of the whole, in logistic 'tail' compared to forward 'teeth' terms they represented a greater loss, more like 50%, because only a small proportion of a typical division actually closes with the enemy. (See Appendix 3.) Such men were irreplaceable. Eighteen months was required to train individual replacements, but the seed-corn of experience had been irretrievably lost. Therefore the conceptual component, the command and leadership of the fighting element of the *Ostheer*, had been grievously injured.

The physical component represents the sum of resources: manpower, logistics, equipment and the training and readiness that makes up the whole. In manpower terms the *Ostheer* had

suffered over half a million casualties, more than three times what it had lost in France. Thirty division equivalents were for practical purposes removed from the order of battle, a loss greater than the size of Army Group North, which had fought itself to Leningrad. A logistic 'trip-wire' had been crossed past which little could effectively be squeezed beyond physical choke-points. War-winning priority equipment — Panzers, artillery prime movers and motorised vehicles — were worn out. There was barely 500km of effective life in them before major overhauls and replacements would be needed to avoid breakdowns. This was hardly sufficient to reach Moscow.

The third and decisive component was the moral, the 'hearts' that sustain the conceptual 'mind'. Losing the cream of its combat leadership affected not only the flexibility, experience and professionalism of the remainder, it also impacted on the will to fight. Most *Landser* were committed and motivated by duty to fight. There was, however, some questioning of the practical ability to reach Moscow, even if it was the last major objective. The debilitating and cumulative impact of stress and physical deprivation was wearing men down. Doubts and scepticism are evident in *Feldpost* letters and diaries that survive from this period at the front. 'Duty' was being eroded to some extent by a moral questioning in some instance of the 'justness' of a cause that was inflicting state-sponsored terror upon the local populace. Interestingly, the official history of the Potsdam-Berlin Infantry Regiment 9 fighting on the Central Front is entitled 'Between Duty and Conscience'.[2] Preaching ideological conflict was not the same as physically inflicting its implications upon a helpless civilian populace. Soldiers feel more at ease with the certainty of a just and clearly identified cause to rationalise the violence they are called upon to execute in battle. A degree of moral degradation was also afflicting the *Ostheer*. Thinking men had to come to terms with the immense cost and ghastly implications of prosecuting an ideological 'Total War'.

The *Ostheer* was bleeding profusely. All three of the primary components constituting its fighting strength were seriously damaged. The assumption that kept the force going was that the Russians were even more grievously hurt. Victory was achievable, it was felt, if the final Soviet field army standing before Moscow could be decisively defeated. Such a catastrophic reversal might indeed provide the catalyst required to convince the Soviet regime to conclude an armistice and allow the occupation of Moscow. Failure was never seriously countenanced, despite the parlous state of the Eastern Army itself. The Wehrmacht had never been defeated in this war, but neither had it sustained such punishment in any previous campaign. It was practically 'victoring itself to death'.

'VICTORY WITHOUT RESULTS'

Left:
'All roads disappear to the horizon,' wrote one German soldier. The long drive to the front.

Below:
A snatched meal for German infantry in Vyazma, apparently oblivious to the blazing destruction around them.

Left:
Two pictures taken during the assault crossing of the River Dniesper prior to Kiev. The soldiers, festooned with equipment, have boarded the crowded assault boat. Two assault pioniers are manning the tiller as the craft surges out into the muddy waters of the river. Shots are passing overhead.

Right:
The cameraman has moved forward as the boat nears the enemy bank. The number 2 machine gunner with the spare barrel slung across his shoulder is clutching boxes of ammunition. All eyes are on the shoreline, a blind spot on the steep slope of the enemy bank. Tension is clearly visible in the faces of alert and apprehensive soldiers.

Left:
An infantry assault group equipped with bags of bundled stick grenades snatch a breather before they are committed to battle. Fatigue and nerves have taken their toll as they apprehensively await the order to move forward.

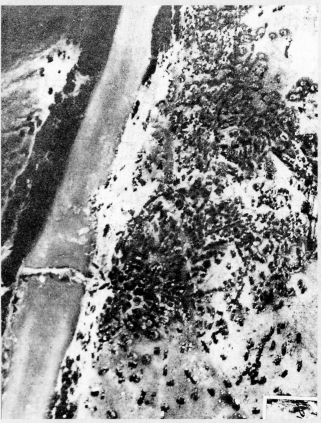

German infantry moving through the centre of Kiev shortly after the city's fall.

Panic on the River Dniester as a traffic jam of marooned Russian vehicles, resembling a swarm of bees from the air, lies helpless beneath German Stuka dive-bomber attacks. The pontoon bridge to the left has been destroyed. Vehicles have driven in all directions to escape the merciless air bombardment.

Operation 'Taifun' was launched in the 'Hitler weather' of an autumn Indian summer at the beginning of October 1941. German infantry here on the march are driving captured Soviet lorries. A German horse-drawn artillery column is following behind. Victories at Vyazma and Bryansk produced this Blitzkrieg-type tempo once again.

Chapter 13
The last victory

'It ought to finish here before the onset of winter. That means the end of this month should see the conclusion [of the campaign].'

German soldier's letter home

DOUBLE ENCIRCLEMENT... VYAZMA AND BRYANSK

Artillery Hauptmann Georg Richter felt the sun on his back as he observed the Russian positions from the heights overlooking the River Desna. It was 1 October, a beautiful autumn day. His unit, Artillery Regiment 74, was in support of the 2nd (Viennese) Panzer Division belonging to Generaloberst Hoepner's Panzergruppe 4. The river lay in the dead ground before him. Scanning the other side, he was able to locate eight Russian bunkers. Both sides were harassing each other with sporadic artillery fire.

Richter wrote in his diary that night, 'I believe the attack will start the next day; in my opinion it will be the last big operation this year.' The woodland on the heights 'was just like an exercise area where another track opens up as soon as a vehicle goes by'. It was a fragile peace. Mines were going off intermittently. Only 150m away a gun exploded as it was being guided into its firing position. Shortly after, a platoon prime mover (artillery towing vehicle) also blew up on a mine. There had been time while all this was going on to review the future. Doubts were less about whether the objective would be reached, but rather how the eventual victory would be played out.

'The question is: will Moscow be included in the huge pocket about to be created, or would the ring close immediately in front of the towers of the capital?'[1]

Unteroffizier Helmut Pabst, serving with Ninth Army, declared, 'We don't yet know when it will start,' but it would obviously be soon. 'Somebody has seen the tanks,' he said, 'the yellow ones which were meant for Africa.' All sorts of weapons — SP assault guns, Nebelwerfer multi-barrelled rocket launchers and heavy guns — were appearing in his sector. 'It's piling up inexorably like a thunderstorm,' he observed. News was pieced together by the soldiers 'like bits of a mosaic'. The front was showing all the signs of impending developments. Pabst and his men perceived 'the veil over the calm getting thinner, the atmosphere gathering tension'.[2] The storm was about to break.

At 04.40 hours the next morning — and 'a hot day', commented Richter — at least 20 batteries of artillery opened up around him in a 'dazzling display of fire'. Simultaneously, 'Stuka squadrons appeared from our rear and began to fly in huge circles', awaiting direction for targets. A Focke-Wulf twin-fuselage reconnaissance aircraft curved by and appeared to transmit the objective to the Stukas, 'who dived, huge detonations testifying to the power of their bombs'. Richter watched as directed artillery fire began to straddle the bunkers. 'To our left a noticeable series of hissing reports captured our attention' as Nebelwerfer rocket salvoes streaked out toward the Russian positions — 'long trails of white smoke across the sky'.

'Any war film would pale by comparison,' commented Unteroffizier Pabst. He counted about 1,200 tanks, not including assault guns, advancing on a 2km front. After the artillery preparation he watched as 'assault guns and motorised infantry come on without a pause'. Roads appeared across fields which 15 minutes previously had been a featureless expanse. He remarked the assault was 'far bigger than the one on the frontier defences' the previous June. 'It will be some time before we see a picture like this again.' The Russian defensive crust had first to be broken. Georg Richter monitored the forward movement closely through binoculars. 'White Very signals indicated the front line,' he said, 'and red was a request to shift [artillery] fire in depth.' Red lights were constantly arcing across the terrain to their front.[3] Operation 'Taifun', the final attack towards Moscow, was under way.

Guderian's Second Panzer Army to the south had the greater distance to cover and had begun its offensive from the Gluchow area on 30 September. This was within four days of the officially announced conclusion of the Kiev battle. He pushed north-eastward against the Bryansk–Orel line with five Panzer divisions, four motorised infantry, one cavalry and six foot-marching infantry divisions. To the north, and on the left flank of Second Panzer Army, eight infantry divisions belonging to Second Infantry Army began to move forward to complete an encirclement of Soviet forces in the Bryansk area. A second pocket was foreseen around Vyazma. Left of Second Army, and further north, Hoepner's Panzergruppe 4 in concert with Generalfeldmarschall von Kluge's Fourth Army provided the *Schwerpunkt* for the attack with 15 foot divisions, five Panzer and two motorised infantry divisions.

They were to advance due east from Roslavl to Moscow with their left flank on the upper Dnieper river east of Smolensk. The northern flank of Army Group Centre held Strauss's Ninth Army with Panzergruppe 3 (Hoth) under command. It contained 18 infantry divisions, three Panzer and two motorised infantry divisions. Attacking north-east of Smolensk, their task was to penetrate Russian defences north of the Smolensk–Moscow road and cover the flank along the upper Volga river. Army Group Centre had been reinforced by an additional seven 'fast' divisions from Army Group North. Its sister formation, Army Group South, had placed one further Panzer, two motorised infantry and five foot divisions under command.

As envisaged in the original 'Barbarossa' concept, Panzergruppen 4 (Hoepner) and 3 (Hoth) were massed on the outer flanks of their respective infantry armies. Both Panzer forces were to drive eastward first then turn inwards, this time to encircle Vyazma. Subsidiary encirclements would be executed by the infantry armies as in the first battles east of the Bug, loosely enclosed by the pincers of the larger Panzer envelopments. Once the rings were closed the Panzers would leave the infantry armies behind to subjugate the pockets while they pushed on, maintaining maximum strength and tempo in the direction of Moscow. The Luftwaffe IInd and VIIIth Fliegerkorps had committed over nine fighter and nearly 15 fighter-bomber Geschwader, with eight Stuka, a Bf110, and intermediate- and long-range reconnaissance Geschwader and

Staffeln in support. On the ground the Ist and IInd Flak Corps provided anti-aircraft and ground-role anti-tank assistance. The offensive took the Russians completely by surprise. They had felt it was too late in the year to launch another campaign.

Hauptmann Richter's opening day of the offensive was beset by worries over the effectiveness of Russian mines. The third vehicle of his artillery column was abruptly blown into the air as they changed location to support the forward advance. His diary recorded it as the fourth mine strike in only two days. He quickly reached the damaged vehicle to recover the driver, who appeared uninjured, but 'his face was as white as snow and he was shaking all over'. Richter drove through several villages toward the previously observed enemy bunkers. En route they saw 'only a few curious inhabitants staring out of the doors'.

Soviet resistance along the line of bunkers was as tenacious as ever. Assault pioneers had directed artillery and Panzers in the direct-fire role and heavy infantry weapons close-up to embrasures and entrances, to no visible effect. Grenade after grenade was tossed in and one of Richter's over-zealous NCOs was wounded in the process. Huge detonations reverberated but, as soon as the smoke cleared, pistol shots rang out as entry was sought. One captured Russian was motioned inside a bunker to persuade the crew to surrender. After disappearing from view a single shot rang out. 'He didn't come back,' observed Richter. Artillery again commenced smashing at the entrance and more grenades were tossed in,, and still German casualties occurred as they attempted to break in. In exasperation the assault group sprinkled petrol across the entire bunker mound and set it on fire. Deprived of air, three Russian soldiers hesitantly emerged. 'Several of our men were so frustrated and enraged they wanted to mete out summary justice,' said Richter. 'We quietened them down, conceding that we had at least emptied the bunker, but it had cost time.' Fighting carried on throughout the night:

'There was shooting everywhere. Soon the village was on fire. Enemy tanks had shot it into flames, with our own men returning fire. A Russian artillery piece boomed out near us. Explosions and machine gun fire banged and rattled out uninterruptedly from all directions around us until dawn. One round shot by close over our heads. The glare from the flames of Suborowo lit up the sky.'

Richter's final diary entry on this opening day of the new offensive echoed Hitler's order of the day. 'Today,' it read, 'the decisive battle against the Russian has begun.' His opinion was 'it ought to be all over before winter'.[4] They had broken through the defensive crust along the River Desna.

As the momentum of the advance increased, combat transitioned to a series of rapid meeting engagements as the Panzers sought to build up an irrepressible tempo. On 4 October the advance elements of the Kampfgruppe 'Koelitz' spearheading the 2nd (Vienna) Panzer Division paused at a track junction, having broken through the Desna line. So engrossed were they in attempting to interpret their poor maps that they were taken aback by the sudden 'tank alarm' which immediately overrode their navigational dilemma. Three armoured vehicles had been spotted 300m to the right. These were immediately engaged and hit, but surprisingly to no effect. Especially hardened shot was loaded and could be seen striking their targets but still there was no response. An infantry Oberleutnant seeking to solve the mystery approached the tanks from the rear by motorcycle,

and was seen standing and laughing amid the enemy vehicles. He shook the 'barrel' of the nearest, which resulted in the entire structure collapsing in on itself. The German advance had been delayed by masterfully constructed tank-target decoys.[5]

The prevailing mood along the Army Group Centre front was buoyant. 'There is a tremendous pressure to get moving forward,' wrote a Panzer division officer, describing the initial three days' fighting.[6] By the second day of the attack Guderian's Second Panzer Army had penetrated 130km into the enemy hinterland, reaching the Orel–Bryansk road. Thereupon, Panzer spearheads began to turn inwards, to the north. Orel, a city of 120,000 inhabitants sitting astride a strategic road and rail junction, fell on 3 October. The 4th Panzer Division, forming part of this sweep, covered a 240km stretch from Gluchow to the objective in four days. The fuel and rations captured at Orel were sufficient to keep Second Panzer Army resupplied for two weeks. On 5 October, 18th Panzer Division captured Karatschew, and on the following day 17th Panzer took Bryansk and the Desna river bridge. This created a huge pocket south of the city, which was to contain elements of three Soviet armies: the Third, Thirteenth and Fiftieth. Meanwhile Panzergruppe 4 formed the thumb of a hand closing on Vyazma from the south.

The fingers enveloping the pocket from the north were provided by the armoured columns of 7th Panzer Division from Panzergruppe 3. Motorcyclist infantry from 10th Panzer entered the city of Vyazma on 7 October. A second huge pocket was thereby formed around the Sixteenth, Nineteenth, Twentieth and Thirty-second Soviet armies. The *Ostheer* now had the last well-equipped Soviet field armies standing before Moscow in its grasp.

Newly promoted tank commander Feldwebel Karl Fuchs with the 7th Panzer Division relayed the triumphant news to his wife. At last the whole front was moving again:

'I'm sure that you must have heard the special radio announcements about our battle achievements. Yes, you can find me somewhere on this front near Moscow! The Russians didn't believe that we would attack at this time of the year when the cold weather is setting in.'[7]

Another officer in the same division reflected, 'there is a mood among the troops that we have not seen since the Suwalki [the start of 'Barbarossa'] days. Everyone is pleased we are finally moving forward again in our sector.' The commander of the 6th Panzergrenadier Regiment directed 'full speed ahead' as his half-track column steadily overtook a line of Russian vehicles on the same road. Cloaked in swirling dust, the Russians were unaware of their predicament until vehicles failing to give way were promptly shot off the road. Panic dispersed the rest. Panzergrenadier Regiment 6 was the first German unit to reach the 'Autostrasse' which led from Vyazma to Moscow. A private soldier riding in the half-tracks jubilantly exclaimed, 'everything was rolling like in the good old days; only one order remained — get moving forward with everything available!' He continued:

'We were calling the shots once again in the advance. It made a tremendous impression on us! Wherever the enemy had convinced himself he had erected an invisible barrier to hold us up, we drove over it hardly noticing. We penetrated kilometre after kilometre further eastward and soon we were well in the rear of the enemy.'

The 7th Panzer Division War Diary described the closure of the Vyazma pocket on reaching the Moscow road as 'a race between the 25th Panzer Regiment and the reinforced Panzergrenadier Regiment 6'. Following up the 'fantastic success' of the spearhead units, the infantry commander remarked, 'we were surprised at the long columns of Russian PoWs marching against us towards the rear'. He reflected on the numerous roadside bunkers and anti-tank ditches which they passed one after the other. 'They ought to have made our advance impossible — but they hadn't used any of them.'[8]

Leutnant Wolfgang Koch, advancing pell-mell in the lead half-track of Schützen Regiment 52 on Orel, with the 18th Panzer Division, recalled the men playing Tchaikovsky's choral music on a gramophone in the back of the vehicle. It was just like France in 1940. The Luftwaffe bombed and burned villages ahead while they followed up in the Panzers. Eventually the grenadiers became tired of endless Russian mass choirs. Unlike France, the gramophone represented the only worthwhile booty they had picked up during the entire advance. After hours of ceaseless and monotonous motoring they found they could still bear the 'Nutcracker Suite'.[9]

Following close behind came the foot infantry, visibly boosted by the sight of the damage and carnage wreaked by the Luftwaffe and Panzers leading ahead, 'In brief — *Sieg und Heil!*,' declared a Leutnant with the 123rd Infantry Division with heady optimism, 'the Red Front has been smashed.' He jubilantly added, 'a feeling of profound good fortune has gripped us all, victory celebrations are almost within our grasp'.[10] An artillery Gefreiter supporting the 23rd Infantry Division announced: 'we have been actively moving forward here after holding this bloody front for almost two months'. They were now 'storming ahead'. The tempo of the advance had meant he was unable to wash or shave for eight days. His battery alone from Artillery Regiment 59 had taken 1,200 prisoners. Victory beckoned.

'During the weeks before 2 October we had constantly seen Russian bombers and fighters, now they seem to have blown away. Either they are frightened or they haven't got any left and the last few are being held for the fellows in the Kremlin's towers. Instinct tells us that Russian resistance will soon be at an end. Only fought-out remnants will be left after that and those can be swiftly settled.'[11]

A German propaganda company reporting the closure of the Vyazma pocket alongside the 2nd Panzer Division sensed the momentous achievement they were witnessing.

'We don't know how many divisions, how many armies, how many guns and numbers of tanks are stuck in these large forests, the edges of which we can now see with our own eyes. We only know that for them there is no escape.'[12]

Oberst von Manteuffel, the commander of Panzergrenadier Regiment 6, had a less sanguine view of the situation. His predecessor had been killed in action only six weeks before. He suspected what might be coming. As soon as all his units had reported that they were set around the crucial eastern sector of the Vyazma ring he issued a simple instruction: 'Dig in up to your necks!'[13] It was to prove a prophetic directive. Inside the loosely held pocket rings were 67 Soviet Rifle divisions, six cavalry divisions and 13 tank brigades. Once again the German 'fast' divisions had 'a tiger by the tail'.

Meanwhile to the north, in the Panzergruppe 3 sector,

XXXXIst Panzer Corps, spearheaded by the 1st Panzer Division, were ordered to attack beyond the forming pockets north-west towards Kalinin on the River Volga. After it had captured Staritza, north-west of Rzhev, resupply difficulties — evident even during the assembly area phase — made themselves felt. Non-combat vehicles were ordered to remain behind to husband sufficient fuel to reach the River Volga. Petrol was siphoned from these non-combatant types and reallocated to Panzers, half-tracks and artillery prime-movers. These ad hoc measures maintained the operational tempo and achieved absolute surprise, reflected in a buoyant radio transmission from the 1st Panzer operations officer to the Corps Chief of Staff, Oberst Hans Röttiger. 'Russian units, although not included in our march-tables, are attempting continuously to share our road space' between Staritza and Kalinin, it read. Mischievously, Röttiger was informed the intermingling of Russian with German vehicles was 'partly responsible for the delay of our advance on Kalinin. Please advise what to do.' The 1st Panzer Division was boldly advancing with completely open flanks. Its supporting 36th Motorised Infantry Division was languishing to the rear, held up by bad roads and fuel shortages. Oberst Röttiger offered an equally euphoric solution to the problem posed. 'As usual,' his message stated, '1st Panzer Division has priority along the route of advance — reinforce traffic control!' In short, the unit was invited to ignore the risks and drive on.[14]

Trams were still running in the streets of Kalinin as the leading elements of the Panzer division rumbled into the city. Furious street-fighting erupted once armed Russian factory workers, still dressed in civilian overalls, realised who they were. Flamethrower Panzers drenched machine gun nests with fiery petroleum while German motorcycle soldiers were pinned down in the streets by Russian roof-top snipers. Seeking to capture the Volga river bridge intact, the lead element of a Panzergrenadier company from Regiment 113 drove at it. Both civilian and Russian military traffic could be seen streaming over the crossing. An intense battle developed for possession of a canal bridge that appeared unexpectedly before the main span. It was smoked off during the fighting by German mortars and the company commander from Regiment 113 suddenly found himself across.

As the smoke cleared, the superstructure of the 250m bridge-span beckoned. A solitary Russian sentry stood with his back towards him on the road. It was one of those bizarre incidents of war that can occur even during the most intense fighting. He was attired in a simple khaki cape and alone, his comrades having long since fled. Unable to bring himself to shoot this unsuspecting and vulnerable individual, the German officer called out: 'Hey you! Hop it!' He later recalled the Russian 'obviously did not understand German, but he turned around and for a few seconds was rooted to the spot, mouth agape'. Suddenly he sped away. The German advance guard, lying around catching their breath on the south side of the bridge, let him go. 'A race with death' followed as they hesitatingly broke into a run to reach the other side. Facing them on the northern bank was an artillery piece, a machine gun bunker and infantry positions. 'We received heavy fire,' said the company commander, 'but it was not possible to pause.' At every running step they winced in anticipation that the bridge might be blown up. It was not. By the evening of 14 October, Kalinin was in German hands.[15]

The *Kesselschlachten* (pocket battles) at Vyazma and Bryansk were to last 10 days. Fighting raged in woods, villages and over strategic road junctions and around lakeland to finish off the last effective remaining Soviet armies before Moscow. As in earlier encirclement battles at Minsk, Smolensk and Kiev, the initial burden of the fight fell upon the motorised infantry and motorcycle battalions of the Panzer divisions. Schützen Regiment 6 belonging to the 7th Panzer Division was ordered to hold 6km-wide battalion sectors, which was two or three times greater than the norm. This could only be practically achieved by establishing interlinked strongpoints. These covered wide stretches of front with limited or often no depth. Support weapons and artillery would then attempt to dominate the inevitable gaps by fire. Mobile Panzer units were employed in a 'fire brigade' capacity as reserves. As 7th Panzer Division commented:

'Inevitably it happened as it had to! With no centralised control, the Russians massed against our positions and stormed them day and night. The enemy successfully broke through several times at night. Initially with small bitterly fighting sub-units and later with dynamically led complete formations, they got through our positions. In such cases they even penetrated battalion headquarters and artillery positions, where hand-to-hand fighting broke out.'[16]

Feldwebel Karl Fuchs, commanding a Czech 38,T light tank on the edge of the Vyazma pocket, declared, 'for days now the enemy has tried to break out of our iron encirclement, but their efforts have been in vain'. Ground mist was beginning to complicate the subjugation of a foe using every ruse to break out. Fuch's Panzer platoon of four tanks was ordered to scout and foil such attempts occurring between infantry strongpoints. After they had destroyed two Russian tanks and beatien off a third, the fog rose from the valley feature they were covering. 'We really let them have it with every barrel,' he wrote to his wife, 'tanks, anti-aircraft guns, trucks and the infantry fired on everything in sight.' Inevitably a price was paid. The motivation driving the exhausted German soldiers was their perception this was likely to be the final battle of the campaign. Fuchs wrote sadly three days later that 'my brave, young friend Roland just died of severe wounds'. He reflected with frustration 'why did he have to give his life now, with the end practically in sight?'[17]

Further sacrifices were required of the 7th Panzer Division. One of the private soldiers in its 7th Infantry Regiment claimed companies could now field only two platoons. These weak units were required to hold sectors 3.5km wide, a battalion task. 'One attack after the other was broken up by the infantrymen and supporting weapons,' he said. Forty of his comrades from the 'Schleevoigt' Platoon were overrun and killed with their platoon commander at the head, having 'fought to the last round'. Vyazma became a battle of annihilation, pursued with the pitiless ferocity of men intent on finishing the war here. Leutnant Jäger from the same regiment described the bizarre lengths Russian tank, infantry and even cavalry took to puncture the thin German lines. His men held fire until the last possible moment:

'The first bursts caused huge losses of people and matériel. Their attack was absolutely unbelievable. Whole columns were on the move with artillery, horse columns and lorries in between coming out of the woods behind Shekulina. Without deviating they came directly at us. What targets they presented our forward artillery observers! The sent salvoes of artillery, without pause, one after the other into the enemy hordes. It caused a practically unbelievable destruction.'

Following the assaults, which continued throughout the night, the German infantrymen lay in their foxholes, virtually out of ammunition. 'They waited, nerves at breaking point, for whatever was to come next.'[18] Soviet corpses were strewn all around.

The 2nd Panzer Division had converged on Vyazma from the south with Panzergruppe 4. On 10 October the anti-tank guns of the Kampfgruppe 'Lubbe-Back' were spread about 150m apart with infantry from Regiment 304 dug in between. They awaited the inevitable attacks from the interior of the pocket. At daybreak Panzers would relieve them. As the sun descended, the landscape was transformed to a dark grey, always a tense time. Panzerjäger H. E. Braun recalled, 'the woods and shrubs in the foreground appeared to change shape from minute to minute'. Light eventually deteriorated into a misty darkness. 'Everyone paid sharp attention' to the scene ahead; 'they were reliant now on hearing alone.' Braun said:

'They could hear the sounds of battle within the pocket. The sky to the west slowly changed to a red hue. Villages must be on fire. Now and then a sharp detonation could be picked out. Tension increased and pulses beat faster.'

Braun shared this acute anticipation. At first indiscernible, and then gradually more clearly, strange noises wafted toward the anti-tank and infantry positions. At about 22.00 hours the fires in the west had died down. Total darkness reigned and in the blackness the noise in front of the perimeter perceptibly increased. A horse would whinny, wagon wheels creaked and engine noises could be heard. 'The tension was unbearable,' said Braun as the first Very lights burst in the night sky.

'Their blood froze in their veins at what the light showed. Hundreds, no, thousands of Russians were approaching their thin positions. Cossack cavalry were attacking too between vehicles and columns of lorries. A staccato noise of shots and strikes rang out . . . the monotonous automatic bapp-bapp-bapp-bapp of 20mm cannon in the ground role was constantly superseded by lighter sharp reports from the 37mm PAKs and the heavy bell-like sound of 50mm anti-tank guns. In between heavy and light machine guns were rattling away, intermixed now and then with several mortars and heavy-calibre infantry guns.'

From this point onward the fighting troops, Braun explained, lost all sense of time. 'Several times the attacking Russians were shot to pieces directly before the positions.' The rest were thrown back. Piles of bodies appeared in wave-like mounds before the German positions as the Russians stacked their dead to chest height to seek cover from fire. Complete Russian company groups tortuously crawled through heaps of their own dead to attempt sudden rushes against the German trenches. Little could be seen from these positions although the shrieks of the mortally wounded and appeals for help could clearly be heard. Russian lorries and armoured vehicles were hit until more light was provided from a petrol-laden carrier that burst into flames. The furious battle raged all night. Braun remembered how startled soldiers were when checking watches during a pause. They saw they had been fighting uninterruptedly for five hours. As dawn approached the fires on the burning lorries finally went out.

The coming light brought a sense of relief, for with it would come the reinforcing Panzers. Soldiers allowed themselves a chance to relax. 'Suddenly the dead in the foreground started to move again,' realised Braun with some alarm. Even though they were raked by a combined weapons barrage, 'a sea of Red Army soldiers' bore down on their positions. The impact of the merciless defensive fire dreadfully shaped the approaching mass, chopping parts away so that Braun described it resembling 'the head of a huge Hydra, with ever new earth-brown forms'. With a nerve-shattering 'Urrah-scream' the Red Army soldiers swept in waves across the German positions. Braun and his comrades ,fearing for their survival, glanced anxiously 'at the dark red colouring on the muzzle brakes of their anti-tank guns', now glowing from the heat of constant firing.

'Like a storm flood the [Russian] flow began to trickle over the embankments into ditches. Then small breaches were torn aside until finally the unstoppable wave flooded into the hinterland. Brave [German] infantrymen and in places even the anti-tank teams with guns were trampled into the ground by the mass of humanity driven by the certainty of death to seek an escape to the east.'

Isolated 'islands' of resistance held out, shooting in all directions. 'Now the time came for the logistics men and the staff,' Braun said. 'Cooks fought weapons in hand from their kitchens and the rear-area drivers fought for their naked lives.' Panzer reinforcements in the next village drove into the counter-attack, plunging and firing into the mêlée with machine gun and main armament fire. 'They fired without aiming straight into the mass,' said Braun, 'hitting Red Army men who had broken through and their own men.' Dozens of *Panje* carthorses galloped around out of control, 'whinnying pitifully'. Russian platoon vehicles, completely festooned with men hanging on for dear life, rolled over the living and the dead. 'Russian lorries raced by at full speed, completely full of soldiers,' Braun observed, 'lit only by the flash of weapon reports'.

On the position, the infantry fought with pistols, spades and grenades to gain space. Even the company commander fought with a smoking-hot machine pistol from his trench, fed full magazines by his orderly. Braun, fighting nearby, opened fire on Russians running toward him with their hands up. He had noticed the grenades. A huge detonation followed after the Russians pitched to the ground.

Finally it was over. 'With tracks whirring and loud engine noises our Panzers from Regiment 3 approached their island of resistance from the rear.' Steadily the steel-grey Panzers moved through their position on the final mopping-up. Russian survivors raised their hands and were formed into small columns to be marched off. Braun noticed their dumb, beaten-looking expressions as they were waved on.[10] It appeared had momentous victory had been achieved.

The Panzers did what they could to hold the porous perimeters in support of their own motorised infantry, who were quite literally bled white. Generalfeldmarschall von Bock, well aware of these losses, cajoled and pushed his infantry divisions forward.

'The performance of the infantry,' he reflected in his diary on 3 October, 'has been almost unbelievable.' More, however, was required. Three days later he was to remind General Strauss of the Ninth Infantry Army 'that its most important task was quickly to send strong infantry forces after the tanks'. Road conditions were atrocious. Driving along the Roslavl–Moscow highway he saw 'things are a mess'. He described how 'four to five columns side by side, with unauthorised Luftwaffe elements wedged in between them, clog the road on which the entire supply effort, including deliveries of fuel for the tanks, depends'.

Four days later the Vyazma pocket, still fighting furiously, was dwindling in size. Guderian's Second Panzer Army was having difficulty containing the Bryansk pocket. Von Bock's diary charted the steady compression until by 13 October the Vyazma *Kessel* was beginning to collapse amid fanatical resistance. Bryansk, meanwhile, was disintegrating into lesser pockets, which remained troublesome and indeed unpredictable. On 15 October a German regiment from the 134th Division was surrounded on all sides in the southernmost pocket.[20] Two more sub-pockets were pinched out between 17 and 18 October.

An officer from Schützen Regiment 7 with 7th Panzer Division described the plight of its first battalion, before being rescued by the Panzers of Regiment 25:

'It was actually worse than Jarzewo [Yartsevo — a bloody sector on the Smolensk perimeter]. Then, the enemy attacked mainly in battalion strength. This time we had to hold back several divisions, but with motorised infantry companies spread over a 12km sector. What use are numerous heavy weapons and favourable terrain in a few positions on the whole of the left sector, when everything is only held together by a series of strong-points?'

Hauptmann Schroeder's Panzer Abteilung reached the right flank of the threatened battalion in the nick of time. They were totally sobered by what they found. All around them lay large numbers of the 3rd Company, strewn about their positions on the heights north of Bogowodjiskije.

'In several foxholes there were four or five dead interspersed with one or two survivors standing among the bodies of their own, rifles at the ready. Several of the machine guns were completely shot-out and nobody in the company had any ammunition left. A badly wounded Feldwebel was still crouched at the ready in his trench. My impression was that the soldiers of the 3rd Company had actually fought to the limit of sustainable endurance.'[21]

Schroeder, visibly affected by the scene, was to remind his battle group constantly during the bleak days ahead of the example they had witnessed that day. The price had been paid by men convinced that one final effort would conclusively break Russian resistance. The end justified the means. Panzer commander Karl Fuchs also lost a close friend.

'We hard-hearted soldiers have no time to bemoan his fate. We tie down our helmets and think of revenge, revenge for our dead comrades. The battle of Vyazma is over and the last elite troops of the Bolsheviks have been destroyed.'[22]

The Soviet pockets at Bryansk, however, held on. On 14 October two battalions from the 'Grossdeutschland' Infantry Regiment were ordered to conduct a night attack on Annino, to prevent further seepage by Soviet forces from the beleaguered pocket. Nobody relished the prospect of a night attack. Both battalion commanders were depressed, knowing casualties would be heavy. Company commanders registered disquiet in their own indirect way through repeated radio requests for confirmation that the attack was to go ahead. 'No man can adequately describe the feeling that prevails before a major attack,' admitted one eyewitness. 'The troops sat there [during the briefings] with their notes and inner battles.' Leadership was applied and feelings of insecurity suppressed.

Oberleutnant Karl Hänert, a veteran Knight's Cross holder, wounded three times, represented the steadying influence that kept soldiers moving despite nervous stress. He was 27 years old and his orders were 'cold and clear'.

'The possibility of a failure on one of the attack's wings was thrashed out mathematically and without feeling. He issued his orders no differently than on a peacetime exercise. Everyone knew what he had to do. Beyond that, everyone knew as well what he could do.'

After the attack went in, reports came back one after the other of company commanders killed or wounded. Hänert was shot in the head by a Soviet sniper. Another company commander, in post barely four weeks before, also died. The news of Hänert's death was passed on by a weeping aide. 'No one spoke a word,' said the witness. 'We didn't look at each other. Everyone had been floored by the news.' Shock enveloped them. 'I am not sure what happened in the next hour,' he said. The carnage continued. Several other officers were killed the same night. 'It was difficult to comprehend that they were gone,' reflected the witness. 'Surely at any minute they must come up and say something to us!' Annino was successfully taken, but during the following night another officer was killed and a second seriously wounded. They were mistakenly shot by their own sentries.[23] The drain on the veteran leadership of the *Ostheer* was constant and unremitting.

Operation 'Taifun' was launched by Army Group Centre with 14 of the 19 Panzer divisions in theatre, and eight of 14 motorised infantry divisions. These 'fast' divisions were supported by a force of 48 infantry foot divisions marching up in depth. Twenty-five infantry divisions were reducing the Vyazma and Bryansk pockets while a further seven continued the advance to the east. Nine infantry divisions were deployed securing the flanks. Nine of the 'fast' divisions (six Panzer and three motorised) were intensively committed to pocket fighting, leaving six (four Panzer and two motorised infantry) continuing towards Moscow, moving west to east. A further three divisions (two Panzer and one motorised) sought to disengage from the Bryansk battles and advance on Tula and Moscow beyond on a north-easterly axis. The success of this strategy was dependent upon the destruction of the six to eight last-remaining Soviet field armies now in their grasp, standing before Moscow. Generalfeldmarschall von Bock announced in an Order of the Day on 19 October that:

'The battle at Vyazma and Bryansk has resulted in the collapse of the Russian front, which was fortified in depth. Eight Russian armies with 73 rifle and cavalry divisions, 13 tank divisions and brigades and strong artillery were destroyed in the difficult struggle against a numerically far superior foe.'

Booty was calculated at 673,098 prisoners, 1,277 tanks, 4,378 artillery pieces, 1,009 anti-tank and anti-aircraft guns, 87 aircraft and huge amounts of war matériel.[24]

To be successful, the strategy now required a Russian capitulation. This was anticipated. Von Brauchitsch had confided to von Bock during the heady days of the initial 'Taifun' success 'that this time it was different from Minsk and Smolensk, this time we could risk pursuing immediately'. Panzergruppe 3 was the only sizeable element of Army Group Centre still pushing eastward towards Moscow. Bock declared, still remembering his frustration at the decision prematurely to form pockets at the outset of 'Barbarossa':

'I am of the view that it was just as possible at Minsk and Smolensk and that we could have saved blood and time if they hadn't stayed the army group's hand back then. I am not in total agreement with the drive to the north by Panzergruppe 3. Perhaps it will be spared me, for the heavy blow inflicted today may result in the enemy, contrary to previous practice, yielding opposite my front as well; some signs point to that.'[25]

The double encirclement battles at Vyazma and Bryansk rivalled the achievement at Kiev. It represented perhaps the final and decisive Cannae. Tank commander Feldwebel Karl Fuchs was euphoric:

'The last elite troops of the Bolsheviks have been destroyed. I will never forget my impression of this destruction. From now on, their opposition will not be comparable to previous encounters. All we have to do now is roll on, for the opposition will be minor.'[26]

This view was clearly reflected in letters sent home across the front. An Unteroffizier with the 6th Infantry Division, jubilantly describing taking thousands of prisoners, said that 'some are even coming voluntarily — a sign of the approaching resolution of the issue . . . And we are already being bombarded by press reports stating: "[Soviet] Annihilation is just around the corner!"' Another artillery NCO with Army Group South predicted that, by the time his wife read his letter, 'bells throughout Germany will be proclaiming victory over the mightiest enemy civilisation has ever faced'. He was totally confident. 'It cannot last longer,' he predicted; in fact, 'we are puzzled what will become of us here now — are we coming back to Germany or will we stay on as occupation troops?'[26]

It was anticipated, as in the case of the battle fought by Napoleon at Borodino, before Moscow in 1812, that the Russians might surrender their capital city, following the destruction of their field armies. If they chose not to, it would be difficult for the *Ostheer* to impose an armistice because only a fraction of its striking force was still moving eastward. Some 70% of the infantry divisions belonging to Army Group Centre were mopping up the pockets and securing its rear and flanks. Only seven divisions appeared to be still advancing. The 'fast' divisions had been bloodied yet again and only 40% of these were still pushing toward Moscow. Moreover, they had entered the battle at only two-thirds of their established strengths. Von Bock wished to exploit his victory. 'If the weather holds,' he wrote on 7 October, 'we may be able to make up for much of what was lost through Kiev.' He constantly chivvied his subordinates to keep the momentum going. A week later, the battle at Vyazma had been fought to a successful conclusion and the pocket at Bryansk was soon to be extinguished, but the intense fighting and awful road conditions meant Guderian's north-east advance faltered. 'A success for the Russians' resistance,' Bock concurred, 'whose stubbornness paid off.'[28]

An event occurred at the beginning of the second week of October which was to be recorded in virtually every letter or diary account maintained by German soldiers serving on the 'Ostfront'. Unteroffizier Ludwig Kolodzinski, serving with an assault gun battery in the Orel area with Second Panzer Army, remembered it well. He was shaken from a deep sleep at 02.00 hours on 8 October by his radio operator, Brand. 'Hey, Ludwig,' Brand whispered urgently, 'open your eyes a moment and come outside with me!' Kolodzinski quickly pulled on a

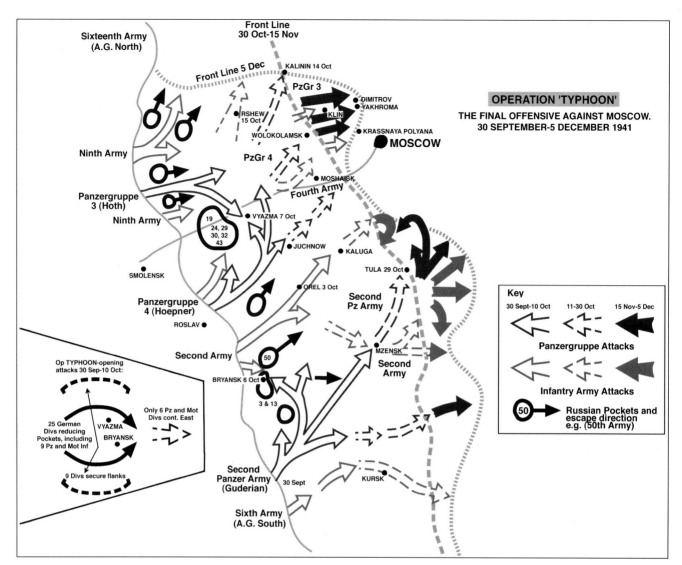

Above: The final German victories at Vyazma and Bryansk utilising favourable autumn conditions appeared to herald a final Blitzkrieg that would overcome Moscow itself. The final Russian field armies facing Army Group Centre before Moscow were surrounded and annihilated at Bryansk and Vyazma. It was a success comparable to Kiev. The German press claimed final victory even as the much weakened Panzer pincers were brought to a standstill by autumn rains and mud, and an ominously undiminished bitter resistance. The weather denied the tactical mobility thereby gained. In reality, however, the *Ostheer* was itself mortally wounded and in the throes of 'victoring itself to death'.

jacket and was abruptly jerked to his senses by an icy flurry of wind and something whipping into his face as he looked out.

'It was snowing! The wind drove thick clouds of snow-flakes across the earth and the ground was already covered in a thin sheet of snow. Even the assault guns parked outside on the road had taken on a curious appearance. They were completely white as if covered in icing sugar!

'I recorded this first snowfall in my diary and went back inside to lie down again. When I awoke in the morning and glanced outside, the snow had already gone. But as a consequence the road was covered in mud and the land around totally soaked.'[29]

Major Johann Adolf Graf von Kielmansegg was driving forward with the 6th Panzer Division. 'On 8 October the battle of Vyazma concluded,' he said in a postwar interview. 'The aim and objective of this battle had been to kick in the gates of Moscow.' But conditions changed. 'On 9 October, as we started to move in the north, centre and south towards Moscow, the temperature dropped and the rain began.'[30] The onset of poor weather affected the infantry also. 'Yesterday we had the first snow,' wrote an NCO with the 6th Infantry Division on the same day.

'Not unexpectedly it was primarily rain, which had the additional disadvantage of soaking the roads. The muck is awful. Luckily the issue can't last much longer. Our main hope at the moment is that we are not kept behind in Russia as occupation troops.'[31]

'The roads, so far as there were any in the western sense of the word, disappeared in mud,' remarked Major Graf von Kielmansegg. 'Knee-deep mud, in which even the most capable overland tracked vehicles stuck fast.' The Russians, faced with the same problems, avoided the German tendency, through inexperience, to drive through the same ruts. Ordered to bypass Moscow to the north, 6th Panzer Division remained stuck fast in the mire for two days once the rain began. 'The division was strung out along 300km,' von

Kielmansegg remarked, 'whereas the normal length of a division column then was 40km.' One soldier summed up the development thus:

'Russia, you bearer of bad tidings, we still know nothing about you. We have started to slog and march in this mire and still have not fathomed you out. Meanwhile you are absorbing us into your tough and sticky interior.'[32]

THE GREAT ILLUSION

The colossal victory at Kiev at the end of September rekindled German public interest in the eastern campaign previously thought deadlocked. It resurrected thoughts that the war may be over before the winter. Two Russian cities had consistently held the public's attention. Leningrad, the birthplace of the Bolshevik ideology, was anticipated to fall soon. Letters from the front stimulated rumours that the other, Moscow, had already been targeted by German *Fallschirmjäger* units, which had dropped east of the capital. Moscow was the lofty prize that would signify the war's end. Kiev had already been compared to the World War 1 victory at Tannenberg, and public expectation was raised even further by the news of the latest Army Group Centre offensive.

'German Autumn Storm Breaks over the Bolsheviks', announced the *Völkische Beobachter* newspaper on 2 October. This was followed by the Führer's announcement that 'the enemy is already broken and will never rise again'. Rumours began to circulate that a new pocket battle for Moscow had started and that its fall was imminent.[1] Front letters appeared to confirm the press line. Infantryman Johann Alois Meyer, writing to his wife Klara, said, 'you will have heard the Führer's speech yesterday' announcing the opening of the final offensive. 'It ought to finish here before the onset of winter,' he assessed. 'That means the end of this month should see the conclusion.' Meyer, however, hedged his bets like everyone else when he ended: 'give thanks to God that it does come and pray to God above all else that we come through it sound in mind and limb.'[2]

Radio programmes in the Reich were interrupted during the evening of 8 October with the dramatic announcement: 'we expect an important special announcement in a moment'. These *Sondermeldungen* had always presaged momentous events: the capitulation of Warsaw, victory in the Low Countries, the French Armistice and fall of Paris and Belgrade. Brass fanfares had played for the fall of Crete, entry into Athens, the storming of Smolensk and the battle of annihilation at Kiev. Loudspeakers were turned up in expectation in cafés and restaurants. Guests were forbidden to speak and waiters to serve. 'Das Oberkommando der Wehrmacht gibt bekannt,' — "The High Command of the German Armed Forces announces' — (the precursor to all such statements), 'the final victory which the decisive battles in the East have led to, has arrived!' Adolf Hitler declared during a speech to the German people the following day:

'In a few weeks three primary industrial areas will be completely in your hands. You have taken over two to four million prisoners, destroyed or captured 17,500 tanks and over 21,600 artillery pieces, 14,100 aircraft have been shot down or destroyed on the ground. The world has never witnessed its like before.'

Dr Dietrich, the Reich Press Chief, announced this news to the world's press and accredited diplomats. Rumours immediately circulated throughout Berlin that Moscow had already fallen, that Stalin was seeking an armistice and the troops would be home for Christmas. A Berlin post official from the post office in Nürnberger Strasse sent a housewife home when she requested 'front postcards' claiming, 'you will not need them any longer'. Sausage was given away free by a butcher in Hausvogteiplatz. On 10 October the *Völkische Beobachter* claimed, 'the eastern offensive has achieved its aim: the annihilation of the enemy', adding triumphantly, 'Stalin's armies have been wiped from the face of the earth'.[3]

SS Home Front reporters monitoring the situation observed, 'the various phases of the final battle were followed with utmost tension'. Newspaper banner headlines announcing German troops were already far beyond the Vyazma and Bryansk pockets reminded the public of the previous year. 'One saw parallels between the advance of German troops on Moscow and the taking of Paris, which was followed soon after by the French Armistice,' stated observers. The press had whipped the Reich into a fervour of anticipation. One housewife wrote to her husband at the front on 14 October:

'Dear Fritz! Write to me again when the issue in Russia is definitely over . . . How happy I was to hear that things in Russia are at an end and you can both [including her son Hermann] *return home again in good health. Ach dear Fritz, I know you always said at the beginning of the war that it would not last long. You will need to get home quickly if you want to take something else* [ie employment] *on. You have certainly had about as much as you can take, and know what war is all about. A typical mother's view, eh?'*[4]

Autumn rains were slashing across the 'Ostfront'. The natural phenomenon upon which Stalin had relied to deter the final German offensive had arrived. One disgruntled *Landser* wrote home:

'We can't go on. There is no more petrol and nothing is coming up behind us. The route is long and the roads even worse over the last few days. The snow has melted and worsened the muck. Rations still do not arrive and we sit in filth the entire day.'

An infantryman in Second Army recorded, 'early on 10 October it began to rain and the rain turned to sleet. The difficulties soon set in,' he said, 'the roads turned into knee-deep mud and were unbelievable.' It proved particularly heavy going for the artillery. 'The so-called "*Rollbahn*" upon which we are marching is a sea of knee-deep mud,' complained an artillery unit with the 260th Infantry Division. 'Vehicles sink up to the axle and in many places the morass is up to the bellies of the horses.'[5]

The headlines back home in the Reich followed a similarly tortuous path as disillusionment set in. 'The momentous hour has struck: the Eastern campaign is at an end,' crowed the *Völkische Beobachter* newspaper on 10 October. The following day it proclaimed 'The Breakthrough in the East is widened'. Then on 12 October it claimed, 'The Annihilation of the Soviet Army is almost finished', and on the 13th 'The Battlefields of Vyazma and Bryansk are far behind the Front'. A degree of temporisation was introduced by a clearly exhausted press, seeking to maintain the morale tempo, when on 14 October the headline read 'The Movements in the East are proceeding according to plan'. The next day there was a simple acknowledgement that 'The Fighting in the East is running to plan'. This was followed by a resounding silence on

16 October when the headlines limply changed the subject to 'Torpedo boats sink six freighters from a Convoy'.[6] The point was not lost on the politically astute population of Berlin, always quick wittily to expose press inconsistencies. A joke was circulated whereby it was assessed the 'BZ' (an abbreviation for the *Berliner Zeitung* newspaper) was the only newspaper remaining worth reading. The explanation being, 'it only lied between "B and Z" while all other newspapers lied from "A to Z"!'.[7]

Leutnant Heinrich Haape recalled watching how 'the first snow fell in heavy flakes on the silently marching columns' of Infantry Regiment 18 two days after leaving Butovo. 'Every man's thoughts turned in the same direction as he watched the flakes drop on the slushy roads.' Winter had arrived. It was late afternoon and the temperature dropped, causing the snow to fall more thickly until the countryside assumed 'a white mantle'. Haape remembered, 'we watched it uneasily'.[8]

Greatcoats were a problem. Not all soldiers even had the temperate issue. During the attack it hampered movement. On dismounting, infantrymen left them behind in their vehicles. Jackets had to suffice. Leutnant Koch serving with the 18th Panzer Division recalled that, just prior to the second (November) phase of Operation 'Taifun', his battalion commander ordered all greatcoats to be left behind with the logistic train at Orel. Unlike many other formations, their issue had arrived, but they were not allowed to take them.[9] Leutnant Haape's men in Infantry Regiment 18 resorted to other methods. 'In order to keep warm they put on all their spare clothes and slept dog-tired, in full battledress.' Whereas previously there had been time to wash and change clothing during the static 'inter-regnum' period before 'Taifun', 'now the poor fellows were constantly on the move' and sleeping in louse-infected houses. There was no time to wash their clothing and scant opportunity to change it. Ingenuity was employed to stay warm. As Leutnant Haape explained:

'Newspapers in the boots took up little space and could often be changed. Two sheets of newspaper on a man's back, between vest and shirt, preserved the warmth of the body and were windproof. Newspaper round the belly; newspaper in the trousers; newspaper round the legs; newspaper everywhere that the body required extra warmth.'[10]

Soldiers for the first time in this war positively enthused over propaganda publications. Sheets of it could be put to good use.

Roads resembled muddy moonscapes with metre-deep craters which filled with water. Thousands of trucks were stranded. Supply and construction troops laboured to produce log-wood roads and other repairs, but to little effect. Rain or sleet fell incessantly after the night of 7–8 October. Tracked vehicles moved with difficulty, wheeled transport not at all. It was taking 24 to 48 hours to negotiate a short 10km stretch of road. Second Panzer Division reported 'it was virtually impossible to supply the troops with the necessary combat and life support'. Junkers Ju52 transport aircraft dropped supplies from the air and landed fuel containers from towed gliders. 'Each day our bill of fare,' the report continued, 'was two crackers, some sausage and a couple of cigarettes.'[11]

Little could be requisitioned from the local population, who were already short themselves. Only light artillery could be moved, at speeds of a kilometre an hour despite superhuman efforts. Von Bock observed, 'in some cases 24 horses are required to move a single artillery piece.'[12] Heavy guns remained where they were. Carriage wheels for light guns had often to be removed and carried by hand through the mud. The 1st Artillery Abteilung supporting the 260th Infantry Division made dispiriting progress.

'The gun crews, with coats smeared in wet mud up to their hips, had been in this mud bath for days without taking their boots off. They were clustered around wheel spokes and hanging off ropes. On the signal "Heave!" ten pairs of hands pulled with a loud "huh!" and "get going!" across the barrier. A battery needed one, two or often three hours to overcome such an obstacle. Often it appeared a vehicle had hopelessly sunk in the mud or that a half-destroyed bridge was irretrievably repairable . . . A sharp easterly wind brought with it the sound of grumbling artillery fire, indicating our comrades in the forward battalion were already in action against withdrawing Russians.'[13]

The simplest task required Herculean effort. Emaciated horses collapsed in the mire, unable to continue. Fähnjunker Karl Unverzagt serving with a Panzergrenadier unit said, 'there was hardly ever an opportunity to get the mud off'. Not that it really mattered because 'it provided the most ideal camouflage you might imagine!' Von Bock, passing a 5th Division artillery regiment on the road, commented 'it is hard to recognize the men, horses and military vehicles as a military column under their crust of dirt.'[14]

Leutnant G. Heysing with Panzergruppe 4 observed the 'fast' motorised divisions started to be overtaken by the foot infantry. 'Even if the soldiers of the Panzer divisions are more or less powerless against the mud,' he wrote, 'this deluge has its master too; the soldiers of the German infantry divisions appear on the scene, drawing closer on anything that can in any way be referred to as a path.' The infantry, having successfully concluded the double encirclement battles, was moving up.

'They came marching in endless columns from the west from morning to night, taking advantage of every minute of the few hours of late autumn daylight. Tens and hundreds of thousands, endless and unlimited, with arms and munitions hanging on them, just as soon as they became available from the battle of Vyazma . . . These infantrymen, all with the same expression under their faded field caps, stamp silently through the mud, step by step to the east. The loamy liquid runs into the top of their boots . . . The coats also are wet, smeared with clay. The only things dry and warm are the glimmering cigarette butts hanging from the corner of their mouths . . . If the path is not wide enough to walk in columns, they march in long rows.'

This gritty propaganda piece of reportage intended for the Reich press glorified the aura of invincibility raised by the German infantry, which was sincerely believed by the population at home. Heysing reported the situation on 25 October:

'The tanks are out of fuel, the guns are nearly out of shells, and again and again we have had to take leave for ever from many dear comrades. It is practically impossible to get our boots dry again, and the uniforms are turning yellow and getting threadbare. But none of us lying here stuck in the mud in the midst of the enemy have lost our courage. The frost has to come some time and the terrain will become passable again.'[15]

Although Heysing wrote with convincing authenticity, his optimistic view was not shared by all at the front. Unteroffizier Wilhelm Prüller was wrestling with the greatcoat dilemma. 'Which is better?' he reflected at the beginning of October, 'to be moving and to sweat more *with* a greatcoat and then to shiver less when you're quiet, or to go on as we've been doing, without one?' His commanding officer, like Leutnant Koch's from the 18th Panzer Division, said, 'we can't move as well in a coat.' There was little debate. 'His is the bigger pay packet,' Prüller ruefully admitted, 'so it's no coats for us!' His diary chronicled the cumulative and depressing impact the appalling wet weather in Army Group South's sector had on the troops. It lasted almost three weeks.

On 6 October he observed after it had 'rained in torrents all night' that 'at night it gets really cold now, and we all think that it can't go on much longer'. With the baggage train marooned somewhere behind on the rutted roads, no food or spare dry clothing got through. The next day saw a snowstorm which did not settle 'but the wind whistled through every nook and cranny of our hut'. Still it rained. By 13 October rain alternated with snow. 'It only freezes at night,' commented Prüller, 'when it's cold, but at 07.00 in the morning it thaws out again.' No mail could reach the troops or was collected because the supply trains 'can't catch up with us through the mud'. Four days later, 'there's still no trace of our baggage train'. Changed weather conditions resulted in different march routines. 'There's no point in trying to move during the day; the mud would not allow it,' said Prüller. 'We can make it only during the night, when the earth is frozen hard.' At the end of the week depression became evident, reflected in much shorter diary entries. 'The rain stops only for a few hours at a time,' he wrote, and 'everything is grey, dark and impenetrable. The whole of Russia is sunk in mud.'

On 28 October Prüller was marching 'in driving snow-cum-rain'. On the eve of the attack on Kursk, the last day of the month, 'the night was simply freezing,' he complained. 'We froze, particularly since we had neither blankets nor overcoats.' Kursk, as a consequence, was an objective well worth attacking, because it could provide accommodation. 'The rain has stopped, and the streets are frozen solid,' commented Prüller as the advance got underway.[16] There seemed no end to their misery.

Leutnant Georg Richter with Artillery Regiment 74, driving through light snow conditions in mid-October, fervently wished the light frost, that periodically hardened the roads, would last longer. But when it did, treacherous slides resulted. One sudden halt resulted in a pile-up involving every single vehicle in the column. Two were totally written off. 'We spent the night in our vehicles either side of the road and almost froze half to 'death,' he commented. Depressing circumstances invariably bred hopeful rumours. 'A common opinion was that our division would still be relieved before the winter and we would most likely be sent to Africa,' he mused. Shelter was at such a premium that soldiers were prepared to fight for it. Every time they drove into a village at the end of the day it was 'always the same old picture', he complained. 'Every house completely filled up with soldiers, and all over were staffs and baggage trains.'[17]

On the road to Kalinin, Unteroffizier Helmut Pabst marched 55km during a frozen period on 12 October between 08.00 hours and 02.00 the following day. 'We didn't find any billets,' he ruefully commented when they finally reached their distant objective. Freezing temperatures forced them inside, and 'the boys warmed themselves in the overcrowded rooms, determined to get warm even if it meant standing', as was often the case. The infantry endured wretched conditions. 'My boots were still so wet this morning,' Pabst complained, 'I could only get into them in my bare feet.'[18] Their feet, constantly soaked, in temperatures just above freezing, were susceptible to 'immersion' or 'trench foot'. Such chilling interrupted the blood flow to these extremities and could cause tissue damage akin to superficial frostbite. Close-fitting wet clothing and saturated shrunken boots exacerbated the symptom, as also did protracted standing in wet and cold conditions. Damage was often not recognised, and dismissed as aching feet, occurring as it did in conditions above freezing. Not seen since World War 1, 'trench foot' and hypothermia (body chill) took a steady toll of the sick, further increasing the vulnerability of under-nourished soldiers to face even harsher conditions to come.

Prevailing dull wet weather with driving sleet and rain, together with the social pressures of a crammed existence in crowded foul-smelling accommodation, produced bad tempers. This, combined with the persistent anxiety of impending combat, frayed nerves and tested leadership. 'War began to sap the soldiers' nerves,' recorded the official history of the 9th Potsdam Infantry Regiment:

'Many were too tired to take cover or even throw themselves to the ground when the whistle of enemy shells was heard. Sleeping in foxholes remained by necessity perfunctory, as they were always on the look out for some danger.'[19]

Overcrowding in cold, wet and unsanitary conditions produced colds, influenza, disease and lice. Unteroffizier Pabst, packed into a small baker's house on the Kalinin road, complained, 'the nine of us can hardly move.' The billet was crawling with lice.

'Our little Viennese was unwise enough to sleep on the stove last night; he's got them now — and how! Socks which we put there to dry were white with lice eggs. We've caught fleas — absolute prize specimens.'[20]

Lice were the scourge of the Eastern Front, an irritant contributing to ill-health and cumulative psychological depression. Painstakingly picked off the body, they could only be killed with certainty by cracking them between fingernail and thumb after they were gorged with blood. Machine gunner Joachim Kredel with Infantry Regiment 67 embalmed one in hot candle wax on his mess tin, and sent it home in a match box as a souvenir, 'so that they might at least see one louse!' he explained.[21]

At home, the cinemas were showing a noteworthy scoop — the fighting around the old Napoleonic battlefield at Borodino. The implicit parallel was that this event preceded Napoleon's entry into Moscow in 1812. In 1941 it formed part of the Mozhaisk defence line, the outer ring of concentric barriers protecting the capital city, stretching almost 300km from Kalinin to Kaluga. This line was attacked by the spearhead of Panzergruppe 4: the 2nd SS 'Das Reich' and 10th Panzer Divisions. The newsreel portrayed unprecedented realism, narrated by war reporter Hugo Landgraf as he participated in the actual attack. His report 'on the battlefield at Borodino' was conducted with an immediacy typical of present-day TV media coverage. It caused quite a stir among cinema audiences.[22]

'I am sitting at the radio operator's post inside a heavy-duty [PzKpfwIV] Panzer and will be filming the attack from here,' says Landgraf on the film. 'Against us are heavily armed and well equipped new groups of Soviet reserves just outside Moscow.' Bucking images taken through the dark surround of the vision slit recreated the uncomfortable cross-terrain ride of a Panzer sweep. 'You can hear the clack-clack of artillery and machine gun fire on three sides,' he said. His armoured group trades fire with enemy positions 'for hours' in a 'fierce battle' illustrated by images of burning houses and hayricks with momentary glimpses of accompanying Panzers jockeying for and shooting from fire positions. 'Our tank shakes with mortar rounds landing all around us,' he reports. Eventually resistance is beaten into submission and Landgraf comments, 'our gun barrels are becoming hot from continuously firing round after round for so long'. The scene changes to night shots of tracer arching away from the tank into an indiscernible gloom. They have managed to advance several kilometres.

'It snowed overnight,' Landgraf continues — an ominous statement for cinema audiences concerned at the onset of winter and fearful of the consequences for their menfolk at the front. Accompanying infantry had dug trenches between the Panzers. 'The battle continues,' says Landgraf as groups of infantrymen, stooping under the weight of heavy machine guns and ammunition, move by. Many characteristically have cigarette butts or pipes dangling from their mouths. The flat landscape broken up by woods has been totally transformed by a light covering of snow. Panzers and half-tracks starkly silhouetted against the whiteness are engaged in an intense fire-fight. Smoke spurting from squat 50mm tank barrels is accentuated in the freezing air. They have encountered 'a wall of resistance' and among fleeting groups of running German infantry 'our tanks can only inch their way forward' over a landscape dotted with burning village houses. Luftwaffe dive-bombers are seen to engage enemy artillery positions ahead, but the war reporter dramatically interjects 'as soon as one battery is defeated another takes its place . . . Dusk falls again,' he reports as the metallic concussions of turret machine gun fire ring out. The camera tracks the lines of tracer beyond the vehicles, bursting on indistinguishable targets in the distance.

Daylight revealed, 'we are standing directly before a wooded area containing one of the main Soviet defence lines'. Up ahead, houses are blazing furiously. 'The camouflage covering the Soviet bunkers,' cunningly concealed underneath the wooden houses, 'has caught fire'. Landgraf next provides commentary to an 88mm Flak gun crew feverishly working and firing their gun in thick falling snow. 'On the third day,' he said, 'anti-aircraft artillery is brought in to assist us in the decisive blow.' Puffs of smoke indicating air-bursts are seen detonating over the wooded objective. Meanwhile the Flak gun crew are becoming covered in thick wet snow. 'We manage to break through over a wide front,' he says. Panzer PzKpfwIIIs and IVs silhouetted against the white background drive past a trio of dead Soviet soldiers sprawled untidily across the snow. The Panzers are shooting the infantry onto the objective as 'we move in from the flank to attack the middle of the Soviet defence line and break it down in a series of bloody skirmishes'. It is all over. 'Over there you can see the Bolsheviks coming out of their trenches,' Landgraf triumphantly announces, 'we have successfully broken down the enemy defence lines.'

Much was made of this example of realistic war-reporting, which proceeded to show the extent of the defences overcome on this position either side of the Moscow road. A diagrammatic survey shows automatic flamethrowers, zig-zag trenches and wide anti-tank traps covered by artillery and spiky 'hedgehog' tank obstacles constructed from sections of railway track. Heavy concrete bunkers covered by intermediate positions housing heavy weapons and artillery formed the core of the line. The camera lingered over the broken bodies of the Russian defenders. The film was in stark contrast to the clarion special announcements by the Reich Press Chief, Dr Dietrich, and newspaper headlines declaring the war was just short of being decisively won. It was shown in German cinemas at the end of October, coinciding with SS Secret Service observations of 'a certain public disappointment' at events. 'The collapse of the Bolshevik system was anticipated in a few days' and the public's interpretation of this was that 'it was unlikely large scale actions would occur at the front'. Reports such as Landgraf's demonstrated this was not the case. Confusion turned to cynicism. It was obvious major fighting was still going on.[23]

This was grimly apparent to soldiers at the front. Leutnant G. Heysing, writing about the same battle at Borodino with Panzergruppe 4, reported the town of Mozhaisk on the strategic Moscow defence line was taken on 18 October, but that 'autumn rains have set in, depriving German soldiers of the fruits of the victory they have already won'. His assessment was, 'the German assault is stuck knee-deep in the mire'. The 10th Panzer Division spearheading the advance 'is spread far apart between forest and swamp, the mud reaching the vehicles in some instances up to the loading area so that supplies cannot get through'. He concluded, 'try as we may, we cannot go on.'[24] Both the 10th Panzer and the 2nd SS Division 'Das Reich' in support suffered heavy losses during the Borodino fighting. The 'Der Führer' Infantry Regiment was down to 35 men per company, compared to a normal complement of 176 soldiers. They were over-stretched. 'Every objective given the regiment was reached,' declared its official historian, 'even if it required unspeakable effort.' The regiment's first battalion and motorcycle battalion had fought the Soviet 82nd Motorised Rifle Division for possession of Schelkowka, an important crossroads on the advance.

'The 18- to 20-year-olds had repulsed two Soviet battalions in close combat with spades, hand-grenades and bayonets. Many of the young SS men were killed, and all were bare-foot in their boots in 15° below freezing.'[25]

Expectations had been high that the *Sondermeldungen* trumpeting the victories at Vyazma and Bryansk heralded the end of Russian resistance. This was the great illusion. Cynicism now began to set in. Unlike the previous Borodino battle, the gates of Moscow did not swing open, nor had an armistice been offered. General Günther Blumentritt described the bitter realisation:

'And now, when Moscow itself was almost in sight, the mood both of commanders and troops changed. With amazement and disappointment we discovered in late October and early November that the beaten Russians seemed quite unaware that as a military force they had almost ceased to exist. During these weeks enemy resistance stiffened and the fighting became more bitter with each day that passed.'[26]

At the end of October only a small part of the Reich's population believed the war in the east would end that year. Observers commenting on recent reports of progress and fighting against stubborn and bloody Soviet resistance had 'clearly led to an intensification of public scepticism over the propaganda of the preceding few weeks'. By early November 'there were signs of impatience that clarion announcements of successes were not forthcoming'. Continued reports of bitter Soviet opposition led to frustration. The interpretation of the public mood read: 'one simply cannot understand why the German troops do not suddenly swiftly advance after destroying 260 of the best-equipped Russian divisions.' This feeling had changed to 'resignation' by the middle of November. 'The conviction that a decisive outcome to the war is unlikely to occur this year is becoming even more pronounced,' read another secret SS report.[27] A similar view was emerging at the front.

'One began to hear sarcastic references to the military leaders far away in Germany,' commented Blumentritt. 'The troops felt that it was high time our political leaders came and had a look at the front.'[28] Unease permeated the motivation sustaining fighting power at the front, especially among the infantry. Harald Henry's infantry regiment in Ninth Army marched at night, when the mud temporarily froze over. Between 17.45 hours and 02.00 the following morning 'we were outside in a snowstorm, apart from a short break,' he said.

'My things were gradually saturated as the water soaked through my greatcoat to my body, which was frozen stiff. Everything was dripping and the weather was freezing. My stomach and bowels were in a state and cold temperatures dropped off the scale — and the lice! The frost penetrated the weeping sores on my fingers.'

Henry's company was ordered to sweep a wood. The snow, over knee-deep, soon filled his boots with a slushy mess. As they painstakingly clambered across frozen marshland they occasionally broke through the ice, immersing their feet in freezing water.

'My gloves were so wet I could not bear the ache [of his infected hands] any longer. I could have wept with pain as I bound my useless hand with a handkerchief. My contorted face was streaked with tears, but I was in a trance-like state. I plodded forward, babbling incoherently, feeling I was asleep and reliving a nightmare. All the others were in the same state. There was shooting and one threw oneself into the snow, formed a half-circle, made ready and waited for orders. It was a cycle of non-ending misery.'

Wood-clearing was tedious, frustrating, exhausting and dangerous. By nightfall the sweep was over. 'Then came an order that said the operation had been unsuccessful and we had to do the whole thing again from the beginning.' Just as they started, another radio message was received ordering a withdrawal. This meant a 10–15km march, which was to last nine hours. Much of it was spent waiting in column, as the company made tortuous progress through the trees. It was a physical ordeal which left them:

'Standing hour after hour in the open, wet and frozen with hands wrapped [in bandages], lashed all the time by the unbelievable weather. Our boot soles froze sticking to the ground. We were wet through and had simply to stand, stand, stand, wait — march a bit — and stand again.'

At 02.00 hours they reached a village where they were told they could rest. 'All of us are ill and absolutely worn out to some degree or other.' Their joints were stiff. 'Every fibre in my body is broken,' complained Henry. Early the next morning it would probably start all over again. The awful weather, however, precluded any further movement. Men lay on the floor, some 30 to a small room. 'Liquid excrement ran through the middle of the hut between our ponchos and packs,' said Henry. 'We all had diarrhoea and stomach cramps.'[29] There seemed no end to the suffering.

Soldiers grew increasingly sensitive to the 'hurrah-patriotism' they heard on the radio and read in the press. 'One can only shake one's head at what you hear on some radio programmes, or in some propaganda company reports,' complained an artillery Leutnant with the 131st Infantry Division. 'We're not too influenced by such shitty stories,' he said, 'but it is no good singing about it.' Morale was being eroded. 'After four months,' concluded the officer, 'one has had enough.'[30]

'Morale has dropped,' reported IIIrd Corps with Army Group South, particularly after the optimistic propaganda 'which contradicts their experience on the battlefield'. Troops enduring the hardship that produced the victories were unsparing with their comments. One said, 'the capture of Odessa, Kharkov, or anywhere else makes no impression at all if you yourself are lying in the shit.'[31]

Warfare on the Eastern Front had changed from attaining strategic objectives to fighting for the next shelter. Oberstleutnant von Bose, commanding an infantry battalion with the 98th Division, took a delivery of rations on a particularly cold night on 16 October and found they were frozen solid. He radioed his regimental headquarters and said, 'we're freezing and want to attack'. Back came the mystified response: 'Attack where?' Von Bose retorted, 'It doesn't matter where — we need accommodation!' An order followed to capture the village of Awdotnja, which the battalion took in a surprise attack. All night the battle raged against repeated Soviet counter-attacks, desperate to regain their lost shelter.[32]

The German soldier at the front felt keenly the disappointment of having the chalice of victory dashed from his lips, more so than the population in the Reich. Unteroffizier Helmut Pabst summed up the feeling in mid-October when he wrote, 'what a country, what a war, where there's no pleasure in success, no pride, no satisfaction, only a feeling of suppressed fury now and then.'[33] Harald Henry exclaimed:

'How much longer should this go on! There should surely eventually be a stop to it, or at least a relief. We have acquitted ourselves magnificently, and with heavy losses, in all the great Army Group Centre pocket battles: Bialystok, Minsk, Mogilev, Roslavl, the Desna river, Vyazma and Bryansk. In the final resort we ought to be allowed at least some rest. We can't take much more.'[34]

The *Ostheer* had delivered all that had been demanded of it, and more. The last remaining identified Soviet field armies were destroyed in the twin encirclement battles at Vyazma and Bryansk. Operating beyond logistic range and bled white in the process, the German armies had inflicted a further devastating blow on the Russians. But still the enemy fought on. Moreover, whatever the result of the victory, a two- to three-week delay was being imposed by the mud of the autumn rains. General Blumentritt remarked, 'the troops not unnaturally now resented the bombastic utterances of our propaganda in October.'[35]

Chapter 14

'The eleventh hour'

> **'The state of our forces must not, "for heaven's sake", be overestimated in future . . . they must be clear that as far as this attack is concerned it is "the eleventh hour".'**
>
> *Generalfeldmarschall von Bock*

MOSCOW . . . A DEFENCE CRUST FORMS

The Soviet leadership was taken aback at the 'Autumn Storm', triumphantly announced by the German press, that burst upon them. Panzergruppe 4 drove a wedge between Maj-Gen Petrov's Fiftieth Army and the Forty-third Reserve Front Army, and Second Panzer Army entered Bryansk on 6 October, at which point Moscow lost contact with its forward Army Groups. Major Ivan Schabalin, an NKVD staff officer with Fiftieth Army, jotted 'we are surrounded' in his diary on 4 October.

'The entire front, three armies, have been embraced — and what do our generals do? "They think about it." . . . As ever, we lose our heads and are incapable of taking any active measures.'

Schabalin assessed the front staff had lost all initiative from the very moment the German attack began. Two days later he despairingly admitted, 'history has never witnessed anything like the defeat of the Bryansk Front'. The front command irretrievably lost control, 'it's rumoured the idiots are already on their way back to Moscow,' the disillusioned officer complained.[1]

At noon on 5 October a reconnaissance pilot from the 120th Fighter Squadron reported that he could see a 24km-long Nazi armoured column moving along the Warsaw highway from Spas-Demensk toward Yukhnov. This was about 160km south-west of Moscow. Nobody would believe him. He was ordered to fly back and confirm. Now the undisturbed German column could be seen approaching Yukhnov itself. A degree of authentication was provided by the damage the aircraft received from anti-aircraft fire. Colonel Sbytov, Air Commander of Moscow Military District, decided this was proof enough and passed the urgent report on. He was immediately accused by the NKVD of 'encouraging panic', and his staff was threatened with court martial and execution. A third reconnaissance report confirmed the column had actually entered the town. Stalin was informed. There were no Russian forces on the Warsaw highway between Yukhnov and Moscow. Units in the capital were placed on alert and an ad hoc force hastily assembled to hold up the German advance until major reserves could be committed.[2]

The next day, with the front before Moscow apparently falling apart, General Georgi Zhukov was recalled from Leningrad and ordered to report to the capital. On 10 October, he was appointed Commander of the West Front, responsible for all the defences west of the Soviet capital. He was to have a decisive influence on the approaching battle.

Zhukov's immediate priority was to stabilise the front. He requested Stalin to begin transferring large reserves toward Moscow. The State Defence Committee, the Party's Central Committee and the Supreme Command took measures to halt the enemy advance. Troop movements began on 7 October, reinforcing the concentric defence belts facing west. A total of 14 rifle divisions, 16 tank brigades and more than 40 artillery regiments were taken from the supreme Headquarters Reserve and adjoining fronts.[3] They totalled some 90,000 men. Remnants of units that had cut their way out of the German double encirclements were filtered into the same defence lines.

In addition, existing West Front air forces were reinforced by Maj-Gen Klimov's 6th Fighter Corps, all the fighter squadrons from the Moscow Military District, several long-range fighter divisions and four newly formed squadrons. On 13 October the State Defence Committee issued order number 0345, calling for maximum effort from the highest commander to the lowliest Red Army private. 'Cowards and panic-mongers' — any soldier who gave up a position without authorisation — would be 'shot on the spot' for crimes against the state.[4]

The power of the Communist Party lay in the cities. Its instruments of state reached out to control the geographical expanse of Russia from these political vantage-points. This explains the superhuman effort made to defend centres such as Leningrad, the cradle of the Bolshevik ideology, and Moscow, the capital of the Soviet apparatus — and later Stalingrad, the city that bore Stalin's name. Hitler's own totalitarian ideological convictions granted intuition that enabled him to discern the intrinsic value of such objectives. To despatch a rival ideology with lethal certainty necessitated the destruction of the primary cities of the Soviet Union: to blockade them, level them to the ground and disperse the populations. In choosing to conduct a *Vernichtungskrieg* (war of annihilation) the German regime ignored the possibility of exploiting home-grown dissatisfactions with the Soviet system, evident in rural areas. The Teutonic hordes portrayed in Eisenstein's film *Alexander Nevsky* playing in Russian cinemas, with images of German Knights burning babies alive, was perceived in the Russian nationalist psyche as being not far from the truth.

The opportunity to exploit internal political contradictions, which the German staff achieved in 1917 by aiding Lenin, was forgone in 1941. Major Ivan Nikitowitsch Kononov, the commander of the Russian 436th Rifle Regiment, cut off in the Vyazma pocket, claimed 'an atmosphere of panic reigned within [Nineteenth] Army . . . the soldiers only attacked under considerable pressure from the political apparatus.' This negative view of resistance inside the pocket was shared by his army commander, Lt-Gen Lukin. In his view, shared with his German captors after being wounded and taken prisoner, the infantry 'did not demonstrate the necessary will to break out. They would rather go into captivity'. They were 'driven' into offering themselves in their thousands as victims 'time and again' in failed break-out attempts. A number of high-ranking Soviet generals captured at this time were eventually to switch loyalties against the communist cause. Lukin explained:

'The farmer wants land, the worker a part of the industry he was promised . . . If misery and terror reign and above all a cheerless existence, then you could understand that these people would positively welcome being freed from Bolshevism.'

An alternative regime to Stalin was therefore conceivable. One could justifiably fight against 'the hated Bolshevik system,' claimed General Lukin, 'without thereby compromising one's claim to be a Russian patriot'.[5] No such options were offered to the Soviet front soldier.

'We have not seen a single one of our own aircraft in the last few days,' wrote Major Schabalin with the Soviet Fiftieth Army on 7 October. 'We are giving up cities with practically no resistance.' Within three days he was on the run from pursuing German forces inside the pocket. His health was deteriorating and now it was snowing heavily. 'Masses of cars and people' were on the roads, mute testimony to the defeat and disintegration of the Russian armies. A colleague from the 217th Rifle Division told him that they had suffered 75% casualties. Resistance was collapsing all around. 'Where are the rear areas and where is the front?' he wrote on 11 October. 'It is difficult to say,' he reflected, 'the noose around the Army is being drawn ever tighter.' Two days later the situation had become even more tenuous.

'The enemy has pressed us together in a circle. All around was the uninterrupted sound of gunfire, an unbroken barrage of artillery duels, mortars and machine guns — danger and fear for practically the whole day.'

Life was reduced to short snatches of rest during lulls, in woods, marshes and night bivouacs. He was soaked and cold. 'I have not slept since 12 October,' Schabalin complained, 'or read a newspaper since the 2nd.'[6]

Pocket fighting was an unremitting nightmare for the Soviet soldier. Anatolij Tschernjajew, an infantry platoon commander, said, 'the worst was when the Germans sent over their reconnaissance groups at nights into villages where we were accommodated, and threw grenades inside.' This was generally the precursor to liquidation.

'Then they went into the attack, practically surrounding the village, rolling tanks right up to us. That was truly a catastrophe, because we had absolutely nothing to use against them, no anti-tank guns or anything!'[7]

On 15 October Major Schabalin was 'staggering about, bodies all around, constantly under fire'. His army 'had been completely annihilated', and he spent his final days filling in diary entries around a wood fire with soldiers he did not know. Schabalin's body was recovered in light rain in a small village south-west of Paseka. There were no entries after 20 October. The importance of the little book was recognised by the searching German soldiers, who passed it on to the Second Army staff. Schabalin was one of thousands who failed to escape the pocket.[8]

Capture was worse than defeat. Vladimir Piotrowitsch Schirokow witnessed a column of 15,000 Soviet prisoners being driven from Vyazma to Smolensk.

'Most of them could hardly keep going and despite that they were constantly cudgelled. They simply broke down and remained lying on the ground. If someone from the local population threw them a loaf of bread they would be beaten or even directly shot on the spot. The edges of the road were covered with bodies, which were left lying for days. Only 2,000 of these 15,000 prisoners survived their arrival at Smolensk.'[9]

Even von Bock, the army group commander travelling the same road on 20 October to check supply difficulties, stated:

'The impression of the tens of thousands of prisoners of war, who were scarcely guarded, marching toward Smolensk, is dreadful. Dead-tired and half-starved, these unfortunate people stagger along. Many have fallen dead or collapsed from exhaustion on the road.'[10]

Small wonder the Soviet soldier, despite being aware of the shortcomings of his own totalitarian regime, opted to fight to the death.

The rapid German advance, which resulted in the occupation of further towns and cities, was an unmitigated disaster for all that lay in its path. Panzergruppe 3 achieved the maximum progress: 400km compared to a minimum of 220km marched by Ninth Army.[11] Fifteen-year-old Alexander Igorowitsch Kristakow, in a village near Vyazma, had lived a simple and happy life up to this point. The family had geese, chickens, two pigs and a cow. After receiving instructions to herd their livestock to a collective farm near Gorki, 'the Germans,' Kristakow said, 'time and time again attacked us with low-flying aircraft'. He survived the experience and returned in time to witness the arrival of the Germans at the beginning of October. 'All the chickens and geese were taken away and eaten,' he said. Their sole cow was taken the following year. The day after he was liberated by returning Russian troops, Alexander Kristakow stepped on a mine and was blinded.

On 15 October the Germans reached Rzhev. 'That was it so far as employment was concerned,' said 33-year-old postmistress Jelena Gregoriwna. This was a tragedy. She had already lost her second husband at Leningrad. 'I had to sit there with four children with nothing to eat.' They made their way into the cellar where they hid throughout the German occupation. Four days previously the town had been bombed, prior to German entry. 'It's awful,' confided Nina Sernjonowa to her diary, 'what is going to happen?' It became impossible to sleep at night. 'Gestapo people came persistently asking the same question — "where have all the Communists disappeared to?" If they were not given up, the family would be shot. A German officer billeted nearby boasted that Leningrad and Moscow had been occupied by the Germans. 'I said nothing — I did not believe him.' Nina Sernjonowa grew to detest the Germans once the executions started and soldiers took all their food. She was not to survive the occupation.

Kalinin had fallen on 14 October and, Nikolaj Antonowitsch Schuschakow said, 'the Germans were given full freedom over five days to plunder everything.' Moreover, 'they freed the convicted criminals and got them to join in.' In all 155 shops in the town were looted and then torched. Two weeks later Alexandra Scholowa and her friend Lobow Karalisowna entered the city. 'My God, it was a sight!' she exclaimed. She had lived in the city before 'but I could hardly recognise it again'. All around, the houses were in ruins, trams stood forlornly, hollow shells, with their cables dangling grotesquely into the street. There was no light or electricity. They saw there were Panzers parked around the railway station. Soldiers had pulled the statue of Lenin from its plinth in Lenin Square and were smashing it into sections to the accompaniment of laughter. A huge swastika flag hung in its place, which a young Russian tried to remove the following day. Caught in the act,.

he was hanged, head down, from the very plinth he had sought to clear. 'He took two days to die,' remarked Scholowa, 'which served only to harden our resolve to resist.'[12]

From the beginning of October and continuing into November, Luftwaffe air formations attacked transport, military installations and other targets in and around Moscow. Natalya Pavlicheva, a factory worker, remembered air raid warnings sounded mostly at night. They never went home.

'So a group of us from the home defence brigade would run up on to the rooftops. We then ran around and simply threw off the fire bombs . . .Nobody wants to die and of course it was frightening — especially when you were only 17 — but you can get used to anything, can't you?'

Anastasia Egorova animatedly gesticulated during the same interview as she said:

'Of course we were frightened. These phosphorus fire bombs were blazing and throwing off sparks and you had to go right up to them, pick them up and run off and find somewhere to put them out. Sparks could quite easily hit, you know, because they were flying off in all directions. It was terrifying, of course, but after a while we got very fierce. We'd pounce on the bombs, grab them by the tail, and stick them straight in [a bucket of] *water.'*[13]

The fall of Kaluga on 13 October and Kalinin the following day unhinged the defence belt south and north of Moscow. The weak defence line from Volokolamsk to Mozhaisk and Maloyaroslavets that lay in between was breached in several places. In Moscow there was little knowledge about what was going on. Actress Maria Mironowa remembered how 'we listened to the radio the whole time, poring over the news'. It was all they lived for. 'But it was a time full of worries. Nobody could get away from it, even a famous artist.' In the factories workers slept in rows inside following a 12-hour day. Sixteen-year-old Natalie Shirowa, making parts for Katyusha rocket launchers, recalled: 'We often thought of Moscow as already surrounded and did not even bother to go home after work.'[14]

The Communist Party Central Committee and State Defence Committee decided to evacuate a number of government agencies and the entire foreign diplomatic corps to Kuibyshev, a city 850km further east on the River Volga. The evacuation — nicknamed the 'Big Skedaddle' — began during the night of 15/16 October and witnessed scenes of stampeding at railway stations. These signs of collective panic, accompanied by some looting, represented the nadir of fortune for the Communist regime. Lorries loaded with families and their possessions began to move through the streets. Officials sought to leave without permits, and traffic jams developed on the eastern outskirts of Moscow. Rumours proliferated that surrender was imminent. Offices and factories stopped working. Trains entering stations were swamped by masses of passengers.

'16 October was an awful day for Moscow,' recalled journalist A. Maluchin, observing the panic at Kasaner station. 'Trains were not just made up from passenger wagons,' he said, 'but also goods wagons and underground carriages.' He noticed the trains were going only one direction — eastwards. 'Trains set off without automatic safety governors [ensuring they were set distances apart], they departed in dense rows separated only by visual distance.'[15] Even Lenin's coffin was removed from its Red Square Mausoleum to be transported to safety. Stalin remained.

Stalin's presence in the capital was a stabilising factor. Outside the city, reports of flight were causing unease. Gabriel Temkin, digging anti-tank ditches on the defence belt, said: 'the gloomy news had a devastating effect on the morale of our labour battalion, creating a mood of complete apathy.' Digging came to a virtual halt. There appeared little point. 'People were grumbling, "our fortifications are just another exercise in futility",' he said. The morale-boosting talk from their *Politruk* (political party official) was seen as 'hollow' and he quickly left. 'He knew everybody detested his speeches.' Life for Temkin, like many others, deteriorated into a series of personal crises that quickly dwarfed the strategic events being conducted around them. As the weather got worse the left sole of his boot fell off. It could not be replaced and, worse still, with winter approaching, his underwear was stolen on one of the rare occasions the battalion received a shower. Temkin almost tangibly felt, as the weather got colder, his survival chances ebbing away.[16]

On 19 October General Zhukov declared Moscow to be under a state of siege and placed the capital and its population under martial law. Breakthroughs of the Mozhaisk line between Kalinin and Kaluga and another threatened breach in the Naro-Fominsk area, the third in-depth line in front of Moscow, were creating a bulge directly threatening the Soviet capital. Zhukov repeated the emergency measures he had previously enacted in front of Leningrad. Extensive defences were ordered to be constructed in depth, covering the main approaches to Moscow. Engineering work was already underway behind the first echelon of the West Front to erect anti-tank barriers in all sectors potentially vulnerable to an enemy armoured advance. Every morning and until it was dark, nearly 70,000 women and children and 30,000 factory workers marched out from the suburbs, wretchedly clothed and equipped only with hand tools, to work on the outskirts of the city. Vera Evsyukhova dug anti-tank ditches.

'They were huge, about 8m wide and 10m deep — as big as that. It was mostly us women that did the work, and it was hard labour. We had to light fires to thaw the earth before we could dig into it. On top it was frozen solid, but deep down it was not so hard.'[17]

Within three weeks they had dug 361km of tank ditches and erected 366km of tank obstacles with 106km of 'dragons' teeth' (tooth-shaped concrete buttresses) protected by 611km of barbed wire. They needed little encouragement. Gabriel Temkin remembered the atmosphere of unease that had permeated his labour battalion. 'Everyone felt a nervous chill, listening to radio news about the Red Army again and again abandoning cities and territories,' he said. 'The Germans were coming closer and closer.'[18]

Bridges were prepared for demolition on all approaches, rivers and streams mined, and huge earth embankments raised, interspersed with one-metre deep 'fish-bone' pattern ditches, impassable to heavy vehicles. Anti-tank barriers, consisting of ditches covered with rows of barbed wire, and star-shaped iron 'hedgehogs', made from six jagged iron rails welded into clusters, were concreted into vital street intersections, to prevent the passage of tanks. Concrete bunkers covered these obstacles with machine guns, anti-tank and artillery pieces.[19]

The work was not allowed to continue totally unmolested. A 25-year-old cotton weaver, Olga Sapozhnikova, ordered to dig trenches alongside a crowd of other factory girls, remembered, 'we were all very calm, but dazed and couldn't take it in.' On the first day they were strafed by a low-flying German fighter: 'Eleven of the girls were killed and four wounded,' she said.[20]

They could sense the proximity of the approaching Germans. 'They were strange, those nights in Moscow,' said Elizaveta Shakhova. 'You heard the guns firing so clearly.'

'It was freezing cold, a terrible frost, but you had to keep digging. They made us dig. We had to do it, and we did, we kept digging.'

Through it all 'they were bombing us all the time,' said Evsyukhova. Rumour and uncertainty reigned. 'The Germans dropped leaflets on us stating "Surrender — Moscow is kaputt!" But we did not believe it.'[21]

There was no sign — at any stage — that Moscow would ever have surrendered. The decision to transfer the most important Soviet ministries and agencies to Kuibyshev had already been taken, and the evacuation of vital industrial assets to the Urals continued. Over a number of weeks from mid-October, 498 industrial operations were transported eastwards, carried in 71,000 freight cars.[22] Stalin had clearly resolved to fight on, a view echoed by Soviet diplomat Valentin Bereschkow who learned later that all Moscow bridges and many public buildings, including the Kremlin, were prepared for demolition with delayed-action mines. 'If the Germans had marched into the city,' he said, 'they would have experienced a lot of surprises.' The tactic had already been employed in other overrun cities such as Kharkov and Kiev. Explosive charges fired after the occupation demolished entire buildings, killing many Germans in the process. 'The mines were supposed to explode as the installations were occupied,' Bereschkow explained, 'hopefully causing heavy casualties among the military headquarters staff, expected to be the first to occupy them.'[23]

Communist Party activists formed workers' battalions in every city borough. Within a few days of the crisis Moscow scraped together 25 ad hoc companies and battalions numbering 12,000 men, most of them Party or Young Communist League members. Another 100,000 workers began military training in their spare time, while 17,000 women and girls were trained as nurses and medical assistants. Journalist A. Maluchin recalled lorried convoys full of these volunteers rolling westwards, passed by refugees streaming out of the eastern exits of the city. These reinforcements were hastily incorporated into the Western Moscow defence zone. In all, 40,000 volunteer troops formed rudimentary militia divisions. By the end of October, 13 rifle divisions and five tank brigades were despatched to create a measure of stability to the threatened Volokolamsk sectors on the River Nara and Aleksin on the River Oka. By the middle of November the STAVKA was to provide the West Front with 100,000 men, 300 tanks, 2,000 artillery pieces and numerous anti-tank guns. They were redirected to the threatened sectors.[24]

Mud and Soviet resistance had checked the German offensive at the end of October along a line running from Kalinin on the Volga, through Turginovo, Volokolamsk, Dorokhovo, Naro-Fominsk and Aleksin on the River Oka and south to the outskirts of Tula. Army Group Centre had bitten off a linear strip of 230–260km penetrating into the Russian interior. Some units were within 120–140km of Moscow. Army Group North meanwhile had retained its stranglehold on Leningrad in the north, while in the south Generalfeldmarschall von Rundstedt's Army Group South was successfully maintaining its drive along the Azov coast toward Rostov. Sebastapol might hold out but the Crimean peninsula seemed about to fall. Harsh early winter sleet and rain alternating with freezing night conditions, which thawed again by day, brought the front to a standstill for three weeks. During this interlude Soviet reserves achieved a degree of stability in the threatened areas, enabling the Moscow labour force to erect an extensive series of fortifications and obstacles across the likely future route of the German advance.

General Zhukov was summoned to Stalin's Supreme Headquarters on 1 November and questioned whether the traditional October Revolution Anniversary parade could be held on 7 November. Holding it would send a strong and politically tangible message to the international community and Russian population, demonstrating the ability of the regime to survive despite recent setbacks. Stalin had consulted General Artemev, the Moscow District Commander, the day before to assess its practicality. Alexei Rybin, a member of Artemev's security team, recalled the general's fear of a Luftwaffe bombing raid. 'In the first place,' Stalin admonished, 'you will not let a single plane through to Moscow.' Reality suggested, however, it could still conceivably happen. If that was the case, Stalin instructed he should 'clear away the dead and wounded and continue with the parade'.[25] Zhukov, appreciating this resolve, advised that although there was unlikely to be a major German ground offensive, the Luftwaffe could interfere. Additional fighter squadrons were transferred from nearby fronts to minimise the chances of this happening.

In wartime Russia every official utterance, particularly a speech from Stalin, was awaited with enormous expectation. The speeches and the October Revolution Parade delivered in the dramatic setting of Red Square, with the Germans virtually at the gates of Moscow, were to make a lasting impression on the population and world community alike. Artillery Cadet Mark Ivanikhin marched across a desolate Red Square on 7 November, the 24th anniversary of the October Revolution.

'It was winter or rather it was November, but the snow was bitterly cold and it was dark. As we paraded across Red Square I was somewhere on the fifth line on the right flank, with my eyes facing right. I was surprised to see Stalin looked so short in his hat and ear flaps, not at all like the man we had seen in the portraits everywhere.'

Stalin adapted himself to the nationalist mood, making a considerable impression on both the army and workers. He reminded those present of previous invasions: the Tartars, French and Poles, and played upon the population's deep feeling of insult aroused by this latest incursion. The Germans had lost four and a half million men in the last four months, he claimed.

'There is no doubt that Germany cannot stand this strain much longer. In a few months, perhaps in half a year, maybe a year, Hitlerite Germany must burst under the weight of her own crimes.'

Ivanikhin, crunching through the snow as he was marched off the square, was as unimpressed by Stalin's speech as he was by his size. 'At the bottom of my heart I felt a little dubious when he said that the war would be over in six months to a year.' It was likely to last a lot longer than that. Actress Maria Mironowa, living in Moscow, said, 'everybody paid attention when Stalin spoke on the radio, because he rarely spoke and when he did it was not for long'. Everybody sat still and listened because 'despite this, his remarks were treated as gold dust'. Stalin's nationalist propaganda was appealing but the population saw through it. Like many soldiers and Cadet Ivanikhin, Maria Mironowa had her doubts.

'We knew our land was becoming smaller. It didn't matter what Stalin said, because the Germans were forever advancing.'

The thoughts emanating from the serried columns marching across Red Square were also of little consequence because after the parade they continued directly on to the front.[26]

On the same day, the snow turned to rain across the main part of the Central Front. All roads, except in the German Ninth Army area further north, remained impassable. During the evening of 10 November, there was snow and a light frost, but it was not accompanied by any appreciable improvement in the state of the roads. Conditions marginally improved the following day but 12 November produced clear blue skies and freezing weather. The OKW War Diary reported 'clear, frost, roads negotiable with deep ruts in places'. Temperatures fell to −15°C and dropped to −22° the following day. 'There was frost across the entire Army Group Front,' the War Diary recorded. 'All routes are frozen hard and drivable.'[27] Winter had arrived and was to last for four months. The German offensive could resume.

DILEMMA AT ORSCHA

General Halder, the Chief of the German General Staff, arrived at Army Group Centre's headquarters in Orscha, near Smolensk, on 13 November. There was a conflict of opinion between OKW in Berlin and staffs at the front over the future conduct of the campaign. All three Panzergruppen commanders — Guderian, Hoth and Hoepner — were concerned at their ability to push their spearheads to the final objective. The perception gap between front and rear was increasing.

Generalfeldmarschall von Bock was concerned about his Army Status reports. Although the 95th Infantry Division belonging to Second Army had reached Kursk at the end of October, part of it still remained at Kiev, dispersed over 500km. The Führer was questioning Fourth Army's progress, slowed down by appalling weather and road conditions. 'He probably refused to believe the written reports,' commented von Bock, 'which is not surprising, for anyone who hasn't seen this muck doesn't think it's possible.'[1]

At Orscha the army group chiefs of staff — Generalmajor Sodenstern from South, Brennecke from North and von Greiffenberg from Army Group Centre — were summoned to discuss the feasibility of continuing the proposed advance. Should the *Ostheer* commit itself to a final dash, or dig in for the winter months before resuming the offensive in the spring? Army Groups North and South were blocked and overstretched and wished to halt. Army Group Centre's Generalmajor von Greifenberg accepted 'the danger that we might not succeed must be taken into account'. But, he said, 'it would be even worse to be left lying in the snow and the cold on open ground only 50km from the tempting objective.'[2] This was precisely the conclusion the Führer and Halder sought. The offensive was to be resumed.

Behind von Bock's decision to continue was his belief that 'the enemy was at the end of his combat resources', even though he 'still retained his determination'. Von Bock was buoyed by the conviction that 'the enemy has no more depth and is certainly in a worse position than ourselves'. Soviet reinforcements had appeared at the front but this was interpreted as 'a last-ditch effort', and, being volunteer worker battalions, were likely to be of dubious quality.[3]

The decision to attack was taken following painstaking appreciations in early November of relative opposing strength ratios across all three fronts. German infantry divisions were assessed at two-thirds their normal strength and artillery not quite so bad. If sickness, casualties and vehicle losses were brought into the equation, infantry divisions were considered to be at 65% of their combat potential. Panzer divisions had

lost 40% to 50% of their effectiveness and were down to about 35% their normal strengths. The 101 infantry divisions, 17 Panzer and 13 motorised infantry divisions of the *Ostheer*, according to these equations, represented only 65 infantry, eight Panzer, eight motorised infantry divisions and two other regiments in real terms. In summary, a 'paper' battle strength of 136 divisions had been reduced to a much fewer 83 in reality. Despite shortcomings, the risk was considered acceptable because it was felt the Russians were worse off.

Soviet forces in December were calculated to total 200 rifle and 35 cavalry divisions, with 40 tank brigades. They could be reinforced with a potential 63 rifle and 6.5 cavalry divisions and possibly 11 tank brigades from the Russian interior. German planners were not intimidated by this data. 'The combat strength of the majority of the Russian units is small at the moment,' OKW rationalised, and 'they are insufficiently equipped with enough heavy weapons and artillery'. Significantly, reports assessed 'previously unidentified units now rarely emerge', which appeared to indicate 'that integrated reserve units are no longer available in appreciable numbers'. Although units might appear from the interior, they 'were not expected to appear for the foreseeable future'.[4]

The actual extent of the mauling the Soviet Army had received since the invasion was suspected but misappreciated. Soviet figures released after the war reveal the significance of the damage. The Russian Army, which maintained an average field strength of 3.3 million men, lost an 'irrecoverable' 2.1 million casualties between June and the end of September, and 676,694 sick and wounded. They were to prove the highest losses to be sustained by Russian forces throughout the rest of the war.[5] The figures included 142,043 officers and 310,955 senior NCOs (or sergeants) with some 1,676,679 men, representing 18.9% of the average monthly strength of the army. This fell to 8.9% in the next quarter, a reflection, among other factors, of the diminishing impact of the surprise occasioned by the initial invasion.[6] Strengths were, nevertheless, laboriously maintained.

Daily losses during the early border battles had been stupendous, confirming Wehrmacht claims. From 22 June until 9 July 23,207 soldiers were lost *each day* on the Belorussian front, which amounted to 341,000 irrecoverable losses from 625,000 soldiers committed to battle. At Smolensk 12,063 men were killed or irretrievably injured each day from 10 July until 10 September, ie 486,171 irrecoverable losses from a committed strength of 581,600. The reeling Russia colossus was dealt a further crushing blow at Kiev when 8,543 men fell on average each day, which was 616,304 from a combined defeated armies total of 627,000.[7]

Losses in material were equally appalling. On the Belorussian front, 4,799 tanks were destroyed at a rate of 267 per day from the start of the invasion until 9 July, alongside 9,427 artillery and mortar pieces captured or knocked out at 524 per day, and 1,779 aircraft shot down or hit on the ground at 99 per day. At Smolensk 1,348 tanks were lost in two months between July and September at 21 per day, 9,290 artillery and mortar pieces at 147 per day and 903 aircraft at a daily destruction rate of 14. Fewer tanks were operable by the time of the Kiev encirclement battle, but 411 were knocked out at five per day between 7 July and 26 September. Artillery and mortars provided the main Russian fire power in the pockets and 28,419 guns were lost, picked off at 347 per day with 343 aircraft.[8]

The double encirclement battles at Bryansk and Vyazma cost the Soviet field armies caught either in the pockets or on the retreat some 9,825 soldiers per day. By the end of November their losses were to total 658,279 men. Soviet tank losses from the beginning of Operation 'Taifun' were running at 42 per day and were eventually to total 2,785. Artillery and mortar losses reached 3,832 pieces at 57 per day, and, despite the poor weather, four aircraft were being lost on average each day.[9]

Stupendous though these losses were, the Red Army was not persuaded or indeed reduced sufficiently to advise Stalin and the Communist regime to sue for peace. Officer and senior NCO losses were serious but absorbed by a centralised structure, which — unlike the *Ostheer* — was not reliant upon initiative. Contrary to the German *Auftragstaktik* style of leadership, Soviet formations were committed to battle as large closely supervised blocs. German contemporary accounts constantly dwell on the 'unpredictability' such methods conferred. General von Mellenthin, a panzer commander, emphasising this characteristic, remarked 'today he is a hero attacking in great depth — tomorrow he is completely afraid and not willing to do anything'.[10] Panzer General Hermann Balck was to comment after the war:

> 'The Russians are astonishingly unpredictable and astonishingly hard for a Westerner to understand. They are a kind of herd animal, and if you can once create panic in some portion of the herd it spreads very rapidly and leads to a major collapse. But the things that cause the panic are unknowable.'[11]

It was this 'unknowable' element that clouded German intelligence thinking. Having survived the shock of the initial onslaught, the Soviet Army was relying upon space and its considerable manpower resources to buy the time necessary to develop the experience that would eventually reduce casualties. In short, the *Ostheer* had to deliver a knock-out blow to win. The Russian Army, by contrast, had merely to remain standing to achieve eventual victory. It was this apparently inhuman capability to endure punishment and losses that German planners were never able to quantify. They applied their own psychological and rational parameters, irrelevant to the Russian context of waging war.

General Balck, observing the steady dissipation of German strength with some concern, admitted, 'when we advanced on Moscow, the general opinion, including my own, was that if we take Moscow the war will be ended'. This was the logic applied by the German General Staff in pursuing its final reckless push against the city. Soldiers at the front, facing the reality of continued and sustained bitter resistance, thought otherwise. 'Looking back in the light of my subsequent experience,' Balck concurred, 'it now seems clear that it simply would have been the beginning of a new [phase in the] war.'[12]

The perception of the *Ostheer*, the field army, differed from that of planners at OKW in Berlin academically assessing relative strengths. There were disagreements over objectives as a consequence. Second Panzer Army was, for example, allocated Gorki, 500km east of Moscow, as an attack objective. Its Chief of Staff, Oberstleutnant von Liebenstein, frustratedly retorted, 'This is not May again and we are not fighting in France.' He changed the objective to Wenjew, 50km north-west of Tula, considered to be the maximum achievable objective for the Second Panzer Army.[13] Von Bock acknowledged 'the attack cannot become a great strategic masterpiece'; rather the aim was 'to conduct the thrust in concentration at the tactically most favourable points'. This was a clarification of earlier statements which suggested the best that might be achieved was the creation of conditions for a future encirclement of Moscow. 'Our planned interim objective is Moskva and the Moskva-Volga canal and the capture of its

crossings,' he said, warning 'it is not impossible that the state of the attack forces units may force us to halt on this line.'

There were too many conflicting pressures to overcome. Plans were deteriorating to the status of a gamble. Von Bock was only too aware of the situation:

> 'Conditions have thus forced the Army Group to work with very short-range objectives. I cannot suggest waiting longer than is necessary to attack . . . because I fear that the weather conditions will then thwart our plans . . . if we get deep snow, all movement is finished.'

Hitler and Halder had achieved their intention, the acceptance of a last gamble: a *Flucht nach Vorn* (headlong dash) against Moscow in the hope it might succumb. Halder privately admitted, 'the time for spectacular operational feats is past . . . the only course lies in purposeful exploitation of tactical opportunities'. Generalmajor von Greiffenburg returned from Orscha and reported to von Bock, 'all that remains of the recently propagated distant objectives opposed by the army group is that the army groups are to do what they can.'[14]

Fundamental shortcomings that had applied at the end of September prior to Operation 'Taifun' were even more apparent. The *Ostheer* had attacked, despite serious logistic sustainability shortfalls, to annihilate what it perceived to be the last Soviet field armies before Moscow. These logistic and manpower shortages reduced the latest attempt to rush Moscow to the status of combined raiding forays. Mortally wounded, the *Ostheer* was at the end of its strength. Second Panzer Army reported on 17 November:

> 'The army has favourable attack conditions for the moment from the situation perspective, the strength of the enemy and 'going' over terrain and roads. It cannot, however, exploit this advantageous situation because of constant train and supply delivery problems. Responsible army staffs are unable to replenish divisions with fuel. The fuel situation today is such that the attacking Panzer divisions have about 60–90km worth of fuel . . . Likewise the motorised [infantry] divisions have not received their allocation and as a result have been static within their locations for several days.'[15]

This was a snapshot of the extent to which the previous 500km 'trip-wire' hurdle had worsened at the 1,000km point. It was now a positive barrier. The 1,000km distance to the Reich frontier was served by only two main rail links (Warsaw–Minsk–Smolensk and from Brest through Gomel and Bryansk). Both were frequently cut and harassed by partisan groups. Distribution from railheads was through the available *Grosstransportraum* of lorried transport. Many of these had been stuck fast for three weeks with mud up to their axles. When the mud froze they were hauled out but hundreds were severely damaged in the process. By the middle of November, 50% of the Army Group Centre lorry fleet was out of action. Fourth Army had been reduced to one eighth of its original complement of trucks. Panzergruppe 4, which had relocated from the Leningrad front to the centre, had only half its motorised transport running, even before Operation 'Taifun' at the beginning of October. Many vehicles failed to receive timely deliveries of anti-freeze and broke down. Meanwhile the Minsk–Moscow 'Autobahn' had its concrete covering stripped away between Smolensk and Vyazma during the difficult weather. A whole infantry division was required to expedite sufficient repairs to get traffic moving again.[16] Artillery soldier Franz Frisch with Panzergruppe 4 summed up the problems:

'We started the offensive on Moscow with dilapidated equipment, and we lost a lot of it. 30% of the leaf [suspension] springs in our trucks broke later in the cold, robbing them of braking power. There was such confusion that even officers started to question the logic of pushing ahead despite transportation problems. "What stupidity is this — starting an attack with units whose trucks will not move, and ammunition trucks with cold brakes and no springs?"'

Nobody questioned Hitler's determination. As Frisch explained, 'he was absolutely crazy, but everybody was saying "Heil Hitler".'[17]

Resupply by rail, vital to sustain any operational advance of consequence, began to disintegrate in freezing conditions. Ninth Army received only four fuel trains between 23 October and 13 November, while Second Army gained only one of three required from late October. As temperatures plummeted to minus double figures, 70% to 80% of German steam locomotives, whose water pipes — unlike Russian types — were outside their boilers, froze and burst. This provided the prelude to a transport crisis that dwarfed all those that had preceded it. Virtually no trains reached Second Army between 12 November and 2 December and only one fuel train reached Ninth Army between 9 and 23 November. When the latter arrived, its contents could not be distributed because waiting lorries were also out of petrol. Despite awesome difficulties, it was these lorry columns that kept units intermittently resupplied. Von Bock complained as early as 11 November that the number of trains reaching his army group was down to 23 per day. If the 30 originally promised could not be maintained, he assessed that stockpiling 'even for an attack with limited objectives, cannot be contemplated before 11 December; that means in my opinion the attack will not take place!' At the end of November only an average of 16 trains per day were reaching the army group.

During the Orscha conference, Major Otto Eckstein, the staff officer responsible for the organisation of Army Group Centre's logistic resupply, briefed a totally pessimistic logistic picture, along with the senior army group quartermaster arguing against the resumption of the proposed offensive. Von Bock chose not to support him. The prospect of going forward with even an outside chance of seizing Moscow was preferable to a freezing halt just before it. The supreme irony was von Bock's protest at this particularly difficult moment over several logistic trains which had been held to the rear of the army group to give priority to an equal number transporting Jews from Germany to the same area. *Vernichtungskrieg* knew no conventional bounds.[18]

'THE ELEVENTH HOUR'

The final phase of Operation '*Taifun*' was launched on 16 November with both wings of the army group making surprisingly good progress. Panzergruppen 3 and 4 moved on Klin to the north of Moscow and Second Panzer Army to the south bypassed Tula, where it had been blocked for weeks, and moved north-eastward. Even as Guderian's much reduced force of 150 Panzers moved off (it had numbered 400 at the end of September),[1] a Soviet attack crashed into Fourth Army immediately to its left, cutting contact and exposing his flank. A double envelopment of the Moscow defences was soon under way. Zhukov's last line of defence, the Mozhaisk position, barred the way, stretching between the 'Sea of Moscow' reservoir in the north to the River Oka in the south. At first the Russians were unable to stop the German thrust on any broad front. Nevertheless, the pressure of Soviet attacks on the German Fourth Army forced elements of it to come to a

standstill and go over to the defensive, forming a 'sack' in between the two enveloping Panzer prongs. Pressure on their flanks correspondingly increased as these advanced.

General Halder remarked on 19 November that 'this has been a good day again', and 'heartening progress' was being made the following day. Reports about the poor condition of the German troops were not taken too seriously. Optimism clouded objective reasoning once again. 'Guderian had someone call up in the afternoon to report that his troops are on their last legs,' Halder recorded on 21 November, but with the strategic objective in sight the Chief of Staff did not take the concern seriously. He reasoned:

'It is true, they did have to fight hard and a very long way; and still they have come through victoriously and pushed back the enemy everywhere. So we may hope that they will be able to fight on, even against the repeatedly reinforced enemy [new Siberian divisions] until a favourable closing line is reached.'[2]

On the northern flank of the advance, the Russians struggled to consolidate a defensive line along the Volga canal and the Sea of Moscow. Klin fell to Panzergruppe 3 on 23 November as Panzergruppe 4 entered Solnechnogorsk. The former now began to pick up a Blitzkrieg momentum as Russian forces steadily retreated before its advance. Ninth Army in support penetrated as far as the canal line and Panzergruppe 3 reached it just south of Dimitrov.

The reality of the advance did not, however, correspond to the symbols that General Halder's staff moved on maps. One of the regimental commanders with the 98th Infantry Division supporting Hoepner's Panzergruppe 4 submitted a confidential personal report to Generalmajor Schroeck, his division commander, outlining his concerns. 'Without a meaningful replacement of fallen officers, NCOs and weapon specialists,' it read, 'and a reorganisation and issue of clothing, equipment, weapons, vehicles and horses, and unless urgent measures are taken to restore the fighting power of his troops, his command would have no combat value.' A battalion commander in the same division questioned whether all the other units were 'as pathetically battered as ours? And still we are optimistic!' Company Feldwebel Schiff, in one of the infantry regiments, gave his pessimistic overview on 2 November from the soldier's perspective.

'The beards on our faces make us all look like U-Boat crews and our hands are encrusted with filth. When was the last time we washed our clothes or had a bath? It seems to have been months. Joints are commonly stiff from lying in holes all day long. One can hardly feel one's feet because of the cold! But you can feel the tormenting lice. And where are our dear friends, all those that had marched and fought with us?'

Where indeed? The regiment had lost 50 officers and 1,673 NCOs and men — two-thirds of its officers and over half its men — since the beginning of the campaign. Overall, 98th Infantry Division had lost 5,881 men, one-third of its total strength but more than half of its actual fighting men.[3]

The consequence of massively costly victories was all-apparent at front level. Operation '*Taifun*' alone had cost the army groups 114,865 casualties. This represented a further 6.8 division equivalents completely removed from the order of battle. The significance can be measured against the fact there was only one division left available for the Army Group Centre

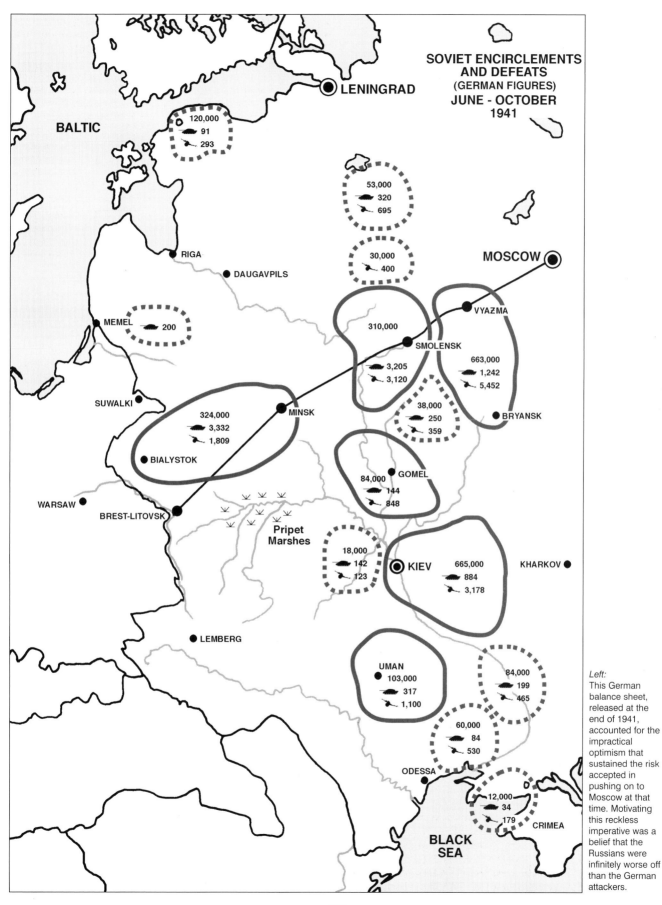

SOVIET ENCIRCLEMENTS
AND DEFEATS
(GERMAN FIGURES)
JUNE - OCTOBER
1941

BALTIC

LENINGRAD

120,000
91
293

53,000
320
695

30,000
400

RIGA

DAUGAVPILS

MOSCOW

MEMEL

200

VYAZMA

310,000

SMOLENSK

663,000
1,242
5,452

SUWALKI

MINSK

324,000
3,332
1,809

3,205
3,120

38,000
250
359

BRYANSK

BIALYSTOK

84,000
144
848

GOMEL

WARSAW

BREST-LITOVSK

Pripet
Marshes

18,000
142
123

KIEV

665,000
884
3,178

KHARKOV

LEMBERG

UMAN

103,000
317
1,100

84,000
199
465

60,000
84
530

ODESSA

12,000
34
179

CRIMEA

BLACK
SEA

Left:
This German
balance sheet,
released at the
end of 1941,
accounted for the
impractical
optimism that
sustained the risk
accepted in
pushing on to
Moscow at that
time. Motivating
this reckless
imperative was a
belief that the
Russians were
infinitely worse off
than the German
attackers.

reserve. Officer casualties in October were 3,606, enough to man seven division equivalents; the 22,973 NCOs who perished or were wounded amounted to the same comparable ratio.[4]

The physical impact of these losses seriously eroded fighting power at the front. An assessment of a typical German infantry division structure[5] reveals that from an average strength of 16,860 men about 64% — some 10,840 — could be classified as 'fighters'. The remaining 36% was the logistic support 'tail' that sustained the 'teeth' or combat elements forward. This provides the explanation for the small numbers of soldiers infantry companies were actually committing to battle. Morale and instinctive self-preservation continued, remarkably, to hold these much reduced bands of men together. An Oberfeldwebel in a 260th Division infantry regiment remarked, 'we have 49 dead and 91 wounded in the company' which would have had a theoretical combat strength of 176 men. Only 36 men who had started the campaign would still be serving in its ranks. Despite this he claimed 'our heads are always held high, even when the going is rough'. They had penetrated to within 80km south of Moscow and still believed 'eventually we will definitely destroy the Russians'.[6]

Panzer regiments were even worse off. Prior to the second phase of 'Taifun' they had been assessed as being at 35% of their normal strength. This meant an overall average of 50–70 Panzers per division, normally 180–200 strong (with about 350 armoured vehicles altogether).[7] Helmut von Harnack, serving with a Panzer regiment, wrote at the end of October:

'The last few months have not passed without leaving their mark on the old veteran crews, many of whom have already been knocked out once within their Panzers.'

He was an officer and amazed at the 'zest for life' displayed by his 19-year-old crews, commenting on 'the flush of victory in their eyes'.[8] But it was a truism that the highest losses were among units who had fought the most successful actions, and they were losing their best men. Second Panzer Army had been reduced from 248 tanks on 16 October to 38 by 23 November. Panzergruppe 3 likewise dropped from 259 to 77 over the same period.[9] These losses at the 'teeth' end of Panzer divisions were more significant than the infantry because just under half of the 13,000–14,000 armoured troops deployed were actually 'fighters'. Most casualties would be forward, far exceeding losses among considerable specialist and logistic units forming the 'tail' to the rear.

Artillery Leutnant Hubert Becker graphically illustrated this gap between front and rear, describing a return journey from leave.

'On the rare leaves, departing Berlin the train was absolutely full of soldiers with field packs, in clean uniforms, deloused, going back to the front. All were sad at parting and fully packed. The compartments were so full you could hardly move. But in spite of that we were in good spirits and cracking jokes.

'And the trip took three days, four days, five days... to the East. 'The further the train travelled eastward the more space there was inside. By the time we got to our former eastern territories the train would be half empty. When we got to the end of the line, 40km behind the front, the compartment would be empty. You'd get off completely alone and you'd ask: "Well — who's fighting this war?"'[10]

The offensive fighting power of the infantry and Panzer divisions in the attack was, in reality, reduced to the level of heavy raiding battle groups. The combat 'teeth' ratio to logistic

and specialist 'tail' structures of both infantry and Panzer divisions was breaking down. The development could not necessarily be remedied by drafting 'specialists' forward to join the fighting troops. Results when this was attempted were generally catastrophic. General von Mellenthin, a Russian front veteran, remarked after the war that there 'is a difference between "infantry minded" officers on the one hand and "armour minded" officers on the other'. This applied also to soldiers. 'Either capability acting alone,' he said, 'has a value significantly less than 50% of their combined effectiveness.'[11] General Balck, referring to combat attrition in front of Moscow, said, 'we wound up with valuable tank crews fighting in black uniforms in the snow as infantrymen — and being totally wasted.'[12] A tank soldier with the 20th Panzer Division admitted:

'The shortage of tanks was a worrying thing for the Panzer crews. The division formed a so-called "tank-crew" battalion from the men in the regiment who no longer had tanks or wheeled vehicles, or were unable to be transported in any other way. It had four companies with no heavy weapons. Many of the 21st [Panzer Regiment] crews hanging on hopes of a long rest and recuperation on an exercise area [in Germany] and being re-equipped with a bigger tank than the Panzer III soon had them buried.'

Tank crews performed as best they could fighting as infantry, but, as their division history commented, 'they lacked the training basis required to fulfil their task'. By the beginning of January 1942 only 18 soldiers from one company had survived from the 160 men that had formed up in the middle of November. They quickly realised that 'employment as infantry required totally different needs from those of Panzer combat'. Living and digging foxholes in ice and snow was not comparable to crewing a Panzer. 70% of the losses were from frostbite.[13] General Balck conceded:

'Casualties in the tanks themselves were almost always quite light. However, once the tank crew had to abandon their tank, we often had to employ them immediately as infantry. And at this point we took unheard-of losses among the tank crews because they had no infantry skills.'

Combing the rear area was not a solution because, Balck explained, 'the division organisation must be maintained, because it is the basis for the training and the feeding and the command and control of the unit.'[14] Luftwaffe personnel from Flak, signals and other grand units were employed as infantry as the crisis worsened. Even pilots whose aircraft were out of action and highly trained specialists were put into the line on the orders of Generalleutnant Baron von Richthofen, the commander of VIIIth Fliegerkorps. A diary entry revealed his total ignorance of the implications of his directive. 'People will enjoy the opportunity to have a go again at the enemy,' he said, 'from 150m with a rifle.'[15] Many infantry veterans would not have relished the prospect, never mind totally untrained Luftwaffe ground crews.

These draconian measures, employing unprepared specialists, began to break up the infrastructure of some divisions, further reducing their effectiveness in the line. General Balck explained the penalty of committing artillerymen, tank crews and resupply troops forward as infantry. 'Where you simply have to insert these people,' he said, 'the losses among them are terrible if they are not trained.' Because, he explained, 'the "hero" of the communications zone is rarely a front-line hero.' It was an impractical measure. 'People who could do their maintenance or supply tasks perfectly in the midst of the heaviest bombing or artillery attacks failed miserably.' In short, Balck pointed out, 'the results were quite shocking.'[16] Problems already apparent in September were getting worse. As the *Ostheer* 'victored itself to death', the very fabric of its Blitzkrieg structure, the synergy and coherence of the specialist organisations that had previously given it a battlefield edge, were coming apart.

As the final advance gathered momentum in the middle of November, units became increasingly aware of an intangible yet icily apparent foe, the Russian winter. 'We hadn't been deployed as regiments or companies for quite a while,' revealed Panzer commander Karl Rupp with Hoepner's Panzergruppe 4:

> *'My battle group consisted of two PzKpfwIII medium tanks, three PzKpfwII light tanks, about 40 or 50 riflemen and one 88mm. We were all dog-tired. The young men slept in any position whenever they got a chance. For weeks, we only got out of the tank for minutes at a time. Our breath condensed on the metal, so that everything you touched inside the tank was covered with ice. It was –40° to –50°C outside. Most of the time even the rations were frozen. At night we had to start up the tanks every two hours to keep the engines from freezing up.'[17]*

Snow and ice conditions changed the nature of the fighting on the Eastern Front. Both sides were subjected to the same conditions but the *Ostheer* was disadvantaged by the unfamiliar environment. Paradoxically the intensity of fighting, and as a consequence casualties, diminished, due to the physical difficulties of manoeuvring and fighting in adverse weather. Formations on both sides had, in any case, been much reduced by attrition. Flexible and mobile operations were no longer achievable, further blunting the *Auftragstaktik*-based leadership edge the *Ostheer* enjoyed relative to its more inflexibly led foe in the summer months. The *Ostheer* was neither trained, equipped nor psychologically prepared for winter operations. These, by physical necessity, were degraded to man-against-man frontal attacks, as conditions denied flanking options, favouring the Russian defender more conditioned to the climate in which he lived. German tactical expertise could no longer compensate for the technological superiority of heavy Russian tank types. German casualties, likewise, meant fewer experienced officers and NCOs available to exploit rapid-moving situations, leading to an imperative to control and centralise assets in the hands of the few who could.

By the end of October von Bock was complaining about serious officer shortfalls in the army group. 'More than 20 battalions are under command of lieutenants,' he lamented. Battalions, traditionally led by majors and lieutenant-colonels, were being led by lieutenant platoon commanders. Despite their combat experience, these men were trained to lead a few score men, not hundreds, and operate in close co-operation with tanks, artillery and aircraft — a demanding task. On 16 November von Bock informed his commanders he was down to a single division reserve and as a consequence 'they would have to get by with their own forces'. Freedom of action, in particular taking operational 'risks', was reduced. Units would have to fight their own way out of difficulties individually. 'I further reminded them,' von Bock emphasised, 'that the forces were to be held together and not jumbled up — as is the case with Fourth Army, which admittedly is fighting under very tough conditions.'[18] These were not fertile conditions to practice *Auftragstaktik*, which depended upon personal initiative in order to flourish.

In summary, these German raiding formations had limited physical options as they sought to grasp Moscow in a double envelopment. The former tactical and technological superiority conferred by Blitzkrieg was constrained, having to deal with superior and heavier Soviet tanks, often frontally without the benefit of Luftwaffe air support, much degraded by the weather. By contrast, the Soviet air force, served by permanent air bases in and around Moscow, was increasing its activity.

Karl Rupp, commanding a light PzKpfwII with the 5th Panzer Division with the northern envelopment moving toward Moscow, recalled the most important addition to these small battle groups of five to six tanks was the inclusion of one or two 88mm anti-aircraft guns. 'These alone could measure up to the Russian T-34 tanks, which were shooting up our tanks like rabbits,' he said. 'We were powerless to do anything about it with our light guns.'[19] One PzKpfwIII crew reported striking a T-34 four times at 50m and again at 20m with special upgraded 50mm *Panzergranate 40* projectiles which 'did not penetrate but sprayed off the side'. By contrast, a strike from the 76mm T-34 gun could be devastating. 'Time and time again our tanks have been split right open by frontal hits,' complained a Panzer commander. Commanders' cupolas on both PzKpfwIIIs and PzKpfwIVs 'have been completely blown off', read a report, 'proof that the armour is inadequate and the attachments of the cupolas faulty'.

German tank crews felt increasingly vulnerable. The Panzer officer reflected that the former elan of the Panzer force 'will evaporate and be replaced with a feeling of inferiority, since the crews know they can be knocked out by enemy tanks while they are still a great distance away'.[20] They were reduced to firing carefully aimed shots against the rear drive sprocket, along with chance strikes on the turret ring, rather than a rapid shot into the centre of mass. German tank crews had to light fires beneath their hulls in order to cold-start engines. A T-34 driver had a pair of compressed air bottles at his feet to help turn the diesel engine in particularly cold weather. Continuing German success against these superior tanks, despite the need to confront them head-on, was maintained primarily because of the fifth additional crew man, the radio operator. Every German tank in the division had a radio. 'As a result,' concluded one senior Panzer officer, 'our tanks were able to defeat tanks that were quite superior in firepower and armour.' A communications system was provided which enabled a German division commander to direct operations from any point on the battlefield within the division — an option not available to their Soviet opponents.

German infantry anti-tank vulnerability was officially recognised at the end of the French campaign, but not resolved. Shortfalls became apparent again in front of Moscow. The previous effective combined arms support, which had compensated for weaknesses during the summer, was annulled by the onset of winter weather. Infantry felt naked when faced with tanks, as one graphic veteran assessment testified:

> *'Use your rifle? You might as well turn round and fart at it [the tank]. Besides it never comes into your head to shoot; you just have to stay still as a mouse, or you'll yell with terror. You won't stir your little finger, for fear of annoying it. Then you tell yourself you may be lucky, perhaps it hasn't spotted you, perhaps its attention has turned to something else. But on the other hand perhaps your luck's right out and the thing is coming straight for you, till you lose sight and hearing in your hole. That's when you need nerves like steel wire, I can tell you. I saw Hansmann of the Ninth get under the tracks of a T-34, and he hadn't dug his hole deep enough; he had been too bloody tired to shovel. The tank just turned*

a bit off its course, that skidded just enough of the ground away. It had him. The next minute there he was flattened out like a bit of dog-shit you accidentally put your foot in.'[21]

Leutnant Adolf Stamm, serving with Flak artillery, recalled, 'the cry from heavily pressured infantrymen, "Bring up the Flak!" happened ever more frequently these days, because we, with our 88mm guns, were practically the only weapon which could still halt the Russians.' But the 88mm was cumbersome to bring into action. Despite excellent penetration, it was, in the opinion of another Panzer veteran, 'really large, quite immobile and hard to handle'. It was designed to be set up in the anti-aircraft role from a fixed static position, not engage in the mêlée of mobile meeting engagements. Getting the gun into action at vulnerable points with flexibility restricted by ice and snow, or dragging it into hasty positions among the wooded areas pronounced at this stage in the advance on Moscow, was labour-intensive and cost time. It was not a tank. Yet there were few alternatives. Adolf Stamm pointed out, 'the other weapons and even the hard-pressed infantry had scant capability to halt the attacks'. As a result, 'from morning until evening the infantry would repeatedly call *"Flak Vorn!* Flak Forward! Bring up the Flak!"'[22]

Luftwaffe support began to fall away with the onset of bad weather and the effects of the resupply crisis. Generalleutnant Baron von Richthofen assumed command of Army Group Centre's air support with Luftflotte 7 when Generalfeldmarschall Kesselring was withdrawn, along with all his Luftflotte 2 units, to Italy, to shore up the Axis effort in North Africa and the Mediterranean. Von Richthofen's command post moved from Smolensk and was eventually established at Jemelyanovo, 125km west of Moscow. Resupply became so critical that long-distance communications cable was flown forward by air transport. Aircraft fuel, bombs and ammunition requirements were not being met. Roads were constantly churned up by trucks, and delays ensued. 'The entire stretch between Rzhev and Kalinin was precarious,' von Richthofen explained, 'because Soviet infantry and even tanks and artillery were always crossing the roads.' Additional Junkers Ju52 air transports were brought in from Norway to fly air supply sorties in support of the army group.

Winter weather applied its own peculiar attrition rate through adverse conditions and accidents, which resulted in a decline of the sortie rate. The 2nd Stuka Geschwader reported in November: 'winter weather; sleet; only dive-bombers fly at 100m altitudes against a Soviet tank counter-attack into the flank of the 110th Infantry Division'. On 7 November the temperature fell below –20° and the Ju87 Stuka engines failed to start. Major Hozzel, the Geschwader commander, wrote in his diary that 'in spite of the efforts of all personnel, we can only sortie on a few days'. As a result, only one dive-bombing attack was mounted on 13 November, another on 18 November and some others on the 26th and 28th, when four sorties were flown. At the end of the month another sortie was mounted in support of Panzergruppe 4 about 20km north-west of the outskirts of Moscow.[23] Support deteriorated almost completely at the beginning of December when temperatures plummeted to –30°. Oberleutnant Hans Rudel, a Stuka pilot, declared 'a sudden cold snap of below –40° freezes the normal lubricating oil. Every machine gun jams'. He ruefully commented, 'the battle with the cold is tougher than the battle with the enemy'.[24] German airstrips were hardly usable, whereas the Russians used permanent Moscow bases. Russian sources claim a five-fold sortie superiority rate of 15,840 against 3,500 German during the three-week period 15 November–5 December.[25]

Artillery Leutnant Georg Richter with the 2nd Panzer Division repeatedly referred to Russian air attacks in his diary. They appeared to climax at the end of November, coinciding with the reduction of Luftwaffe support. Richter, routinely commenting on a wide range of issues, pointedly emphasised the significance of the development. On 26 November he observed, 'there are heaps of Russian aircraft around — our own very seldom!' The following day, 'Russian aircraft totally dominate air space' over Panzergruppe 4, and as the advance got under way he declared, 'Russian flyers dominate the air and the ground'. Repeated references to Russian air superiority and strafing attacks are made on 29 November and 2 and 3 December. Every attack killed or wounded small numbers of artillerymen and began significantly to disable increasing numbers of artillery-towing vehicles.[26] Russian air dominance had a cumulative and negative impact on morale. Attacks were more effective in winter than summer because men and vehicles were unable to get quickly off roads, hemmed in by piled snow from clearance, and funnelled by the wooded terrain through which they advanced.

The advent of winter caused soldiers to take the 'Mot' abbreviation used to describe motorised units and substitute it with a sardonic 'Hot' label. The *Ostheer* was becoming increasingly reliant on horse power for transport and infantry manpower to maintain progress. Infantry were shouldering an increased burden of the *'Flucht nach Vorn'*. They were completely unprepared for the conditions they encountered. Temperatures of –10° to –15°C deteriorated even further. Winter on the Western Front in 1940 had also been severe, but then it had been *Sitzkrieg* (Phoney War). There was no possibility of sitting out the present winter in bunkers, and the weather was becoming progressively worse.

Gefreiter Joachim Kredel with the 9th (Potsdam) Infantry Regiment naïvely felt with the onset of the first snowstorms that 'now the war will stop, you can't fight in the snow'.[27] He was wrong, but it was a justifiable error of judgement, shared by many others. Winter conditions up to this point were the worst they might have experienced in Germany, in which case they would have ceased training and returned to barracks. Training had not prepared them for such conditions. On 21 October a Flak regiment Unteroffizier wrote home:

'How long we remain here is dependent upon the course of this operation. Of course the greatest pleasure for us would be to load up and be off to Germany. We may perhaps need to stay, even over the winter. We don't know.'

Another Unteroffizier in 167th Infantry Division spoke of 'diverse rumours with varying content'. He explained, 'one says we will be out of here before Christmas, the other that we are to occupy winter quarters at Riesana, 150km from Tula'. In any event, 'by Easter we ought to get some home leave'. All this ominously suggested the campaign would last longer than anticipated. A transport battalion NCO wrote with some exasperation in early November:

'One cannot fundamentally grasp why we have not received any winter things . . . I believe that [the French] in 1812 were better equipped against the winter than we are . . . Surely . . . the "men at the top" can't be aware of this, otherwise they would certainly have helped us.'[28]

Logistic decisions taken in good faith by the staff were being unravelled by events and bad weather. Throughout the summer, campaign diaries and official records indicate staffing activity was ongoing to prepare for the approaching winter. Assumptions concerning the predicted outcome of the campaign were to prove massively wrong. It was anticipated that, following a rapid conclusion of the 'Barbarossa' invasion phase, an occupation army of 56 divisions would remain in Russia. Two-thirds of the *Ostheer* would be likely to return to the Reich, leaving the bulk of their matériel for an occupation force, which would almost certainly occupy winter quarters. At the beginning of September it dawned on planners that the number of trains would have to be increased by 50% to clothe 750,000 men and care for 150,000 horses. Not until mid-December did it become ominously apparent that the mass of units would not only stay in Russia but would be engaged on active operations in winter field conditions.

Without prior notification, economic production was unable to remedy the shortfall. The Quartermaster-General set up numerous production lines in the Reich and occupied territories to produce — in addition to bathtubs, fire-grates and other equipment — 252,000 towels, 445,789 articles of woollen underwear and 30,000 snow camouflage jackets. An appeal (code-named 'Bögen') was set in motion for the German civilian population to provide winter clothes and skis for troops at the front. Trains were loaded with clothing, accommodation materials and winter sports equipment and sent forward, only to become snarled up in sidings at Warsaw as greater priorities were given to fuel and ammunition. The railway logistic network meanwhile ground to a frozen halt as a result of the weather and partisan attacks.[29]

Results at the front were catastrophic. 'One started to look for things to use,' said artillery forward observer Hans Mauermann, outside Leningrad. White sheets were stolen from Russian houses for use as camouflage 'to produce covers, not so much for warmth, but so one was not so starkly visible in the snow'. Only chalk was available to whiten helmets. 'That was the practical sum of our winter preparation,' he said.[30] During the heat of the summer campaign most infantry soldiers had cut off the legs of their 'long johns', the only type of Wehrmacht underwear issued. As a consequence, soldiers froze with only shorts beneath their trousers, supplemented by a thin issue temperate coat and a poncho, a waterproof sheet that could be joined with others to make a bivouac tent. By the middle of November alternating frost and thaw conditions were replaced by permanent ice and snow.

Temperatures hovered between −8° and −22°C on average, offering little respite. A higher than usual number of logistic trains arrived in the Army Group Centre area on 24 November. This shipment of 24 trains permitted the first winter clothing issue to be distributed. On average one man from five received an overcoat. They were not issued to the men of the rear services. Russian tank driver Benjamin Iwantjer on the Central Front wrote on 17 November, 'the Germans are still wearing summer clothing'. They had captured a 'thin, dirty and hungry' 18-year-old German soldier who told his captors all they wanted to know when questioned with a map. When offered his freedom, Iwantjer said, 'he would not go for anything in the world'. So far as the German was concerned 'the war was over' and 'he was content to be a prisoner and still alive, because he believed we would shoot him.'[31]

'The wind was forever howling and blowing in our faces,' recalled German machine gunner Walter Neustifter, causing 'ice to crystallise all over our faces, in front, behind, and on the nose'; the cold was all-pervasive. Weapon systems began to malfunction and vehicles did not start. 'It is freezing again,' declared Leutnant Georg Richter on 5 November, 'Will the campaign now go on?' All the wheels of his artillery towing vehicles had frozen fast, with 'mud frozen like granite between the wheels and brake drums'. Hard work was required to clear it. They tried to dig bunkers around the artillery positions when a failure of fuel resupply obliged a halt. 'It's not so easy to stay outdoors without gloves and head protection,' Richter commented. He noted the average temperature was −15°C, and the ground had frozen hard to a depth of 20cm.[32] By 16.00 hours — late afternoon — it was dark. General Guderian, speaking with soldiers from 167th Division on 14 November, observed:

'The supply situation was bad; snow-shirts, boot polish, underclothes and above all woollen trousers, were not available. A high proportion of the men were still wearing [summer] *denim trousers, and the temperature was eight degrees below zero!'*

He continued on to the 112th Infantry Division, 'where I heard the same story'. Around him stood soldiers wearing captured Russian overcoats and fur caps. 'Only the national emblem showed that they were Germans.' Driving on to a Panzer brigade he saw only 50 tanks were left of the 600 which had originally been available to three divisions. 'Ice was causing a lot of trouble,' he remarked, because calk grips needed to prevent tracks skidding had yet to arrive. 'The cold made the telescopic sights useless' and the optic salve to remedy this had also not been delivered. Fires were burning beneath the Panzers in preparation for starting them up. 'Fuel was freezing on occasions,' he was told, 'and the oil was becoming viscous . . . This unit, too, lacked winter clothing and anti-freeze mixture'. Guderian left feeling depressed.[33]

Soldiers tackled their problems through self-help. In the 2nd Panzer Division, hides, old furs and felt boots were stolen from Russian cottages. Fur collars were wound around necks and used as gloves and ear protectors, and boots were stuffed with straw and felt. Platoons commandeered up to four coats apiece to enable sentries to use them in turn as they came on duty. General Guderian wrote on 17 November:

'We are only nearing our final objective step by step in this icy cold and with all the troops suffering from the appalling supply situation . . . Yet the brave troops are seizing all their advantages and are fighting with wonderful endurance despite all their handicaps. Over and over again I am thankful that our men are such good soldiers.'[34]

Tikhvin, east of Leningrad, fell to von Leeb's Army Group North on 9 November. A stranglehold had been placed on any Soviet hope of resupplying the city, now condemned to starvation. Repeated Russian attacks were mounted against the Tikhvin salient in order to open the railway north of Lake Ilmen to break the blockade. A German push from the salient toward Lake Ladoga stopped 56km short. Army Group North was now increasingly dependent upon the progress of the Moscow offensive in the centre to stabilise its increasingly vulnerable salient east of Leningrad. Cold weather arrived earlier in the north. 'Sometimes it was −40° sitting there in a bunker,' declared Rolf Dahm, a radio operator in an infantry battalion besieging Leningrad. Everything was difficult. 'There was the problem of washing and going to the toilet in extremis,' he said, interjecting, 'You try coming out and dropping your trousers when it's 40° below zero!'[35]

The immense breadth of front that had to be secured by the shrinking *Ostheer* is placed in sharp relief by Generalfeldmarschall von Bock's comment on contrasting weather conditions between fronts. On 1 November he complained:

'The situation is enough to drive one to despair and filled with envy, I look to the Crimea, where we are advancing vigorously in the sunshine over the dry ground of the steppe and the Russians are scattering to the four winds.'

'It could be the same here,' he exasperatedly declared, 'if we weren't stuck up to our knees in the mud!'[36] An unseasonably cold period soon set in to the south, which by mid-November was recording lower temperatures than even Army Group Centre.

Army Group South, spearheaded by the 1st SS Division 'Leibstandarte Adolf Hitler' took the city of Rostov on 21 November. Rostov, at the confluence of the River Don and Gulf of Taganrog, was the communications gateway to the Caucasus. Jubilation followed in the German press over this notable but, unbeknown to them, dangerous achievement. The IIIrd Panzer Corps was soon subjected to attacks in and around Rostov from across the frozen River Don in the south and the open steppe to the north. On its left, elements of three Soviet armies battered away at XIVth Panzer Corps. Within 24 hours von Kleist, the commander of First Panzer Army, realising he had insufficient forces to resist this onslaught, ordered the evacuation of the city. The order was countermanded by Generalfeldmarschall von Brauchitsch, Commander-in-Chief of the German Army. Giving it up would have military and 'far-reaching political consequences'. Hitler had been staging a publicity spectacle for the renewal of the 1936 Anti-Comintern Pact, the cornerstone of the Rome–Berlin–Tokyo Axis. With Rostov lost, Leningrad isolated and Moscow in imminent danger, the Soviet strategic position looked worse than ever.

By 28 November there were 21 Soviet divisions aligned against IIIrd Panzer Corps at Rostov. The corps commander, General der Kavallerie Eberhard von Mackensen, had reported even 10 weeks earlier that his two divisions, the 'Leibstandarte' and 13th Panzer, were worn out and short of everything from socks to anti-freeze. They were down to two-thirds of their normal strength. Fighting power had been reduced in much the same way as the German divisions struggling toward Moscow. The IIIrd Corps reported, 'any actions which are undertaken are borne by non-commissioned officers and a few die-hards'. Their strength was at an end. 'The bulk of the men go along only because of their training and the basic decency in their bones.'[37] On 28 November the corps evacuated Rostov and pulled back behind the River Mius. It was the first German retreat of the war.

On the Central Front, Panzergruppen 3 and 4 attacks beyond Klin and Solnechnogorsk opened a 45km gap between Dimitrov on the Moscow–Volga canal and the village of Krassnaya Polyana, just 18km north of Moscow. To the south, Second Panzer Army's 17th Panzer Division pushing toward Kashira had begun to form a deep pocket around Tula, placing their enveloping spearhead 100km short of the southern outskirts of Moscow. These pincer arms, however, did not possess the power they had enjoyed at Smolensk, Kiev and Vyazma. They were weak. Von Bock on 23 November enjoined both von Brauchitsch and his Chief of Staff, Halder, 'for heaven's sake' not to overestimate the strength of his forces. Staffs 'must be clear,' he said, 'that as far as this attack is concerned it is "the eleventh hour"'.[38]

Army Group Centre was making only slow progress. 'Are we to be pitied or admired?' asked a soldier in the 260th Infantry Division. 'Without winter clothing and with no gloves, and footwear in need of repair, we live in the open, lying if necessary in foxholes.'[39] During clear evenings the advancing infantry could see flashes from Flak and ghostly searchlight beams above the city of Moscow. It was within their grasp. The German effort had reached crisis point. Panzergruppe 3 at Krassnaya Polyana was within 20km of the suburbs.

Locomotives puffing sparks and huge clouds of steam into the frozen night air slowed and clattered their way into the sidings and railheads at Yakhroma and Ryazan, north and south of Moscow. Goods wagons and passenger carriage doors were freed of ice and knocked open. Soldiers leaped down onto tracks, raising clouds of condensation; stretching, urinating and slapping themselves for warmth. Quickly rounded up in the normal pandemonium of military activity with shouting, whistle blasts, vehicles drawing up and flashing lights, they were formed up and marched off into the darkness. Unloading vehicles took longer. There was ceaseless activity as trains shunted in, unloaded and puffed out of the railhead again. It was bitterly cold. Deep snow impeded the movement of the troops as they set off to their new assembly areas. Many of the soldiers had endured cramped conditions inside these trains for the nine, to ten-day journeys that had brought them from as far afield as Ulan, Siberia and the border with Mongolia and China.

New armies were being formed and assembled in areas just behind the front. At Yakhroma, north of Moscow, First Shock Army began to coalesce in freezing conditions toward the end of November. In the centre was Twentieth Army, and Tenth Army was around Ryazan to the south. Stalin had closely questioned Zhukov two weeks before on Moscow's survival prospects. 'Are you sure we are going to be able to hold Moscow?' he asked. 'Tell me honestly, as a member of the Party.' Zhukov believed 'there is no question that we will be able to hold Moscow' but it was dependent upon the arrival of reserves he had requested on being appointed commander of the Moscow Front. 'Two more armies and two hundred tanks,' he said. Stalin had answered, 'They will be ready by the end of November, but we have no tanks for the time being.'[40] Meanwhile the front was to be held with what there was.

The number of tanks on the Russian West Front increased from 450 to 700 between 1 October and 15 November. In addition the STAVKA had reinforced and covered projected German attack avenues, providing eight rifle and seven cavalry divisions, four rifle brigades, an airborne corps and independent tank and specialist units at the end of November. Further armies were also forming up: the Twenty-eighth, Thirty-ninth, Fifty-eighth, Fifty-ninth, Sixtieth and Sixty-first armies. In total, 194 divisions and 94 brigades had been newly created since the beginning of the war, which had started with 291 divisions.

Russian intelligence was informed by Richard Sorge that Japan might be verging on an offensive so vast in scale and remote from Russian territory that substantial Russian units could be risked transferring from Siberia to the west. The Sorge spy network was eventually compromised with his capture and execution. Even so, 27 of the new divisions (comparable in size to Army Group North at the outset of 'Barbarossa') came from the Far East, Central Asia and the Transcaucasus.[41] This amounted to the creation of a second strategic echelon not yet identified by Luftwaffe reconnaissance. Although the new armies were inexperienced and short of artillery and tanks, they were fresh. They would not hesitate in the attack, unlike the assaulting veteran but weak German divisions, until they, too, knew what it was like to be bloodied. The potential to administer a strategic counter-blow was crystallising in the very Arctic conditions that would make their sudden deployment in the teeth of their exhausted foe quite devastating.

Chapter 15
The spires of Moscow

'They could count the number of days required to reach Moscow on the fingers of one hand. The spires of the city were visible to the naked eye in the clear cold weather.'

SS infantry officer

'FLUCHT NACH VORN'

Flucht nach Vorn (the desperate German rush against Moscow's defences) was predicated on the belief that Soviet forces were verging on collapse. Von Bock was reminded by General Halder, 'we must understand that things are going much worse for the enemy than for us and that these battles are less a question of strategic command than a question of energy.'[1] It was not energy driving soldiers, more a desire to conclude the campaign. Unaware of the true situation, they instinctively felt a 'decision' achieved in front of Moscow or the capture of the city itself would bring a form of respite, a lull in the fighting, at minimum some shelter, at best the end of the war. 'Moscow' became the dominant theme of *Feldpost*, diaries and unit accounts. Time and distance was measured in terms of proximity to the city.

Von Bock lamented on 21 November, 'the whole attack is too thin and has no depth'. Unit symbols on his 'green table' belied the true situation; the ratio of forces was no more unfavourable than before, except 'some companies have only 20 and 30 men left'. He accepted 'heavy officer losses and the over-exertion of the units in conjunction with the cold give a quite different picture'. Alois Kellner, a despatch rider journeying between divisions near Naro-Fominsk, about 70km from Moscow, saw the picture only too clearly. 'The frozen bodies of *Landser* were stacked next to the roads like timber,' he said. These grisly constructions, 'shaped like huts, might include between 60 and 70 bodies, frozen stiff'.[2] Officer losses were especially high. 'Many second lieutenants are leading battalions,' von Bock recorded, 'one first lieutenant was leading a regiment' (a weak brigade of three battalions).[3]

Panzer commander Karl Rupp remembered, 'our last push was through wooded terrain'. He was advancing with the 5th Panzer Division some 20–25km from Moscow.

'The spearhead consisted of two PzKpfwIIs and two PzKpfwIIIs. At the end of the column was another PzKpfwII with riflemen in between. The lead tank was knocked out with no survivors. I was in the second tank. There was no way to get through, we had to pull back.'

They passed a Moscow tram stop on the city route. At night they could see Flak engaging German aircraft over the city.[4]

Panzer thrusts were in reality probing raids. Progress was characterised by a series of short, confused, hotly contested meeting engagements with the enemy. Both protagonists had scant knowledge of the overall situation. Gerd Habedanck, waiting with infantrymen securing a wintry forest road, 'suddenly heard tracked vehicles driving towards them at frantic speed from the rear'. Three Soviet T-34s abruptly rushed by, spraying up snow from the back. 'Behind each turret,' said Habedanck, 'lay a barely identifiable group of spectre-like Soviet infantrymen, who had jumped onto the back of the tanks hoping to break through to Moscow.' They pressed tightly up against each other, heads burrowed down into brown greatcoats, to secure protection against the wind. A flurry of wild shooting broke out and two of the Russians toppled from the tanks into the road. 'Then the last tank drove into a shell crater where it was struck by an anti-tank shell,' reported the correspondent. 'It managed to get out and then disappeared down a small wooded track, streaming smoke as it went.' Shortly after, a thick black pall of smoke began to rise above the tree-tops. A PzKpfwIII then clattered into an ambush position at the edge of the wood. Its first victim was a Russian armoured car travelling toward Moscow, which received a direct hit and was bulldozed from the road. On examination it was discovered there was only 476km on its speedometer. This brand-new vehicle had barely been delivered to the city.[5]

These skirmishes fought in the wooded areas on the outskirts of Moscow were conducted with pitiless ferocity. Much was at stake. Peter Pechel, a forward artillery observer riding with a column of nine tanks moving toward Volokolamsk, 60km from Moscow, had a 'queasy stomach and difficulty breathing'. The rest of his crew felt the same. 'Are we going to get it today?' he considered.

Some T-34 and not so new BT tank types belonging to M. E. Katukov's 1st Guards Tank Brigade were operating in the same area. They had been ordered to set ambushes along the same highway, with an infantry and anti-aircraft battalion in support. The infantry were already partially surrounded. 'Four of the [German] tanks crawled along the highway' and 'were set on fire' by two hidden T-34s, said Katukov.

'All hell breaks loose,' observed Pechel as the Panzer column came under fire from several directions. Intent on manoeuvring behind the enemy, the Panzer *Keil* had unluckily placed themselves directly in front of the Russian anti-tank positions. 'The lead tank is on fire,' said Pechel, and then 'the tank in front of me takes a direct hit on the turret hatch'. With no chance of returning fire, Pechel's tank was hit next.

'There is a brief roaring sound. I can't see. Blue stars dance in front of my eyes. Then I feel two quick blows to my right arm and left thigh. My radio operator cries out, "I'm hit!" Suddenly everything turns quiet inside our tank — horribly quiet. I squeeze my way out, shouting, "Quick, get out!"'.

Only two others scrambled from the smouldering wreck. Looking around, Pechel saw five tanks already hit and burning with wounded and dead crews scattered alongside. The entire right side of their Panzer had been shot away by the T-34's 76mm shell. 'My arm and thigh begin to hurt,' he said. 'There is blood on my face which sticks to my eyes.' His broken right hand flapped uselessly from his wrist and soon developed a blue tinge from the −14° temperature outside the tank. Pechel slipped into shock as the carnage carried on around him. 'Those who have already been wounded once are being hit a second and third time,' he said. Crackling incoming fire became interspersed with the whimpering from the wounded.

'The commander of the tank in front of me has taken a bullet in the head, and his brains are running down his face. He's running around in grotesque circles crying "Mother, mother". Finally, and almost mercifully, he is hit again by shrapnel and falls to the ground.'

Russian counter-attackers swarmed through the woods alongside Pechel, who began to consider his possible fate.

'Oh God, only four days ago I saw the dead of another one of our companies. I saw the poked-out eyes, the severed genitals, the horrible, tortured, distorted faces. Anything but that.'

Russian soldiers did not differentiate between black SS uniforms and Panzer crews. Any uniform bearing the 'death's-head' insignia at the collar (which Panzer troops might also wear) was inviting retribution 'When you're so young, and have been at war since the age of 19, you really haven't had much of a life. I *don't* want to die,' reflected Pechel, contemplating suicide.[6] At this moment German reinforcements coming up behind his initial probing attack crashed into the Russian positions. He was recovered and transported to the rear for treatment.

Katukov's two T-34s covered the fighting retreat of the Russian infantry. German soldiers clambered atop one of the tanks shouting to the Russians inside to surrender. The sister T-34 observing this threatening development 'used his machine gun,' said Katukov, 'to clean the enemy off his friend's tank'. Fire was returned from the other tank, which scythed through more enemy infantry who had meanwhile attempted the same.[7]

Despite the technical superiority of the T-34, they and inferior Russian models continued to endure fearful losses. Mortally wounded tank driver Ivan Kolosow wrote a final letter to his wife Warja at the end of October, revealing, 'I am the last of three tank drivers [from his platoon] still alive'. Seriously wounded, he regretfully wrote, 'we will never see each other again.' Nurse Nina Vishnevskaya, a medical orderly with a Soviet tank battalion, recalled fearsome burns and the hard physical effort required to pull injured crews from their confined fighting compartments. 'It's very difficult to drag a man, especially a turret gunner, out from the hatch.' She described the emotional trauma of caring for the hideously mutilated crewmen.

'Soon, of course, when I had seen burnt overalls, burnt hands and burnt faces, I understood what war was. When tank men jumped out of their burning machines, they were all ablaze. Besides, they often broke their arms or legs. They were serious cases. They would lie and beg us, "If I die, please write to my mother or wife"'.[8]

Russian resistance in German eyes alternated between the fanatical and the bizarre. An infantry officer with 7th Panzer Division, breaking into fortified villages near the Llama river, described 'resistance of such bitter intensity, it can only be seriously comprehended by those who had been through it themselves'. During these Panzergruppe 3 battles in the third week of November, 'Red Army soldiers continued to shoot from blazing houses even when their clothes were on fire.'[9] Such intense fighting was costing the Germans their best NCOs, the very men who led from the front in order to keep the lesser-motivated going. Feldwebel Karl Fuch's vulnerable Czech 38,T light Panzer was finally knocked out near Klin in an unequal skirmish with Russian tanks on 21 November. He was killed. A photograph taken by his comrades examining the destroyed tank reveal its 37mm gun bent in several places like a toy. Frau Fuchs received the death notice

from Leutnant Reinhardt, his company commander. It read: 'I hope it will be a small consolation for you when I tell you that your husband gave his life so that our Fatherland might live.' This was probably scant compensation. 'We commiserate and are saddened that fate did not allow Karl to see his little daughter,' wrote the Leutnant. He was not to know that the child that had been born after his father left for the front was in fact a son. Reinhardt had doubtless written countless similar death notices. Feldwebel Fuchs's only child had been five months old nine days before.[10]

Towards the end of November the division's Panzergrenadiers observed Alsatian dogs loping toward their armoured half-tracks with strange packages attached to their flanks and back, secured by wide leather girths. They opened fire immediately. Each dog appeared to trail a wire like an extended leash. These lines ran to Russian foxholes. The animals were trained to duck under vehicles or jump inside the fighting compartments. Red Army soldiers looking on would yank the line to arm the detonator mechanically which would then explode on contact with a surface. The German regimental commander had briefed his men to be wary of such tactics but in reality had already dismissed the bizarre warning as 'the usual latrine rumours'. He commented, 'One could never know or indeed imagine what new bestial methods the Russians would dream up next.' A virtual 'hare-shoot' followed, reported another witness, 'there were no checks on opening fire and a great many dogs were shot'. When the advance continued, the regimental commander's radio operator counted 42 'mine dogs' pathetically scattered about in the snow. 'I did not hear of a single case in our attack area when this Red Army trick worked,' added the regimental commander.

Three days after this incident the Panzergrenadier regiment had reached the Kalinin–Klin–Moscow road with the 'Von Rothenberg' Panzer regiment in support. That afternoon, they were attacked by Russian cavalry, an epic scene from a bygone age. Oberstleutnant von der Leye, the officer in charge, was a keen rider and wistfully regarded the oncoming riders with some regret. He was the third commander appointed since the beginning of the campaign and had no intention of taking any chances. 'Must we shoot at them?' asked a machine gunner alongside. He nodded in the affirmative. A storm of fire descended on the charging cavalry, cut to pieces in the co-ordinated fire of their modern Panzer counterparts. The advance continued on and it soon became apparent that the enemy for once was retreating steadily, not even torching the villages they vacated.[11]

At dusk on 27 November, Kampfgruppe 'Von Manteuffel' reached the Astrezowo–Jakowlewo area, 4km north-west of a bridge spanning the Moscow–Volga canal. A raid was ordered to capture it intact. The canal was the last defence obstacle before the city itself. Roads marked on maps would not be used, to avoid the likelihood of bumping into Russian resupply convoys. Von Manteuffel approached the bridge, detouring through surrounding woodland and bypassing villages en route. Engineer troops equipped with motorised saws were at the head of the column to cut pathways through the trees sufficiently wide for Panzers, half-tracks and heavy weapons to transit. Dismounted infantrymen moved either side of the column for security as it snaked its way through forest areas. Once clear, they accelerated along icy paths and across snow-covered fields toward the south-east. Shortly before darkness, the head of the column penetrated thick woods and came out in the village of Astrezowo.

No German troops were allowed to approach the wooded outlets on the Yakhroma town side for fear of compromising the raid. The battle group commander moved forward to the heights above the town where he was able to discern the iron girder bridge, the objective, silhouetted north of the town in the gathering winter dusk. Many of his officers and men, acutely aware of the vital significance of this bridge for any future advance, urged its immediate capture by *coup de main*, while it was still intact. Von Manteuffel refused to be drawn piecemeal. Equipment and additional units were still arriving and the Panzers would require more fuel if they were to be able to range around the sizeable bridgehead needed on the other bank. Orders were given for a dawn attack. They were meticulously briefed because few men had actually seen the objective. As one soldier remarked, 'we had not been able to see the approach terrain to the bridge so the commander painted a precise picture of the ground and axis of advance'. This was so accurate that 'despite pitch darkness not one foot was out of place during the pre-planned move to the bridge'. Villagers in Astrezowo were rounded up and locked away in a few houses as a security measure. Fires were strictly monitored as also orders for opening fire in the event of an unexpected enemy appearance. They were now set to go.

At 02.00 hours on 28 November a selected company of volunteers under Oberleutnant Reineck stealthily overpowered the guards on the bridge, and crossed without a shot being fired. The Moscow–Volga Canal was a deep stonework construction with steep sides which cut through the wintry landscape like a vivid scar. There was a road along both sides and a railway line on the eastern edge. Breathless German infantrymen were soon scaling the steep slopes of the high ground on the east bank, carrying or towing heavy weapons and ammunition. Enemy foxholes on the far side were reached and penetrated. As the first Russians came forward with their hands raised to surrender, they were shot down by their own men behind.

A Panzer group under Hauptmann Schroeder clattered across to the other side and the bridgehead swiftly began to take shape. Pandemonium resulted when a Russian armoured train appeared on the railway line and a group of several Russian T-34s began to attack German infantry digging in on the east side. A German Panzer company shot the armoured train into a flaming wreck. Smoke poured into the sky now growing lighter with the dawn and swirled about at ground level, smudging the snow. Very quickly three T-24s were hit, motionless and burning. At this moment a taxi cab drove incongruously onto the bridge and its surprised occupants were taken prisoner by the headquarters staff of Regiment 6. Inside was a Soviet officer with written orders and maps for the defence of the canal. Von Manteuffel remarked, 'He was amazed to be told to get out because he had no idea we had already broken through the canal defensive positions and that the bridge was in our hands.'

Complete surprise had been achieved. Nobody in the town of Yakhroma realised anything was wrong. At about 07.00 hours, workers poured into the factories and even at 08.00 the huge bread factory was at work. When it became lighter, realisation dawned what was going on and the town's noisy bustle resumed as the factories closed. Yakhroma's citizens — such as 19-year-old Valentina Igorowna Belikowa — had previously 'dug tank ditches so that the Panzers would not get through'. It was already too late. She said:

> 'We suddenly heard engine noises during the night of 27/28 November 1941, but they were from a direction we would have never thought possible. They came with motorcycles and started searching immediately for partisans all over the town.'

Von Manteuffel, the battle group commander, strode across the Yakhroma bridge, grim-faced and seemingly oblivious to the shouted cries of congratulations from his men. They appreciated the significance of their achievement. Indeed,

Generalfeldmarschall von Bock, on hearing the news, wrote, 'I had been preoccupied with the idea for days; its execution might bring about the collapse of Moscow's entire north-eastern front provided we simultaneously kept the advance by Fourth Army's northern wing going . . . But,' he added, 'that is not yet assured,' hence Manteuffel's grave expression. His men had driven a wedge across the canal, forming a bridgehead within ideal defensive terrain on the other side. Transmissions picked up on his own radio net confirmed his own worse fears. 'I realised,' he said, 'that apparently there were no worthwhile combat units quickly following up, to exploit this surprising success.'

First Soviet Shock Army, one of three armies building up for the proposed counter-offensive, had its concentration area nearby. It had yet to be identified by German forces. Von Bock noted in his diary later that day, 'I was given further cause to consider when, toward evening, Panzergruppe 3 reported heavy attacks against the bridgehead at Yakhroma.' He ordered the bridgehead to be held 'at all costs' but with 'no unnecessary casualties'. Von Manteuffel, meanwhile, began to piece together a troubling intelligence picture. An ominous report from a recently shot-down Russian pilot disclosed that the roads leading from the capital, over which he had just flown, 'were completely filled with marching Russian columns'; and they were heading his way.[12]

On the same day, 2nd Panzer Division came to a virtual standstill 30km south at Krassnaya Polyana, 18km north of Moscow. to their right was General Hoepner's Panzergruppe 4 with 11th and 5th Panzer, the 2nd SS Division 'Das Reich' and 10th Panzer Division groups all probing and stretching fingers out to Moscow, but unable to grasp a hold. They were battering their way head-on into the minefields and fiercely defended earthworks ringing the city. Behind and in echelon were the 23rd, 106th and 35th Infantry Divisions seeking to move either side of the 2nd Panzer Division in support. Von Kluge's Fourth Army northern flank was likewise making hesitant progress. Hoepner's Panzer battle groups were stretched so thinly they were barely able to maintain contact. Second Panzer Army, meanwhile, was enlarging its substantial bulge south of Tula.

A thrust north to Kashira was drawing swarms of Soviet cavalry and tanks upon the doggedly advancing, but now vulnerable, 17th Panzer Division. A decision point had been reached. Army Group Centre was poised to 'do or die'. As von Bock, its commander, expressed it: 'If we do not succeed in bringing about the collapse of Moscow's north-western front in a few days, the attack will have to be called off.' He was emphatic in his resolve not 'to provoke a second Verdun'.[13] This was the direction from which pressure was to be applied. The focus of the advance now began to shift south of 7th Panzer Division as the fingers of the laboriously advancing Panzer division battle groups scraped at the outer defensive crust north-west of Moscow.

THE FROZEN OFFENSIVE

At the end of November there were indications that the cold snap was coming to an end. Although frost, fog and some snow continued, temperatures rose to 0°C. This appeared to offer some physical respite. Meteorological statistics stretching as far back as the 19th century gave no reason to expect heavy snow and extreme low temperatures before mid-December. Until now, weather conditions had resembled the worst one might anticipate on an exercise during a bad winter in the Berlin area. Difficulties were encountered because of the lack of winter training. Units generally occupied warm barracks in such weather, sallying out to train for only short periods. On 1 December temperatures plummeted. The 2nd dawned sunny and clear but with temperatures at –20°C. A north-west European winter began now to give way to the merciless embrace of its Asian variant. Until this point OKW *Kriegstagebuch* (war diary) entries had referred only to frost and snow in its daily weather summaries, with occasional reference to comparable western European extremes. Now it was different. Temperatures slipped to –25°C on 4 December and then –35°C and –38°C on subsequent days. 'General Winter' had entered the field.

By the light of a freezing moon, which had already risen by 17.00 hours on 1 December, armoured half-tracks of the 6th Panzer Division infantry regiment combat group began to crawl forward laboriously through frozen snow. Ahead, their objectives were the villages of Ipleura and Swistuela, north-east of Moscow. Vehicle after vehicle began to break down in the freezing conditions. Before long, 15 had fallen by the wayside, left behind with skeleton and watchful crews. Most of the soldiers had already spent three complete nights in the open in conditions for which they were totally unprepared. The Division Supply Officer (1b) had already noticed that 'the lack of fat [in their rations] is having a detrimental effect upon the soldiers' body resistance'. They had received barely two days' equivalent (60 grams) over the previous 10 days. The last PzKpfwIV heavy tank in Panzer Regiment 11 also broke down that day in temperatures of –22°C.[1]

Soldiers require a substantial calorific intake to fight in these temperatures, otherwise they become increasingly lethargic. This, combined with living unprotected in the open, sapped physical and mental resilience. Winter clothes had still to be issued. The 98th Infantry Division had received only 'some winter coats and some gloves', and these had been set aside for drivers. 'It was like a drop of water on a hot stove,' commented one witness.[2] Winter warfare clothing layers need constant adjustment to control body temperature when undergoing strenuous tasks. Sweat clogs the airspace in material with moisture, reducing its insulating qualities. Perspiration when it evaporates chills the body and can cause freezing in extreme conditions.

Lethargic and tired soldiers tend not to take the trouble to adjust their clothing or regulate layers. The normal reaction is to add more clothing, which compounds the problem. During combat or when marching, soldiers perspire, get wet and then chill. At the end of November the 2nd Panzer Division anti-tank battalion received only a partial issue of winter clothing, enough for only one greatcoat per gun crew.[3] Fighting ability decreases with temperature and slows the rate of operations. After it drops below a bearable point, survival replaces the previous combat imperative. Organised manoeuvre involving combined activity becomes correspondingly difficult. Even today, NATO armies with high-tech lightweight 'breathable' and layered clothing reduce training activity at temperatures below –25° and virtually cease at –35°C, when survival is declared the paramount consideration. Training stops, snow holes are dug, mobility is reduced or troops return to accommodation. Conditions in front of Moscow began to vary between these two parameters, both judged unacceptable for operations other than war today. German soldiers possessed little to combat the cold. Their Russian counterparts were more fortunate, receiving padded clothing, ear muffs, gloves and felt boots. Zhukov pointed out, 'by the middle of November our soldiers were a great deal more comfortable than enemy troops, who wrapped themselves in warm clothes confiscated from local residents.'[4] Oberleutnant Ekkehard Maurer, serving with the German 32nd Infantry Division, declared:

'I felt terribly angry. We had no gloves, no winter shoes — we had no equipment whatsoever to fight or withstand the cold.'[5]

Inexperience in such sub-Arctic conditions was lethal. The body can lose liquid at an exceptional rate in freezing temperatures. Soldiers bundled themselves up in as many layers of clothing and materials they could find and became dehydrated, not imagining such conditions might exist aside from hot and humid weather. Infantry officer Heinrich Haape 'had gathered together an assortment of clothing,' he said, 'that kept me reasonably warm'. On his feet he wore outsize boots with two pairs of woollen socks wrapped in flannelette. The soles were padded with newspaper. He wore two pairs of 'long john' woollen underpants, two warm shirts, a sleeveless pullover, a summer uniform temperate overcoat and, over all this, 'a special prize' — a loose leather greatcoat. His hands were protected by an inner layer of woollen gloves, with leather gloves on the outside, and he wore two woollen caps. String was tied around his wrists to prevent the wind blowing up his sleeves. Any violent movement by the non-acclimatised German soldiers resulted in a bath of perspiration. Liquid was further lost breathing in cold air which, on being heated to body temperature inside the lungs, absorbs large amounts of moisture which is then expelled as body fluids. Soldiers ate snow because there was rarely time or opportunity to boil it: 17 times the volume of snow is required to produce an equivalent volume of water. Body 'cores' became chilled taking in snow, which often initiated diarrhoea.

Dysentery was an *Ostfront* affliction caused by poor food, unhygienic conditions and lice bites, and was a death sentence in certain conditions. Leutnant Heinrich Haape, a medical officer intent on keeping his men in the line, recognised 'these poor fellows' who, despite being badly weakened, attempted to keep up with their comrades as best they could. 'If they exposed themselves more than three or four times a day to the demands of nature,' he said, 'they lost more body warmth than they could afford to lose.' Soiled clothing might cause frostbite and death. A crude remedy was instituted:

'Without regard for the niceties, therefore, we cut a slit 10–15cm long in the seats of their trousers and underpants so that they could relieve themselves without removing their garments. Stretcher bearers or their own comrades then tied up the slit for them with a string or thin wire until the operation had to be repeated. All the men had lost weight so the trousers were roomy enough to permit this solution.'[6]

All these afflictions impaired fitness. Considerable energy was burned simply struggling through deep snow, burdened with heavy weights. An inadequately protected and exhausted man might freeze to death in his sleep. Unfit soldiers were more susceptible to cold injuries and frostbite. The latter occurs when blood supply to chilled areas of the body diminishes. Dehydration and the adrenaline surges that frightened soldiers experience in combat inhibit blood flow. All these conditions applied to the inadequately equipped German soldiers advancing on Moscow. 'People seemed to go grey overnight,' commented infantry soldier Harald Henry. 'Our best strength was murdered here on these snow fields,' he wrote in front of Moscow at the beginning of December.[7]

If the chilling process is brief, only minor damage occurs to flesh tissue, sometimes termed 'frost-nip'. Complete constriction leads to a discolouring of flesh and, if not treated, tissue damage resulting in gangrene. This might, at worst case, necessitate amputation. A steady trickle of such casualties began to occur. The 3rd Battery of Artillery Regiment 98 recorded, 'Ten men were passed on to the field hospital' on 8 December, 'including four men with second-degree frostbite'.[8] It was infinitely worse for the infantry forward. Walter Neustifter, a machine gunner, claimed 'most soldiers froze to death in temperatures under −30°C; they were not shot, simply frozen'. Icicles, he graphically described, would form around nasal passages, and 'fingers!' (he demonstrated with a sharp tap of the hand) 'would drop off! Real shitty!'[9]

Arctic temperatures brought planned operations to a frozen impasse. The 6th Panzer Division war diary recorded a temperature drop of −32°C on 4 December and −25°C to −32°C the following day, dropping to −35°C at night. Cold injury casualty figures were passed by radio, not in writing, to corps headquarters, so as not to alarm the soldiers unnecessarily about the true situation. Infantry companies down to 30 men needed three reliefs of sentry per hour to cope with the biting cold. Five soldiers standing guard meant 'half of the company was on duty while the other half got some rest'. On 5 December the operations officer reasoned:

'As a consequence, combat effectiveness, even security, was practically impossible to achieve. Twenty cases of frostbite were appearing in the battalions on average each day. The care of weapons and their maintenance for readiness is a matter of considerable urgency but difficult to accomplish. At times about two-thirds of the artillery guns are unable to fire because their barrel brakes and recoil mechanisms are frozen up. Feverish work is required to free them. Both infantry regiments are organised and maintaining their fighting strength . . . but in both regiments the available companies cannot be maintained at acceptable strengths.'[10]

Other complications were caused by the intense cold. Shock from wounds developed more quickly and was more lethal; cases of snow blindness increased in incidence. Carbon monoxide poisoning and eye irritations resulted from constant confinement in lice-ridden, ill-ventilated and overcrowded smoky hut and bunker conditions. Compressed living space in unhygienic conditions, coupled with winter darkness and the depressing attrition rate of dead and wounded, frayed nerves and shortened tempers. The cumulative impact this had on fighting power is difficult to quantify. Morale in general was maintained, but not easily. Opinions varied in relation to the proximity of the front. Panzer soldier Götz Hrt-Reger reflected with hindsight:

'In my opinion I believe the advance would have been a lot quicker with more material. Given fresh divisions and in sufficient numbers we could have reached Moscow before winter. Because of this we had delays. The troops were — let's say — overtired with the effort. There were heavy losses but, despite that, morale was "tip-top" — first class. Nobody wanted to [carry on the advance], that was another story, but you can't say the troops had no morale. In my opinion it was good, up to the zenith of the high point — otherwise it could not have lasted so long.'[11]

This high point was reached at the beginning of December. There were alternative opinions. Artillery soldier Josef Deck argued, 'our morale was actually in a catastrophic state, because constant combat with its incessant changes of accommodation grated on the nerves.' Infantryman Harald Henry held a similar view, declaring, 'A tremendously deep hatred, a resounding "No" collected in our breasts — *Ach*, it was so awful!' In order to counter collective dismay, officers and NCOs had to exercise their leadership qualities more often. In practical terms this meant more exposure to the enemy, and their casualties rose in order to maintain the momentum of the advance. Oberleutnant Ekkehard Maurer, fighting in the Leningrad area, described the inertia that had to be overcome.

'We could hardly take care of our own wounded, not to mention dealing with the enemy. We were afraid to become wounded and become the prey of the very bad winter climate, as much as the prey of the enemy. We had seen enough of the enemy to know that in cases like that prisoners were hardly ever taken, so a good many people, when it came to a decisive moment, opted not to stick his head out as far as he might have done otherwise.'[12]

Casualty reports reflected this drain on the junior leadership. The 6th Company of the IInd Battalion Schützen Regiment 114 reported being led by its sole surviving officer, an artillery observer, on 2 December. That day, nine men died and three were officers, as also one of 10 wounded. Total battalion losses had been 11 dead and 24 wounded.

While 7th Panzer Division clung to its tenuous bridgehead across the Moscow–Volga canal, on its right the 6th Panzer Division pushed on ahead. Gefreiter vom Bruch, advancing with Shützen Regiment 4, watched the explosions of bombs dropped from high-altitude Soviet bombers on the hilly wooded areas on the German side of the canal in bright freezing sunlight. As they entered the village of Goncharowo, he asked a little girl standing amid the ruins how far it was to the canal, Panzergruppe 3's objective. '11km to the canal and 12 to Yakhroma,' she said. 'And Moscow?' enquired the corporal. '60km,' was the reply.[13] Fighting began again in earnest as they penetrated the village of Bornissowo. Arctic temperatures were producing weapon malfunctions, which impeded operations with depressing regularity. Metal becomes brittle with intense cold and this, combined with the rapid increases of temperature by working parts during firing, caused breakages. Machine guns, in particular, needed substantially more spare parts. Belt-fed weapons had their feed pans regularly snarled up with snow, or fired intermittently due to the difficulty of controlling the gas flow to produce rapid rates of fire. Repeated reference is made in the 6th Panzer Infantry Regiment war diaries to heavy casualties caused by machine guns seizing up. Weapon stoppages and casualties among junior leaders attempting to remedy them were endemic across the front. Karl Rupp, commanding a PzKpfwII with Panzergruppe 4, recalled that, apart from the distraction of constantly turning over his tank engine to keep it working:

'One night the riflemen noted with horror that, on top of everything else, our machine guns had frozen up. If the Russians had attacked, they could have finished us without the least problem.'[14]

The Panzer spearheads continued falteringly to reach out thin fingers towards Moscow. On 2 December the 6th Panzer Division experienced 'a light parachute-drop scare' to its rear. Russian bombers were resupplying partisans but there were also parachute infantry insertions. German vehicles were shot at on the Klusowo road bridge in the division rear as the lead elements reached Kulowo. The 1st Panzer Division took Bely-Rast on 3 December with a tank/infantry attack. They were 32km from the Kremlin.[15]

The unfortunate Russian population was caught between German spearheads and Red Army resistance. They were exposed to the same −40°C temperatures described by Josef Deck with Artillery Regiment 71.

'Bread had to be chopped with hatchets to make it smaller. First aid packs set as hard as wood, petrol froze, optical instruments failed and the skin from hands remained frozen to rifles. The wounded froze to death within minutes in the

snow. Only a few people these days had the fortune to thaw out a Russian body to get his clothes.'[16]

Non-combatants caught in the path of the Army Group Centre advance suffered enormous privations. The *Landser*, insufficiently supplied, fell upon the populace like a horde of ravaging locusts. Valentina Judelewa Ragowskaja remembers the Panzers clattering into Klin on 23 November. The family hid in the cellar, 'dreadfully frightened', until German soldiers stamped on their cellar lid with jackboots. 'A soldier came down the cellar steps with a stick grenade in his hand — "Out!" he cried, "all Russians out!" They demanded "bread and sugar Mother!" making smacking noises with their lips. Two loaves of bread and a pair of turnips had been saved for the children. They were handed over.' One loaf was devoured before their eyes, the other tossed up out of the cellar to others. 'I went up and saw about 300 soldiers outside.' They were making fires with furniture gathered up from the houses to keep warm. Water and meat was then demanded. Ragowskaja's two hens were snatched up, their necks broken and flung on the fire, complete with feathers. 'Once the feathers were burned off, they stuffed themselves with chicken meat, as simple as that!' When she complained to the German commander she was haughtily informed, 'German soldiers do not take foreign property!' Total catastrophe ensued when the Germans slaughtered their one cow. 'It was our only cow and a young one at that, she produced a lot of milk,' said Ragowskaja. 'I cried and threw myself on the carcass of my dead cow.'

Forty years after the conclusion of the war, journalist Paul Kohl travelled the Army Group Centre route to Moscow during an academic pilgrimage to research Russian eyewitness accounts of the invasion and occupation. Cold War still reigned in Europe. Although it was difficult to avoid the 'Great Patriotic War' rhetoric, and it was a long time after the event, there was little doubt, despite exaggeration, that this had been an emotionally searing experience for those he met. Perceptions, like propaganda, can have the same impact as the truth. Inhabitants living in the communities on the approaches to Moscow suffered dreadfully. 'The way they treated us!', exclaimed Vera Josefowna Makarenko, from Klin, 'they hardly regarded us as human beings!' Her house was burned to the ground and her husband hanged. 'Right on the first day,' she wept. 'Five days he hung there, and they did not allow us to take him down . . . When they came, they took everything,' she said. There was nothing to eat or drink and it was forbidden to fetch water. Their bucket was shot full of holes to make the point. All their felt boots were stolen, despite it being the middle of winter. 'Our legs were frozen,' complained Makarenko.

'If only this war had not happened we would have had an excellent life. But the war destroyed all that, everything, it ruined us.'

Her young niece was taken away for questioning. 'Your father,' they asked, 'where is your father? Is he defending the homeland at the front? Or is he a partisan?' The little girl's finger was cut off during the interrogation.[17]

Istra — 30km from Moscow — was captured by the 4th SS Regiment 'Der Führer', alongside infantry and tanks from the 10th Panzer Division. Fighting raged against elements of the 78th Siberian and Manchurian units between 23 and 26 November through Istra cathedral, situated west of the river, and around a surrounding complex of six large ecclesiastical building ringed by a stout 5m-high wall. The 'Der Führer' companies were reduced to 25-man companies in the process.[18] Sixteen-year-old Ludmilla Romanowna Kotsawa described the impact on its hapless

inhabitants. 'Many had already fled into the woods,' she said, 'and they stayed in holes dug in the ground in ice and snow with temperatures at −20°C for days and nights.' Her music teacher, Michailow, was held up by soldiers in the street and robbed of her coat. 'You bandits!' she screamed at them. Kotsawa watched as 'one of them cold-bloodedly shot her in the mouth'. Istra typified what could happen to a town in this theatre of operations. It remained occupied for only two weeks before it was back again. Only 25 children were found in its cellars from a former population of 7,000. 'Istra was a beautiful green town,' Kotsawa wistfully remembered, but the population had been driven out. During December and January its ruins were infested with wolves. A rebirth did not occur until the re-establishment of its school in 1943.[19]

Josef Deck recalled the surreal scene by night, observing the approaches to Moscow from the forward positions of Artillery Regiment 74.

'As far as one could see the horizon stood out in flames. The Russians, using linked incendiary mines, were beginning to create a cleared "dead" security zone. Engineers over there were emulating an earlier self-inflicted solution that had been applied to Moscow in 1812 when Napoleon and his Grand Army saw only a blazing city on their line of advance.'[20]

Hatred arose among the scenes of unbelievable destruction visited by both sides upon the Russian population. Vera Josefowna Makarenko knew whom to blame:

'Just consider it for a moment. From over there came foreign people from a land which we believed were our friends. We had read their Goethe and Heine. And now they come and want to destroy us. Can you understand that?'[21]

'THE SPIRES OF THE CITY' . . . MOSCOW

The 1st and 2nd Panzer Divisions with the 23rd Infantry Division in between were the nearest German units to Moscow on 3 December during the final phase of the assault. There had already been some withdrawals as von Bock straightened his line on the Moscow–Volga canal to secure his northern flank before penetrating the city.

The 7th Panzer Division received the order to pull back from the Moscow side of the Yakhroma bridgehead at 02.15 hours on 29 November. It was a depressing development for the hard-pressed troops fighting on the enemy side, who had, in the words of their commander General Frhr von Funck, expended 'sweat and blood'. They recognised the underlying negative implication for any future advance on the city. Von Funck described it as 'an evil flash of lightning illuminating the great turning point of the campaign and, with it, the whole war . . . From now on one heard the oft-repeated expression "there are insufficient forces" with increasing frequency.' Forward riflemen were told at about 04.30 hours that the bridgehead had to be evacuated by daylight, which would be in one and a half hours' time. Heavy weapons and Panzers would have to recross the canal before they could be picked out in the murk. A sharp crack reverberated through the frozen air at 07.30 hours and an ominous black column of smoke rose from the centre of the bridge. It was regarded attentively and wistfully by the soldiers of the 7th Panzer Division. Only the centre part of the bridge span collapsed because there had been insufficient explosive. At 19.00 hours that night the Russians blew the remainder.

Explosives were also unavailable to burrow new defence positions into the west bank. Houses by the canal edge were fortified instead. Both sides appreciated the implications of this latest development. First

Shock Army, forming up nearby in preparation for the forthcoming Soviet counter-offensive, had applied unremitting pressure to the bridgehead. Soviet artillery fire began to range in on the newly established German positions. Air attacks increased. On 2 December the 7th Panzer staff ominously reported, 'Sixteen air attacks today!'[1]

Forty years later, Soviet artillery soldier Pjotr Jakowlewitsch Dobin, observing the canal bridge, reflected on the intensity of the fighting.

'I fought then to prevent the Germans from crossing the canal. They were actually successful in getting across, but only for a day. For two days there was awful fighting here, on 28 and 29 November 1941, a hideous bloodbath in ice and snow. We then forced them back onto the west bank. I'm still astonished today that I managed to survive it all.'[2]

Many Germans remember the fateful bridge detonation early on the morning of the evacuation. 'We were missing Unteroffizier Leopold,' said one witness:

'He had been sleeping and now made his way back, with long loping strides across the ice covering the canal. The sound of the explosion had been the first thing to wake him up. He was quite literally the last man to come back from "over there".'

With victory no longer an option, the surge of morale that originally accompanied the capture of this Moscow entry point suddenly dissipated and reaction set in. There was nothing left to transcend the physical discomforts and threat. Fighting continued in driving snowstorms against a build-up of enemy attacks, which had to be opposed with faulty frozen machine guns. There were complaints 'that urgently required warm winter clothing had still not arrived', and these 'became even more pronounced'.[3] Now that Moscow was denied them, survival became the primary concern.

Gefreiter vom Bruch was attacking forward further south of the 7th Panzer Division; he was with Infantry Regiment 4, part of 6th Panzer Division and 7km from the canal. His squad, protecting the forward artillery officer of the battery in support, 'soon ran out of ammunition.' Caught on exposed flat ground, the company suffered appalling casualties. On 3 December they occupied the village of Jasikowo but were ejected by a surprise attack at midday by 10–15 Russian tanks which suddenly emerged from the wood. Vom Bruch described the pandemonium as they burst upon them.

'We were overrun and could only flee. Many ran simply to conserve their naked lives. Equipment and various items fell into Russian hands. Some 20–30 men were missing from the battalion, including the battalion commander and two of the company commanders, who could not be saved.'

That night, with temperatures down to –32°C, their orders of several days, standing remained unchanged — 'hold the ordered line'.[4]

The 1st Panzer Division had meanwhile advanced 5km east of Bely-Rast, placing it 32km north of Moscow. Below them the bulge created by the 2nd (Vienna) Panzer and 23rd Infantry Divisions was creeping south-eastwards toward the Moscow suburbs. The 2nd SS Division 'Das Reich', with its 4th 'Der Führer' Regiment, was further south of the Istra–Moscow road and had reached the western outskirts of Lenino, 17km from Moscow. Russian Worker's Militia volunteers were thrown against them. 'Moscow was near enough to touch,' announced Otto Weidinger, one of its commanders.

'The men of the Regiment were convinced they could count the number of days required to reach Moscow on the fingers of one hand. The spires of the city were visible to the naked eye in the clear cold weather. A forward 100mm battery placed harassing fire on the city.'[5]

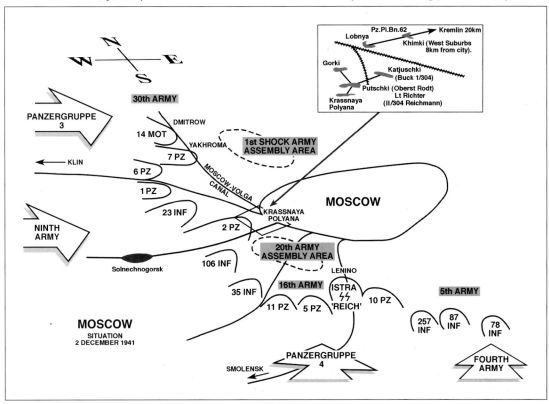

Left: The 2nd (Vienna) Panzer Division [inset diagram] was the closest unit to the Kremlin on 2 December 1941. To claim to be in sight of Moscow had the same epic significance to German soldiers as claims of being at Dunkirk or Arnhem had to Allied soldiers. One reconnaissance unit penetrated as far as Khimki — a 15-minute drive from the Kremlin — in the western suburbs of Moscow. This was the high point of *Ostheer* success during the eastern campaign. It was powerless to achieve more.

Legends abound concerning which German unit penetrated the nearest to Moscow. Its suburbs may well have been reached and were frequently easily observed. To be within visual sight of Moscow during this attack was in German eyes of epic significance, comparable to other 'glorious' failures at Dunkirk or (later) Arnhem for the British. Little glory remained to an advance which had deteriorated to one of groping progress. A young SS 'Deutschland' Regiment officer wrote, 'We are approaching our final goal, Moscow, step by step.' But, as he recounted, there were supply difficulties and weapon malfunctions. 'The day is coming,' he said, 'when the soldiers will not only be at the end of their strength, but companies will have lost their fighting strength due to the loss of numerous wounded, frozen and dead.' This was no final sally at a crumbling fortress. On the contrary:

'These fighting half-frozen German front-line troops stand and lie in a pitiless cold which occasionally drops below –45°C. They only wear regulation uniforms with normal leather boots, and are without gloves, overshoes or scarves while exposed to merciless combat and winter conditions.'[6]

North of the 2nd SS Division 'Das Reich', Unteroffizier Gustav Schrodek with Panzer Regiment 15 reflected in his diary: 'the capital Moscow is our attack objective — will we reach it?' He was a Panzer commander advancing with the 11th Panzer Division and was stalled by enemy action a few kilometres beyond the village of Krjukowa. 'I saw a signpost,' he said, 'which read "MOSKWA 18,5 km". His Panzer was abruptly reversed by its alert driver, just as a 76mm shell from a hidden T-34 whooshed by the turret.

'But to our right another vehicle in the company was knocked out by a direct hit to the turret. I saw the commander and driver clamber out while I traversed my turret to take aim, but he had already disappeared. Only later did I realise the Panzer commander lost his legs and the driver's hand had stuck, tearing flesh on the frozen track. Our ranks are thinning. Every day we lose a couple.'

Burying the dead in the frozen ground was hardly achievable with picks and shovels. 'We could only create a shallow ditch using hand-grenades,' he remarked. Temperatures had dropped to –35°C, and they were unable to advance further. Moscow was merely one hour's drive by Panzer, but with no accompanying infantry, they had to leaguer up in the snow and wait. They felt isolated, virtually abandoned.[7]

The closest finger niggling at the Russian defences on the outskirts of the city was the 2nd (Vienna) Panzer Division. Its anti-tank battalion was becoming increasingly dismayed at the ineffectiveness of its 37mm guns against the increasing numbers of Soviet T-34s its battle groups were encountering as they advanced south-eastwards along the Solnechnogorsk–Moscow road. A lucky shot striking the machine gun aperture of a T-34 from only 10m during an attack at Turicina had set one tank ablaze. It suicidally carried on to crush its 37mm assailant. At Strelino four English 'Matilda' tanks were despatched by Panzer Regiment 3. They had all been recently manufactured and had 'September 1941' stamped on their engine plates — an indication of Allied resolve and urgency to stem the Axis advance. On 28 November American tank types were knocked out. As the Kampfgruppe 'Decker' rolled into Oserezkoje on 1 December soldiers remarked on the appearance of Moscow Omnibus line stops. A combat group of Panzers, infantry, artillery and engineers commanded by Oberst Rodt of the 304th Regiment occupied the three villages of Krassnaya Polyana, Putschki and Katjuschki on 30 November.

Another battalion (the IInd) from the same regiment under Major Reichmann secured Gorki, nearby. A small salient had been driven into the area of Sixteenth Soviet Army, 17km from the outskirts of Moscow and only 27km from the Kremlin.[8]

They had been preceded, unknown to themselves, the previous day by motorcycle patrols from Panzer Pionier Battalion 62. Temperatures had now risen slightly to 0°C, which produced light wet snow and patchy fog. Utilising these conditions, General Hoepner commanding Panzergruppe 4 detached these motorcyclists from 2nd Panzer Division and ordered them forward to raid the railway station at Lobnya and conduct a fighting reconnaissance south of it. In one of those bizarre episodes of war, as the Russians fell back from Solnechnogorsk and the 2nd Panzer Division pushed its battle groups south-eastwards in search of an unopposed route into Moscow, the motorcycle raid found it. Hunched behind their BMWs and machine-gun-mounted sidecars, the force thrust forward, encountering no opposition until it reached Khimki, a small river port in the north-west suburbs of Moscow. They were within 8km of the city and 20km of the Kremlin, only a short drive away, a distance that could be covered in minutes. Panic ensued among the startled local inhabitants. 'The Germans are in Khimki!' was the cry. The motorcycle detachment, having had no substantial contact with Soviet troops, feeling vulnerable at the depth of their incursion and seeing the obvious agitation they had caused, turned back. They needed to report this unopposed thoroughfare. Support would not be at hand if they drove into resistance and, feeling over-extended, they retraced their route. Incredibly the unit drove back through the German lines without a shot being fired.[9]

Not surprisingly a flurry of activity resulted on the Russian side. Soviet General Konstantin Rokossovsky, whose Sixteenth Army was located just west of Moscow, received an unwelcome reminder of Stalin's resolve. He said:

'Comrade Stalin called me during the night. The situation was pretty difficult and our units had already fallen back in a number of areas. We knew that the Commander-in-Chief would give us such a dressing down we would feel sick. So I picked up the receiver with the special line with some trepidation. He asked me one question "Are you aware, comrade Rokossovsky, that the enemy has occupied Krassnaya Polyana, and do you realise that if Krassnaya Polyana is occupied it means that the Germans can bombard any part of the city of Moscow?"'[10]

Rokossovsky could only agree. Counter-attack orders were issued. Sixteenth Army had already been forced to pull back from Solnechnogorsk, 'giving rise to a serious situation,' as General Zhukov later explained. Units were moved into the area from the Supreme Headquarters Reserve. The Russian line was bending in an arc commensurate with German pressure, but did not buckle. Zhukov in early December was beginning to detect 'from the nature of the military operations and from the attacks of the enemy forces that the offensive was grinding to a standstill and that the Germans had neither the manpower nor the arms to continue their drive'. Michael Milstein, an officer on Zhukov's staff, recalled, 'we were able to capture German staff documents in front of Moscow and all these indicated that Soviet reserves appeared to be exhausted, and there would be no more available.'[11]

The Russian Supreme Command inserted forces sufficient only to hold the line while they amassed forces for a counter-offensive immediately behind the front. Soviet tank driver Benjamin Iwantjer remarked on the extent of the casualties they had already suffered. 'Standing before those who have already died in this war leaves us remaining alive with a sense of almost unbearable guilt,' he admitted.[12] General Zhukov, however, had no compunction in exacting whatever price was necessary to create the necessary conditions for his planned counter-stroke. The Soviet West Front continued to be reinforced with two newly formed armies — the First Shock and Tenth Armies — as well as a number of other units combined into a third, named Twentieth Army. Still the Germans suspected nothing.

Zhukov was a master of military deception. He applied measures similar to those he had conducted as commander of the First Mongolian Army Group in 1939 after the Japanese invasion of Mongolia. The formation successfully encircled and destroyed a Japanese force in a surprise assault on the River Khalkhin Gol. Although Zhukov's force had been 644km from the nearest railhead he clandestinely organised massive deliveries of matériel, assembling a huge tank force which subsequently overwhelmed the Japanese in a totally unexpected attack. These same deception measures were re-enacted on the Moscow front to give the impression that the Russians were intent on defence rather than offence. Soviet artillery observer Pawel Ossipow, preparing for the attack, recalled:

'We had to dig ditches at temperatures of –30°C with the ground frozen hard to a depth of 60–70cm. There were only picks, crow bars and shovels available to do the job. The work was done mostly at night because we would have been seen by day. It took about two days before we were dug in. On 1 December we occupied the fire positions. A few days later the warm clothing was brought up, fur jackets, gloves, mittens, padded trousers and felt boots. It was already much better after that, because we had to sleep in the snow next to the guns, on top of the ammunition boxes. It was uncomfortable but we did not freeze and we remained combat-effective.'

Soviet soldiers were prepared to endure whatever was necessary to win this war. Lew Kopelew, a junior officer, pointed out, 'a lot of people forget the fact that we fought voluntarily, many of us, millions — and we *wanted* to counter-attack.'[13]

Zhukov transposed this Mongolian experience to camouflage preparations for the pending counter-offensive. Transport movement from the interior was cloaked in secrecy. Extensive reconnaissance was conducted alongside meticulous planning to enable the passage of large formations from their assembly areas to attack points. Strict security was applied to briefings on a 'need to know' basis. Bogus signals, radio traffic and other disinformation methods were used to cloak the intent of the operation. Pamphlets had even been issued during the Mongolian operation which offered Soviet soldiers advice on defence and were left in situations where they might be found by the Japanese. Concentrations and all regrouping activity were conducted by night. Officers carried out reconnaissance dressed in soldiers' uniforms and used lorries rather than distinctive cars and jeeps. Tanks, heavy weapons and other equipments were painstakingly camouflaged and dispersed. Artillery barrages were fired to disguise the noise of marching units and other methods were employed to dampen engine noise.

The attack orders were not issued until the last possible moment for fear of compromising security,[14] after which routes needed to be cleared of snow. This strategic deception was based on a fine balance between concentrating the mass of overwhelming strength at a given point and not dissipating its impact through compromising surprise. Applying barely sufficient and piecemeal resources to counter local German penetrations contributed to the overall deception. German units had become accustomed to strong local counter-attacks, and never realised the sinister implication behind these probes. As a consequence, the steady Soviet build-up was misinterpreted as 'last-ditch' efforts to retain key ground. The 7th Panzer Division front line reports, for example, gave little indication that its bridgehead across the Moscow–Volga canal was clashing with the newly formed First Shock Army. Likewise, 2nd Panzer Division, pushing forward a salient in the Krassnaya Polyana area within striking distance of Twentieth Army — similarly expanding and preparing to attack — misconstrued increasing resistance as fanaticism.

Soldiers from the 2nd Panzer Division occupying the villages of Katjuschki and Gorki near Krassnaya Polyana on 4 December soon found 'it was possible to observe everyday life in the capital using scissor-telescopes'. The distance as the crow flies to the edge of the city was 16km. Much to their frustration, they were unable to engage Soviet soldiers daily disembarking at Lobnya station in sight, because their supporting artillery was out of ammunition. Kampfgruppe 'Buck' from Infantry Regiment 304, in taking these villages had placed themselves within 'cannon range' of the Moscow city limits. Conditions were harsh. Layers of jackets of temperate issue coats offered the only protection against an icy east wind. Movement was so difficult that it was decided lightly wounded soldiers should be kept with the battle group rather than sent to the rear. Partisan activity and snowstorms had converted administrative and resupply runs into perilous activity. Nightfall came abruptly and as early as 15.30 hours in these wintry conditions, at which point whoever was not on guard or building defences disappeared inside a dwelling for shelter.[15]

A number of German probes were conducted toward the city outskirts. One combat group from 240th Infantry Regiment, supported by a 52nd Flak Regiment unit, worked its way forward in temperatures of –40°C to the Krjukowa railway station. This was a stop on the local Moscow suburban railway line. They passed a signpost at a road intersection, barely visible in light snow, reading '22km to Moscow'.

Leutnant Heinrich Haape, moving forward on a liaison visit to the 106th Infantry Division south of 2nd Panzer, found the optimism in the rear was greater than that at the front. 'We were told that the great final attack on Moscow would begin within the next few days,' he heard. 'Morale was at peak level and everyone seemed confident that the city would fall before the year was out.' Spiritual momentum alone seemed to be maintaining the advance. 'The troops argued,' observed Haape, 'that rain, mud, snow and frost had failed to stop them; they had earned Moscow and now it must fall to them.' Haape's view encapsulated what every soldier felt: the culminating point of this battle was fast approaching. 'Moscow, a city that had haunted our thoughts during the long, marching kilometres, and which now seemed to be approaching us like a city in a legend,' he wistfully reflected, 'screened from us by seven veils'. Haape was close to the city centre. 'It was a sobering, almost frightening, thought that if one continued at this speed for only 15 minutes we would be in Moscow itself, and a further 15 minutes would bring us into Red Square or to the walls of the Kremlin.'[16]

Across the front there were repeated glimpses of the tantalising prize. The combat diary of the 87th Infantry Division reported its 173rd Infantry Regiment was manning positions in temperatures of –30°C on 3 December on the edge of the forest of Masslovo, at the confluence of the Istra and Moskva rivers. They were 'no more than 20km from the outskirts of Moscow, whose towers are already in sight'. The report's author felt able to 'boast with pride that they were among those German soldiers in World War 2 who came nearest to the capital of the Russian empire'.[17]

Back home in the Reich, the gulf between expectation and reality had become even greater. Wehrmacht High Command reports were no longer effusive. There were no more *Sondermeldungen*. On 25 November it was officially reported, 'the attack in the central sector of the Eastern Front is enjoying further success.' Four days later, 'further progress has been made in the attack on Moscow'. On 1 December it was announced that 'infantry and Panzer formations are advancing closer to the capital', 'deep penetrations' on 'a broad sector' were reported the next day and 'gains' on 3 December. The population suspected developments of greater significance than these frugal statements. Newspapers tended to give more space to 'smaller' successes achieved by minor Wehrmacht units, which were regarded as insignificant compared to previous epic results. Public opinion was convinced the reportage was masking unannounced important developments. A brief stir was created by the capture of Solnechnogorsk, 50km north-west of Moscow, which appeared to indicate the Wehrmacht's determination to prosecute the advance whatever the weather.

There was further anticipation by 1 December that Moscow may yet fall. Much popular news was concerned with the 'tragic' deaths of well-known Nazi personalities. The Luftwaffe general and stunt-flying film star Ernst Udet died, as did top-scoring fighter ace and Spanish Civil War veteran Werner Molders. This offered some distraction from the dramatic events being played out around Moscow. Winter thus far in Berlin had been reasonably mild, averaging 2°C. Only 14 days had been recorded below freezing. The 'Frozen Offensive' seemed a long way away indeed.[18]

When Leutnant Haape reached the forward positions of the 106th Infantry Division, temperatures had dropped to double figures below freezing. Russian positions were pointed out on the ground. Nearby was a solitary Moscow tram stop, which was wistfully regarded by Haape and his companions. They were so near, yet so far. The fall of Moscow could mean the end of the war. The tram stop was barely 16km from the capital.

'We stopped and stared at the wooden seats on which thousands of Muscovites had sat and waited for the tram to clang down the road from Moscow. There was an old wooden bin attached to the wall. I felt inside and dragged out a handful of old tram tickets. We picked out the Cyrillic letters which by now we knew spelled "Moskva".'[19]

The forward triangle of villages and towns around Krassnaya Polyana occupied by the 2nd (Vienna) Panzer Division was the nearest *Kiel* that had been driven toward the Moscow suburbs. Katjuschki, held by the Kampfgruppe 'Buck' from 134 Regiment, formed part of an integrated defence position mutually supported by Gorki, held by Kampfgruppe 'Decker' to its north-west and Putschki to the rear. Oberleutnant Georg Richter's battery from Artillery Regiment 74 was in Putschki with Kampfgruppe 'Rodt' from 2nd Regiment. It was 'a big town, practically a city with factory blocks and store-houses', Richter explained, writing proudly in his diary, that they 'were the furthest forward of all the divisions operating on the *Ostfront*'. Now wearing Russian felt boots, the artillery officer felt the rate at which temperatures were falling merited daily inclusion in his diary. Starting at −15°C on 3 December, he plotted a daily decrease to −28°C on the 6th. The battle had become merciless in his opinion, sustained by the inescapable logic that 'what you took once, even with weak forces, was held' because 'if you give it up, it could only be retaken with very heavy casualties'. His artillery battery, not even directly in the forward positions, had already suffered a notable 12 dead and 20 wounded. 'One learned what was meant by fear,' he observed, because, in the face of such losses, 'people who earlier commanded respect were exposed as panic-mongering cowards'. Doubts over whether they would actually take Moscow began to surface. 'We were asking ourselves more often,' he admitted, 'whether we would truly break through this ring'. The frequency of local counter-attacks also perceptibly increased.

'The enemy is particularly lively with his attacks today,' he announced on 2 December, 'he has received reinforcements.' It was a steady build-up, 'first a battalion, the next day a regiment, two regiments, one division, two divisions' and so on.[20]

The day before, Generalfeldmarschall von Bock accepted, 'the fighting of the past 14 days has shown that the notion that the enemy in front of the army group has "collapsed" was a fantasy'. His forces were now dangerously over-extended. He complained to Halder, the Chief of the General Staff, that the seriousness of the situation appeared not to have been briefed to Hitler. 'It was astounding,' he said to Halder, 'how little the highest levels of command were informed of my reports.' The General Staff had retained a mystical faith in the resilience of the *Ostheer*, paralleled by a firm conviction that the Russians must be at their last gasp. Halder confided to his diary later that day:

'I emphasize that we, too, are concerned about the human sacrifice. But an effort has to be made to bring the enemy to his knees by applying the last ounce of strength. Once it is conclusively shown that this is impossible, we shall make new decisions.'[21]

On a clear sunny day on 2 December, the men from Kampfgruppe 'Buck', occupying positions dug in the Katjuschki village graveyard, received their first hot food from the rear in many days. Previously they had endured snowstorms and the temperature was now −15°C. As they commenced eating, the forward outposts yelled '*Alarm!*' The German battery outside Putschki immediately opened fire, sending salvoes whooshing over their heads to cascade in a series of crackling detonations on the edge of the wood south of the village. Crouching in their stand-to positions, the German infantry were acutely aware their hot food was going to waste, until Russian counter artillery fire interspersed with Katyusha rocket strikes, burst all over their positions.

Activity was apparent inside the wood. Trees were being snapped off and broken down like matchwood, until, with a series of deep-throated diesel growls, Russian T-34 and BT-7 tanks dashed aside the last trees and swung into an extended line and moved toward the German positions. Russian infantry were labouring through the deep snow behind them. 'Like a steel Phalanx,' the Russian armour bore down on the village of Katjuschki. As the Russian artillery switched fire to the rear onto Putschki the rumble of German artillery ceased. Low-flying bombers and thick-bellied 'Rata' Soviet fighters swept by and strafed and bombed the German artillery positions. Leutnant Richter had already developed a healthy respect for these attacks which produced a stream of casualties and 'catastrophic' damage to vehicles. 'Enemy pilots,' he recorded on 2 December, 'kept our arses warm, as the *Landser* would say, throughout the day.'

The T-34s and BT-7s grew steadily larger within the sight telescopes of the two German 50mm anti-tank guns hidden among headstones in the graveyard on the southern edge of Katjuschki. Having lost artillery support, everything depended upon the detachment commander, Unteroffizier Hentsch, a cold-blooded veteran of many actions, to fight them off. Hentsch, aware of the T-34's armoured protection, chose to open fire at the last possible moment and use all his stock-piled ammunition at close range. All were versed in the tactics: drive the accompanying infantry to cover and then engage the tanks. Any that broke through the position were to be left to infantry anti-tank teams who would attack them with hand-held explosive devices. The Russian tank commander, intent on his objective, failed to notice he had outstripped his infantry, who were pinned down by German small arms fire. Kicking up great clouds of snow, the tanks drove directly at the German positions.

The lead tank exploded on a mine as it entered the obstacle belt and ploughed to a shuddering halt, the first of several 50mm rounds slamming into its flank. It suddenly burst into a slurry of flame and black oily smoke. Three tanks were disabled, one after the other, by the solitary 50mm anti-tank gun. Thick clouds of dark smoke pouring out of the wrecks soon disorientated the remaining tanks, which abruptly changed course and began to bypass the village, moving in the direction of Putschki. Hentsch immediately began shooting into their rear as they moved off.

Three tanks remained in front of the graveyard, seeking the anti-tank gun causing so much damage. They machine gunned the positions and grave plots in a reconnaissance by fire. Another BT-7 erupted, metal, boxes and equipment flying off the decks of the tank as the internal pressure of the explosion flung the hatches open. Unteroffizier Braun, observing the action, saw:

'A dappled-camouflage T-34 with a red flag in the turret [probably the commander] now knew exactly where the gun was. Having got through the mine belt he accelerated at full speed toward the anti-tank gun. The huge tank was 60 — 50 — 40 — 30 — 20m away. All the time the anti-tank gun fired back. Ricochets bounced high into the air from the forward sloping armour of the T-34. A few metres from the position the tank swung slightly left and rolled over the infantry and crew positions. The endangered soldiers dived out of the way as quick as a flash.'

Narrowly missing Braun, the tank churned around like an enraged dinosaur, smashing into the corner of a barn, which collapsed upon it. 'It then disappeared into a cloud of snow,' he said. The remaining tank meanwhile slowly traversed its gun onto the now clearly identifiable solitary PAK, whose fate appeared sealed. A single 50mm projectile slammed into the side of the T-34 at 823m per second. It did not move as a further four rounds tore into the smouldering carcass until it burst into flames. The twin supporting 50mm gun of the pair manned by Unteroffizier Becker had been moved from the other side of the graveyard as soon as the Russian artillery fire had switched to the rear.

Inside the village the surviving T-34 was playing 'cat and mouse' with a 37mm anti-tank gun. The latter was eventually cornered and the crew fled as the tank crushed the gun and bulldozed into a cottage directly behind it, the building collapsing to the ground. Stuck fast in a civilian shelter, its see-sawing motion and bellowing diesel engines indicated it could not get out. An anti-tank mine was flung onto its engine deck and the single crack of its detonation reverberated around the village, signifying the end of the action. Clouds of smoke spilling across the snow to the rear of the village also indicated the demise of the tank attack on Putschki. The solitary tank that had evaded the two anti-tank guns had been despatched by a direct-fire hit from the artillery battery.[22]

To the north-west the 23rd Infantry Division sought, with steadily declining strength, to continue its advance to the Moscow–Volga canal. They laboured forward in more than knee-deep snow, 35km from Moscow. Feldwebel Gottfried Becker with Infantry Regiment 9 was ordered to extract a beleaguered company that had been ambushed 5km further east, outside the village of Choroschilowo. The mission was only partially successful. The remnants were rescued but the wounded had to be left behind. Becker delivered his report, much troubled by his conscience. It was received without demur by the battalion commander; these things happened. They remained holding their positions at Staroje, enduring the bitter cold in a totally cheerless landscape. Soon they lost all sense of time. Every two hours a reconnaissance patrol was despatched to check the woodland bordering the village. The veterans were uneasy. There was a collective perception that a

Russian attack was pending. A patrol returning that night reported 'something going on, you can hear loud noises'. Snow began to fall heavily, which reduced visibility to 200–300m. Nobody wanted to do more. Becker was exhausted and his men were tired. They would investigate further in the morning.[23]

Russian probing attacks continued against the 2nd Panzer Division vanguard in the Krassnaya Polyana area. Leutnant Georg Richter gloomily observed that being only 30km from Moscow meant 'the enemy could move his troops up to the front in trams'. The supporting artillery battery outside Putschki was experiencing problems because 'its guns could only be traversed with considerable difficulty'. Lothar Fromm, another artillery observer, described the impact of these Arctic conditions:

'The weapons did not work any more. Let me tell you about the recoil mechanism of the guns. Minus thirty degrees was seen as the lowest temperature at which efficiency could be maintained. They were frozen up. Crews stood there and tried to make them work time, and time again. It didn't happen. The barrel would not come back and the recoil mechanism was unable to move. That was really depressing.'

By contrast, as Richter complained at Putschki, 'It was unbelievable what ammunition the enemy had stacked up next to his positions to blast out every calibre'. As a consequence, 'the factory buildings,' he wrote, 'were burning for the umpteenth time.' Nerves were feeling the strain. 'The extent of fear and cowardice,' the dispirited Richter admitted by 3 December, 'is catastrophic — the cooks won't come out and cook because they are ducking inside their shelters the whole time.' Prospects did not appear good. In Richter's opinion it was 'senseless' to try and hold onto the villages of Gorki and Katjuschki.[24]

Generalfeldmarschall von Bock was of like opinion. He instinctively felt the army group had approached the end of its strength. Corps commanders were telexed during the night of 2 December 'that the undoubtedly serious moment of crisis that the Russian defenders are facing must be exploited wherever the opportunity presents itself.' But he did not believe it, because he confided, 'I have my doubts whether the exhausted units are still capable of doing so.' That night von Bock was presented with a document from the city of Smolensk thanking him for liberating it from Bolshevism. Three months before, Army Group Centre had stood at the pinnacle of success. As he considered the document, von Bock probably reflected all this was virtually an age ago.[20]

Two days later Leutnant Richter was overseeing a gun-position change at Putschki. They were pulling back. Every single vehicle needed to be tow-started in temperatures of –25°C. Many vehicles, in particular the 6.5-ton 'Tatra' heavy lorries, had to be abandoned. Their wheels would not turn and the steering was frozen solid. An NCO shouted a warning:

'"The Russians are attacking. Don't you see the white ghosts? We have got to open fire, now, now!" For a while I could not see anything, although a burning haystack lit up the surrounding area to some extent, sufficient to shoot. But then, yes, I could see running spectre-like figures; ghosts, one might say. Our men have not got so many white camouflage smocks — they must be Russians.'

They were indeed. Another soldier, writing home that day, encapsulated what was going on in a simple terse statement:

'The Russians are fielding everything they've got, because around here at Moscow — the devil is loose.'[26]

'THE SPIRES OF MOSCOW'

Left:
Once the autumn rains began, initially only tracked vehicles could keep moving.

Below:
Presently, as one soldier wrote, 'vehicles sink up to the axle and in many places the morass is up to the bellies of the horses'. The front, as shown here, came to a virtual standstill at the very time victories at Bryansk and Vyazma had restored tactical mobility to Army Group Centre. Exertions such as these killed the horses upon which much of the infantry were reliant for artillery and logistic support.

Right:
A PzKpfwIII from Panzergruppe 4 stranded in the mud of the autumn 'Rasputzia'. Its lighter counterpart, a PzKpfwII, is attempting to tow it free. When the ground froze over, considerable damage resulted from trying to free vehicles from its vice-like grip.

Left:
An infantry section snatches a brief rest during a lull in the battle. They have crudely fashioned civilian bed linen into snow camouflage capes.

Right:
As the German logistic system faltered, food became shorter at a time when the intense cold required the infantry to have an even greater calorific intake. As the visage of this infantryman suggests, endemic ill-health and increased cold casualties resulted.

Above:
At the end of November 1941, tired units from Panzergruppe 3 move through the streets of Klin wearing temperate issue greatcoats. Note the crude white sheet hung across the armoured car. Only chalk was available to whiten helmets.

Left:
White sheets were plundered from Russian houses, as in the case of this anti-tank gun crew, to provide rudimentary snow camouflage.

Left:
A historic picture of German Panzers moving in tactical formation toward a blazing Russian settlement near Gorki, on the Moscow road, 16km north-west of the city outskirts. The view shows the wooded terrain typical on the western approaches to Moscow. The Kampfgruppe 'Decker' held these positions, the nearest point to the city, from 1 to 7 December 1941.

Below:
The Russian counter-offensive was crudely conducted, as exemplified by this typical mass infantry assault which produced heavy casualties. It achieved total surprise and swept the Germans from the gates of Moscow. Army Group Centre was defeated, but was eventually to survive the onslaught and stabilise the front further to the west.

Left:
The aftermath of just such a costly Russian assault.

Below:
This German infantryman still manages a grim bravado, retreating before Moscow still wearing summer uniform.

Bottom:
The 7th Panzer Division 'hardly looked like a military formation any longer,' wrote one soldier. Men rode, were sledge-borne — as in the case of this 20mm cannon — or marched on foot. Only 10 armoured fighting vehicles were still running in the division at the beginning of December. Villages were torched, as seen in the background, as they fell back.

Left:
The horizon was lit by the glare of burning villages.

Below:
On the retreat west of Subzow. One German soldier said, 'We would pick up anything warm left lying behind by the dead, or our comrades.'

Above:
'*Vorwärts Kameraden, wir müssen züruck!*' —
'Forward men, we have to get back!' was the
sardonic catch-phrase used by German
infantry rearguards constantly required to
fight rearwards and westwards in order to
survive. They endured appalling hardships.

Right:
Many, as in the case of this solitary German
soldier, did not make it. The *Gulaschkanone*
(mobile soup kitchen) was the company
rallying point, where meals were shared, mail
exchanged and where casualties and
survivors might congregate to regenerate
following disaster. This man has died a
solitary death, frozen on the blizzard-swept
steppe as he sought succour from the dying
heat of the company kitchen fire.

Chapter 16
The devil loose before Moscow

'The German soldier does not go "kaputt!"'
Halder, Chief of General Staff, German Army

THE SOVIET COUNTER-OFFENSIVE

Soviet 'Shock Armies' were originally conceived as being particularly heavy in armour, motorised vehicles and automatic weapons. First Shock Army to the east of Yakhroma and the others created during the winter of 1941–42 were not so well equipped. When Kuznetsov, the First Shock Army commander, took over on 23 November, he expanded it from a single rifle brigade to one division, nine rifle brigades, ten independent battalions, a regiment of artillery and a contingent of Katyusha rocket launches. About 70% of the soldiers were over 30 years old. Likewise Twentieth Army was brought up to a similar strength. Tenth Army was approximately 100,000-strong, consisting of seven reserve rifle divisions recruited from the Moscow region. It had been on the march by rail and foot from Syzran on the Volga, some 480km away. Four other newly formed reserve armies were brought forward from the line of the River Volga at the end of November. Twenty-fourth, Twenty-sixth and Sixtieth were placed east of Moscow and Sixty-first was newly located behind the right flank of the south-west front.

Stalin passed over control of the newly formed strike element — First Shock, Twentieth and Tenth Armies — from STAVKA Supreme Command to Zhukov on 29 November. Even without the addition of the reserve armies, the Soviet forces opposite Army Group Centre on 5 December were greater than when Operation '*Taifun*' began, two months before. The German army group had been unable to replace its considerable losses in troops, equipment and especially leaders. Soviet armies in the Moscow sector, by contrast, acquired one third more rifle divisions, five times more cavalry divisions, twice as many artillery regiments and two and a half times as many tank brigades by 5 December than they had on 2 October.[1]

Zhukov's Chief of Staff, Lt-Gen V. D. Sokolovskiy, calculated the West Front armies numbered over a million men, slightly under the German figure (ie 1,100,000 against 1,708,000), but the latter also included its rear area elements. Massive losses of German 'teeth arm' personnel, tanks and weapons had seriously depleted the combat strength of its divisions. Artillery and mortar numbers were similar at 13,500 as also were 1,170 Panzers to tanks, but fewer were running on the German side. The Soviets had an overwhelming preponderance of 1,370 aircraft to about 600 German, with the further advantage of hardened Moscow airfields.[2]

The Soviet plan was to attack either side of Moscow and bite off the encircling fingers of the German advances from the north-east and south-east. Having eliminated the threat to the Moscow–Volga canal, First Shock Army was to strike west toward Klin and, in conjunction with the Thirtieth and Twentieth Armies, attack Panzergruppe 3 and the German Ninth Army in the north. Twentieth Army, supporting First Shock and combined with Sixteenth Army, was to assault from Krassnaya Polyana and Bely-Rast towards Solnechnogorsk (see map on page 225), capture it from the south and drive towards

Volokolamsk. Guderian's Second Panzer Army salient would be attacked by Fiftieth Army in combination with the Tenth, which were to drive due west, south of the River Upa. The initial intent was to eliminate the immediate German threat to the Soviet capital: as expressed by Lt-Gen Sokolovskiy, 'to break up the enemy's attack conclusively and give him no opportunity to regroup and dig in close to our capital'.[3] Just under half the Soviet tank strength, 290 of 720 tanks, was placed at the main point of effort against Klin, Solnechnogorsk and Istra — the nearest German penetrations to Moscow. The Russians were not totally confident of success; a major Russian counter-offensive had yet to succeed in this war. There was, however, an instinctive appreciation that the enemy was probably sufficiently exhausted to be caught off balance.

This lack of balance was hinted at by Generalfeldmarschall von Bock, who declared on 3 December, 'if the attack is called off then going over to the defensive will be very difficult'. The last card had been staked on Moscow's fall. In fact, von Bock admitted, 'This thought and the possible consequences of going over to the defensive with our weak forces have, save for my mission, contributed to my sticking with this attack so far.' Within two days Panzergruppe 3 reported 'its offensive strength is gone'. It could only hold its positions if the already decimated 23rd Infantry Division remained under command. Von Bock was also informed by General von Kluge, the commander of Fourth Army, that Hoepner's planned attack with Panzergruppe 4 should not go ahead.[4] Late that same day Generaloberst Guderian advised that his Second Panzer Army should 'call off the operation'. He said the 'unbearable cold of more than –30°C was making moving and fighting by the tired, thinned-out units extremely difficult'. German tanks were breaking down while the Russians, did not.

Oberstleutnant Grampe, commanding a tactical headquarters with the 1st Panzer Division, reported the same day that his Panzers had been put out of action by low temperatures, which had dropped to –35°C. 'The turrets would not revolve,' he stated, 'the optics had misted up, machine guns could only fire single rounds and it took two to three crew members to depress tank gun barrels, only achievable if they stamped down on the main barrel where it joined the turret block.' His unit was not equipped to cope with such conditions. Cases of first- and second-degree frostbite were beginning to emerge. 'The division,' he assessed, 'was practically immobile.'[5] The German front went over to the defensive, frozen inert at the very moment the Russian offensive was about to strike. Temperatures plummeted from –25°C on 4 December to –35°C on the 5th and to –38°C the following day. Co-ordinated operations appeared impractical. German troops sought only shelter.

The new Soviet armies had been assembled together for only two to three weeks. They were a mixture of fresh Siberian units, burned-out veteran formations and briefly trained militia or reservists. Many lacked equipment and there were shortages of ammunition. Officers and NCOs were inexperienced. Tanks were dispersed among about 15 tank brigades with about 46 machines in each. A high proportion of the units were fresh and unbloodied in battle, and, unlike the enemy, they were warmly clad. Their motivation was superior to that of the German, whose moral component of fighting power had bled profusely, perhaps mortally, since September. As in the case of the original 'Barbarossa' invasion, Soviet counter-stroke formations had deployed in such numbers that, even if they were discovered, the difficulty of moving troops and equipments to oppose them was impractical. A 'checkmate' configuration had been created in these Arctic conditions. They possessed massive local superiority and, above all, total surprise.

In mind-numbing, freezing conditions during the early morning hours of 5 December, the Soviet Twenty-ninth Army attacked across the ice-covered Volga west of Kalinin. They penetrated the German Ninth Army line for up to 10km before they were checked. On the following morning, which dawned clear with temperatures of −38°C, the soldiers of the West and South-west Fronts went over to the offensive. Drifting snow and near-Arctic conditions seriously impeded the final build-up, resulting in piecemeal attacks which gradually achieved a cumulative and unstoppable momentum.

The IInd Battalion of Schützen Regiment 114, part of 6th Panzer Division, in the village of Stepanowo immediately east of the Moscow–Volga canal line, reported on 6 December:

'During the course of the morning there were signs of unrest among the civil population. The explanation — that Stepanowo would be taken by the Russians, and that the Germans would leave — was laughed at by the German soldiers. Radio enquiries, however, confirmed the opposite. Soon part of the 7th Panzer Division was coming back along the Stepanowo–Shukowo road.'

A visit by General Model, the corps commander, to 6th Panzer Division headquarters at 10.00 hours, 'produced a surprising direction,' admitted the operations officer (1a). Model assessed Panzergruppe 3 had insufficient strength to hold the present line 'against an enemy who had introduced an astonishing infusion of strength' and was directing his main efforts against the north-eastern flank. 'As a consequence,' Model directed, 'the front must be shortened.' Engineer rear area route and obstacle reconnaissance was ordered 'at once'. The logistics (1b) officer was told to ferry back wounded and to begin the necessary reorganisation of the logistic rear support services.[6] Model's corps was about to embark on its first retreat of the war. It was the third disappointment the 6th Panzer Division had experienced short of victory. They were halted at Dunkirk in 1940 and again before Leningrad in September 1941. Moscow was also to be denied them.

Artillery soldier Pawel Ossipow took part in the barrages that preceded the Russian attack on 6 December. As the infantry moved forward, their inexperience became increasingly apparent. 'Particularly the youngsters,' he said, 'were exposed to a lot of blood and witnessed the horror of war for the first time as wounded men died in deep snow at temperatures of −30°C.' Pjotr Weselinokov also recoiled at the sights of 'our first battle'. He likened it to an abattoir. 'The worse thing of all,' he reflected, 'were the freshly killed bodies of soldiers left steaming' where they lay in the frozen temperatures. 'The air was filled with the peculiar stench of flesh and blood.'[7]

On the second day of the offensive, attacks gathered momentum. Thirty-first Army joined the stalled Twenty-ninth Army grappling with the German Ninth Army to the north, on the Kalinin front. They failed to force a passage across the Volga south of Kalinin. Thirtieth Army, however, made a deep

12km penetration into the Panzergruppe 3 flank north-east of Klin. First Shock and Twentieth armies crashed into both Panzergruppen 3 and 4 on a front from Yakhroma to west of Krassnaya Polyana. Some gains were made south of the latter in desperate fighting. Tenth Army, meanwhile, struck Second Panzer Army at the east point of the Tula bulge with one rifle division and two motorised infantry regiments. The rest of the army was still marching up from Syzran. South-west Front's Second and Thirteenth armies began to apply pressure at Yelets at the southern base of the Tula bulge.

Michael Milstein, attached to Zhukov's staff, remembered that 'gradually confidence came, the first counter-attacks were showing results'. But this was at considerable cost. Artillery soldier Pawel Ossipow said:

'There were many wounded, particularly among the [hand-towed] *machine gun crews. While all the others had to keep moving forward, nobody could help them. We detached one of our men, who had to administer first aid, to report them to the rear area services, so that the motorised unit following behind could pick them up.'*

'One could actually see signs,' said Michael Milstein, 'that it may be conceivable the Hitler Army might be defeated.' This was not expressed in the typical inflated 'Great Patriotic War' rhetoric. Milstein, a staff officer, objectively assessed the achievement as being 'no miracle', rather 'it was the result of planned operational preparation . . . Certainly there were losses and disadvantages,' he concluded, 'but it was a properly executed operation.' Lieutenant — and later historian — Dimitrij Wolkogonow, observed that the German Army 'appeared out of breath,' and that 'the Soviet Army counter-offensive was fully unexpected'. This was also the case for the civilian population. Pawel Ossipow grimly pointed out, 'we also saw a lot of dead civilians, old women and children.' They were completely caught out by the sudden resurgence of operations in such terrible weather. 'Many of them ran naked into the open during the attack,' said Ossipow. 'It was awful.'[8]

On 5 December German medic Anton Gründer was on duty until 06.00 hours in the Ninth Army sector.

'As I was making something to eat, all hell broke loose outside. Everything was pulling back, Panzers, artillery guns, vehicles and soldiers — singly or in groups. They were all in shock. There were no more orders; everybody took up the retreat and looked no further forward than what he felt he might reach. Most vehicles didn't start because of the terrible cold; despite that we were able to take most of the medical supplies with us. We tried to keep together with the remnants of the company so far as possible, but whoever fell out, was lost.'

Caring for the wounded in the confusion of the retreat was an almost unsupportable burden. 'Dreadful scenes were played out before our eyes,' admitted Gründer. Many wounded presented themselves for treatment with emergency bandages that had been applied more than a week before.

'One soldier had an exit wound through the upper part of his arm. The whole limb had turned black and the puss was running from his back down to his boots. It had to be amputated at the joint. Three soldiers smoked cigars throughout the operation because the stench was so unbearable.'[9]

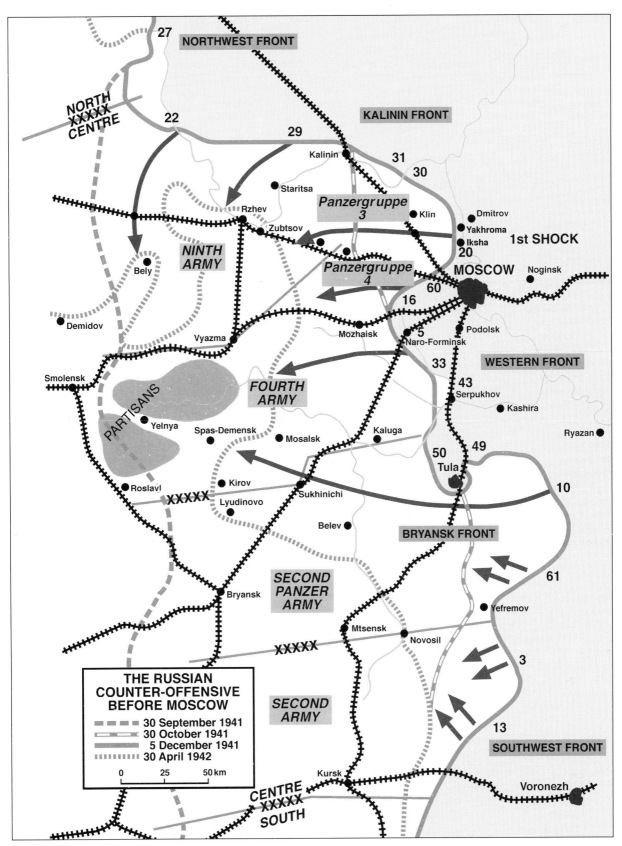

THE RUSSIAN
COUNTER-OFFENSIVE
BEFORE MOSCOW

30 September 1941
30 October 1941
5 December 1941
30 April 1942

0   25   50 km

The Soviet counter-stroke before Moscow in December 1941 achieved complete strategic and operational surprise. By Christmas the Germans had lost all the ground they had won during the final drive following the Orscha conference. The first phase of the Soviet counter-offensive cleared the Germans before Moscow, but the second phase did not succeed in destroying the *Ostheer*. Soviet operational inexperience resulted in some reverses before a tortuous yet continuous German front was shored up by April 1942. Army Group Centre had lost its offensive capability.

The German retreat took many forms, varying between disciplined order and panic-driven flight. Whatever the recriminations and debates between army group and higher headquarters over its extent, it continued to run. Motorised formations, which had achieved the glory of the advance, were fortunate in being able to withdraw to a plan of sorts. They had a chance. The infantry, who through sheer brute strength and willpower had underpinned the offensive and arrived last, were the most exhausted. Being foot-borne, their survival chances were correspondingly less. Caught in the open, with no prepared bunkers to their rear, many perished anonymously in hard-fought rearguard actions.

Leutnant Heinrich Haape's leave train was halted, just as he was departing for Germany. 'Every man is to return at once to his unit and report for duty,' they were told. Muttered protests stopped when it was announced the Russians had broken through at Kalinin. 'There was silence among the men now,' Haape recalled, 'nobody swore — the matter was too serious for swearing even.'

'And where are the Russians?' asked Haape, when he rejoined his division. 'Everywhere,' was the response, 'nobody seems to know precisely where.'[10]

In the north the deepest Russian advance was made by General Lelyushenko's Thirtieth Army. It soon reached the Moscow–Leningrad highway, jeopardising the link between Panzergruppe 3 and von Kluge's Fourth Army. On 13 December Klin was reached, threatening a partial encirclement with First Shock Army advancing due west. It took two days of fierce fighting to clear the town. Sixteenth and Twentieth Armies, meanwhile, captured Istra on the original Army Group Centre axis of advance toward Moscow. Solnechnogorsk was abandoned by the Germans on 12 December. South of Moscow, Guderian's main supply artery, the Orel–Tula line, was menaced by advancing Soviet forces as the Fiftieth and Tenth Armies succeeded in separating Second Panzer Army from von Kluge's Fourth Army to its north. During the first phase of the Soviet counter-offensive, which lasted until Christmas, the Russian armies took back all the ground the Germans had won during their final drive on Moscow after the Orscha conference.

Pawel Ossipow pondered the cumulative impact of successive German setbacks:

'On the second or third day of the counter-offensive, on 7 or 8 December it dawned on us that our attack was going successfully, morale amongst all the soldiers, sergeants and officers soared. From then on we pushed forwards in order to overtake the Germans before they could set villages on fire. As a rule they torched everything before a withdrawal.'[11]

Devastating villages was universal practice across the front for both sides. It had already occurred during withdrawals around Leningrad. Gefreiter Alfred Scholz, with the 11th Infantry Division, had participated in the systematic wasting of territory whereby 'civilians were pitilessly set outside in cruel freezing temperatures down to −30° and −40°C'.

'I personally saw,' he admitted, 'Russian women and children lying frozen in the snow.' As the withdrawal started in the central sector, the excesses visited on the population during the advance were repeated during the retreat. Obergefreiter Wilhelm Göbel, with Infantry Regiment 215 (part of 78th Division) south-west of Moscow, recalled the pain of constant withdrawals. 'While accommodated in these villages,' he

admitted, 'the Germans were taken in hospitably by the civilian population. They washed our underclothes, cleaned our boots and cooked potatoes for us.' When his IInd Battalion commander, Major Käther, received the order 'to burn down various villages and pollute wells,' he remonstrated, stating that he 'disagreed with such senseless destruction.' But duty and an in-bred sense of order and discipline overcame his doubts. 'An order is an order,' he resolved. 'We had to do our duty as soldiers and had strictly to obey.'[12] Each rearguard was instructed to torch villages as it withdrew. When Pawel Ossipow reached his own village near Volokolamsk he found his own house had been burned to the ground and his family had fled. There was some compensation in the fact that 'liberated villagers always welcomed us and offered hospitality, which pleased us'.[13]

The Russians were winning and beginning to realise it. Infantry platoon commander Anatolij Tschernjajew, contemplating the pitiful state of German prisoners, assessed 'to a certain extent they had been unprepared for a war against Russia'. In his view:

'The popular picture of the German Army had altered starkly during the course of the war. The summer and autumn offensives had been conducted against a back-drop of an invincible, mighty and colossal strength. Now when we saw them miserable, half-naked and hungry in front of Moscow we realised that this army had been defeated.'[14]

The moral initiative was passing to the Russians. It was coincidental with a diminution of the moral component of German fighting power. A reversal they themselves were beginning to recognise.

THE GERMAN SOLDIER DOES NOT GO 'KAPUTT!' . . . THE CRISIS OF CONFIDENCE

By 7 December von Bock had appreciated that 'the orders for the ruthless pursuit of the enemy' were justified only if 'the ultimate sacrifice' demanded by his Army Group 'was against the very last of his forces'. This was demonstrably not the case, and this 'mistake' had forced his army group to go over to the defensive 'under the most difficult conditions'. On the telephone the normally ebullient Generaloberst Guderian had described his situation 'in the blackest of terms'. He told von Bock that 'a crisis of confidence was taking hold' among the troops and NCOs. When closely questioned against whom, he declined to answer, but constantly asked his C-in-C whether OKH and OKW were being given a clear picture of what was happening at the front. Visibly affected by this exchange, von Bock passed on his concerns to General Halder a few hours later. The Chief of Staff told him 'not to take Guderian's comments to heart'. When von Bock admitted he could not stand off a determined attack anywhere on his front, Halder speculated it was likely that the Russians were using cadres and untrained troops which they would otherwise have held back until the spring. 'I suspect,' he said, 'that it will continue until the middle or end of the month and then tail off into a quieter period.'

'By then,' remonstrated von Bock, aghast at Halder's insensitive appreciation of what was going on, 'the Army Group will be *kaputt* [finished].' Halder coolly responded: 'The German soldier does not go *"Kaputt!"* Von Bock ordered his planners to begin working on the practicality of a 100–150km withdrawal along a line stretching from Rzhev through Gzhatsk to Kursk.[1]

Guderian was merely articulating the moral transformation that had occurred from the *Ostheer*'s high point at the beginning of 'Barbarossa' to the present crisis before Moscow. He viewed it in physical terms. 'We are faced with the sad fact,' he wrote on 8 December, 'that the supreme command has over-reached itself by refusing to believe our reports of the increasing weakness of the troops and by making ever new demands on them.' A typical product of the analytical German General Staff, Guderian concentrated on the tangible manifestation of the physical component of fighting power. They were insufficient in numbers and not equipped for the cold. Even after failure at Rostov, Guderian complained, 'the same old business went on as before'. His criticism was directed at a failure of the General Staff to present clearly an accurate picture to the political leadership, Adolf Hitler. His men, meanwhile, carried the burden. He complained:

'Then my northern neighbour broke down; my southern one was already very weak, and so I was left no alternative but to break off my attack, since I could hardly roll up the whole Eastern Front by myself, let alone at a temperature of −32°.'[2]

The ordinary German soldier, who had awaited the order to attack on the eve of 'Barbarossa', was not the same man being ordered to fall back from Moscow now. Of his nine peculiar characteristics identified at the beginning of the operation,[3] six were transformed in the crucible of the campaign. Change had accelerated between September and the end of the year. Success in previous campaigns had created an idealistic zeal that diminished with casualties. Atrocities across the front drove a wedge between those who retained decent personal standards versus a peer pressure to conform with National Socialist ideology. Resistance to the Commissar Order had come from liberal Weimar-educated older officers and NCOs who had been decimated by casualties or retired through illness brought on by physical and nervous exhaustion. Confidence following near-victories at Leningrad and Rostov ebbed with the realisation of failure. The surge in the size of the Wehrmacht following its victorious campaigns in the west had diluted previous quality, which was parcelled out among smaller but more numerous Panzer divisions. Casualties by September, followed immediately by crippling losses in the autumn and winter offensives, had removed the cream of the combat-effective and experienced leadership. The 'teeth' had suffered in disproportionate terms to the specialist 'tail', breaking up the combined operations characteristics of divisions. The 'seed-corn' of Blitzkrieg was dead.

The characteristics that had not changed during this process of disintegration were those related to the continued existence of the Nazi totalitarian state. Its 'endless pressure to participate' and its acceptance of 'order and duty', regimentation and acute sense of responsibility to 'orders' was holding the core of the army together during this crisis. Faith in the Führer remained, but would be increasingly questioned in the future on both the home and fighting fronts as the fortunes of war deteriorated.

The Russian war was to prove a catalyst for the German nation. There would now be a certain intangible conflict between those who clearly fought for the Führer and Nazi ideology, and those who did their duty for their country. Men who had been prepared to storm Warsaw, Rotterdam, Paris, Athens, Belgrade and now Smolensk and Kiev, questioned whether Moscow was really worth the price. The decline of the moral component of the *Ostheer*'s fighting power can be charted within Halder's Diaries, adding weight to Guderian's assertion that the signs had clearly been evident, but the Supreme Command, over-confident in its assessment of German fighting power, had 'over-reached' itself. As early as 3 November Halder was admitting that Army Group South was 'pessimistic' and losing drive, and that 'some energetic persuading would be in order to kick them'. On 22 November he assessed that the troops on the southern wing and centre of Fourth Army 'are finished'. The commander of the 13th Panzer Division 'and one of his ablest regimental commanders have had complete nervous breakdowns,' he observed on 1 December. Nine days later he commented on Guderian's 'serious breach of confidence' in the field commands, and that the 'commanding General of the XXVIIth Corps is said to have failed completely'.[4]

The crisis of confidence is also reflected within the *Feldpost*. Soldiers, aware of censorship in the Nazi State, were still wary of free expression when they sent letters home. Gefreiter Fritz Sigel, complaining of frostbite in the fighting around Tula in temperatures of −32°C, echoed his commanding general's concern when he wrote on 6 December:

'My God, what is this Russia going to do to us all? Our superiors must at least listen to us on one occasion, otherwise, in this state, we are going to go under.'[5]

Gustav Schrodek, stalled with the 1st Panzer Division one hour's Panzer drive from Moscow, had written four days previously in his diary that 'the troops' trust in the higher command had quickly disappeared'. In his view, 'morale has collapsed'.[6] Failure to reach Moscow, which the troops keenly felt to be their due by virtue of casualties and pain, was deeply disappointing. One Leutnant from 258th Infantry Division claimed their lead unit had penetrated to within 30km of the city, 'an indication of the heroism and readiness and effectiveness of our soldiers'. Casualties were not unexpected, and those that were lost 'were all loved'.

'But when nothing of use comes from the attack then that is something to think about. I have no clue or opinion why it should be so, but, despite all this, what a real shame. A pity! The end effect was that on 3 December we went back to the start point during the night. In some places there were merely remnants from previously strong companies.'[7]

Front letters covered a myriad concerns, primarily discomfort, survival and an emotional reaching of hands back home. Most accepted the abrupt reversal with resignation. But the fire of June 1941 had gone. 'The retreat has taken a lot out of us,' wrote a Gefreiter with the 262nd Infantry Division, 'with constantly over-stretched nerves, sometimes I do not want to go on.' He longed for a little peace at Christmas and particularly 'my post!' But he would fight on. 'My dearest,' he continued, 'some very hard days lie behind us, but now we have overcome all that.' Realising his letter was unlikely to arrive home until the New Year, he concluded on an optimistic note. 'The political situation nevertheless is now crystal clear,' he wrote, 'it can only result in victory!' Whatever the blind faith, the Soviet offensive had come as a brutal surprise. Soldiers were irritated that the 'higher-ups' could have got them into such a mess. Oberleutnant Karl Moltner, a Panzer corps staff officer, stated indignantly in a postwar interview:

'We were in no way equipped for such a winter with temperatures of −36°C. There was not even any winter clothing at this time. I can truly say we only had our so-called "summer" coats and, whoever might be lucky, a motorcyclist's greatcoat.'[8]

There was now a parting of ways. The moral component would never be restored to its original state of June 1941. One fought for survival or the Führer, occasionally together, but never with the same idealistic purpose with which the campaign had begun. As the retreat gathered momentum only one objective preoccupied the German soldier — to live.

THE GERMAN ARMY IN RETREAT

The potential for the complete destruction of German divisions was unprecedented in this war and the deep Soviet penetrations of Army Group Centre's flanks either side of Moscow threatened to achieve just that. Leutnant Georg Richter, having departed Putschki, 30km from Moscow, on 6 December, recorded two days later, 'until now, the retreat is proceeding to plan.' It was easier for vehicle-borne troops. On the road moving west with Panzergruppe 4 there was constant danger from their northern flank that Russian spearheads would break through in the direction of Klin. Temperatures varied between −6°C and −15°C, with fog and snowfalls. Petrol shortages necessitated frequent halts. Richter observed 'a seemingly endless column of vehicles stretching before him' on 13 December when they came across lines of blackened German vehicles, burned out during a recent Russian breakthrough. From the edge of the wood, Richter was suddenly aware of a sinister 'Urra! Urra!' sound.

'Brown figures poured out of the woods and a stream of German soldiers, drivers and vehicle crews came back towards me along the road. At first I did not know what I ought to do, I couldn't grasp it. One couldn't hold back the fleeing men who had been gripped by panic and shock. Most of them had not even held onto their rifles. There were also probably Russian tanks. I saw one had already driven across the road and on to the other side.'

Some of his own men were crawling back along the roadside ditch. 'One of them, the oldest man in our battery, was shot and killed, it was a sorry affair.' Richter gathered about 10 men together and tried to fight back, but the German armoured cars escorting the convoy 'did not show their brave side'. They merely 'blazed away from where they were,' according to Richter, 'at the edge of the wood, where there were no more Russians'. The group fell back to a neighbouring village. Nothing could be done. After darkness fell it was suddenly illuminated by the flash of an exploding ammunition lorry, which had been smouldering for hours. 'We could not rescue our vehicles,' said Richter, 'at least 25 others were littered about, criss-cross around the road.'

The following day the route was reported as fought clear. Passing the ambush site they noticed food and other items scattered about the road. 'Anything usable had been taken by the Russians,' Richter observed, 'or snatched up by our own *Landser* passing by.' The march continued over subsequent days. Abandoned vehicles were burned where they stopped. 'It was such a shame,' Richter commented. 'One often saw how the crew would gather together the essentials and then set off on foot.' He was especially depressed, as an artillery officer, by the abandonment and destruction of guns.

Superhuman effort had been expended to get them this far. 'In front of Petrowskoje is a sea of vehicles,' he wrote on 16 December. They had driven out of the town and parked in columns. 'At first there were 10 rows, then 15 and so on, with the 5th Panzer Division, the 1st Panzer Division, 2nd Panzer Division, 14th Infantry Division and everything else all in between.'

Air attacks became increasingly persistent as the march continued. 'Single and very daring Ratas grazed the treetops and then turned and dived on us, this time with twinkling machine guns blazing at us.' Everyone sought cover until the infantry mustered courage to fire back with machine guns. 'One stood with his legs apart, his companion placed the machine gun on his shoulder and "*rattattatt*" a Rata is shot down,' said Richter. Traffic jams built up around vehicles which broke down either because of the cold or lack of petrol. They were burned. 'Why has the column stopped?' Richter would ask. 'It was always the same, one went forward to investigate and found, after walking past a kilometre of vehicles, the driver asleep in his cab.'[1]

Opinion concerning the retreat varied with individual experience. Horst Orlov, a Panzer company commander who had been close enough to Moscow to see its towers 'lit by the sun', was emphatic about the disciplined nature of the retreat. He declared during a postwar interview:

'I can only say that in my area of responsibility, where I was committed, the retreat was conducted in an orderly manner. There were naturally losses in matériel and also personnel, but to speak of a flight would be overstating it.'

Leutnant Adolf Stamm with the Flak artillery recalled 'awful days in front of Moscow, suffering in temperatures below −35°C and sometimes even −40°C'. But he remembered the retreat was generally under control.

'On 6 December, it was already St Nicholas's Day, we received the order to clear our positions and conduct the retreat using available resources. The withdrawal was not a flight or a panic-stricken rush. Rather, positions were vacated platoon by platoon from village to village. What was particularly difficult to master was to get the vehicles started and then move back through the deep snow.'[2]

There was total unfamiliarity with the tactical handling of a withdrawal. The German Army had never practised it in the prewar period and until now had never experienced the need to execute it. Scenes observed by Leutnant Richter, retreating with Panzergruppe 4, were repeated along Panzergruppe 3's route. 'Discipline is beginning to let up,' the latter observed in a later operations report.

'There are more and more soldiers separated from their commands walking westward, without weapons, leading cattle by ropes or pulling walking sledges filled with potatoes. Men killed by air bombardment are no longer buried . . . A psychosis, bordering on panic, has gripped the baggage trains, unaccustomed to this retreat, being only used to a rapid advance. Service troops, too, are without rations and are cold. They are retreating in utter confusion. Among them are those wounded who could no longer be sent to the rear . . . Traffic control elements working day and night can hardly cope any more. The Panzer Group's most difficult hour has begun.'

Leutnant Richter's unit, moving steadily westwards, had begun to speed up by 17 December. 'But one misses the orderly hand of the High Command,' he stated. Everything was mixed up. 'Every vehicle is from another unit, another division.' Morale was falling. 'One heard the private soldiers often asking: "Where are the commanders? Will nobody create some order here?"' Richter felt they had a point because 'you seldom saw a high-ranking officer'. His sentiment was echoed by the Panzergruppe 3 headquarters staff:

'The High Command can hardly know what things look like out here at the front. The seriousness of troop reports is not fully appreciated; perhaps they do not want to understand.'[3]

High Command was barely able to interpret and cope with a constant stream of reports across the front, all identifying previously unreported new Russian units. An advisory OKH letter was despatched to staffs to counter alarmist reports. It read: 'The large number of enemy units identified sometimes had a paralysing effect on our leadership,' and instructed, 'the leadership must not be allowed to fall into a numbers psychosis'. More assessments were required. Staffs were directed to measure the combat power of often poorly trained and equipped Soviet reserve units instead of counting off the quantities, while ignoring the underlying qualities of opposing divisions. 'Intelligence officers must be trained to be discriminating,' the report insisted. Troops at the front meanwhile felt neglected. Leutnant Richter complained, 'the trouble is that nobody feels responsible if the Russians come.' When they did, 'we're off! was the solution'.[4]

Still the ragged German columns fell back. One 7th Panzer Division officer said 'we had set off from Suwalki on 22 June 1941 with three complete battalions (*Abteilungen*) numbering 270 tanks, now we have only 10 fighting vehicles led by the regimental commander himself.' There were no heavy PzKpfwIVs: 'the last one had broken down and was blown up'. The signals battalion had lost 70 vehicles since the campaign began. Its second company had only 10 of 23 signal detachments left, the rest lost through breakdown or enemy action.[5] Another veteran claimed the division 'hardly looked like a military formation' marching back on 10 December. Some men rode, others were on *Panje* sledges, the mass were on foot. The Panzer regiment had converted some tank crews to infantry. Only the bare necessities were carried: emergency rations and a rifle. Many fell out of the line with frostbite. One infantry officer from the 6th Schützen Regiment described the exhausting routine resisting constant Russian attempts to cut the Klin–Jaropoletz road near the River Llama.

'Dead-tired, we went from village to village. Time after time it was "Halt! Occupy positions! Prepare to move — march!" One did not even consider rest.'[6]

Another Panzer officer ruefully admitted, 'this breaking contact with the enemy and then retreating through a region long regarded as the administrative rear zone was not to the taste of the German soldier.' Morale plummeted because, as the 20th Panzer Division officer explained, 'being required to fall back long distances created fertile ground for encouraging panicky and disturbing rumours.'

The lot of motorised formations paled into insignificance compared to that endured by the infantry. 'One look at the infantry,' declared a 20th Panzer Division soldier, 'was enough to change our minds if we ever felt compelled to complain.' He added:

'It was astonishing what was expected of and done by them. Worst was the cold. Temperatures could change from four days at −15°C to −20°C by day and −35°C at night and then go up and be followed by a snowstorm. Those who endured it would remember it for the rest of their days. They lay in the open and were unprotected on the roads.'[7]

Infantry Unteroffizier Rolf Müllender said 'nobody had reckoned on' the sudden counter-offensive on 6 December. His unit north of Moscow was quickly bypassed. 'A ski battalion whooshed by and we did not have a clue what had happened,' he said.

'Then came the order to pull back along the road toward Solnechnogorsk and Klin. We began marching with 26 men who remained from about 833 that had started the campaign as rearguard for the infantry marching ahead. One could say we were the last men in front of the enemy. Although skimpily dressed with summer coats and head warmers, we would pick up anything that could make one warm left lying behind by the dead, or our comrades. We put it all on to withstand the temperature. Weapons operated badly for the most part, especially the machine guns.'[8]

Infantry rearguards, such as the remnants of Leutnant Haape's Infantry Regiment 18, faced formidable problems. Strongpoints were established around villages and some attempt made to interlock weapon systems. Soldiers adapting to extreme conditions realised that weapons, once thawed out and dry-cleaned of lubrication, could fire more reliably. Small arms were kept warm in village ovens until needed. 'In any case,' a wiser Haape assessed, 'it's damned difficult for troops to attack over open snowfields in the face of an alert enemy.'

These more effective German tactics contributed to rising casualties among attacking Soviet units. Russian officers and NCOs were tactically amateurish compared to their German counterparts. Commanders tended to assign wide frontages, as much as 9–14km for a rifle division, dispersing forces, equipment and tanks evenly across the front. Tanks were placed in support of infantry, in preference to concentrating on narrow breakthrough areas or massing on main advance routes. Such shortcomings diluted combat power and weakened the Russian capacity to strike swiftly into German rear areas with sizeable mobile forces. Snow, ice and near-Arctic conditions impeded cross-country mobility. The consequence was frontal headlong assaults against flimsy German positions, which could have been infiltrated or simply bypassed.

The Russians were well aware that 'the German soldier was poorly clad for winter operations'. A later staff report observed, 'he sat most of the time in warmed shelters or in buildings prepared for defence; he preferred to die in the warmth than to die in the cold.'[9] Russian artillery was generally employed to demolish this essential shelter. But the inevitable bunching of infantry on the objective, a feature of inexperience, was severely punished by the interlocking fire systems the Germans faultlessly created. General Zhukov felt obliged to issue a curt directive to West Front commanders within three days of the offensive to desist from profligate frontal attacks. 'Especially created shock groups had been drawn into heavy and bloody frontal attacks,' he later complained. The advance of the Thirtieth and First Shock Armies was held up in the Klin area due to such tactics. He called on commanders 'to persuade their troops to bypass strongpoints of the enemy and pursue him relentlessly'.[10]

Primitive attempts to encircle German units often missed, or breakthroughs were not followed up by commanders fearful of German counter-measures on their flanks. The strongpoint system maximised German resources and experience, effectively networking their automatic weapons and artillery with a few Panzers in a way the Russians could not. Many German units owed their subsequent survival, despite a considerable mauling, to Soviet tactical failings and inexperience at the higher operational level to combine resources effectively enough to create successful encirclements.

German soldiers were driven by a stark philosophy simply to survive. Leutnant Haape's regimental commander explained:

'A soldier must learn that death is always by his side. And if we don't want death to have complete power over us we must take it for granted that he may strike at any moment — either at us or our comrades. And we must take it as a matter of course. It's up to every soldier to develop that attitude, or he's not worth calling a soldier.'[11]

A 'scorched-earth' policy was conducted as rearguards retreated from village to village behind Kalinin. 'The falling darkness was lit from the bright flames of burning villages,' observed Werner Pott, writing a letter home, 'in a house which would be up in flames in half an hour.' His unit was holding 'a long thin wedge' sticking out into the enemy line.

'For weeks we have been in action without a rest or break. Day after day ,marching to another quarter through snowstorms at −25°C, with frozen noses and feet so bad it makes you cry out when you take your boots off.'

'Filth, vermin and other unpleasantries' pervaded their lives. But beyond this it was the sight of the civilian population condemned to death by hunger or freezing that affected Pott the most, as they burned all villages through which they retreated. He described the scene:

'Red tongues of flame shot greedily upward as if they wished to devour the heavens — the world is on fire!
'Stooping old men and mothers with tiny children hasten by, a small bundle on their backs, carrying their last belongings. Behind us engineers are blowing bridges and houses.
'Back home somewhere is a Christmas tree, twinkling with familiar decorations. Much loved people are singing beautiful carols. It is better not to think about it.'

Werner Pott, a 19-year-old former Hamburg student, concluded his philosophical letter with a terse statement. 'Now we're off again to fight on; the village is already burning from end to end.'[12]

Wilhelm Göbel with the 78th Infantry Division witnessed the same gloomy spectacle. 'The nights presented an awful sight,' he said, 'with the entire horizon glowing red from the fires of burning villages.' He recalled an Unteroffizier Müller from Infantry Regiment 215, who had been given a stinging rebuke for not entirely burning the village of Dolginino, north of

Mozhaisk, 'because the weeping and crying had become too much for him'. Göbel was emphatic: 'every rearguard had the order to burn the village to the ground as it left.' The consequence for the inhabitants left behind with no shelter in near-Arctic conditions was clear. 'They were thereby totally delivered to the mercies of the cold,' Göbel admitted.[13] Leutnant Haape described what these −45°C temperatures were like. 'Every time we inhaled the frozen air our bodies lost heat,' he said, 'and the cold seemed to penetrate the marrow of our bones until walking became a stiff and awkward business.' Nevertheless, Infantry Regiment 18 continued to burn villages as it fell back from Kalinin.

'Nothing had to be left to the Red Army — and nothing was left. We marched with flames licking our footsteps, marched day and night, with only short halts, for we well knew that we were the rearguard . . . there were no troops between us and the pursuing Russians . . . Like Mummies we padded along, only our eyes visible, but the cold remorselessly crept into our bodies, our blood, our brains. Even the sun seemed to radiate a steely cold and at night the blood-red skies above the burning villages merely hinted a mockery of warmth.'[14]

Christmas was a sentimental time for the German soldier. Twenty-two-year-old infantryman Harald Henry with Ninth Army sought anxiously to deliver a letter to his parents in time for Christmas. He was concerned that the 'dry reports' they were getting in Germany were not the true picture, and admitted that his 'Christmas letter' written on 3 December 'says too little also'. On 7 December he told them he was in poor health, with dysentery and septic lice bites, but 'I am alive,' he continued, 'and uninjured, which gives me some hope to keep going'. Despite the pressures of everyday front life, Harald Henry felt an imperative to write home and stay in touch. 'Greetings from 11.12,' he wrote, 'impossible to write — Harald.' Another short note followed on 13 December and he managed a further letter on the 21st which included these last few lines:

'Dear Parents!
Unfortunately still no chance to write. Only the growing certainty of perhaps actually escaping this "dog's breakfast", because I appear to be the last single survivor from the whole company.'

The fighting strength of a company was normally about 176 men. On the day before Christmas Eve, Harald Henry was shot in the stomach during a tank infantry battle north-west of Moscow. The young man who had held a brief doctorate at Berlin University did not survive his wounds.[15]

Panzer officer Helmut von Harnack, already twice wounded, managed to extricate an infantry battalion under intense Russian pressure with his company of mixed Panzers and self-propelled guns. 'It was unforgettable,' he wrote, 'the battalion commander, out of breath, kept calling out "My best Christmas present ever!"' On Christmas Eve von Harnack received the gift of life himself. As he climbed down from his Panzer to check over one of his broken drive wheels 'my Panzer was rammed by a heavy Russian tank'. His elation was, however, short-lived. Within a month he was dead.[16]

The German sentimental view of Christmas lay in cruel juxtaposition to, and starkly emphasised, the reversal of fortunes compared to the more successful previous year. Panzer

Leutnant F. W. Christians admitted, 'Christmas was a particularly emotional experience for us German soldiers in such conditions.' The Russians, according to artillery soldier Pawel Ossipow, made the most of it also.

'We know that the Germans would want to celebrate Christmas between 24–25 December. There were indications of this from the Christmas trees and other decorations we found in the villages we liberated. The enemy's alertness would be correspondingly reduced indulging in such niceties so we tried to pursue them even more quickly during this period. It was, however, particularly tiring for our troops to advance 15km in a day.'[17]

Will Thomas, a German infantry NCO platoon commander, wrote to his wife on the second day of Christmas, cynically describing 'the best Christmas Day of my life', during which:

'The enemy attacked in overwhelming strength the entire day, using tanks, against which we had no defence. The entire position was reduced to soot and ashes and we crawled out from under the rubble. It was icy cold. The entire company was torn to pieces. Leutnant Wufert was killed! There was little rest that night, but in the morning it will start up again . . .'

The unit was surrounded. Thomas ended his letter with a prescient confirmation of his love, writing 'even in death we will never be apart'. He was killed the following month.[18]

Atrocities continued unabated. Ludwig Frhr von Heyl, a reconnaissance patrol commander, assessed that the campaign was certainly 'no gentleman's war'; it was in fact more like a 'punitive' expedition. 'What was the point of it all?' he asked.

'Human life appeared cheaper than shovels. One did not kill people it was "the enemy", something impersonal. What was also particularly shocking was how little worth the Russians appeared to ascribe to life.'[19]

Both sides were guilty of this. Gefreiter Vetter's unit was surrounded by Russians on the second day of Christmas, in temperatures of −35°C. Nevertheless, 3,000 Russian PoWs were taken out of their prison camp at nearby Kaluga and driven toward Roslavl. Vetter observed:

'Many, weak with hunger, fell onto the road and were shot. After the road was empty again of prisoners one saw countless dead lying by the sides. A number of the prisoners were seen carrying bits of human bodies [an arm, or foot etc] *in their pockets* [to eat]. *If one fell the others would immediately fall on him to strip him of clothing and take anything to eat. They all appeared starved and in terrible condition and had an animal look about them.'*[20]

Soviet prisoners were transported to the rear by rail, in open goods wagons, even after the retreat had started. Exposed to cold, rain and snow, up to 20% perished before they reached their destination. One-fifth of 5,000 Russian PoWs transported over 200km from Bobruisk to Minsk between 20 and 21 November froze to death. Obergefreiter Franz Wesskallnies, with 161st Infantry Division, saw Soviet prisoners arriving at Ebenrode in East Prussia in mixed open and enclosed goods wagons in temperatures of −18°C. 'The cars were so overfilled the prisoners could not lie down, and had to sit there [in the open] for six days with no food.' They were so hungry and thirsty that they subsisted on snow and grease scraped from the wagon wheels. 'Several lorries,' Wesskallnies said, 'were required to take away the bodies' of Red Army men found in every compartment. When they arrived at the camp there was no accommodation ready. Prisoners were obliged to dig holes inside the perimeter to gain protection against the elements.[21]

German soldiers caught up in the retreat reaped the whirlwind of these excesses. Quarter on the Eastern Front was rarely given or, for that matter, anticipated. At the end of December the port town of Feodosia on the Crimean Peninsula was overrun by a surprise Russian amphibious assault. The resident German 46th Division hurriedly evacuated, abandoning 160 severely wounded cases in the Feodosia hospitals. When the town was recaptured in February 1942, the ice-blackened corpses of these wounded littered the beach alongside the hospital by the Black Sea. They had been thrown out of second floor windows onto the sand and hosed down with water so they froze to death in the sub-arctic temperatures.[22]

During the early morning hours of 27 December Amadeo Casanova, a member of the Spanish 'Blue Division', was defending a position with German troops north of Novgorod. One of the Spanish companies was attacked and encircled by the Russians. A rapid counter-attack was mounted to extract them, and during this fighting a Spanish lieutenant and four soldiers were wounded and had to be left behind. 'Shortly after,' Casanova testified, 'we found them dead. In all cases the Russians had nailed their heads to the ground with pickaxes.'[23]

There was dread throughout the retreat at the prospect of capture by the Russians. Eye gougings, genital mutilations and arbitrary shootings continued. 'Fear of what would happen if captured by the Soviets,' remarked one regimental history, 'was what kept the German soldier on his legs'; adding, 'no small number shot themselves when in doubt.'[24] It was another nagging fear eroding morale and gnawing at nerves, magnifying further the desperate situation the troops felt themselves to be in. On 20 December Oberarzt Hans-Georg Suck's battalion, retreating with Guderian's Second Panzer Army, had fallen back to Plawsk, south of Tula. Lights had not been allowed within the column, which was being pursued by Soviet ski troops. As they moved through an unknown village the *Panje* wagons being used for the wounded and ammunition began to skid and slide over an uneven part of the road. Such an expanse of sheet ice was unusual in a village main street and merited investigation. Suck shone his pocket lamp on the surface of the road and recoiled in horror. A naked corpse stared back at him through the shimmering ice. 'We found several naked bodies lined up next to each other' under the ice, he said. There was no time to investigate the scene minutely because the enemy was in hot pursuit and closing. They realised they were German 'because there were pieces of German uniform scattered by the roadside'. The soldiers were much depressed and alarmed by this gruesome discovery in temperatures of −42°C to −48°C. 'Our comrades,' he surmised, 'must have had to undress in the road, were made to lie down in the street, and then covered with water so as to construct a stretch of road!'[25]

Fear and comradeship kept German units intact. Leutnant Haape, retreating with Infantry Regiment, 18 said:

'We had our cowards in the earlier fighting but they had been weeded out, for it was better to be one man short than to have a man who might start in a panic . . . At some time or another we had all been ready to run in blind fear, but the natural impulse was to stick it out with everyone else.'[26]

Leutnant Erich Mende concurred, stating, 'only one thing steadied the nerves, and that to a lesser or greater degree sustained you, and that was a sense of comradeship.' Everything else was otherwise subsumed in the 'awful automation of war'. He said:

'You knew you had a friend to your right and another to the left. If you were hit, they would help. If he was hit, you would go to him. And when someone shot at you, you fired back. One didn't think about it, that one killed or was killed. The motto was: "you or me." Either one killed or was killed in turn.'[27]

More than simply a will to survive was required to weld the German front together. As the army group fell back, a vitriolic debate raged between the operational army groups staffs and the strategic (OKH and OKW) level staffs to identify a way out of the crisis. By the third week in December, deep Soviet penetrations on both flanks of Army Group Centre were threatening to develop into a double envelopment of the entire German Central Front. There was a stark choice: retreat or fight. The former was the course currently being conducted and favoured by German field commanders, a prompt and extensive withdrawal to a suitable defence line. This had been identified as roughly the line between Kursk, Orel and Gzhatsk. The risk, and this was occurring in some sectors, was that enemy units thrusting between retreating German columns might inflict a sudden moral collapse. At the very best, considerable matériel would be lost and lines of abandoned guns and vehicles testified to this fact.

To stand and fight was, in the eyes of field commanders, a suicidal option. Success in this scenario was achievable only if German defensive endurance was superior to Soviet offensive capability. The present weakness of German fighting units seemed to preclude that. Moreover, such a course of action would result in the overrunning of units, and their loss would forfeit any opportunity of husbanding resources for a spring offensive in the central sector. Field commanders and the staff preferred the risk of a winter retreat to the certainty of annihilation if they stood their ground in the face of the Russian assault. Adolf Hitler provided a characteristic solution to this dilemma in a Teletype to Army Group Centre on 18 December.

'Commanding Generals, commanders and officers are to personally intervene to compel troops to fanatical resistance without regard to enemy that may break through on their flanks or in the rear.'

The instruction was an uncompromising 'stand and die' order. 'This is the only way,' the Führer added, 'to gain the time necessary to bring up the reinforcements from Germany and the West that I have ordered.' Two days before, Hitler had telephoned von Bock to order Army Group Centre to cease all withdrawals and defend in its present position. German soldiers would take 'not one single step back'.[28]

General Günther Blumentritt, the Chief of Staff to Fourth Army, was in conference with his Commander-in-Chief and other corps commanders in mid-December. They were totally engrossed in co-ordinating the move westward of their increasingly vulnerable army. A steadily widening gap had opened between von Kluge's Fourth and Guderian's Second Panzer Army. There were no reserves to restore the increasingly dangerous situation on the southern flank, which threatened to cut Fourth Army's single supply line to the rear. One motorised division was already marching westwards to Yukhnov. The withdrawal of Fourth Army units south of the Moscow–Smolensk highway was being discussed when Blumentritt was summoned to the telephone to speak to his personal friend and counterpart at Army Group Centre, Chief of Staff General von Greiffenberg. 'You'd better make yourself comfortable where you are,' he said. 'A new order has just arrived from Hitler. Fourth Army is not to retreat a single yard.' Blumentritt was aghast:

'According to every calculation, it could only mean the destruction of the Fourth Army. Yet this order was obeyed. Units already moving westwards were turned about and brought back to the front. Fourth Army prepared to fight its final battles, only a miracle could save it now.'[29]

Adolf Hitler had personally assumed the mantle of Commander-in-Chief of the Army. The Ostheer would fight where it was and, if necessary, perish.

Chapter 17
The order of the frozen flesh

'Vorwärts Kameraden, wir müssen züruck!'
(Advance men — we've got to get back!)

German infantry humour

'NOT ONE SINGLE STEP BACK' . . .THE HOLD ORDER

'This retreat order has reduced me to dumb resignation,' admitted an officer in the 198th Infantry Division. 'I don't want to think about it any more,' but he appreciated that, in order to survive, 'thinking and forethought is more necessary than before'. Obergefreiter Huber from Infantry Regiment 282 recalled 'unforgettable days battling on the Nara, with long nights, the cold, snowstorms — grey sinister days with artillery impacts and a constant racket among the smoke and crackling explosions of the fearsome "Stalin organs"'. The interminable retreat depressed the infantry officer. He was uneasy.

'Awful weeks of withdrawing through the thick snow-covered countryside and impenetrable woods stood before us. Short insecure pauses in empty half-destroyed villages, a harassed existence in icy cold with driving snow and long hours of darkness. Will it be possible to rebuild a front? Will substantial combat-ready units ever turn up? Will we be able to hang on?'[1]

When the 'hold' order was received at battalion level in the Fourth Army sector, it was met with incredulity. Infantry Regiment 9, part of 23rd Infantry Division, heard:

'The High Command has ordered that the present withdrawal movements around the Llama [river] are to be halted, and the division is to concentrate on both sides and now go firm. The Llama position must be defended to the last man!'

Commanders were to be held personally responsible for the order's execution. Feldwebel Gottfried Becker's initial reaction when told to dig was, 'OK, OK we hold the position, but could someone please tell me which one?' His commander, Leutnant Bremse, pointed to a hole in the ground partially filled with snow. 'It was not completely prepared,' he agreed, 'but they could do it now.' Each man in Becker's platoon had the same unsettling thought: 'He has got to be kidding!' They had completed a seemingly endless march through snow and ice with no sleep, and fought countless rearguard actions. Now they were instructed to dig a position virtually from new, in rock-hard frozen ground. Mindful of the Soviet approach, they commenced digging. Becker shovelled snow out of the half-constructed trench, complaining that 'those at the "top" had to be nuts'. Bremse was not sympathetic. 'That's it,' he said, 'shut your mouths and get on with it — now! Dig!'[2]

Obergefreiter Huber from the 98th Division reached his objective at 02.00 hours on Christmas Eve.

'Christmas morning dawned and now we had to occupy the edge of a wood. Thirty hungry spectres groped their way back to the position with shrunken cheeks, wearing summer uniforms with threadbare coats in temperatures of below –30°C. They had torn gloves, boots with holes and many wore laced-up shoes. Balaclava head-overs were soaked in sweat beneath chalk-smeared helmets. Stomachs were empty. They had two machine guns still in working order and some rifles. The route took them across fields, meadows, ditches and holes, into which the unsteady stumbled. Finally they arrived at the "position" at the end of the wood — a pair of holes half full of drifted snow. An icy wind cut through the position, quickly coating helmets and balaclavas from top to bottom with a thin coating of ice.'[3]

Adolf Hitler had confounded the plans of his military advisors. Viewing an impending collapse of the front with dismay, he resolved to relieve his generals of command initiative. He took pride in his proven ability to master and profit from a crisis. The ailing Generalfeldmarschall von Brauchitsch, the German Army Commander-in-Chief, followed the hapless von Rundstedt from Army Group South into retirement. Von Brauchitsch became the scapegoat both for the failure of 'Barbarossa' and the present winter crisis. Next came Generalfeldmarschall von Bock, who, in predicting disaster unless his Army Group was allowed to retreat, received a much earned 'rest' on 20 December. Generaloberst Guderian, evading orders to 'stand fast', was relieved from active duty on 26 December. General Erich Hoepner, the aggressive commander of Panzergruppe 4, enraged Hitler in early January as he retreated westward to avoid encirclement. Stripped of command, rank and privileges, he was forbidden to wear uniform in retirement. Strauss, the commander of Ninth Army, was cashiered one week later, and von Leeb, the Commander of Army Group North, was relieved on 17 January. During the subsequent winter, over 30 generals, corps and division commanders and senior officers were removed from command. They were the leaders that had brought the *Ostheer* with dramatic success to the very gates of Moscow. Now they were gone. Hitler, in removing them, completed the physical and moral transformation the *Ostheer* had been undergoing since June 1941. The last vestiges of Weimar and General Staff influence were gone. The *Ostheer* and Wehrmacht became the military arm of a National Socialist Reich.

Cashiering so many senior commanders in the midst of the winter crisis had an inevitable impact upon the flow of operations. Hitler's aim was indeed to minimise fluidity. His instinctive reaction, grounded on his veteran World War 1 experience, was that soldiers in a fast-moving crisis or retreat are more easily controlled when instructed to stand fast. An unequivocal 'stand and fight' order, whatever the seriousness of the situation, removed immediate uncertainties. Soldiers crave decision and clarity of intent at times of crisis. The German soldier sought clear direction and 'order.' Panzer Leutnant F. Wilhelm Christians later explained:

'Don't ask me if we complained, or if we had a mind of our own. What remained for us to do? There was no freedom of action, or indeed even the idea of it! Nobody debated whether he would participate! Such issues were never raised. We were given a mission and we took orders seriously.'

This resolve was not simply a mindless adherence to duty. 'A feeling of comradeship sustained us also,' said Christians, 'right up until entry to a Soviet concentration camp.'[4] Soldiers did what was required to live.

The next impact of the turmoil created by the extensive command changes was to stultify initiative at the front. The *Ostheer* was asked to perform the unthinkable, and elements would need to be sacrificed to achieve it. Hitler did not want his commanders to think; they were required to obey. As a result, strategic and operational control went to the supreme commander, virtually by default. An important source of advice and professional assessment was silenced in the process. The very command philosophy of the German Army, *Auftragstaktik*, designed to confer maximum initiative in accomplishing assigned tasks, was compromised. In one of those bizarre parodies of warfare, centralisation was imposed on the German military machine at the very time its opponents began to realise the virtues of decentralised control. The Wehrmacht had already demonstrated that the war-winning edge conferred by Blitzkrieg was dependent upon it.

The first phase of the Soviet counter-offensive clearly drove the Germans back from Moscow but did not destroy the bulk of the Panzer forces. Zhukov's original concept had been to gain space in front of Moscow, but the near-total collapse of the Army Group Centre front exceeded even the most sanguine Soviet expectations. As the three main German infantry armies were locked in combat, the beginnings of a possible double envelopment began to form. This encapsulated the area of Rzhev and Ninth Army in the north and a developing split between Fourth and Second Panzer Army creeping towards Vyazma in the south. Having planned and configured for a shallow set-piece battle, the Russians were unable to sustain wide-ranging penetrations without further supplies, replacements and fresh units. Momentum petered out as the distance between the advancing armies and their supply bases widened. Hitler coincidentally decided at the same moment that Army Group Centre should stand its ground and fight. A crucible of experience resulted from this decision for which a special German Winter Medal entitled *'In Osten 1941–42'* was struck. German soldiers, with typical black humou,r immediately labelled it 'The Order of the Frozen Flesh'.

Feldwebel Gottfried Becker, holding on the Llama river line with Infantry Regiment 9, was driven from his bunker by artillery fire on Boxing Day. Shelter was crucial for Becker and his men, but they had no idea of the overall situation as they fell back to a village. There was no way of knowing which houses were enemy held, and which by German troops. It was not until his rifle slipped involuntarily from his grasp that Becker realised, in a moment of heart-stopping panic, that he had left his gloves behind in the bunker. All feeling had gone from his hands and he could not even hold his weapon. Frostbite had already reached the tissue-damaging stage. Becker had no option but to follow scores of walking wounded and struggle back through 20km of deep snow to seek treatment in the rear. He trudged through the snow accompanied by another lightly wounded soldier, towing on a sledge a more serious casualty shot through both knees. The man's knees had swollen to the size of 'two children's heads' but he displayed 'immense stoicism', Becker said. 'He did not complain once despite being tipped several times into deep snow.' Morale in the rear was low. There was a reluctance to accept the sledge-borne casualty at the division aid post, but Becker did at least manage to purloin some food and drink. He decided to continue on foot alone to seek treatment for his badly frozen hands.

After walking several kilometres Becker felt the need to urinate. This posed a dilemma because he was physically unable to unbutton his trousers because his hands were thickly bandaged. What could he do? Perform the action in his pants? If he did so, he realised with sinking heart that his trousers would freeze rock hard in the extreme temperatures and cold injuries would result. A vehicle appeared ahead which he urgently flagged to a halt. Inside was a lieutenant at the wheel, who looked at him enquiringly. 'Could you help me undo my trousers?' Becker asked, gesticulating with bandaged hands. 'What's wrong?' asked the officer. On realising, he responded 'you poor bugger' and got out of the vehicle and led Becker to the roadside, where he extracted his penis, enabling him to pass water. The officer acted as if it was the most natural thing in the world, and apologised for not offering a lift; he was required at the front. He wished him well and departed. Becker had been unlucky. One moment's lack of concentration in the fighting around the bunker had within minutes cost considerable damage. He placed his hands wrapped in socks under his armpits and continued on his way.

The intense cold caught many inexperienced soldiers unprepared. An artillery radio operator from the 400th Artillery battalion, working alongside inadequately clothed soldiers from the 'Grossdeutschland' Regiment around Gorodok in temperatures of −40°C, related just how inhibiting the cold could be. He described a Soviet attack:

'Next to me stood a grenadier. His hands were in his pockets and his rifle was leaned against the fence as he watched the approaching Ivans. I asked him why he didn't shoot, and all he said was "No, you go ahead!" So I took off my headset, stood up, snatched up the rifle, took off my old mittens — they were little more than tatters anyway — adjusted the sight from 500m to 300m, poked the rifle through the fence and fired three shots. I doubt that I hit anything. Then it was all over for me; I was simply unable to insert another clip of ammunition; my hands were white and stiff. Now I was just as powerless in the face of the attacking Russians as my chum from the infantry. I felt what it was like to be unable to do anything when I knew that I should and must do something.'[5]

Becker reached a clearing station for the wounded and was placed in a straw-covered railway goods wagon. This took him to Vyazma, a journey lasting two to three days. A remorseless itching had begun to irritate from beneath his bandages after the second day. Somebody helped him to remove his pullover to relieve the itching he felt all over his body. It was infested with lice. With some revulsion he realised what the irritation beneath his bandages portended. They were rationed and looked after at Vyazma, but the dressing was not replaced. A further train journey followed to Smolensk, lasting several more days.

By now, the badly wounded soldiers lying in the straw-covered goods wagons were in a distressed state. Becker had to walk to hospital on arrival at the city, where a doctor examined his hand. The right one had turned almost completely black. 'We must take it off,' was the doctor's diagnosis. Becker declined, pleading, 'it would heal some time,' which drew a disinterested, 'do as you wish' from the much harassed doctor. Nobody bothered to delouse him and his injured hands were hurriedly rebound. Two days later a hospital train left for the West with Becker on board. It took 10 days to reach Warsaw. The Feldwebel had lost all feeling in his hands. Driven to distraction by the lice he pleaded to his doctor, 'I can stand it no longer, please, please take away these bloody bandages.' As the sister cut away the dressings he saw a sight that would remain with him the rest of his life: a triple layer of lice were crawling over 'the suppurating flesh of his hands'. Becker, in tears, had his hands disinfected and rebound. He was transported back to Germany where he spent four months recovering in a clinic. It took nine weeks before he was able to hold a spoon. Recovery came, but slowly.[6]

Becker's comrades with the 23rd Division were ejected from the Llama position and had to retreat 50km to west of Rzhev. Panzer Hauptmann Schroeder with the 7th Panzer Division recalled operating alongside them once again 'with the whole front slipping'. They were described as 'decimated but unbroken'. Feeling guilty with the realisation that the Panzers increased his chances of survival well beyond that of the hapless infantry, he said:

'I tried to support the infantry with my pair of Panzers but there was nothing more I could do. These brave men ran about with threadbare summer coats, no gloves and defective boots. They simply could not hold open ground in these freezing temperatures. Nearly all of them were afflicted by various grades of frostbite.'[7]

During the latter part of December both sides sought to reinforce their battered forces. Hitler ordered the despatch of 17 fresh divisions to the Eastern Front from other parts of German-occupied Europe.[8] They would take considerable time to arrive. Meanwhile Stalin saw the opportunity to apply an even more ambitious counter-stroke, encouraged at the success of the initial phase of the offensive. Phase two opened during the first two weeks of January and included another attempt to raise the siege of Leningrad, combined with an offensive by the south and south-west fronts. Amphibious landings were mounted by the Caucasus Front in the Crimea. In the Central sector the Kalinin, West and Bryansk Fronts attempted a double envelopment from Rzhev in the north and Sukhinichi from the south to close on the main Moscow highway at Vyazma. Hitler was obliged to order a withdrawal to a line approximating to the original '*Taifun*' start point the previous October. Many German units were surrounded during the withdrawal, but the move shortened the front, which freed units for counter-attacks able to seal the worst gaps torn in the front line. Another Soviet attack swept in from the north in a wide arc that sought to capture German-held Smolensk. Although the German strongpoint belt was penetrated in several areas, it soon became apparent the Soviet second stage objectives had been over-ambitious. The Russians had insufficient strength and resources to achieve a decisive victory as the drive was dispersed over too many objectives. German armies were not only spared decisive encirclement, they began to isolate over-extended Soviet thrusts which were mopped up later when reinforcements arrived. Second Shock Army under General A. A. Vlasov penetrated the rear of the German Eighteenth Army but became isolated in forest and marsh with its supply lines cut. Eventually its nine divisions and several brigades capitulated in June 1942. The Soviet Thirty-third Army with an integrated mobile cavalry group was cut off near Vyazma, as also the Twenty-ninth Army near Rzhev. This strategic spread of forces, weak in artillery and short of ammunition, enabled the ragged but still lethal forces remaining with Army Group Centre to bite back savagely. By the end of February, Stalin's great offensive had run its course.

German armies, partly reinforced by fresh divisions, re-established a continuous front in the centre. The line, tortuous in shape, reflected the limits of Russian offensive and opposing German defensive endurance.

FROZEN FLESH

The stamina of the *Ostheer* was tested to breaking point, an experience many would have difficulty coming to terms with mentally in later life. 'Our division was in reality decimated in Russia,' declared a distressed Walter Neustifter, 'perhaps up to 80% of its strength.'

'My comrades — [a heavy weapons] company was 220 men strong with mortars, heavy mortars, heavy machine guns and two light infantry [heavy-calibre] guns. It must have been during an attack when we had two infantry guns in support. They received a direct artillery strike and the complete crew was wiped out — totally. Ten men were cut down. This didn't just happen once [visibly upset], it must have happened a hundred times until there was nothing left.'[1]

Killing the enemy engendered a spectrum of emotions unique and peculiar to each man. German soldier Benno Zeiser, newly arrived at the shifting front, described his feelings:

'I got the leading man in my sights and clenched the bucking machine gun hard. If anybody got a dose of my stuff he was not going to get up again. You actually had the feeling you could hear the bullets go plonk into a man's body, yet you didn't really feel you were killing, or destroying human lives. On the contrary, you got a regular kick sometimes out of that sensation of the sploshing impact of the bullet. I must say I had always thought killing was much more difficult.'[2]

The majority of soldiers suppressed their feelings automatically, adjusting to whatever was required of them. Artillery observer Helmut Pabst, fighting near Rzhev at the end of January, saw that 'counter-attacks have all failed'. Night after night the infantry had gone into the attack despite enduring days in the open. 'They knew full well,' he said, 'the effort was hopeless.' One night a platoon of Pioniers, an officer and 42 men, mounted an attack. 'The officer came back ashen-faced with 15 men.' Eleven had been killed, and nine seriously and seven lightly wounded. Six days later the same officer, shot through the arm, fought his way out of Russian encirclement with only two of his original 15 men. Pabst bleakly observed, 'no more prisoners are being taken in the front line.'[3]

The health of the soldiers deteriorated to an alarming degree. An assessment by the senior medical officer with 167th Infantry Division highlighted concerns at the beginning of January 1942.

'Something like 80% of the fighting troops are undergoing medical treatment especially for stomach and bowel, catarrh, frostbite, skin diseases and fever. The level of health and overall condition is extremely bad, lowering the body's resistance in coping with illness and wounds. Death is often resulting from slight wounds with blood loss. Total physical and psychological collapse threatens not only the NCOs and men but the majority of officers as well.'[4]

The front was held by such men. Conditions in the fighting line itself were almost untenable. Gefreiter Rehfeldt recalled:

'The lice drove us practically insane. Our underwear was black with them, crawling not only inside our clothes but even onto our coats outside. This revolting feeling accompanied by itching could drive the most composed people to distraction. We have already scratched ourselves bloody — and the whole body, especially legs, looks scabby and lacerated. Frost injuries have developed into deep septic and bloody holes on both legs . . . When we have to go out to relieve a sentry post, I have to stagger along 40 minutes before the others . . . In the evenings, following the relief, I get in half an hour after them, wheezing from the pain . . . Taking off boots is only achievable at the second attempt accompanied with unbelievable effort and pain. Life is a total misery.'

Two weeks later Rehfeldt complained he had been three days without rations and 'practically everyone has the shits on an empty stomach'. They felt as 'weak and miserable as dogs,' and above all there was 'the unbelievable cold!' His frostbitten feet were becoming more swollen and septic with the passing of each day. 'Nothing heals in this cold,' he despairingly wrote.[5]

Leadership combined with draconian measures kept men in the line. Unteroffizier Pabst commented on near-hopeless counter-attacks mounted near Rzhev on 28 January. 'The front line dug-outs,' which had been lost, 'will be reoccupied,' he wrote; and 'any man leaving his post will be court-martialled and shot.' The mood in their shelter was 'extremely sombre'. Pabst, however, admired his company commander, Leutnant von Hindenburg — 'from an old family' — who kept them together.

'Strain has drawn rings under his eyes. In moments when he thinks he is not being watched, a great tiredness overtakes him and he grows quite numb. But as soon as he takes the receiver in his hand, his quiet, low voice is clear and firm. He talks to his platoon commanders with such convincing warmth and confidence that they go away reassured.'[6]

Comradeship mattered to the exclusion of all else. It sustained both sides. Leadership qualities were the cement binding it together. Discipline and mutual suffering bonded men together in an inexplicable, intangible way. Oberleutnant Beck-Broichsitter held a 4km-wide sector with 200 men from the 'Grossdeutschland' Regiment. (It was normally a task for two battalions numbering 1,400 men.) His men had been required to march the whole night and occupy hastily dug and inadequately prepared positions against Russian attacks. While crossing a stream, moving up, some of his men had broken through the ice and had been soaked in waist-deep water. 'They had then to stand around outside for ten hours in frozen trousers . . . Exhaustion,' the company commander wrote, 'was hindering his leadership.' When checking his perimeter a few days later Beck-Broichsitter stumbled across an amazing scene. One of his grenadiers was manning a single foxhole surrounded by 24 dead Russians sprawled all around. He had shot them all with his rifle.

'He had remained completely alone at his post during a snowstorm. His relief had not turned up and despite dysentery and frost-bitten toes he stayed there a day and night and then another day in the same position.'

'I promoted him to Gefreiter,' said the impressed company commander. Another of his NCOs 'had three children and also dysentery and frostbite.' Exercising compassion, the officer suggested he might wish to serve a period with the logistics element to the rear. 'No, no,' responded the soldier. 'Somebody else will only have to do it — I'll stay here.' The position was held for 20 days following a punishing routine, according to the company commander, of 'one hour's sentry and three hours' rest in an overcrowded lice-ridden area, during which most had to prepare new positions'. His battalion commander consistently asked him whether he could hang on, posing the eternal leadership dilemma.

'I wanted to help my company and should have said "no" and hope we would be relieved, but nobody wanted to admit it. So I said "yes" — and not only that — but that the soldiers' morale and resolve were firm.'[7]

It made him feel guilty.

If leadership alone did not suffice then the ultimate price was exacted from flagging men. Oberleutnant Sonntag, a battalion commander with the 296th Infantry Division, felt duty-bound to report on Oberfeldwebel Gierz, a senior NCO, to his regimental commander. Gierz appeared incapable of keeping his men in the line. Accused of cowardice, the hapless sergeant and his men were driven back into their position. The battalion commander despaired what to do next because, as he said, he was convinced, 'the next time the enemy came, they would run again'. He agonised over the decision. 'It wounds my heart,' he later wrote, 'when one has to consider it is German soldiers we are dealing with.' The inevitable happened. 'I am ashamed to report, Herr Oberstleutnant,' he wrote, explaining, 'I was obliged to implement draconian measures, and ordered the company to implement the order.' Gierz was shot.[8]

Infantry Leutnant Erich Mende appreciated the powerlessness of the individual to make an impact in such circumstances. 'I had extraordinary casualties,' he said, defending a railway station south of Kaluga. 'Of my original 196 men, 160 were dead, wounded or missing by the end of January.' Reflecting on this experience after the war, he mused, 'the soldier is a tragic figure'.

'During war he must shoot at other soldiers and in extremis kill them, without knowing or hating them. He follows orders from people he knows and bitterly dislikes, who do not have to fire at each other. In front of us was the Red Army, defending themselves, while we in the Wehrmacht were ordered to attack them. Deserting to the Red Army was no solution for the soldiers when faced with pressure. But when we retreated, or left our position, then along came military policemen and we were up before a Court Martial.'[9]

Meanwhile, at home in the Reich, the appeal to collect winter clothes received massive support but created uneasiness. Information was filtering back, but there was no substance to it. Wehrmacht broadcasts and announcements appeared to concentrate on apparently insignificant local actions. Many soldiers imposed a form of self-censorship in their letters, indicating they were alive but deliberately avoiding subjects that might arouse concern. Leutnant Heinrich Haape, fighting for his life, applied a certain circumspection to everything he wrote. 'When I wrote to Martha,' (his wife) he admitted, 'I mentioned little of the fighting, for the people at home had not yet been conditioned to realise what a serious change had come over the situation on the Eastern Front.'[10] Sceptics were beginning to guess. SS Secret Service Home Front reports remarked on the contradiction between press and film reports, showing warmly clad troops at the front and the call for winter clothing. It concluded, 'the appeal is clearly confirmation of the authenticity of the soldiers' stories on front leave and *Feldpost* letters pointing to the shortage of equipments suited to the Russian cold.'[11] Armaments Minister Albert Speer said after the war:

'We were all quite happy about the success of the German armies in Russia, but the first inkling that something was wrong was when Goebbels made a big "action" in the whole of Germany to collect furs and winter clothes for the German troops. We knew then something had happened which was not foreseen.'[12]

Hildegard Gratz, working as a relief school-teacher at Angerburg in east Germany, felt uneasy teaching children 'about a hero's death' when she clearly saw 'sitting in front of me were children whose fathers would never come home'. The children were required to participate in the 'Winter Relief' programme, collecting or knitting warm clothing. These activities aroused 'anxious, despairing and forbidden thoughts,' she said.[13]

Then came the startling news that the Führer had assumed overall command of the army. This 'elicited the utmost surprise', commented SS Secret Service observers. 'Amazement bordering on dismay prevails among much of the population that the change in the Army High Command should occur just when the fighting was at its fiercest on all fronts, and, of all times, just before Christmas.'

There was increasing unease that the war was perhaps not going too well. People said they would rather be told about a withdrawal or failure than be denied a clear picture of what was going on. 'A certain mistrust over official reports' resulted, fuelled further by letters and reports from soldiers on leave. Rumours suggested German troops had been driven back 150km from the line originally reached due to the introduction of the excellently equipped Soviet Far Eastern Army. Faith in the Führer remained but 'it was becoming ever more apparent,' commented the SS reports, 'that the war had become a matter of life and death for Germany, and everyone would need to be prepared to offer himself up as a victim if necessary'.[14]

This development was crystal clear to those engaged in the pitiless struggle at the front. The German soldier had experienced defeat and a retreat and had survived. 'It was the first time,' one veteran noted, 'that our soldiers remarked on the dark shadows of the coming times.'[15] Friedebald Kruse wrote back from the front on 23 December that 'yesterday's news that Brauchitsch had to go and today the Führer has

taken on the High Command of the Army affected me'. It was to him an inauspicious development: 'the first time that faith in the army had been questioned.' Many soldiers dismissed the news as a 'palace revolution' resulting from military failure.[16] Staff officer Bernd Freytag von Lorringhoven, working at Guderian's headquarters, viewed it from a more sombre perspective.

'The atmosphere following the defeat practically in front of Moscow was deeply depressing. On the one hand, the war was probably — Ja — virtually lost, and could only be prosecuted beyond with great difficulty. On the other side there developed at that time, a deep bitterness over the measures that Hitler ordered, dismissing these well qualified people.'[17]

'Having to retreat from Moscow,' declared another Eastern Front veteran, 'meant the Russian people and soldiers must realise it is possible to defeat the German Army'.[18] Panzer Major Johann Graf von Kielmansegg agreed. 'It was the first time in this war,' he said, 'that German soldiers had been defeated somewhere en masse.'[19] It produced a measured celebration on the Russian side. Actress Maria Mironowa, living in Moscow recalled, 'the mood during the New Year festivities was bad, it was not celebrated.' They drank a little to coming victory 'but we certainly had no idea it lay so far in the distant future'. There had been too much suffering. 'The war,' she said, 'was like a natural catastrophe and had an impact on us like an earthquake.' But despite all this, Soviet platoon commander Anatolij Tschernjajew recognised, 'it was an enormous turn around of events, this feeling that an offensive, a victory and finally even a turning point in this war were again possible.'[20]

The German soldier enjoyed a certain black humour, even in defeat. During the retreat a cynical motto was introduced. It was often preceded by a comic reversing of the helmet or field cap, and the exclamation — frequently when threatened by Soviet encirclement — 'Vorwärts Kameraden, wir müssen zürück!' In short: 'Advance men, we've got to get back!' One soldier in the 2nd Panzer Division, on hearing the exhortation admitted, 'in spite of the serious situation, one had to laugh.'[21] This ability to recuperate suddenly and lash out again against the foe was time and time again to stun Allied armies thinking they held the initiative during the final stages of World War 2. 'That explains the huge trauma and shock,' Russian platoon commander Anatolij Tschernjajew explained, 'when six months later the German Army was advancing even further, against Stalingrad!'[22]

The war was far from over yet.

Postscript — 'Barbarossa'

'Only rarely did I weep . . . There is no point weeping, even when confronted with the saddest scenes.'
German soldier

'The world will hold its breath,' announced Adolf Hitler when on 22 June 1941 three million German soldiers and their allies launched a surprise attack across the Russo-German border. Operation 'Barbarossa' committed the largest and finest army the German nation had ever fielded. Tempered by success in previous campaigns, the *Ostheer* had every expectation of victory, yet within four months its fighting power had been irretrievably sapped. Success was degraded to a reckless and rapid advance, driving into an enemy of indeterminate strength, to gain shelter before the onset of a pitiless winter. The final assault on Moscow was more a gamble than a considered operational plan. A number of factors contributed to this eventual débâcle, and these are considered in turn.

Surprise was the paramount feature of this initial campaign of the Russian war. Both populations were stunned at the precipitate nature of the attack. Most German soldiers were informed about the impending assault a mere 24 hours before their relatives at home. The Russian population was at first dismayed, then indignant at this blatant disregard of a Non-Aggression Pact that had promised so much two years before, with a fanfare of political rhetoric. War occasioned mutual surprise. Unlike earlier adversaries, who logically surrendered if outmanoeuvred and encircled, Russian armies fought on to the death. 'Don't die without leaving a dead German behind you,' exhorted hopelessly surrounded Russian soldiers at Brest-Litovsk in June.

Soviet planners, checkmated by their strategic compromise between an offensive and defensive stance on the German border, were stunned by the Blitzkrieg pace of advance forced on their confused armies. They were outwitted at each strategic development by massive encirclements unprecedented in military history, first by the sudden change of direction south into the Ukraine away from Moscow, and then by the timing of Operation 'Taifun'. This was unexpectedly launched at the capital well into the autumn, despite the impending winter. The German General Staff likewise underestimated the extent of the 'Russian Colossus'. A potential Russian strength of 200 divisions had to be reassessed at 360 within two months of the invasion.[1] 'Kick in the door and the whole rotten edifice would come crashing down' was the loose ideological underpinning of the plan to prosecute the campaign approved by Adolf Hitler.

Despite the maligned and shabby 'workers' paradise' portrayed in jeering German newsreels, cinema audiences in the Reich were soon to see film of the massive Dnieper dams and shipyards at Nikolaev on the Black Sea, contrary to the primitive society claimed. German soldiers further experienced a technological shock on encountering hitherto unknown heavy tank types. There was no reliable anti-tank defence against these, other than static, high-velocity anti-aircraft guns hurriedly employed in the ground role. Soviet Katyusha M13 multi-barrelled rocket launchers also had an unprecedented and devastating effectiveness, and on German morale, again demonstrating this opponent was unlike all others that had preceded it.

Surprise impacted in other ways. As well read as the German Army was on the historic invasions of Russia by Charles XII of Sweden in 1707 and Napoleon in 1812, they were still mentally unconditioned for the vastness and extremes of climate in Russia. The fan-shaped German advance widened to 2,800km within four months and was over 1,000km deep. To maintain a conventional continuous front would require 280 divisions. But only 127 divisions participated in the original invasion. Partisan warfare across this wide expanse and in such depth had never been experienced before. German soldiers were unprepared for the physical extent of the undertaking. Phrases used to describe the phenomenon in *Feldpost* letters reflect this perception of inadequacy. Unit fighting contributions were likened to 'a drop of water on a hot stove' or to 'a stone cast into the sea'.

Operation 'Barbarossa' became the longest campaign in the war. Blitzkrieg or 'lightning war' had until then offered speedy conclusions to operations. This one was anticipated to last eight to ten weeks. At the six-week (or successful French Armistice of 1940 point) German forces were still battling to close the Smolensk pocket. It also coincided with the period of the heaviest casualties during the war. The final surprise was in not winning. No German Army had been defeated en masse since the beginning of the war. Zhukov's counter-stroke in front of Moscow may have been primitive in its delivery, but it brought the *Ostheer* to its knees. This should perhaps not have been totally unexpected. Defeat had already been insidiously inflicted in a cumulative manner by the bloody Pyrrhic pocket-battle victories up until September.

The need to fight encirclements to annihilation had not happened before in this war. It broke the tempo of Blitzkrieg. An ominous portent of the future had been the vicious battle for the citadel at Brest-Litovsk in the first days of the campaign. This action on the border cost the division that fought it more casualties in one week than it lost during the entire operation in France, lasting longer than the western campaign in its entirety. Encirclement battles at Minsk and Smolensk consecutively tied down more than 50% of the offensive potential of Army Group Centre. In the west, creative General Staff planning had split and outmanoeuvred the allied armies, which capitulated. The Russians doggedly fought on, whatever the cost. Inspired manoeuvre alone would not suffice to win battles on the new Eastern Front. The savaged opponent had first to be finished off, a time-consuming and costly affair. German 'fast' motorised or Panzer divisions were not configured for this development and were unpractised in defence. They were badly mauled penning their fanatical opponents, waiting for the arrival of the infantry who were to administer the *coup de grâce*. Infantry 'will' became as important as Panzer 'skill' in pursuing battles of attrition. Infantry operations required willpower, less appropriate arguably to Panzer formations required to excel in manoeuvre warfare, not the static defensive battles they were involuntarily obliged to fight. Throughout the 'Barbarossa' offensive phase, often described as Blitzkrieg, one is struck by the quantity of soldiers' accounts that describe costly defensive actions, not fast-moving meeting engagements.

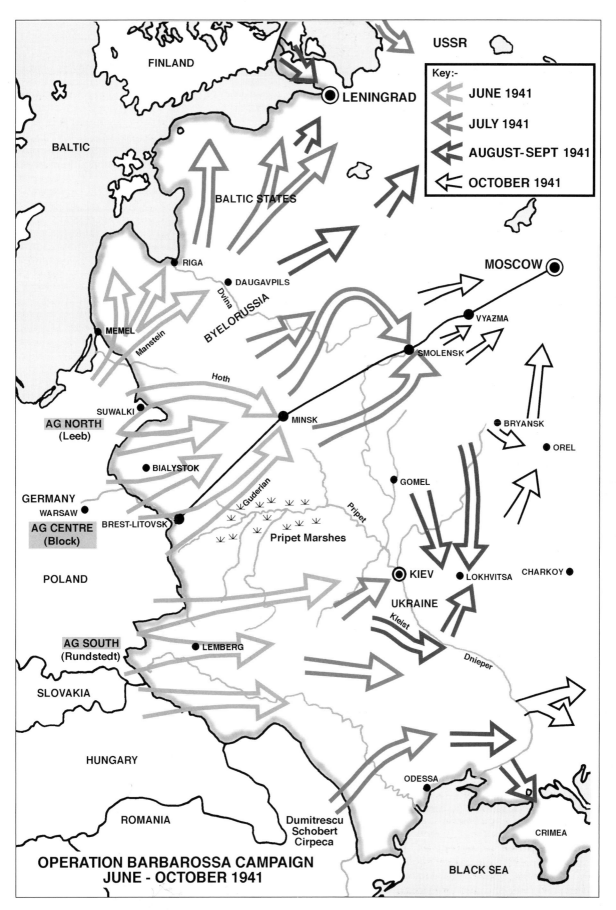

FINLAND

USSR

BALTIC

Key:-

	JUNE 1941
	JULY 1941
	AUGUST-SEPT 1941
	OCTOBER 1941

LENINGRAD

BALTIC STATES

● RIGA

● DAUGAVPILS

Dvina

BYELORUSSIA

MOSCOW

● VYAZMA

MEMEL

Manstein

● SMOLENSK

Hoth

● BRYANSK

SUWALKI

● OREL

AG NORTH
(Leeb)

● BIALYSTOK

● MINSK

Guderian

● GOMEL

GERMANY

WARSAW ●

Pripet

AG CENTRE
(Block)

BREST-LITOVSK ●

Pripet Marshes

POLAND

● KIEV

● LOKHVITSA

CHARKOY ●

UKRAINE

Kleist

AG SOUTH
(Rundstedt)

● LEMBERG

Dnieper

SLOVAKIA

HUNGARY

● ODESSA

ROMANIA

Dumitrescu
Schobert
Cirpeca

CRIMEA

**OPERATION BARBAROSSA CAMPAIGN
JUNE - OCTOBER 1941**

BLACK SEA

Operation 'Barbarossa' was unlike previous campaigns because the Wehrmacht made war on the Russian civilian population. Fighting in the west had, of course, not been prosecuted in a vacuum. Civilian centres had been bombed, such as Rotterdam, and Warsaw and other towns and cities were fought over. But there was a vicious ideological thread within the new campaign that saw operations being actively prosecuted against civilians by certain elements within the armies. During the invasion the Reich population read about developments in their newspapers, listened to the radio or watched *Wochenschau* newsreels. The Russian population was *in* the fighting. This was to have an impact upon the moral component of the fighting power of both sides. German infantryman Robert Rupp confessed to his wife:

'Only rarely did I weep. Cryin___ ___way out when you are standing amid these event___ ___back again with you and able to unwind in ___ ___e will need to cry a lot and you will ___ ___ ___nd your husband. Here, there is ___ ___ven when confronted with the sadde___ ___ng of human pathos and guilt is gra___ ___everyone. A deep shame develops. Some___ ___med even to have been loved.' [2]

Whereas ___ moral seepage occasioned by cruelties was to have a corrosive impact on German motivation and fighting power, it increased the will of the Russian soldier to resist at all costs.

A central theme of this book has been the recognition of the extent to which German fighting power had been degraded by the Pyrrhic victories of summer encirclement battles. September 1941, according to this hypothesis, represents the key watershed of the 'Barbarossa' campaign, rather than the collapse of the Army Group Centre front in the face of the Russian counter-offensive before Moscow in December. 'General Winter' was not responsible. Rather the ferocity and doggedness of Russian resistance, despite the hideous human cost, was instrumental in reducing the three components of German 'fighting power' to an almost terminal state.

Fighting power according to modern British military doctrine can be crudely broken down into three inter-related aspects: the physical, moral and conceptual. The physical part is concerned with the manpower and resources to execute the mission. The 'moral' is the 'hearts' aspect, requiring willpower and determination to enact it, while the conceptual aspect is the 'minds' or intellectual input. This is the plan or strategy required to achieve the objective. By the end of September the *Ostheer*, while inflicting three to four million casualties on the enemy, had suffered half a million in so doing itself. This loss represented 30 division equivalents, and a like strength of officers and NCOs to man 37 from 117 divisions. These totals were greater than the sum strength (26 divisions) of Army Group North at the outset of the campaign. Leadership losses, representing probably one-third of the total, were key. Both these and soldier casualties came from the 'teeth' or fighting elements of divisions. They were the cream, the veterans forged in battle. As training times varied from six to 18 months, they were irreplaceable. A typical infantry division was 64% 'teeth' compared with its non-combatant 'tail'. Panzer division combat elements represented just under half its nevertheless essential 'specialised' and logistic 'tail', made up of technical experts. Overall, the losses constituted half the fighting element of divisions. Motorised vehicle and Panzer states were in no less parlous a state at the end of September. In general only half

were still operating, and much of the remainder were good for only another 200km, barely sufficient to reach Moscow.

Inextricably linked to this equation was a logistic 'trip-wire' impediment. This invisible motor transport shuttle line stretching 500km beyond the Reich frontier meant a rail network had to be quickly established beyond to bring fighting divisions up to their full logistic combat supplements. With half the lorry fleet out of action and no capability quickly to reconfigure Russian railway gauges, an intangible logistic hurdle was created stymieing any further strategic advances on Moscow. Adverse weather — first mud and then sub-arctic temperatures — ensued, preventing practical and sustainable logistic support. An irretrievable breakdown of the *Ostheer*'s logistic ability to support an offensive was the result. Wheeled and rail transport was unable to cope.

The 'physical' component of fighting power was directly linked to the 'conceptual', in that losses rendered the Blitzkrieg mode of war fighting inoperable. Leadership losses by the end of September burned out the nucleus of the veteran capability practically to execute fast-moving and joint operations beyond the breakthrough achieved at the beginning of October. A paucity of reserves robbed the *Ostheer* of its *Auftragstaktik* flexibility, reliant upon initiative. It was emasculated by the inability to pass on risks to higher formations, who traditionally influenced the outcome of battle by deciding when reserves should be committed at the right place and moment to win. Lack of reserves necessitated a centralisation of the fewer available assets. Less risk-taking denied tactical flexibility. No one could salvage the daring commander who over-committed himself. It preceded the greater control that Adolf Hitler was later to impose on assuming the mantle of Commander-in-Chief in December. Likewise, the breakdown of 'teeth to tail' ratios robbed divisions of their combined arms synergy. Close co-ordination between Panzers, infantry, air and artillery was dependent upon the 'specialists' who made it work. Once these technical tradesmen and Panzer and Luftwaffe crews were employed as infantry, current and future professional expertise was squandered, and with it the implicit war-winning superiority of German combat structures. The conclusion of the battle of Kiev at the end of September coincided, therefore, with two watersheds on the Eastern Front. Firstly, it was the point at which German experience began to lose its edge, relative to Russian learning capacity. Secondly, the impetus conferred on German formations by surprise was lost. With Leningrad encircled and Kiev taken, both sides could see that Moscow would be the next objective.

The 'moral' component of fighting power — willpower and motivation — lies at its core. At the outset of 'Barbarossa' the *Ostheer* was committed to its duty to the Reich, and confident of achieving its objectives. Large segments were convinced of National Socialist ideals in a loose 'peer pressure' sense. Casualties and the morally corrupting influence of officially sanctioned violence against the Russian Army and populace began to erode this core. Momentum was sustained despite losses during the battles at Smolensk and Kiev because the Panzers were always winning up ahead. The infantry instinctively realised from its French experience that heavy casualties may result in the short term, but the long-term result is cheaper if the momentum is sustained.

They fought on. Battles at Kiev and Vyazma and Bryansk during Operation '*Taifun*' were appreciated for the gambles they were, but the men had faith in their Führer. 'Those at the top' had yet to be proven wrong in this war. Cynicism, however, developed in tandem with losses. Domestic pressure increased from anxious relatives at home, questioning the cost and mistrustful of propaganda. A frustrated feeling of betrayal arose after the successful encirclement battles at Vyazma and Bryansk. The German press crowed that Soviet capitulation would follow, but it was not delivered.

It is interesting to observe the extent to which SS Secret Service reports focused on the opinion of women in the Reich. During an era of male dominance, only beginning to change with the increasing employment of women in industry required in 'Total War', their opinion was canvassed and accorded immense respect. Their views were totally uncompromising and voiced like lions, as they gradually perceived the extent of the suffering of their men-folk at the front. From Smolensk onwards, women in the Reich expressed concern at casualties and the likely impact of the approaching winter.

Excesses committed by the *Einsatzgruppen* and other state-sponsored terror committed against Russian prisoners and civilians had a cumulative moral impact on German soldiers. Although orders were not overtly questioned, many became increasingly uncomfortable at the 'justness' of their cause. Complicity was variable and depended upon individual standards of human decency. More recent conflicts in Europe, notably the Balkans, reveal the extent to which complicity, viewed through nationalist, UN, NATO and political-ideological filters is not clear-cut. *Vernichtungskrieg* in Russia was becoming increasingly transparent.

A string of campaign setbacks created further unease. One had lived with the disappointment of the 'half' result at Dunkirk because it had been followed by the French Armistice. They were to be followed, however, by reverses at Leningrad, Rostov and finally the débâcle before Moscow. The totally unexpected Soviet counter-offensive crashed into an *Ostheer*, which saw the cream of its generals abruptly removed in the throes of a crisis. Faith in the Führer remained, but 'those at the top' had badly let the men down. The German General Staff, whatever the political pressure, was equally mesmerised by the ultimate prize to be had at Moscow. Its fall came to symbolise a likely end to the war. With the veterans dead and the chalice of victory snatched dishearteningly from its lips, there was a real crisis of confidence. The *Ostheer* subsequently fought almost to the death in front of Moscow, not for Hitler or duty, but to survive.

The final theme to emerge is a failure of German command, a lack of OKW perception. This was firstly its misappreciation of the Russian foe, and secondly its inability to recognise the effect the campaign was having on the very fabric of the *Ostheer* itself. Russian casualties during the first six months, at three to four millions, dwarfed the imagination. Stupendous though they were, they were never sufficient to persuade the Soviet regime to sue for peace. As a consequence, Russia had only to weather the initial shock of invasion to survive. In time it could exploit its superior demographic and economic resources to win. Cities tended to be avoided by the Führer and the General Staff for tactical not ethical reasons. It was decided at Leningrad to starve the metropolis into submission. But they were equally significant as Communist Party centres, the focal points from which it extended its power and influence into the immense interior of the state. They were, therefore, strategic targets. Hitler's acute perception of what was ideologically important influenced his judgement on objectives such as Leningrad, Moscow and, later, Stalingrad — 'Stalin's City'. Russia may not have been militarily defeated, but the Communist Party power base resided in the cities, which were vulnerable to military action but whose vulnerability was not exploited. The consequences of racial war were to prove a salvation for the Communist Party, enabling it to harness Russian nationalism as a panacea to the crisis.

The second failure of German Command was OKW's inability to recognise the extent to which German fighting power had actually eroded by September. The force fighting on the approaches to Moscow was tangibly different from the one that had crossed the demarcation line in June 1941. Expanding the number of new Panzer divisions using the same number of equipments but with manpower increases diluted the quality of the Wehrmacht instrument that had Blitzkrieged its way through Western Europe. None of the fundamental shortcomings that emerged from the French campaign, notably insufficient motorised vehicles and effective infantry anti-tank defences, were properly addressed during the pause between operations. 'Mot', the German military abbreviation for 'motorised', was replaced by 'Hot', a sardonic *Landser* label describing the extent to which motor vehicle losses were replaced by horse power.

As the German armies 'victored' themselves to death, all the negative aspects of linkage between the three identified components of fighting power came together. The very 'Verdun' that von Bock sought to avoid at the gates of Moscow occurred before he arrived. The *Ostheer*'s momentum was halted within 20km of the Kremlin. Blind faith in the invincibility of the Wehrmacht, maintained during every campaign in this war to date, was finally shattered in the snow-covered fields and forests of the western approaches to Moscow. They had sacrificed the seed-corn of Blitzkrieg to get this far. Many of those responsible for the planning and conduct of the advance were removed from command as part of the price. The cream of the army, the last vestiges of Weimar influence and the majority of World War 1 veterans had disappeared, dead or broken men. The German soldier had now ostensibly to fight for the Führer, the man to whom they swore allegiance as the Head of State and now Commander of the Army. Most, having witnessed the depredations visited on the civilian population and prisoners of war, whether they were accomplices or not, feared an inevitable retribution. They would reap the whirlwind. The war, all sensed, had reached a turning point. They would now have to fight for their comrades, their families and, above all, themselves.

Between 9 and 11 May 1942 the 7th Panzer Division was relieved in the line and sent back to France to recuperate. In June 1941 one of its units, Infantry Regiment 6, had been transported from the Cologne area to East Prussia in 12 trains in preparation for the invasion. One train was sufficient to achieve the move less than one year later.[3]

Germany's borders might one day be under threat. Now, it was a matter for survival. This imperative was to become corrupted with further setbacks and the passage of time to a sardonic *Landser* motto, adopted during the eventual retreat of the German armies. 'Enjoy the war while you can,' it enjoined, 'because the peace will be terrible.'

Notes to Text

Introduction
1. Kohl, Paul: *Ich wundere mich, dass ich noch lebe*, Gütersloh, 1990.
2. Interview *'Mein Krieg'*, German TV documentary, 1991.
3. Newspaper interview: *'Die Zeit — Forum'*, 3 March 1995.

Chapter 1: 'The world will hold its breath.'
Saturday, 21 June 1941
1. Buchbender, O. and Sterz, R.: *Das Andere Gesicht des Krieges Deutsche Feldpostbriefe 1939-1945;* Verlag C. H. Beck, 1982 (henceforth referred to as *Feldpostbriefe)*; p68 Letter 12/18 Regt, 21 Jun 41.
2. Letter 21 Jun 41. Bähr, H. W., Meyer, H. J. and Orthbandt, E.: *Kriegsbriefe Gefallener Studenten 1939-1945;* Rainer Wunderlich Verlag, 1952 (henceforth referred to as *KGS)*; p34-5.
3. Letter 19 Jun 41. *KGS* p40-1. He was killed on 25 June.
4. Letter 21 Jun 41. *KGS* p35. He was killed during the assault of Brest-Litovsk.
5. *Feldpostbriefe* p65.
6. Interview Jan Szcepanink ZDF TV 1991 documentary. *Steh auf! es ist Krieg.*
7. Knappe, S.: *Soldat; Reflections of a German soldier 1936-49*; Dell, 1993 (henceforth referred to as *Soldat)*; p198-200.
8. Glantz, D. M.: *The Initial Period of War on the Eastern Front*; Frankcass & Co, 1993; p30.
9. Knopp, G.: *Der Verdammte Krieg*; C. Bertelsmann Verlag, München, 1991; p31.
10. Ibid p37.
11. Letter 13 Jun 41. Golovchansky, A., Osipov, V. , Prokopenko, A. , Daniel, U. and Reulecke, J.: *Ich will raus aus diesem Wahnsinn — Deutsche Briefe von der Ostfront 1941-1945 aus sowjetischen Archiven*; Rowohlt Verlag Hamburg, 1993 (henceforth referred to as *Soviet Feldpostbriefe)*.
12. Kuby, E.: *Mein Krieg; Aufzeichnungen aus 2,129 Tagen*; Deutscher Taschenbuch Verlag, 1977; p105.

'Forget the concept of comradeship'
1. Halder, F.: *The Halder War Diary 1939-42*; Ed. Burdick, C. and Jacobsen, H. A., Greenhill Books, 1988; 31 Jul 40 p244.
2. Ibid, 30 Mar 41 p346.
3. a. *'Behandlung feindlicher Landeseinwohner im Operationsgebiet des Unternehmens Barbarossa.' Geheime Kommandosache Mai 1941. Az. Gen sb vb, ob d.H. Nr 75/41. G.Kdos. Chefs.* Issued to 2, 4, 6, 9, 11, 16, 17 and 18 Armies and those in Norway.
   b. *'Richtlinien für die Behandlung politischer Kommissare.' Anlage zu OKW/WF St/Abt. Liv/Qu. Nr 44822/41 g. K. Chefs.*
4. Hoeppner to Panzergruppe 4. Quoted from Murray W.: 'Barbarossa', *Quarterly Journal Military History*, Spring 1992; p10.
5. Heydorn, V. D.: *Der sowjetische Aufmarsch im Bialystoker Balcon bis zum 22. Juni 1941;* Verlag für Wehrwissenschaften; München, 1989; p82.
6. 'First hand account of Leo Scharf' from Dills, K. W.: *German War Art 1939-45;* Bison Books, 1983; p150.
7. Halder op cit 15 Oct 40 p263.
8. Interview 'The World at War — Barbarossa.' Thames TV 1973.
9. Speer, A.: *Inside the Third Reich*; Sphere, 1971; p257.
10. Halder op cit 16 Nov 41 p283.
11. Extract from *Die Deutschen im Zweiten Weltkrieg* SWF German TV 1989.

'The Führer has got it all in hand'
1. Letter Lt P.G. Inf Ers Btl 2 151 Div 7, Mar 41. *Feldpostbriefe* p65.
2. Ibid Letter 27 Mar 41 p66.
3. Halder op cit 14 Mar p330, 30 Apr p378, 9 Jun 41 p403.
4. Stahlberg, A.: *Bounden Duty — The Memoirs of a German Officer 1932-45*; Brassey's UK, 1990; p155.
5. Knopp op cit p40.
6. Interview *Der Verdammte Krieg* ZDF German TV 1991.
7. Interview Harriet Eder, Thomas Kufus, *Mein Krieg* WDR German TV 1988.
8. Stahlberg op cit p156.
9. Interview *Steh auf es ist Krieg* ZDF German TV 1991.
10. *Feldpostbriefe* Letters 30 Apr, 19 Jun 41 p62 and 68.
11. Thilo's Diary Entries, 21 Sept and 2 Sept 40, quoted Glanz p292.
12. Westphal, S.: *The Fatal Decisions*; Michael Joseph, 1956; p34.
13. Halder op cit 29 Jan 41 p314-5.
14. Westphal op cit p34.
15. *Militärgeographische Angaben über das Europäische Russland. Generalstab des Heeres, Berlin 1941. Wallets: Mappe E. 'Weißrussland', G. 'Zentral-Russland', H. 'Moskau'.*
16. Westphal op cit p34-5.
17. Historical quotations Bain and Belloc from Cooper, L.: *Many Roads to Moscow*; Hamish-Hamilton, 1968; p55 and 150.
18. Halder op cit 5 Dec 40 p383.
19. Ibid, 26 Apr 41 p376, 5 May 41 p383.
20. Interview *'Der Marsch in den Krieg'* from *Die Deutschen im Zweiten Weltkrieg.* SWF German TV 1989.

Tomorrow 'we are to fight against World Bolshevism'
1. Knopp op cit p44.
2. Interview *'Der Krieg im Osten'* from *Die Deutschen im Zweiten Weltkrieg* SWF German TV 1989.
3. Interview *Der Verdammte Krieg* ZDF German TV, 1991.
4. Interview *Mein Krieg* WDR German TV, 1988.
5. Interview *Der Verdammte Krieg* ZDF German TV 1991.
6. *Feldpostbriefe* Letters 30 Apr 41, 4 May 41, p66.
7. Interview *Der Krieg im Osten* SWF German TV, 1989.
8. *Feldpostbriefe* 2 Jun 41 p67.
9. Ullrich, K.: *Wie ein Fels im Meer — Kriegsgeschichte der 3.SS Panzerdivision 'Totenkopf'*; Munin Verlag, Osnabrück, 1987; p99.
10. Zieser, B.: *In Their Shallow Graves*; Elek Books, 1956; p23.
11. *Soldat* p204.
12. Luck, H. von: *Panzer Commander*; Praeger NY, 1989.; p56-7 and 64.
13. Interview *Steh auf! es ist Krieg* ZDF German TV 1991.
14. Diary entry 21 Jun 41. Dollinger, H.: *Kain, wo ist dein Bruder?*; Fischer Verlag, 1987; p78-9.
15. *Geheimer Bericht des Sicherheitsdienstes der SS zur innterpolitischen Lage, Nr. 185. (Auszug)* from Piekalkiewicz, J: *Die Schlacht um Moskau — Die erfrorene Offensive*; Gustav Lübbe Verlag, 1981; p38.
16. Letter Rheydt 17 Jun 41. The letter had been apprehended by the Russians. *Soviet Feldpostbriefe* p15.
17. Letter Berlin 6 Jun 41. *Soviet Feldpostbriefe* p13.
18. Letter M. Gladbach, 17 Jun 41. *Soviet Feldpostbriefe* p16.
19. Interview *Der Krieg im Osten* SWF German TV, 1989.
20. Letter 21 Jun 41 *Feldpostbriefe* p68.
21. Pabst, H.: *The Outermost Frontier*; William Kimber, London, 1957; p11.
22. Interview *Steh auf! es ist Krieg* ZDF German TV 1991.

Chapter 2: 'Ordinary men' — The German soldier on the eve of 'Barbarossa'
'Endless pressure to participate'
1. Zieser op cit p9. On joining the army 12 May 1941.
2. *KGS* 31 Jan 41 p34.
3. Interview *Steh auf! es ist Krieg* ZDF German TV 1991.
4. *War of Extermination: Crimes of the Wehrmacht 1941-44;* Exhibition Hamburg Institute for Social Research, 1995.
5. Interview. *Der Verdammte Krieg* ZDF German TV 1991.
6. Steinhoff, J., Pechel, P. and Showalter, D.: *Deutsche im Zweiten Weltkrieg*; Bastei-Lübbe Verlag, Gladbach, 1989; p718. Conclusion of a group of modern German historians.
7. Kuhnert, M.: *'Will We See Tomorrow?' — A German Cavalryman at War 1939-42*; Leo Cooper, 1993; p2.
8. For example the American experience of the Republic of South Vietnam during the Vietnam conflict.
9. *Soldat* p138.
10. Interview *Die Zeit* 3 Mar 95.
11. *Soldat* p138.
12. 'Voices from the Third Reich' p51.
13. Interview *Die Zeit* 3 Mar 95.
14. Stahlberg op cit p159-160.
15. Prüller, W. *Diary of a German Soldier*; Faber & Faber, 1963; p63.

'Order and Duty' and the Führer
1. Metelmann, H.: *Through Hell for Hitler*; Patrick Stephens, 1990; p14 and p19.
2. Interview *Mein Krieg* WDR German TV 1988.
3. Interview. Ibid.
4. Becker: pen name. Becker, H.: *The Devil on my Shoulder*; Jarrolds, 1955; p16-7.
5. Interview *Mein Krieg* WDR German TV 1988.
6. Ibid.
7. Metelmann op cit p21, p14 and p15.
8. Steinhoff, Pechel and Showalter op cit p35.
9. 'Voices from the Third Reich' p24.
10. Ibid p50.
11. Ibid p56.
12. Interview Georg Buchwald. Vol 5. *Purnell's History of the Second World War*; p2000.
13. Steinhoff, Pechel and Showalter op cit p125-6.
14. Ibid p88.
15. Ibid p150.
16. Becker op cit p16-7.
17. 'Wovon kann der Landser denn schon träumen— Urlaub und Urlaub-Maschen.' Article Hanns-Karl Kubiak. *Band 3. Der II. Weltkrieg* 1976. p26-9.

'Prepared . . . to face what is coming!' The German Army June 1941
1. Fourth Army Assessment 28 June 1940. Lewis, S. J.: *Forgotten Legions*; Praeger Special studies, 1986; p106.
2. XXXVIII Korps Report Aug 10, 1940. Ibid p112.
3. Ibid p103.
4. *Erfahrungsbericht* Aug 18, 1940. Ibid p107.
5. *AOK 4. Mar 20, 21, 1941.* Ibid p132.
6. Ibid p64.
7. May 15, 1940.
8. OKW KTB Vol 1. p87, quoted Lewis p121.
9. Glantz op cit p398.
10. Lehmann, R.: *The Leibstandarte — 1 SS Panzer Division Leibstandarte Adolf Hitler*; Vol II, Fedorowicz Publishing, 1988; p277.
11. Hinze, R.: *Hitze, Frost und Pulverdampf; Der Shicksalweg der 20. Panzer Division*; Heinrich Pöppinghaus Verlag, 1981; p19.
12. Gareis, M.: *Kampf und Ende — Der Frankisch-Sudetendeutschen 98. Infanterie-Division*; Podzun-Pallas-Verlag, 1956; p78.
13 Ibid p80.

Chapter 3: The Soviet frontier
'There was no information'
1. Suvorov, V.: *Who Was Planning to attack Whom in June 1941, Hitler or Stalin?'* R.U.S.I. Jun 85 p54.
2. Mackintosh, M.: 'The Red Army Before Barbarossa', Purnell's *History of the Second World War*; Purnell; p654.
3. Quoted Suverov p50.
4. Ibid p51.
5. The 18th, 19th, 20th, 21st, 24th, 28th, 16th and 22nd Armies. Ibid p51.
6. Ibid p52. Quoted from *History of Kiev Military District*, Moscow, 1974; p162.
7. Suverov's view, p83.
8. Subsequent interrogations of Soviet POWs appear to confirm this according to Volker Dietlef Heydorn in *Der sowjetische Aufmarsch* p79-80.
9. Heydorn op cit p83.
10. Glantz op cit p227.
11. Ibid p325.
12. *Der Angriff auf die Sowjetunion; Militärgeschichtliches Forschungsamt in Freiburg*; p327 (Henceforth referred to as *Freiburg*).
13. Ibid p320.
14. Hinze op cit p23-5.
15. Guderian, H.: *Panzer Leader*; Michael Joseph, 1952/70; p153.
16. Interview *Steh auf! es ist Krieg* ZDF German TV 1991.

'We've never had such a situation . . . Will there be any instructions?'
1. Starinov, I. G.: *Over the Abyss — My Life in Special Operations*; Ivy Books NY, 1995; p165.
2. Interview *Der Verdammte Krieg* ZDF German TV 1991, additional material from *Steh auf! es ist Krieg* ZDF German TV 1991.
3. Starinov op cit p167-9.
4. Heydorn op cit p149.
5. Knopp op cit p27.
6. *Purnell's History of the Second World War* p674-5. Popel's personal account.
7. Interview *Steh auf! es ist Krieg* ZDF German TV 1991.
8. Heydorn op cit p178.
9. Danishevsky, I.: *The Road of Battle and Glory*; Foreign Languages Publishing House, Moscow, 1964; p13.
10. Heydorn op cit p155.
11. Ibid, quoted p150.
12. Danishevsky op cit p14-5.

Chapter 4: H-Hour 0315
The River Bug . . . Brest-Litovsk
1. Habedanck, G.: 'Bei Brest-Litovsk über die Grenze', *Die Wehrmacht*, 1941, p233.
2. Gschöpf, R.: *Mein Weg mit der 45. Infanterie Division*; Oberöstereichischer Landesverlag, 1955; p146-7.
3. Guderian op cit p146-7.
4. These were 125 Rifle Regiment to the NW, 333 Regiment in the Citadel, 84 Rifle Regiment in the SW and 44 and 455 Rifle Regiments from 42 Rifle Division. This section is based on Heydorn, op cit, p118 and 120-122 and *Auswertung der alten Unterlagen aus dem Weltkrieg über die Festung Brest-Litovsk.* AOC 4 lc, 9 May 41.
5. *Divisionsbefehl für den Angriff über den Bug.* 45. Div. Op. Nr. 1/41. 16 Jun 41, and Heydorn, op cit, p161-3.
6. Interview with author 3 Oct 95.
7. Material extracted from Wechtler video history of 45th Division.
8. Gschöpf op cit p149.
9. *Die Wehrmacht* p233.

Air strike . . . First light
1. Bekker, C.: *The Luftwaffe War Diaries*; Macdonald & Co, 1966; p217-8 and Haupt, W.: *Sturm auf Moskau 1941*; Podzun-Pallas Verlag, 1986/90; p63.
2. Knoke, H.: *I Flew for the Führer*; Corgi, 1956; p44-5.
3. Döring, A. quoted in *The War Years 1941-1945*, Marshall Cavendish, p82, and H. Vowinckel *KGS* p44-5.
4. Halder op cit 17 Feb 41 p320.
5. *Freiburg* p342-3.
6. Ibid, Chart p362.
7. Halder op cit 22 Feb 41 p322.
8. *Freiburg*. p348.
9. Halder op cit 27 Feb 41 p324.
10. Kesselring, A.: *The Memoirs of Field-Marshall Kesselring*; Greenhill, 1988; p89.
11. Ibid p90 and Bekker op cit p218.
12. *Freiburg* op cit p348-9.
13. Döring op cit p82.
14. Berlin material from Goebbel's Diary. Sat, 21 Jun 41.
15. 0830, 22 Jun 41. 'Combat Documents of Soviet Western Front Armies 22-30 Jun 41', *Journal of Soviet Military Studies* Sept 91 p515 (Henceforth referred to as Soviet Combat Docs). Note Russian time was one hour ahead of German.
16. Knoke op cit p45.
17. Guiness, *History of Air Warfare*; p114.
18. Döring op cit p81.
19. Bekker op cit p219.
20. Döring op cit p81.
21. Interview *Mein Krieg* WDR 1988.

The shortest night of the year . . . H-Hour
1. Haape, H.: *Moscow Tram Stop*; Collins, London, 1957; p13-4.
2. Interview *Der Verdammte Krieg* ZDF German TV 1993.
3. Stahlberg op cit p160 and 162.
4. Interview Knopp op cit p44.
5. Kuby op cit p106-7.
6. Westphal op cit p46-7.
7. Hinze op cit p25.
8. Haape op cit p14.
9. Letter. Kuby to his wife op cit p106.
10. Haape op cit p15.
11. Dollinger, H.: *Kain, wo ist dein Bruder?*; Fischer Verlag, 1987 p79.
12. Interview Knopp op cit p56.
13. *Soldat* p205.
14. Adamczyk, W.: *Feuer!' — An Artilleryman's life on the Eastern Front.* Broadfoot Pub Co, 1992; p64-5.
15. Interview *Mein Krieg* Basis-Verleih film 1991.
16. Kurowski, F.: *Panzer Technik 1939-45*; p223-4. Carell, P.: *Hitler's War on Russia*; p24-5.
17. Nayhauss, M. Graf von.: *Zwischen Gehorsam und Gewissen'.Potsdamer Infanterie-Regt 9*; Bastei-Lübbe, 1994; p130-1.
18. Knopp op cit p53.
19. Nayhauss op cit p131-2.
20. Interview. Mein Krieg.' 1991.
21. Nayhauss. p132-3.
22. Interview *Der Verdammte Krieg* ZDF German TV 1993.
23. Interview Knopp op cit p57.
24. *Kriegstagebuch XII Armee Korps* 04-55. 22 Jun 41.
25. Rudel, H. U.: *Stuka Pilot*; Bantam, 1979; p17.
26. Interview *Der Verdammte Krieg* ZDF German TV 1993.
27. Interview Ibid.
28. Interview Knopp op cit p47.
29. *Kriegstagebuch XII Armee Korps* 06.15. 22 Jun 41.
30. Knopp op cit p69.

Daybreak. . . Berlin
1. Based on interviews with V. Bereschkow and E. Sommer. Knopp op cit p42-3.
2. Goebbels Diary 22 Jun 41 p424.
3. Knopp op cit p42.
4. Ibid p43 and p45.
5. Goebbels Diary 22 Jun 41 p425.
6. Pabst, H.: *The Outermost Frontier*; William Kimber, London, 1957; p12.
7. Deck, J.: *Der Weg der 1000 Toten*; Badenia Verlag Karlsruhe, 1978; p44.

Chapter 5: The longest day of the year

The first Soviet pocket is formed — Brest-Litovsk

1. Kohl, P.: *Ich Wundere mich, dass ich noch lebe;* Gütersloher Verlaghaus Gerd Mohn, 1990; p27.
2. Soviet Combat Docs 22-30 Jun 41 p519.
3. Kohl op cit p27.
4. Ibid p30.
5. Interview *Die Deutschen im Zweiten Weltkrieg* SWF German TV 1985.
6. Article *Die Wehrmacht*, 1941 p233.
7. Gschöpf op cit p149.
8. 14/IR130 *Kriegstagebuch H. Wild* 22 Jun 41. Linzer Turm Sept 73. Taken from Wechtler docs.
9. Gschöpf op cit p150.
10. Article *Die Wehrmacht*, 1941 p233.
11. Quoted Gschöpf op cit p155.
12. *XII Korps Tagesbericht* p34. 00.30 hours 22 Jun 41. Also Carell, op cit, p22-3.
13. Diary 22 Jun 41 Linzer Turm 73.
14. *Bericht Sturmboot Unternehmen Inf Regt 130. Anlage 4.* 22 Jun 41.
15. *Kriegstagebuch H. Wild* 22 Jun 41.
16. Interview *Der Verdammte Krieg* ZDF German TV 1991.
17. Kohl op cit p28.
18. Interview *Steh auf es ist Krieg* ZDF German TV 1991. M. Wechtler claims no aircraft supported the German ground assault.
19. Ibid.
20. Interview *Der Verdammte Krieg* ZDF German TV 1991.
21. Interviews Yangchuk and Timovelich *Steh auf es ist Krieg* ZDF German TV 1991.
22. Interviews Makarow *Der Verdammte Krieg* ZDF German TV 1991 and Karbuk Kohl op cit p27.
23. *XII Korps Tagebuch* reports: 04.00 Uhr, 04.17, 04.42, 06.23, 07.20, 08.35, 08.50 and 10.50.
24. Gschöpf op cit p155-6.
25. *Gefechtsbericht über die Wegnahme von Brest-Litovsk.* 45 Div Stabsqu 8 Jul 41 p2-3.
26. Ibid p2-3.
27. Gschöpf op cit p156-7.
28. *Gefechtsbericht 45 Div* p3-4.
29. Gschöpf op cit p54.

'Only 1,000km as the crow flies to Moscow'

1. Hammer, I. and zur Nieden, S.: *Sehr selten habe ich geweint' — Briefe und Tagebücher aus dem Zweiten weltkrieg von Menschen aus Berlin.* Schweizer Verlaghaus, Zurich, 1992; p74.
2. Letter 22 Jun 41 Dollinger op cit p79.
3. Hammer/Nieden op cit p226-7.
4. *Soldat* p205.
5. Malaparte, C.: *The Volga Rises in Europe;* Alvin Redman Ltd, London, 1957; p26-7.
6. Glantz op cit p232-3.
7. Letter 22 Jun 1941 Lt P.G. 9/IR721 Inf Div 714 22 Jun 41 *Feldpostbriefe* p72.
8. Letter 22 Jun 41 Oblt. G.K. IR365 Inf Div 211 *Feldpostbriefe* p71.
9. Letter 22 Jun 41. FW H.M. 9/IR226 Inf Div 79 *Feldpostbriefe* p71.
10. Knopp op cit p61.
11. Becker op cit p22.
12. Manteuffel, H. E. V.: *Die 7. Panzer-Division im Zweiten Weltkrieg;* Podzun-Verlag, 1986; p135-6.
13. Fuchs, K.: *'Sieg Heil!'— War Letters of Tank Gunner Karl Fuchs 1937-41.* Archon Books USA 1987; p114.
14. Manteuffel op cit p137.
15. Ibid p137-8.
16. Kuby op cit p107.
17. Manteuffel op cit p27-8.

Where was the Red Airforce?

1. Interview with author Oct 95.
2. Knoke op cit p46 and 48-9.
3. Letter 23 Jun 41 *Feldpostbriefe* p71.
4. Rudel op cit p16.
5. 'I flew with them', from *Signal* magazine reproduced in Mayer, 'Ed S. L.: *Years of Triumph 1940-2;* Bison Books.
6. Article Gerhard Meyer *Der Adler*, Heft 4, 1941.
7. Interview *Die Deutschen im Zweiten Weltkrieg* SWF German TV 1985.
8. *Rudel op cit p16-7.*
9. Combat Report 24 Jun 41 Soviet Combat Docs p517.
10. Fourth Army HQ to COS Western Special Military District 22 Jun 41 Soviet Combat Docs p520.
11. Heydorn op cit p169.
12. Kesselring op cit p90.
13. Bekker op cit p221.
14. Rudel op cit p17, Knoke op cit p49.
15. *Freiburg* p737.
16. Kesselring op cit p90.
17. *Freiburg* p738.
18. Ibid p739.
19. Halder op cit 1 Jul 41 p440.
20. Halder op cit 3 Jul 41, *Freiburg* p740.
21. Bekker op cit p220 and Miller, R.: *The Soviet Airforce at War;* Time-Life, 1983; p84.
22. *Freiburg* p740.
23. Döring op cit p82.

Dusk . . . 22 June 1941

1. Haape op cit p20.
2. Halder op cit 22 Jun 41 p413.
3. Ed. Schramm, P.; *Kriegstagebuch des OKW* 22 Jun 41 Vol 2 p491.
4. Hammer, I. and zur Nieden, S.: *Sehr selten habe ich geweint' — Briefe und Tagebücher aus dem Zweiten weltkrieg von Menschen aus Berlin.* Schweizer Verlaghaus, Zurich, 1992; p227.
5. Heydorn op cit p164.
6. *Kriegstagebuch des OKW* 22 Jun 41 Vol 2 p490, Halder Diary 22 Jun 41 p411-2.
7. Haape op cit p20-1.
8. Halder op cit 22 Jun 41 p412-3.
9. Haape op cit p30-1.

Chapter 6: Waiting for news

The home fronts . . . Victory will be ours! Germany

1. *Feldpostbriefe* Frau A.N. 22 Jun 41. p70.
2. Ibid p70-71.
3. Interview *Der Verdammte Krieg* ZDF German TV 1991.
4. Hünermann, C.: *Chronik 1941;* p106.
5. Interview *Der Verdammte Krieg* ZDF German TV 1991.
6. *Feldpostbriefe* Oblt IR365 211 Div 22 Jun 41 p71.
7. Interview *Der Verdammte Krieg* ZDF German TV 1991.
8. Kuby op cit p107-8.
9. Interview. Knopp op cit p57.
10. *Meldungen aus dem Reich Nr 197.* 26 Juni 1941 p2440 (henceforth *Meldungen*).
11. *Glantz op cit p110.*
12. Mayer, S. and Schultz, E.: *Wie wir das alles geschaft haben;* p150-1.

Victory will be ours! Russia

1. Holliday, L.: *Childrens' Wartime Diaries;* p251 and 139.
2. Ibid p251.
3. Boll, H. and Kopelew, L.: *Warum haben wir aufeinander geschossen?'* Lamuv Verlag, 1981; p16.
4. Interview *Der Verdammte Krieg* ZDF German TV 1991.
5. Extracts from Molotov's speech quoted from Werth, A.: *Russia at War 1941-1945;* Pan Books, 1964; p162-3.
6. Interview *Der Verdammte Krieg* ZDF German TV 1991.
7. Interview *The World at War* Thames TV 1973.
8. *Quoted from H. Dollinger op cit p80.*
9. Simonov, K.: *Kriegstagebücher;* Bellestristik, Berlin, 1979; p6.
10. Interview *Steh Auf! es ist Krieg* ZDF German TV 1991.
11. Ibid.
12. Lidow's Diary from Bähr, H. W.: *'Die Stimme des Menschen' Briefe und Aufzeichnungen aus der ganzen Welt.1939-45.* R Piper & Co. Verlag, München, 1961; p93-4.
13. Interview 'Blockade. Leningrad. 1941-44.' Film by Thomas Kufus 1991 (p161-2 supporting book *Docukumente und Essays*).
14. Interview *Steh Auf! es ist Krieg* ZDF German TV 1991.
15. Danishevsky op cit p36-7.
16. Krylov, I.: *Soviet Staff Officer;* Falcon Press, 1951; p115.

'Don't die without leaving a dead German behind you' . . . Brest-Litovsk

1. Interview. Knopp op cit p60.
2. Gschöpf op cit p157.
3. *45 Div Gefechtsbericht* 23 Jun 41 p5.
4. Interview *Steh Auf! es ist Krieg* ZDF German TV 1991 and quoted Kohl op cit p26.
5. Ibid.
6. Ibid.
7. *XII Korps Tagebuch* reports 24 Jun 16.00, 21.40 Uhr.

Across the Dvina . . . Army Group North

1. Combat Report No. 3. Third Army HQ. Forest SE of Lunno. 1230 hours 24 Jun 41. Soviet Combat Docs p518-9.
2. Erickson, J.: *The Road to Stalingrad;* Weidenfeld, 1975/93; Chart p133.
3. Heydorn op cit p168.
4. Figures from Haupt, W.: *Leningrad. Wolchow. Kurland;* p11-2.
5. Haupt, W.: *Die 8. Panzer-Division im 2.Weltkrieg;* Podzun-Pallas, 1987; p138.
6. Ullrich, K.: *Wie ein Fels im Meer — Kriegsgeschichte der 3.SS Panzerdivision 'Totenkopf';* Munin Verlag, Osnabrück, 1987, p100.
7. Jäger, G.: *'Division Brandenburg', Der II. Weltkrieg Band 4;* p334-7.
8. *Steinhoff, Pechel, Showalter op cit p177.*
9. Jäger op cit p337.
10. Steinhoff, Pechel, Showalter op cit p178-9.
11. Ibid p178-9.
12. Haupt, *Die 8. Panzer-Division im 2.Weltkrieg*, p146-150.

No news
1. Goebbels Diary p426-9.
2. *Meldungen Nr. 197* 26 Jun p2440, 2441; *Nr. 198* 30 Jun p2458.
3. Ibid p2461-2.
4. *Soviet Feldpostbriefe* 29 Jun 41 p19.
5. Ibid 28 Jun 41 p18-9.
6. Bock, F. von: *Generalfeldmarschall Fedor von Bock — The War Diary 1939-1945*; Schiffer Military History, 1996; 23 Jun 41 p225.
7. Letter *Die Deutschen im Zweiten Weltkrieg* SWF German TV 1985 p95.
8. Goebbels Diary 23 Jun p426, 25 Jun p430.
9. *Soviet Feldpostbriefe* 29 Jun 41 p20.

Brest-Litovsk . . . 'I wonder how it is I am still alive!'
1. Interview *Steh Auf! es ist Krieg* ZDF German TV 1991.
2. Kohl op cit p26.
3. Interview. Knopp op cit p60.
4. *Gefechtsbericht Nr 1. 4. Zuges. Kampf um die Zitadelle von Brest-Litovsk* 25 Jun 41.
5. *Gefechtsbericht 45 Div* p7-8.
6. Interview Kohl op cit p30.
7. Bock op cit 25 Jun p226.
8. Kohl op cit p30-1.
9. *Gefechtsbericht 45 Div* 27 Jun 41 p8.
10. Ibid p9.
11. Interview *Steh Auf! es ist Krieg* ZDF German TV 1991.
12. Interview Ibid.
13. Interview Kohl op cit p31.
14. Interview *Steh Auf! es ist Krieg* ZDF German TV 1991.
15. Zentner, K.: *Nur Einmal Konnte Stalin Siegen;* Gruner Verlag Hamburg, 1952; p8.
16. Goebbels' Diary 30 Jun 41 p437.
17. *Meldungen Nr 198* 30 Jun p2458, 2463.

Chapter 7: Blitzkrieg
The 'smooth' period . . . The Panzers
1. Bock op cit p228.
2. Major Kielmansegg was destined to become a NATO four-star general. Taken from interview in: Eichel, M., Pagels W., Reschl, W.: *Der Unvergessene Krieg;* Verlagsgesellschaft Schulfernsehen-Vgs, 1981; p64.
3. Interview Glantz op cit p112.
4. Eichel, Pagels, Reschl op cit p64.
5. *'Drei Tage Panzer Vormarsch', Signal;* Heft 16 2 Aug 41.
6. Halder op cit 24 Jun 41 p418, 420.
7. Erickson, J.: *The Road to Stalingrad;* Weidenfeld, 1975/93; p33.
8. See charts in: Stolfi, R. H. S.: *Hitler's Panzers East;* Alan Sutton, 1992; p158-9 and *Freiburg* p225.
9. Deck op cit p67.
10. Interview *Decisive Weapons — T34. Queen of the Battlefield* BBC TV Sept 96.
11. Macksey, K.: *Tank Facts and Feats;* Guiness Publishing; p116.
12. SS Secret report. *Meldungen Nr. 197* 26 Jun 41 p2444.
13. The 6th Panzer Division 1937-45 from Zaloga, S. and Sarson, P.: *T34/76 Medium Tank 1941-45;* Vanguard 28, Osprey, 1994; p18.
14. Letter 28 Jun 41. Fuchs op cit p115.
15. Despatch 2 Jul 41 from: Malaparte, C.: *The Volga Rises in Europe;* Alvin Redman Ltd, London, 1957; p42.
16. Letter 5 Jul 41. Fuchs op cit p116.

Frontier tank battles
1. Grimm, A.: *'Die erste Panzerschlacht im Ostern', Signal;* Heft 15. 1 Aug 41 p11-13.
2. Glantz op cit p114.
3. Interview *Decisive Weapons — T34. Queen of the Battlefield* BBC TV Sept 96.
4. Ibid Grimm and Ritgen accounts. Lingendahl interview from 'The Eastern Front 1941-43', British Army Dept C1591 Documentary Film Series Part 1. 'Barbarossa. The Invasion' (Henceforth Army Dept C1591).
5. Kielmansegg interview Glantz op cit p114, 116.
6. *Signal* Heft 15. p13, and Radciekov: *Die II. Panzer Division. Gespensterdivision;* p124-132.
7. Interview Army Dept C1591.
8. Ibid.
9. Danishevsky op cit.
10. Soviet Documents. Op. Rpt No. 01. 24 Jun 41 p525.
11. Simonow op cit p15-6.

Panzer vanguard
1. *Signal* Heft 16 2 Aug 41.
2. Interview *Die Deutschen im Zweiten Weltkrieg* SWF German TV 1989.
3. Letter 28 Jun 41. Fuchs op cit p115-6.
4. Becker op cit p22-3.
5. Ullrich op cit p99-100.
6. Manteuffel op cit p141.
7. *'Mit dem Stählernen Pfeil in das Herz des Feindes'; Die Wehrmacht* Band III 1941-2 p18-9.
8. Manteuffel op cit p141.
9. Grimm, A.: *'Verwegener Handstreich', Signal;* Heft 16 2 Aug 41.
10. Manteuffel op cit p143.
11. Glantz op cit p324.
12. *'Drei Tage Panzer Vormarsch', Signal;* Heft 16 2 Aug 41 — *'Der Zweite Tag'*.
13. Diary 24 Jun 41 Central Front near Minsk in Dollinger op cit p80-1. See also p4 of this book.
14. Malaparte op cit p51.
15. Ibid p42.
16. Glantz op cit p396-7.
17. *Signal* Heft 15 Aug 42, article referring to the 1941 period. Statistical data is from Hünermann op cit p214.
18. Glantz op cit p397.
19. Hinze op cit p65.
20. Interview *Mein Krieg* German WDR TV 1988.

On to Smolensk
1. Westphal op cit p48.
2. Spaeter, H.: *The History of the Panzercorps 'Grossdeutschland';* Vol.1, Fedorowicz Canada, 1958/92; p185.
3. Bock op cit 2 Jul 41 p235.
4. Ibid 8 Jul 41 p243. Figures also based on: Haupt, W.: *Die Schlachten der Heeresgruppe Mitte 1941-1944;* Podzun-Pallas, 1983; p44.
5. Letters *KGS* 29 Jun and 11 Jul 41 p45-7.
6. Interview *Mein Krieg* German WDR TV 1988.
7. Haupt op cit p56.

Finale: Brest-Litovsk.
1. Kohl op cit p131.
2. Film material provided by ex-Lt M. Wechtler, interview with author 3 Oct 95 and Gschöpf op cit p158.
3. *Gefechtsbericht 45 Div* 29-30 Jun *Erfahrungen* p9-12
4. Figures Gschöpf op cit p142 and p158.
5. Heer op cit p49.
6. Name withheld.
7. Hammer and zur Nieden op cit p128-9.
8. Kohl op cit p31 and Carell op cit p44.

Chapter 8: Smolensk.
The infantry.
1. Westphal op cit p47-8.
2. Ibid p49.
3. *KGS* Diary 23 Jun 41 p69.
4. Haape op cit p35.
5. *KGS* Diary 23 Jun 41 p69.
6. *Signal* Heft 21 1 Nov 42.
7. *KGS* Diary 30 Jun p69.
8. *Signal* Heft 21 1 Nov 42.
9. *Soldat* p213.
10. Haape op cit p52-3.
11. *Signal* Heft 21 1 Nov 42.
12. *KGS* Diary 4 Jul 41 p71.
13. *Signal* Heft 21 1 Nov 42.
14. *Soldat* p214.
15. Nayhauss, M. Graf von.: *Zwischen Gehorsam und Gewissen'.Potsdamer Infanterie-Regt 9;* Bastei-Lübbe, 1994; p143 and 148.
16. Haape op cit p55.
17. Buchner, A.: *Das Handbuch der Deutsche Infanterie;* Podzun-Pallas, 1987; p103-4.
18. Gareis op cit p84.
19. *KGS* Diary 4 Jul 41 p71.
20. Ibid 30 Jun 41 p69.
21. Haape op cit p65.
22. *KGS* Diary. 30 Jun and 4 Jul 41. p69-70.
23. Haape op cit p66.
24. Interview *Mein Krieg* German TV 1991.
25. *KGS* Diary 30 Jun 41 p70.
26. Ullrich op cit p102-3.
27. Aaken, W. van: *Hexenkessel Ostfront;* Erich Pabel Verlag, 1964; p27.
28. Interview *Mein Krieg* German TV 1991.
29. Ullrich op cit p103-4.

The Smolensk pocket.
1. Hammer, zur Nieden op cit p240.
2. Manual published in Dec 40. Wray, T. A.: *Standing Fast. German Defence Doctrine on the Russian Front during World War II;* p20.
3. Spaeter op cit Vol 1 p185.
4. Bock op cit 20 Jul 41 p255.
5. van Aaken op cit p13-4.
6. Bock op cit p256.
7. Manteuffel op cit p153.
8. Bock op cit 21 Jul 41 p258, 23 Jul 41 p260.
9. Spaeter op cit p188.
10. Kister account from van Aaken op cit p35-6.
11. Ibid p45-7.
12. Bock op cit 25 Jul 41 p262.
13. Ibid 26 Jul 41 p263.
14. Halder op cit 8 Jul 41 p457.
15. Bock op cit 29 Jul 41 p266-7.
16. Manteuffel op cit Chart p167.
17. Fuchs op cit 5 Jul 41 p116.
18. Ibid 11 Jul p117 and 17 Jul 41 p119.
19. Manteuffel op cit p167-8.
20. Halder op cit 1 Aug 41 p491.
21. Spaeter op cit p192.
22. Bock op cit 5 Aug 41 p273-4.
23. Spaeter op cit p221.

'Do not cry' . . . Soviet defeat in the West
1.   Holliday op cit p253.
2.   Krylov op cit p119.
3.   Soviet Combat Documents 22-30 Jun 41 p532 and 534.
4.   Knopp op cit p65.
5.   Letter 10 Jul 41 Dollinger op cit p88.
6.   Knopp op cit p65.
7.   Front letter 18 Jul 41 from: Bähr, H. W.: *Die Stimme Des Menschen*; p126.
8.   *Kriegstagebücher* p11 and 14.
9.   Knopp op cit p64.
10. Starinov op cit p184.
11. Kohl op cit p131.
12. Starinov op cit p187.
13. Knopp op cit p65.
14. Kohl op cit p57.
15. *Ibid p50.*
16. Ibid p59.
17. Ibid p66 and 68-9.
18. Ibid p117.
19. Interview *Steh auf es ist Krieg* ZDF German TV. 1991.
20. Interview *Red Empire* Yorkshire TV 1990.
21. Extracts from Stalin's speech from Werth op cit p165-8.
22. Halder op cit 8 Jul 41 p457.
23. Holliday op cit p254.
24. Interview *Der Verdammte Krieg* ZDF German TV 1991.
25. Knopp op cit p65.

Chapter 9: Refocusing victory conditions
The longest campaign
1.   Bock op cit 28 Jul 41 p265.
2.   Ibid 24 Jul 41 p261.
3.   Kuby op cit 11 Aug 41 p160.
4.   Letter 9 Aug 41 *Soviet Feldpostbriefe* p27.
5.   Halder op cit 2 Aug 41 p492-3.
6.   Bock's op cit 2 Aug 41 p270-1.
7.   Soldier R. K. 14/Inf Regt 111 35 Inf Div *Feldpostbriefe* 10 Aug 41 p77.
8.   Ibid, 10 Aug 41. Nachsch Btl 563 p77.
9.   Ibid, 11 Aug 41. 8 /Inf Regt 55 17 Inf Div p78.
10. Prüller, W. *Diary of a German Soldier*; Faber & Faber, 1963; 4 Aug 41 p89-91.
11. Kuhnert op cit p75.

Conditions for victory
1.   Townsend, C. and E.: *Der Überfall*; Hoffman & Campe Verlag, Hamburg, 1984; p80.
2.   Halder op cit 1 Aug 41 p506.
3.   Interview *Der Verdammte Krieg* ZDF German TV 1991.
4.   Halder op cit 22 Aug 41. p515.
5.   Interview *Der Verdammte Krieg* ZDF German TV 1991.
6.   Stahlberg op cit p172.
7.   Interview. *Der Verdammte Krieg* ZDF German TV 1991.
8.   Adamczyk, W.: *Feuer!'* — *An Artilleryman's life on the Eastern Front.* Broadfoot Pub Co, 1992; p143.
9.   Haape op cit p88.
10. Keegan, J.: *The Second World War*; Arrow Books, 1990; p194.
11. *Feldpostbriefe* 8 Aug 41 p77.
12. Ibid p77.
13. Ibid Inf Regt 73 p77.
14. Ibid 22 Aug 41 Inf Regt 459 p79.
15. Ibid Inf Regt 481 p79.
16. *KGS* p50.
17. *KGS* Diary entry 22 Aug 41 p75.
18. Soviet *Feldpostbreife* Letter 28 Aug 41 p29.

19. Quoted Werth op cit p164.
20. Interview *The World at War* Thames TV.
21. Rürup, R.: *Der Krieg gegen die Sowjet-Union 1941-45*; p170-1.

A city 'pulsing with life' . . . Leningrad
1.   Interview *Der Verdammte Krieg* ZDF German TV 1991.
2.   Diary 17 Aug 41 Dollinger op cit p93-4.
3.   Statistics taken from Keegan op cit p197.
4.   Clark, A.: 'Leningrad', *War Monthly*; Vol. 1. Issue 2 p13.
5.   Interview *Der Verdammte Krieg* ZDF German TV 1991.
6.   Ibid.
7.   Diary entries 29 Aug 41, 25 Jun 41. Taken from Dollinger op cit p81-2, p94-5.
8.   Interview *Der Verdammte Krieg* ZDF German TV 1991.
9.   Knopp op cit p143.
10. Interview ZDF German TV 1991.
11. Halder op cit p458.
12. Ibid, 5 Sept and 12 Sept 41 p524 and 528.
13. Knopp op cit p147.
14. *Vortragsnotiz Leningrad. Abteilung Landesverteidigung des Wehrachtfuhrungstabes OKW* 21 Sept 41 from: Leetz, A. and Wenner, B.: *Blockade. Leningrad. 1941-44*; Rowohlt 1992; p99-101.
15. *Kriegstagebuch der Heeresgruppe Nord* 01.15 Uhr. 12 Oct 41 from: Leetz and Wenner op cit p100-1.
16. Knopp op cit p147.
17. *Kriegstagebuch der Quartiermeister Abteilung des 18. Armee* 3 Oct 41 19.30 Uhr, 5 Oct 41. 21.30 Uhr.
18. *Kriegstagebuch der Heeresgruppe Nord* 01.15 Uhr 12 Oct 41.
19. Harald Brand Interview *Der Unvergessene Krieg*. Eickhoff/Pagels/Reschl. p75. Historische Stichworte WDR German TV 1982.
20. *Kriegstagebuch der Heeresgruppe Nord* 24 Oct 41 07.00 Uhr. Report on visit to 18th Army Sector by Ia [ie Ops staff offr].

Chapter 10: A war without garlands
'Better three French campaigns than one Russian'
1.   Dollinger op cit p92.
2.   Diary 12 Aug 41 Kuby op cit p167.
3.   *Deutsche Wochenschau* shown early July 1941.
4.   Official Census Summer 1939. Quoted in Paul op cit p65-6.
5.   'Ordinary Men. Police Battalion 101 and the Final Solution in Poland' p46-8.
6.   *Kriegstagebuch der Heeresgruppe Nord* 07.00 Uhr 24 Oct 41.
7.   Interview *Mein Krieg* German TV. 1991.
8.   Interview *Die Deutschen im Zweiten Weltkrieg* SWF TV 1985.
9.   Heer op cit p10.
10. 'Images of War' op cit p187.
11. Heer, H. and Naumann K.: *Vernichtungskrieg — Verbrechen der Wehrmacht 1941-4*; Hamburg 1995 p265-7.
12. Helmut Schmidt, later Chancellor of the Republic of West Germany, in an interview in *Die Zeit* newspaper 3 Mar 95 p14-20.
13. Interview *Mein Krieg* German TV 1991.
14. Ibid.
15. Hannes Heer op cit p9.
16   Interview *Mein Krieg* German TV 1991.

The pressures on the German soldier
1.   Zieser op cit p15-6 and 24.
2.   Adamczyk op cit p109.
3.   Dills op cit p150.
4.   Zieser op cit p166.
5.   Adamczyk op cit p115.
6.   Zieser op cit p167-8.
7.   *Das Reich* 'A popular German newspaper. 3 Aug 41.
8.   Heer and Naumann op cit p448-9.
9.   Ibid, Letters Sporrenberg 17.7.41, Egon Kolbenhoff 13.10.42. and other quotations p450.
10. Interviews with Ostfront veterans *The World at War* Thames TV.
11. Letter 2 Sept 41. *KGS* p112.
12. 'Diary of a German Soldier'. 1 Jul p69, 5 Jul. p75 and 15 Aug 41. p96.
13. *Sieg Heil*! 3 Aug 41. p122.
14. Feldpostbriefe. Nachrichten Regt 501. 9 Jul 41. p73-74.
15. M. Graf von Nayhauss. *Zwischen Gehorsam und Gewissen.* p144-146.
16. Interview *Mein Krieg* German TV 1991.
17. 'The Devil on my Shoulder'. p32.
18. Interview *Mein Krieg* German TV 1991.
19. Testimony of Survivors. *Die Wehrmachts Untersuchungs – Stelle.* Alfred M de Zayas p273-276. Interviews Leutnant Franz Kroning, Oberschutze Wilhelm Metziger from *Kriegsverbrechen Nach der Akten der Wehrmachts Untersuchungsstelle*. Venohr, Vogt and de Zayas. WDR German TV 1983.
20. *Kriegstagebuch* (KTB) *des OKW.* Vol II. 1940-41. P. Schramm. Chart p1120-1121.
21. By 1945 it was down to 20-25%. Kurt Böhme *Die Deutschen Kriegsgefangenen in Sowjetischer Hand.* p49. München 1966. De Zayas p277.
22. De Zayas p277-278 and 280-282.
23. Communication Central Office for Political Propaganda of Soviet 5th Army signed by Maj Gen M. I. Potapov C in C 5th Army. De Zayas p288.
24. De Zayas p289.
25. Report Major Euler. 25 Jul 41. 'Ich Offizier Armeeoberkommando 6'. Ibid p300.
26. Both interviews from *Red Empire* Yorkshire TV 1995 production, presented by Dr Robert Conquest.
27. *Feldpostbriefe* 3 Jul. 41. p73.
28. Ibid 10 Jul 41. p74.
29. Ibid 8 Aug 41. p77.
30. *Meldungen. Nr 201.* 10 Jul 41. p2505.

'Kein Kindergarten Krieg'. Prisoners and partisans
1.   *Under Hitler's Banner*. E. Blandford p127.
2.   Figures were 799,919 rising to 3,350,639 (15,179 officers). KTB des OKW. Vol II P. Schramm. p.1106.
3.   *Die Zeit* German newspaper 'Forum'. 3 Mar 95.
4.   *Soldat* p211.
5.   O. Bartov. 'Eastern Front 1941-45. German Troops and the Barbarisation of Warfare'. Charts 13 and 18 p108.
6.   Martin van Creveld. *Supplying War.* p152.
7.   Interview. *Mein Krieg*. Eder and Kufus. German TV 1991.
8.   Zieser op cit p50.
9.   *Soldat* p211.
10. Blandford, E.: *Under Hitler's Banner*; Motorbooks, 1995; p31.
11. *Soldat* p211.

12. Zieser op cit p50.
13. Blandford op cit p31.
14. *Soldat* p211.
15. Streit *Das Schicksal der verwundeten Sowjetischen Kriegsgefangenen* from Heer and Naumann op cit p78.
16. Ibid p79 and 80.
17. Interview *Mein Krieg* German TV 1991.
18. Zieser op cit p51.
19. Heer and Naumann op cit p327.
20. Bartov, O.: *The Eastern Front 1941-45, German Troops and the Barbarisation of Warfare*; Macmillan, 1985; p111.
21. Zieser op cit p51.
22. Heer and Naumann op cit p328-9.
23. Heer and Naumann Nov 41 op cit p81.
24. Interview *Mein Krieg* German TV 1991.
25. Zieser op cit p53.
26. Bartov op cit p116-7.
27. *Heer op cit p11, p17 and p28.*
28. Bartov op cit p110.
29. Hammer and zur Nieden op cit p127.
30. Heer and Naumann 'Die 62 Inf Div' p300-1 and p325.
31. Adamczyk op cit p144.
32. Hammer and zur Nieden 2 Jul 41 op cit p116.
33. Interview *Mein Krieg* German TV 1991.
34. The Unterstürmführer was subsequently killed in action. Steinhoff, Pechel, Showalter op cit p49.
35. Heer and Naumann 'Korück 582' op cit p325-7.
36. Interview *Der Verdammte Krieg* German TV 1991.
37. 24 Sept 41. 5th SS Viking, following a massacre at Karasnaya, Army Group South, from Neumann, P.: *The Black March*; Bantam, 1958/60; p149.
38. Steinhoff, Pechel, Showalter op cit p202-3.
39. Interview *Der Verdammte Krieg*. German TV 1991.
40. Neumann op cit p131.
41. Browning, C. R.: *Ordinary Men — Reserve Police Bn 101 and the Final Solution in Poland;* Harper Perennial, 1992, looks at how ordinary men in Reserve Police Battalion 101 were transformed into active participants of the 'Final Solution' in German occupied Poland.
42. Heer op cit p22 and p37.
43. Knopp op cit p126.
44. Bamm, P: *The Invisible Flag*; Faber & Faber Ltd, London, 1956; p44-5.
45. Heer and Naumann op cit p272-3.
46. Interview *Die Deutschen im Zweiten Weltkrieg* SWF German TV. 1983.

Chapter 11: *'Kesselschlact'* — victory without results
Cannae at Kiev
1. Strawson, J.: 'Kiev 1941', *War Monthly*; Marshall Cavendish; Vol 2 p30.
2. Stolfi, R. H. S.: 'The Greatest Encirclement in History', *RUSI Magazine*; Dec 96.
3. Malaparte op cit p61.
4. Ibid p55-7.
5. Ibid p51 and p61.
6. Interview *Der Verdammte Krieg* ZDF German TV 1991.
7. Knopp op cit p111.
8. Ibid p119.
9. Strawson op cit p28.
10. Halder op cit 28 Aug 41 p519.
11. Haupt, W.: *Die Schlachten der Heeresgruppe Süd*; p83.

12. Williamson, G.: *The blood soaked Soil*; Blitz Editions, 1997; p60.
13. Bock op cit 30 Aug p299, 2 Sept p301, 4 Sept p303, 5 Sept p305.
14. 'With the 97th Infantry Division Personal Account' Dills op cit p151.
15. Haupt, W.: *Die Schlachten der Heeresgruppe Süd*; p74. Halder op cit 28 Aug 41 p519 states an average of 50%.
16. Stolfi op cit p64-72.
17. Bock's op cit 12 Sept 41 p310-1.
18. Becker op cit p26-7.
19. Kuhnert op cit p91.
20. Dills op cit p152.
21. 'Geschichte der 3. Pz Div' from Haupt, W.: *Die Schlachten der Heeresgruppe Süd*; p84.
22. Stolfi op cit p72.
23. Haupt, W.: *Die Schlachten der Heeresgruppe Süd*; p84 and Knopp op cit p119.
24. Bock op cit 15 Sept 41 p313.
25. Source Hanson, V. D.: 'Cannae', *Quarterly Journal Military History*; Vol 2 No 4 1990 p60.
26. Haupt, W.: *Die Schlachten der Heeresgruppe Süd*; p84.
27. Russian figures of average daily losses Kiev Strategic Defensive Operation 7 July–26 Sept 41. Quoted from Krivosheev, G. F.: *Soviet Casualties and Combat Losses in the Twentieth Century*; chart p114.
28. Guderian op cit p219.
29. *KGS* Letters 18 Aug and 2 Sept p110-2.

The reduction of the Kiev pocket
1. Bähr op cit p126-7.
2. Interview *Der Verdammte Krieg*. ZDF German TV 1991.
3. Bähr op cit p127.
4. 15.30 hours 4 Sept 41.
5. Becker op cit p226.
6. Kesselring op cit p94.
7. Temkin, G.: *My Just War — The Memoir of a Jewish Red Army Soldier in World War II*; Presido, 1998; p37-8.
8. *Freiburg* p752-3.
9. *Diary 12 Sept, 22 Sept Dollinger op cit p96-8.*
10. Gschöpf op cit p179-180.
11. Kuhnert op cit p96.
12. '2 cm-Flak bezwingt T-34' from *Der Deutsche Fallschirmjäger* 5 Sept/Oct 1984 p15-6.
13. Gschöpf op cit p179-184.
14. Kuhnert op cit p96-8.
15. Ibid p97 and Gschöpf p185.
16. Prüller, W. *Diary of a German Soldier*; Faber & Faber, 1963; p106-7.
17. Werth op cit p203 and Knopp op cit p121.
18. Temkin op cit p42-3.
19. Bähr op cit p129.
20. Blandford op cit p122-3.
21. Haupt, W.: *Die Schlachten der Heeresgruppe Süd*; p96.
22. Krylov op cit p178-9.
23. Figures based on articles by: Strawson, J. 'Kiev 1941' p32, Keegan, J. 'Barbarossa' p109 and Krivosheev op cit p114.
24. Kuhnert op cit p98.
25. Gschöpf op cit p186.
26. Newspapers 26 Sept and 27 Sept 1941.
27. *Meldungen Nr. 217* 4 Sept 41 p2724.
28. *Meldungen Nr. 222* 22 Sept 41 p2787, and Nr. 223 25 Sept 41 p2795.

29. *Feldpostbriefe*. Diary Schwarzenbach nr Nürnburg 22 Sept 41 p81.
30. Ibid, 11/IR290 19 Sept 41 p80.
31. Ibid, 7/IR208. 24 Sept 41 p82.
32. Ibid, 13/IR105. 22 Sept 41 p81.
33. Bock op cit 20 Sept 41 p315, Sept 24 p318.
34. Letter 24 Sept 41. Meyer, E. V.: *Briefe 1938-1941*; Berlin & Düsseldorf, 1976; p125.
35. Personal account Dills op cit p152.

Chapter 12: 'Victored' to death
Objective Moscow
1. Bock op cit 26 Sept 41 p319.
2. Figures: Paul op cit p122 and Krivosheev op cit p118.
3. Paul op cit Chapter 2
4. Paul op cit p121.
5. Halder op cit 4 Apr p350, 26 Jul p485 and 11 Aug 41 p506.
6. Ibid 11 Aug 41 p506.
7. Quoted Paul op cit p119.
8. Bartov op cit p20. *'Totsiegen'* literally 'victoring to death'.

A logistic 'trip-wire'.
1. 88 divisions; info from Creveld, M. van: *Supplying War — Logistics from Wallenstein to Patton;* CUP, 1977; p145.
2. Automotive Technical Reports: vehicle situation 13 Oct 41. Reported 10 Dec 42. Lehmann, R.: *The Leibstandarte* Vol II, p147, 277 and 279.
3. Conference points for visit of von Kleist to III Corps. 17 Oct 41. Lehmann op cit p141.
4. Lehmann op cit p87.
5. Creveld op cit p146 and p150.
6. Ibid p157 and p153.
7. Soviet *Feldpostbriefe* 20 Sept 41 p32-3.
8. Lehmann. p97-100.
9. Kuhnert op cit p105.
10. Creveld op cit p153.
11. Ibid p157 and p160; eg. Army Group North: one in ten trains could reach Dunaburg.
12. Ibid p161.
13. Temkin op cit p36-7 and p44.
14. Creveld op cit p170-1.
15. *Freiburg* op cit p658.
16. *Meldungen aus dem Reich* Nr 214.
17. Halder op cit quoted Stolfi op cit p174.
18. *Freiburg* op cit p657-8.
19. Paul op cit p143.
20. Buffetaut, Yves: *Objectif Moscou*; p86. Burkhart Muller-Hillebrand: *Das Heer*, Band II: *Der Zweifrontkrieg*; p20. Halder op cit 28 Aug p519. Freiburg op cit p657-8.
21. Article Röttiger, H.: 'XXXXI Pz Corps during the battle of Moscow in 1941 as a Component of Panzergruppe 3', from *German Battle tactics on the Russian Front 1941-45*; Ed. S. H. Newton, p16-17 and p53.
22. Memoirs [Kesselring] p95.
23. Figures from Halder's Diary 6 Sept 41. p525-526.
24. Memoirs [Kesselring] p95.

'Totsiegen' . . . *victored to death.*
1. The establishment of one infantry division was 518 officers.
2. 3.3 to be precise. See Appendix. Based on *Kriegstagebuch des OKW 1940-41 Vol II Anlage 5 Jan 42. 'Personelle Verluste'.* p1120-1.

3. Losses were 19.5%. Bartov op cit and Charton p19 and p20.
4. Bamm op cit p9.
5. Interview *Mein Krieg* German TV 1991.
6. Ibid.
7. Buchner op cit p130.
8. Interview *Mein Krieg* German TV 1991.
9. Bamm op cit p24 and p30-2.
10. See Appendix 1 Casualties.
11. Halder op cit 24 Jun 41 p418 and 6 Jul 41 p454.
12. Stöhr, A.: '*Wie war das mit der Tapferkeit?*' from *Der Zweite Weltkrieg. Tief im Feindesland.* Vol 1. p116.
13. Lehmann op cit Vol II p141.
14. Schrodek, G. W.: *Die 11. Panzerdivision 'Gespensterdivision'*; Podzun-Pallas-Verlag, 1984; p308-9.
15. *KGS* Diary 23 July 41 p209-1.
16. '*Sehr Selten Habe Ich Geweint*' Hammer and zur Nieden. Diary account: 12 Jul p235, 14 Jul p236, 27 Jul p239 and 24 Aug 41 p248.
17. Soviet *Feldpostbriefe* 5 Sept 41 p31-2.
18. Diary 10 Sept 41. *KGS* p76.
19. Stöhr op cit p116.
20. Ibid.
21. Kuby op cit p189.
22. Lehmann op cit p85. Summary of medical report by SS Unterstumführer Babel, unit doctor of the supply services, covering the first nine months of the Russian campaign.
23. Bamm op cit p35. Klaus von Bismarck quoted from article: *Die Zeit* '*Forum*' 3 Mar 95.
24. Haape op cit p135.
25. Soviet *Feldpostbriefe*. 21 Sept 41 p34-5. A letter apprehended by Soviet Soldiers.
26. Article '*Wovon kann der Landser denn schon traumen*' From *Der Zweite Weltkrieg. Tief im Feindesland.* Vol 1 p29.
27. Letters 15 Sept and 19 Oct 41. Dollinger op cit p97 and p102.
28. *Meldungen Nr 218* 8 Sept 41 p2740.
29. Interview *Der Verdammte Krieg* German ZDF TV 1991.
30. *Meldungen Nr 214* 25 Aug. p2684-5, (Nr 218) 8 Sept 41 p2739.
31. Townsend, C. and E.: *War Wives*; Grafton Books, 1989 p303.
32. *Meldungen Nr 231* 23 Oct 41 p2914-6.
33. Townsend op cit p303.
34. *Meldungen Nr 221* 18 Sept 41 p2772.
35. *Meldungen Nr 222* 22 Sept 41 p2787-8 and KTB OKW Vol 2. 1940-41 '*Personelle Verluste.*' Chart p1120-1121.
36. Otto Kumm. *The 4th SS Panzergrenadier Regiment 'Der Führer' 1938-45.* Otto Weidinger. p71.
37. Conference points for the visit of the commander Pz Gruppe I to Commander III Pz Corps. 17 Oct 41. R. Lehmann 'The Leibstandarte'. Vol II. p141.
38. Feldpostbriefe. Artillery Regiment 255. 21 Sept 41. p81.
39. *KGS* Diary. 6 Oct 41. p71.

A dying army.
1. *British Defence Doctrine*. 6:2. Joint Warfare Publication 0-01. MOD CS(M)G London 1996.
2. *Zwischen Gehorsam und Gewissen*. Mainhardt Graf von Nayhauss. 1994.

Chapter 13: The last victory.
Double encirclement . . . Vyazma and Bryansk.

1. Diary 30 Sept 41. '*Angriff und Rückzug vor Moskau 1941-42*'. Miteilungsblatt Kameradschaft Wiener Pz Div. 4/1995. Henceforward referred to as 'Richter's Diary'.
2. *The Outermost Frontier* p29.
3. Richter's Diary 1 Oct and 2 Oct 41 and *Outermost Frontier* p30.
4. Richter's Diary 1 Oct 41.
5. *Friedens und Kriegserlebnisse Einer Generation*. History of Pz. Abt. 38(SF) 2. (Wiener) Panzerdivision. F. J. Strauss. p89.
6. H. Manteuffel. *Die 7. Panzerdivision im Zweitenweltkrieg*. p189.
7. Letter 9 Oct 41. *Sieg Heil!* p140.
8. Quotations H. Manteuffel *Die 7. Pz Div*: p188, 193 and 194.
9. W. Paul. *Die Schlacht um Moskau 1941-42*. p147.
10. *Feldpostbriefe* 10 Oct 41. 418 Regt. p83.
11. Ibid, 10 Oct 41 p83.
12. W. Haupt. *Sturm auf Moskau 1941*. p117.
13. H. Manteuffel. p195.
14. 'XXXXI Pz Corps during the Battle of Moscow in 1941 as a component of Pz Gr 3.' Taken from *German Battle Tactics on the Russian Front 1941-45*. Ed. S. H. Newton p26-28.
15. W. Haupt. *Die Schlachten der Heeresgruppe Mitte*. p95-97.
16. H. Manteuffel p196.
17. Letters 12 Oct and 15 Oct 41. *Sieg Heil!* p142-143.
18. H. Manteuffel p198 –199.
19. H. E. Braun account of the Vyazma Pocket battle between 10-11 Oct 41. Taken from F. J Strauss *Friedens und Kriegserlebnisse Einer Generation*. p90-93.
20. Von Bock's Diary. 3 Oct and 5 Oct 41. p321 and p323. 15 Oct p333.
21. H. Manteuffel. p204.
22. Letter 15 Oct 41. *Sieg Heil!* p143.
23. H. Spaeter. *The History of the Panzerkorps Grossdeutschland*. Vol 1 p235-38.
24. Von Bock's Diary. 19 Oct 41. p336.
25. Ibid, 7 Oct 1941. p326.
26. Letter 15 Oct 41. *Sieg Heil!* p143.
27. *Feldpostbriefe* 15 Oct 41. (Div intelligence unit 6 Div) and 14 Oct 41 (Arty Regt 125) p84.
28. Von Bock's Diary. 7 Oct 41. p326 and 13 Oct 41 p331.
29. Sturmgeschützabteilung 202. W. van Aaken *Hexen Kessel Ostfront*. p80.
30. Interview *Der Unvergessene Krieg*. Eickhoff/Pagels/Reschl. p65.
31. Feldpostbriefe. 9 Oct 41. 12 kp Inf Regt 18. p83.
32. *Der Unvergessene Krieg*. p65.

The great illusion.
1. *Meldungen. Nr 224* 29 Sept 41. p2809 and *Nr 226* 6 Oct 41. p2835.
2. Letter 4 Oct 41. Meyer was killed 10 months later on 18 Aug 42. Quoted G. Knopp *Der Verdammte Krieg*. p116.
3. Quotations from K. Zentner. *Nur Einmal Konnte Stalin Siegen*. p10.
4. Feldpostbriefe. 14 Oct 41. Frau S. Eldagsen/Deister p83.
5. W. Haupt. *Die Schlachten der Heeresgruppe Mitte 1941-44* p91-92.
6. K. Zentner p10.
7. Hans Dieter Schäfer. *Berlin im Zweiten Weltkrieg*. p103.

8. *Moscow Tram Stop*. p140-1.
9. W. Paul. *Die Schlacht um Moskau*. p139.
10. *Moscow Tram Stop*. p182.
11. *Sturm auf Moskau 1941*. W. Haupt p144 and 152.
12. Von Bock's Diary. 24 Oct 41. p340.
13. *Die Schlachten der Heeresgruppe Mitte 1941-44*. W. Haupt. p92.
14. Interview. *Der Verdammte Krieg*. ZDF German TV and Von Bock's Diary. 2 Nov 41. p349.
15. *Die Schlacht um Moskau*. J. Piekalkiewicz. p146-149.
16. *Diary of a German Soldier*. Entries: 6 Oct and 7 Oct p111, 10 and 13.
17. Richter's Diary 14 Oct, 15 Oct and 16 Oct 41.
18. *The Outermost Frontier*. p34-35.
19. *Zwischen Gerhorsam und Gewissen*. M. Graf von Nayhauss p181.
20. *The Outermost Frontier*. p35.
21. M. Nayhauss. p168.
22. 'Auf dem Schlachtfeld von Borodinow'. *Wochenshau* shown 26 Oct 41. *Meldungen Nr 235* 6 Nov 41. p2950.
23. *Meldungen Nr 232* 27 Oct 41. p2916. Author's review and translation of Landgraf Wochenschau war report.
24. *Die Schlacht um Moskau*. J. Piekalkiewicz p120-123.
25. 'Comrades to the End'. History of 4th SS Pz-Gren Regt. *Der Führer*. Otto Weidinger p93 and 95.
26. 'The Fatal Decisions'. *Moscow*. p54.
27. *Meldungen. Nr 233* 30 Oct 41. p2928, *Nr 234* 3 Nov, p2938, *Nr 235* 6 Nov. p2948, *Nr 236* 10 Nov 41. p2962.
28. *The Fatal Decisions*. p55.
29. *KGS* Diary 18 Oct 41. p81-83.
30. *Feldpostbriefe*. 25 Oct 41. Lt. J. H. Arty Regt 131. p85.
31. *The Leibstandarte*. R. Lehmann. p152.
32. *Kampf und Ende*. History of the 98th Div. M. Gareis p139.
33. *The Outermost Frontier*. p35.
34. *KGS* Diary. 20 Oct 41. p83.
35. *The Fatal Decisions*. p55.

Chapter 14: 'The eleventh hour'.
Moscow . . . A defence crust forms.
1. J. Hoffmann. '*Der Angriff auf die Sowjetunion*'. Freiburg. p901, 902.
2. Ibid and W. Paul. *Die Schlacht um Moskau 1941/2*. p164.
3. Shukow *Errinerungen und Gedanken*. Vol II. p18 and Zhukov *Greatest Battles* edited Harrison Salisbury. p34.
4. Freiburg. p904.
5. Ibid p904-905.
6. W. Paul. p195,199 and 213, extracts from Schabalin's diary.
7. Interview. *Der Verdammte Krieg*. ZDF German TV 1991.
8. W. Paul p213-14 and 239-40.
9. *Ich wundere mich dass ich noch Lebe*. pKohl. p140.
10. Von Bock's Diary 20 Oct 41 p337.
11. W. Haupt. *Die Schlachten der Heeresgruppe Mitte*. p122 describing distances covered between 30 Sept to 30 Oct 41.
12. *Ich wundere mich . . .* P. Kohl. Kristakow p151, Gregoriwna p157, Sernjonowa p163, Schuschakow and Scholowa p168.
13. Interviews *Red Empire*. Yorkshire TV 1990.
14. *Der Verdammte Krieg*. ZDF German TV 1991 and book G. Knopp p173 and p180.

15. Ibid, G. Knopp p171.
16. *My Just War*. p46-47.
17. Interview *Red Empire*. Yorkshire TV 1990.
18. *My Just War*. p45.
19. *Sturm auf Moskau 1941-42*. W. Haupt p138-9 and Zhukov. *Greatest Battles*. p61.
20. A. Werth. *Russia at War 1941-45*. p231.
21. Interview *Red Empire*.
22. W. Haupt p139.
23. Interview G. Knopp. *Der Verdammte Krieg*. p169.
24. J. Hoffmann *Der Angriff auf die Sowjetunion*. p906 Freiburg and Zhukov *Greatest Battles*. p906. Maluchin G. Knopp. p171.
25. Interview. 'Russia's War'. *Between Life and Death*. Dir. Igor Grigoriev. IBP Films 1995.
26. Red Army Square. Ivanikhin Interview 'Russia's War', A. Werth *Russia at War*. p238-240, Mironowa Interview *Der Verdammte Krieg*. German ZDF TV.
27. *Kriegstagebuch des OKW. Band II*. Percy E. Schramm. Weather conditions 7-13 Nov. p744-755.

.

Dilemma at Orscha.
1. Von Bock's Diary 31 Oct 41. p347.
2. Quoted J. Keegan. *Barbarossa*. Ballantine. p148.
3. Quoted K. Reinhardt *Die Wende vor Moskau – Das Scheitern der Strategie Hitlers in Winter 1941/42*. Stuttgart. 1972. p132.
4. KTB Des OKW, 1940-41. Vol II *Beurteilung der Kampfkraft des Ostheers. Feindlage* p1074-1076. 6 Nov 41 and 1 Dec 41.
5. Figures are 3,334,400 strength with 2,067,801 'irrecoverable losses'. *Soviet Casualties and Combat Losses in the Twentieth Century*. Ed. Col Gen G. F. Krivosheev 1997. Table 72. p101.
6. Ibid, Table 67. p94.
7. Ibid, Byelorussia table: p111, Smolensk table: p116, Kiev table: p114.
8. Ibid, Table 98. Material Losses p260.
9. Ibid, Table p118 and Table 98, p260-261.
10. Interview BDM Corporation Conference 19/20 May 1980.
11. Interview. Taped conversation Gen Hermann Balck. 12 Jan 79. Battelle Columbus Laboratories.
12. Ibid.
13. K. Reinhardt p140.
14. Von Bock's Diary 11 Nov 41. p354-55 and 14 Nov 41 p358. 'Halder Diary' 11 Nov 41. p556.
15. Quoted K. Reinhardt p145.
16. Dieter-Müller Freiburg p1160 and 1163. And M. van Crefeld *Supplying War*. p173.
17. Article 'A Panzer Soldier's War'. *War Monthly* Sept 95. p56.
18. Dieter Müller. *Freiburg* p1163-64. Von Bock's Diary 11 Nov, 12 Nov 41. p354-356.

.

'The eleventh hour'.
1. *Ausgewählte Armeeoperationen an der Ostfront*. US Historical Division Study p143a, p144.
2. Halder Diary. 19 Nov p557, 20 Nov. p559 and 21 Nov 41. p560.
3. *Kampf und Ende*. M. Gareis p160-162. Schiff belonged to the 4th Kp Inf Regt 290 all part of 98 Inf Div.
4. *KTB des OKW. Anlage: Personelle Verluste*. Band II. p1120. Ed. Percy E. Schramm.
5. See Appendix.

6. *Feldpostbriefe* 11 Kp/Inf Regt 480. 5 Nov 41. p85-86.
7. See Appendix.
8. Letter 21 Oct 41. *KGS* p91.
9. *Sturm auf Moskau*. W. Haupt. p223.
10. Interview. *Mein Krieg*. German TV. 1991.
11. NATO Study. Interview. *Philosophy and Tactics of Armoured Warfare*. Dec 19. 1980 p46.
12. Interview 12 Jan 79. Battelle Colombus Laboratories.
13. *Hitze, Frost und Pulverdampf*. R. Hinze p87. Company was 2 Pz. Sch. Kp. p119.
14. Interview 12 Jan 79 and NATO Study p49.
15. Diary entry 15 Dec 41. Horst Boog. Freiburg p761.
16. Interview 12 Jan 79. p21.
17. *Deutsche im Zweiten Weltkrieg*. Steinhoff, Pechel and Showalter. Interview p199.
18. Von Bock's Diary. 16 Nov 41. p359.
19. Interview. *Deutsche im Zweiten Weltkrieg*. p199.
20. *T34/76 Medium Tank 1941-45*. S. Zaloga and P. Sarson. 'Vanguard'. p14.
21. Zieser op cit Benno Zeiser. p67.
22. Interview Stamm *Die Deutschen im Zweiten Weltkrieg*. SWF German TV 1985 and interview Gen Balck 12 Jan 79. p48.
23. W. Haupt. *Sturm auf Moskau 1941*. p75-77.
24. *Stuka Pilot*. p48.
25. *The Soviet Airforce at War*. R. Miller. Time-Life. p99.
26. Richter's Diary: 26,27,28,29 Nov and 2 and 3 Dec 41.
27. *Zwischen Gehorsam und Gewissen*. M. Graf van Nayhauss. p181.
28. *Feldpostbriefe*. 2 Bttr, Flak Regt 23, 21 Oct 41, p84; Inf Regt 339, 26 Nov 41; p87. Nachsch. BH. 563, 11 Nov 41, p86.
29. Rolf-Dieter Muller. *Freiburg*. p1161-62.
30. Interview. *Der Verdammte Krieg*. ZDF German TV 1991.
31. *Die Stimme des Menschen*. H. W. Bähr. p118.
32. Neustifter interview *Der Verdammte Krieg*. Richter Diary 5, 6, 12, and 17 Nov 41.
33. *Panzer Leader*. p248.
34. Ibid p249.
35. Interview *Der Verdammte Krieg*.
36. Von Bock's Diary. 1 Nov 41. p348.
37. *The Leibstandarte*. R. Lehman. p152.
38. Von Bock's Diary. 23 Nov 41. p368.
39. *Sturm auf Moskau*. W. Haupt. p196.
40. Shukow. *Errinerungen und Gedanken*. Vol II. p31.
41. Joachim Hoffmann. *Freiburg*. p906-907 and 909.

.

Chapter 15: The spires of Moscow.
'Flucht nach Vorn'.
1. Von Bock's Diary. 18 Nov. 41. p362.
2. Interview. G. Knopp. *Der Verdammte Krieg*. p177.
3. Von Bock's Diary. 21 Nov 41. p365.
4. Interview. *Deutsche im Zweiten Weltkrieg*. Steinhoff, Pechel and Showalter. p200-201.
5. PK Bericht. 'Winterkampf vor Moskau'. '*Die Wehrmacht*'. p94-95.
6. Interview. *Deutsche im Zweiten Weltkrieg*. p206-209.
7. *Images of War*. Marshall Cavendish. Vol 1. p211.
8. G. Knopp. *Der Verdammte Krieg*. p190 and *The War Years*. Marshall Cavendish. p86.
9. Combined Schützen Regt 6 and 7. *Die 7 Pz Division in Zweiten Weltkrieg*. E. V. Manteuffel p221.

10. *Sieg Heil!* p157.
11. Manteuffel. p225-227.
12. The Yakhrama raid: Manteuffel p233-36, Von Bock's Diary 28 Nov 41. p372. And P. Kohl *Ich Wundere mich . . .* p176.
13. Von Bock's Diary. 29 Nov 41. p373.

.

The frozen offensive.
1. *Brennpunkte. Die Geschichte der 6. Pz Div 1937-45*. W. Paul p168-169.
2. M. Gareis. *Kampf und Ende*. p163.
3. 19 Nov 41. *Friedens – und Kriegserlebnisse Einer Generation*. D. Strauss p98.
4. *Greatest Battles*. p64.
5. *The War Years*. Marshall Cavendish. p81.
6. *Moscow Tram Stop*. p213 and p233.
7. *KGS*. Letter 1-3 Dec 41. p86.
8. M. Garies. p169.
9. Interview. *Der Verdammte Krieg*. German ZDF TV. 1991.
10. *Brennpunkte*. W. Paul. p173.
11. Interview. *Mein Krieg*. German WDR TV. 1988.
12. Josef Deck Arty Regt 71 *Der Weg der 1,000 Toten*. p105. H. Henry. Letter 1 Dec 41. *KGS*. p86. Ekkhard. *The War Years*. Marshall Cavendish. p81.
13. *Brennpunkte*. W. Paul. p169.
14. 11th Panzer Division. Interview *Deutschen im Zweiten Weltkrieg*. p201.
15. *Brennpunkte*. p170-171.
16. *Der Weg der 1,000 Toten*. p110.
17. *Ich wundere mich . . .* P. Kohl. p174-175.
18. Otto Weidinger. *Comrades to the End. Official history 4th SS Pz-Gren Regt Der Führer 1938-45* p99-100.
19. *Ich wundere mich . . .* P. Kohl. p178.
20. *Der Weg der 1,000 Toten*. p113.
21. *Ich wundere mich...* p174.

.

'The spires of the city' . . . *Moscow.*
1. Manteuffel. p240-242.
2. *'Ich wundere mich...'*. p176-177.
3. Manteuffel. p240-241.
4. *Brennpunkte*. W. Paul. p171-2.
5. *Comrades to the End*. p100.
6. *Sturm auf Moskau. 1941*. W. Haupt. p207-208.
7. W. Paul. *Die Schlacht um Moskau 1941-2*. p313-316.
8. *Friedens und Kriegserlebrusse einer Generation*. D. Strauss p99.
9. Original research by Bundeswehr Panzerschüle (Munster) and Pionierschüle (München). See also P. Carell. *Hitler's War on Russia*. p174-175. Interestingly the S3 (operations) vehicle belonging to Pz. Pi. Brl. 62 was destroyed during the subsequent retreat and all records relating to this period lost.
10. Interview. Film *Russia's War*. 'Between Life and Death'. Directed I. Grigoriev. IBP Films 1995.
11. Shukow. *Erringerungen und Gedanken*. Vol 2. p32. Milstein interview *Der Verdammte Krieg*. ZDF German TV 1991.
12. *Die Stimme des Menschen*. Ed. H. W. Bähr. p119.
13. Interview. G. Knopp *Der Verdammte Krieg*. p218 and Kopelew TV interview. 1991.
14. Shukow. *Erringerungen und Gedanken*. Vol. 1 p186-190.
15. D. Strauss. p102.
16. *Moscow Tram Stop*. p202-203.

17. *Sturm auf Moskau 1941*. W. Haupt. p210.
18. Based on SS Home Front Reports. *Meldungen . . . Nr 240* 24 Nov 41. p3016-17. *Nr 24* 27 Nov 41. p3030. *Nr. 242* 1 Dec 41. p3043. See also W. Haupt p212-13 and *Chronik* Verlag 1941. p214.
19. *Moscow Tram Stop*. p206.
20. Richter's Diary. 29 and 30 Nov 41 and 1 Dec 41.
21. Von Bock's Diary. 1 Dec 41. p376-377 and Halder's Diary 1 Dec 41. p575.
22. *Kampfbericht vom Einsatz des 2. Zuges der 2/Pz. Jäg. Abt. 38 in der Friedhofsiedlung. Katjuschki, sudostwarts Putschki ca. 20 km vor Moskau*. D. Strauss p102-104. Also Richter's Diary 2 Dec 41.
23. *Zwischen Gehorsam und Gewissen*. M. Graf von Nayhauss. p192, 201-202.
24. Richter's Diary 3 Dec 41 and interview from *Der Verdammte Krieg*. ZDF German TV 1991.
25. Von Bock's Diary 2 Dec 41 p378.
26. Richter's Diary 5 Dec 41 and Soviet *Feldpost* letter 4 Dec 41. p47.

Chapter 16: The devil loose before Moscow.
The Soviet counter-offensive.
1. *Moscow to Stalingrad*. E, Ziemke and M. Bauer p60 and 67.
2. J. Hoffman Freiburg p910, W. Paul *Schlacht um Moskau* p312, Zhukov *Greatest Battles* and Ziemke and Bauer assessments.
3. Zhukov *Greatest Battles*. p82 and Ziemke and Bauer p62.
4. Von Bock's Diary 3 Dec 41 p379, 5 Dec 41. p381.
5. W. Paul. *Die Schlacht um Moskau*. p318-319.
6. W. Paul. *Brennpunkte*. p175-176.
7. Interviews G. Knopp *Der Verdammte Krieg*. p218 and ZDF TV series 1991.
8. Interviews ibid. p218 and 213.
9. Ibid p232.
10. *Moscow Tram Stop*. p212 and 214.
11. Interview G. Knopp p234.
12. *Stets zu Erschiessen . . .* H. Heer. p46 and 47.
13. Interview G. Knopp p234.
14. Ibid p206.

The German soldier does not go 'Kaputt!' . . . The crisis of confidence.
1. Von Bock's Diary 7 Dec 41. p384. Kriegstagebuch Heeresgruppe Mitte 8-9 Dec 41. Guderian *Panzer Leader* p260-261.
2. *Panzer Leader*, Ibid.
3. See Chapter Two.
4. Halder Diary. 3 Nov. p552, 22 Nov. p561, 1 Dec p573 and 9 Dec 41. p585.
5. Letter 6 Dec 41. H. Dollinger *Kain, Wo ist dein Bruder?* p111.
6. *Die Schlacht um Moskau*. W. Paul p316.
7. Letter 7 Dec 41. *Feldpostbriefe* p90.

8. Interview *Die Deutschen im Zweiten Weltkrieg*. SWF German TV. 1985.

The German Army in retreat.
1. Richter's Diary: 8 Dec, 13 Dec, 16 Dec, and 17 Dec 41.
2. Orlov and Stamm interviews *Die Deutschen im Zweiten Weltkrieg*. SWF German TV. 1985.
3. Pz. AOK 3. *Gefechtsbericht Russland 1941-42*. 22 Dec. Also Richter's Diary 17 Dec 41.
4. *Beurteiling der Feindlage 17 Jan 41*. OKH. Gen Std H. Chief des Generalstabes Nr. 10/42, and Richter's Diary 17 Dec 41.
5. Manteuffel p252-253.
6. Ibid p256.
7. *Hitze, Frost und Pulverdampf*. R. Hinze. p101.
8. Interview *Die Deutschen . . .'* SWF TV. 1985.
9. Soviet General Staff Study *Battle for Moscow* 1942. Ed. M. Parrish. p44.
10. *Greatest Battles*. Zhukov p88.
11. *Moscow Tram Stop*. p284.
12. Letter 19 Dec 41. *KGS* p223-225. Pott was later killed at Orel in Mar 43.
13. *Stets zu Erschiessen . . .* J. Heer. p47-48.
14. *Moscow Tram Stop*. p286.
15. *KGS*. Letters 1-3 Dec, 7 Dec, 13 Dec and 21 Dec 41. p86-90.
16. Helmut von Harneck was killed at Orchowka Russia on 21 Jan 42. *KGS* Letter 27 Dec 41. p91-92.
17. Interviews Christians and Ossipow. G. Knopp. p245 and p241.
18. Will Thomas was killed on 26 Jan 42 near Rzhev. Letter 26 Dec 41. *KGS* p98-99.
19. Interview. G. Knopp p194.
20. Diary entry 26 Dec 41. *Kain, Wo ist dein Bruder?* H. Dollinger p114.
21. *Ich Wundere mich . . .* Kohl p78 and *Stets zu Erschiessen . . .* H. Heer p45.
22. A. de Zayas. *Die Wehrmacht – Untersuchungstelle*. p308-317.
23. Ibid p325.
24. *Zwischen Gehorsam und Gewissen*. M. Graf von Nayhauss. Inf. Regt 9. p210.
25. Testimony 7 Apr. 78. A. de Zayas p421-422.
26. *Moscow Tram Stop*. p328.
27. Interview G. Knopp p211.
28. 'Weisungen Barbarossa. OKW. Abt. L an H. Gr. Mitte. 18 Dec 41.' Quoted *Kriegsgeschichtliche Beispiele*. Forschungsamt. Freiburg p53.
29. 'The Fatal Decisions'. *Moscow* G. Blumentritt. p65-66.

Chapter 17: The order of the frozen flesh.
'Not one single step back'—The Hold Order.
1. *Kampf und Ende*. 98 Inf Div. was part of Panzergruppe 4 subordinated to Fourth Army. M. Gareis. p173-174.

2. *Zwischen Gehorsam und Gewissen*. M. Graf von Nayhauss. p212.
3. M. Gareis. p174.
4. Interview *Der Verdammte Krieg*. ZDF German TV. 1991.
5. H. Spaeter. *History of the Panzerkorps Grossdeutschland*. Vol 1. p281.
6. Becker was released from hospital in May 1942 after which he achieved his first leave in two years away from home. *Zwischen Gehorsam und Gewissen*. M. Graf von Nayhauss. p212-222.
7. *Die 7. Panzer Division . . .* Manteuffel p259-60.
8. *Das Heer 1933-45* Vol 3. p31. Burkhart Müller – Hillebrand.

Frozen flesh.
1. Interview *Der Verdammte Krieg*. ZDF German TV 1991.
2. Zieser op cit p87.
3. Diary entry 28 Jan 42. *The Outermost Frontier*. p48-49 and 51.
4. *Kriegstagebuch*. Ia. 167 I.D. Anlagen. 4 Jan 42.
5. Diary 9 Jan and 20 Jan 1942. *Kriegsgeschichtliche Beispiele – Verteidigung*. p83. Freiburg.
6. *The Outermost Frontier*. p48.
7. Diary 17 Dec and 20 Dec 41. *Kriegsgeschichtliche . . .* p84. Freiburg.
8. *KTB 296 Inf. Div. Anlagen*. 17 Dec 41. Ibid p85.
9. Interview *Der Verdammte Krieg* ZDF German TV. 1991.
10. *Moscow Tram Stop*. p304.
11. *Meldungen. Nr 248* 5 Jan 42 p3120.
12. Interview. Thames TV. *The World at War*.
13. *War Wives*. C. and E. Townsend. p303-304.
14. *Meldungen. Nr 248* 5 Jan 42. p3120 and 3124. *Nr 249* 8 Jan 42. p3133. *Nr 250* 12 Jan 42. p3151.
15. Interview. Thames TV. *The World at War*.
16. Letter 23 Dec 41. *KGS*. p315-316.
17. Interview *Der Verdammte Krieg* ZDF German TV. 1991.
18. *The World at War*. Thames TV.
19. Interview *Der Unvergessene Krieg*. Eickhoff, Pagels and Reschl. p67.
20. Interviews G. Knopp p243 and p206.
21. *Friedens und Kriegserlebnisse einer Generation*. F. Strauss. p106.
22. G. Knopp. p206.

Postscript — 'Barbarossa'.
1. Halder's Diary. 11 Aug 41. p506.
2. Diary 18 Nov 41. Robert Rupp was killed near Kaschira during a fighting retreat on 4 Dec 41. *Sehr Selten habe ich geweint*. Ed. I. Hammer & S. zur Nieden. p260.
3. Manteuffel. p278.

Appendices

1. German casualties, Operation 'Barbarossa' 1941-2

Monthly totals	Killed	Wounded	Missing
FRANCE 1940			
(10.5–20.6.40)	26,455 (1,253)	111,640 (3,324)	16,659 (329)
RUSSIA 1941			
June (22-30)	8,886 (524)	29,494 (966)	2,707 (50)
July	46,470 (2,443)	125,579 (4,498)	9,051 (169)
August	41,019 (1,563)	147,748 (4,616)	7,896 (153)
September	29,422 (920)	106,826 (2,806)	4,896 (52)
October	24,056 (968)	87,224 (2,577)	3,585 (61)
November	17,806 (802)	66,211 (2,340)	3,122 (45)
December	14,949 (424)	58,226 (1,213)	4,682 (90)
1942			
January	17,544 (656)	59,928 (2,114)	7,875 (110)
February	19,319 (584)	49,398 (1,421)	4,229 (76)

Notes
1. Note the comparison to French campaign figures.
2. Includes entire Ostfront (ie Army Groups North, Centre and South).
3. Figures in brackets are officers.
4. January figures are 1 Jan–10 Feb inclusive.
5. February figures are 10 Feb–10 Mar inclusive.
6. Source: Kriegstagebuch des OKW. 1940-41 (II) P. 1120-21 and 1942 (I) P. 298 and 306.

2. German casualties reflected in Division manning equivalents

Figures are numbers of Divisions

	Officers	NCOs	Soldiers
FRANCE 1940	9.4	12	9.1
RUSSIA 1941			
June	2.9	3.1	2.4
July	13.5	13	10
August	12	15	11.6
September	7.2	10.9	8.3
October	6.8	8.9	6.8
November	6	6.7	5.1
December	3.2	6	4.6
1942			
January	5.5	6.6	5
February	4	5.6	4.3

Notes
1. Figures based on an Infantry Division: 518 Officers, 2,573 NCOs, 13,667 men and 102 *Beamte* (ie Officials/Clerks). Panzer Divisions were less men: 471 officers and 13,255 other ranks.
2. June figures are for 10 days.
3. Fall of casualties from November onwards reflect the impact of weather on the scale and intensity of fighting.
4. NCO casualties rise as they take over officer appointments.
5. Calculated from OKW monthly casualty returns. (See Appendix 1)

3. The fighting elements within a German Division

THE INFANTRY DIVISION

TOTAL PERSONNEL   518 Officers.
2,573 NCOs.
13,667 Men.
102 *Beamte*.

An average total of 16,860 men.

'Teeth' (ie combat element)
Three Infantry Regiments each of: 75 Officers.
493 NCOs.
2,474 Men.
7 *Beamte*

In addition staff, intelligence platoon, cavalry platoon, engineer platoon and anti-tank company.
. . . . .Totalling 9,147 Officers and men.

Reconnaissance Battalion . . . . .623 Officers and men.
Anti-Tank Battalion . . . . .550 Officers and men.
Engineer Battalion . . . . .520 Officers and men.

Between the front line and rear.
Artillery Regiment . . . . .2,872 Officers and men.
Light Infantry 'Column' .30 Men.
Signals Bn . . . . .474 Officers and men.

'Tail' (ie rear area logistic and other support)
Rückwärtige Dienste

Supply Services (*Versorgungsdienste*) — Rations platoon, baker company, Butcher platoon, Military Police and *Feldpost* platoon: . . . . .226 Officers and men.

Logistics column/Train — 6 Columns (3 mot and 3 horse-drawn): . . . . .180 Officers and men.

POL (Petrol, Oil and Lubricants) Column: 35 Officers and men.

Workshop Company: . . . . .102 Officers and men.

Transport Company: . . . . .245 Officers and men.

Medical Services — 2 Medical Companies, 1 Field hospital and 2 medical transport platoons: . . . .616 Officers and men.

One Veterinary Company . . . .235 Officers and men, 890 horses.

In an Infantry Division there are about 10,840 'fighters' or combat elements able to close with the enemy. This represents 64% of the Division.

Source: based on an evaluation of figures taken from Alex Bucher: *Das Handbuch Der Deutschen Infanterie. 1939-45.*

THE PANZER DIVISION
Variable in size but generally: 471 Officers and 13,255 other ranks.

2,685 different vehicles including 357 armoured, mainly tracked, fighting vehicles.

'Teeth'/fighting element

Headquarters . . . . .32 Officers and 109 men.
Panzer Regiment with 3 Panzer Bns
. . . . .69 Officers and 1,592 men.
Infantry Brigade and 2,197 men each . . . .
. . . . . .2 Regiments and 1 Armoured Inf Regt of 61 Officers.
Assault Gun Battalion . . . . .20 Officers and 861 men.
Reconnaissance Battalion . . . . . . .24 Officers and 861 men.
Engineer Battalion . . . . .26 Officers and 958 men.

Between 'Teeth' and 'Tail'

Artillery Regiment of 3 battalions
. . . . .69 Officers and 1,580 men each.
Anti-Aircraft Battalion . . . . .22 Officers and 742 men.
Signals Battalion . . . . .16 Officers and 742 men.

'Tail'/Logistics and supporting services

Division Services . . . . .64 Officers and 1,821 men.

In a Panzer Division just under 50% of the officers and men, on average, actually close with the enemy.

Source: D. Crow: *Armoured Fighting Vehicles of Germany.*

4. A snapshot of Soviet battle casualties

	STRENGTH	IRRECOVERABLE LOSSES	% STRENGTH LOSS
22 June–1 Sept 1941	3.3m	2,067,801	18.79
1 Sep –31 Dec 1941	2.8m	926,002	10.95

Average daily losses 1941

Against German Army Group North:

	MEN	TANKS	ARTY & MORS	AIRCRAFT
Baltic Front — defence Lithuania/Latvia 22 June–9 July 1941	4,845	140	198	55
Arctic and defence of Karelian Isthmus 29 June–10 Oct 1941.	1,295	NK	NK	NK
Leningrad defence operation 10 July–30 Sept 1941	4,155	18	119	20–21

Against Army Group Centre:

	MEN	TANKS	ARTY & MORS	AIRCRAFT
Belorussia 22 June–9 July 1941	23,207	267	524	99
Smolensk 10 July–10 Sept 1941	12,063	21	147	14
Yelnya Salient battles 30 August–8 Sep 1941	3,185	NK	NK	NK
Defence of Moscow 30 Sep–5 Dec 1941	9,825	42	57	4
Counter-offensive Moscow First Phase 7 Dec 1941 –7 January 1942	10,910	13	39	34

Against Army Group South:

	MEN	TANKS	ARTY AND MORS	AIRCRAFT
Defence of Western Ukraine 22 June–6 July 1941	15,414	292	387	81
Kiev battles and Encirclement 7 July–26 Sep 1941	8,543	5	347	14
Don Basin to Rostov 29 Sep–16 Nov 1941	3,277	2	74	5
Rostov Counter-offensive. 17 Nov–2 Dec 1941	2,069	2-3	64	2-3

Source: Ed. Col-Gen G. F. Krivosheev: *Soviet Casualties and Combat Losses in the Twentieth Century*; pp. 101, 110-121 and 260-261.

SOURCES

Published sources

Aaken, W. van: *Hexenkessel Ostfront*; Erich Pabel Verlag, 1964.
Bartov, O.: *Hitler's Army — Soldiers, Nazis, and War in the Third Reich*; OUP, 1992.
—: *The Eastern Front 1941-45, German Troops and the Barbarisation of Warfare*; Macmillan, 1985.
Bekker, C.: *The Luftwaffe War Diaries*; Macdonald & Co, 1966.
Blandford, E.: *Under Hitler's Banner*; Motorbooks, 1995.
Boll, H. and Kopelew, L.: '*Warum haben wir aufeinander geschossen?*' Lamuv Verlag, 1981.
Browning, C. R.: *Ordinary Men — Reserve Police Bn 101 and the Final Solution in Poland*; Harper Perennial, 1992.
Buchner, A.: *Das Handbuch der Deutsche Infanterie*; Podzun-Pallas, 1987.
Buffetaut, Y.: *Objectif Moscou!*; Histoires & Collections, Paris, 1993.
Creveld, M. van: *Supplying War — Logistics from Wallenstein to Patton*; CUP, 1977.
Cooper, L.: *Many Roads to Moscow*; Hamish-Hamilton, 1968.
Danishevsky, I.: *The Road of Battle and Glory*; Foreign Languages Publishing House, Moscow, 1964.
Dills, K. W.: *German War Art 1939-45*; Bison Books, 1983.
Eichel, M., Pagels W., Reschl, W.: *Der Unvergessene Krieg*; Verlagsgesellschaft Schulfernsehen-Vgs, 1981.
Erickson, J.: *The Road to Stalingrad*; Weidenfeld, 1975/93.
Freiburg Militärgeschichtlichen Forschungsamtes.; *Der Angriff auf die Sowjetunion*; Boog/Förster/Hoffmann/Klink/Ueberschär, Fischer Verlag, 1983/91.
—: *Kriegsgeschichtliche Beispiele — Verteidigung*; Freiburg M.F.
Glantz, D. M.: *The Initial Period of War on the Eastern Front*; Frankcass & Co, 1993.
Haupt, W.: *Sturm auf Moskau 1941*; Podzun-Pallas Verlag, 1986/90.
Heer, H.: *Stets zu erschiessen sind Frauen, die in der Roten Armee dienen*; Hamburg, 1995.
Heer, H. and Naumann K.: *Vernichtungskrieg — Verbrechen der Wehrmacht 1941-4*; Hamburg, 1995.
Heydorn, V. D.: *Der sowjetische Aufmarsch im Bialystoker Balcon bis zum 22. Juni 1941*; Verlag für Wehrwissenschaften; Munich, 1989.

Hünermann, C.: *Chronik 1941*.
Keegan, J.: *The Second World War*; Arrow Books, 1990.
—: *Barbarossa — Invasion of Russia 1941*; Ballentine, 1970.
Kohl, P.: *Ich Wundere mich, dass ich noch lebe*; Gütersloher Verlaghaus Gerd Mohn, 1990.
Krivosheev, G. F.: *Soviet Casualties and Combat Losses in the Twentieth Century*; Greenhill, 1997.
Leetz, A. and Wenner, B.: *Blockade. Leningrad. 1941-44*; Rowohlt, 1992.
Lewis, S. J.: *Forgotten Legions*; Praeger Special Studies, 1986.
Marshall Cavendish: *Images of War* and *The War Years 1941-1945*.
Meyer, S. and Schulze, E.: *Wie wir das alles geschafft haben*; Deutscher Tachenbuch Verlag Dtv, 1984.
Miller, R.: *The Soviet Airforce at War*; Time-Life, 1983.
Newton, S. H.: *German Battle Tactics on the Russian Front 1941-1945*; Schiffer Military History, 1994.
Parrish, M. (Ed): *Battle for Moscow — The 1942 Soviet General Staff Study*; Pergamon-Brasseys, 1989.
Paul, W.: *Die Schlacht um Moskau 1941/42*; Ullstein, 1991.
Purnell: *History of the Second World War*; Vols 2 & 5.
Schäfer, H. D. (Hrsg.): *Berlin im Zweiten Weltkrieg*; Serie Piper, 1991.
Stolfi, R. H. S.: *Hitler's Panzers East*; Alan Sutton, 1992.
Townsend, C. and E.: *War Wives*; Grafton Books, 1989.
—: *'Der Überfall'*; Hoffman & Campe Verlag, Hamburg. 1984.
Weltkrieg, Der II, German Series on World War 2. Band 3: *Tief im Feindesland*; Jahr-Verlag, 1976.
Werth, A.: *Russia at War 1941-1945*; Pan Books, 1964.
Westphal, S.: *The Fatal Decisions*; Michael Joseph, 1956.
Williamson, G.: *The Blood soaked Soil*; Blitz Editions, 1997.
Zaloga, S. and Sarson, P.: *T34/76 Medium Tank 1941-45*; Vanguard, Osprey, 1994.
Zayas de A.: *Die Wehrmachts Untersuchungsstelle*; Wilhelm Heyne Verlag, Munich, 1981.
Zentner, K.: *Nur Einmal Konnte Stalin Siegen*; Gruner Verlag, Hamburg, 1952.
Ziemke, E. F. and Bauer, M. E.: *Moscow to Stalingrad.*; Military Heritage Press, 1988.

Unit accounts
Gareis, M.: *Kampf und Ende — Der Frankisch-Sudetendeutschen 98. Infanterie-Division*; Podzun-Pallas-Verlag, 1956.
Gschöpf, R.: *Mein Weg mit der 45. Infanterie Division*; Oberöstereichischer Landesverlag, 1955.
Haupt, W.: *Die 8. Panzer-Division im 2.Weltkrieg*; Podzun-Pallas, 1987.
—: *Die Schlachten der Heeresgruppe Mitte 1941-1944*; Podzun-Pallas, 1983.
—: *Die Schlachten der Heeresgruppe Süd*; Podzun-Pallas, 1985.
—: *Heeresgruppe Nord*; Podzun-Pallas, 1966.
Hinze, R.: *Hitze, Frost und Pulverdampf; Der Shicksalweg der 20. Panzer Division*; Heinrich Pöppinghaus Verlag, 1981.
Lehmann, R.: *The Leibstandarte — 1 SS Panzer Division Leibstandarte Adolf Hitler*; Vol II, Fedorowicz Publishing, 1988.
Löser, J.: *'Bittere Pflicht' — Kampf und Untergang der 76. Berlin-Brandenburgischen Infanterie-Division*; Biblio Verlag, 1988.

Manteuffel, H. E. V.: *Die 7. Panzer-Division im Zweiten Weltkrieg*; Podzun-Verlag, 1986.
Nayhauss, M. Graf von.: *'Zwischen Gehorsam und Gewissen'.Potsdamer Infanterie-Regt 9*; Bastei-Lübbe, 1994.
Paul, W.: *Brennpunkte — Die Geschichte der 6.Pz Div. 1937-45*.
Schrodek, G. W.: *Die 11. Panzerdivision 'Gespensterdivision'*; Podzun-Pallas-Verlag, 1984.
Spaeter, H.: *The History of the Panzercorps 'Grossdeutschland'*; Vol. 1, Fedorowicz Canada, 1958/92.
Strauss, F. J.: *Friedens und Kriegserlebnisse einer Generation — Pz. Abt. 38 (SF) 2. (Wiener) Panzerdivision*; Kurt Vowincliel Verlag, Neckergemünd, 1977.
Ullrich, K.: *Wie ein Fels im Meer — Kriegsgeschichte der 3.SS Panzerdivision 'Totenkopf'*; Munin Verlag, Osnabrück, 1987.
Wagenener, C.: *Heeresgruppe Süd*; Podzun Verlag, Undated.
Weidinger, O.: *Comrades to the End*; *The 4th SS Panzer-Grenadier Regiment 'Der Führer'*; 1938-1945; Schiffer Military History, 1998.

Published personal accounts and letters
Adamczyk, W.: *Feur!' — An Artilleryman's Life on the Eastern Front*. Broadfoot Pub Co, 1992.
Bähr, H. W.: *'Die Stimme des Menschen'. Briefe und Aufzeichnungen aus der ganzen Welt.1939-45*. R. Piper & Co. Verlag, Munich, 1961.
Bähr, H. W., Meyer, H. J. and Orthbandt, E.: *Kriegsbriefe Gefallener Studenten 1939-1945*; Rainer Wunderlich Verlag, 1952.
Bamm, P.: *The Invisible Flag*; Faber & Faber Ltd, London, 1956.
Becker, H.: *The Devil on my Shoulder*; Jarrolds, 1955.
Bock, F. von: *Generalfeldmarschall Fedor von Bock — The War Diary 1939-1945*; Schiffer Military History, 1996.
Buchbender, O. and Sterz, R.: *Das Andere Gesicht des Krieges*; Verlag C. H. Beck, 1982.
Deck, J.: *Der Weg der 1000 Toten*; Badenia Verlag Karlsruhe, 1978.
Dollinger, H.: *Kain, wo ist dein Bruder?*; Fischer Verlag, 1987.
Fuchs, K.: *Sieg Heil!'— War Letters of Tank Gunner Karl Fuchs 1937-41*. Archon Books USA, 1987.
Golovchansky, A., Osipov, V., Prokopenko, A., Daniel, U. and Reulecke, J.: *Ich will raus aus diesem Wahnsinn — Deutsche Briefe von der Ostfront 1941-1945 Aus sowjetischen Archiven*; Rowohlt Verlag Hamburg, 1993.
Goebbels, J.: *The Goebbels Diaries*; Hamish Hamilton, 1948.
Guderian, H.: *Panzer Leader*; Michael Joseph, 1952/70.
Haape, H.: *Moscow Tram Stop*; Collins, London, 1957.
Halder, F.: *The Halder War Diary 1939-42*; Ed. Burdick, C. and Jacobsen, H. A., Greenhill Books, 1988.
Hammer, I. and zur Nieden, S.: *'Sehr selten habe ich geweint' — Briefe und Tagebücher aus dem Zweiten weltkrieg von Menschen aus Berlin*. Schweizer Verlaghaus, Zurich, 1992.
Kesselring, A.: *The Memoirs of Field-Marshall Kesselring*; Greenhill Books, 1988.
Knappe, S.: *Soldat*; *Reflections of a German soldier 1936-49*; Dell, 1993.
Knoke, H.: *I Flew for the Führer*; Corgi, 1956.
Knopp, G.: *Der verdammte Krieg*; C. Bertelsmann Verlag, Munich, 1991.
Krylov, I.: *Soviet Staff Officer*; Falcon Press, 1951.
Kuby, E.: *Mein Krieg*; *Aufzeichnungen aus 2,129 Tagen*; Deutscher Taschenbuch Verlag, 1977.

Kuhnert, M.: *'Will we See Tomorrow?'*— *A German Cavalryman at War 1939-42*; Leo Cooper, 1993.

Luck, H. von: *Panzer Commander*; Praeger NY, 1989.

Malaparte, C.: *The Volga Rises in Europe*; Alvin Redman Ltd, London, 1957.

Meyer, E. V.: *Briefe 1938-1941*; Berlin & Düsseldorf, 1976.

Metelmann, H.: *Through Hell for Hitler*; Patrick Stephens, 1990.

Neumann, P.: *The Black March*; Bantam, 1958/60.

Pabst, H.: *The Outermost Frontier*; William Kimber, London, 1957.

Piekalkiewicz, J: *Die Schlacht um Moskau — Die erfrorene Offensive*; Gustav Lübbe Verlag, 1981.

Prüller, W.: *Diary of a German Soldier*; Faber & Faber, 1963.

Rudel, H. U.: *Stuka Pilot*; Bantam, 1979.

Simonov, K.: *Kriegstagebücher*; Bellestristik, Berlin, 1979.

Starinov, I. G.: *'Over the Abyss' — My Life in Special Operations*; Ivy Books NY, 1995.

Speer, A.: *Inside the Third Reich*; Sphere, 1971.

Stahlberg, A.: *Bounden Duty — The Memoirs of a German Officer 1932-45*; Brassey's UK, 1990.

Steinhoff, J., Pechel, P. and Showalter, D.: *Deutsche im Zweiten Weltkrieg*; Bastei-Lübbe Verlag, Gladbach, 1989.

Temkin, G.: *My Just War — The Memoir of a Jewish Red Army Soldier in World War II*; Presido, 1998.

Zeiser, B.: *In Their Shallow Graves*; Elek Books, 1956.

Zhukov, G. K.: *Shukow. Erinnerungen und Gedanken*; Vols I & II, Militärverlag der Deutschen Demokratischen Republik, 1974

—: *Zhukov's Greatest Battles*; Ed. H. Salisbury, 1974.

Periodicals

Clark, A.: *Leningrad'* Vol 1 Issue 2: War Monthly; 'Der Deutsche Fallschimjäger'. *'2 Cm-Flak bezwingt T 34'*. 5 Sep/Oct 1984

Frisch A. P., and. Jones W. D.: *'A Panzer Soldier's War'*. World War 2 Sep 1995.

Glantz D.: *Combat Documents of Soviet West Front Armies. 22-30 Jun 41'*. Journal of Soviet Military Studies. Vol. 4. No. 3. Sep 91.

German wartime magazine articles taken from:
   'Signal'. 1941.
   'Die Wehrmacht'. 1941.
   'Der Adler'. 1941.
   'Das Reich'. 1941.

Hanson, V. D.: *Cannae'*. Quarterly Journal Military History Vol 2 No 4.

Murray, W.: *Barbarossa*. Quarterly Journal Military History. Spring 1992.

Richter, G.: *Angriff und Rückzug vor Moskau 1941/42; — Ein Tagebuch von Hptm.a.D. Georg Richter AR 74*. Miteilungsblatt Kameradschaft Wiener Pz –Div 4/1995.

Stolfi, R. H. S.: *'The Greatest Encirclement in History'*. R.U.S.I. Dec 1996.

Strawson, J.: *'Kiev'*. Vol 2 *'War Monthly'*.

Suvorov, V.: *'Who Was Planning to attack Whom in June 1941, Hitler or Stalin?'* R.U.S.I. Jun 85 Pp 50-55.

Wray, T.: *'Standing Fast: German Defensive Doctrine on the Russian Front during World War II'. Pre-war to March 1943*. Combat Studies Institute. Research Survey No 5. US Army Staff College. 1986.

'Zeit-Forum': *Die Zeit'* German Newspaper discussion over the role of the Wehrmacht in the Third Reich and World War 2. 3 Mar 95. Pp 14-20.

Filmed and taped interviews

Balck, H. — *Taped Interviews* Battelle Columbus Laboratories; 12 Jan 79 & 19/20 May 1980.

Blockade. Leningrad. 1941-44; Film by T. Kufus. 1991.

Decisive Weapons — T 34 Queen of the Battlefield. BBC TV 1996.

Der Verdammte Krieg. ZDF German TV 1991. G. Knopp.

Die Deutsche Wochenschau. Various German newsreels 1941.

Die Deutschen im Zweiten Weltkrieg. SWF German TV 1989.

The Eastern Front 1941-43. Brit Army Dept C1591. Doc film series.

Kriegsverbrechen Nach den Akten der Wehrmachts-Untersuchungstelle. Venohr, W., Vogt, M. and de Zayas, A. Lubbe German WDR TV 1983.

Mein Krieg. German WDR TV 1988. H. Eder and T. Kufus.

Red Empire. Dr R. Conquest. Yorkshire TV 1995.

Russia's War. I. Grigoriev. IBP Films 1995.

Steh auf! Es ist Krieg. ZDF German TV. H. Kaminski 1991.

Wechtler M. *Video History of the 45. Inf Div*.

The World at War. Thames TV. 'Barbarossa'.

Published documents

'Meldungen aus dem Reich' — Die geheimen Lageberichte des Sicherheitsdienstes der SS 1938-1945.

Boberach (Hrsg). Pawlak Verlag 1984.
   Band 7 — 22 April-14 Aug. 1941.
   Band 8 — 18 Aug-15 Dez 1941.
   Band 9 — 18 Dez-26 März 1941

'Kriegstagebuch des Oberkommandos der Wehrmacht' 1940-41(II) & 1942 (I). P. E. Schramm (Hrsg.) Berard & Graefe Verlag 1982.

Unpublished documents

Kriegstagebücher:
   AOK 4.
   XII Armee Korps.
   HG Nord.
   18 Armee.
   Pz AOK 3.
   167 ID.

'Militärgeographische Angaben über das Europäische Russland'; Generalstab des Heeres, Berlin 1941. *Wallets: Mappe E. 'Weissrussland', G: 'Zentral — Russland', H: 'Moskau'*.

'Wechtler Collection of Documents' Erfahrungsberichte/Gefechtsberichte relating to the storming of Brest-Litovsk June 1941.

Index (Listing of the main people and places mentioned in the text)